Secrecy

AND

Power

Secrecy

AND

Power

The Life of J. Edgar Hoover

Richard Gid Powers

THE FREE PRESS
A Division of Macmillan, Inc.
NEW YORK

Collier Macmillan Publishers
LONDON

The Free Press
A Division of Macmillan, Inc.
866 Third Avenue, New York, N.Y. 10022

Collier Macmillan Canada, Inc.

Printed in the United States of America

printing number

2 3 4 5 6 7 8 9 10

Library of Congress Cataloging-in-Publication Data

Powers, Richard Gid
  Secrecy and power, the life of J. Edgar Hoover.

  Bibliography: p.
  Includes index.
  1. Hoover, J. Edgar (John Edgar), 1895–1972.
2. United States. Federal Bureau of Investigation.
3. Police—United States—Biography.   4. Government
executives—United States—Biography.   I. Title.
HV7911.H6P68   1986   353.0074′092′4   [B]   86–26926
ISBN 0–02–925060–9

For
Eileen, Sarah, and Evelyn

Contents

Acknowledgments

OFFICIALS AT THE FBI were helpful and efficient in fulfilling my requests for files and information. I appreciate the efforts of James K. Hall of the Records Management Division of the Freedom of Information-Privacy Acts Section, Jack French and Ernest Porter of the Research Unit of the Office of Congressional and Public Affairs, and Dr. Susan Falb, FBI Historian, OCPA, who has done great things to justify the ways of SOG (Seat of Government, FBI parlance for Washington) to man. Research in FBI files is inherently difficult, but not, as far as I could tell, because of any obstacles raised by the present-day FBI.

At the National Archives, I was fortunate to have the assistance of Cynthia G. Fox and Michael McReynolds of the Civil Archives Division of the Judicial, Fiscal, and Social Branch, and John Taylor of the Modern Military Division.

I was helped in locating elusive fragments of Hoover's early life by specialists in the history of Washington schools: Richard Hurlbert of the District of Columbia school system; Mrs. Hardy of the system's attendance office; Walton Shipley, Central High School historian; and Hugh Y. Bernard, historian of the George Washington University Law School.

At the presidential libraries I would like to thank Dale C. Mayer of the Herbert Hoover Library, Raymond Teichman of the FDR, Dennis Bilger at the HST, David Haight at the Eisenhower, Nancy Smith at the LBJ, and Megan Floyd Desmoyers and Joan Kennedy at the JFK.

I am grateful for the assistance of Mary Wolfskill of the Manuscript Division of the Library of Congress, Mary Plummer of the Presbyterian National Historical Society, Robin Wear of the Alderman Library of the University of Virginia, and Franz Lassner and Harold Badger of the Freedoms Foundation.

Hoover's nieces, Margaret Hoover Fennell and Anna Hoover Kienest, provided me with many reminiscences of their uncle. Hoover's pastor, Edward L. R. Elson of the National Presbyterian Center, and the historian of the center, Ervin Chapman, gave me insight into the nature of Hoover's religious affiliations. Mr. and Mrs. Rex Collier shared their memories of their long association with Hoover.

Former Attorney General Herbert Brownell, former Associate FBI Director Mark Felt, Assistant to the Director Cartha DeLoach, Assistant Director Courtney Evans, and former Special Agents William Gunn and Milton Ellerin all provided useful information about Hoover and his FBI. Ernest Cuneo and Thomas Troy answered my questions about Hoover and the OSS.

I am grateful for the assistance of many writers whose research has touched on some aspect of Hoover's career: Kai Bird, Ralph de Toledano, Candace Falk, David Garrow, Donald M. Goldstein, Walter Goodman, Gil Green, Robert Hill, Max Holland, Ted Morgan, David Oshinsky, and Scott Rafferty; also Paul Burka, John Cammett, Stanley Coben, John Copp, Lynn Dumenil, Charles Gillieron, Stanley Kutler, J. Fred MacDonald, and Arthur M. Schlesinger, Jr.

At the College of Staten Island, I was given enthusiastic support by President Edmond L. Volpe, Dean Barry Bressler, and Jerome Mardison of the CSI library.

Many friends helped and encouraged me during the years consumed by this project. I am particularly grateful to Frederick Binder, Sandi Cooper, Roy and Cora Hoopes, Jane Kozlowski, Carol Luedtke, Claire and Edward Margolies, Louis Phillips, and Barton L. St. Armand. I am grateful to Seymour Rudin for his pains in correcting errors in the text. From what people tell me, my wife and children did fairly well for themselves while I was tied up with Hoover. I am looking forward to finding out for myself.

No writer could ask for better support than I received from The Free Press at Macmillan. Being exposed to the intelligence of President and Publisher Erwin Glikes was a great experience. Finally, the real credit for whatever merit this book has belongs to my editor at The Free Press, whose good humor, intense concentration, keen insight, and high standards never faltered during a long and intense ordeal: Joyce Seltzer.

Secrecy

AND

Power

PROLOGUE

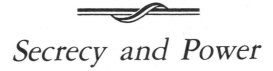

Secrecy and Power

THE J. EDGAR HOOVER FBI HEADQUARTERS, its windows set deeply back behind cast-stone frames, seems to squint suspiciously down Pennsylvania Avenue toward the Capitol and at the Justice Department building across the street. The interior plan of the complex is obscured by heavy barriers of stone and metal. Between protective pillars and behind steep walls only deep shadows can be seen, concealing activities whose nature outsiders can only imagine. The massive FBI headquarters is a concrete monument to the man who ran the Federal Bureau of Investigation for forty-eight years.

Hoover directed the Bureau so long that he seemed fixed in the political landscape of Washington. There was that bulldog face: those tiny, squinting eyes; the clenched jaw; and squashed-in nose—features so distinctive that any decent cartoonist could produce a recognizable likeness with a few strokes of the pen. It was a face of confident power. The wary eyes looked as if they had seen the worst in human nature and expected to see it again. The grim scowl was that of a man who had seen all evil, heard all evil, and could be counted on to warn of any evil that would put the nation in danger.

As chief of federal law enforcement and guardian of domestic security, Hoover moved within the innermost rings of the most powerful circles of government, with critical responsibilities during the greatest political crises and national emergencies of the century. The Bureau he led, powerful, efficient, completely subordinate to his will, was a resource presidents and the public came to depend on for decisive,

1

effective performance under the most sensitive and difficult circumstances.

In his time, the man and his Bureau were cloaked in a selective secrecy and protected by power so formidable that few dared to pry. The secrets—the files on Communists, on spies, the hundreds of millions of fingerprints, the dossiers on the great and the famous—were whispered to have silenced his critics and destroyed his enemies. To those who saw it as a threat to political freedom, Hoover's secret power was a frightening specter that haunted the nation.

Paradoxically, that secrecy and power, so terrifying to some, were what made him a hero to many more, perhaps even most, Americans. Hoover's imposing presence gave much of the country a sense of stability and safety as he gathered to himself the strands of permanence that connected Americans to their past: religion, patriotism, a belief in progress, and a rational moral order. To attack him was to attack Americanism itself. Millions were sure that Hoover's secret power was all that stood between them and sinister forces that aimed to destroy their way of life.

Hoover's crusade against criminals and Communists during the thirties and forties made him a national hero; his stand as a pillar of old-fashioned morality kept him an untouchable political institution. Nixon's eulogy at Hoover's funeral called him "one of the nation's leaders of morals and manners and opinion." The FBI director felt obliged to instruct the nation on family ties, church-going, and deference to authority; he proclaimed these the only effective weapons against crime and subversion, and he denounced any ideas that might obscure the moral significance of private and public behavior. Whether addressing the American Legion or the PTA, he presented himself as an aggressive defender of traditional values and customs. Hoover's reputation was a complex compound of facts, legends, secrets, *and* the endless moralizing, and the public rewarded him with more power, longer, than any other political figure in American history.

Of all Hoover's secrets, the most tightly guarded were his own. Head of what was arguably the most powerful agency in the nation, his influence extending throughout government and society, he managed to block every effort by outsiders to take an independent look at what he was doing and how he was doing it, what he knew and how he knew it. A half century of tightly restricted access made him a figure of mystery and of nervous apprehension; legends grew up about him, and his reputation was haunted by rumors and superstition. Presidents, congressmen, attorney generals, and the public knew only what Hoover wanted them to know about the Bureau and himself.

With his death, the man and the Bureau shrank from mythic to human proportions. Inquiries and exposure stripped away the Bureau's defenses. The record of how the Bureau abused civil liberties poured from the files. The officially approved version of Hoover's career was dismantled and turned into a case study of excessive bureaucratic power run amuck. A last impression is enduring, and so what was remembered was Hoover's illegal surveillance techniques and his secret attacks on unpopular speech and beliefs. The rubble of his reputation buried the man himself even deeper, along with the forces that had produced him.

Hoover's beginnings had vanished into the past even before he died. His family, the church, the school, and the friends were all gone, overshadowed by the later glories, but also forgotten were the first triumphs and disasters that had taught him what was possible and what was not, the great national and international upheavals that gave him his first chance to grapple with communism. When presidents and the public listened to Hoover, they did not hear the echoes of ancient battles only he remembered. Few knew *what* lessons of the past Hoover remembered, and whether, when he spat out the word *Communist,* he meant Gus Hall and Khrushchev and Castro, or was he thinking back to Lenin and Trotsky and Emma Goldman. When he lacerated black radicals, did he mean Rap Brown and Martin Luther King, Jr., or did he mean the whole procession of black leaders beginning with Marcus Garvey, the first he had destroyed, or was he drawing on even older memories, the hates and fears of the segregated Washington of his youth? When he harangued his followers about crime waves, was he thinking of ghetto muggers and looters, or about Dillinger and Machine Gun Kelly? When he slashed away at the pseudo-liberals who protected radicals, did he mean Ramsey Clark and Robert Kennedy, or was he still battling Louis Post and Felix Frankfurter and the other civil libertarians who had thwarted him in 1919 and 1920?

In all nations, people truly live in different centuries and different cities of the mind, even when they seem to be contemporaries. Hoover had, all his life, even as he lived and worked at the epicenter of the capital of the world's most powerful nation, a turn-of-the-century vision of America as a small community of like-minded neighbors, proud of their achievements, resentful of criticism, fiercely opposed to change. As twentieth-century standards of the mass society swept over traditional America, subverting old values, disrupting old customs, and dislodging old leaders, Americans who were frightened by the loss of their community saw in Hoover a man who understood their concerns and shared their anger, a powerful defender who would guard their America of memory against a world of alien forces, strange peoples, and dangerous ideas.

Toward the end, as Hoover thundered against the eternal enemies of the republic—criminals, Communists, and their coddlers—his words had the awe-inspiring quality of those ancient formulas that once called down the wrath of God on sinners and still sent a shiver down the spine. The America Hoover used as a standard to judge the modern world, and from which he drew the power of his fierce convictions, had vanished before most Americans of the sixties and seventies were born. Hoover's thoughts, his feelings, his intentions as he defied presidents and crushed Communists, the roots of the fierce intensity and determination that let him hold onto so much power, so long—the search for these leads to turn-of-the-century Washington, in a quiet city square a few blocks behind the Capitol, where J. Edgar Hoover's story begins.

CHAPTER 1

The Hoovers of Seward Square

As a youth I was taught basic beliefs. Cynics, perhaps, may regard them with derision. For instance, I was taught that no book was ever to be placed above the Bible. Children in my youth were taught the code of the American flag and to defend it against any manner of desecration, as a symbol of life, liberty and justice.

Hoover, November 9, 1959, Austin, Texas

THREE BLOCKS BEHIND the Capitol, where North Carolina Avenue crosses Pennsylvania, is a large, open square bordered by dignified, upstandingly proper Victorian houses that recall the gentility, respectability, and concern for appearances that shaped them a century ago. But a gas station has intruded on the west side of the square now, and a modern brick-and-concrete church of vaguely Romanesque style has carved a chunk out of its southern border.[1] The grass is unkempt and trampled; the trees are few and struggling. Pennsylvania Avenue, which cuts diagonally across the square, has been widened into a major thoroughfare that funnels commuters toward the Capitol in the morning and drains them away in the evening. The old-fashioned houses seem sadly exposed to the traffic that pours by in an unending stream. The square itself has been overwhelmed by mid-twentieth-century Washington's incessant expansion and demand for greater efficiency, convenience, and order.

At the turn of the century, the streets that form Seward Square,

5

Fourth and Sixth streets and the north and south branches of "C" Street, were narrow and cobblestoned, with shade trees and brick sidewalks. Pennsylvania Avenue was a pair of narrow carriage lanes separated by a grassy walkway and lined with trees. The streetcars that ran along the avenue were hidden from the homes by the trees and shrubs, and a cast-iron post and chain fence surrounded the park's well-tended lawns and flowerbeds of calla lilies and dusty millers.[2] It was a quiet neighborhood that had housed the same government-worker families for generations. Proud of its churches, its schools, and its niche in the civil service, it was a secure, self-satisfied community, confident that success and prosperity had proved its way of life worthy of respect—and defense.

Here, at 413 Seward Square, just a five-minute walk from the Capitol, where seventy-seven years later his body would lie in state, John Edgar Hoover was born on January 1, 1895. For forty-three years he would live in this house, to leave only when his mother died in 1938. He would be the last of the many Hoovers who had lived on Seward Square. When he left, the neighborhood, like the world he had known in his youth, had changed, but the values of the old Seward Square itself, those of Southern, white, Christian, small-town, turn-of-the-century Washington, would stay with him the rest of his life.

The vital statistics of the Hoover family were recorded by Edgar in a small notebook during the summer of 1912; he was seventeen years old and about to enter his senior year at Central High School. "On November 21, 1857," he began, "my father Dickerson N. Hoover was born at No. [blank] 6th St. N.W. On Sept 12, 1861 my mother Annie M. Scheitlin was born at Wash. D.C. On Sept 17, 1879, Dickerson N. Hoover married Annie M. Scheitlin at 8.00 in the Presbyterian Church at B and 4 S.E. The day was cool & the night beautiful. Dr. Chester officiated. The church was packed to the doors & steps in fact it was the largest wedding Capitol Hill ever had. My father was 22 and my mother was 19."[3]

Edgar's father, Dickerson Naylor Hoover, grew up in Northwest Washington, about three miles from Seward Square, near the old Central High at Seventh and "O" street N.W. that Edgar would later attend. Dickerson's father, Edgar's grandfather, John Thomas Hoover, worked at the printshop of the United States Coast and Geodetic Survey, where Dickerson himself would earn his living as a platemaker, eventually becoming chief of the printshop. Family tradition held that John Thomas Hoover's father, Edgar's great-grandfather, had worked as a mason constructing the Capitol. Dickerson's mother, J. Edgar's grandmother, continued to live in the Central High neighborhood with her younger son, Halstead Hoover. Halstead, like Edgar, was an unmarried younger son who lived with his widowed mother until her death.[4]

Annie Margaret Scheitlin, Edgar's mother, grew up in Seward Square, where her family had been established since well before the Civil War. Her grandmother and grandfather, John and Anna Hitz, had emigrated from Switzerland around 1820. John Hitz was a mining engineer who had worked in the copper areas of Lake Superior and in the gold mines of North Carolina. In 1853, Hitz, who had settled in Washington, became the Swiss consul (at that time the ranking Swiss diplomatic post in the country). Among his three children were Edgar's grandmother, Mrs. Margaret Scheitlin, and great-uncle, also named John Hitz, who succeeded his father as Swiss consul in 1864, at which time the post was upgraded to the rank of consul general. (Hitz and his father probably maintained dual U.S.-Swiss citizenship.) During Edgar's boyhood, his grandmother Scheitlin lived across the square, and she and his great-uncle were frequent Sunday visitors at the Hoover household. The family often spent Sunday evenings seated around the parlor table, with the white-bearded Swiss consul general leading the Bible reading. Through the Scheitlin side of the family, Edgar was a cousin of District of Columbia Judge William Hitz and distantly related to U.S. Supreme Court Justice Harold Burton.[5]

After their marriage, Annie and Dickerson Hoover moved to a house on Capitol Hill's Sixth Street S.E., near the home of Annie's mother. It was there, according to the young Edgar's notebook, that "On Sept 9, 1880 at 2.30 A.M. on Thursday morning Dickerson N. Hoover, Jr. was born to my father Dickerson N. and my mother Annie M. Hoover. The day was pleasant. The doctor was McKim. He was born at No. [blank] 6th St. S.E."[6] This was Edgar's brother Dick, fifteen years his senior, and in many personal and professional ways the model for his younger brother.

"On Sunday Nov 12, 1882 at 10.00 A.M.," the notebook continued, "my sister Lillian Humphrey Hoover was born to my mother & father. It was a pretty day. The doctor was McKim. She was born at 414 Seward Sq. S.E. at her grandmother's [Margaret Scheitlin's] home," where Hoover's parents had moved before they bought the house directly across the park. Eight years later, after the family had finally moved to its permanent home at 413 Seward Square, another child joined the ten-year-old Dickerson Jr. and the eight-year-old Lillian.

"On Sunday June 2, 1890 Sadie Margeruite [*sic;* actually "Marguerite"] was born to my father & mother at 3.00 P.M. The day was hot and clear. The doctor was Mallan. She was born at 413 Seward Sq. S.E. Wash, D.C."

Three years later, when Dickerson Sr. and Annie were thirty-six and thirty-two, and Dick and Lillian thirteen and eleven, the Hoovers lost three-year-old Sadie. "On Aug 2, 1893 Sadie Marguerite died from Diphtheria at Atlantic City N.J. She is buried in Congressional Graveyard, Wash. D.C." Sadie's grave became a Hoover family shrine, and Edgar's letters and diary mention trips to the graveyard to cut the grass at the cemetery plot.

Less than a year and a half after Sadie's death, and, therefore, conceived just eight months after the tragedy, J. Edgar Hoover was born. Edgar's notebook entry:

> On Sunday January 1, 1895 at 7:30 A.M. J. Edgar Hoover was born to my father and mother the day was cold & snowy but clear. The Doctor was Mallan. I was born at 413 Seward Sq. S.E. Wash. D.C. I entered Brent School in First Grade at 6 yr in Sept 1901 and graduated from Brent at the age of 14 in June 1909. Never kept back once. Had a clean character & high standing in every grade. With the exception of the 7th grade I went to Brent every year. In the 7th I went to Wallack. Transferred from 8th Grade to Central High School. My best Graded [*sic*] teachers were Miss Dalton, 8th Gr. a fine lady who raised me morally; Miss Snowden, 7th Gr., who raised me intellectly [*sic*]; Miss Hinkle, 4th Gr., who raised me in discipline & intellect. I passed 5th highest in the first year high with an average of 93 8/10. I passed 3rd highest in the second year with an average of 96%. I passed first in the 3rd year with an average of 95.8%.

Edgar was the adored and achieving son of doting parents who may never have escaped their feelings of guilt over the summer vacation that had exposed their daughter, the child Edgar replaced, to diphtheria. He was the cherished brother of an older sister and brother who may also have been traumatized by the death of three-year-old Sadie. The future director of the FBI was the pet of the Hoover household, protected by its care and love.

The year Edgar was born, Washington had a population of a quarter-million people and was growing at a rate of 5,000 a year. The half of Capitol Hill that lay north of East Capitol Street was being filled with newly constructed homes, but below East Capitol, the southeast

Washington of Hoover's Seward Square, the neighborhoods had been settled for decades. With its trees and plantings, the area had a prosperous and stable appearance. The public schools and Protestant churches that served the community were well established, and, since 1890, the district had had its own high school, Eastern High, located in Hoover's day a block from Seward Square at Pennsylvania and Seventh S.E.

On his mother's side, Edgar's family may have been more distinguished than most of the lower-level civil servants of the neighborhood. Judging by the Hoovers' home, however, they would not have been among the more affluent. Most Seward Square houses were brick- or stone-faced three-story buildings, but the Hoover family home, like the one Dickerson Jr. would purchase next door, was a modest two-story frame house faced with whitewashed stucco and black trim and shutters. Perched on a high bank above the square, and approached from the street by a flight of seven stone stairs, the house had a one-story front porch with scrollwork brackets. The porch's northern exposure made it ideal for hot Washington afternoons. The sunny, south-facing backyard was filled with Annie Hoover's roses and wisteria. The house had three bedrooms upstairs, and while his sister and brother still lived at home, Edgar slept downstairs in the rear parlor. Like most white housewives in Washington, Annie Hoover had a black maid who came each day to help with meals and cleaning.

Though entirely respectable, the Hoovers' Capitol Hill neighborhood would not have been considered particularly prestigious or wealthy. Seward Square was a microcosm of white, Protestant, middle-class America. There were within its borders few rich and no poor; except for the servants who came each day to do the cooking and cleaning, it was all white. The only religious differences were friendly rivalries among the Lutherans, Presbyterians, and Methodists. A child of Seward Square would have grown up knowing no one who was, in any essential respect, different from himself. The city's more solidly established middle-class families, with several generations separating them from manual labor, would have lived in Washington's northwest, where the wealthy families of Washington's "society" congregated. The black third of the city's population lived in the city's southwest and remote northeast ghettos, or in the nearly invisible "alleys" in the center of white blocks, pockets of poverty scattered throughout the affluent capital city.

Washington was a Southern town where immigrants were scarce and self-abasing, and so the self-assertion of the white Protestant middle class showed itself most clearly in the growing respectability, even conventionality, of racism. The 1890s saw blacks disenfranchised and segregated throughout the South by Jim Crow legislation. It was only a short time before blacks in Washington felt the new wave of persecution and humiliation that was sweeping north. Between 1900 and 1920, from Hoover's fifth to twenty-fifth years, the District systematically institutionalized Jim Crow. By the end of Wilson's administration, the only public accommodations that were not segregated were the trolleys and buses, the public libraries, and the grandstands at Griffith Stadium.[7]

The model for the grandiose civic improvements whose construction fascinated young Hoover during the first decade of the century was the "White City," architect Daniel Burnham's lath–and–plaster neoclassical fantasy at the 1893 Columbian Exposition in Chicago.[8] Washington, in its distribution of power and its exclusion of blacks from the conveniences and amenities of the community, was being turned into another kind of white city in a racial sense as well.

One area in which blacks had always been segregated was the public schools, but now the prejudice expanded to the churches. The few blacks in white churches were made to feel unwelcome, and were banned from white religious conventions and meetings. Black women were asked to leave the Women's Christian Temperance Union and many other philanthropic groups. Segregated washrooms and lockers ("Jim Crow corners") were established for the first time in government offices in 1904. Each year there was more pressure for antimiscegenation laws, Jim Crow cars on the streetcars, and a legal code of residential segregation. In every area of Washington life where blacks had once associated with whites—restaurants, barbershops, theaters, charitable and social organizations—they were now excluded and confined to their own inferior preserves. By 1920, Washington's blacks had come to occupy what historian Constance McLaughlin Green called "The Secret City."[9]

During his infancy, Edgar was largely in the care of his older sister and brother. Dick recalled, "I must have wheeled Edgar a thousand miles around Capitol Hill in one of those old-fashioned, high-wheeled baby buggies that mother bought for him. . . . It was my daily chore to take Edgar out for an airing. I'd tuck his bottle under the pillows of the baby carriage and sometimes we would be gone for hours."[10]

At the turn of the century, the only major public buildings on Capitol Hill were the Capitol itself and the magnificent original facility of the Library of Congress. In 1902, after the publication of a new municipal plan, Washington began a colossal effort to beautify the city, and much of Edgar's childhood was spent exploring it, first by carriage and then on foot and bicycle (in the beginning of the twentieth century, Washington, changing from a hodgepodge of encroachments on L'Enfant's plan into a monumental sequence of public spaces, held no threats to discourage a parent from giving a child the freedom of the city). During the first decade of the century, the Senate and House office buildings were being constructed on each side of the Capitol a few steps from Seward Square. A few blocks farther from Hoover's home, the new Union Station was being built to allow the removal of the train tracks and depots that disfigured the mall. Even more interesting to a growing boy and his dog was the reclamation of Rock Creek Park across town, with its ravines and caves and secret paths. A picture of Edgar around this time shows a husky and rugged boy in sturdy knickers, his bicycle by his side, looking somewhat annoyed at having to pose for the camera. His broad features and stocky body forecast his later appearance, though during his teens and twenties, when he was carving out a place for himself first at Central High and then in the Justice Department, he was sword-slim, with pinched, intense features and piercing intense eyes.[11]

The members of the Hoover family were seldom apart during Edgar's youth. Dick, who lived at home until he married in 1907 at the age of twenty-seven, bought the house next door, where his first daughter was born in 1908. Lillian also lived at home until she married, in 1908, at the age of twenty-five, and then she moved a few blocks away to Tenth Street N.E. near Constitution. Like many close families, the Hoovers tended to cluster within the family circle. It was emotionally difficult for any of them to be apart from the others. This was particularly true for Edgar's father, whose letters when away on business were filled with longing for his wife and youngest son.

In 1904, when Edgar was nine and his father fifty-three, Dickerson Sr. had to travel on business to St. Louis. "My dear Edgar," he wrote,

> I know you would like to hear from Papa, so this morning I will write you a short letter. This is a big city and it is full of people, some parts are very pretty but I don't think you or mama would like it. Everybody is in a rush, but as yet I have not seen any bad people and the police is as scarce as they can be. The Mississippi River is very high and the water is like clay. The drinking water here has to be filtered when it

comes out of the spigot it is very dark. Take good care of Mama and when I come home I will bring you something nice. I must now close as I am got to go out to the Fair grounds its about 4 miles from where I am stopping. Love to all with a kiss for yourself. I have a big favor to ask you it is give Mama a hug and a long sweet kiss. Good Bye, Papa.[12]

A short time later, Annie Hoover took Edgar to St. Louis to visit his father, who had to remain there for a while, and the three of them visited the 1904 St. Louis Fair. When Edgar and his mother returned to Washington, Dickerson Sr. was heartbroken. "Dear old man," he wrote Edgar,

I received your two letters and they were fine. I am so glad to hear that you are much better. Take good care of yourself and don't study too hard. It is cold here and if you was here that big overcoat would just be right to keep you warm. I sleep in your little bed and I wish you were here so that I could fight you in the morning. Mama might think you aint strong but just let her try to fight you and she will find out. I have not seen any of the fair since you and Dear Mama left when I do go around and I see anything I will get it for you. Take good care of Mama. I must now say good night. Be a good boy. With a good big kiss. From Papa.[13]

Annie's letters to Edgar were affectionate but did not show as much emotional vulnerability as her husband's. While on a trip to New York and Boston, probably in October 1906 when Edgar was eleven, Annie wrote a letter to her "Dear little Edgar":

While Mama is writing you this little letter, the Steam Cars are flying past my window, the elevated road passes right by the window, the street cars in front of the door—New York is a very busy place. Yesterday afternoon we took a ride on the sight seeing Automobile all through Central Park, along River side Park and Fifth Avenue, such beautiful houses, it seemed like Fairy Land to see such beautiful places, hope some day when you are older you may be able to see all the wonderful sights in New York.

Annie Hoover was the family disciplinarian who encouraged Edgar with rewards and punishments. The same letter continued with: "Was so glad to hear you were perfect in your spelling and Arithmetic. Study hard both your lessons and your music and try and be a very good boy for Mama wants you to have the trip to Baltimore." She was also the more practical of Hoover's parents: "Take good care of yourself and if you feel badly take some number 10 and if you should have a cold some number 7. Am very glad you are using our room. Take care of everything nicely and don't run the streets. With love and kisses. Yours lovingly Mama."[14]

Annie's interests centered around her family and neighborhood gossip. Servants found her a strict mistress. A letter to Edgar in 1912 describes an altercation with the cook: "And what do you think of Bell this morning she came in and as soon as I came into the kitchen you should have heard her impudence. I waited until she got through and then I told her after she was through with her work she could quit us. I was not paying her for her insolence which surprised her very much and seemed to knock the wind out of her, so when you come home we'll have some one else. I think she has been with us a little too long."[15]

Church membership was an important avenue of social advancement in Washington at the turn of the century. Ambitious young men could signal their commitment to respectability by joining a church. They could also advance themselves socially by seeking leadership positions within the congregation, and then move still higher in social circles by strategically transferring their membership to a still more respectable church when nothing more could be gained from the one left behind. The goal was to arrive at the most socially exclusive church possible, but not so exclusive that one risked rejection by climbing too high. This sort of church politics could also produce a socially advantageous marriage. (For Dick, at least, this was what happened. He met his wife by becoming a prominent member of the Church of the Reformation.)

Edgar's parents were not regular church members (when they did attend, they went to the Metropolitan Presbyterian Church, now the Capitol Hill Presbyterian Church, at Fourth and Independence, one block across Seward Square from the Hoover home).[16] It is quite possible that a blue-collar worker such as Dickerson Sr. might have felt uncomfortable attending churches as genteel and aggressively respectable as Capitol Hill's.

Edgar was very close to his older brother throughout his childhood. Dick often accompanied Edgar on his long walks as he followed the progress of the construction on the Hill and along the Mall where the National Galleries were going up; they also liked to hike along the C&O canal.[17] Dick was a hero and model for his younger brother, and during his youth, Edgar followed closely in his brother's footsteps.

Dick's most important influence on Edgar was to introduce him to the church organizations that absorbed much of his interest during his adolescence. Dick was active in a large number of church organizations and as a young man hoped to become a minister. Edgar joined his brother's Sunday school, attended the lectures his brother regularly gave to church organizations around the city, and may have helped his brother with the missions he ran in the District jail and along the city's waterfront.[18]

The first churches Edgar attended were two neighborhood Presbyterian churches, Eastern Presbyterian at Maryland and Sixth Northeast, and the Metropolitan Presbyterian. These two congregations later merged to form the Capitol Hill Presbyterian Church which now meets in the old Metropolitan Church. The old Eastern Presbyterian church building now houses a black congregation. During his first few years of elementary school Hoover probably attended Eastern's Sunday school, where he received a copy of the New Testament for memorizing Bible texts.[19]

While Edgar was in elementary school, Dick joined the Lutheran Church of the Reformation, which then stood on the site of what is now the Library of Congress Annex between Second and Third Streets at Independence. Edgar followed his brother to the Church of the Reformation, and became the secretary of his Sunday school class in 1907 while Dick was serving as superintendent of the Sunday school. Both brothers were still members of this Lutheran church in September 1907 when the church's minister, John Wiedly, presided over Dick's wedding at his fiancée's home at Quincy Place, Northeast Washington. On Sunday, December 27, 1907, this same Doctor Wiedly baptized Edgar into the Lutheran faith at Dick's house at 411 Seward Square.[20]

In 1908, Dick had his first child, Margaret. Edgar had charge of his young niece and wheeled her around the Capitol in her buggy as his brother had once done for him. Edgar was a hero to young Margaret, just as Dick had been for him. When Margaret was four and Edgar was away visiting relatives in Wytheville (in western Virginia), Annie Hoover wrote him that "Margaret is sitting here while I am writing she says she is writing but I think it would take a Chinese to make it out." A few days later, "If I sent you all the letters Margaret writes I think you would receive one about every hour in the day for she is always writing to Uncle Edgar," and again, "Margaret is counting the days for Uncle Edgar to come home." As a teenager, Margaret would accompany her uncle on streetcar rides across the city to ice-cream parlors, and later, during the twenties, he advised her not to give her right name if she were caught in a speakeasy raid.[21]

Early in 1909, when he was fourteen years old, Edgar resigned as secretary of his Sunday school class, presumably still at Reformation Church, and was then elected corresponding secretary of the entire Sunday school—at his age probably the highest position for which he was eligible. About this time the Hoover brothers may have begun to feel a neighborhood church had little more to offer rising young men like themselves. Dick was beginning to receive promotions within the Steamboat Inspection Service and Edgar had begun to set his sights on attending the more prestigious Central High instead of his own neighborhood's Eastern High. The two brothers began to explore other churches and denominations.[22]

On February 14, 1909, Edgar went to a meeting of Christian Endeavor, a Congregationalist youth organization, and the next day he went to hear Dick give a speech at the Church of the Redeemer. On February 16, Edgar attended a Mission conference at St. Paul's Church, possibly also with Dick. Edgar's diary shows that he continued to attend Sunday school for the rest of 1909, probably at the Church of the Reformation, but by the end of the year he and Dick seem to have made up their minds to change affiliations. Dick transferred from the Lutheran Church of the Reformation to the Old First Presbyterian Church, which was located at John Marshall Place near Judiciary Square at the foot of Capitol Hill in northwest Washington, about an eight-block walk or streetcar ride from Seward Square. On January 9, 1910, he was installed as an elder of this Church. Again Edgar followed his brother's lead, and on September 11, 1910, he recorded in his diary, "I joined the Presbyterian Church & took my first communion from Dr. D. O. M[a]cLeod." It is possible that Dick and Edgar were introduced to Old First by their sister Lillian, whose marriage had been performed by Old First's minister on June 20, 1908. Further evidence of her membership in Old First was her daughter's baptism by MacLeod on June 23, 1910.[23]

In transferring to Old First, the Hoover brothers were moving from a church that had no particular social standing to one that represented the highest level of Capitol Hill's middle-class respectability. Old First was perhaps Washington's most historic church, one of the most famous Presbyterian congregations in the country. Before it acquired its own church building, it held its services in the old Supreme Court chambers in the Capitol, and the congregation had often included presidents, Supreme Court justices, and congressmen.[24] As

money and society shifted farther northwest early in the nineteenth
century, Old First was left with its upper-class reputation but a middle-
class congregation.

Hoover maintained his membership in the Old First and its successor institution, the National Presbyterian Center, for the rest of his
life. He regularly claimed that this church, and the ministers who
served there, had been important influences during his youth, particularly Dr. Donald Campbell MacLeod, pastor of Old First from 1899
to 1913 and, to a lesser extent, John Brittan Clark, who succeeded
MacLeod as pastor of Old First from 1913 to 1926.[25]

MacLeod turned Old First into an "institutional" church with
offerings designed to attract and involve every segment of the congregation. He seems to have been especially successful with activities designed for young boys, and he became well known throughout the
city as an organizer of church-sponsored sports. On September 25,
1909, for example, the young men's class of his Sunday school held
a city-wide Sunday school track meet, with a trophy presented to
the winning team by the *Washington Star*.[26] Edgar was especially
impressed by the baseball teams MacLeod organized and sponsored
for neighborhood youths in the city-wide Sunday school summer baseball leagues, which were the principal vacation recreation for white
Washington youngsters during the first decade of the century.

While Edgar had been an ambitious and dedicated member of
the Sunday school at the Church of the Reformation, he became even
more devoted when he switched to Old First's Sunday school. His
diary mentions teachers' meetings at the church during the autumn
of 1910,[27] and he evidently continued to lead a Sunday school class
throughout his high school years. His friends recall that he regularly
taught his Sunday school class wearing his Central High cadet uniform,
and they considered this an unusual degree of fervor.

Edgar's duties as a Sunday school teacher involved preparing a
weekly lesson based on a Bible text assigned by the national Sunday
school organization, the American Sunday School Union. He was also
charged with preventing defections from Old First's Sunday school
and with attracting new members by maintaining a high level of morale
and enthusiasm.

It is unlikely that he could have enjoyed a high degree of success
as a Sunday school teacher if he had had any reservations about the
school's doctrine, social and political as well as religious, or if he
had any difficulty maintaining order over charges not much younger
than he. The Sunday school by Hoover's time was a venerable national

institution more than a hundred years old with a well-known institutional personality and style. Vast numbers of Americans found its philosophy powerfully attractive; others considered it preposterous. Clearly, Hoover embraced it.

The American Sunday school, like its English model, was founded for secular purposes but was soon taken over by the evangelicals for religious education. To attract and keep the children of the middle class, the Sunday school had to stress its respectability, which made the poor feel uncomfortable within its genteel confines, and emphasize its exclusion of blacks. According to a historian of the movement, "As long as the schools were largely for the children of the poor, mixing the races was no great difficulty. The introduction of an inclusiveness cutting across white class lines made the presence of black children embarrassing and troublesome." By the time Hoover became active in the Sunday schools, they represented a "level of middle-class respectability which some Americans had attained and the rest refused to admit that they could not attain." In the end, "what had begun as an exercise in charity was converted into a prep school for the whole of evangelical America."[28]

From the beginning, the Sunday school saw itself guarding and transmitting a culture under siege. Its earliest mission was to civilize and christianize the West, but the Sunday school organizers soon came to believe that the real threat to Protestantism was not the pioneer but the immigrant. The 1856 Report of the Sunday School Union stated that

> the refuse population of Europe, rolling in vast waves upon our shores, as it passes westward, deposits its dregs upon our seaboard. These congregate in our great cities and send forth their children—a wretched progeny, degraded in the deep degradation of their parents—to be the scavengers, physical and moral, of our streets. Mingled with these are also the offcast children of American debauchery, drunkenness, and vice. A class more dangerous to the community . . . can hardly be imagined. And how are they to be reached? The public school and the church are . . . of no avail.[29]

As nineteenth-century American society grew more complex, many conservatives, among them the leaders of the Sunday school movement, tended to romanticize the America of the past as a lost Eden, peaceful and law-abiding, a land where class hatred and industrial conflict were unknown. The snake in this garden was the immigrant. Although seldom physically present in the Sunday school, his very absence played an important role in developing the Sunday school consciousness. His presence in the outside world explained why *that* America did not resemble the serene and secure society that assembled every week to be inspired to storm out of the church basement to make America over in the image of the Sunday school.

The organizers of the Sunday school, with their "dread of disorder and chaos," came to see their institution as a stronghold against disruptive tendencies in society, as a weapon to be used against the lawless classes. The Sunday school also paid special attention to fortifying teenagers against sexual temptation, which meant, in the minds of many, protecting Anglo-Saxon Protestant youths from the sexually lax example of young immigrants. Among the groups founded for this purpose were Christian Endeavor, founded in 1881 by a Congregational minister in Portland, Maine, and the Epworth League, a Methodist youth group. Another was the Knights of the Holy Grail, whose motto was "Confession, Chastity, Charity." The International Sunday School Convention established a Department of Purity in 1911 to promote what it called, in a phrase perhaps unconsciously connected to feelings about the morals of those darker in complexion than the average Protestant, the "white life," its euphemism for virginity.[30]

By the turn of the century, the Sunday school, with its strong strain of nativism and conservatism, had become an expected part of the Hoovers' middle-class America. Henry Seidel Canby, editor of the *Saturday Review,* recalled the Sunday school of his boyhood: "With clean collar and cuffs and a Sunday suit, one put on decorum and in the calm of the quiet neighborhood the mind relaxed, and when the bells began, the slow march of so many church-goers ranged by families, and dressed for a rite, stirred in the consciousness a sense of immemorial . . . custom."[31]

Edgar and Dick Hoover were not born into the Sunday school; they were, so to speak, converts. For them, Sunday school was not simply an automatic ritual; it was an opportunity to identify themselves with the progressive Protestant drive to impose order on a changing America. The Sunday school plunged Hoover into what some saw as the spirit of the age: "the struggle to organize national life in new patterns . . . the search for a viable collective identity ran all through the era's dynamic growth." He was associating there with men for whom organization "was not just a necessity; it was also the major creative act of life."[32]

The organizational skills and enthusiasm for bureaucratic routine that marked Hoover's later career were also essential to the success of the Sunday school leader. The turn-of-the-century Sunday school borrowed all the methods characteristic of the salesmanship and boosterism of the time. A history of the Sunday school movement notes that for the Protestant churches,

> a loyal Sunday school army was a popular way of maintaining attendance and discipline: "On Time Every Time, A Learned Lesson Every Time, and An Offering for Christ Every Time." An "On Timer's Tribe" had a "pledge to bind and a pin to remind." Local schools had rally days, decision days, children's days, concerts and picnics. National organizations abounded for each age group with headquarters, mottos and special songs.

At the Old First, competition to win prizes by bringing in new members was so spirited that arguments would develop over who should get credit for a recruit when he had been "worked over" by several of his friends.[33]

The leaders of the national Sunday school movement were fascinated by organization per se. One organizer admired "how Tammany divided New York City into districts, each with reliable contacts, so that any 'voter that has to be interviewed' could be reached without fail in twenty-four hours." The Sunday school tried to imitate this technique. The movement claimed that the national head of the Sunday School Convention, like a great detective in charge of a nationwide agency, "could put upon the track of a sinner anywhere in this broad land a Christian worker to speak to him of Christ."[34]

Edgar would have spent his sessions as a Sunday school teacher leading his class in song and drilling his students in biblical memory. (He himself sang in Old First's choir as a boy soprano until his voice changed.) Singing was the best-known and probably the most popular Sunday school activity. The movement produced such famous hymns as "The Bible tells me so," "Shall We Gather at the River," "Hear the Tramp, Tramp, Tramp of the Sunday School Brigade," and "I Am a Little Soldier."[35] One song Hoover would have heard rallied Sunday school children against crime: "Tell him to halt! tell him to halt!/Whatever may be his fault."[36]

The course of Bible study at Hoover's Sunday school stressed memorization and followed a standard curriculum supplied by the national Sunday school organization. The lesson plans chose passages for study based on their supposed appeal to children: Each Bible lesson was organized like a legal brief to lead the class to accept the moral lesson and render a verdict for Jesus. The technique, and the goal, would be much the same in later years when the ex-Sunday school teacher as FBI Director would use John Dillinger and Ma Barker and Harry Dexter White, instead of Cain and Abel, to illustrate his moral lessons.

In 1948, Hoover described the Sunday school as a "crime prevention laboratory."[37] America imagined he meant only the Sunday school's weekly dose of moral maxims, but to him the Sunday school meant much more than that. It mirrored and reinforced an almost-forgotten way of life; it had been a crusade, Hoover's first, to defend traditional America against the outsiders whose real crime was the terror they inspired in the America of Hoover's youth, the America of Seward Square.

In 1906, Dick was twenty-six years old and at an important stage both in his career with the Steamship Inspection Service and in his personal life (he would get married the next year). Nevertheless, he managed to find time to help his eleven-year-old brother put together a neighborhood newspaper. This was a two-page bulletin Edgar called the "Weekly Review, Editor, J. E. Hoover." It sold for a price of one cent to family and neighbors. Dick is listed as the paper's "typewriter," so he must have had the job of typing his brother's collection of jokes, neighborhood gossip, and bogus advertisements. Edgar also listed himself as the "printer." Since the paper was duplicated using the letterpress process that was the standard method for copying documents in government offices at the time, Dick probably let Edgar come to his office at the Steamboat Inspection Service to run it off.[38]

"The Weekly Review" was the world seen through the eyes of the eleven-year-old J. Edgar Hoover, a world that revolved around his family.

Mr. D. N. Hoover, of 413 Seward Square, S.E., will leave on Sunday at 3:33 on some business for the government.

Wanted. A servant at No. 413 Seward Square [apparently Annie Hoover had had another falling out with a cook].

Escaped from death. On Friday, about 12:15 o'clock, Mrs. Hoover, of 413 Seward Square, S.E. came near losing her life. She was frying some eggs for lunch, and the blaze caught to her back, but she managed to put the fire out on her arm, and someone in the kitchen put out the fire on the back.

Found. Mr. D. N. Hoover, of 413 Seward Place, S.E., found a five-dollar gold piece. It was made into a pin. It was found in Chase's Theatre [a favorite vaudeville house of the Hoovers]."

There was news about the Seward Square neighborhood:

A carriage ran into another carriage Tuesday evening about 3:30 o'clock between 4th and 5th Streets, on Pennsylvania Avenue. The man was arrested and paid ten dollars fine. It did seven dollars worth of damage.

An accident happened on the Capital Traction Railway, about 3:00 o'clock Tuesday, between 4th and 5th Streets, S.E. A cartridge was placed on the car track by some boys. It got caught in the slot and broke the plow, so that the car could not run. It caused a great deal of excitement.

Society. A reception was held at Mrs. Griffith's. It was the Hot Air Club that met. They had a very good time.

A regular feature was a series of health tips from "The Brent School Health Club":

The Rules of the Good Health Club of the Brent School. Eat slowly. Don't eat adulterated food. Don't eat too much. Don't eat between meals. Clean your teeth.

Nearly every issue had an article about a historic figure:

Franklin's Life in Brief. Franklin invented the lightning rod to protect houses. He started the first military company, started the first fire engine company, discovered that lightning and electricity were the same, and started the first college, which is now the University of Pennsylvania. Franklin's two-hundredth anniversary was celebrated on Wednesday last. At the Library there were books which he had printed, papers written by him, and the Declaration of Independence, signed by him."

Fond of moral proverbs in his later years, Hoover started quoting them early in a section of "The Weekly Review": "Proverbs: Where there is a will, there is a way. Whatever is worth doing at all is worth doing well." And, since a real paper had advertisements, Edgar included some pro bono ads: "Eat potatoes. Eat Apples. Eat Puffed Rice. Drink Swiss Dairy Milk."

The humor section was entitled "Rich and Racy Jokes": "What is the most difficult surgical operation? If you suddenly saw a home on fire, what three authors would you name? Why is a printer like a postman? (Answers next week)." And "The Hindu. Poor belated Hindu, he does the best he kin do. He follows his cast [*sic*] from first to last, and for clothes he makes his skin do." This last may have been a parody of a song Hoover would have sung in Sunday school: "I am a little Hindoo girl,/Of Jesus never heard;/Oh, pity me, dear Christian child,/Oh send to me His word."[39]

In view of his age, it is not surprising that the young Edgar focused on neighborhood news, though he did make a few exceptions, for example the engagement and marriage of Ned Longworth and Alice Roosevelt (he reprinted their marriage license verbatim). The world beyond Seward Square was filled with calamities: fires, deaths of famous personalities (Marshall Field), and, perhaps because of his brother's career, shipwrecks and nautical disasters. Seward Square was a secure enclave; the world outside was a place of danger. The most controversial neighborhood event to appear in his paper was a tale of unrest at his school: "Salaries: A teacher in the Fourth Division said that she thought the teachers needed more money."

Edgar was not just an observer and a reporter during the first decade of the century. He was active and outgoing, varied and enthusiastic in his interests. Naturally, school took up most of his time. Between 1901 and 1909, he was a student at the Brent Elementary School, the public school at Third and "D," a block down North Carolina from his home on Seward Square. Hoover attended Brent for all but one of his elementary school years; he was at the Wallack school (on the grounds of the Old Eastern High at Seventh and Pennsylvania) for the seventh grade, probably because of overcrowding at Brent, which, as now, was a common reason for transferring students.[40]

The Washington public schools in Hoover's time stressed citizenship and discipline (corporal punishment was not abolished until 1913). Dress was formal: boys wore jackets and ties, knickers in the lower grades, trousers by the eighth grade; girls wore dresses or skirts with middie blouses. Dress was so standardized that students in classroom photographs of the period appear to be in uniform. The schools were also standardized in another way: Since the system was legally segregated, only whites attended Brent.[41]

The curriculum at Brent was demanding, leading, for example, to algebra in the eighth grade; texts in literature were chosen to ensure that the children would be exposed to the American popular classics as well as a smattering of the masterpieces of European literature. Required reading included Shakespeare's *The Merchant of Venice*, a collection of Greek mythology, Defoe's *Robinson Crusoe*, Thackeray's *The Rose and the Ring*, Dickens's *Tale of Two Cities* and *Christmas Carol*, Ouida's *Stories of a Nürnberg Stove*, Hawthorne's *Wonder Book*,

Irving's *The Legend of Sleepy Hollow,* Whittier's *Snow-Bound,* and Bryant's *Thanatopsis.* The day began with a prayer, and the lessons included Bible study.[42]

The curriculum was thoroughly conservative. It was the farthest thing from anyone's mind that a child should be taught to question received ideas or values. The school tried to initiate the student into citizenship by acquainting him with the traditional legends, hallowed words, and scientific wonders that bolstered Western civilization's claim to world leadership. The successful student was one who mastered the circumscribed, coherent system of ideas and values and learned to exhibit this mastery in his work.[43]

When the day's classes were over, Edgar was free to play by himself or participate in organized after-school activities. The diary that he kept between 1908 and 1910 describes his choices: "Went to carpenter shop and I am on my picture frame with William helping me. We got one session." By the time he was fourteen he was exploring the entire city. During July 1909, the Wright brothers were at Fort Myers in Arlington attempting to set a flight endurance record. Edgar spent three days waiting to see a flight, and on July 30 he wrote: "Went to Fort Myers & Arlington. Wright flew to Alexandria & back in 14.2 mi. I [was the] first outsider to shake Orville's hand." And, of course, he continued to monitor the many construction sites around the city, noting in his diary a "walk to the New Union. All tracks used but the West End was not open. No pavement laid and 4 blocks to the cars." Another entry reported that the "House building [was] nearly finished"[44]

His chores around the house included working on his mother's garden and helping her preserve the garden produce. He was fond of recording changes in the weather, sometimes using Southern figures of speech: instead of snow "falling" for Edgar, it was "laying." On February 2, 1908, he wrote "Ground Frog sees shadow. Ground Frog day."[45]

He earned the childhood nickname of "Speed" carrying groceries from the neighborhood market: "I started earning money," he later recalled, "when I was twelve years old by carrying groceries. In those days markets did not hire delivery boys, but I discovered that if one stood outside a store, a customer laden with purchases would happily accept a helping hand and gratefully tip anyone who aided with a heavy load. The first such commission I got was to carry two baskets two miles for which I received a tip of ten cents. I realized that the quicker I could complete each chore, the more money I could earn, so I spent most of my time running. Because I ran back to the market and was outside the Eastern Market every day after school and from 7 A.M. to 7 P.M. each Saturday, I could earn as much as two dollars a day. In those days that was a king's ransom."[46]

His diary has the names of many friends, boys and girls. There were informal visits and formal "calls" in the style of the last century. On Valentine's Day he passed out cards to family and friends.[47]

As he grew older, Edgar began to take more interest in the news, specifically news of crime and disasters: "Estimated report of loss of life in Sicily 200,000 and loss of property $1,000,000,000. Miss Dalton [his 8th-grade teacher] prophecied that there would be an earthquake in the eastern part of Asia & bordering islands at 11.16 today." He noted that she had been wrong: "The time is over a year." (About this time he also read *The Last Days of Pompeii.*) More disasters: "Man killed in the senate building." "Dr. Aippen murderer of Belle Elmore caught about S.S. Montrose by Inspector Dew of Scotland Yard." His developing interest in crime and the law must have been noticed by his family, because they took to mentioning notable cases in their letters. His mother wrote that "the trial of the Allens must have been very interesting. I see by the papers they have caught the last of them in Des Moines. I guess they are not quite as bad as the papers painted them."[48]

He read the popular books of the day, and mentioned several of them in his diary: "Spent day in literary pursuits." "Read Magazines." "Read a little of the *Gospel of Judas Iscariot* (Great book)." "Rested in the morning & read *Circular Staircase* in the afternoon."[49]

Edgar and his parents loved vaudeville, as did President Wilson, who visited Poli's each week. (During the twenties, Hoover became friends with vaudeville performers such as Harry Richman, and during the thirties he enjoyed meeting such show business personalities as Billy Rose.) Edgar's diary often mentions going to Chase's or Poli's theaters. In the summer, when he was away from home, his parents, knowing of his interest, would mention in their letters the new vaudeville shows they'd seen. In 1912, Hoover's father wrote him that "we did not go to Chase's New this week. We went to Poli's 'Checkers' it was very good. Many of the old Thursday night patrons was there and while it was hot the house was crowded and we did not mind the heat. They are doing a good business and I understand that there is over 1200 requests for reservations which they cannot fill." On another occasion, his mother wrote, "Louis Haines has left the Poli Players no one seems to know why the paper merely said he could not learn quickly, am so sorry for we all liked him and last week he was fine."[50]

When in Washington during the summer months, Edgar rode his bicycle to swim at the Tidal Basin: "Took a bicycle ride to the bathing beach in afternoon." But the family also left town during the hot months. In 1910, for example, they visited Cape May: "Arrived at Cape May 6.05 P.M. . . . Went in bathing at 10.30 A.M. Went for a car-ride to Cape May Point & landing. Went to band Concert at 8.00." "Went in bathing at 11:30 A.M. Went to Sewell's Pt & Went to 8.00 P.M. Concert." "Went to Sewell's Point with Mr. Dallas & watched the fishing. Walk to Cape May Hotel & back in the evening with Miss Turiman [?]." "Rode to Cape May Point in the evening with Mom & Pop." "Saw the moon rise out of the water." "Left Cape May at 2.30 and arrived home at 8.05. Had a fine trip."[51]

The young J. Edgar Hoover was aware, alert, convinced of the importance and interest of whatever he saw and did. Protected by concerned, doting parents, brother, and sister, he gained confidence in his own thoughts and abilities at an early age; he took it for granted that his ideas and observations were just as interesting to others as they were to him. He focused on the objective facts of situations, not his emotional reactions. There is a meticulous, exacting quality to his jottings and a sense of concern about the opinions of others.

Because of his dependence on family rather than friends, and because he spent so much time in the company of his elders, he began to act like an adult while he was still a child. Edgar learned early to keep his emotions under restraint even though his family had strong affections for one another. His parents' and brother's care and attention gave him self-confidence and a sense of initiative, but perhaps also an anxiety that he had to live up to their exalted expectations—and his own.

The public schools, like the churches, were sacred institutions for Washington's respectable middle class. Edgar's decision to leave Seward Square in 1909 to go to Central, three miles away, instead of Eastern High, just a block away, where Dick and Lillian had studied, was a deliberate effort to seek out the best opportunities the city had to offer. Central High was the oldest, most prestigious, and best known of the city's public schools. Graduation from there represented a significant achievement in Washington's white middle-class community.

Edgar was not the first Hoover to attend Central. His father's younger brother, Halstead Peirce Hoover, was the head of Central's music department and had been a member of Central's class of 1889. Halstead Hoover still lived near the school with Edgar's grandmother, and while attending Central Edgar would often eat lunch at their house.[52]

At Central, Edgar was one of those young men who seemed to know just what he wanted, and how to get it. He apparently took his academic excellence as a matter of course and regarded it as of no great consequence—he easily compiled an outstanding academic record that earned him election as class valedictorian. Instead, he poured his energy into winning recognition as a student leader. He surveyed the ways to attain that goal at Central by rejecting those activities for which he was unsuited by talent or interest and applying himself with single-mindedness of purpose to those in which he could excel.

Central High was ideally suited to Edgar's ambitions. Founded in 1882, it had been the first white school in the city, and until the branches at Eastern, Western, Business, and Technical were established, it had been known simply as Washington High School. During Hoover's years, 1909 to 1913, the school was located in its original building at Seventh and "O" N.W. Three years after Hoover graduated, the school moved to a fine residential neighborhood at Thirteenth and Clifton Street N.W.—a few blocks from Howard University— where Central filled an entire city block with its academic facilities and playing fields, by far the best in the city.

Washington's public schools were at a high level of academic excellence during Hoover's years. A strong superintendent had provided outstanding leadership and the District administration allocated a budget that allowed the principals to recruit excellent teachers. In fact, the reputation of Washington's public schools, the high schools in particular, was so good, many students from surrounding Virginia and Maryland attended them in preference to their own. From 1902 to 1920, which included the years Hoover was a student there, Central was led by Emory M. Wilson, a principal regarded by the alumni as the finest in the school's history.[53] Wilson assembled an outstanding faculty and he challenged the students (there were 1,060 the year Hoover entered) with a demanding curriculum supplemented by a regular schedule of assembly speakers from official Washington.

School spirit and pride were very high in the Washington area. Students had great enthusiasm for athletics and extracurriculars. They struggled for leadership of the teams and clubs that represented the school in interscholastic competition, and success was rewarded with a heady tribute of praise. A victorious team could count on a school assembly to celebrate the event, featuring a chorus of "Praise God

From Whom All Blessings Flow."[54] Washington regarded Central High's students as the city's young elite, and so achieving distinction there was a prize worth striving for.

As has been said of English public schools, the experiences of many of Central High's students were so intense that it seemed as if nothing in their later lives could ever be as important. One principal said Central was even better than an English public school. "A comparison with Eton or Harrow with respect to distinguished graduates may be permissible," he wrote in 1941, "with the exception . . . that admission to this school is not dependent on rank, wealth, or social position. All may enter and each has an equal opportunity for distinction here and in later life activities." The valedictorian of the class of 1912 (the year before Hoover graduated), told his fiftieth reunion that Central "had all the enthusiasm of a private school. I mean anyone could go there, but out of it came many distinguished citizens—doctors, lawyers, diplomats. Here was a public high school. But it had status. It had a personality, and it had a spirit."[55]

But not quite everybody could go to Central. It was, of course, a segregated school, and the exclusion of blacks seems to have been the principal factor in making Central High's students feel as if they were an elite. Scattered through Central's publications were hints of the school's race consciousness.[56]

The tradition of racial exclusivity and its role in maintaining the pride of Central High were still evident when the school closed in 1950. The Washington school board had imposed tuition on non-District residents attending their schools, and the result was an immediate decline in the number of white students, many of whom had commuted from Maryland and Virginia. The drop in Central's enrollment was so great that the school board decided to turn the facilities over to the colored branch of the still-segregated school system. As soon as the board had acted, and all appeals were rejected, the outraged graduates went on a rampage. They effaced the "Central High" inscription over the door, tore out the cornerstone, ripped the brass seal from the entrance, removed the ornamental trophy cases with their trophies and banners, and purloined the school archives.[57]

Central High was an important symbol of the fact (or illusion) that a white skin was the only passport needed for admission into the privileged ranks of Washington's elite (and, by extension, into the national elite as well). Like the churches and the government bureaucracy, Central High was one of the white middle class's weapons in its drive to cultural, social, economic, and political power. At the

turn of the century it was a palpable expression and vehicle of Seward
Square's sense of moral and racial caste. That, in turn, was sustained
largely by the exclusion of blacks.

Young Edgar thrived at Central. He regularly chose the most challenging electives—Latin, French, four years of mathematics, and phys-
ics. History was his favorite subject, and classmates recall that he
often spent his free periods auditing classes whose topics interested
him.[58]

At Central, however, recognition was based not so much on academic performance as on extracurricular activities, particularly athletics. Edgar's diary shows that he joined the athletic association soon
after entering Central.[59] He tried out for the football team but was
rejected because of his size. Sturdy and stocky as a young boy, Hoover
had grown to nearly his full height of five feet ten inches by his freshman year, but he was extremely thin until his twenties, when he filled
out to 180 pounds. (In later years, his weight fluctuated around 200
pounds, well above his own standards for Bureau personnel.) Instead,
he joined the track team, training for a year under a coach whose
undefeated teams from 1898 to 1921 won four national championships
at the Penn Relays.

By the end of his freshman year, Edgar had shifted his sights
from athletics. In Hoover's day, Central High's debate teams were
the best in the city and even competed against colleges. Hoover attended debates during his freshman year, and mentions one contest
between Eastern and Central in his diary: "Score 2:1 favor Central.
Hurrah with a brecky for Old Central High." (A "brecky" was the
chorus from Aristophanes's *Frogs,* Central's school cheer, traditionally
shouted from the school's front steps.) As a sophomore he joined
the Debate Society, and spent that year participating in intramural
debates, arguing both sides of such topics as women's suffrage. During
his junior year, Edgar was on a city championship team that won
all eleven of its matches.[60] As a senior, he was the team's leading
speaker. No other high school team challenged Central, so the school
claimed its fifth consecutive city championship.

In 1913, Hoover's senior year, the team sponsored a series of intramural debates on the municipal ownership of public utilities and the
primary system of presidential nominations. In order to have some
interscholastic debate experience, Hoover's team debated Baltimore
City College on the question of presidential primaries. The school
paper printed a full account of this match:

> Now a word as to the work connected with debating. The members of
> the team had been preparing their speeches for nearly two months before

the Baltimore City College debate. Besides hours upon hours of research work spent in the Congressional Library, the debaters burned the midnight oil for many nights in composing and recomposing their speeches. During the week or ten days directly preceding the debate, none of the members of the team saw his pillow until far after the witching hour.

Defending the affirmative and taking for its battle cry "We want representation that truly represents," Central opened the debate with Mr. Hoover as the first speaker. He proved that the primary was the natural development of America by showing how the tendency of democracy in this country has rapidly and is still approaching a stage where the will of the people can be respected absolutely and directly. . . . Mr. Hoover spoke in final rebuttal for Central. Gichner's rebuttal for Baltimore was brilliant in every respect but he was unfortunate in being followed by Hoover, whose cool relentless logic overturned point after point.[61]

Afterward, Hoover offered his reflections on the benefits of debate:

Debate offers benefits in many forms. It teaches one to control his temper and free himself from sarcasm; it gives self-possession and mental control; it brings before the debater vividly the importance of clean play, for debate, like other interests, offers loopholes for slugging, but when the referee is a committee composed of three lawyers, slugging in the form of false arguments and statements proves of little use; and lastly, it gives to the high school debater a practical and beneficial example of life, which is nothing more or less than the matching of one man's wit against another; and such is debate.[62]

Edgar had already learned how to lend authority to his opinions by presenting them, not as his own beliefs, but as truths apparent to any serious and honest intelligence. His style of argument can be appreciated in a brief he wrote during his sophomore year.

Brief on Question of Abolition of Capital Punishment (Neg.)
1. The Bible stands for Capital Punishment.
2. All Christian Nations uphold it.
3. The abolition of it would be deplorable in effect on a country.
(Brief made)[63]

There is a brutal force to this argument, which is directed not to the reason but to the loyalty of the judge (in this case the debate referee). The judge must either concur in the argument or admit to a forbidden skepticism about the basic articles of faith that supported his own authority. He must agree or expose himself as disloyal. It was a form of argument that Edgar would later find extremely useful in a much broader arena.

Debate at Central allowed Hoover to explore and develop important traits of his personality. A debater has to enjoy a battle of wits for its own sake. He has to love a good fight. Since, as a matter of course, he has to argue both sides of an issue, he cannot be successful without developing the ability to distinguish between his personal convictions on an issue and the strength of the arguments he will use to support his position. Debating encourages a dispassionate appraisal of the probable persuasiveness of an argument. It teaches that the outcome depends less on belief in the essential rightness of a position than on the facts and logic brought to bear in support of it.

Hoover's debate experience helped develop the combative personality that would fortify him throughout his career. Just as important, it taught him to make a shrewd analysis of both the strengths of his case and its weaknesses. Until his last years, Hoover's characteristic coolness and calculation protected him in his many political confrontations. He often walked away from fights, despite the entreaties of superiors and subordinates, when he thought his position was vulnerable. He was usually the most skeptical and analytic person in any staff discussion, although once he went into battle, he was a committed advocate for his cause.

Debate was one of Hoover's most absorbing interests at Central. The other, which made an equally important contribution to the development of his character, was the Central High School Brigade of Cadets, which he joined during the first week of his freshman year.[64]

Central awarded its highest prestige to the captains of the athletic teams, but a leader of the cadet corps got almost as much recognition. The Central High School Cadet Corps, founded in 1882, the same year as the school, had a long history and rich traditions. The Sousa march, "Washington High School Cadets," was originally written for the Central cadets, and they considered it their official anthem. Each of the Washington high schools had a cadet corps of about three companies; each company contained some sixty cadets organized in four to eight squads. At the beginning of each year the seniors who had been noncommissioned officers the year before took an examination in their knowledge of drill. From these candidates were chosen the captains of the various companies, as well as the colonel and staff of the city-wide cadet regiment to which each of the high school brigades belonged. (The colored schools had their own cadet corps and fielded their own regiment. Their activities were simply ignored by the newspapers and by white Washington.)

Cadets wore their uniforms to school on drill days, and gave their girlfriends ribbons that were the insignia of their companies. They drilled after school every Monday and Thursday, for an hour and a half, on blocked-off streets or, in rainy weather, in a drill room inside Central. The city-wide cadet drill competition was held each spring on the White House Ellipse. This, with its associated parties and dances for each company and the city-wide regimental ball, was considered the social event of the student year. The cadet regiment also staged a mock battle near the White House that was reviewed by members of the cabinet and by army officers.[65]

During his first two years at Central, Hoover was drilled by the junior and senior officers as they practiced maneuvers and developed their "command voice." Diary entries during his freshman year mention getting together with other members of his unit after school: "Went to squad meeting at 1117-G-N.W. Corporal Capt. Lieunt. & serg. all there. Had a great time." At the beginning of his junior year Hoover was named second sergeant in Central's Company B. He was also apparently making his presence felt, because an item in the school paper remarked on the volume of Hoover's cadence counts.[66]

Hoover sat for the regimental and company examinations in October of his senior year and was selected as captain of Company A. One of his fellow captains was Lawrence Jones, a football star and class president who was an all-American football player at West Point and later its head football coach. The third captain, David Blakelock, went on to become a general in the army.[67]

Hoover took his responsibilities as captain very seriously. The cadet brigade customarily marched in the presidential inauguration, and Hoover led his company in President Wilson's inaugural parade in March. Hoover wrote an article in the school paper afterward to refocus his company's attention on the year's real goal: the city-wide drill competition in the spring. He thanked the principal for offering medals to the cadets for excellence in drill and for letting the cadets have a dance at the Cairo Hotel (Hoover's parents were chaperons). He then reminded his men that their real task still lay before them: "Officers meetings are held weekly, convening early in the evening and often adjourning early in the morning. Now that the programs are in our hands, it means work all the time. Attendance, fight and set-up are the three essentials."[68]

At the final drill competition, Hoover's six-squad company placed second to an eight-squad company from another school. Hoover felt that the judges had, as was their right, given extra credit for the added difficulty of training and maneuvering the larger units.[69] After this final review Hoover reflected on his experiences as a cadet captain: "The year has been a most enjoyable one, for there is nothing more pleasant than to be associated with a company composed of officers and men who you feel are behind you heart and soul. The saddest moment of the year was not when I saw the Adjutant turn toward his right; but was when I realized that I must part with a group of fellows who had become a part of my life. And in conclusion, let me say that I want every man of Company A of 1912–13 to look upon me as their friend and helper wherever we might meet after this year."[70]

An enormous expenditure of time is needed to train a group of men to respond precisely to the commands of its leader in a formalized pattern, and its rewards are apparent only to one who finds group solidarity and the techniques of producing it intrinsically satisfying. Hoover did find the process of attaining group cohesion of absorbing interest; to him it was an exercise in group dynamics that was valuable in itself.

Central gave Hoover the opportunity to learn at an early age that he had the ability to motivate men, to lead them, that he enjoyed the process of group organization and leadership. So much of the routine that later consumed Hoover's FBI, and seemed so pointless to his critics, becomes understandable in the light of the youthful Hoover's pleasure in organization for its own sake. Because of his years with the Central High Cadet Corps, Hoover was able to anticipate the rewards, both tangible and psychological, that would be his if he were able to turn the FBI into a highly respected organization of the type he had led as captain of cadets.

Edgar carried away from Central a love of competition in a public arena and the conviction that life is, as he said, "nothing more or less than the matching of one man's wit against another." Throughout his career he loved dispute and looked for opportunities to lock horns with rivals, enemies, even friends. Hoover's opponents usually went into battle against him because some important political issue was at stake, assuming that after a test of strength a mutual accommodation could be reached. Instead, they found themselves committed to an endless and bitter war against an enemy who would keep up the fight even when the point of the contest had been forgotten. Hoover liked to fight; most people do not. And so Hoover would eventually wear them down.

Central High reinforced the sense of self that Hoover had acquired in his early years on Seward Square: that he was part of an elite by virtue of being a middle-class white Protestant in a progressive America. It was a set of personal convictions and values rooted in the outlook of a tightly knit, homogeneous community convinced of its superiority and "civilizing" mission. Central High did nothing to make Hoover question those values. Rather, it permitted him to enjoy a success that depended upon his upholding and expressing the common convictions of the community to which he belonged.

Seward Square knew what it was and what it was not, and the symbol of all it was not was the radical foreigner. Hoover was a boy when immigration surged from 300,000 in 1899 to nearly a million during 1907 alone. It remained above 650,000 each year until the outbreak of World War I.[71] As the numbers of immigrants rose, so did nativist revulsion against the foreigner and his un-American ideas.

The hereditary racism of the capital was exacerbated by the reaction of old-stock Americans everywhere against ethnic and religious outsiders. The expansion of Jim Crow in the first decades of the century was the way Washington's native-born white Protestants expressed their nativist anxiety and aggression. Outside the South, where there were few blacks, the immigrant was the enemy.

All the institutions the young Hoover joined—Sunday school, church, Central High—regarded themselves as defenses against the immigrant threat to the country's ethnic homogeneity, its character as an all-but-officially Christian nation, and to the national leadership of the old-stock American. Not content with a defensive posture, the Protestant churches created a network of institutions to carry on the work of safeguarding the Christian character of American culture. The expansion of the Sunday school into the elaborate enterprise the young Hoover joined, together with the WCTU, the Anti-Saloon League, the YMCA, and the Student Volunteer Movement, were all part of Protestant America's defense against the immigrant threat. The new "institutional" church that was so appealing to Hoover was another response to the influx of foreigners as the church tried to provide a substitute within its walls for the lost dream of America as a Christian commonwealth, a beachhead for a new drive to "Christianize" America.[72]

It was not merely the foreigner's strange appearance, abhorrent customs, and infidel religion that terrified the Seward Squares of America. Old-stock Americans were so sure of the eternal validity of American institutions that any serious dissatisfaction with American society was assumed to have a foreign origin. The labor strife in the coal fields of Pennsylvania during the 1870s and the nationwide railroad strike of 1877 were both blamed on the Irish-born members of the Molly Maguires, the underground branch of the Ancient Order of Hibernians. In 1880, the revolutionary wing of the Socialist Labor party endorsed the anarchist program of Bakunin,[73] and when a bomb exploded during a radical demonstration in Chicago's Haymarket Square in 1886, the courts blamed eight self-proclaimed "anarchists" and hanged four of them.

Haymarket made "anarchist" mean anyone advocating, or suspected of advocating, violence as an instrument of economic or political change, particularly after the anarchist Alexander Berkman tried to kill Henry Clay Frick of the Carnegie Steel Company in 1892; then another anarchist, native-born Leon F. Czolgosz, managed to assassinate President McKinley in 1901 (and implicated the anarchist leader Emma Goldman during the course of his interrogation). In the myth of the foreign origin (and hence un-American character) of American radicalism, small-town America was imagined as being corrupted by old-world evils smuggled in by the foreign radical, "a ragged, unwashed, long-haired, wild-eyed fiend, armed with smoking revolver and bomb—to say nothing of the dagger he sometimes carried between his teeth." A student of the antiradicalism of the period says that "no nativist image prevailed more widely than that of the immigrant as a lawless creature given over to violence and disorder."[74]

There was an automatic search for a foreign culprit whenever the repose of conservative America was disturbed. "There is no such thing as an American anarchist," wrote one editor. "The American character has in it no element which can under any circumstances be won to uses so mistaken and pernicious." In 1886, the Reverend Theodore T. Munger wrote that "anarchism, lawlessness . . . labor strikes, and a general violation of personal rights" were something that "the Anglo-Saxon race has not witnessed since Magna Carta. . . . This horrible tyranny is wholly of foreign origin." Woodrow Wilson, in a speech during his preparedness campaign, charged that immigrant radicals had "poured the poison of disloyalty into the very arteries of our national life. America has never witnessed anything like this before. . . . Such creatures of passion, disloyalty, and anarchy must be crushed out."[75]

A child would find Seward Square a safe and secure haven. As he grew older, though, he would learn that there was a danger against which the Old First Church, the Sunday school, Central High, and Seward Square itself stood guard. The threat was the foreigner and the un-American ideas he carried with him like an infectious disease.

During the years of Hoover's youth, other members of his generation were assimilating the ideas of Karl Marx, Sigmund Freud, George Bernard Shaw, and H. G. Wells and using them to explode the inherited pieties of the Victorian era. In *A Preface to Politics,* published the year Hoover graduated from Central, Walter Lippmann argued that "no moral judgment can declare the value of life" and that government, instead of trying to stamp out "badness," should try to channel the impulses behind it toward worthwhile goals. Government, he said, should "add and build and increase the facilities of life. Repression is an insignificant part of its work."[76] Such young intellectuals as Max Eastman, Floyd Dell, Van Wyck Brooks, and John Reed, many the same age as Hoover, were unknown to him, and he would not learn of them until he was helping enforce the laws that would make many of them criminals. In the opening decades of the twentieth century, Seward Square seemed far removed from such dissent. In the face of skepticism and change, it nourished belief in progressive America's white Christian vision of good and evil. It was this vision—nurtured on Seward Square, in Sunday school, and at Central High—that Hoover carried with him as he left his neighborhood to begin his career in official Washington.

CHAPTER 2

The Alien Enemy Bureau

Attached hereto are the files on the case of Udo Rall, age, 24. . . .
An investigation conducted by the American Intelligence Bureau
showed that Rall belittled the United States; talked against the War;
spread pacifist propaganda and wrote against conscription.

 The United States Attorney recommends that Rall be interned
for the duration of the war and the above facts are submitted to you
for your consideration in acting upon his recommendation.

J. Edgar Hoover, January 2, 1918,
Memorandum to John Lord O'Brian

J. EDGAR HOOVER was, figuratively, born into the federal bureaucracy. He grew up learning the dead-ends and shortcuts of federal employment the way a country boy soaks up the lore of willow whistles and grapevine cigars. Hoover's father and grandfather spent their lives in the printshop of the Coast and Geodetic Survey. His brother worked his way up the Steamboat Inspection Service to the rank of chief inspector. There were other relatives throughout the federal and district bureaucracy; on his mother's side there was a District of Columbia judge, William Hitz, a friend of Louis Brandeis and Woodrow Wilson.[1]

 When Hoover graduated from Central in 1913, Washington was, as it still is, a company town, and the company was the federal government. Then, as now, taking advantage of the opportunities Washington offered depended on personal relationships with the entrenched bureaucrats who controlled access to government employment. Direct entry into the higher, policy-making levels of the bureaucracy was largely restricted to the allies and protégés of elected officials. In Hoover's Washington, those families tended to congregate in northwest Washington and Georgetown.

While admission to the upper reaches of government was generally beyond its grasp, Seward Square did exert a jealous watch over the lower, entry-level positions in the federal bureaucracy. The Hoovers were part of an almost hereditary order of families who knew their way in and about the federal agencies. By virtue of his family, his neighborhood, and his training, J. Edgar Hoover was a full-fledged member of this caste.

For families like the Hoovers, the government was not simply an abstract principle or a vague symbol, nor was it an oppressive force or an instrument to be shaped and manipulated. It was the family's source of employment, of pride, and of its sense that its values were the official morality of the nation and state. To Seward Square, the federal government was an extension of itself. The permanent bureaucracy was made up of people like themselves who came from similar neighborhoods throughout the city.

By the time he graduated from Central, Hoover had his sights set on a career in law. Beneath his yearbook photo was the caption: " 'Speed' intends to study law at college, and will undoubtedly make as good in that as he has at Central." Hoover probably had a career with the government already in mind: With the example of his grandfather, father, and brother before him, it would have seemed the logical move.

But while committed to the government, Seward Square was alienated from politics. It was one of the threatening and unsettling forces that periodically threw the bureaucracy into fits of insecurity—and nobody is less secure than the long-term bureaucrat. Besides the conservatism inspired in Seward Square by its white middle-class Protestantism, its intimate and familial connection to the federal bureaucracy made the advocacy of any kind of change dangerous and terrifying.

Hoover never joined a political party. As a Washington resident he never voted, and he used his disenfranchisement as evidence of his distaste for corrupt politics. Even after home rule and the Twenty-third Amendment (1961), he continued to boast that he had never cast a ballot, a prudent course for a non-Civil Service appointee dependent on the elected politicians of both parties who were regularly swept in and out of office as the political currents shifted.

As a young man, Hoover had a significant advantage over his

rivals in government service. As a native of Seward Square, he knew exactly how to prepare himself for a government career. Besides his knowledge of the bureaucracy and the confidence he had acquired at Central, he knew that prestigious credentials were a waste of time and money for entry-level work. The vita of a native Washingtonian in government service who grew up in the District before, say, 1950, is almost predictable: the public schools—probably Central, but sometimes Western or Eastern—and then night school at George Washington University. Out-of-towners who moved to the capital during either World War I or II often came to the same conclusion: Once the federal connection was made, it should never be broken, certainly not for anything as superfluous as an education. The sooner one became part of the great chain of seniority that was federal civil service, the better. A law degree might be essential, but an early start and continuity of service were even more important. The most common solution was George Washington University's night school. That was Hoover's path, as it had been his brother's and as it would be his niece's and many of his top assistants' at the Justice Department and its Bureau of Investigation.

George Washington University was essentially a pragmatic solution to the career needs of the federal bureaucracy. During its early years, it survived precariously on tuition, its student activities run on a shoestring. Founded as Columbian College in 1821 in hope that it would become the "national" university envisioned in L'Enfant's plan for the District, the university for years existed in a makeshift collection of buildings near McPherson Square in downtown Washington. In 1912, the undergraduate college moved to its present location in Foggy Bottom, now a most desirable neighborhood but at that time an area "miscellaneous in character [that] gave a distinct impression of decadence." When the rest of the school moved, the law school stayed behind on the second floor of the Masonic Temple at the triangle formed by Thirteenth Street, New York Avenue, and "H" Street N.W. It was a convenient location for a student with his eye on government work—the Justice Department was then located a few blocks away at "K" Street and Fifteenth.[2]

The GWU Law School was not particularly prestigious, but it was by no means disreputable and was one of the founding members of the American Association of Law Schools in 1900. In strictly academic terms, it was overshadowed in the Washington area by Georgetown and the University of Virginia. Its real attraction was that it was one of the few law schools in the country (and the only one in

Washington) where it was possible to obtain a degree as a "late afternoon student." Another attractive feature was that a student could skip the undergraduate degree and enter directly into the three-year bachelor of law program, with an additional year's course work in practices and procedures for the master of law degree. This was the route Hoover followed.

To support himself, Hoover took a job at the Library of Congress, just down Pennsylvania Avenue from Seward Square. He began work in the order division on October 13, 1913, at a salary of $360 a year. He was a junior messenger, the lowest rank on the staff.

In 1913, the Library of Congress was in the process of being transformed into the nation's foremost research collection by the remarkable Herbert Putnam, an early example of the bureaucratic empire builder that was later typified by such men as Robert Moses, Hyman Rickover, and Hoover himself.[3] Putnam's professional expertise, academic reputation, organizational ability, and, not least, his skillful manipulation of congressmen had won him a large degree of immunity from the political interference and patronage demands that wrecked the efficiency of most government agencies. His personal reputation and the effectiveness of his administration convinced his congressional overseers to approve his budgets each year just as he submitted them. At the Library Hoover was in a position to observe a rare example of an efficient unit of the federal bureaucracy. He was able to study how Putnam won personal security and bureaucratic independence through his reputation for efficiency and by skillfully handling congressional requests for service.

Putnam filled the Library's professional positions on the basis of merit, but at the nonprofessional level, where Hoover joined the staff, political sponsorship was necessary. Perhaps Hoover got his job through his brother, or through the senator Dick worked for while studying law at George Washington. The law school may also have had connections with the Library, since it was a common employer of GWU law students. (The historian of George Washington University Law School worked at the Library while attending law school, as did Hoover's niece Margaret, who got her law degree at GWU in the 1920s.)[4]

Hoover spent his four and a half years at the Library (from 1913 to 1917) in the order department, except for a period in late 1915 when he was detached to the cataloging division. His pay rose steadily. From an initial salary of $30 a month in October 1913 (about the same as he had earned delivering groceries while in high school),

Hoover's pay had increased to $70 a month by the time he finally left the Library on July 31, 1917. There have been suggestions that Hoover's experience at the Library proved to be invaluable when he organized the index files at the General Intelligence Division in 1919; however, the Justice Department had long had an efficient system of cross-referencing its case files, as had every organization that dealt with large masses of information in the days before computers. If Hoover's experience at the Library had any significant influence on him, it was that it gave him the opportunity to observe how a government agency could be managed according to sound administrative principles.

Hoover's routine at the Library was to work from 9:00 A.M. to 4:30 P.M. and then travel across town to GWU for evening classes from 4:50 to 6:30. During the summer, his classes ran from 7:50 to 8:40 in the morning, before the heat grew oppressive, and then he spent the rest of the day at the Library. In the few hours this demanding schedule left him for study, he filled twenty-six bound notebooks, each between one and two hundred pages, with notes on his lectures and reading assignments. He obtained some practical experience working with the Legal Aid Society, and even managed a social life despite his work and studies. There was no age difference between the undergraduates and the law students at GWU, so students of the law school were able to join the college fraternities, even play on the varsity teams. Hoover became a member of Kappa Alpha, a predominantly Southern fraternity that originated at William and Mary. For a while after graduation he maintained this connection, and even was president of the fraternity during the early 1920s.[5]

Hoover finished his bachelor of law degree in 1916 (without honors)[6] in the minimum period of three years. He kept his job at the Library while he spent an extra year at GWU taking the courses required for the master's degree in law.

On April 2, 1917, Woodrow Wilson delivered his war message to Congress. On June 5, all men between the ages of twenty-one and thirty-one had to register for the draft. Hoover was twenty-two years of age and in excellent physical condition, just what the army needed, so in early June, besides receiving his master's degree and sitting for his bar examinations, he filled out his selective service forms. On July 3, 1917, he was notified that he had passed the bar and was admitted to practice before the Supreme Court of the District of Columbia.

Photographs of Hoover at this time show a young man with a thin, intense countenance, one of almost grim determination, perhaps a result of the pressure brought on by a crisis that had been developing at home. On April 17, 1917, Hoover's sixty-year-old father, who had been ailing for some time and needed medical attention, had to retire from the Interior Department. (He evidently suffered from mental illness; one of Edgar's nieces later recalled a "nervous breakdown of some sort.") This reduced the family's income by $2,000 a year. The support of their ailing father and their mother (Dickerson Sr. would live until 1922, Annie until 1938) would now depend on Edgar and Dick. And since Dick had a wife and three children, the burden of supporting the parents and coping with the father's illness fell on Edgar's shoulders.[7]

Yet Edgar's family was a resource he could draw on in this domestic emergency. His uncle, William Hitz, had been a special assistant to Attorney General Thomas Gregory during 1916, doing work in the court of claims, which sent him to Boston and to Portsmouth, New Hampshire. Though Hitz left the Justice Department on November 15, 1916—he was appointed associate justice of the District of Columbia Supreme Court—his experience there made him a likely source of information about job opportunities with the department. According to one of Hitz's other nephews, Hoover's cousin Harold Burton, later United States Supreme Court Justice, Hoover was quite close to Hitz,[8] and being thus connected to a successful Washington jurist certainly had to have been of value to Hoover when he looked for work at the department.

Lawyers begin their practical legal education only when they leave law school and enter into practice, so they often choose their first job more for its value as legal training than for the pay. (In later years, Hoover usually described his first job as that of a clerk, and there is a reference in his official FBI personnel file to his being a "clerk in the files division."[9] It was not a job that required or utilized legal training.) Hoover's starting salary at the Justice Department was $990 a year, more than the $840 he had been earning at the Library of Congress, but still a very low-paying job, though it carried with it exemption from the draft. To put this in perspective, the U.S. attorney general earned $15,000 a year, and his highest subordinates, the solicitor general and the special assistant for war work, earned $10,000 each. A politically well-connected Washington lawyer such as A. Mitchell Palmer earned $200,000 a year in private practice at the outset of the war. While this kind of income was far beyond

Hoover's reach, even with the expectation of early promotion, he still would have done better in private practice.

Hoover was in fact promoted to the rank of "attorney" in less than a year.[10] This paid $1,800—about double what he was getting, and just about what he needed to replace his father's $2,000 a year. It is likely that his uncle's influence was what gave him the assurance that he would get special attention.

Not only did Hoover's uncle William Hitz know Gregory; he was also a good friend of the man who would be Hoover's superior, John Lord O'Brian, whom he had known at Harvard. During the month of July 1917 (Hoover entered the department on July 26), Attorney General Thomas Gregory was laying plans for the War Emergency Division of the Justice Department, an agency he would formally establish in late summer. O'Brian, an eminent Buffalo, New York, attorney, was the man Gregory had in mind to head this division. O'Brian had just finished successful prosecution of the government's first important domestic security case, the antitrust prosecution of the German propagandist Franz von Rintelen.[11] O'Brian accepted the appointment to head the War Emergency Division in the fall of 1917, so he was in communication with Gregory about it during the same summer Hoover was looking for a job.

O'Brian was in the habit of attending Judge Hitz's Saturday luncheons at the Cosmos Club, to which they both belonged. Hitz had an important part in introducing O'Brian to important members of the Washington legal community, and many years later O'Brian gratefully remembered that Hitz "had a good part in shaping my own life in those early days." It is possible that at one of those Cosmos Club luncheons O'Brian had mentioned to Hitz that he needed lawyers for his new division at the Justice Department, and that Hitz had told him he had a nephew who had just finished George Washington Law and needed a job. His uncle's line to O'Brian might also have made Hoover confident that he had a good chance of being rescued from the file room, because unless someone brought Hoover to O'Brian's attention, it is unlikely that a man so close to the top of the Justice Department would have noticed a clerk who was so near the bottom, even one as hard-working as Hoover.[12]

One puzzling note on Hoover's early days at the Justice Department is a reference to him as a "special agent," raising the possibility that Hoover's initial appointment (perhaps only as an administrative formality) was with the department's detective unit, the Bureau of Investigation, rather than with the Justice Department proper. John

Lord O'Brian's first official mention of Hoover (on December 14, 1917) refers to him as a "special agent,"[13] but since many of the Bureau of Investigation's detectives were working outside the Bureau on the department's war work, on clerical tasks similar to Hoover's, O'Brian could easily have been mistaken about Hoover's appointment. He could not have been expected to be fully acquainted with the precise details of his various clerks' departmental status.

On the other hand, the 1919 Washington City Directory also lists Hoover as a "special agent" with the Justice Department. This edition would have been compiled early in 1918, and would have been based on information Hoover or his parents gave to the canvassers. The reason Hoover may have first joined the Justice Department as a special agent in the Bureau of Investigation was that the Bureau had recently (July 1916) gotten a special appropriation to hire more agents, so it was the branch of the department that had the most job openings in July 1917. Later, Hoover might not have wanted to have this known by his subordinates because of the unsavory reputation of the pre-1924 Bureau. It also might have diminished his authority if his subordinates had thought of him as someone who had once taken orders in the Bureau, as well as given them. In any case, if Hoover had once been a special agent, he certainly kept it a secret the rest of his life.

As J. Edgar Hoover rode the trolley from Seward Square across town to "K" Street N.W. on July 26 for his first day at the Justice Department, the forces that would shape his future were just making themselves felt. The Bolsheviks, who had helped overthrow the czar in February, were preparing to seize control of the Russian revolution. Left-wing members of the American Socialist party, excited by the developments in Russia, were still two years away from leaving the Socialists to form the Communist and Communist Labor parties. Emma Goldman and Alexander Berkman had been convicted of obstructing the draft on July 9 and were in prison—Goldman in Jefferson City, Missouri; Berkman in Atlanta, Georgia. John Dillinger was a fourteen-year-old apprentice machinist in Indianapolis, Indiana.

The United States had been at war for four months when the twenty-two-year-old Hoover joined the Justice Department. Those had been four months of war hysteria, and Justice was at its center.

The Justice Department that Hoover joined was rapidly expanding because of the war, but it was still an old-fashioned place and Gregory was an old-fashioned attorney general. His 1917 budget listed an expense of $12 for a new pole for his carriage. Out of the $2,486.44 spent by the department to maintain its transportation equipment, all but $1.80 went for the upkeep of the department's horses, its victoria, and its brougham—the odd $1.80 was spent fixing a broken bicycle.[14]

The Justice Department's offices were in a collection of leased buildings clustered around the headquarters at Vermont and "K" Street at McPherson Square. Not until 1934, when the Justice Department moved into its present quarters at Pennsylvania and Ninth, would it be centralized in a building of its own.[15]

Thomas W. Gregory, the first of the nineteen attorney generals Hoover would serve, was a Mississippi-born Texan. One of Woodrow Wilson's earliest supporters, he was credited with persuading the indispensable Colonel House to back Wilson for the presidency. Gregory took charge of the Justice Department in 1914, succeeding the politically inept James C. McReynolds after Wilson elevated him to the Supreme Court. Gregory quickly ended the department's traditional alliance with industry in labor struggles, and redirected the Justice Department's energies toward enforcement of the antitrust laws. As a progressive-era reformer, he also had the Bureau of Investigation emphasize enforcement of the federal white slave law (the Mann Act), in those days regarded as a progressive cause.[16]

Like many of President Wilson's early supporters, Gregory was instinctively in sympathy with reform and reformers. He urged Wilson to appoint Louis Brandeis to the U.S. Supreme Court, saying that "one radical in nine is not such a bad thing on the Supreme Bench."[17] Wilson had such respect for Gregory's character and intellect that he wanted to appoint him to the Supreme Court when Justice Charles Evans Hughes resigned in 1916 to seek the presidency, but Gregory disqualified himself because he was almost deaf. So, Wilson's cabinet, which was soon to preside over atrocious assaults on civil liberties, entered the war with at least two civil libertarians, Attorney General Gregory and Secretary of Labor William B. Wilson, to help stem the stampede to repressive policies.

Hoover's quick promotion from "clerk" to "attorney," and the responsibilities he was immediately given, were unusual for someone his age, but he was still not involved in any significant policy-shaping or decision-making during the war. He *was* in a position to observe a major government drive to eliminate political dissent. While his assignment was to help administer the department's supervision of German aliens, the Justice Department itself was committing some of the most egregious violations of civil liberties in American history. For example, it used a major political trial in Chicago in April 1918 to destroy the country's most militant radical organization, the International Workers of the World (IWW). It also prosecuted and convicted Emma Goldman, Alexander Berkman, and Eugene Debs, the perennial Socialist presidential candidate, for opposing the draft.

The Bureau of Investigation, recently enlarged to 300 agents and augmented by detectives borrowed from the Immigration Service, was led by A. Bruce Bielaski, another GWU Law School graduate. To supplement its own small staff, the Bureau joined forces with a civilian force, the American Protective League (APL), an army of 260,000 amateur spy-hunters organized in March by Albert M. Briggs. The Bureau supplied the APL with badges identifying them as Justice Department auxiliaries, and turned them loose to hunt for spies and disloyal neighbors. The Justice Department also used the APL to help enforce the draft by allowing them to round up huge numbers of draft-age men on suspicion of being "slackers."[18]

It was ironic that the Justice Department's repressive wartime policies were directed by officials as committed to civil liberties as Thomas Gregory and John Lord O'Brian. During the wartime emergency, Gregory and O'Brian tried their best to preserve constitutional processes in the overheated atmosphere of the war emergency, and to ensure that wartime restrictions of individual rights would only be temporary. Things could have been much worse if Gregory's first advisor on war legislation, Assistant Attorney General Charles Warren, had had his way. An extreme nativist, Warren saw the war as a chance to settle old scores with the country's enemies. He had always regarded immigrants as a major threat to American society, and so was one of the five founders of the small but influential Immigration Restriction League, organized at a meeting in his home in 1894.[19] Warren and other superpatriots lunged at the chance to use the rough rules of war against alien "reds," a broad category that included anyone who was dissatisfied with the established order.

The Justice Department was the command center of the government's drive to maintain support for the war and foster national conformity. Hoover could observe the struggle between constitutionalists determined to protect individual rights and those bent on fostering tribal unity by using the war regulations to repress anyone who disturbed the status quo.

The most visible Justice Department operation in the summer of 1917 was the department's war against German spies, really more of a public relations campaign to persuade the country that the government was dealing competently with a greatly exaggerated spy threat. Related to this was a bureaucratic battle between Gregory's Justice Department and its rivals in Treasury (the Secret Service) and War (the Military Intelligence Division) for jurisdiction over loyalty and espionage cases.

Within the Justice Department there was also a struggle by Gregory and John Lord O'Brian to preserve due process and to prevent the use of war regulations to wage a battle against unpopular beliefs and groups. Assistant Attorney General Warren was the chief proponent of repression in the department. Though held in check by Gregory and O'Brian, Warren's point of view was shared by many subordinate members of the department. (After the war, when Warren, Gregory, and O'Brian had all left the department, views similar to Warren's became Justice Department policy when, in 1919, A. Mitchell Palmer became attorney general.)

When Wilson signed the declaration of war against imperial Germany on April 6, 1917, the U.S. had, beginning in August 1914, experienced almost three years of war news and war propaganda, most of it calculated to inflame the country against Germany. The nature of the sea war—British control of the ocean's surface countered by German submarines—had made it inevitable that when there were American casualties, it would be the Germans who were responsible, as in the sinking of the *Lusitania* in May 1915 and the French passenger ship *Sussex* in 1916. And while both German and British agents in the U.S. ignored American sovereignty, only the acts of German agents alarmed the public. This anti-German prejudice was also exacerbated by the administration's extreme pro-British bias.

Secretary of the Treasury William McAdoo had his Secret Service agents investigate "German intrigues," and they had produced spectacular disclosures about the German underground. One such exposé was a supposed German plot with Mexican revolutionaries against American interests in Mexico. Then, in July 1916, the public's fear of German agents had swelled to a panic when ammunition stored at a munitions depot on New York Harbor's Black Tom Island exploded. While the German government's responsibility for the explosion was not legally established until decades later, at the time it was still universally assumed that German agents were to blame.

Three years' worth of stories about German intrigues convinced much of the public that enemy agents had organized vast numbers of aliens, particularly Germans and Austro-Hungarians, into a secret army poised to sabotage the nation's defenses. By April 1917, when Wilson delivered his war message, according to one analysis,

> many Americans believed that a declaration of war would transform the United States into a battlefield, with every one of the million resident German aliens an agent of the Kaiser. Mexicans in league with Germany would march north, retake Arizona and New Mexico, and cut off California from the rest of the country. Japanese would then land on the Pacific Coast and invade California. In the East, German submarines would shell New York. Sabotage would be particularly widespread in the heavily industrialized Northeast. Spies, of course, were believed to be everywhere.[20]

Hoover's first months in the Justice Department put him in the middle of this hysteria over traitors, spies, and saboteurs. In March 1917, the War Department began to ostentatiously guard public utilities and railroad bridges and distribute weapons to factory owners. On the West Coast, public opinion was even more out of control. Power plant owners surrounded their facilities with barbed wire and electric fences, gun clubs mobilized to protect their neighborhoods, and citizens were warned to arm themselves. On March 25, 1917, the War Department imposed a blackout on all news of military movements, and in the absence of hard news about military preparations, rumors ran wild about enemy agents.[21]

Under these circumstances, those government officials who refused to give in to the hysteria risked being accused of failing in their duty. Within Wilson's cabinet only a few stood their ground. Secretary of State Robert Lansing and Secretary of the Treasury McAdoo were in favor of a sweeping roundup of aliens, but Secretary of War Newton D. Baker and Attorney General Thomas Gregory remained skeptical that there really was any critical internal threat.[22]

Despite the repugnance Gregory felt for wholesale infringements on political rights, certain factors impelled him to swim with the repressive current. Most important was his loyalty to the administration, in which he was a leading figure, and to a president he greatly admired. With the country and the press screaming for government action against the alien threat, inactivity would have been political suicide. Gregory also deeply distrusted Secretary of the Treasury McAdoo and his Secret Service, and if the Justice Department appeared lax against aliens, the result would have been to cede control of the internal security field to Treasury. Gregory felt that, eventually, McAdoo's irresponsibility would discredit the government and the administration.

At the beginning of the war, Gregory had to rely for advice on
Charles Warren, who had impressed the Department by his ingenuity
in resurrecting the old 1798 Alien Act as the legal basis for Woodrow
Wilson's April 6 proclamation on "Alien Enemies." (The phrase is
taken from the 1798 law.)[23]

Warren's virulent anti-immigrant prejudices colored his search for
disloyalty among aliens, and helped foster the attitude of suspicion
towards foreigners that pervaded the Department when Hoover joined
it. Gregory and O'Brian finally had to force Warren out of the Department on April 19, 1918, when he lobbied in congress for a bill that
would have turned espionage investigations and trials over to the Army,
even though he knew the president and the attorney general were
both opposed. "One man shot, after court martial, is worth a hundred
arrests by this Department," Warren had written Gregory.[24]

Hoover's first assignment in the Justice Department was to handle
the flood of paperwork generated by the regulations governing German
aliens. Since 1914, the Justice Department had been preparing lists
of aliens considered dangerous. "Prior to the passage of the joint
resolution of Congress of April 6, 1917," Gregory reported, "elaborate
preparation was made for the arrest of 63 alien enemies whom past
investigation had shown to constitute a danger to the peace and safety
of the United States if allowed to remain at large." There were 295
aliens arrested by June 30, 1917; 895 by October 30. By the end of
the war, 4,000 alien enemies had been arrested by the Justice
Department.[25]

On April 6, immediately after signing the declaration of war, President Wilson issued the proclamation Warren had drafted invoking
the 1798 Alien Act. The principal statute (Section 4067 of the Revised
Statutes) held that:

> whenever there is declared war between the United States and any foreign
> nation or government . . . and the President makes public proclamation
> of the event, all natives, citizens, denizens or subjects of the hostile nation
> or government, being males of the age of fourteen years and upwards,
> who shall be within the United States, and not actually naturalized, shall
> be liable to be apprehended, restrained, secured, and removed, as alien
> enemies. The President is authorized, in any such event, by his proclama-
> tion, thereof, or other public act, to direct the conduct to be observed,
> on the part of the United States, toward the aliens who become so liable;
> the manner and degree of the restraint to which they shall be subject,

and in what cases, and upon what security their residence shall be permitted, and to provide for the removal of those who, not being permitted to reside within the United States, refuse or neglect to depart therefrom; and to establish any other regulations which are found necessary in the premises and for the public safety.[26]

There were twelve regulations that prohibited "alien enemies" from possessing guns or explosives, radio transmitters, and documents "printed in cipher or in which there may be invisible writing." They were banned from coming within half a mile of military installations or munitions plants as well as other zones—for example, the capital and the Port of New York—and were barred from entering or leaving the United States. Wilson's proclamation gave notice that all alien enemies would have to register at a later date and threatened prison if "there may be reasonable cause to believe [an alien] may be aiding or about to aid the enemy." There was almost superstitious dread of enemy propaganda during the war, and the regulations also sought to silence this:

> An alien enemy shall not write, print, or publish any attack or threats against the Government or Congress of the United States, or either branch thereof, or against the measures or policy of the United States, or against the person or property of any person in the military, naval, or civil service of the United States, or of the States or Territories, or of the District of Columbia or of the municipal governments therein.[27]

Wilson gave the attorney general the responsibility of enforcing these regulations and of drawing up procedures for alien registration. On April 16, Gregory gave alien enemies until June 1 to leave the prohibited zones, but he also instructed his marshals to issue permits to those aliens whose presence posed no danger and who needed to stay in these areas. United States attorneys were to send him names of alien enemies they felt should be summarily arrested under the terms of the proclamation. Gregory warned that no arrests should take place until approval had been obtained from Washington unless it was extraordinarily dangerous to allow the alien to remain free.

Gregory instructed his department that his "plan" was to "take up the case of each individual alien enemy arrested separately and decide . . . what disposition the interests of the country and of justice required." His orders required that field agents should transmit information about permit applications to the "Permit Officer, Department of Justice, Washington, D.C." Even at this early date the department was hard put to cope with the work generated by the department's authority over alien enemies.[28] At the time Hoover was recruited for the War Emergency Division, he was, along with many other clerks, performing the duties of "Permit Officer."

Hoover's first four months in the Justice Department in 1917 are, on the whole, undocumented. His name first surfaces in a letter John Lord O'Brian submitted to Attorney General Gregory on December 14 in which O'Brian described the organization of the new War Emergency Division. The substance of O'Brian's proposal had already been informally approved by Gregory on December 4, so it may be assumed that sometime before December 4 O'Brian chose Hoover to be part of his division's Alien Enemy Bureau. It is probable that Hoover had been working on alien affairs for several months before O'Brian formalized his assignment.

The reason so many of the department's resources were directed to alien affairs was that Gregory was able to delegate almost all of his other war-related work to U.S. attorneys or to the APL. It was only the control of alien enemies that presented the department with an uncontrollable flow of paper. President Wilson's proclamation—which first applied only to German and Austro-Hungarian males over the age of fourteen—gave the attorney general the "duty of execution."[29] Gregory was immediately inundated with thousands of appeals from German aliens who wanted exemptions from the prohibited zone regulations so they could keep their jobs and homes.

The paperwork mounted fast: Red Cross regulations required that all interned enemies be registered. Forms had to be prepared to allow them to apply for parole. Aliens who resided or worked in the forbidden areas, which included many large concentrations of the foreign-born, had to register with the department to apply for permission to remain where they were. A complete registration of all German male aliens—and later, German females (there were, in all, 480,000 German alien enemies in the country, as well as nearly 4 million Austro-Hungarians)—was deferred at the outset because of the need for extensive preparations. Since a severe labor shortage was already developing, employers were desperate to have their interned alien workers released, and so the department had to begin processing parole applications almost as soon as the internments started, and Hoover was put to work on this task.[30]

When John Lord O'Brian arrived at the Justice Department, his first task had been to reorganize the staff that had been assigned to war work. O'Brian's plan[31] called for the establishment of an Emergency War Division or a "Temporary War Division or . . . some other similar title" and for setting up four bureaus within it:

1. Supervision of litigations, special arguments in aid of the United States Attorneys, supervision of liquor and vice zones and miscellaneous business chiefly relating to litigation, Mr. Bettman, special assistant to Attorney General, aided by Mr. Mothershead, attorney.
2. Registration of Aliens, Mr. Sprague, special attorney, assisted by Mr. Blanchard, special agent; other subordinates to be named.
3. Supervision of water-front protection in connection with the Army authorities to be assigned to Mr. _____. (For the present in charge of Mr. Kenefick, attorney.)
4. All work relating to the internment and parole of enemy aliens and supervising issue of permits, etc., to them, to be handled by a subordinate "Alien Enemy Bureau" in charge of Mr. Storey, as attorney."

Within this Bureau, work to be sub-divided as follows:

All subordinates reporting to Mr. Storey and Mr. Storey reporting directly to Mr. O'Brian, namely:

(a) Questions effecting arrest and internment of alleged alien enemies, Mr. Storey.
(b) Questions relating to the parole of men in detention including the important work to be done in connection with the Department of Labor, relating to interned seamen, Mr. Saxon, assistant to Mr. Storey, aided by Mr. Hoover, special agent.
(c) Questions effecting permits for aliens, barred zones, supervision of United States Marshals, etc., including miscellaneous correspondence, Mr. McGuire assistant to Mr. Storey.[32]

By December, departmental correspondence shows that Hoover had become part of the Alien Enemy Bureau routine. He was reviewing cases, summarizing them, and then submitting them to O'Brian with a recommendation for action. Most of the cases were very clear-cut. An eighteen-year-old German named Ernest Loehndorff was arrested in El Paso, Texas, as he was trying to enter the U.S. from Mexico. "Loehndorff stated that he reported to the German consul in each city and offered his services on behalf of his country. He also refused to promise that he will not aid enemy and states that 'if there is anything any of the high officials tell me to do, I shall try to do that thing even if it costs me my life.' " Hoover summarized the case and wrote that "the facts in this case lead me to recommend that Ernest Loehndorff be detained for the duration of the war."[33]

O'Brian's practice was to intern an alien for the duration of the war whenever anyone in authority had reasonable doubts about his reliability. He nearly always overruled pleas for clemency, evidently on the grounds that the law required the internment of any alien who gave the slightest appearance of posing a danger.

For the most part, Hoover simply submitted to O'Brian the U.S. attorney's recommendation without comment. In many cases, however, Hoover and his immediate superior, Special Assistant Attorney General Charles W. Storey, recommended action less severe than open-ended internment. In most of these instances Hoover was overruled, and these cases offer some insight into his attitude about his work at this time. On December 28, 1917, Hoover wrote O'Brian about a German seaman who had been refused permission to work on shipboard or near the waterfront after hostilities began. The German then violated regulations by signing on a coastal vessel as a deckhand. Hoover noted that "the attitude of this alien enemy is stated to be sullen and uncommunicative. The Special agent in charge recommends that Diedricks be interned for the duration of the war." All the same, Hoover recommended that "in view of the circumstances of the case a parole may be safely granted at the end of thirty days, provided the limits of such are restricted to a rural community." Charles Storey disagreed vigorously: "A willful violation of our most important regulation. I see nothing to do but recommend detention for the war. Resp. CES. P.S. This is in line with our regular policy in these cases." O'Brian concurred: "Intern for War."[34]

In another case, a German was arrested for "selling liquor to soldiers in uniform and soliciting men for immoral women." Hoover's comment was that "this is a case in which parole may be safely granted, provided Schachman is able to secure a competent supervisor and furnish a bond of not less than $1,000." Storey concurred: "If the man were a spy he would hardly have acted the way he did in regard to petty larceny and women. I fancy he is harmless in this respect and am inclined to recommend we remove him from the Naval Base and parole him in some inland town on a bond as stiff as he can put up." Albert Bettman, special assistant to Attorney General Gregory, disagreed, noting that "I think he should be interned for duration [of the] war. Has violated laws passed to further war." O'Brian's decision was to intern him for the duration. In a third case, Hoover recommended parole for a German train conductor who had said, "It is a shame that the best blood of the United States should be sent to Europe to fight England's war."[35] Again he was overruled.

There were also cases where Hoover recommended treatment more severe than his immediate superiors, although in these cases also O'Brian's final action was to intern the alien for the duration of the war. In one case, an Otto Mueller called President Wilson "a cock-sucker and a thief"; later, when asked how he liked America, he answered, "fuck this god damned country." Hoover characterized these as "various vulgar and obscene remarks about the President" and "the most pronounced Pro-German expressions," and endorsed the decision of the United States attorney who "recommends that Mueller be interned for the duration of the war, in which recommendation I concur." Charles Storey disagreed with Hoover, saying that "Mueller has unquestionably overstepped the rights of free speech but still his offense is no more than a failure to keep his mouth shut, and I feel that internment for the war for mere talk is rather severe. Three or four months in jail will be equally effective."[36]

Another time that Hoover's recommendation was more severe than his superiors' involved a German who, Hoover reported, "engaged in a conversation with a negro in which he indulged in pro-German utterances and in derogatory remarks regarding the United States Government. He also made disloyal statements to other parties." Hoover passed along without comment the U.S. attorney's request for the permanent internment of the alien. Storey protested that the alien had been in the country for thirty years. He agreed that speaking "in this manner to a negro lends color to the idea that he was trying to influence the latter against the United States," but he recommended that the alien be given a month or two in prison followed by parole. "The additional facts that this man is a drunkard and abuses his wife cut two ways and I do not feel that they should be considered in this case." O'Brian interned him for the duration.[37]

There is a faint pattern discernible in these cases. O'Brian was determined to base his internment decisions only on the specific actions of the accused, or on the fact that someone with firsthand experience of the alien thought him dangerous. Hoover, by contrast, displayed a desire to probe the beliefs and attitudes of the aliens for mitigating or aggravating circumstances. Hoover was willing to excuse illegal actions by well-meaning aliens, but he was vindictive toward those whose actions might be innocuous but whose opinions indicated disloyalty.

Hoover continued to summarize the case files of interned alien enemies until April 1918. During this time, he also fielded administrative problems arising from the November 16, 1917, registration of German males.

On April 19, 1918, the department issued regulations requiring the registration of German females. This is the first time Hoover appears to have been deeply involved in the actual planning as well as administration of a departmental operation. He may even have directed this project. On July 3, 1918, he sent O'Brian an editorial from the *New York Sun* that praised the "efficient work of the Department in the registration of alien females." If Hoover was calling attention to the success of this operation, it may have been because he was in charge of it.[38]

Beginning in the summer of 1918, letters begin to appear in the files with O'Brian's signature but bearing Hoover's "JEH" initials, meaning Hoover was the attorney who had drafted the letter and that replies should be routed back to him. Most of these documents deal with the registration of German alien females, and they show that Hoover was being permitted a fair measure of personal discretion in his decisions, a remarkable advance in view of his age (twenty-three in 1918).

There are also signs that Hoover had become known to his superiors as someone who was reliable and efficient, because they were giving him assignments outside his area of formal responsibility. When the Justice Department became anxious about the number of German aliens living on Staten Island, close to the prohibited area of the Port of New York, Hoover collected data to make an estimate of the size of Staten Island's German population, and he obtained the names and precincts of the police officers supervising the aliens.[39]

By mid-summer 1918, Hoover was no longer simply summarizing files and attaching his tentative recommendations. He was evaluating cases from a legal standpoint and furnishing final decisions to his superiors for their signature. He was no longer merely reporting to Charles Storey, but was also working for Albert Bettman, who was in charge of war litigation for O'Brian. Since Hoover had earlier reported to one of Storey's assistants, this would indicate that he had moved up at least one echelon in the Justice Department bureaucracy.

The assignment that carried with it Hoover's promotion to the rank of attorney on June 8, 1918, was "reviewing aliens who volunteered for military duty and wanted to become citizens." This law went into effect on May 9, 1918.[40] By the end of September, Hoover was also providing O'Brian with opinions on complicated cases involving travel permits for German aliens; he now handled difficult cases from all areas within the Alien Enemy Bureau, although he still kept his hand on his old job, so that Armistice Day (November 11) found him still compiling registration statistics on alien enemies.

Both Gregory and O'Brian had notified President Wilson that they wanted to leave government service at the end of the war. O'Brian, alarmed that Gregory and Secretary of Labor William Wilson had asked Congress for the power to deport dangerous interned aliens, stayed on long enough to review the files of all interned aliens to make sure they would not be placed in jeopardy by still being in jail if a new law went into effect. He released all of them except some German seamen who had refused repatriation during the war and about 150 aliens who had been convicted of violations of wartime regulations. He also reviewed all the convictions he had obtained under the Espionage Act, and obtained three pardons and 102 commutations from President Wilson.[41]

Hoover's wartime experience in the Alien Enemy Bureau did more than simply give him a foothold in the Justice Department. It accustomed him to using administrative procedures as a substitute for the uncertainties and delays of the legal process. The enemy status of the aliens Hoover supervised had stripped them of the protection of the Constitution, and so he got his first taste of authority under circumstances in which he could disregard the normal constitutional restraints on the power of the state.

Hoover had spent a heady year and a half as a novice lawyer with freedom or prison his to grant with the stroke of a pen. The war emergency had given his personal judgment the force of law when determining the loyalty or disloyalty of alien enemies. His latitude to decide the fate of those whose papers were before him was limited only by his sense of responsibility and the review of his superiors. After the end of the war Hoover would no longer be supervised by O'Brian and Gregory, with their scrupulous regard for civil liberties. They would be replaced by ambitious politicians, such as A. Mitchell Palmer, who were all too willing to use the administrative techniques of the Alien Enemy Bureau in a postwar campaign to repress unpopular political beliefs.

CHAPTER 3

The Red Years: The Lessons of Success

The Red Army already exists in Russia; the Red Army soon will exist over all of the world. . . . In 1919 was born the Great Communist International. In 1920 will be born the Great International Soviet Republic.

The First Congress of the Third International, 1919, quoted
that year by Hoover in his legal brief on the Communist Party

THE YEAR 1919 was the first of what the Italian left dubbed the *biennio rosso,* the "red years," when the Communist revolution surged out of Russia to topple governments throughout Central Europe, terrifying the rich, the powerful, and the respectable everywhere before being thrown back by the unexpectedly resilient and ruthless forces of conservatism. By the end of 1920, it was clear that the revolution had been confined to Russia for the foreseeable future, and that the international Communist movement had become an instrument of Russian policy. However, between 1919 and 1920, when J. Edgar Hoover began his battle against radicalism, a worldwide revolution seemed not only possible but imminent. Hoover's anticommunism never lost the flavor of those years when, in John Dos Passos's words, "Lenin was alive, [and] the Seattle general strike had seemed the beginning of the flood instead of the beginning of the ebb."[1]

While Hoover was processing his last, meaningless cases in the expiring Alien Enemy Bureau, all of Europe

seemed to be turning to Lenin's banner. In October, 1918, revolutions broke out in Hungary, Austria, and Bulgaria. A month later came the revolution in Germany which deposed the Kaiser and trembled on the edge of eliminating the Junkers. In Hungary, Finland, and parts of Germany soviets were declared, and while all went down to quick and bloody defeat no one could suppose that in any of these countries the impulse to revolt had been exhausted. Mutinies ravaged the French army; workers in the major Italian cities seized the factories; a radical shop steward movement grew rapidly in England.[2]

Meanwhile, Hoover was watching his Justice Department career wind down as the Alien Enemy Bureau was liquidated after the armistice. The expertise he had acquired in dealing with aliens during the war would not be needed in the peacetime department; aliens would once again become the responsibility of the Immigration Bureau, a section of the Labor Department.

Almost all the men Hoover had worked with in the wartime Justice Department, the people who knew his energy and talents, were leaving government service. By May 1, 1919, Gregory, O'Brian, Warren, and Bielaski (who resigned on February 10, 1919), would be gone, and the new attorney general (Palmer took office at the beginning of March) could not be expected to show any interest in a low-level holdover like Hoover.[3]

Early in 1919, Hoover, along with the rest of the country, was subjected to a barrage of hysterical warnings from pulpit, rostrum, and editorial page that the institutions of government and property in America were under attack by international revolution, and that the American radical movement was the Red conspiracy's cutting edge in the United States. During the first few months of 1919, when the Red tide was running highest in Europe, Hoover was in no position to form any independent impressions of what was happening, and so he, like the rest of the public, had to rely on accounts in the rabidly anti-Communist press. A few months later, though, as head of the antiradical division within the Justice Department, he would be in a position to collect and study the whole written output of the radical movement. To Hoover, this material would seem authoritative confirmation of the worst fears of the right-wing press and conservative politicians.

The background of European violence made the wave of strikes that broke out in the United States in 1919 seem part of a worldwide class war between capital and labor. Strikes had been prohibited during the war, and there was still a lingering public sentiment that any kind of work stoppage was disloyal. The media had little difficulty frightening the country when some 4 million American workers went out on 3,600 strikes in 1919. In February alone there were three major strikes with radical overtones—in Lawrence, Massachusetts; Butte, Montana; and Seattle, Washington.

For years employers had appealed for government and public support in labor disputes by charging that workers were not simply seeking economic advantages but were instead out to destroy the basic economic institutions of society. The mainstream unions learned to defend themselves against this charge of radicalism (which was often a pretext for government intervention in strikes) by explicitly rejecting any goals except economic ones: "Pure and simple unionism" had become the formula for survival of Samuel Gompers and the moderate unions of the American Federation of Labor (AFL). When radical unions like the IWW struck for avowedly political goals, the mainstream unions joined business and government in attacking them. The Wobblies's doctrine that "every strike is a small revolution and a dress rehearsal for the big one," was precisely the argument labor's enemies used when they called on the government to suppress strikes. By 1919, the nonradical labor union movement had essentially conceded antiunion forces their essential premise: that any demands beyond improvements in wages and hours were illegitimate, even criminal. "For wages or for bolshevism" was the test strikes had to pass.

The Seattle general strike seemed to be for bolshevism. It began with a walkout of 35,000 shipyard workers on January 21, 1919; it spread when the Seattle Central Labor Council voted to shut down the city to support the shipyard workers. The conservative press, seeing the general strike as the beginning of a revolution, ran headlines that screamed: REDS DIRECTING SEATTLE STRIKE—TO TEST CHANCE FOR REVOLUTION. On February 6, 60,000 more workers joined the walkout, closing schools, public transportation, businesses, and stores. Mayor Ole Hanson said that the general strike was an act of war by radicals who "want to take possession of our American Government and try to duplicate the anarchy of Russia." Hanson got federal troops from a nearby army base and, riding in a flag-draped auto, led the march into the city himself. With soldiers to back him up, he told the strikers to resume work or have the soldiers take their jobs. The strikers were now under fierce attack from their own national unions for abandoning pure and simple unionism, and after only four days gave up and called off the strike. Hanson's role in crushing the strike made him a national hero, perhaps giving Hoover and Palmer an idea of what could be gained from militant anticommunism in the crisis atmosphere of the times. Meanwhile, Hanson turned his reputation into cash by resigning and taking to the lecture circuit.[4]

The Seattle general strike raised suspicions that there was a Red flag hidden behind every picket sign. Since there were 175 strikes in the U.S. in March 1919, 248 in April, 388 in May, 303 in June, 360 in July, and 373 in August, that was a fearsome prospect. The wartime assumption that strikes were unpatriotic, even pro-German now shifted to the view that they were pro-Soviet, and so still quasi-treasonous. Hoover would have heard politicians in early 1919 call industrial America a battlefield in an international class war, requiring the continuation of the wartime measures that controlled union activities.

In both Europe and the United States, veterans who felt threatened by revolutionary ideology organized themselves to defend against the revolution. The most violent was the German *Freikorps,* which put down the German revolution and killed Karl Liebknecht and Rosa Luxemburg. In the U.S., the leaders and members of the wartime American Protective League, disbanded after the armistice by order of the Justice Department, begged to be allowed to regroup to oppose bolshevism and, in isolated instances, this offer was informally accepted. In an uncomfortably close parallel to the *Freikorps,* the American Legion was founded on May 5, 1919; one of its avowed purposes was to aid the government in the fight against communism. In November 1919, there was a pitched battle between members of the IWW and the American Legion in Centralia, Washington, in which one of the IWW members, Wesley Everest, himself a World War I veteran, was castrated, hanged, and shot to death by a mob of Legionnaires.[5]

While Hoover sat on the sidelines in the Alien Enemy Bureau, newspapers claimed there was an international radical plot to assassinate world leaders. Those rumors seemed to have been proved true when a bomb was delivered to the home of Ole Hanson on April 28, 1919. (It was detected and disarmed.) The next day, another bomb blew off the hands of a maid at the Atlanta home of former U.S. Senator Thomas Hardwick. Over the next few days, thirty-four more bombs were discovered and intercepted before reaching their intended victims, public figures such as Frederick C. Howe (the commissioner of immigration at Ellis Island), Senator Lee Overman (who had chaired a sensational senatorial hearing on Bolshevism), Supreme Court Associate Justice Oliver Wendell Holmes, Jr., Postmaster General Albert Burlson, and Judge Kenesaw Mountain Landis (who had sentenced Victor Berger and Big Bill Haywood). Others were sent to Attorney

General A. Mitchell Palmer, Secretary of Labor William Wilson, John D. Rockefeller, and J. P. Morgan.[6]

The April bombs were sent to both friends and foes of immigrants and radicals, but few at the time doubted the senders were radicals celebrating a slightly premature May Day, marked that year by Red-flag parades, riots in scores of American cities, and mob assaults on Socialist party headquarters. Years later, when the Red Scare had run its course, there were suspicions that the bombers may not have been radicals after all, but right-wing provocateurs hoping to touch off violence against radicals.[7]

The unrest of 1919 might not have led to such insistent calls for action against radicals if the public were not already so predisposed. This prejudice had been greatly intensified during the war by Justice Department prosecution of radicals under the Espionage and Sedition acts, which branded anyone who opposed the war as "pro-German." Nearly all of the country's ethnic, religious, and cultural minorities had embraced the war as a way into the American mainstream, so when radicals conspicuously rejected the call for national unity it set them apart from and against the rest. During the period of Hoover's wartime service in the Justice Department, the belief spread among self-consciously patriotic Americans that radicals, anarchists, Communists, and Socialists were all un-American, unpatriotic, and even treasonous.[8]

As soon as the war was over, conservatives demanded radicals be held accountable for their wartime disloyalty. The process was begun, almost inadvertently, by Alien Property Administrator A. Mitchell Palmer, Hoover's future chief at the Justice Department. In 1918, Palmer charged that Senator Boies Penrose, a political enemy from his home state of Pennsylvania, had accepted political contributions from the brewing industry. Palmer claimed that since the brewing industry was pro-German and disloyal, Penrose was disloyal for accepting its money.

A subcommittee of the Judiciary Committee headed by Senator Lee Slater Overman was appointed to investigate Palmer's charges. The Overman Committee soon broadened its investigation into the general phenomenon of "pro-Germanism."[9] Bureau of Investigation Director Bruce Bielaski helpfully informed the committee that his men had made an extensive study of the subject and had concluded that pro-Germanism was sweeping America like an epidemic (based on the assumption that anyone who opposed Wilson's neutrality or war policies was a German sympathizer). The Overman Committee made itself a forum for irresponsible charges against prominent professors, journalists, and government officials whose real offenses were unorthodox political opinions, but the committee was discredited when many of the victims easily refuted the unsubstantiated charges. The armistice of November 11 seemed to cancel the committee's mandate, and, embarrassed by the pro-German fiasco, most of the members were content to go quietly out of business.

At this point, one of the committee's witnesses, New York lawyer Archibald E. Stevenson, showed the senators a way to shift from flogging the dead horse of pro-Germanism to tormenting the increasingly lively Bolsheviks. During the war, Stevenson had chaired the Mayor's Committee on Aliens in New York and had worked for the Justice Department as a special agent investigating enemy propaganda. After the war, he had made a study of radical aliens for New York's Union League. On January 22, 1919, he informed the Overman Committee that bolshevism "is the result of German propaganda" and that "German socialism . . . is the father of the Bolsheviki movement in Russia, and consequently the radical movement which we have in this country today has its origin in Germany." By linking antiradical sentiment to the hatred of Germans, Stevenson's testimony gave the Overman Committee a reason to request a new mandate from the Senate to investigate American radicalism. The hearings on bolshevism began on February 11, 1919, and lasted until March 10, capitalizing on the panic generated by the Seattle general strike. The senators grilled radicals like John Reed and his wife, Louise Bryant, gathered estimates from White Russian refugees on the number of American troops needed to overthrow the Soviet regime (50,000 was not an untypical guess), and listened to lurid accounts of Bolshevik atrocities.[10]

Stevenson's testimony was a recapitulation of everything conservative Americans believed about radicals: Reds were dangerous troublemakers; they subscribed to unpatriotic and irreligious ideas; and they could not be trusted around decent women. They were almost always aliens; if they were Americans, they belonged to an effete class that had abandoned true Americanism for European decadence. What was new in Stevenson's story was his description of Russian bolshevism as a malevolent force that unified (and controlled) radicals everywhere. "So long as the Bolsheviki control and dominate the millions of Europe, so long . . . [they will] be a constant menace and encouragement to the radical and dissatisfied elements in this country." The committee listened to proposals for new laws, such as "no person should enter this country unless he is a white man—and Anglo-Saxon—for the next 10 years," that "bars should be put up to exclude seditious literature," and that "American citizens who advocate revolution should be punished under a law drawn for that purpose."[11]

The Overman Committee thesis that bolshevism was pro-Germanism simply confirmed what many already believed. When the Bolsheviks had pulled Russia out of the war in March 1918, freeing Germany from the necessity of fighting a two-front war, many Americans had been convinced that the Bolsheviks were allies of the Germans, in effect if not in intent. By the crude logic of wartime patriotism, this meant that anyone who sympathized with the Bolsheviks should be regarded as a German sympathizer as well. This was devastating to the public image of the American radical movement, because enthusiasm for the Bolshevik revolution united almost all American leftists in 1918 and 1919. Eugene Debs, the most prominent Socialist in the country, proclaimed that "from the crown of my head to the soles of my feet I am Bolshevik, and proud of it."[12]

After the armistice, the government continued to press for punishment of radicals convicted under wartime statutes, and even initiated new prosecutions. In January 1919, Victor Berger, the former Socialist congressman from Wisconsin, was convicted under the Espionage Act. Eugene Debs, convicted under the same act on March 10, 1919, exhausted all avenues of appeal when his case was rejected by the Supreme Court, and he entered prison two weeks later. These cases had to have reinforced Hoover's assumption that radicals were criminals and traitors.[13]

State and local loyalty crusades also contributed to the sense of crisis to which Hoover and Palmer responded in 1919. The New York State Assembly had ordered an investigation of radicalism in response to Archibald Stevenson's Union League report of March 13, which was filled with wild allegations that such prominent New York liberals as social workers Jane Addams and Lillian Wald, historian Charles Beard, editor Oswald Garrison Villard and Ellis Island Commissioner Frederick Howe were covert radicals.[14] This was the notorious Lusk Committee, chaired by State Senator Clayton R. Lusk, with Stevenson its chief counsel.

The Lusk Committee began its hearings on March 26, 1919, and provided more headlines about the radical threat. Throughout the spring and summer of 1919, the Luskers hammered away at the idea that radicals were disloyal and dangerous, and that the strikes and bombings of that year were actually the beginning of the Bolshevik revolution in America.

On the evening of June 2, a month after the May Day bombs, a blast destroyed the front of Attorney General Palmer's home in northwest Washington. The explosion killed the bomb-thrower, and in the grisly debris was found a leaflet threatening violence against the "capitalist class"; it was signed "the Anarchist Fighters." Neither Palmer nor his family were injured, but according to Palmer's neighbor, Assistant Secretary of the Navy Franklin D. Roosevelt, the attorney general was so rattled that he reverted to his Quaker childhood usage of "thees" and "thous." It was this blast, never solved, that provoked the Justice Department's 1919 drive against radicals, and launched the FBI career of J. Edgar Hoover.[15]

The dust had hardly settled when Palmer recruited Francis P. Garvan, his old chief investigator from the Alien Property Bureau, and William J. Flynn, the former head of the Secret Service and a renowned private investigator, to help plan a Justice Department response to the bombing. On June 4, he announced he had appointed Garvan as his assistant attorney general to deal with the radical threat. He made Flynn the director of the Bureau of Investigation, and appointed Frank Burke, who has been head of the Secret Service's New York branch and also of its Russian division, as Flynn's assistant director, with the title "chief." (Titles of the Bureau's top ranks were now being regularized; the head of the Bureau, heretofore sometimes called "director" and sometimes "chief," was now designated as the "director," while his second-in-command was known as "assistant director and chief.")[16]

With these men as his advisors, Palmer began drawing up plans for an all-out attack on radicalism. He asked Congress for an additional appropriation to investigate radicals, claiming he had certain information that there was soon to be an "attempt to rise up and destroy the government at one fell swoop." At an all-day meeting on June 17, the Justice Department decided on its strategy: a mass roundup and deportation of alien radicals.[17]

Hoover probably attended this June 17 meeting, and it was either then or shortly thereafter that Palmer and his advisors decided to put Hoover in charge of the drive. On July 1, Palmer promoted Hoover to the rank of special assistant to the attorney general, reporting to

Garvan; the promotion was accompanied by a raise in salary, from $1,800 to $3,000. (By way of comparison, the director of the Bureau of Investigation, William Flynn, was earning $7,500 a year, while Chief Burke's salary was $4,000.) Shortly thereafter, Hoover's name appeared for the first time in the table of organization of the Bureau of Investigation.[18]

At the time Palmer promoted him, Hoover was, in effect, hanging onto his job by virtue of John Lord O'Brian's recommendation to Palmer (probably in March or April). According to O'Brian, "at the end of the war, at the time of the Armistice, [Hoover] told me he would like to continue in the permanent side of the Department of Justice, and I took that up personally with the new Attorney General, A. Mitchell Palmer."[19] O'Brian's recommendation would still have been fresh in Palmer's mind when the bomb went off and he needed the help of someone who knew something about aliens.

O'Brian's recommendation might have impressed Palmer for personal reasons. Despite the many differences between the two men (Palmer was a power within the national Democratic party; O'Brian an influential Republican), they had many friends in common. Palmer was closely associated with J. Harry Covington and Edward B. Burling, who later founded the powerful Washington law firm of Covington and Burling. These two men were friends of Hoover's uncle, Judge William Hitz; it was Hitz, at one of his Cosmos Club luncheons, who introduced his friend O'Brian to Covington and Burling, whose law firm O'Brian joined much later in 1944. It is quite likely, therefore, that when O'Brian mentioned Hoover to Palmer he would also have mentioned that Hoover was related to Judge Hitz, a friend of Covington's.[20]

Hoover's most valuable credential for his new job was his wartime experience dealing with undesirable aliens. With the departure of Gregory and O'Brian, Hoover was, despite his youth, the Justice Department's resident alien expert. He was the only man in the Justice Department who had experience in working with the Labor Department's Immigration Bureau to use deportation statutes as a way of dealing expeditiously and extrajudicially with aliens. (The Washington staffs of the Labor Department's Immigration Bureau and the Justice Department's Alien Enemy Bureau had been practically merged during the war.) When it became necessary to reestablish relations with the Labor Department in order to conduct a large-scale operation against aliens, Hoover was the logical, indeed the only available, choice for the job.

Hoover's enthusiasm for tracking down foreigners, fueled by the suspicion of aliens nurtured in his youth, may have become known throughout the department. This is what John Lord O'Brian may have meant when, on the day of Hoover's death, he said that Hoover had always had an "active interest in alien activities." Hoover joined the Masons around this time, and that may also have been connected to his attitudes toward immigrants; World War I had been a watershed in the history of Freemasonry, when it became active in nativist politics, and many lodges became involved in the campaign against radicalism and for immigration restrictions. (In joining the Masons, however, it is possible that Hoover was simply following the lead of his brother, Dick, who was an avid member.)[21]

Hoover's youth (he was just twenty-four in the spring of 1919), may actually have been one more reason Palmer chose him to direct the anti-Communist campaign. While Palmer was personally religious and publicly moralistic, he was politically corrupt—a type not infrequently attracted by the ruthlessness and recklessness of young, clean-cut subordinates—with a lifelong suspicion of foreigners and radicals.[22] He was avaricious and up to his elbows in political profiteering. His Alien Property Bureau was a conduit for transferring German wealth to his political allies in the Democratic party. By 1919, Palmer had few scruples or fixed political beliefs. He wanted desperately to win the 1920 Democratic nomination for president, which he felt was almost within his grasp. He was willing to do anything to achieve this end, and he may have seen in Hoover an aggressive, self-confident young operative who would give him the issue he needed to become president.

With his straitlaced morality, his energy, intelligence, and his complete lack of self-doubt, Hoover was the very model of the young middle-class crusader, obsessed with the crimes and failings of the lower orders, and suspicious of those in the upper classes who pampered them. This combination of youth, intelligence, and energy might have been attractive to Palmer, whose own capacity for hard work and concentrated thought was limited. (He was prone to nervous collapse in times of stress.)

Not only did Hoover have enormous energy and ambition, but he had a dauntless confidence in his organizational and leadership abilities based on his experience in the Alien Enemy Bureau and his earlier successes at Central High. He carried with him a sense of self–assurance that came from membership in a local elite, accompanied, perhaps, by a resentment of both the undeserving lower orders and the idle rich, whose solicitude for those below them mocked middle-class ambitions and respectability. Hoover's commitment to a government career, at a time when able lawyers in the department were eager to leave and resume their peacetime legal practice, also made him stand out from his competitors in the department, who, by self-selection, would not have been the most ambitious and energetic members of the profession.

Hoover probably would have had a successful career no matter what the circumstances, but the unsettled state of public opinion, the radical movement's uncontrollable and uncontrolled sense of imminent triumph, the spectacular bombings directed against the attorney general and other prominent officials, created an opportunity for which he was perfectly suited by background, experience, and personality. Perhaps every great career depends on an improbable run of good fortune. At this critical moment in his life, Hoover had the luck to be at the right place, at the right time, with the right aptitudes, credentials, and confidence.

Once Hoover was installed at the head of the Justice Department's antiradical campaign, Palmer turned to other pressing concerns. Inflation had surged after the armistice and the public demanded government action. Palmer and the Justice Department had the hapless job of policing regulations against the "high cost of living," as well as settling disruptive strikes in basic industries. Toward the end of the year, Palmer's heavy work load, and the probability that President Wilson's stroke made Palmer the leading contender for the 1920 Democratic presidential nomination, reduced him to a state of nervous prostration. His doctors described his condition only in the guarded euphemisms of the day, and sent him away for several weeks of vacation. Hoover found himself left to his own devices during the height of the department's preparations for its antiradical drive.[23]

Except for the decision to restrict the anti-Communist drive to aliens—a policy with which he was unlikely to quarrel since his reputation as an alien expert had gotten him the job—Hoover was in complete charge of planning the attack on radicalism during the summer and fall of 1919. He selected the targets of the antiradical campaign, both individuals (Emma Goldman, Alexander Berkman, and Ludwig Martens) and groups (the Union of Russian Workers, the Communist party, and the Communist Labor party). He wrote the briefs that justified the deportations, and personally presented the government's case at the deportation hearings. He organized the Radical Division's research facilities, hired its experts and translators, and directed the Bureau of Investigation in beginning the files on the Communist movement that have been the foundation of the FBI's domestic security apparatus to the present day.

In terms of his career and the future of the FBI, the most important thing Hoover did during that summer of 1919 was to immerse himself in the words and ideas of the Communist movement as it went through the most dynamic and self-confident period in its history. Hoover's research during his hectic first months as head of the Radical Division, cutting out and pasting together hair-raising passages from Communist journals, manifestos, and propaganda, gave him fixed convictions about the nature and intentions of Communists that supported his anti-Communist fervor the rest of his life.

Hoover's first task was to organize the Radical Division, which he would direct until his appointment as head of the Bureau of Investigation in 1924.[24] The Radical Division (Hoover would rename it the General Intelligence Division, or GID, in 1920) was primarily a research operation, the kind of work that appealed to Hoover and for which his experiences at the Library of Congress and the Alien Enemy Bureau had prepared him. Initially, Hoover's salary as special assistant to the attorney general showed that he ranked third in the Bureau, behind Director Flynn and Assistant Director Burke, but within a year he would be making $4,500 a year—still with the same title—which put his salary higher than the assistant director's (still $4,000). In terms of salary, then, he would in effect be the second-ranking official in the Bureau of Investigation at the age of twenty-five, earning almost as much as Director Flynn, who was one of the best-known detectives in the country.

Despite his youth, Hoover's appointment to head the Radical Division put him in charge of what quickly became by far the largest section of the Bureau of Investigation, and made him independent of the authority of anyone in the Bureau. Though his position made him formally subject to Director Flynn, Hoover did not report to him; instead, he reported to Flynn's immediate superior, Assistant Attorney General Francis Garvan. Thus, from August 1, 1919, to August 1921 (when he officially became assistant director of the Bureau), he was able to operate as part of the Bureau of Investigation's chain of command when he wished, but also to act independently of the Bureau as part of the Justice Department. This situation afforded him unusual autonomy, which he would later demand as his due.

Under Hoover, the Radical Division was an interdivisional task force with its own budget and administrative staff but able to call on the operational resources of the Bureau and the other branches of the Justice Department. Hoover's operational orders to Bureau agents working on Radical Division cases were usually issued in the name of Flynn or Burke, particularly at the beginning, but the agents' reports on radicals were routed directly from the field to him. His orders to Justice Department personnel or U.S. attorneys were usually issued in Palmer's name. Requests from Bureau or department officials to use his facilities or to borrow his subordinates had to be submitted to Hoover for his approval.[25]

At the outset, Hoover's activities were exclusively "general intelligence" in nature (the term refers to the gathering of background information for a general understanding of a situation, as opposed to an investigation to produce a case for criminal prosecution). By December, however, his mastery of the facts on radicalism had given him effective operational control of the department's antiradical campaign as well.

Hoover prepared for his antiradical operations by collecting information on radical publications, organizations, and individuals in his central files in Washington. By November, his division had completed a classification of over 60,000 "radically inclined" individuals. He reported that "one of the first matters receiving the attention of the Radical Division after its organization were the various societies in the United States adhering to anarchistic doctrines." He organized and trained a team of forty translators, assistants, and readers to monitor 471 radical periodicals published in this country and abroad. Like the competitive debater he had been, he gathered all available material on his opponent's case, mastered its contents, and then prepared thoroughly for the eventual confrontation. Within a year, Hoover had assembled a vast collection of research materials on the "ultraradical movement." Congress was informed that "the work of the General Intelligence Division necessitates a large amount of research and the study of the various ultraradical movements theoretically and historically. . . . The nucleus for an excellent working library has been procured." A year after the organization of his division, Hoover had at his disposal a Publications Section that scanned 625 papers for information on the radical movement, and a card catalog of 200,000 entries on "various subjects or individuals."[26]

The Radical Division described its "general intelligence" function in a report probably written by Hoover himself: "It is clearly recognized that the present unrest and tendency toward radicalism arise from social and economic conditions that are of greater consequence than the individual agitator. An intelligent investigation of the agitator, of his work, and of the results of his work, therefore, demands an understanding of social and economic conditions as a whole. With no social or economic theories to exploit, but with the simple desire to work intelligently and effectively, the division is steadily training a group of its agents to take in account these larger factors at the same time that they are investigating individuals."[27] This closely resembles, in substance and style, the description Hoover wrote for the Central High newspaper about his plans for training his Cadet Company for its end-of-year competition.

Hoover was preparing, by virtue of his files, to function as the government's expert on radicalism so he could be more definite and convincing in his analysis than any rival. The facilities of the Radical Division gave Hoover a semi-monopoly over a sort of information so difficult to obtain, so extensive in coverage, and so commonly inaccessible as to make its independent verification almost impossible. He had put himself in a position, as he had when he debated for Central High, of being able to overawe and overwhelm his enemies, and of being indispensable to his friends because of his intense preparation and study. The Radical Division, and Hoover's skill at organizing it, turned him into the government's first authority on communism, a position he jealously guarded the rest of his life.

From the start, Hoover had a reverence bordering on idolatry for the "fact" as conclusive and self-explanatory in itself, and a belief that since facts carried their own persuasiveness, other people should see the same significance in them as he did unless they were deliberately and perversely obtuse. He exhibited a pronounced tendency to equate the facts themselves with the interpretation he made of them. And, because he possessed more "facts" than anyone else, and could point to his files to prove it, he had absolute confidence in the validity of his opinions.

The Justice Department had been under pressure to do something about alien radicals even before the bombings. As early as February 1919, Attorney General Thomas Gregory had announced the department's plans to deport between 7,000 and 8,000 "alien anarchists and trouble makers." In March, Congress criticized Gregory for not having done enough to combat radicalism.[28]

Early in 1919, the Immigration Bureau of the Labor Department, facing the same kind of pressure, particularly from West Coast officials, increased its efforts to use the deportation laws against radicals. On February 6, agents of the Immigration Bureau loaded a railroad car in Seattle with thirty-six alien Wobblies. This "Red Special" got enormous publicity, and immigration officials promised there would be many more such trainloads. When the "Special" arrived at Ellis Island, Secretary of Labor William Wilson (an immigrant himself) stepped in to review the Wobblies's deportation orders. He released twelve of them on March 14, and two more a few days later. Five voluntarily accepted deportation. Of the remaining seventeen, six had their orders confirmed by the court, and the rest dismissed. By the time the Immigration Bureau had concluded its IWW deportation efforts, 150 had been arrested but only twenty-seven deported.[29]

Attorney General Palmer rationalized the Justice Department's focus on *alien* radicals by claiming (with statistics furnished by Hoover) that "the results of investigations made by this Department into the ultraradical movement during the course of the last year has clearly indicated that fully 90 per cent of the communist and anarchist agitation is traceable to aliens."[30] There were also practical reasons for Palmer and Hoover to move first against aliens. No law then in effect permitted the Justice Department to attack radical citizens for their beliefs and associations, but only for criminal acts, and such criminality was hard to prove. In no instance, for example, was the department able to build a case against anyone for the bombings that had touched off the 1919 drive.

However, it *was* possible to attack aliens for their beliefs and associations. The Immigration Act passed in 1918 had given the government a weapon of enormous power to use against radical aliens. Aliens were subject to deportation if they believed in anarchism or political violence, or if they belonged to organizations that advocated political violence or anarchistic principles.

Radical citizens could be punished only after being convicted in court proceedings in which they were protected by constitutional safeguards. Under the tortured logic of immigration rules, deportation was viewed as an administrative action, not as a punishment, so an alien in an immigration hearing was not entitled to any of the constitutional protections he would have had at a criminal trial. The rules of evidence, the right to counsel, the right to a speedy trial—none of these applied. The alien was protected only by the Immigration Bureau's own regulations, which were thoroughly skewed against the alien "to protect the rights of the government," in the Immigration Bureau's quaint phrase.[31]

The immigration laws also held out the possibility of proceeding against alien radicals *en masse* rather than individually. As Hoover's thinking on the subject evolved, he worked out a procedure in which he would simply obtain a ruling that an organization fell within the class of those proscribed under the 1918 law (advocating anarchism or the violent overthrow of the government). That accomplished, he felt he should be able to deport aliens simply by producing evidence that they were members—membership cards, dues books, or testimony that they attended meetings—without any direct evidence about their personal beliefs.

By concentrating on radical aliens, Hoover and Palmer had adopted a practical course, but not a strictly legal one. Since 1871, the Justice Department's authority for conducting investigations had been contained in its appropriation bill, which authorized the expenditure of funds only for the "detection and prosecution of crimes against the United States." Many members of Congress expected the department to follow this restriction literally; when William Burns, President Harding's director of the Bureau of Investigation, requested that this language be extended to include "prevention" of crime, Congress rejected the idea. No broader investigative authority for the Justice Department had been granted in the new appropriation Palmer had obtained to investigate the radical bomb plots, and it is unlikely that he could have obtained broader authority without a political struggle.

The legal fiction that made deportation such an attractive strategy against radicals—that deportation was not punishment for a crime but only an administrative procedure—was based on the second fiction that the offense for which the alien was being deported was not a crime. This meant that an investigation intended to produce a deportation was, by definition, *not* an investigation of a crime and therefore not authorized under the Justice Department's appropriation. Hoover himself later admitted there was "no authority under the law permitting this Department to take any action in deportation proceedings relative to radical activities." The Justice Department had maneuvered itself into a legal dilemma: Its loose and arbitrary procedures against aliens were justified by the legal pretense that the proceedings were not criminal, while the language of its appropriation very specifically limited the department to investigations of criminal matters. Nevertheless, what the Department was doing was no secret to Congress, so Hoover and Palmer were not overly concerned about their technical misallocation of funds.[32]

As soon as Hoover took charge of the Justice Department's antiradical drive, the government's efforts—heretofore scattered and uncoordinated—were turned into a unified program that had a long-range goal that transcended the immediate objective of deporting a few thousand aliens. Hoover and Palmer were working to whet the appetite of the public and Congress for an extension of the drive to include citizen members of radical organizations. They hoped that the 1919 deportation campaign would result in new legislation already being prepared by Justice Department lawyers. This was a peacetime sedition law that would give the Justice Department as powerful a weapon against radical citizens as the 1918 immigration law had given it against radical aliens.[33]

Palmer and Hoover never hid their real aim in 1919, which would have been truly "radical": a permanent alteration in American political culture by the setting of strict legal limits to allowable political dissent. Palmer later described the deportation drive as not "a mere matter of punishing, by sending out of the country a few criminals or mistaken ultraradicals who preach dangerous doctrines, but rather as a campaign against—and I have felt that was the purpose of the country—a growing revolutionary movement which sought by force and violence to undermine and injure, and possibly destroy our Government." Since the ultimate goal was "to rid the country of the Red agitators," the Justice Department regarded the deportation raids, while valuable in themselves, as a stopgap measure until legislation to "punish the citizen for the offenses of which the penalty for an alien is deportation" could be prepared.[34]

Palmer and Hoover were hardly alone in their desire for a new weapon against radical ideas. Most of the government was in a frenzy against radicalism. In one of his last speeches before his stroke, President Wilson himself had denounced "the poison of disorder, the poison of revolt, the poison of chaos [that is] . . . in the veins of this free people," and then, in his annual message to Congress in December 1919, recommended passage of the Justice Department's new sedition law.[35]

Late in 1919, the Justice Department's proposal for a sedition bill was introduced into the House by Congressman Martin Davey of Ohio. It contained provisions directed specifically against aliens, but the substantive portion of the bill applied to all persons, citizens and aliens alike. It offered a definition of sedition that seemed to grow broader with each clause:

> Whoever, with the intent to levy war against the United States, or to cause the change, overthrow, or destruction of the Government or of

any of the laws or authority thereof, or to cause the overthrow or destruction of all forms of law or organized government, or to oppose, prevent, hinder, or delay the execution of any law of the United States, or the free performance by the United States Government or any one of its officers, agents or employees, of its or his public duty, commits, or attempts, or threatens to commit, any act of force against any person or any property, or any act of terrorism, hate, revenge or injury against the person or property of any officer, agent or employee of the United States, shall be deemed guilty of sedition.[36]

A second, and still more drastic, section defined the offense of "promoting sedition":

Whoever makes, displays, writes, prints, or circulates, or knowingly aids or abets the making, displaying, writing, printing, or circulating, of any sign, word, speech, picture, design, argument, or teaching, which advises, advocates, teaches, or justifies any act of sedition as hereinbefore defined, or any act which tends to indicate sedition as hereinbefore defined, or organizes or assists, or joins in the organization of, or becomes or remains a member of, or affiliated with, any society or organization, whether the same be formally organized or not, which has for its object, in whole or in part, the advising, advocating, teaching, or justifying any act of sedition as hereinbefore defined, or the inciting of sedition as hereinbefore defined, shall be deemed guilty of promoting sedition.[37]

The Red Scare raids were part of the political struggle to enact this legislation. Hoover prepared testimony for Palmer in which he described to Congress the sort of citizens who would be liable under the new law:

Most of the individuals involved in this movement are aliens or foreign-born citizens. There are some, however, of unquestioned American extraction. Some of the leaders are idealists with distorted minds, many even insane; many are professional agitators who are plainly self-seekers and a large number are potential or actual criminals whose baseness of character leads them to espouse the unrestrained and gross theories and tactics of these organizations. If there be any doubt of the general character of the active leaders and agitators amongst these avowed revolutionists, a visit to the Department of Justice and an examination of their photographs there collected would dispel it. Out of the sly and crafty eyes of many of them leap cupidity, cruelty, insanity, and crime; from their lopsided faces, sloping brows, and misshapen features may be recognized the unmistakable criminal type.[38]

(The legislation passed the Senate, but was still being considered in the House when the Red Scare drive collapsed under the weight of congressional investigations, and so was never brought up for a vote in that chamber.)

With the blueprints for the Radical Division drawn, its personnel chosen, and the ultimate purpose of the drive clearly in mind, Hoover next had to locate specific candidates for deportation. For the antiradical drive to have any real impact on public opinion, there would have to be large numbers of deportees, and at least some of them would have to be well known to the public. Once this was accomplished, Hoover and the department would be able to claim that they had driven the "brains" of the radical movement out of the country.

Hoover's wartime experience had accustomed him to a wholesale brand of justice that could dispense with due process by dealing with defendants administratively. The alien enemies that he had then supervised had been considered guilty because of their group membership (their nationality) until proven innocent. Thus, Hoover knew fully well what would be needed to mount an effective operation: agreement by the relevant authority (the Labor Department) that the target organizations fell within the language of the 1918 immigration law; then he would use the Immigration Bureau's procedures to bypass the cumbersome legal processes.

In August 1919, however, Hoover was in the frustrating position of being one step ahead of the radicals. He was ready to deport them as soon as they had joined formally organized groups, but, for the most part, they had not yet done so. The radicals he most wanted to attack, the American Socialists who were in sympathy with Russian bolshevism, had not yet declared their independence from the nonrevolutionary Socialist party. The IWW, the Workers International Industrial Union, and the Left Wing of the Socialist party were all regarded by the Russian Communists as potential allies, but the Left Wing, which contained the largest number of aliens, had not yet organized itself into an American Communist party. It remained part of the American Socialist party, which was formally and actually committed to parliamentary methods and opposed to "direct action."

As soon as he took over the Radical Division, Hoover had the Bureau director initiate a search for organizations that could be proscribed under the 1918 immigration law for advocating anarchy or the forcible overthrow of the government. On August 12, 1919, Director Flynn sent instructions (probably drafted by Hoover) to his special agents requesting that they give Hoover any information they could discover in this regard. "The bureau," Flynn wrote, "requires a vigorous and comprehensive investigation of anarchistic and similar classes, Bolshevism, and kindred agitations advocating change in the present form of government by force or violence, the promotion of sedition and revolution, bomb throwing, and similar activities." Admitting that there were no federal laws under which citizens might be effectively prosecuted for merely advocating such acts, Flynn stated that "in the present state of the Federal law this investigation should be particularly directed to persons not citizens of the United States, with a view of obtaining deportation cases." With new sedition legislation in the offing, however, Flynn told his agents to also keep an eye on citizen radicals "with a view to securing evidence which may be of use in prosecutions under the present existing State or Federal laws or under legislation of that nature which may hereafter be enacted."[39]

Hoover had Flynn explain to his agents why they needed the membership rolls of these radical groups. "With the character of the society or organization definitely established," Flynn wrote, "a general groundwork for deportation is furnished, affording in all instances deportable cases upon proof of alienship and membership in or affiliation with the organization." He admitted, however, that "investigations heretofore conducted have not disclosed instances of many bodies, associations or groups of anarchists that can be regarded as organizations. Real anarchists are usually associated together, if at all, simply in groups or gatherings which have no constitution or by-laws and no officers other than a secretary-treasurer."[40]

At the outset, Hoover saw three potential targets for his drive: El Ariete, a group of Spanish anarchists in Buffalo, New York; l'Era Nuova, an organization of Italian anarchists in Paterson, New Jersey; and the Union of Russian Workers (UORW). These three seemed clear-cut examples of organizations that professed belief in the violent overthrow of the government. The Justice Department used El Ariete as a test case to see if radicals could be prosecuted under the seditious conspiracy act of the Penal Code, but the case was dismissed on July 24, 1919, on the grounds that the statute, which dated back to the Civil War, was intended to apply to the actual use of force, not its advocacy. It did not ban, according to the judge, "the overthrow of the government . . . by the use of propaganda." Then l'Era Nuova was raided in January 1920, but since the total combined membership of both El Ariete and l'Era Nuova was thirty-six, they clearly did not constitute an impressive target.[41]

The Union of Russian Workers, founded in 1907 and with national headquarters in New York, was ideal—having from 4,000 to 7,000 members in 1919 (estimates vary). Furthermore, the work of having it proscribed had already been done. In 1918, a Labor Department conference consisting of Anthony Caminetti (commissioner general of the Immigration Bureau), John W. Abercrombie (solicitor general of the Labor Department), and A. W. Parker (counsel to the Immigration Bureau), had decided that mere membership in the Union made an alien liable to be deported. Flynn's August 12, 1919, letter to his agents singled out the Union as the only group that had already been determined to fall under the provisions of the 1918 law, and in the fall of 1919, a conference of officials from Labor and Justice decided to make the Union the deportation campaign's first target.[42]

According to Assistant Secretary of Labor Louis B. Post, who eventually signed the orders deporting the UORW's members, two clauses in the Union's constitution made it vulnerable: that the masses would "take possession by forcible social revolution of all the wealth of the world," and that "having accomplished such an overthrow" and "having destroyed at the same time all institutions of state and authority, the class of the disinherited will have to proclaim a society of free producers." It did not mitigate the offense that this constitution, which dated back at least to 1911, was written with reference to the overthrow of the czar's regime in Russia, and that the top leadership of the Union had returned to Russia after the revolution in 1917, leaving behind a rank and file for whom the Union's principal attraction was its Russian-speaking milieu. In actual practice, most of its members had not been required to familiarize themselves with the vexations clauses or any other part of the constitution as a condition for membership. The Union was for most a place to meet with other Russian immigrants, to study English in night school classes (perhaps to qualify for citizenship), and to drink with friends from the old country.[43]

Since the Labor Department had already determined that membership in the Union of Russian Workers was a deportable offense, Hoover made it his business to gain possession of the organization's membership books and records. On July 30, 1919, two days before the official birth of the Radical Division, Hoover wrote Caminetti to ask him to look at the exhibits from an Akron, Ohio, deportation hearing to see if they contained membership records, informing him that he was "at present endeavoring to obtain detailed information concerning [the UORW]."[44]

The next week Hoover asked Caminetti to reopen a deportation hearing in Baltimore so he could obtain an affidavit from a UORW member that "the red membership card is in fact the official membership card of that organization." Two weeks later he told Caminetti he was still "desirous of establishing the anarchistic nature of the Union of Russian Workers," and asked his assistance in examining the transcript of another hearing to see if it might contain the admission he needed that the "red card is, in fact, the official membership card."[45]

It is likely that during the last two weeks of October Palmer began pressing Hoover for results after all the poking and probing into the radical movement. On October 14, the Senate unanimously passed the so-called Poindexter Resolution, which required Palmer to report on his progress in solving the spring bomb plots and on his investigation of radicals. The resolution broadly defined radicals as anyone who

> attempted to bring about the forcible overthrow of the Government of the United States . . . preached anarchy and sedition . . . advised the defiance of law and authority, both by the printing and circulation of printed newspapers, books, pamphlets, circulars, stickers, and dodgers, and also by the spoken word; and . . . have advised . . . the unlawful obstruction of industry and the unlawful and violent destruction of property . . . to destroy existing property rights and to impede and obstruct the conduct of business essential to the prosperity and life of the community.[46]

On October 17, the *New York Times,* responding to unsettled world conditions, criticized Palmer for not acting more quickly and effectively to counter the radical menace.[47]

Once Hoover had satisfied himself that a UORW membership card or a name in a UORW membership book would be enough to build a deportation case, he was ready to act. He gave the Labor Department the names of 600 members of the UORW and asked that warrants for their arrest be issued. On November 7, 1919, a date chosen because it was the second anniversary of the Bolshevik revolution, teams of local police and Bureau of Investigation agents broke into the meeting places of the UORW in twelve cities. They ransacked the premises, arrested everyone in sight, and carried away anything that could conceivably be turned into evidence. Hoover's apologists later claimed he was still playing only "a liaison role between the Department and its field agents during the roundups," but Hoover himself said that his office had been "permitted . . . to handle the Union of Russian Workers' raid and the Communists' raids, both of which had been conducted so far as I know with no adverse criticism."[48]

Many more than the 600 for whom warrants had been issued were arrested. In New York City, for instance, there were only twenty-seven warrants, but 200 were arrested; in Newark, there were thirty-six warrants with 150 arrests. If similar proportions obtained in the other ten cities, several thousand were detained in the raid, with most released soon after questioning. Eventually, 452 of the 600 Labor Department warrants were executed, and after a month's delay, orders were signed for the deportation of 246 of them, 184 on the *Buford*. [49]

The principal raid was in New York City at the Union's national headquarters, the Russian People's House. The raid was commanded by the head of the New York City Police Department's "bomb squad," which then usually meant the antiradical division of a police force, and many of those arrested were beaten with makeshift clubs ripped from the stair rails. The raiders carried away "several tons" of literature in "several trucks." Doors were torn down, carpets ripped up. Surviving photographs show smashed typewriters and other office equipment, with office records strewn about the room, evidently with the intention of further disrupting the organization. Of the 650 arrested in New York, the Bureau had evidence to hold only thirty-nine after their initial interrogation. [50]

The next day, the New York police, directed by the State Assembly's Lusk Committee, carried out raids on seventy-three more radical centers, arresting another 500 persons. Local Red squads across the country carried out similar raids in coordination with the federal operation. Some of those arrested were added to the crowd of potential deportees being assembled on Ellis Island. The primitive level of coordination that existed between the Immigration Bureau and Hoover's Radical Division led to some unconscionable delays in dealing with the detainees. The worst situation was in Hartford, Connecticut, where ninety-seven aliens were held, practically in solitary confinement, for five months before the situation was discovered by Assistant Secretary of Labor Post, who transferred the aliens to Boston's Deer Island prison. [51]

The November raids turned Palmer into a hero for much of the country. Letters flooded his office congratulating him and demanding similar action against the IWW, the Communist party, and even the American Federation of Labor. The November 7 raids also were an opportune time for Palmer to release his reply to the Senate's Poindexter Resolution. He used the occasion to recommend passage of his peacetime sedition law and to describe the fine work done by Hoover's Radical Division. On December 3, the *New York Times* responded by endorsing the sedition bill. Palmer, however, may have read of the problems Hoover's campaign would cause in the future in a letter from the National Civil Liberties Bureau (renamed the American Civil Liberties Union, or ACLU in Jaunary 1920) in which they protested that prisoners taken at the Russian People's House had been beaten by the raiders.[52]

If the public had been able to see the record of the interrogation of the radicals arrested in the November sweep, it might have agreed with Assistant Secretary of Labor Post, who wrote that the " 'red' crusade" was a "gigantic and cruel hoax."[53] One of the aliens arrested in Hartford was asked (through an interpreter):

> "The Union of Russian Workers teaches anarchy—do you believe in anarchy?"
> "Never. I never heard of it."
> "They advocate the overthrow by force or violence of any form of organized government. Do you believe in that?"
> "I did not hear of that." . . .
> "Did you ever read the Constitution of that Union?"
> "No." . . .
> "Are you an anarchist?"
> "No."
> "Do you understand what anarchism is?"
> "I don't know what it is."
> "Then why do you say you are not an anarchist? . . . Does the Union of Russian Workers approve the Lenin and Trotsky regime?"
> "Some members approve it—some don't."
> "What is your personal opinion?"
> "I don't know either of them." . . .
> "What would you do if you were told you are a member of an organization which advocates the overthrow of organized government by force or violence?"
> "I would just drop it and leave." . . .
> "Have you ever had a venereal disease?"
> "No."[54]

An affirmative answer to the last question would have made the alien deportable for health reasons, an expedient sometimes resorted to when the evidence for a political deportation was insufficient.

Once the aliens had arrived at Ellis Island, the operation began to bog down because the commissioner of immigration there, Frederic C. Howe, refused to be hurried into departing from the normal pace of deportation procedures. On November 22, the House Committee on Immigration, outraged by Howe's obstructionism, launched an investigation of his administration. The committee announced its findings that of the 600 aliens arrested as anarchists from February 1917 to November 1919, only sixty had been deported. Howe was subjected to more pressure when the Justice Department raided the Russian People's House again on November 25 and announced that it had discovered a secret "bomb factory." When the "bomb," a dangerous-looking iron sphere, mysteriously disappeared after being placed in a pail of water for safekeeping, there was some sarcastic speculation that the anarchists had discovered how to build a water-soluble infernal machine. At this point Howe resigned, and his successor as head of Ellis Island, Byron Uhl, quickly fell in line with the wishes of the Immigration Bureau and the Justice Department.[55]

Hoover made sure his first shipment of deportees included some celebrity radicals. The Justice Department was able to describe the alien members of the Union of Russian Workers as fearsome in the aggregate, but individually they were rather pathetic: poor, mostly ignorant of English, and certainly illiterate in that tongue. Few of them were guilty of anything more than membership in proscribed organizations—organizations that were, in fact, proscribed after the aliens had joined them. Hoover needed aliens with star quality, radicals with names and faces known to the public; the "star" deportees would lend a fearsome personality to the anonymous rabble who made up the bulk of the aliens Hoover was labeling the Red Menace.

It was inevitable that Hoover's attention would fall on Emma Goldman—dubbed the "Queen of the Reds" or "Red Emma" by reporters—and her longtime associate, Alexander Berkman. Born in Russia in 1870, Goldman had arrived in the United States in 1889 at the age of sixteen. A feminist, an anarchist, a birth control reformer, a crusader for the liberation of the individual from servitude to the state, she had a charismatic personality with energy and a level of commitment to her cause at least as strong as Hoover's was to his. In the fall of 1919, Emma Goldman was fifty years old. Her pince-nez glasses and stern expression gave little hint of her remarkable powers as a spell-binding orator who could rouse or quiet an audience with a word or gesture. In an era when the word *anarchist* was a generic label for everything alarming to the middle class, Emma Goldman had already been proudly proclaiming herself an anarchist for more than two decades. Deporting Goldman would give the Justice Department drive instant credibility, so during the summer of 1919 Hoover wrote a legal brief in support of the Immigration Bureau's deportation case against Goldman. This amounted to an abbreviated account of her life, surely one of history's more unusual conjunctions of biographer and subject.[56]

Goldman and Berkman had both been imprisoned during the war for offenses against the conscription act, and while they were still "sojourning in the custody of the federal authorities" (in Hoover's words), he conferred with the Immigration Bureau and confirmed that both were deportable: Berkman because he was an admitted alien, and Goldman because of a technical defect in her naturalization. Hoover therefore notified his superiors in the Justice Department that he was putting together a case against them, calling them "beyond doubt, two of the most dangerous anarchists in this country, and if permitted to return to the community [it] will result in undue harm."[57]

Hoover knew that the public could not hate a faceless enemy, and so he used Goldman to give a human element to the radical conspiracy he claimed to be exposing (as he would later use Dillinger, Ma Barker, Alger Hiss, the Rosenbergs, and the Berrigans). Hoover did not have to exert himself to inflate Emma Goldman into a symbol. She had done that herself with the cooperation of a press enchanted by her flair for the dramatic. Hoover could capitalize on the popular impression that Goldman was the leader of the radical movement to transform the anonymous mass of the deportees—a disorganized, helpless rabble—into the image of a revolutionary army.

In building a case against Goldman, Hoover and his energetic investigators in the Publications Unit of the Radical Division followed the same pattern they had with the Communist movement in general. They gathered a library of incriminating materials from Goldman's career as agitator, speaker, and founder and editor of *Mother Earth,* a journal she started in 1906 as the anarchists' answer to the Socialist review, *The Masses.* They even intercepted mail addressed to Goldman and Berkman in jail, forwarding photostats of incriminating material to the Immigration Bureau.

Emma Goldman was Hoover's first big case, and he threw himself into it with a commitment that went far beyond the normal eagerness of a prosecutor in pursuit of his prey. Years later, on the occasion of Hoover's appointment as director of the Bureau of Investigation, a magazine story (probably based on an interview with Hoover) claimed that Hoover had

> pitched camp in the very heart of the enemies' stronghold. Emma Goldman, queen of the Reds, who had held sway in the United States since her spectacular rise in the Chicago Haymarket riots thirty years prior to this, and with her power of speech and pen from which had flowed

a number of books on anarchism and free-love and kindred, had gathered
to her a strong and dangerous following, and her paramour, Alexander
Berkman, were his first thoughts. He went to their place of living; read
and studied Emma Goldman's books and writings; attended her lectures
and talked over her philosophy with her and sounded out the feelings
and sentiments of those gathered about her until after six months of
thought and investigation he had thoroughly established the fact that
they were really enemies of our established government and worked out
the legal way of deportations.[58]

Since Goldman was in prison (from February 1918 until September
1919) and then immediately left on a speaking tour of the Midwest,
not to return to New York for her deportation hearing until the end
of October, it is highly unlikely that Hoover actually did attend Goldman's lectures and argue with her. However, the remarks Goldman
and Hoover exchanged on board the *Buford* do hint that their acquaintance went beyond Hoover's appearances at Goldman's deportation
hearings (where Goldman did not speak at all, much less argue with
Hoover).[59]

The Immigration Bureau, cooperating closely with Hoover, issued
a warrant for Goldman's arrest on September 18, to take effect upon
her release from prison. (A warrant for Berkman's arrest had long
been in effect.) On September 27, Goldman was released from the
penitentiary in Jefferson City, Missouri, and the warrant was served.
When Goldman's deportation hearing was held in New York on October 27, Hoover wrote the government's brief against Goldman, and
presented the government's case himself.[60]

The first part of Hoover's brief refuted Goldman's claim that she
had acquired citizenship through her father and her husband. Since
she was twenty-four years old when her father was naturalized, Hoover
argued, she was not eligible to acquire citizenship in that manner,
which applied only to minors. He then held that her marriage to an
American was invalid according to Jewish law (and therefore American
law), since it was performed not by a rabbi but by a "Rev." Kalmon
Bardin, a *shochet,* or ritual slaughterer. Even had the marriage been
valid, Hoover argued, Goldman still was not a citizen because in 1909
the immigration authorities had canceled her husband's naturalization
on the grounds that he had not been a resident in the country the
required number of years before applying.[61]

Hoover then turned to the crucial argument that Goldman merited
deportation under the Immigration Act of October 16, 1918. He first
contended she had been guilty of behavior that could be characterized

as "advocation of violence." One piece of evidence was the July 1914 issue of *Mother Earth* in which Goldman had printed a number of sympathetic comments on the deaths of three anarchists in a July Fourth explosion at a radical bomb factory in New York and had announced that the ashes of the three dead anarchists would be displayed at the magazine's offices. Goldman herself had contributed a message (signed also by her lover at the time, Ben Reitman) that "We honor the memory of our dead comrades, the victims of the capitalist system and the martyrs of labor." Hoover asked the immigration commissioner (who was in effect the judge at the hearing) to take "particular note" of the fact that Goldman's telegram spoke of the three anarchists as "dead comrades," and that she was "honoring their memory."[62]

Hoover's next exhibit was Goldman's reaction to the dynamiting of the *Los Angeles Times* in 1911. He showed that the two dynamiters (members of the AFL, who had astounded radicals by confessing to the bombing) were friends of Goldman's, had been at her home, and that the evidence needed to convict them had been obtained by an informer who had wormed his way into Goldman's confidence. He attached as an exhibit a copy of *Mother Earth* that praised the two bombers as "martyrs to their cause."[63]

The lengthiest section of the brief was devoted to the interrogation of Leon Czolgosz, McKinley's assassin, to prove that Goldman, though admittedly not directly implicated, nevertheless had inspired the impressionable assassin. Czolgosz admitted he often went to a club in Cleveland, Ohio, where he had met Goldman and he had heard her say that she "didn't believe in government." When he was asked, "Who was the last one you heard talk?" (on the subject of assassination), he answered, "Emma Goldman."[64]

Hoover showed that Czolgosz had read articles by Goldman in which she wrote: "I have never opposed force or propaganda by deed, either publicly or privately. . . . I demand and acknowledge the right of an individual or a number of individuals to strike back at organized power and defend themselves against invasion." She went on: "I am a revolutionist by nature and temperament and as such I claim the right for myself and all those who follow with me to rebel and resist invasion by all means, force included, consequently, a destructionist. But I am also an anarchist, and as such a constructionist. In order to construct a new sanitary building for human beings to live in, I must, if I do not find clear ground, tear down the old, rotten, decayed obstacles which stand in the way of that beautiful and magnificent mansion called 'anarchy.' " Hoover commented that this was "a sample of the literature read by Czolgosz, and it apparently molded his ideas along the lines of determining to commit the act of murder." Hoover concluded this portion of his argument by stating that "even though it be conceded that Emma Goldman was not a direct party to his crime in the assassination of President McKinley, yet she was instrumental in helping to form the unnatural ideas which Czolgosz held toward government and authority." Hoover noted that Goldman had dedicated the October 1906 issue of *Mother Earth* to Czolgosz.[65]

There are suggestive hints in the Goldman brief about what it was in radicals that most alarmed Hoover. Although atheism was not one of the charges against Goldman, Hoover included a mass of material documenting Goldman's attacks on religion. He included his own observation that Goldman's "Philosophy of Atheism and the Failure of Christianity" exemplifies "the typical anarchist doctrine of the non-necessity of God and the Church," and he quoted her opinion that "religion is a superstition that originated in man's mental inability to solve natural phenomena. The church is an organized institution that has always been a stumbling block to progress. . . . It has turned religion into a nightmare that oppresses the human soul and holds the mind in bondage."[66]

With his own family's relationship to the federal bureaucracy, and his attraction to such institutions of authority as the family, church, and school, Hoover found Goldman's denunciation of the state, of nationalism, and of patriotism personally offensive. Commenting on Goldman's "Anarchy on Trial," Hoover wrote that "particular attention is called to this article as being one setting forth principles and ideas entirely contrary to those upon which this Government was founded and upon which its present institutions exist." From Goldman's "What I Believe" (July 19, 1918) he quoted her statement that "government, organized authority, or the State, is necessary only to maintain or protect property and monopoly. It has proven efficient in that function only. As a promoter of individual liberty, human well-being and social harmony, which alone constitute real order, government stands condemned by all the great men of the world." He called attention to another of Goldman's attacks on patriotism, which she called "a superstition artificially created and maintained through a network of lies and falsehoods; a superstition that robs man of his self-respect and dignity, and increases his arrogance and conceit."[67]

One of Hoover's fixed ideas was that political radicalism and criminal behavior both grew out of what he called "the eternal rebellion against authority," so he quoted a passage by Goldman that could be interpreted as a defense of criminality:

> Break your mental fetters, says anarchism to man, for not until you think and judge for yourself will you get rid of the dominion of darkness, the greatest obstacle to all progress. Anarchism therefore stands for direct action, the open defiance of, and resistance to, all laws and restriction, economic, social, and moral. But defiance and resistance are illegal. Therein lies the salvation of man. Everything illegal necessitates integrity, self-reliance, and courage.[68]

One of Goldman's worst heresies in Hoover's opinion was her claim that radicalism was not alien, but a normal part of American character that sprang naturally from American conditions. Thus he quoted her defense of Leon Czolgosz that "in vain have the mouthpieces of wealth denounced Leon Czolgosz [despite his name a native-born citizen] as a foreigner; in vain they are making the world believe that he is the product of European conditions and influenced by European ideas. This time the assassin happens to be the child of Columbia, who lulled him to sleep with—'My country, 'tis of thee, Sweet land of liberty, etc.' " Another incriminating piece of evidence was something that sounded like an endorsement of McKinley's assassination: "Poor Leon Czolgosz, your crime consisted of too sensitive a social conscience."[69]

Hoover's arguments against Goldman prevailed, and on November 29 the Immigration Bureau announced its decision to deport her. After her attorney obtained a writ of habeas corpus to free her from confinement, a hearing on the government's motion to dismiss the writ was held in New York on December 9. Hoover was present (along with the Bureau of Investigation director, William Flynn) to assist Francis G. Caffrey, the U.S. attorney who presented the government's case. Assistant Secretary of Labor Louis Post had signed Goldman's and Berkman's deportation orders with the proviso that they be deported to "Red" Russia, so Hoover assured the judge that the Immigration Department had already made arrangements to that effect; however, he refused to tell Goldman or her attorney when the sailing would take place, or exactly what the destination would be. Federal Judge Julius M. Mayer voided the writ of habeas corpus, saying that "the court views both of these defendants as enemies of the United States. . . . They have consistently and systematically done everything to destroy the welfare, stability and integrity of the government. Their actions were as bad and as inimical as the actions of the common enemy, the German Empire." Goldman at first filed an appeal to the Supreme Court, but then, feeling that her eventual deportation was a foregone conclusion, withdrew the appeal to avoid what might have been a prolonged wait in prison for the final disposition of her case.[70]

Early in the antiradical campaign, probably before the November raids, Hoover and Anthony Caminetti had asked the War and State departments for a troop transport to carry the deportees back to Europe. On November 25, the Labor Department wrote the War Department again, this time specifying it needed a ship capable of carrying 200 deportees, and obtained the U.S.S. *Buford.* On December 17, with the sailing of the *Buford* only four days away, Hoover obtained maps of northern Russia from the War Department so that he could meet any possible objections to the deportees' port of disembarkation. Communications between Hoover and the State Department show that he had not only taken charge of the sailing of the *Buford,* but had worked out arrangements for the deportees' treatment once the boat reached Europe. In a letter in which he lightheartedly referred to the "celebrities" on board the *Buford,* Hoover notified the State Department that the ship should stay at port until "assurances had been received from the local authorities that the deportees had actually been turned over to the Soviet forces." Hoover felt this would "eliminate any assumption of bad faith upon the part of the government."[71]

Of the 249 aliens Hoover sent to Russia aboard the *Buford,* 184 were members of the Union of Russian Workers (on the grounds of advocating the violent overthrow of the government) and fifty-one were anarchists deportable under the 1918 law for not believing in any form of government. The remaining fourteen were deported for having been convicted of various crimes, for pauperism, or for having entered the country illegally.[72] In itself, with the exception of Berkman and Goldman, this was not an especially impressive haul, except that Hoover and the Justice Department instructed the press and the public to regard the *Buford* as only the first in a long procession of "Soviet arks" to follow.

On December 21, the day the *Buford* sailed, the Justice Department tried to whip up enthusiasm by releasing Hoover's brief against Goldman. It got front-page coverage, and the *Washington Post*'s story ran beneath headlines that reminded the public of Goldman's reputation as the "Mentor of Czolgosz, McKinley's Slayer." It identified Hoover, "special assistant to Attorney General Palmer," as the author of "the confidential reports on Berkman and Goldman." The story characterized Hoover's brief as "most painstaking" and reported that it provided "proof in the form of documents and testimony" that Goldman was "instrumental in helping to form the unnatural ideas of Czolgosz," and that "she is not and never has been an American citizen. . . . Although she was in the United States nearly 34 years, she worked only eighteen months and spent most of the past 25 years denouncing the United States government, teaching anarchy and disrespect of authority, advocating violence and obstructing the law."[73]

Congressman William Vaile of Colorado put an eyewitness account of Hoover at the *Buford*'s sailing into the *Congressional Record:*

> At midnight at the barge office there were a good many people, mostly men. Mr. Hoover, that slender bundle of high-charged electric wire, the prosecutor of the Department of Justice, told us that these were mostly agents of his department, brought here for this particular job. . . . In company with Mr. Hoover, I talked a little with Miss Goldman. . . . She was quite bitter against Mr. Hoover because he had not given notice to her counsel, Mr. Weinberger, of the time of the departure. The world knows, of course, that she had had her day in court, and many such days, and that every possible recourse had finally been tried in vain, but apparently she still had some hopes that the courts would have protected her. Mr. Hoover asked: "Haven't I given you a square deal, Miss Goldman?" "Oh, I suppose you've given me as square a deal as you could," she answered. "We shouldn't expect from any person something beyond his capacity."[74]

Hoover gave the *New York Tribune* his own account of the sailing of the *Buford*.[75] "The three women in the party," Hoover told the reporters,

> are traveling first-class. The men are traveling with the same accommodations the American army had en route to and from Europe. Goldman had several trunks and half a dozen suit cases filled with her belongings and she took with her a lot of money she has collected from her followers in America. Berkman and most of the others had plenty of money. Just before we left the island, one of the men wanted me to cash a check for $3000. I refused and suggested he send it to some of his friends remaining in this country and have them get the money. He said he wouldn't trust the check into our hands for transmission. "All right," I said, "take it to Russia and trust the Bolsheviki."
> The crowd was very cocky Saturday night, and full of sarcasm for the Department of Justice and immigration agents. When we got them

out about 4 AM and they saw the number of soldiers and guards on hand they were thoroughly cowed. They showed no pep. Berkman bossed all of the others. He was strutting around wearing high Russian boots, khaki and a sombrero hat. I went to pay my respects to Goldman after she and the other two women were put in their stateroom. She was very bitter in her remarks about the United States and about the Department of Justice activities. "I'll be back before long," she declared, "and I'll give you plenty more work to do." Berkman's uncle is one of the leaders under Lenin and Trotsky and Berkman told me he expects to join the two and help govern Russia just as soon as he arrives.

Berkman declared we were making a mistake in sending back most of those being deported. "They are not anarchists," Berkman said, "but they will be by the time I've talked to them a few times on the way back to the old country."

The government saw to it that all of the deportees were warmly clothed and well treated. Many people may think they didn't deserve such consideration, but the department considered the matter in a more generous light. After the crowd disembarks at the Russian port they will receive each several days' supply of food—enough to see them through until they can make arrangements.

When reporters asked whether there were enough guards to handle this dangerous crew, led by the "brains" of the revolution, Hoover assured them that "it isn't likely the deportees will mutiny. There is on board ship a guard of 200 soldiers, each carrying, besides his rifle, two pistols. Berkman is expected to start trouble. In that event he will be put in solitary confinement."

Hoover told the press, "The Department of Justice is not through yet, by any means. Other 'soviet arks' will sail for Europe, just as often as it is necessary to rid the country of dangerous radicals." The *Herald* took this to mean that more were to sail that same week. There was a statement from Director Flynn that the *Buford* had rid the country of "the brains of the ultra-radical movement."[76]

Hoover was in such high spirits over the success of his operation and the amount of personal publicity he had received that he began to keep a scrapbook of his newspaper clippings. His clippings about the *Buford* included not only stories about himself, but others that recalled the carnival atmosphere of the Red Scare. (This was the beginning of a collection that eventually filled three dozen binders Hoover kept in his office.) One was a poem that began, "I saw fair Emma leave our shores, and crepe was festooned on her lid; she sailed with many other bores who talked too much, as Emma did."[77]

On Christmas Day of 1919, Hoover was well pleased with the

world and his place in it. His twenty-fifth birthday would come on New Year's Day. Over the past six months, he had turned himself into one of the more powerful men in Washington. He was already known throughout the federal bureaucracy as the mind and will behind the most highly publicized program of the federal government. He was even being watched by anxious anti-Communists overseas: The Justice Department would soon be asked by the Serbo-Croatian Legation for its advice on anti-Bolshevik tactics, information Hoover "took pleasure" in sending.[78]

Hoover could also feel confident that this success was just the beginning. He had already scheduled another radical raid that would dwarf the Union of Russian Workers operation, and it was just a week away. In a few days his Radical Division would begin a massive publicity campaign to put the antiradical message in front of the country's lawmakers and opinion shapers. It had been an astonishing year.

To leaf through the mass of letters, memos, and orders that flowed from Hoover's desk during the last half of 1919 is to realize that only a near-demonic energy could have produced them. (It is also sobering to realize that with the aid of computers even an ordinarily industrious person today would be able to do the same thing.) Hoover was planning large and complicated operations that spanned the continent at the same time that he was putting together a bureaucracy where none had existed before and guiding an untried and unusual policy through the thickets of established legal practices and requirements. Nevertheless, he still had the will and energy to oversee the most minute details of every phase of the operation: the legal work, the administrative work, and the public relations work.

The intensity of Hoover's determination to make sure his plans and orders were carried out can still be felt in files he filled during the 1919 campaign. There are dozens of memos badgering the Immigration Bureau to raise the bail of radicals, to sign warrants, to expedite hearings. During the Ellis Island hearings on the *Buford* radicals, he kept up unrelenting pressure on the officials whose performance was vital to his plans. He peppered Ellis Island with complaints that security was lax. He demanded that the radicals' visitors be searched, and he objected to their attorneys' being able to enter the hearing exhibits room without supervision. When the detainees went on a "talk" strike and refused to respond to questions, he demanded that the immigration authorities amend their procedures to permit photos to serve as affidavits of identification. No detail was too small for his attention, no lapse could escape his notice and complaint. At twenty-four, overseeing subordinates twice his age, he was already the alert and unforgiving taskmaster he would be for the next half century.[79]

Hoover's friends and enemies were already learning that he was not a man to be crossed with impunity. In December, Hoover was demanding that an attorney who had criticized the November raids be banned from immigration hearings. When he learned that an interpreter at the Immigration Bureau's Pittsburgh office was sympathetic toward the Russian prisoners and had criticized the deportation campaign, he insisted that she be fired, and kept up the pressure until she was.[80]

What emerges from Hoover's obsessive attention to the details of the radical cases is how much they meant to him, not just as the ingredients of his success, but as moral issues in themselves. These cases really *mattered* to him. In the cynical world of the professional politician, this intensity made Hoover a useful but unsettling ally, and a dangerous enemy. It was surely Hoover who fed Palmer the phrases "moral rats" and "scum of the earth," which the attorney general used to smear the Socialists he was driving from the country in 1919. It was also Hoover who would excuse a UORW member from deportation because he was an army veteran, but would also specify that he "be warned to conduct himself properly in the future."[81] This intensity of personal involvement in the details of enormous enterprises is precisely what prevented Hoover's operations, then and later, from drifting into lethargy, the normal state of bureaucracy.

Hoover was already demonstrating an intuitive grasp of how popular psychology operates and how it can be manipulated. His Central High drill and debate experience had given him a keen insight into the means by which men might be motivated and led, but now it was the nation whose ideas and attitudes he was trying to shape. In his brief on Emma Goldman he had used the same technique as in his debate notes on capital punishment, a technique of stigmatizing the opponent by making him (or, even more dramatically, her) seem a threat to the shared values of the speaker and his audience.

Hoover's 1919 antiradical drive was aimed directly at discrediting and destroying new values that threatened Seward Square. He was providing the nation with dramatic representations of those threats, a menacing crowd led by well-known individuals; then he banished those enemies from the nation, a modern version of a ritual that had ancient roots. With the nation troubled by a vague dread of change, Hoover had identified the source of evil as those who were different in appearance, culture, and belief—groups who were alienated from the old truths and pieties of nostalgic America; he then drove these despised aliens from the community in a demonstration of the power of the state and the powerlessness of its enemies, a purgative ritual of national solidarity.[82] From the very beginning, Hoover showed an insight into and creative grasp of the principles of political melodrama, and he understood them far better than the politicians who were his superiors.

Hoover's performance in 1919 might be interpreted as a variation on a technique developed by the Pinkerton Agency in the nineteenth century: "Every group was assumed to be led by a tight inner circle of conspirators whose program and tactics were closely held secrets. These insiders were, in theory, surrounded by an outer ring of followers, many of them unaware of the criminal purposes of the leaders." By treating Goldman and Berkman as the "tight inner circles of conspirators," the Justice Department was able to draw on popular beliefs about the nature of radicalism to create the impression that the pathetic rabble of deportees on the *Buford* constituted the "outer ring of [their] followers," and that Goldman, Berkman, and their shipmates represented a microcosm of the Red Menace.[83]

When Hoover incorporated the 1919 raids and deportations into the fabric of a broader political campaign to influence public opinion against communism and to press passage of new sedition legislation, he was rehearsing the techniques he would perfect during his later career. As he had learned to do as a Sunday school leader at the Old First, he was forever looking past the job at hand to see how he could turn it into a moral lesson for the benefit of his national audience.

According to the scanty record that survives, Hoover had been somewhat of a lone wolf during his days in the Alien Enemy Bureau and his first months in the Radical Division. He remained aloof from the other clerks and attorneys and passed his free time leafing through magazines in the reading room of the University Club. This changed on October 27, 1919, when he brought Thomas Franklin Baughman into the Radical Division. Baughman was a twenty-two-year-old army captain just out of army artillery.[84] He was a student at George Washington University (Bachelor of Law, 1922; Master of Law, 1923), and belonged to the same fraternity as Hoover, Kappa Alpha. In Baughman, Hoover found a friend who would be his inseparable companion for the next ten years.

Soon after joining the Bureau, Baughman's "TFB" initials begin to appear on Hoover's correspondence, meaning that he was drafting some of his friend's mail. During the first few weeks of 1920, Hoover and Baughman were so swamped with the work of the January raids that they set up a secretarial assembly line, with each grabbing whatever letter was on top of the "In" basket and dictating a reply to a team of stenographers.[85]

After work, Baughman and his widowed mother would call on Hoover and his mother at Seward Square to play a social game of bridge while the two young men exchanged anti-Communist confidences. It may have been about this time that Baughman presented Hoover with the dashing-looking photograph of himself that was found among Hoover's belongings after his death. It was inscribed:[86]

To "Speed" Hoover:
　　With Much Affection.
　　　　Thomas Franklin Baughman.

CHAPTER 4

The Red Years: The Lessons of Failure

Now we see and we feel that we are not so near the goal of the conquest of power, of the world revolution. We formerly believed, in 1919, that it was only a question of months and now we say that it is perhaps a question of years.

Leon Trotsky at the Third Congress
of the Comintern, July 1921

THE PERSONAL TRIUMPH of the *Buford* let Hoover taste the rewards early in his career that come to one bold enough and imaginative enough to satisfy the country's needs at a time of crisis. The experience might have made him reckless except that it was immediately followed by a disaster on just as grand a scale. The *Buford* operation showed Hoover what the results could be when an audacious plan unfolded as expected. The raids he orchestrated against the two American Communist parties in January 1920 demonstrated how hidden flaws in preparations and unforeseen errors in execution could not only destroy great plans but their planners as well.

Throughout his career, caution was as much a mark of Hoover's style as boldness. He always knew that events could not be relied on to conform to expectations, that worthy goals could not be achieved without control of all contingencies and certainty of overwhelming political support. His success in 1919 and 1920 taught him to be ambitious and daring in setting his goals; the final collapse of the

antiradical campaign taught him it was just as important to be modest
and realistic in his immediate plans and meticulous in his planning.

While Hoover was planning the raids against the Union of Russian
Workers, he was waiting impatiently for the American Communists
to give him the kind of target he could legally attack. In August 1919,
this did not yet exist.

Soon after the Bolshevik revolution, a militantly revolutionary and
internationalist "Left Wing" caucus had begun to emerge as a powerful
faction in the American Socialist party. It was particularly strong in
Brooklyn and Chicago, and in November 1918, it established the Communist Propaganda League in Chicago. The Bolshevik revolution had
captured the imagination of immigrants from the old Czarist empire,
and they were largely responsible for the party's growth from 80,379
in 1917 to 104,822 in 1919.[1] Immigrants were also responsible for
the growth of the Left Wing within the Socialist party. The old Socialist
party of Eugene Debs, long the refuge of native American noncon-
formists of every stripe, entered 1919 with its largest and most enthusiastic faction an excitable collection of aliens, few of whom spoke English. These foreign language Socialists were so intent on lending moral
support to the Russian Communists that they were hardly aware of
the very different circumstances in the United States that made a
similar revolution improbable.

On March 4, 1919, the Third International (the "Comintern")
was established in Moscow, and on March 8, it issued its manifesto.
It was this document that gave Hoover the basis for his case against
the American Communist parties. For the most part, the manifesto
was a violent attack on the "state" Socialist parties of Europe that
had supported their countries' war efforts and helped repress communism after the war, collaborating, for instance, in the murders of Luxemburg and Liebknecht. In the United States, there had been no significant prowar Socialist group, but this fact was lost on the militant
American Left Wing in its eagerness to mimic the Bolsheviks in every
way, including "splitting" from an official party.

The Comintern manifesto concluded with a call to revolution that
the American Left Wing found irresistible:

> the Third International is the international of open mass action of revolu-
> tionary realization. Socialist criticism has sufficiently stigmatized the bour-
> geois world order. The aim of the International Communist Party is to
> overthrow it and raise in its place the structure of the socialist order.[2]

Even before the Comintern manifesto, the Left Wing faction of the New York Socialist party, excited by plans for the Congress of the Third International, issued its own manifesto on February 16, 1919. This called on Socialists to spurn parliamentary tactics and to struggle for an immediate revolution in alliance with the Russian Communist party, and gave Hoover a prize exhibit for his legal attacks on the Communist parties: "Revolutionary Socialists do not believe that they can be voted into power. They struggle for the conquest of power by the revolutionary proletariat." Hoover later helpfully explained that "it is conceded by all parties concerned that the reference to the bourgeois state refers to the Government of the United States, as at the present time there is but one state existing in the United States, namely, the Government."[3]

In the American Socialist party elections that spring, Left Wing candidates, headed by John Reed, overwhelmingly defeated the national officers of the party and elected twelve out of the fifteen members of the national executive committee. The incumbent officers of the party were terrified. Facing the very real prospect that the Justice Department's proposed peacetime sedition law would make criminals out of members of any party advocating violence, the old leadership refused to turn over their offices to the new leaders. Instead, Morris Hillquit and the other right-wing Socialist leaders held a meeting in Chicago that lasted from May 24 to May 29, and expelled 40,000 radicals from the party. Between January and July of 1919, the National Executive Committee of the Socialist party expelled two-thirds of the membership for trying to turn the party into a revolutionary movement.[4]

On June 21, the Left Wing held a conference in New York that called for the formation of a new party; however, they could not agree on an immediate strategy. This meeting produced yet another manifesto and gave Hoover more fiery phrases for his attacks on the Communists: "Revolutionary Socialism must use these mass industrial revolts to broaden the strike to make it general and militant; use the strike for political objectives, and finally develop the mass political strike against capitalism and the state," and again, "revolutionary Socialism does not propose to 'capture' the bourgeois political state, but to conquer and destroy it."[5]

On August 31, the Left Wing formally seceded from the Socialist party when the Socialists, meeting in Chicago, failed to adopt a sufficiently revolutionary platform. The following day, the foreign-language groups within the Left Wing decided to form their own Communist party under the leadership of Louis Fraina, Nicholas Hourwich, and Charles Ruthenberg. The English-speaking members of the Left Wing then assembled at the Chicago IWW hall on September 3 and organized themselves as the Communist Labor party under John Reed, Benjamin Gitlow, and William Bross Lloyd. Eugene Debs and Morris Hillquit retained control of what remained of the nonrevolutionary Socialist Party of America.

Thus, at the end of August 1919, the Communists finally provided Hoover with what he needed to proceed under the immigration laws. There were now 40,000 to 70,000 radicals in organizations that openly advocated the violent overthrow of the government. Most important, about 90 percent of these Communists were aliens.

It was at this stage that Hoover began his research on Communism. He could not actually move against the alien members of the new Communist and Communist Labor parties until he persuaded the secretary of labor that they were deportable under the Immigration Act of 1918. To accomplish this, Hoover began work on a set of legal briefs during the fall of 1919, completing them in December. There was one brief for each of the two parties, and a third brief that urged the deportation of the unaccredited representative of the still-unrecognized Soviet government, Ludwig C. A. K. Martens.

Hoover threw himself into the preparation of these briefs with his usual intensity. He had no specific knowledge of Communist history or theory before he began his research, but everything in his background predisposed him against what he would find when he began mining revolutionary Marxist literature for evidence. Hoover began his study of communism at a unique moment in Communist history. Communists were never more confident of their imminent triumph than they were in mid-1919, immediately after the first congress of the Comintern, when revolutionary events in Europe buoyed their hopes. Had Hoover done his research a year earlier or a year later, the impact of his reading would have been far different, because in 1919 the Communists were not talking about triumphing in decades or years, but in months or weeks. A year later, events forced the Communists to revert to the traditional article of faith that "eventually" their day would come. In 1919, it seemed to be at hand.

Never before or after did Hoover have to exert himself so energetically in any intellectual exercise, and so nothing ever made as deep an impression on him as this research in 1919. Communism might change, but Hoover's ideas about it would never. Hoover claimed ever after that these three briefs were the "first" official government assessments of communism. They gave him and his Bureau a claim to be the government's official authority on anything involving Communist activities. Hoover's 1919 studies of communism were, with little exaggeration, fundamental texts in the evolution of the anticommunism that was American orthodoxy for the next fifty years. Half a century later, Hoover was still citing these papers, written when he was twenty-four years old, as the essential blueprints for the "nation's response to communism."[6]

Hoover's research into communism was, of course, not prompted by idle curiosity. He had a very specific purpose: to provide a factual and logical basis for ruling that the two American Communist parties fell within the scope of the Immigration Act of October 16, 1918, which provided that

(1) aliens who disbelieve in or advocate or teach the overthrow by force or violence of the government of the United States shall be deported;
(2) aliens who are members of or affiliated with any organization that entertains a belief in, teaches, or advocates the overthrow by force or violence of the Government of the United States shall be deported.[7]

The critical section of Hoover's brief on the first of the two parties argued that each member of the Communist party should be held responsible for the doctrines of the organization.

> From the examination of . . . the manifesto of the Communist International and the manifesto of the Communist Party of America, we find advocation of doctrines to the overthrow of the Government of the United States, not by parliamentary action but by direct action or mass action, which, as above shown, means force and violence. Thus the Communist Party of America stands indicted under the act of October 16, 1918. However, in order that there may be no doubt as to the responsibility of individual members of the Communist Party of America, we have but to examine the application for membership which each member must sign upon entering the organization. The following is a statement taken from the application: "The undersigned, after having read the constitution and program of the Communist Party, declares his adherence to the principles and tactics of that party and the Communist International; agrees to submit to the discipline of the party as stated in its constitution; and pledges himself to actively engage in its work."[8]

Although Hoover's purpose was to present a vigorously persuasive argument that members of the Communist party could be deported simply on the grounds that they were members, he did not pass up opportunities to suggest that they were responsible for much of the nation's social and economic unrest. Referring to the national steel strike (which began September 22) and the national coal strike (which started November 1), he quoted from the American Communist Party manifesto that "there is a more vital tendency . . . to start mass strikes—strikes which are equally a revolt against the bureaucracy of the unions and the capitalists. The Communist Party will endeavor to broaden and deepen these strikes, making them general and militant, developing the general political strike." Hoover remarked that this was "of particular significance due to the fact that in the great coal and steel strikes which have been existing in the United States for the past several months . . . the Communist Party has been actively engaged in its propaganda in fomenting industrial unrest, a doctrine specifically advocated in its manifesto and to which, as I will later show, each and every member of the Communist Party pledges himself to adhere."[9]

Hoover intended simply to blacken the reputation of the Communist party, but this obviously also suited the purposes of the steel corporations and mine owners. Their basic strategy was to convince the public that bolshevism was the real issue in the strike, and not the economic struggle between capital and labor, even though William Z. Foster, the future Communist party leader, who led the steel strike as an official of the American Federation of Labor, was denounced by the Communists themselves for his tactic of "pure and simple unionism"—of favoring economic over political goals.[10]

There is nothing in these briefs to suggest that Hoover had any motive besides "pure" anticommunism, but by linking strikes to communism he provided others with a convenient weapon to use to destroy economic enemies. The steel and coal strikes were both broken by federal action—the steel strike by the army occupation of Gary, Indiana; the coal strike by an injunction obtained by Palmer. They were disasters from which organized labor did not recover until the thirties; the Red smear had been the employers' winning weapon, and it had been largely handed to them by the Justice Department's noisy drive against radicals.[11]

Hoover's brief on the Communist party ended with his claim that

the Communist Party of America and persons members thereof fall within the provisions of the act of October 16, 1918, in that it openly advocates the overthrow of the Government of the United States by force and violence.

Respectfully submitted.

J. E. Hoover

Special Assistant to the Attorney General.[12]

Hoover then turned his attention to the Communist party's rival, the Communist Labor party. Since the Communist party's membership of 60,000 was 90 percent alien, it represented by far the more attractive target for the deportation drive. The Communist Labor party numbered perhaps only 10,000 and most of its members were English-speaking, although many of them were foreign-born.[13]

Hoover's brief on the Communist Labor party was shorter than the Communist party document. Since he claimed the practices and principles of both parties were "practically the same," it followed exactly the same format as the Communist brief—except for one crucial difference. In the Communist party brief, Hoover had quoted the Party's membership application in full: in the Communist Labor brief he merely paraphrased the application, stating that "the applicant pledges himself to be guided by the constitution and platform of the Communist Labor party."[14] When the two application blanks are compared, the explicit nature of the Communist party pledge (in the first brief) made the Communist Labor party's application (omitted from the second brief) seem vague, general, almost theoretical. The Communist party application required that members read the constitution and program of the party, but the Communist *Labor* party application merely required that the member be "guided" by the constitution. While the Communist party application pledged the member's loyalty to the Communist International and included a full description of the Comintern's program and manifesto, which the applicant was required to read, the Communist Labor party required no such explicit pledge of agreement with the ideas of the Communist International.

It was probably because the application for Communist Labor party membership was far weaker proof of an individual's agreement with the professed ends of the organization that Hoover did not include it in the main section of his brief. (It *was* one of the attached exhibits.) However, this difference between the formats of the two briefs may have been what later alerted Secretary of Labor William Wilson to look at the application form itself to refute Hoover's argument that the two parties were, as far as the Immigration Act was concerned, identical. The discrepancy between the application forms for the two parties proved to be the fatal weakness in the legal underpinnings of Hoover's deportation drive, the flaw that eventually led to the collapse of the entire campaign.

The third brief Hoover wrote in 1919 concerned Ludwig C. A. K. Martens, the Soviet representative to the United States. It advanced the thesis that anyone who had any connection, or even expressed any sympathy for the Russian revolution, stood in violation of American laws against advocacy of the violent overthrow of the government—federal laws where aliens were involved, state sedition laws for citizens of states with such statutes.

Martens was a German citizen born in Russia of German parents. He had participated in the Russian revolution of 1905 and had come to the United States in 1916. An engineer by training, he worked as the American representative of a Russian steel firm. After the Bolshevik revolution, Martens was given Russian citizenship by the Provisional regime (a procedure not recognized by American law) and opened the Russian Soviet Government Information Bureau in New York, with a staff of thirty-five. Until 1919, Martens concentrated on establishing trade ties between the United States and the Soviet Union. In 1919, the Soviets directed him to organize a diplomatic mission to the United States. His efforts to do this brought him to Hoover's attention. Hoover decided to take Martens at face value as the "Bolshevist Ambassador," and make him one of his celebrity deportees.[15]

As in his two earlier briefs, Hoover's strategy was to prove that Martens was a member of an organization advocating the violent overthrow of the American government. In this instance, however, the organization Hoover sought to proscribe was not an American party at all, but the Russian Communist party.

Hoover's reasoning was that the Third International's call for worldwide revolution compelled the Russian Communist party, as a member, to advocate the overthrow of the United States government. And since Martens was a member of the Russian Communist party, he fell within the provisions of the deportation regulations.

Hoover's brief on Martens, if endorsed by the secretary of labor (who had to determine which organizations were covered by the 1918 Immigration Act), would establish an important precedent. Not only would it allow Hoover to deport representatives of the Soviet government and trade organizations, it would also put him in a position to launch proceedings against all recent immigrants from Russia on the grounds that they might have been Party members in the Soviet Union. (In January, Hoover actually did begin to ask the Immigration Bureau to arrest members of the Russian Communist party that his agents had managed to locate on the West Coast.)[16] By stretching a point, Hoover's argument in the Martens brief would let him move against any aliens in sympathy with the Comintern, and, when a new sedition law was passed, against any citizens as well. In the meantime, Hoover could turn citizens' names over to states that had already passed sedition laws. Enthusiasm for the Comintern was so widespread among radicals in 1919 that they all would have been vulnerable in an expansive application of Hoover's arguments against Martens.

In the course of the Martens brief, Hoover felt compelled to make one peculiar digression. To demonstrate the fundamental opposition between communism and traditional Americanism, Hoover stated that "one of the fundamental principles of communism is the international character of the same," while the American government, on the other hand, was founded on the basis of "nationalistic sectionalism."[17]

Hoover's theory may have been that the underlying conflict in the revolutionary era was the clash between the ideologies of nationalism and internationalism, perhaps even drawing on Wilson's Fourteen Points' doctrine of national self-determination as a reason to oppose the internationalism of the Comintern. Secretary of Labor Wilson, who would rule on the Martens case, was a fervent believer in the special mission of America to democratize the world, so Hoover might have thought describing communism as a threat to nationalism would have special appeal to the Secretary. Isolationists naturally would be alarmed by Communist contempt for national independence, while Wilsonians would bridle at the Communists' presumption in offering the world a model of internationalism that did not follow the American lead. Thus Hoover's final indictment of Communism in the Martens brief was that "with the existence of communism, patriotism disappears and the Utopian idea of the Communist is for one great international proletarian State."[18] Hoover was obviously groping for a formula that would allow him to demonstrate that communism was the antithesis of Americanism.

On December 15, Hoover sent his brief on the Communist party to the Immigration Bureau's commissioner-general, Anthony Caminetti; on December 22, he shipped Caminetti the names of 2,280 Communist party members, and requested that warrants be issued for their arrest;

he promised Caminetti another 441 names for the next day, assuring him that the affidavits were based on "careful and thorough investigation of the activities of the individuals . . . you will note it is stated that they are aliens, members of the Communist Party of America, and that that party is an organization advocating the overthrow of the government of the United States by force and violence." On December 24, Hoover sent Caminetti his brief on the Communist Labor party, enclosing the names of forty-seven of its members and a request for warrants for their arrest. His cover letter stated that the two parties were "exactly" alike, with a difference "only in leadership."[19] On Christmas Eve, 1919, therefore, the Labor Department had Hoover's request for 2,768 warrants of arrest; this was not accompanied by probable cause proof of each individual's guilt, but by briefs holding that the Communist parties fell within the definition of the 1918 immigration law, and affidavits that the aliens were members of those organizations.

On the basis of Hoover's December 15 Communist party brief, Acting Secretary of Labor John Abercrombie had already deported an alien named Marion Bieznuk who had been arrested in the UORW raids but had been found to belong to the Communist party as well. At that time, Abercrombie evidently authorized the Immigration Bureau to deport anyone in the same category as Bieznuk—that is, any alien found to be a member of the Communist party.[20] But when Abercrombie unexpectedly received Hoover's massive package of 2,741 warrant requests on December 22 and 23, he suddenly realized this was far beyond the scope of anything he had intended when he had routinely approved the Bieznuk case. Abercrombie knew he would have greatly exceeded his authority as acting secretary if he permitted such a major operation without notifying the secretary of labor that something out of the ordinary was happening, and so he requested a meeting with Wilson.

While Hoover waited for a Labor Department decision on his Communist and Communist Labor party briefs, he pressed Caminetti for information on the status of the Immigration Bureau's rule which regulated aliens' access to counsel during deportation proceedings ("Rule 22"). On March 13, 1919, Secretary of Labor Wilson had significantly expanded the rights of aliens threatened with deportation by revising the language of this rule to give aliens the right to legal counsel at the very outset of proceedings against them. On November 19, Hoover began pestering Caminetti about whether the old or new Rule 22 was going to apply during the proceedings generated by the raids he was planning. He complained that the presence of lawyers had caused "difficulty" in dealing with the members of the Union of Russian Workers who had been arrested during the November 7 raids. (Their lawyers had advised the aliens to refuse to answer any questions at deportation hearings.) Hoover renewed this request in a letter dated December 17. On December 31, Abercrombie finally approved a request from Caminetti that the original language of Rule 22 that denied aliens early access to counsel be restored.[21]

The meeting between Abercrombie and Secretary of Labor Wilson took place on Christmas Eve, 1919. At Wilson's request, Assistant Secretary of Labor Louis B. Post also attended. It is certain that at this meeting Wilson, at the very least, authorized arrests of alien members of the Communist party; it is also probable that he approved the arrests of members of the Communist Labor party. In any case, Hoover proceeded on the assumption that Wilson had been persuaded in both instances.[22]

Once Hoover was sure that the Labor Department would uphold his cases against the Communists, he rushed events to a conclusion. On December 27, Abercrombie signed more than 3,000 warrants, a number that included the names Hoover had forwarded before Christmas and an additional 202 Communists and fourteen members of the Communist Labor party that Hoover had sent Caminetti that day. On December 31, he forwarded a list of another 185 members of the Communist party and twenty-nine more Communist Labor party members. On December 27, Chief Frank Burke of the Bureau of Investigation ordered the Bureau's agents to prepare to round up members of the two parties, and notified them that the raids would occur on the night of January 2.[23]

In planning raids of such enormous scope (six or eight times as large as the November raids), Hoover had two concerns. He wanted first to ensure that the dragnet would have the greatest possible impact on public opinion and radical morale; therefore the numbers arrested had to be large enough to be sufficiently dramatic. His second concern was to prevent the destruction of the membership records vital to the mass deportation strategy, so the raids had to be fast and tightly synchronized. However, the size and speed of the operation also meant the Justice Department would have no effective control over the behavior of the raiders. There were only 579 agents in the Bureau at the time even though there had been a recent expansion. Since the raids were going to span the continent, with hundreds of separate raids in thirty-three cities (in 23 states), the Bureau had to recruit help from local police and volunteers from anti-Communist groups, specifically the recently disbanded American Protective League. These auxiliaries could not be restrained from venting personal animosities and local prejudices against the aliens, and this made abuses of the aliens' rights inevitable.[24] Hoover's failure to maintain control over all the participants in his operation, which led to inhumane treatment of the aliens, would provide the campaign's critics with all the ammunition they needed to throw the Justice Department and Hoover on the defensive.

On January 2, Hoover notified the chief clerk of the Justice Department to hold the offices open all night and to expect heavy use of the telephone lines because "there will be made this evening throughout the entire country arrests totaling over 3,000 persons charged with being communists who will be held for deportation."[25] That night, while Hoover and Baughman manned the telephones in the Bureau offices at the Justice Department, Bureau agents led raids on Communist meeting halls across the nation (the Bureau had urged its informants to schedule meetings and other gatherings that evening). They herded the radicals into detention centers where other agents waited with warrants.

At least 4,000, and possibly as many as 6,000, radicals were taken to detention centers that night and over the next few days. According to a procedure developed by Hoover, those individuals whose names appeared on the warrants were immediately arrested, others were released. Many aliens, however, were neither released nor formally arrested but simply held in illegal limbo while the field agents wired their names to Hoover. He would then forward their names to Caminetti with an unsupported affidavit that they were members of one or the other Communist party, and request that telegraphic warrants be wired to the detention centers. From January 3 through January 28, a blizzard of requests for telegraphic warrants flew out of Hoover's offices to Caminetti. All were dictated by either Baughman or Hoover. Between the two of them, they wrote 291 memoranda to Caminetti containing 2,705 names.[26]

Hoover's agents and their auxiliaries raided saloons, poolrooms, and in some instances simply broke into the aliens' homes and dragged the suspects out of bed. In the most notorious instance of official misconduct, authorities in Boston handcuffed the detainees, chained them together, and led them along sidewalks filled with jeering spectators to the Deer Island prison. In Detroit, 800 detainees were cooped up for days in a windowless corridor without toilet facilities. Similar makeshift centers across the country produced inadequate and unhygienic conditions. The Justice Department invited reporters to view and photograph the unkempt, dirty, bearded Reds the agents claimed had been on the verge of overthrowing the United States government. A federal judge investigating the conditions at one of the detention centers reported that "conditions were unfit and chaotic. No adequate preparations had been made to receive and care for so large a number of people. . . . For several days the arrested aliens were held practically incommunicado . . . confusion and the resultant hardship to the arrested aliens . . . [had] some additional terrorizing effect upon the aliens."[27] There is every reason to suppose this situation was typical.

The inhumane and illegal handling of the aliens galvanized the opposition of civil libertarians and enabled Hoover's critics to shift public attention from the alleged offenses of the aliens—which were vague, theoretical, and seldom based on overt acts—to the cruel and illegal behavior of the raiders—which were thoroughly documented in photographs and direct testimony. In this way the enemies of the antiradical drive were able to seize the initiative from Hoover and Palmer and halt the antiradical campaign before it attained its ultimate objectives: more mass deportations, a peacetime sedition law, and a drive against citizen radicals.[28] Out of a combination of inexperience and overconfidence due to the success of the November raids, Hoover had failed to organize a command system adequate to the scale of his operations. As soon as the raids began, events were out of his control.

In the January raids Hoover had planned and executed one of the boldest government operations in American history, so audacious that for a short time the opposition was stunned into silence. The raids were so outrageous, however, and so contrary to all notions of decency, legality, and fairness, that after the initial period of consternation an alliance of lawyers, clergymen, and civil libertarians rushed to expose the Justice Department's excesses, and so brought Hoover's crusade to a halt. For a while, however, Hoover could bask in a glow of a triumph even greater than the November raids and the sailing of the *Buford*. For the moment, the raids had given another boost to Palmer's presidential hopes, while newspapers applauded the Justice Department with such headlines as: ALL ABOARD FOR THE NEXT SOVIET ARK."[29]

While Hoover and his assistants tried to keep up with the flood of requests for warrants from the field offices, his briefs on the two Communist parties were released to the press. On January 4, the headline in the *New York Times* promised: RAIDERS WILL SERVE ALL OF THE 4,000 WARRANTS ISSUED. And it went on to carry Hoover's threat that he was going to GET PARLOR BOLSHEVIKI:

> Briefs had been submitted by J. E. Hoover, special assistant to Attorney General Palmer, demonstrating that both the Communist Party and the Communist Labor Party had as their aim the destruction of the American Government and supplanting it with Soviet control. . . . American citizens taken in the raids will be handed over to State authorities for prosecution where the States in which they were arrested have anarchy laws broad enough to apply to these particular cases. . . . No warrants were issued against any persons known to be American citizens, but a number of those caught with aliens have been found to be such, many of them of the "parlor Bolsheviki" type.[30]

Hoover seems to have been dreaming of a spectacular roundup of these parlor Bolsheviki, the "limousine liberals" of the day; they would have been a tempting target for an ambitious young man with Hoover's modest social and educational credentials. In December and again in January, Hoover tried to get the radical section of the U.S. Post Office to send him a list of "certain wealthy women who are giving financial aid to various radical publications."[31]

On January 2, 1920, Assistant Secretary of Labor Louis B. Post received Hoover's brief on Ludwig C. A. K. Martens, which Hoover was also circulating elsewhere throughout the government.[32] This brief was dated December 29, 1919, and Post reviewed it during the first week of January 1920.

On the basis of Hoover's brief, Post decided that he *would* sign a warrant for Martens's deportation. He suspected, however, that if Martens were "to fall into the hands of the secret-service auxiliary of the Department of Justice . . . there was a certainty, judged by the spectacular performances of that industrious and ingenious group . . . that he would be made the subject of humiliating newspaper publicity." Post decided not to allow Hoover's men to arrest Martens because he thought such an arrest would be "a species of public entertainment for which the Department of Labor could not decently allow itself to be responsible." He irritated Hoover by arranging for Martens's lawyer to bring his client to Post's office, where a warrant was served and parole granted. Subsequently, Secretary of Labor William Wilson permitted Martens to return to Russia and then canceled the arrest warrant so that if diplomatic relations were later established,

Martens might return to the United States; an actual deportation would have kept him out forever.[33]

Hoover was sure that in a matter of weeks he would be able to deport all the Communists he had arrested. Concerned about keeping them available for processing and shipment, he urged the Immigration Bureau to set high bail to keep them in jail, and he protested when he thought the bail was too low.[34]

Hoover was initially euphoric about the raids and decorated his Washington office with mementoes his agents took from the Communist offices they raided. He wrote the U.S. attorney in New Jersey, and said he had seen

> the most interesting [picture] taken by the Pathe Weekly of the evidence collected by you in the raids in Newark, N.J. In this photograph, I observe several life-size pictures in frames of Trotsky, Lenine [sic] and some of the other most noted Bolsheviks.
>
> I am endeavoring to place upon the walls of my office here a representative collection of Communists, and if you could forward to me some of the larger photographs of the world-wide Communist movement, I would greatly appreciate it, likewise any interesting banners which could be used for interior decorating would also be appreciated.[35]

A week later Hoover sent thanks for some "banners." He said he had given four of them to Palmer's secretary, presumably for Palmer, and that he was still waiting for the photographs of the Russian leaders. The U.S. Attorney in New Jersey had also sent something Hoover called a "small coin collector" for the assistance of victims of the czar. For some reason, Hoover found this object particularly obscene, and he asked for more of them: "I find that by giving samples of such materials to the Senators, Congressmen and newspaper men that call at this office, that they begin to realize the extent to which the propaganda of the pernicious forces in this country has gone."[36] Hoover was obviously learning to ingratiate himself with Congress and the press.

Along with his other work, Hoover had the job of answering the many letters of praise Palmer was receiving for the raids. He assured Palmer's admirers that "it is particularly gratifying to receive words of commendation from loyal American citizens upon the stand taken by this department in such matters."[37]

In January 1920, Hoover began to edit a newsletter initially called the *Bulletin of Radical Activities*—at first biweekly, then, after June, on a weekly basis. In August, Hoover changed its name to the *Bureau*

of Investigation General Intelligence Bulletin, the name by which it
was known until its demise, apparently in October 1921.[38] The *Bulletin*
was marked "confidential" and its circulation was restricted to key
government officials.

In a style remarkably similar to the *Weekly Review* he had edited
when he was eleven, Hoover filled the *General Intelligence Bulletin*
with a miscellany of items he thought might interest and encourage
the anti-Communist community. There were summaries of the activities of "leading radicals"—a category that included such figures as
Morris Hillquit, American Civil Liberties Union founders John
Haynes Holmes and Roger Baldwin, and the progressive Catholic
labor advocate, Msgr. John A. Ryan,—and denunciations of the enemies of the anti-Communist drive—men like Assistant Secretary of
Labor Louis B. Post, federal judge George Anderson, and columnist
Walter Lippmann. Hoover used the *Bulletin* to disseminate tips, instructions, and warnings throughout the anti-Communist movement.
For instance, he warned raiders to look out for booby traps in Communist meeting halls:

> Caution: usually, in the halls of the Russian clubs which have been visited
> by agents of the Bureau, there is a room,—generally a "soft" bar, in
> which is kept a stock of fruit, candy, etc. A report comes from Providence
> that some of the fruit has been poisoned purposely,—the intention being
> to cause the death of agents who, during a raid, eat any of the fruit.
> All agents should be cautioned to exercise particular care,—especially
> if it has been their practice to indulge in the refreshments of their
> "hosts"—and in cases where city, state, or other officers accompany them,
> to impress upon the latter a strict observance.[39]

Hoover used the pages of the *Bulletin* to call attention to patriotic
groups like the Knights of Columbus, the American Legion, and the
Fraternal Order of Eagles of Philadelphia. He reported the Eagles
were "one of the first fraternal bodies in the country to open a drive
against Bolshevism." He also noted with approval that "in some locali-
ties 2 minutes each day is given to the teaching of American ideals
in the schools of the State, and the idea is spreading."[40]

To generate public and press support for the antiradical campaign,
Hoover also produced documentary material for use by the mass media.
A pamphlet entitled *The Red Radical Movement* displayed photostats
of the more blood-curdling radical publications seized by his raiders.
He released this to the press and also sent it to members of the Senate
Judiciary and Immigration committees, and probably other congress-

men as well. Attorney General Palmer alluded to this publication at a House hearing, and advised the lawmakers that "it is not good reading late at night when you are at home in your own house. It gives you the creeps a little."[41]

Hoover's cover letter that accompanied the *Red Radical Movement* pamphlet was written in the flamboyant style Hoover would employ in his own speeches and articles, though it was signed by Palmer. Addressed to "the leaders of thought in this country," it proclaimed the Justice Department's goal of using the antiradical campaign to turn public opinion against radicalism. "I recognize that there can be no real effectiveness or saving in our legal prosecutions of sedition," the letter stated,

> unless those prosecutions are backed by the systematic and hearty efforts of all elements of good citizenship. There is a menace in this country. It may not be the menace of immediate revolution [a surprising concession from the department, which was predicting an uprising for May Day]. No harm, however, can come to the American people from intelligent contemplation of the situation in Russia and the woe that has been brought upon three hundred millions of people. . . . My one desire is to acquaint men like you with the real menace of evil-thinking which is the foundation of the red movement.[42]

The cover letter continued with the Radical Division's thumbnail sketch of bolshevism, which claimed that communism "advocated the destruction of all ownership in property, the destruction of all religion and belief in God. It is a movement organized against Democracy, and in favor of the power of the few built by force. Bolshevism, syndicalism, the Soviet Government, sabotage, etc., are only names for old theories of violence and criminality."

Hoover's most elaborate analysis of radicalism during 1919–1920 was a "popular survey" entitled *The Revolution in Action.* Prepared after the February 1920 meeting of the Communist International in Amsterdam, and shortly before Palmer's June 1920 appearance before the House Rules Committee, it captures the anticommunist hysteria of the period, and shows how deeply Hoover had been struck by the Bolsheviks' belief in 1919 and 1920 that revolution in one country could not survive and that the revolution would have to spread everywhere if it were going to last anywhere.[43]

Hoover's *Revolution in Action* drew a picture of a world where armed Communists were poised in every country and colony of the world awaiting Moscow's word to begin the final drive to establish an international dictatorship of the proletariat. The preliminaries for the revolution had already begun. "In the latter half of 1919," Hoover's Radical Division began, "all these protagonists and helpers of the international revolutionary scheme, the I.W.W., the communists, the Communist Labor party, the anarchists, the radical associations of rebellious schools, and unaffiliated Reds, and parlor Bolsheviks, fired by the enthusiasm thrown across the seas by flaming Russia and the glowing torch of the third international, began to work, hammer and tongs, 'to beat anvil blows,' the revolutionary poets would say, for an actual revolutionary uprising in the United States." The general strikes in Winnipeg and Seattle, the coal strike, the bomb plots, were all parts of this uprising. The Radical Division made a particular point of Communist propaganda directed at American blacks, calling this "perhaps the most contemptible and wicked performance of our American revolutionary fanatics."[44]

Hoover's survey of radicalism ended with this apocalyptic warning:

> Civilization faces its most terrible menace of danger since the barbarian hordes overran West Europe and opened the dark ages.
> We have furnished a picture now of the revolutionary thought and of the revolutionary presence. It remains to see the social-industrial problem as it is, apart from our hopes or fears, and to win sight of the ways and means of preventing international collapse.[45]

The "ways and means" may have referred to the Justice Department's proposed sedition legislation. By this time, there were many bills prohibiting revolutionary speech or beliefs in Congress. (By mid-November 1919 there were about seventy.) On January 10, the Senate passed the extremely repressive Sterling Sedition Bill. The House was considering the Graham Bill, which was closely modeled on the Sterling legislation. These measures aroused the violent opposition of the AFL's Samuel Gompers, who suspected that the Justice Department, which had already intervened in the steel and coal strikes against labor, would use the new legislation as a weapon against strikers. Attorney General A. Mitchell Palmer began to sense that his strike-breaking activities were losing him the political advantage he had gained from his war on radicalism, which conservative labor leaders such as Gompers had supported. He urged Congress to pass, instead of the Sterling or Graham bills, the somewhat milder sedition legislation drafted by the Justice Department and introduced by Martin L. Davey of Ohio. (Nevertheless, Gompers decided to oppose this as well.) As part of his antiradical duties, Hoover spent a good deal of time preparing Palmer for his House testimony in favor of the Davey sedition bill.[46]

To make sure his antiradical campaign had the advantage of the very latest intelligence, Hoover continued to search out new materials for his growing collection on radicalism, with particular attention given to fast-breaking events in the international Communist movement. He asked the State Department to send its complete set of Russian press releases to him directly instead of simply sending them to the files division at Justice. "I find that some things go astray. In view of the great value of these releases to my work, I would like to feel that I was receiving everything that was being forwarded." He also arranged to trade copies of his division's Russian newspapers for materials gathered by the State Department's Russian Division, informing the State Department that he was giving "particular attention" to developments in the Communist movement in Moscow. He asked the State Department to send him twelve copies of a document he variously described as "Ten Protocols" or the "Jewish Peril" for "my information and use." Evidently, Hoover had just heard for the first time about the *Protocols of the Elders of Zion,* a forged early-twentieth-century Russian document purporting to reveal a Jewish plan for world domination, and wanted to add it to his files. He had U.S. attorneys send him records of cases and opinions for the department to use in its briefs against Communists, and he collected transcripts of trial testimony for the information they contained on radical organizations and activities. He likewise sent materials to local prosecutors to use in preparing cases against radicals under state sedition laws; he gave New York prosecutors evidence against Benjamin Gitlow, whose "activities," he wrote, were "fully covered in the Bureau files."[47]

Hoover's requests to other government agencies for specific and obscure information on communism show that by 1920 he had become thoroughly acquainted with both the broad outlines and the details of the movement. He wrote the State Department that "Trotsky's famous order charging Arlov with the enforcement of discipline in the Red and Labor armies by arresting the relatives and friends of deserters, is understood to have been published in *Bednota,* date unknown. [*Bednota* was a newspaper for the peasantry published by the Central Committee of the Russian Communist Party.] I am anxious to procure a certified copy of this particular issue of the publication." Hoover asked for the text of one of Gorky's attacks on Lenin in the Menshevik party paper *Novaya Zhisn* that had a reference to "the

large number of persons who have been killed and the fact that the
enormous loss of life would not affect Lenin in trying his experiment."
In July, he asked the State Department and Military Intelligence to
give him information about the Second International Congress of Communists then meeting at Petrograd, particularly on the Americans
attending the meeting.[48]

Hoover had grandiose plans for still more radical raids. On February 21, 1920, he wrote Bureau Chief Frank Burke that he was putting
together a brief arguing that alien members of the IWW should be
deported because it advocated the "unlawful destruction of property."
He told Burke that if the secretary of labor accepted his arguments,
he intended to

> pick out five hundred (500) of the leading alien agitators of the I.W.W.,
> perfect the cases against them, and then have warrants issued for the
> specific 500. This would result in taking out of the organization leaders
> and if it did not have a salutary effect upon the organization after a
> month had elapsed another 500 would be taken.[49]

By February a gathering storm of criticism was swirling around the
Justice Department, and a cautionary note started to enter Hoover's
communications; he complained to Burke that the department would
have to proceed cautiously in planning the drive against the alien
Wobblies. "One of the difficulties we are facing at the present time
in connection with the communists," he wrote,

> is that there is an extensive propaganda on foot that many ignorant
> Russians were taken in the raid who knew nothing of the organization.
> While this is not entirely true, yet it has proved meat for propaganda
> and as the deportation policy must be supported solely by public opinion,
> I feel that a dragnet raid would be detrimental.[50]

Hoover was about to learn how vulnerable he was without his
own power base of public support. The backing of superiors such as
Attorney General A. Mitchell Palmer was useful while they maintained
their own political power bases, but if they should lose their power,
Hoover would be left at the mercy of his enemies. In view of Palmer's
growing political weakness during the spring of 1920, his support
would not have been of much value to Hoover even if the attorney
general had been a braver man than he was.

Hoover's statement to Burke that the antiradical program "must
be supported solely by public opinion" shows that Hoover already

understood the political realities. His survival depended ultimately on public support, which could be translated into political protection in the administration and on the Hill. He probably realized that the department may have exceeded the mandate granted it by public opinion, so he and Palmer were now vulnerable to counterattack.

Early in January, Secretary of Labor William Wilson began to have misgivings over the decision that had unleashed Hoover's raids.[51] He decided to hold formal hearings on the question of whether the Communist parties actually did come under the provisions of the 1918 Immigration Act. The hearings would give both sides in the dispute, the Justice Department and the Communists, a chance to air their arguments.

The first hearing was on a test case involving Englebert Preis, an alien facing deportation for his Communist party membership. On January 21, 1920, Hoover presented the Justice Department case at the Preis hearing in which he defended the legal basis for the January raids. The newspapers treated Hoover's testimony as an authoritative statement of the government's aims in the antiradical campaign. The *New York American* reported that Hoover's thesis was that "the literature, periodicals and manifestoes of the party show it advocates the use of force and violence. He sought to establish a relationship between the party and the Soviet Government in Russia."[52]

The *New York World* reported that Hoover made a "vigorous" case against the Communist party. "Reading the manifesto of the party, he pointed out the section in which it urged that strikes be broadened and deepened, making them general and militant. 'Certainly the word "militant" carries with it at first blush the thought of violence,' he declared."[53] The newspaper accounts of his appearances described him as performing confidently, brashly, even flamboyantly as he mocked the pleas of self-styled revolutionists seeking protection from the force of the law.

Despite his growing apprehension about the fairness of the raids, on January 25, 1920, Wilson decided against Preis, and in a ruling intended to apply to the thousands of Communist party members Hoover had arrested, Wilson stated that the Communist party, because of its goal to "conquer and destroy the government of the United States, not by parliamentary processes, but by direct conflict," was an organization that came under the terms of the 1918 immigration law.

Wilson's ruling encouraged Hoover to promise the press that "deportation hearings and the shipment of the 'Reds' from this country will be pushed rapidly. . . . Second, third, and as many other 'Soviet arks' as may be necessary will be made ready as the convictions proceed . . . and actual deportations will not wait for the conclusion of all the cases."[54]

Not everything had pleased Hoover at the Preis hearing. He had been infuriated by the behavior of Swinburne Hale, the lawyer who represented Preis and the Communist party. Hoover asked Military Intelligence to see if it had any derogatory information about Hale, who had been in Military Intelligence during the war. Hoover complained to his friends in the army that Hale "is now actively engaged in the defense of radicals, who find themselves in difficulty in New York State." Hoover told the head of Military Intelligence, General Marlborough Churchill, that "I noted the somewhat peculiar attitude of Captain Hale upon the elements involved in the discussion and I would therefore appreciate it if you could supply me with his past history and connections."[55] Hoover suspected that there must be something in the man's past to explain his defense of such dangerous radicals.

The Preis hearings were only the beginning of Hoover's troubles with Secretary Wilson and the Labor Department. On January 26, Wilson again changed Rule 22, reinstating the liberal policy originally instituted on March 13, 1919, again permitting aliens access to counsel at the beginning of the deportation process. Hoover learned of this on February 2 and demanded, "in view of the burden which same will no doubt place upon the government," to know the reason for the change. He complained that "the courts have time and again held the original Rule 22" to be constitutional.[56]

These were minor irritations. On March 5, 1920, there moved into a post of authority in the Labor Department the man who would destroy Attorney General Palmer's reputation, and very nearly Hoover's career. This was Assistant Secretary of Labor Louis Post, who took over Abercrombie's responsibilities for the deportation cases on that date. This put Post in a position to end what he called the "gigantic and cruel hoax" of the "deportations delirium."[57]

Post was seventy-one years old and had been assistant secretary of labor for seven years. Before joining the Wilson administration he had edited a liberal weekly entitled *Public,* and had befriended many radicals. He and his wife had entertained Emma Goldman in their home and had defended her and other radicals during the wartime free-speech battles. Circumstances had given Post the unwelcome job of signing Goldman's deportation papers in 1919, and she had written, bitterly and unfairly, that by doing so "Post had covered himself with ignominy."[58] With his wild hair, unkempt moustache, and Van Dyck beard, Post looked like the popular stereotype of the radical, and when he called a halt to Hoover's deportations Palmer accused him of being the Bolshevik he resembled.

Since Wilson had twice ruled that members of the Communist party were subject to deportation, Post felt it was his duty to sign their deportation orders. He was determined to do this, however, only if there was evidence that "each individual alien charged with being a member of the Communist Party was so in fact."[59] Despite Hoover's plea that a membership card or a name on a Communist party membership roll should be enough to deport an alien, Post decided that each individual case required scrutiny to ensure that the alien had indeed voluntarily become a member and that he had been fully aware of what he was doing. Post was concerned that many of the Communist party's membership had been "automatically" transferred from the foreign language groups associated with the Socialist party's Left Wing when the leaders of those groups joined the newly established Communist party, and that the individual members were not cognizant of what had happened.

In addition to thousands of Communist party members, the Immigration Bureau was holding about 300 members of the Communist Labor party. Post made a personal examination of Hoover's brief on that party, making the critical discovery that, despite Hoover's statements, there were significant differences between the two Communist parties in the degree of knowledge a member was required to have of the organizations' purposes. Post decided that there was no prima facie case for deciding that an individual member of the Communist Labor party was deportable solely because of his party membership, and so he deferred decision on all such cases until Wilson could personally take another look at the situation.[60] Ignoring the protests of Caminetti and Hoover, Post released the members of this party on their own recognizance until Wilson could make decisions on their cases.

The effect of Post's actions was to shift the focus in the deportation proceedings from the theoretical danger of the Communist movement in general to the actual threat represented by the individual Communist in particular. By insisting on evidence of personal guilt, contrary to the intent of the 1919 immigration law, Post destroyed the momentum and reduced the scale of Hoover's drive. By showing the public the enormous discrepancy between the Justice Department's propaganda about the Communist threat and the pathetic and harmless individuals

Hoover had rounded up, he exposed the fundamental gap between the plausible theory and the cruel fact of the Red Scare.

In the eighteen months from July 1, 1919, to January 1, 1921, the Immigration Bureau had issued 6,328 warrants against alien "anarchists." Of these, Post reported that "somewhat within 6,000 warrants of arrest were issued for alien 'reds' by the Department of Labor at the instance of the Department of Justice detectives." Out of this number some 4,000 were actually arrested, although the order was usually reversed—first the arrest, then the warrant. Of this 4,000, Post related (with no little satisfaction) that "3,000 were cancelled after hearings, nearly if not quite all by myself." To refute charges that his practice was simply to turn loose any Bolshevik brought before him, Post pointed out that "out of less than 1,000 deportations ordered after hearings, more than 500 were ordered by me."[61]

Post knew he had to be careful because "detectives for the Department of Justice, law clerks in the Department of Justice, and politically alert members of Congress inspired by special interests, together with coadjutators in the Department of Labor itself, were vigilantly scrutinizing every case in which my decisions were favorable to accused aliens." He therefore took pains to observe all legal forms and procedures, despite the great number of cases he had to decide and the chaotic state of the files when he began his work. He was pleased that not one of his decisions was reversed because of legal error despite Hoover's contention that the immigration law did not require examination of the actual status of an alien's membership in a proscribed organization. All Hoover could do was to complain in his *General Intelligence Bulletin* that "the cancellations of warrants by Mr. Post continue as usual," and try to sustain public support for the antiradical drive with more hair-raising reports on the Red Menace.[62]

Soon Hoover became aware an even greater disaster was developing in Boston. In April, the federal judge, George Anderson, was conducting a hearing in that city on a writ of habeas corpus for eighteen radicals arrested in the January raids and confined to the Deer Island prison. (The case was *Colyer* vs. *Skeffington*. The Colyers were British citizens; Skeffington was the chief of the Boston Bureau of Immigration.) Anderson was growing outraged over what he had learned about the behavior of Hoover's agents and auxiliaries during the raids. The tenor of his criticism of the Justice and Labor departments during the hearings made it clear to Hoover and Palmer that they could expect an adverse decision in the *Colyer* case. This would have a devastating impact on the legal status of their other cases, and so

Hoover was dispatched to Boston to assist the U.S. attorney's presentation of the government's defense.

By now, Hoover's reputation as the government's leading Red hunter was such that his arrival was greeted with excitement by the Boston press. Although Hoover seems to have merely lent advice and moral support to the government team, he received a great deal of attention in news accounts of the hearings. The *Boston Post* reported that

> considerable comment has been made by lawyers and others in attendance at the radicals' hearing in the Federal Court on the appearance of extreme youth of John E. Hoover, special assistant to Attorney-General Palmer, who is here during the trial of the habeas corpus case. Despite his boyish looks, however, I am informed that Mr. Hoover is regarded as one of the ablest men connected with the department in Washington.[63]

The *Boston Globe*'s story noted the red neckties worn by Colyer's supporters, one of whom was Harvard law professor Felix Frankfurter acting as a friend of the court. Frankfurter would later meet with Anderson at the judge's home to help draft the decision in the case.[64]

As soon as the *Colyer* hearings were over, and while both sides were waiting for Anderson's decision, Hoover had to hurry back to Washington to argue for the government at another test of the antiradical drive. Secretary of Labor Wilson had agreed with Louis Post that the Communist Labor party could not be put in the same deportable class with the Communist party unless it were first given a chance to object at an open hearing. Again Hoover represented the Justice Department, again the radicals were represented by Swinburne Hale. Armed with Judge Anderson's caustic criticism of the Justice Department's tactics during the raids, Hale repeated Anderson's charge that the government, through agents provocateurs, "operates some part of the Communist party in this country." Hoover fired back that Anderson's statement was "an unjustifiable misconception of the facts." He called it a construction "which the most perverted mind could not put upon the evidence."[65] This was strong language for a twenty-five-year-old attorney to use in reference to a federal judge.

Never one to settle back on the defensive, Hoover resumed his attacks on the radicals at the Communist Labor party hearing. He said that the Party was "a gang of cutthroat aliens who have come to this country to overthrow the government by force. Fifty percent of the influence behind the recent strikes," Hoover said, "was directly traceable to the communist organizations."[66]

On May 5, Secretary Wilson stunned Hoover and the Justice Department and threw the antiradical campaign into disarray by ruling that membership in the Communist Labor party was not a deportable offense because members were not required to know of or subscribe to the Party's goals or tactics as a condition of membership; he flatly rejected Hoover's brief and argument on the subject. Three hundred members of that Party who had been rounded up in the dragnet were freed.[67]

Hoover's campaign was rapidly collapsing as such powerful national figures as Post, Wilson, and Anderson mounted murderously effective attacks on him and his division. Palmer's general ineffectiveness was compounded by his confusion at the sudden unfavorable turn of events and by his preoccupation with his presidential plans. Hoover was left to defend the antiradical campaign on his own. Despite his age and the odds against him, he showed no trace of discouragement. He stubbornly tried to keep the drive alive and to keep the cases against the arrested aliens moving, while slashing back against his critics by attacking their patriotism. Hoover kept up the pressure on the Immigration Bureau to process the Communist party members whose deportation still seemed possible, prodding Caminetti to take action against those members arrested in the January raids not yet deported. He wrote Caminetti angry letters about inaction on individual cases and demanded the Immigration Bureau explain its failure to complete the deportation processes he had initiated. Despite his mounting frustration, Hoover continued to defend his plans and policies, giving back as good as he got.[68]

On May Day, there had been another setback. Based on Lenin's promise of a worldwide Soviet state by the summer of 1920, Hoover's Radical Division spewed out predictions during the final days of April that there would be a wave of assassinations, general strikes, and bombings on the first of May.[69] In many cities, including New York and Boston, the police forces went on alert to await the Red assault, but nothing happened. The radicals had never been quieter. The Red Scare was beginning to look ridiculous.

On June 23, Hoover's anti-Communist campaign finally collapsed. Judge Anderson issued his decision in the *Colyer* case, ruling that *neither* the Communist party *nor* the Communist Labor party was an organization whose alien members were subject to deportation. Anderson's decision was promptly overturned on a Labor Department appeal, but the conflicting opinions effectively halted deportations pending a decision by the Supreme Court—which never ruled on the case. Meanwhile, Louis Post continued to find, in case after case, that there was "no lawful proof to sustain the charges in the warrants of arrest under any provision of the immigration statutes."[70]

The tide had definitely turned against the Justice Department, but Hoover still fought back against his critics. He searched his files for proof that Post was a radical sympathizer and furnished Palmer with allegations that Post, as Palmer told Secretary of State Robert Lansing, was a "Bolshevik himself."[71] Palmer complained to the press and to Congress about Post, and finally, on April 17, got the House to look into the possibility of impeaching him. Hearings began on April 27, but the Rules Committee could find no basis for prosecuting Post, and instead voted on sending a resolution to the House censuring Post's leniency in the deportation cases. Post refused to accept the insult and demanded his day before the committee. When he appeared, his performance was so impressive, his indictment of the Justice Department so straightforward and convincing, that the investigation collapsed, and he turned all of the charges back against Palmer and the Justice Department. The committee voted to suspend all further action, including further deliberations on the peacetime Sedition Law that had been the goal of the Justice Department all along.

The attempt to impeach Post backfired in another way. As part of Post's defense against impeachment, his lawyer launched an investigation of the Justice Department's performance in the raids. The investigation was cosponsored by the National Popular Government League and aided by the newly named American Civil Liberties Union (before January 1920 the National Civil Liberties Bureau). When the investigation was completed, the report was sent to members of the legal community opposed to the raids. When the sixty-seven-page report appeared late in May, it bore signatures of twelve prominent lawyers.[72] Two of these, Frank P. Walsh and Swinburne Hale, were frequently associated with radical causes, and one of them, Jackson Ralston, was Post's attorney. The rest included some of the most distinguished members of the American bar, including Zechariah Chafee, Jr.; Ernst Freund; Francis Fisher Kane; Roscoe Pound; and Felix Frankfurter.

The lawyers' *Report Upon the Illegal Practices of the United States Department of Justice* charged that for six months there had been a "continued violation of [the] Constitution and breaking of . . . Laws by the Department of Justice . . . under the guise of a campaign for the suppression of radical activities." The lawyers accused the Justice Department (meaning Hoover's Radical Division) of levying cruel and unusual punishments, of making arrests without warrants, of unreasonable searches and seizures, of the use of agents provocateurs, of forcing witnesses to incriminate themselves, and in what was indirectly a charge of misusing an appropriation, of conducting an illicit propaganda campaign. In this last regard the *Report* made an observation that would be permanently relevant to Hoover's later activities. The lawyers pointed out that "the legal functions of the Attorney General are: to advise the Government on questions of law, and to prosecute persons who have violated federal statutes. For the Attorney General to go into the field of propaganda against radicals is a deliberate misuse of his office and a deliberate squandering of funds entrusted to him by Congress." The indictment concluded by saying that the behavior of the Justice Department involved "no question of a vague and threatened menace, but a present assault upon the most sacred principles of our Constitutional liberty."[73]

Palmer, reeling from Post's accusations and the attacks in the lawyers' *Report,* demanded a hearing before the House Rules Committee to refute the charges against him and the Justice Department. Hoover spent late May coaching the attorney general for his testimony before the committee; when the hearing began on June 1, Hoover sat by Palmer's side.

A memorandum from Hoover to Palmer on May 25 showed Hoover planning the attorney general's strategy during this crisis. Hoover told Palmer that he and Assistant Attorney General Francis Garvan thought Palmer's statement to the committee should be prepared in advance. The Justice Department would then furnish it to the reporters "so that the press might have something concrete upon which to formulate their articles." Hoover urged Palmer not to "mince words" but to regard the hearing as "an excellent opportunity not only to answer these specific charges but also to tell the committee and the country the real story of the red menace, both the International and National phase of the same, the efforts of the Department of Justice to specifically curb the spread of Bolshevism, and the results obtained from these efforts and finally the consequences following the action of the Assistant Secretary of Labor in cancelling the warrants." Hoover gave Palmer a massive memorandum that tried to answer all the charges made against the department. Hoover's strategy was to seize the initiative from Post by focusing the committee's attention on the threat the country had faced and how the department had defeated it. Palmer's entire testimony before the Rules Committee, together with all attached exhibits, can be regarded as a J. Edgar Hoover production.[74]

That production, however, was not well received. Palmer's attempts to refute the overwhelming evidence collected by Post and the lawyers in their *Report* amounted to little more than an emphatic denial that he had done anything wrong, supplemented by affidavits from the Bureau's agents that they had done no wrong, either.

Despite the generally unfavorable reaction to Palmer's testimony, Hoover put the best face on the situation and argued that Palmer had cleared the department of all charges. He refused to accept the general assessment that the raids had been a mistake, and continued to promote the notion that they had been a rousing success. He even tried to describe Palmer's appearance before the House committee as another triumph for the Justice Department. He sent congressmen and other influential officials transcripts of Palmer's testimony, together with copies of the Radical Division's newest publication, *The Photographic History of the Bolshevik Atrocities,* which, he said, showed "the acts indulged in by the present authorities of Soviet Russia."[75]

Despite Hoover's best efforts, however, Palmer's poor performance before the House, along with the May Day fiasco, convinced the congressmen that the Red Scare was a dead issue; the Rules Committee decided to halt all further investigations without censuring anyone. Hoover's only revenge against Post was a typescript poem he pasted in his scrapbook of souvenirs. It had a hand-colored red crayon frame around it, and was placed next to a newspaper photo of Post, likewise hand-colored in red. Hoover may have been the artist, perhaps even the poet.

The Bully Bolsheviki

Disrespectfully dedicated to "Comrade" Louie Post

1.
The "Reds" at Ellis Island
Are as happy as can be,
For Comrade Post at Washington
Is setting them all free.

2.
They'll soon be raising hell again
In every city and town
To bring on Revolution
And the old U S A to down.

3.
But Uncle Sam will clinch his fist
And rise up mighty strong

Take hold of Comrade "Louie"
Send the "Reds" where they belong.

4.
It's awfully nice of Comrade "Louie"
Of his position to make the most
The "Reds" all cheer when ere they hear
That sweet sounding name "ach Louie dear."

5.
But don't forget, he'll get his yet
For this is the land of the brave
He'll fail in his plan to rescue
Not one of the Reds will he save.

6.
And when he's lost his nice fat job
And is looking around for some work
They'll ask him to come to Russia
With the Bolshevikes he'll lurk.

7.
Nick Lenine will gladly greet him
In dear old Petrograd
He'll be a "Bullshevki" sure
Because he got in bad.

8.
His whiskers they'll grow longer
On that "Bullshevikie" bull
If you don't believe me, watch them
After he has lost his pull.

9.
So then all hail, dear Comrade Post!
With all his ways so tricky
And ponder well, that it was only he
Who saved the "Bullsheviki"[76]

Palmer was still running for the Democratic nomination for president during all this, uttering such wisdom as "I am myself an American and I love to preach my doctrine before undiluted one hundred percent Americans, because my platform is, in a word, undiluted Americanism and undying loyalty to the republic."[77] The failure of Palmer's predictions about a Bolshevik uprising in America now counted against him, as did the hostility of organized labor. Palmer did poorly in the primaries, and by the time he got to the San Francisco convention in June, his campaign had been mortally wounded. The winner of the Democratic nomination found it politically advantageous to repudiate the Red Scare campaign.

To heap further humiliation on Hoover and Palmer, when Congress reconvened for a lame duck session after the election, Senator Thomas Walsh of Montana prodded the Senate Judiciary Committee to hold hearings on the charges against the Justice Department. These were held from January 19 to March 3, 1921, before a subcommittee chaired by conservative Republican Thomas Sterling of South Dakota. Sterling managed to protect Palmer from some of Walsh's attacks, and he blocked Walsh's efforts to have the committee issue a report on the charges against the Justice Department. Nevertheless, the hearings did subject Palmer, with Hoover sitting by his side, to another grilling over the abuses committed during the raids and their aftermath. They placed in the record Palmer's references to Hoover as the person "who was in charge of this matter." Sterling managed to bottle up the committee's report, and so it was not until 1923 that Walsh was able to read his conclusions into the *Congressional Record,* a no-holds-barred indictment of the entire antiradical crusade.[78]

Hoover himself ever afterward displayed an ambivalent attitude toward his Palmer raid days. He did his best to disassociate himself from the raids themselves, having the Bureau issue outright lies to minimize the importance of his role. In his later version of the events he claimed he was little more than an errand boy for Palmer, Garvan, and Flynn. On the other hand, he did refer proudly to having gotten rid of Goldman, Berkman, and Martens, and to having written the briefs on the two Communist parties.

There was no indication that the disasters of the spring of 1920 had the slightest effect on Hoover's confidence in himself. He put a quotation from Goethe in his scrapbook: "[T]he important thing in life is to have a great aim, and to possess the aptitude and perseverance to follow it."[79] To all appearances, Hoover still had his "great aim," and he was to display no lack of the "aptitude and aim to follow it." But if he needed to take refuge in such consolations, the Red Scare failure may nonetheless have bruised his spirits. If so, he gave no outward sign. Its only lasting effect was to make him forever wary of putting himself in a position where he had to depend on anyone except himself or men completely subject to his control. Hoover learned from the disaster and went on with his life. Other men might have been destroyed.

Despite the end of the Red Scare, Hoover did not relax his General Intelligence Division's surveillance of the radical movement. He kept his agents watching Communists, his librarians cataloging their literature, his translators searching through foreign periodicals. He maintained his liaisons with Military Intelligence and state anti-Communist agencies even though by the summer of 1920 the public had grown perceptively tired of the Red Scare. It had become old news. The new news was the surge of popular amusements and entertainments: baseball and Babe Ruth, boxing and Jack Dempsey—an era later stereotyped as the Roaring Twenties.[80] The shift in mood was epitomized, perhaps, by Warren G. Harding's election as the symbol of "normalcy." Hoover's crusade against radicalism dropped out of sight.

The most important factor in the decline of the Red Scare in 1920 was the world situation. It had been the possibility of revolution throughout Europe in early 1919 that had made Americans see their own strikes and political violence as local manifestations of a terrifying international conspiracy. By late 1919 that analysis no longer seemed convincing, or even plausible. Not only had the revolution failed to spread during 1919, but it lost the footholds it had gained outside of Russia.

Although Hoover was unconvinced that the Bolsheviks had changed their strategy, the Soviets decided that any further encouragement of revolutionary adventures in Europe would place them in danger at a time when they should be consolidating what they had won at home. During the spring of 1920, Lenin wrote *Left Wing Communism, An Infantile Disorder*[81] and told Western Communists to participate in parliamentary politics. He denounced conspiratorial activity as dangerous romantic escapism that disarmed communism for the long struggle it faced in the future.

In 1919, Communists and anti-Communists alike had been overwhelmed by the success of the Russian revolution. By 1920 and 1921, the overwhelming fact of contemporary politics was the failure of the revolution outside Russia.[82] Moderate Americans sensed that the danger, if there ever had been a danger, had passed. Although the anti-Communist lobby struggled throughout the twenties to keep the spectre of communism alive in the American imagination, they met with little success. Hoover, who had learned the danger of acting without being assured of overwhelming public backing, warily resisted their efforts to enlist him in their cause.

But to say that the raids of 1920 ended in a personal failure for Hoover is not to say that they failed to inflict severe damage on American radicalism. Many forces besides Hoover's were operating to weaken the Communist parties in the United States during the 1919–1920 period. Factional conflict and subservience to Moscow were already decimating Communist membership even before January 1920, so Hoover's raids were directed against a Communist movement already losing its mass base. Nevertheless, Hoover's campaign has to be considered a major cause of the precipitous drop in Communist party membership, from perhaps 60,000–88,000 in September 1919 to 5,700 in December 1920.[83]

Hoover's campaign had demonstrated that it was dangerous to belong to the Communist parties. He had shown that they were already illegal for aliens and soon might be made illegal for citizens. That certainly terrified the less committed Communists. Communist Labor party organizer Benjamin Gitlow bravely asserted that "the raids helped the communist party separate the wheat from the chaff," but those few die-hards who stayed in the party were self-selected to belong body and soul to Moscow. The incredible vacillations and reversals of Russian policy over the next decades made staying abreast of Russian developments so important to a Communist's party career that his thinking inevitably acquired (or never lost) a foreign accent. European Communist parties suffered parallel disasters in the early twenties; thus Irving Howe and Lewis Coser, in their authoritative history of the Party, say only that "it is a moot point as to which did more to shatter the early Communist movement: the government's harassments or the furious inner squabbles of the Communist sects. Mass arrests, underground existence, and the sustained sectarianism had completed their isolation from American life and turned the entire movement into an arena for political cannibalism."[84]

For his part, however, Hoover had no doubt that he and his raids had prevented the spread of bolshevism to America. In a report Hoover almost surely drafted, Palmer said that "the result of the arrests of January 2, 1920, was that there was a marked cessation of radical activities in the United States. For many weeks following the arrests the radical press had nearly gone out of existence in so far as its communistic tendencies were concerned. Meetings were not held of the organizations and an examination of their subsequent literature shows that they had been completely broken by the activities of the Department of Justice."[85]

After Palmer's June 1920 appearance before the House, Hoover's General Intelligence Division largely abandoned its pursuit of publicity. The declining interest in the Bolshevik threat, Palmer's political demise, and congressional hostility toward the Justice Department all cautioned against any repetition of the large-scale operations of the previous year. But perhaps most importantly, organized revolutionary communism had collapsed as a significant political force in the United States. Hoover's Radical Division was organized to conduct large-scale assaults on major radical groups; even if conditions had permitted a continuation of the 1919–1920 drive, by late 1920 there was hardly anything left for the Justice Department to attack.

One illustration of the public's loss of interest in radicalism was its reaction to the bomb blast at the corner of Wall and Broad streets in New York City on September 16, 1920. This explosion, in the heart of New York's financial district, killed thirty-three people, injured 200 others, and damaged the headquarters of J. P. Morgan and Company. Even though this blast was far more damaging than the June 1919 explosions, Palmer and Hoover could not convince the press or public to regard it as part of what they called "a gigantic plot to overthrow capitalism."[86]

Hoover took personal charge of the Wall Street bombing; his authority was very clearly no longer confined to "general intelligence" operations. He and his superiors regularly referred to the Wall Street blast as a reason to continue funding anti-Communist investigations. Now and then he would alert the newspapers that there was a new development in the case, but like the June 1919 bombing of Palmer's house, it was never solved.[87]

Another sign that the Justice Department saw nothing to gain in continuing its antiradical campaign after the collapse of the Red Scare was its reluctance to get involved in the great radical cause of the twenties, the Sacco-Vanzetti case. The trial, conviction, and execution of Nicola Sacco and Bartolomeo Vanzetti, two Italian radicals, for the April 15, 1920, slaying of a shoe company paymaster and guard in Braintree, Massachusetts, became an international sensation because of the radical politics of the suspects and the obvious political and ethnic bias of the Massachusetts establishment—just the sort of case that might have been irresistible to Hoover. The Justice Department and Hoover's General Intelligence Division stayed out of the case even though the governor of Massachusetts tried to relieve himself of political pressure by turning it over to Washington. The Bureau of Investigation did, however, share routine information on the case with Massachusetts authorities, and had contingency plans for deportation proceedings against Sacco and Vanzetti if they had been acquitted.[88]

Hoover's four years under attorney generals Thomas Gregory and A. Mitchell Palmer had given him political experience, a taste of power, and an understanding of how that power was won and lost. In his essential values, however, he hardly changed from the boy he had been at Central High and Old First.

Defending the values of Seward Square was now, for him, a matter of attacking whatever threatened them. After his encounter with communism during its exuberant days of 1919, the Communists were forever after the symbols of that threat. Hoover was now a committed anti-Communist, but of a uniquely pure variety. In Hoover, one hardly ever caught a glimpse of the ulterior motive that was standard equipment for the general run of anti-Communist crusaders. He scarcely seems to have had any economic ideology and hardly ever showed any interest in the clash of Socialist and Communist economic institutions. He did not oppose labor unions or strikes for themselves, but only when he detected in them the influence of communism at work (though in practice this was a distinction that made little difference).

The exception to the purity of Hoover's anticommunism, however, was his instinctive antagonism toward black protest. In most of Hoover's radical investigations, he made some distinction between the Communist minority in an organization and the non-Communist majority. Usually it was apparent that he was motivated by his hatred of communism, not the cause communists were trying to control. In his Communist party brief, however, Hoover quoted a section of the Party's manifesto that "the Communist Party will carry on among the negro workers agitation to unite them with all class conscious workers." His comment, which went far beyond the evidence (and far beyond what he had said about the strikes), was that in communism "we see the cause of much of the racial trouble in the United States at the present time."[89]

Hoover was already forming the dangerous conviction that Communist agitation, and not the objective racial situation, was the cause of unrest among American blacks. In 1919, the Jamaican-born Marcus Garvey, arguably the most important black leader between Booker T. Washington and Martin Luther King, Jr., was organizing the Black Star Steamship Line as the cornerstone of the independent black economy he hoped to build. Hoover wrote his superiors that while "unfortunately" Garvey had not yet violated any federal laws that would permit his deportation, perhaps a fraud case involving Garvey's promotion of the steamship line might be a way of getting him out of the country. Hoover continued his investigation of Garvey for the next two years, and finally convicted him of mail fraud in June 1923. After serving his sentence, Garvey was deported to Jamaica in 1925.[90] In this case, the desire to destroy Garvey as a black leader came first, the search for a crime came later.

Marcus Garvey was the first black leader who felt the impact of Hoover's hostility toward racial change. By the end of 1919, Hoover had already defined political movements within the black community as a permanent field of investigation for his Radical Division. In 1920 he circulated a pamphlet entitled *Radicalism and Sedition Among the Negroes as Reflected in Their Publications,* the first of his many "exposes" of radical influence within the black community.[91] His determination to destroy Garvey and other black leaders by any means available, including the Red smear, may have had its origin in the rigid Jim Crow mores of his boyhood. In any case it revealed a racial hostility so strong that it could overwhelm any sense of fairness or justice.

Hoover emerged from his early days at the Justice Department the consummate professional who had learned to his pain the danger of slack management and loose control. What made him more than a bloodless bureaucrat, however, was the moralistic fervor he could bring to his efforts in matters of organization and discipline. Passionate in his beliefs, uncorrupted in his motives, and professional in his methods, Hoover had also acquired formidable political skills. During his time at Palmer's side he had acquired a taste for the excitement that comes from competition at the highest levels of national leadership. He had learned how to build alliances with his natural constituency— the conservative congressional establishment and the network of patriotic organizations that stretched across the country. And he had seen how he could direct his operations from a safe position behind an ambitious political figure, letting someone else take the major share of glory so that he would also absorb the punishment when political fortunes changed, as all political fortunes eventually do. Though Hoover had not been personally destroyed by the investigation of the Palmer raids, he had come close to disaster, close enough to know that failure was always possible.

Having lived through defeat, for the rest of his life he carried the knowledge that, in politics, he had to play to win but be prepared to lose. He had learned to remain the "objective" expert even in the heat of ideological battle. By furnishing facts and letting others draw their own conclusions, he could walk away from the wreck if his luck went bad. He was as ambitious as ever, but the experience of defeat had also made him cautious. Never again would he be in the position of wagering his entire career on one irretrievable political gamble.

CHAPTER 5

The Assistant Director

Make out an appointment for Colonel George R. Shanton and take it down to Mr. Holland and tell him that this is the man that Mr. Husted has been after us to put on—Mr. Husted of the Appropriations Committee.

I have seen the man and talked with him and he is a very high class man and we want to start him in at $8.00 a day. . . . I wish you would also note the Attorney General's memorandum to me on my desk telling me that Senator Gooding of Idaho has two men, I think their names are Day and White. The Attorney General says to put one of them on; we will therefore put Day on. [1]

Memo from William J. Burns,
Director, Bureau of Investigation,
to J. Edgar Hoover, Assistant
Director, May 5, 1922

IN LATER YEARS, Hoover told the story of his tenure as the Bureau's assistant director during the Harding administration as a parable of corruption and redemption, three years under a corrupt attorney general and a compliant Bureau director when the Justice Department gained a popular reputation as the "Department of Easy Virtue." He described himself as keeping clear of the corruption while he observed at close range how easily detectives could go bad when discipline was lax, and stored up lessons to be applied when and if he ever got the chance to clean house.

For the first half of 1921, the holdover director from the Wilson administration, William Flynn, hung onto his job despite the change in administrations. Lewis J. Baley, a former assistant attorney general, remained as assistant director and chief, a position he assumed when Frank Burke resigned in July 1920. On August 18, 1921, the new attorney general, Harry M. Daugherty, finally fired Flynn. To run the Bureau Daugherty chose a boyhood friend from Ohio, the famous detective and founder of the detective agency that bore his name, William J. Burns—like Flynn, Burns had first achieved fame as a detective in the Secret Service. On August 22, 1921, Daugherty named twenty-six-year-old Hoover the assistant director and chief at a salary of $4,000 a year. Since the assistant director had charge of all administrative matters and supervised the day-to-day functions of the agency, the position called for someone of Hoover's bureaucratic abilities and familiarity with Bureau routine.

Hoover's three years as assistant director did not demand the kind of effort and involvement he had displayed during the Red Scare, so he was able to develop more of a social life. He took up golf at the Columbia Country Club, where he stayed an active member until 1936. He also broadened the scope of his activities in Washington's Masonic network. On November 9, 1920, Hoover was raised to the Sublime Degree of Master Mason in Federal Lodge Number 1; in April 1921, he obtained the various degrees of Royal Arch Mason. Three months later, he joined the Washington Commandery Number 1, and on March 1, 1922, he was made a member of Almas Shrine Temple. Hoover also joined the University Club, and became a member of the National Geographic Society to be able to use the Society's reading rooms. In 1922, he obtained a reserve officer's commission in the army's Military Intelligence Division, and during his years as assistant director he held the rank of captain, which gave him credentials in his regular contacts with Army Intelligence, which was heavily involved in domestic surveillance during the twenties.[2]

Hoover was still living at 413 Seward Square with his parents. Dickerson Sr. had been suffering from emotional instability, perhaps depression, ever since retiring from government service in 1917 and had to be institutionalized for a time at a sanatorium in Laurel, Maryland. When he returned home his spirits had changed, and he was cross and abrupt with his family. In 1922, Dickerson Hoover, Sr., died. Later, Hoover hung in the foyer of his house in northwest Washington the classic photograph of President Lincoln and his son Tad. The picture might have reminded Hoover of his stricken father who had once written such touching letters to his "Little Edgar."[3]

Perhaps in an attempt to help his mother cope with loneliness, in 1924 the Hoovers took in Dickerson Jr.'s older daughter, Margaret. This allowed her to finish school at Eastern High without having to commute from Maryland, where Dick had recently moved his family. Margaret continued to live at 413 Seward Square while she attended teachers' college and then law school at George Washington University. Like her uncle, Margaret worked at the Library of Congress to support herself and her studies.[4] Margaret and her younger sister, Anna, remember their grandmother running a strict, well-ordered, sparkling clean house for their uncle Edgar, with a parquet floor in the dining room that "was kept waxed to within an inch of your life."

Both mother and son had strong personalities, with occasional tests of will. Annie Hoover liked to keep the shades drawn, Edgar preferred sunlight in the rooms. As soon as he got home Hoover would raise them, then go to his room to work on the papers he carried home every evening. Hoover's niece said, "It was a kind of battle of wits on the part of two very intelligent people." Mrs. Hoover would prepare breakfast each morning with the help of a maid, and it would have to be ready when Edgar came down, and prepared just the way he liked it or it had to be done over. He would take a few bites of his poached egg on toast, then set the plate on the floor for the Airedale, Spee Dee Bozo. After breakfast he walked the dog to Pennsylvania Avenue to get the paper for his mother; he took the dog out again after work.[5]

The Bureau had been in existence for thirteen years when Hoover became its assistant director. Since its establishment in 1908, it had operated in that highly charged political arena where national leaders struggle over basic definitions of national values. Neither at its inception nor at any time after was the Bureau's function in American politics adequately defined by the clause in the Justice Department's annual appropriation which had simply authorized the department, since 1871, to expend funds for the detection and prosecution of crimes against the United States.[6]

The Bureau's operations have ranged so far afield from law enforcement, and have been so controversial, that writers on Hoover and the FBI have looked for explanations in the anthropology of secret societies, the psychology of voyeurism, and the political function of popular mythology. It is hard to avoid these digressions because the FBI has always been as concerned with morality as with law, with sin as with crime. In actuality, the Bureau of Investigation from the beginning had two purposes not strictly confined to law enforcement: to provide the president with an authoritative source of sensitive information, and to give him a dramatic means of exercising presidential power when faced with unavoidable (or sometimes irresistible) challenges to his authority.

For the three years before the establishment of the Bureau in 1908, Theodore Roosevelt and Congress had been locked in a feud over presidential use of Secret Service agents. Until then, the practice had been for the different departments, including Justice, to use their funds appropriated for the investigation of crimes to borrow Secret Service agents from the Treasury Department. In this manner, Roosevelt had used Secret Service agents attached to the Interior Department to collect evidence to convict a senator and a congressman from Oregon of land fraud. Naturally, Congress resented having its members investigated by the executive branch, and on May 27, 1908, attached a measure to an appropriations resolution that would suspend from the Service any Secret Service agent who accepted assignments outside the Treasury Department.[7]

Roosevelt charged Congress with obstructing justice, and authorized his attorney general, Charles J. Bonaparte (nephew of Napoleon III), to organize a new force of investigators. Bonaparte did so on July 1, 1908, with personnel drawn from the Justice Department's twelve "examiners" (who audited the accounts of U.S. attorneys, marshals, and clerks), thirteen employees who had been working on land frauds and peonage cases, and nine Secret Service agents who had been attached to the Justice Department under the old rules. Congress correctly saw the new Bureau as an enormous expansion of executive power and attacked Roosevelt for setting up "a system of spying upon and espionage of the people, such as has prevailed in Russia." Despite these complaints, the president now had his force of investigators, and on March 16, 1909, Bonaparte's successor named it the "Bureau of Investigation"; Chief Examiner Stanley Finch was chosen as its first "chief."[8]

The controversy between the executive and legislative branches over the Bureau was serious because it involved a congressional effort to resist the expansion of presidential power that was occurring under

Theodore Roosevelt. The refusal of Congress to let Roosevelt use the Secret Service to investigate the land frauds threatened the president's ability to act as public defender against those he had branded public enemies—the despoilers of the public's natural heritage. Roosevelt had to restore that power or abandon his role as national protector and leader. The Bureau gave him a way of projecting his office into popular controversy to demonstrate that he and the public stood together against evil.[9]

Despite the Bureau's small size (even today it numbers only 8,700 agents), it could have a significant impact on the country because its actions could reduce complex problems to understandable dramas of crime and punishment. The Bureau's cases were important not so much for any effect they had on the crime rates but as a way of reinforcing the public's perception of the president as the ultimate public defender.

Before World War I the Bureau's most spectacular operation was its role in the White Slave Scare of 1910, when press hysteria had managed to convince the public that organized prostitution was a menace to national survival. Chief Finch told Congress that unless a woman were "actually confined in a room and guarded, there was no girl, regardless of her station in life, who was altogether safe. . . . There was need that every person be on his guard, because no one could tell when his daughter or his wife or his mother would be selected as a victim." In response, Congress passed the Mann Act, which outlawed the interstate transport of women for immoral purposes. This was interpreted by the courts to include (in Hoover's words) "personal escapades." The Bureau got the juicy assignment of enforcing this law and garnered sensational headlines by arresting celebrities, like black heavyweight boxing champion Jack Johnson for crossing a state line with his white mistress. The Bureau's war on prostitution put the federal government on the right side of an issue of intense public concern, which Hoover later called "the problem of vice in modern civilization." Mann Act cases were such an important part of the Bureau's work that on April 30, 1912, the Attorney General designated Finch as Special Commissioner for the Suppression of White Slave Traffic, with a special force of "White Slave" officers drawn from the ranks of the Bureau. A. Bruce Bielaski replaced Finch as chief of the Bureau of Investigation. The two Bureaus were reunited in 1914 after the White Slave scare had run its course.[10]

During World War I, there was as much alarm over "slackers," or draft dodgers, as German spies. The Bureau's job was to prove that the selective service laws were being rigorously enforced. From April 1918 to September 1918, the Bureau and its volunteer auxiliary, the American Protective League, rounded up thousands of draft-age men and held them until they could produce their draft cards—only a tiny proportion proved to be slackers. As before, the Bureau was the government's instrument for defusing a deep-rooted public anxiety, this time over whether the country was adequately prepared for war. The tactic was to attack a symbolic enemy (the draft dodger). The Mann Act, the Slacker dragnets, and, of course, the Red Scare raids all displayed the Bureau's role as the federal government's champion in the battle against public vice, just as the Oregon land fraud cases had shown the Bureau used as a presidential weapon for disciplining his enemies.

The Bureau was not simply the creation of one particularly pugnacious and publicity-conscious president. The relationship between president and nation had been permanently changed when the new media of communications and improved transportation created a "national" public consciousness. Twentieth-century presidents had to assume responsibility for a range of issues formerly considered local in nature, but now seen (sometimes accurately, sometimes not) as causes or symptoms of national problems. Increasingly, local crime was becoming one of these new areas of presidential responsibility. Astute politicians sensed that they would have to respond to public alarm about new "dangers" or forfeit public confidence in their leadership.

In fact, government authority in America remained as decentralized as before despite public perceptions: Since there was no public support for a true unification of local and federal law enforcement, the national government could do little more to respond to public concern over crime than make occasional theatrical gestures against symbolic enemies. The Bureau's little band of investigators (346 in 1921; the average was fewer than 400 a year until the mid-thirties) was pathetically inadequate to police a nation of 106 million (in 1920), no matter how liberally the Bureau's mandate of investigating "crimes against the United States" was construed, but the tiny Bureau was ideally suited to act in the political theater of symbolic politics.

Partly for reasons of political theatrics, Hoover's two predecessors at the Bureau, William Flynn and William Burns, were appointed largely because of their reputations as great detectives. Both had done great things in the Secret Service (Flynn as its head); both had solved famous cases that had made them national celebrities. When Attorney General A. Mitchell Palmer named Flynn to head the Bureau of Investigation in 1919, he called him "the leading, organizing detective of America. . . . Flynn is an anarchist chaser . . . the great anarchist expert in the United States." Flynn's successor, William J. Burns was even more famous. He had been in charge of the Secret Service agents attached to the Interior Department who had solved the Oregon land frauds case, so he was indirectly responsible for the establishment of the Bureau of Investigation. He founded the William J. Burns National Detective Agency in 1909, and, after he solved the sensational *Los Angeles Times* bombing case, the *New York Times* wrote that Burns was "the greatest detective certainly, and perhaps the only really great detective, the only detective of genius, whom this country has produced."[11] When Burns became director of the Bureau, he was the most famous American detective since Allen Pinkerton, a celebrity and a prominent figure in New York City's nightlife. Burns was also a popular lecturer, the subject of countless feature stories, and the author of a series of stories about his most celebrated cases (as well as two novels, *The Argyle Case* [1913] and *The Crevice* [1915]).

Since crime stories were popular entertainment, it was natural for great detectives (or their ghost writers) to provide the public with true crime stories. Like Burns, Allen Pinkerton had also been a very popular storyteller. From 1873 until 1886, he published eighteen volumes of casebooks. And William Flynn edited a crime magazine called *Flynn's Weekly,* and Hoover eventually followed in their footsteps with such books as *Persons in Hiding* and *Masters of Deceit.*

When Hoover entered the top ranks of the Bureau of Investigation, he was moving into a role shaped by strong public expectations, and these expectations were formed as much by popular entertainment as by the famous detectives who had preceded him. And as a leading detective, Hoover could expect to be compared (or contrasted) to such fictional heroes as Old Sleuth, Cap Collier, and, most popular of all, Nick Carter.

The public's fascination with law enforcement and crime entertainment was part of the intense politicization of crime in American society. The drama of crime and punishment had long functioned as a social ritual of solidarity, like elections and even wars, to strengthen the bonds of community.[12] The Bureau Hoover joined had provided these rituals of solidarity in the past, and so the media expected its director to act like a detective hero. No one, however, could have resembled traditional detectives like Flynn and Burns (affable, extroverted, in some senses stereotypical Irish cops) less than intense, abstemious Hoover, but even he would eventually have to adapt himself to fit the public's expectations about detective heroes. As assistant director from 1921 to 1924, however, Hoover's job was to stay behind the scenes and manage the details while "Billy" Burns loped through the headlines solving crimes and threatening criminals.

The Daugherty-Burns era lasted until the spring of 1924 when both men had to resign during the Teapot Dome scandal. Bureau correspondence shows Hoover as the dutiful administrator, translating the commands of his superiors into operational orders to agents. Where the field agents of the Bureau engaged in obviously illegal activities, Hoover later defended himself by claiming that Washington's control over agents was then so loose that headquarters often did not know where the agents were or what they were doing. (The system of command Hoover later established ensured that his agents never escaped his control when they were detached to U.S. attorneys and other federal law enforcement agencies.)[13]

Hoover continued as head of the General Intelligence Division after his appointment as assistant director, and continued to keep close watch on radical activity. Presumably, he was the source for the dire warnings about the radical threat Burns delivered during his annual testimony before the House Appropriations Committee. Nevertheless, the collapse of the Palmer deportation drive led to a dramatic decrease in the size of the Bureau—from a peak of 579 agents (1,127 total personnel) in 1920 to 441 agents (657 in all) in 1924. Most of the decline came at the end of 1920, when the department abandoned its plans for further drives against radicals.[14]

Despite its smaller size, the General Intelligence Division was still a going concern. In addition to maintaining already existing division files on national and international Communists, Hoover arranged with Military Intelligence to share the fruits of the army's investigations of radicals and for the General Intelligence Division to pass on to the army any information uncovered in the course of its investigations.[15] He also continued to collect information from other government agencies and to share this information with the rest of the intelligence community.

Hoover refused to forgive and forget those who had derailed his anti-Communist crusade: he ordered investigations of the Federal Council of Churches of Christ, and continued his investigation of Swinburne Hale; he provided help to a Harvard alumnus who wanted to get Zechariah Chafee fired from Harvard, and circulated what he considered incriminating evidence about Louis Post's radical tendencies. Not only did these fights appeal to Hoover's naturally pugnacious disposition; they also let friends, potential enemies, and subordinates know that if they crossed him they would have a dangerous enemy the rest of their lives.[16]

Although Hoover continued to investigate radicals such as Kate Richards O'Hare and Marcus Garvey, the focus of his antiradical activities after 1920 shifted to cooperation with those states that had passed sedition laws during the war and Red Scare periods. On December 9, 1922, the Bureau claimed it had helped the states obtain 115 political convictions, and Hoover pasted a newspaper clipping about the conviction of Benjamin Gitlow under the New York State Sedition Law into his scrapbook. And on April 10, 1923, the Bureau bragged it had helped the state of Arizona eradicate radicalism in the city of Globe.[17]

Hoover's most important attack on American radicals while he was assistant director was the raid on the convention of the Communist party in Bridgman, Michigan, on August 22, 1922. The Party's leadership, after taking elaborate precautions to avoid detection, had gathered at a farm near Lake Michigan to debate whether the Party should stress legal political activity or illegal covert operations. Acting on information from Hoover's General Intelligence Division, William Burns sent the Bureau's top antiradical agent, Jacob Spolansky, to Michigan, where he discovered the Communists masquerading as a foreign singing society. While Spolansky was hiding in the woods awaiting reinforcements he was spotted, and the alarm was given by William Z. Foster, who had joined the Party as liaison with the labor union movement. The Communists buried the Party's records and the transcript of the convention and tried to escape, but Spolansky and his agents arrived before they could all get away and captured, among other Party leaders, the future (1930–1945) head of the Party, Earl Browder. One of the Communists they arrested was the Bureau's undercover agent, Francis Ashworth, known to his superiors as "K-97," who had infiltrated the Party leadership and had helped organize the convention. Ashworth was able to show Spolansky where the records were buried; later K-97 was the government's principal witness at the Michigan sedition trials of Charles Ruthenberg (secretary of the Communist party), William Z. Foster, and others. (Ruthenberg was convicted, but died before his appeal could be heard. The case against Foster ended in a hung jury.)

During the Bridgman trial Hoover began a practice he would follow the rest of his career, that of making the Bureau's research facilities available to friendly journalists and writers who could be counted on to produce materials that would aid him in his objectives. He helped Richard Whitney, director of an anti-Communist pressure group called the American Defense Society, write a series of articles on the case for the *Boston Evening Transcript.* Whitney acknowledged that he had based his essays on "photostatic copies of documents . . . taken in the Bridgman raid supplemented by talks with William J. Burns and Mr. Burns' associates, John Hoover and George Ruch." In 1924, Whitney turned his newspaper articles into a book, *Reds in America,* which again thanked Hoover, Ruch, and Burns for their "helpful . . . advice and friendly criticism."[18]

Because a violation of state sedition law like the Bridgman affair was not a crime against the United States, the Bureau's critics protested that the Justice Department had exceeded its authority. Since the Bridgman case was within Hoover's area of responsibility, it was probably he who coached Burns to tell the House Appropriations Committee that the Bureau had refused to explain its authority to the ACLU except to say "very courteously" that "we had ample reasons under the law for taking the action we did."[19]

By 1922, Hoover's campaign against the American Communists, beginning with the deportation raids and culminating in the raid on the Bridgman convention, contributed to a decline in the size of the Party to 5,000–6,000 members. Hoover was later to watch it slowly grow again to a peak in 1943 of about 80,000 strategically situated members. The experience of seeing a seemingly dead Communist party revive before his eyes made him permanently suspicious whenever afterward he received reports from his own agents or anyone else that the Party was again expiring.[20]

Also in 1922, Burns and Daugherty drew Hoover into the Justice Department's successful campaign to break the national railroad strike, which had began on July 1 when employers announced a 24 percent wage cut. On September 1, 1922, Attorney General Daugherty obtained an injunction against the strike that prohibited any word or deed by a worker that hampered the operation of the railroad. The wording of the court order was so broad that both Secretary of State Charles Evans Hughes and Secretary of Commerce Herbert C. Hoover protested and called it "one of the most sweeping and drastic injunctions ever issued in the United States."[21]

Bureau Director William Burns had long experience as a strike-breaker from his private detective agency days, and gave the Bureau the job of collecting evidence to prosecute strikers for violating the injunction. Hoover, as the operational head of the Bureau, dispatched the agents to the picket lines and collected their reports. The department used Hoover's reports to persuade judges that the strike was Communist-inspired. Twelve hundred workers were arrested as a result of the Bureau's investigations, a major factor in breaking the strike.[22]

The Justice Department's reputation under Daugherty and Burns was so bad that afterward Hoover tended to steer the discussion away from the more notorious activities of the Bureau and toward his investigation of the Ku Klux Klan in Louisiana, particularly when he was criticized, as he frequently was, for lack of enthusiasm in enforcing civil rights laws. Hoover's case against the Klan began in September 1922 when a Louisiana newsman came to him with a message from the governor of that state that the Klan had become so powerful that it was monitoring the governor's mail and tapping his phone. Hoover told the governor to go directly to the president. Harding, acting under the provision in the Constitution that authorized the president to suppress domestic violence, then directed the Justice Department to investigate. Bureau agents found evidence implicating the Klan in a series of murders, but Klan-dominated local grand juries refused to indict. Blocked in this direction, Hoover found an indirect route to his goal: He collected information about the sexual practices of the Klan's leader, Imperial Kleagle Edward Y. Clark, which led to Clark's conviction on March 10, 1924, for violating the Mann Act.[23] In later years, the fact that the Bureau's most important early civil rights successes had resulted from morals investigations may have accounted for Hoover's instinct to start searching bedrooms whenever confronted by a difficult problem in the field of civil rights.

The Teapot Dome scandal, which destroyed the pre-Hoover Bureau, first touched the Justice Department in January 1924 when Senator Burton K. Wheeler of Montana charged Attorney General Harry Daugherty with blocking the investigation of Secretary of Interior Albert B. Fall's sale of the navy's oil reserves at Teapot Dome, Wyoming. Daugherty retaliated by having Burns send Bureau agents to Montana to collect incriminating evidence on Wheeler in order to discredit him. The department used the Bureau's findings to draw up a hasty indictment of Wheeler for representing a constituent before a federal agency, a violation of federal statutes. Wheeler *had* represented his client in state courts; the charge that he had done so before a federal agency was untrue.[24]

Wheeler's trial began on March 25, 1924. There were, according to Wheeler, twenty-five to thirty Bureau agents in Great Falls, Montana, making nightly phone calls to Hoover in Washington about the progress of the trial (Wheeler was eventually acquitted). Wheeler and his attorney, Senator Thomas Walsh, were convinced that Hoover played a major part in the attempt to frame Wheeler, but Wheeler later changed his mind and accepted Hoover's explanation that Assistant Attorney General William Donovan (Hoover's World War II intelligence rival as head of the OSS) was actually responsible for the vendetta. Hoover probably just did what he was told, and did it with his usual efficiency. Hoover later claimed that, during his time as assistant director, agents were frequently "detached from the Bureau" for use by the department and "I didn't know even where the Accountants or Special Agents were . . . I did not . . . assume direction of their investigative work nor see any of their reports nor know what they were doing."[25]

When Hoover wanted to dramatize the corruption of the Daugherty-Burns Justice Department, and his own role in cleaning it up, he usually told the story of Gaston B. Means, the rogue agent who was Hoover's symbol of the corruption he had to contend with when he took over the Bureau in 1924.

During the 1930s, Hoover, with the help of a ghost writer, turned Bureau history into mythology; he made the Bureau's great cases demonstrate the virtues the FBI defended, the vices it warred against, and the irresistible power of its scientific crime-fighting methods. Means held a special place in this allegorical wax museum as Hoover's prime symbol of police corruption.

Hoover wrote that he first met Means in 1921 "when, as a newly appointed Special Agent of the Bureau of Investigation, he lumbered into the Department of Justice where I then was a subordinate and immediately began to investigate everything within reach. A bulky man, with heavy body and long, gorillalike arms, there was about him the air of a person eternally reaching a climax [sic]. It was all simulation. Underneath his excited exterior, Gaston Means was cool and cunning and crafty."[26]

Means's record as a confidence man went back to 1911, when he cut the supports on his Pullman berth and sued Pullman when the bed collapsed. In 1914, he married a rich widow, took her hunting, and carried her out of the woods, claiming she had accidentally shot herself in the head. Before World War I, Means worked for German intelligence and teamed up with William Burns, who was working for British intelligence, to furnish each other with information to sell to their respective employers. When Burns became director of the Bureau he brought Means with him and signed him up as a special agent.

Means went into business selling information from the Bureau's files, and he spread the word to his underworld contacts that he could fix cases. Means's activities became so noisome that they disgusted even Attorney General Daugherty, who had a notably strong stomach. After he was fired from the Bureau in August 1922, Means started taking orders from bootleggers for "B Permits," which were official permissions to withdraw impounded liquor from government warehouses for sale overseas. During the Teapot Dome scandal, Means claimed he had documents that would expose the entire mess in Washington. At the last moment he announced that all his records had been stolen.[27]

For the rest of his life, Hoover told Gaston Means's story to show the corruption that had infected the Bureau before he became its director, saying that "the man always had disgusted me. A subordinate at that time, I had determined that if ever I became Director, I would end all possibility of the Bureau again being sullied by such a person. That became my first big endeavor when I received my appointment."[28]

When President Harding died on August 2, 1923, the scandals involving his cabinet members had not yet reached the public. The Senate hearings on Teapot Dome, with Montana Senator Thomas Walsh acting as chairman, began on October 22. The full story of Secretary of the Interior Fall's corruption came out on January 24, 1924, followed, a week later, by Senator Burton K. Wheeler's call for Daugherty to resign for failing to investigate the Teapot Dome affair. On March 28, President Coolidge fired Daugherty and appointed Harlan F. Stone, the dean of Columbia Law School, to succeed him.

Next to go was Billy Burns. On April 10, 1924, the Bureau director had admitted to a Senate panel that he had remained silent when Daugherty had lied about sending agents to Montana to investigate Wheeler. After that, Stone went looking for the right man for the job of director, and he mentioned his problem to the cabinet. Secretary of Commerce Herbert Hoover told his confidential assistant, Larry Richey, about Stone's problem. Richey was something of a detective buff: He had done undercover work for the Secret Service when he was only thirteen, had joined the Service at age sixteen, and had served in the presidential guard before leaving to work for Herbert Hoover. With this background, it is not surprising that Richey had become a friend of his boss's namesake at the Justice Department. Richey told his chief that J. Edgar Hoover could do the job.[29] The secretary of commerce passed the word to Stone, who had also gotten a good report on Hoover from the Justice Department attorney in charge of Prohibition enforcement, Mabel Willebrandt. She had told

Stone that Hoover was "honest and informed and one who operated like an electric wire, with almost trigger response." Despite recommendations that he appoint Elmer Irey, an Internal Revenue investigator, Stone decided that Hoover was his man.[30]

A few days later, on May 9, Stone asked for Burns's resignation and sent word to Assistant Director Hoover that he wanted to see him the next day. On May 10, 1924, Harlan Stone named Hoover acting director, and gave him the job he would hold for the rest of his life.

CHAPTER 6

The Progressive Years

I am determined to summarily dismiss from this Bureau any employee whom I find indulging in the use of intoxicants to any degree or extent upon any occasion. This, I can appreciate, is a very drastic attitude and I shall probably be looked upon by some elements as a fanatic. . . .

This Bureau cannot afford to have a public scandal visited upon it in the view of the all too numerous attacks made . . . during the past few years. I do not want this Bureau to be referred to in terms I have frequently heard used against other government agencies. [1]

Hoover to Special Agents in
Charge, May 1925

WHEN J. Edgar Hoover took over the Bureau in the spring of 1924, Coolidge's housecleaning was sweeping through the administration. Harding's people, tainted by the corrupt connection between business and politics revealed in the Teapot Dome scandals, were being replaced by ostentatiously apolitical appointees. Harlan F. Stone was representative of the kind of men the Coolidge administration needed, but the perfect example and model of the new breed of nonpolitical, scientific managers was the "other Hoover," Herbert C. Hoover, the holdover secretary of commerce, who was the very image of the progressive-minded businessman-in-politics. (There was no family connection between the two Hoovers.) Herbert Hoover's progressivism, in fact, furnished J. Edgar Hoover with a guide for his administration of the Bureau during the next nine years.

In 1924, Herbert Hoover's prestige was enormous because of his much-admired work as wartime food administrator and head of postwar European relief. He was known as the "Great Engineer," and his scientific approach to organizational administration was the model for thoroughly modern administrators. An astute bureaucrat—like J. Edgar Hoover—who followed Herbert Hoover's lead could expect to share in the Great Engineer's prestige. By adopting Herbert Hoover's ideas, J. Edgar Hoover identified himself as one of the new breed of progressive managers who were applying the methods of science to the old problems of government. J. Edgar Hoover's success in adapting these methods to police work during the twenties not only influenced his administrative style the rest of his career, but made him a lifelong symbol and spokesman for the gospel of scientific law enforcement.[2]

J. Edgar Hoover's appointment was popular with the press because his education, brains, memory, even his game of golf were all seen as marks of the progressive business manager, who shared with the progressive movement a fascination with problems of organization, efficiency, and control. The hallmark of this movement was the tendency, within both the political parties and the business community, to look to research for solutions to the problems of social waste and inefficiency.

The moral fervor J. Edgar Hoover brought to the technical problems of his Bureau's organization and discipline was only one of the many ways he resembled the progressive civil servants who had begun to enter the government early in the century. To a remarkable degree, these men shared a common background: They were the young, well-educated offspring of the beleaguered middle class, and they usually came from old-stock families who wanted to restore "a kind of civic purity that was . . . believed to have been lost" through urbanization and industrialization.[3]

The progressive movement gave Hoover a positive model to follow; it also gave him a clear idea of what he should avoid. The progressives saw themselves as the antidote to the old-style corrupt politician, and nobody fit that negative image better than William Burns. Without knowing very much at all about Hoover, reporters simply described him as the negation of the disgraced Billy Burns. Papers advised him to "make a careful study of the official acts, utterances and purposes of William J. Burns. Study them and study them and study them.

Memorize them. Second: Do those things Mr. Burns did not do; refrain from doing those things which he did do."⁴ For a start, at least, all Hoover had to do was not be Billy Burns. He might not exactly be Herbert Hoover, at least not yet, but he could certainly manage not to be William Burns.

Billy Burns had so discredited the image of the old-style detective that Hoover was even praised for *not* being a detective, for having "scrapped the old 'gum shoe, dark lantern and false moustache' traditions of the Bureau of Investigation and substituted business methods of procedure." Burns was remembered as the "reincarnation of Old Sleuth," a man "who knew the ways and the wiles of criminals as well as any man in the world. He had been brought up with his nose to the ground." Hoover was seen as "the disciple of Blackstone," belonging to "the new school of crime-detection" and "as clean as a hound's tooth . . . furthermore, he plays golf. Whoever could picture an 'Old Sleuth' doing that?"⁵

In their eagerness to paint a dramatic contrast with the old Daugherty-Burns regime, reporters gushed about the wholly different aims and abilities the new director brought to his tasks. The public wanted a new departure, a break with the legacy of Palmer and Burns, and Hoover seemed to fit the bill.

> Young Mr. Hoover, who succeeds the unlamented Burns as head of the Department of Justice's Bureau of Investigation, was trained under former Attorney General Palmer and was active in the work of deporting some of the Palmer undesirables. It is interesting to note that Attorney General Stone, who has given this promotion to Mr. Hoover, was one of the men most active in fighting the hysteria developed in Washington by Mr. Palmer's red crusade. We hope that Mr. Hoover will be able to forget the teachings of Mr. Palmer under the more intelligent leadership of Mr. Stone. It would be worth a great deal to the American people to be assured that the Department of Justice is what the name signifies and not a Department of Hysteria and Intolerance.⁶

The Bureau of Investigation was a shambles when Hoover took over on May 10, 1924. There was even talk of putting it out of its misery, transferring its functions to the Secret Service, thereby getting the Justice Department completely out of the detective business. During the Palmer era, Hoover's new boss, Attorney General Harlan Stone, had been a vigorous critic of the Bureau's role in the alien raids. He had joined a committee of protest against Justice Department illegality in 1921 and had called for a congressional probe of the Bureau. Nevertheless, Stone believed that the Bureau was "a necessary instrument of law enforcement." This was, however, a weak endorsement, and in light of Stone's well-known doubts about the Bureau's conduct, Hoover could not have taken too much comfort from it.[7]

If Stone was not going to abolish the Bureau, he was going to let it continue only on a completely different basis. He drew up a strict set of guidelines to serve as a constitution for reorganization. Stone told Hoover to limit the Bureau's activities "strictly to investigations of violations of law, under my direction or under the direction of an Assistant Attorney General regularly conducting the work of the Department of Justice." He ordered Hoover to slash the size of the staff, removing "those who are incompetent and unreliable." In the future, he was to hire only "men of known good character and ability, giving preference to men who have had some legal training."[8]

A strict limitation of the Bureau's activities to investigations of "violations of law" meant an end to the General Intelligence Division and to the investigation of political beliefs and associations. To ensure that there was no misunderstanding, Stone repeatedly stated that "the Bureau of Investigation is not concerned with political or other opinions of individuals. It is concerned only with their conduct and then only with such conduct as is forbidden by the laws of the United States." Hoover announced a new hands-off policy toward radicalism: "Our bureau carries on no investigations of matters that are not contrary to federal statutes. There is no federal statute against entertaining radical ideas, and we are wasting no time collecting information that we cannot use." Hoover even said he was refraining from speaking out against communism because if he were "to start making speeches enlarging on the 'red menace' the agents of the Bureau naturally would take the cue and begin looking for radicals all over the place."[9]

Stone's guidelines effectively halted Hoover's systematic domestic surveillance activities, and they remained suspended until FDR ordered their resumption in 1936. In 1924, ACLU Director Roger Baldwin visited Hoover and Stone to make sure the Radical Division really had been abolished. After talking to Hoover, Baldwin wrote his colleagues at the ACLU that

> we were wrong in our estimate of his attitude. That estimate was based upon some of the unfortunate performance of the Bureau in a previous administration in which Mr. Hoover doubtless played an unwilling part. What he told me of the details and changes made in the administration of the Bureau all indicate that the reorganization meets every suggestion

any of us could possible make, and that it has already been carried out
faithfully in accordance with [Stone's] stated policy.[10]

Perhaps amused at Baldwin's portrait of Hoover as a civil libertarian, Stone wrote Hoover that "this may be embarrassing praise,
but I suppose we will have to endure it like the hot weather." The
good impression Hoover made on the hierarchy of the ACLU during
the twenties lingered for many years; for the rest of his career he
could count on endorsements from ACLU luminaries like Roger Baldwin and Morris Ernst when he was attacked by civil libertarians,
even when the attackers were other members of the ACLU.[11]

If the ACLU was pleased by the Bureau's abandonment of the
antiradical cause, the powerful anti-Communist lobby was not. For
the next twelve years, anti-Communists unsuccessfully begged the
White House, the attorney general, and the director to reactivate the
General Intelligence Division. Restoring the Bureau's anti-Communist
activities was, in fact, one of the private anti-Communist lobby's highest priorities for the next decade.[12]

Hoover had finally achieved his ambition of running the Bureau of
Investigation, but with its staff slated to be slashed to the bone, it
was a Bureau stripped of its most important responsibilities. (From
441 agents in 1924, the Bureau declined to 402 in 1925 and as low
as 339 in 1929.) It was an unpromising situation, however, that Hoover
was able to turn to his advantage. The same passion for order that
had made Hoover such an effective agent of repression under Palmer,
made him a tirelessly innovative bureaucrat committed to solving organizational problems of efficiency and control. He devoted himself
wholeheartedly to the task of making the Bureau a textbook example
of a perfectly organized and totally controlled bureaucracy and showed
as much enthusiasm for this as he had for ridding the country of
radicalism. His capacity to focus his energies, skills, and resources
on the business at hand, which had characterized him in adolescence
and then in the Alien Enemy Bureau and the Radical Division, were
now applied to the progressive and scientific management of a complex
bureaucracy.

The highest value in Herbert Hoover's progressivism was efficiency,
and in pursuit of this goal, Herbert Hoover created a new role for
the federal government: He would use its good offices to enable interest
groups, professional associations, and local governments to exchange

ideas and set standards to regulate their conduct. This policy of using independent, often private, organizations to carry out nationally planned programs was known as associationalism, and was the major theme of Herbert Hoover's New Era politics during his tenure as secretary of commerce under Harding and Coolidge; it was also his goal, despite the depression, as president.[13]

J. Edgar Hoover's administration of the Bureau during the twenties was in the spirit of this New Era. J. Edgar Hoover made the Bureau of Identification a national clearinghouse for fingerprints much as Herbert Hoover had created a Division of Simplified Practice in the Commerce Department.[14] Both men were working to turn the federal government into a progressive force for spreading the gospel of efficiency and professionalism.

J. Edgar Hoover also shared with the progressives a muckraking approach to social problems; he believed that exposing evil to the gaze of the respectable majority was tantamount to eradicating it. Historian Richard Hofstadter understood muckraking also to include the belief that corruption was everywhere and that social problems can "be interpreted simply as a widespread breaking of the law." Therefore, "if the laws are the right laws, and if they can be enforced by the right men, the progressive believed, everything would be better." Like the muckrakers, Hoover turned his exposés of crime into "appeal[s] to universal personal responsibility." He used them to demonstrate that social problems had their cause in the personal guilt of individuals. "The Progressive mind," said Hofstadter, "was pre-eminently a Protestant mind."[15]

There was also a dark side to progressivism: It saw in the immigrant the cause of the complexity, ignorance, and nonconformity that confounded the progressive agenda; and it was repressive, particularly toward the targets of its benevolence. The progressives' impatience with waste and corruption made them intolerant toward cultural pluralism, and so they looked for ways to impose a uniform moral discipline on an unruly society. "In practice . . . social-control progressives often unwittingly employed progressive means that subverted progressive ends," wrote Hofstadter. "The demand for order seemed all too often to encourage physically improved but depersonalized working and living conditions, and to be incompatible with . . . participatory democracy."[16]

J. Edgar Hoover's first speech as head of the Bureau (in July 1925) was a description of its Identification (Fingerprint) Division in terms that applied the ideas of associationalism to law enforcement.

He told the International Association of Chiefs of Police (IACP) that
this division was

> due to a recognition on the part of the members of this Association
> that any real development and progress in crime detection and punishment
> must, if the modern criminal and latter-day crime is to be successfully
> combatted, be founded upon the rock of universal cooperation. This is
> not a strange or novel discovery or doctrine. The entire history of human-
> kind is simply the record of the development of the idea of universal
> cooperation."[17]

Because of the "development of science and invention," he told
the police chiefs, the country had to face "the necessity for the uniting
of the forces of the guardians of civilization in the face of the common
danger." He asked the law enforcement community to join him in
an effort to bring science's aid to "the guardians of civilization in
the face of the common danger." Even this early, Hoover had a vision
of the Bureau becoming a national nerve center for the coordination
of the law enforcement community. "The mighty, irresistible current
of world-wide, cosmic forces, have created the necessity and impetus
for the inception and growth of an organization which will serve to
centralize and crystallize the efforts of those who would meet the
exigencies of our changing times by a pooling of all of the wisdom
and power of the guardians of civilization, the protectors of Society."

Hoover thrived under Stone's new progressive regimen. Ever since
his days as a cadet captain and Sunday school teacher, Hoover had
been fascinated by problems of leadership, control, and group motivation. Now, at the age of twenty-nine, he was in charge of an organization of some 650 employees (441 agents), and he was determined to
make it work effectively and efficiently. He became engrossed with
the mechanics of administering a bureaucracy, just as interested in
the technique of power as in possession of it.

Stone had ordered Hoover to reduce the cost and size of the Bureau
to the bare minimum, and on May 16, 1924, six days after taking
charge, he wrote Stone that "I have already commenced an examination of the personnel files of each of the employees of the Bureau
and have already recommended a number of Special Agents whose
services may be discontinued for the best interests of the service."[18]
Hoover pursued this policy of personnel reductions with enthusiasm
because one source of the Bureau's problems in the past had been

headquarters' inability to properly supervise all its employees. Initially, therefore, reducing the size of the Bureau simplified Hoover's task of establishing strict control over the organization. Hoover knew that the Bureau had no really important responsibilities. Since the Coolidge and Hoover administrations had no pressing need for the services of the Bureau, he could not expect any great credit for his achievements, though he would certainly suffer for any mistakes.

Furthermore, the abysmal reputation of the Bureau made firing agents in itself a reform, and served to distance Hoover from the misdeeds of the old regime. Each year, Hoover's section of the attorney general's report boasted about further reductions in the size of his staff. By the end of his first year Hoover had let sixty-one employees go (including Gaston Means) and closed five out of fifty-three field offices; he was also able to return $300,000 of his $2.4-million appropriation. At the end of the decade, his staff was down to 581, 339 of them agents, far below the Bureau's peak figure of 1,127 (579 agents) in 1920, and he had reduced the number of field offices to thirty. At the end of 1932, the number of field offices would reach a low of twenty-two.[19]

As a scientific manager, Hoover immediately set about to experiment with methods of improving his agents' efficiency. Educational credentials were part of the progressive mystique, and Hoover emphasized the requirement (long in effect) that new agents have training in either law or accounting. Out of necessity, waivers from this requirement were (and still are) given, but they were given very quietly. Early in 1925, he established a training school in the Bureau's New York office, supervised by the special agent in charge (SAC; the Bureau designation for the chief of a field office). In a small outfit like the FBI, however, a full-scale school was an enormous drain on resources, so he soon substituted a policy of assigning all agents directly to field offices to be trained by the special agent in charge. Belatedly, Hoover realized how valuable the school was, not only for indoctrinating agents in appropriate behavior and uniform procedures, but also for creating a public image of the Bureau's elite status, and so, in November 1928, he reestablished the training school (originally in Washington) that the Bureau now maintains in Quantico, Virginia.

One of the earliest newspaper stories about the Bureau was a 1930 feature on the training school written by Hoover's close friend Rex Collier of the *Washington Star*. Collier described Hoover's Bureau not only as the "most secretive of all investigative agencies of the Government," but "the most exclusive, for only college graduates are

eligible to become its operatives." Collier called the training school
"Uncle Sam's detective university" and a few paragraphs later described it as "Director Hoover's university." The image of the special
agent as a college-educated "scholar and gentleman," trained in specialized and exclusive techniques, followed from Hoover's view of reform
as the achieving of middle-class respectability. So did the strict code
of personal behavior Hoover imposed on his agents when he assumed
the directorship, which included a ban on the use of liquor during
Prohibition, even off duty.[20]

Hoover projected an image of the Bureau as a bastion of progressive
Protestant reform. An involvement in such Protestant causes as the
YMCA was common among Hoover's early appointees, although there
were always a few Jews and Catholics among Hoover's top aides.
Hoover was the first non-Catholic director in some time, and this
was noted with approval in respectable circles.[21] The Irish cop had
a shabby image, and Hoover's predecessor was almost a caricature
of that stereotype. Although there is no evidence that Hoover was
overtly anti-Catholic or anti-Semitic, it is clear that his Protestant,
Masonic, Sunday school image represented, in his own eyes and in
the opinion of others, a considerable step up the ethnic status ladder
for the Bureau.

While the number of agents in the Bureau declined under Hoover's
belt-tightening measures, the attention paid to supervising them increased—enormously. Hoover's complex system of record-keeping and
supervisory machinery, which would seem so onerous to outside observers and disaffected agents, had its origins in these early years. A
survey of the administrative machinery installed during this period
reveals Hoover restlessly tinkering with his system of controls, experi-
menting and fine-tuning strategies that would allow him always to
know what every one of his agents was doing wherever he might
be.

He increased the authority and accountability of the special agents
in charge by making them completely responsible for all agents in
their areas, including the antitrust examiners and the agents working
for U.S. attorneys, neither of whom had previously been directly supervised. SACs were required to visit the U.S. attorney in their district
at least once a month to remind them that the special agents detailed
to assist in investigations were really working for Hoover. In 1924,
he instituted the Bureau's famous policy of regular field office inspections by a special Inspection Division of the Bureau located in
Washington.[22] This eventually included taking inventory, every six
months, of Bureau property.

The format of agents' reports was also systematized. In September 1927, Hoover equipped each agent with a loose-leaf manual of instructions that specified standard procedures to follow in investigating and reporting results; later the agents were furnished with printed investigation report forms. In 1929, agents were furnished with a new Manual of Rules and Regulations and Instructions, and in July 1930, this was completely revised.

On July 12, 1925, Hoover formally established strict safeguards over use of the Bureau's files by prohibiting their withdrawal except by agents actively working on investigations, and then only with the approval of the special agent in charge, with a written record of the transaction.[23]

Hoover had inherited a decentralized system that had nine field divisions, each headed by a division superintendent who had authority to transfer and reassign the special agents and special agents in charge of his division's field offices. On February 20, 1925, Hoover replaced this system with six divisions located in Washington, each with a different function or with responsibilities for a specific class of investigations. This put the supervisors in Washington in immediate command over all SACs, while Hoover, of course, oversaw the headquarters staff.

Every year there were more rules, more regulations. Agents were trained and retrained. To many of them it seemed that the bulk of their time was taken up in submitting reports to Washington and defending themselves against inevitable violations of Hoover's regulations. The point, of course, was to make sure Hoover never found himself answering for anything he had not personally approved. In later years, he would be fond of saying "no single individual built the Bureau, but one individual can destroy it."

By the end of the decade, Hoover may well have constructed a perfect system of control, but given the small size of the Bureau, and the pressure placed on his employees, some of the human materials began to crack. There had already been small-scale revolts against his authority in the twenties, and they would continue to occur throughout his career.

One of these revolts occurred in 1929, when an agent resigned and sent Attorney General William D. Mitchell a twenty-six-page memorandum on his grievances against Hoover.[24] The agent charged that Hoover was wasting money transferring agents from one office to another for disciplinary purposes. More money was wasted because of the frequent resignations of expensively trained agents, as "few self-respecting men will tolerate the Director's tyrannical treatment."

This high turnover occurred, the agent charged, despite the "intensely interesting" nature of the work. He accused Hoover of favoring applicants who were politically connected, who lived in Washington, and who were fellow graduates of George Washington University Law School. There was, he said, a high-salaried force of inspectors hired for the sole purpose of "spy[ing] upon field personnel." Hoover had deemphasized investigative work in favor of producing statistics and controlling agents, he said:

> Under Hoover, investigative work, which is the real work of this Bureau, has had little supervision from Washington. This is probably because his training has been clerical rather than investigative work. His predecessors were investigators with field experience, which Hoover lacks. . . . His employment of an accountant to act as Inspector reflects that statistics and not investigative work is uppermost. . . . Since Hoover took charge in May, 1924, practically all instructions by him have been repressive and directed against the personnel rather than against the criminal. . . . The matters mentioned above, and many others of which I know are illustrative of bureaucracy gone mad.[25]

Discounting the personal abuse of Hoover ("at least 75% of the personnel intensely dislike the Director, who appears to demand merely personal loyalty, and seeks to obtain this by threat, disciplinary action and frequently cruel and inhuman treatment"), the agent's complaints confirmed Hoover's success in transforming a corrupt, uncontrollable Bureau into one in which the problems were caused by too much, rather than too little, discipline.

Attorney General Mitchell responded to this diatribe by writing the White House that nothing in the agent's charges had shaken his faith in Hoover: "I have confidence in Mr. Hoover and believe that he is administering the Bureau well." Hoover took the charges seriously enough to submit to Mitchell a sixty-page rebuttal, and he rallied his friends in the law enforcement community to his defense. The International Association of Chiefs of Police passed a resolution that complained about the "unjust, unwarranted and unmerited attacks . . . on Mr. J. Edgar Hoover" and voted to give him "its unqualified support." The attorney general was deluged with almost identically worded resolutions from other law enforcement agencies, indicating that in his typically efficient way Hoover had coordinated a defense against his ex-employee's charges.[26]

Occasionally, other reports surfaced about Hoover's harsh treatment of his employees. In 1932, a Washington paper ran the headline HOOVER TERMED RUTHLESS SLAVER over stories about an employee tricked into taking a drink of medicinal alcohol and then fired; other employees complained that Hoover kept the heat turned low because of his theory that "they'll do more work if they're uncomfortable."[27]

This discontent was a symptom of an organizational imbalance that had developed in the Bureau: the training, discipline, and controls had reached a state of elaboration out of all relation to the job at hand. The Bureau's organizational structure was not yet directed toward any operational goal commensurate with its potential. At the end of the decade, perhaps in recognition of this problem, Hoover's organizational priorities shifted from control to motivation and morale. He started employee newspapers and social clubs and fielded athletic teams that captured awards for the Bureau in competition with other federal agencies.

In many organizations there comes a time when discipline has been so perfected that the leader has to provide action and publicity for his followers if he is to maintain morale. The Bureau of Investigation was reaching that point, although Hoover would have to wait several more years before he received assignments that would let him exercise the new capabilities with which he had equipped his organization. It was a system Hoover had instituted partly out of progressive commitment to scientific management, partly to protect himself against the misdeeds of his agents, and partly—perhaps mostly—because of that restless determination, evident at every stage of his life, to impose his will and ideas on an ever-widening sphere of influence. Without action and glamor, however, the harsh regulations, the anxiety, and the boredom would have taken a toll on the perfect organization Hoover had created.

Long after fingerprint identification had become thoroughly familiar to the public, Hoover continued to trumpet the Bureau's collection as its proudest achievement, even its trademark. That was because it was the first and best symbol of the leadership role he had created for himself and the Bureau. It was through the Bureau's fingerprint facilities that Hoover first managed to place himself at the head of a law enforcement community drawn into a cooperative network by the professional standards he promoted and the scientific facilities he maintained for the local police. Long before he became known to the general public, Hoover's control over the national system of criminal identification had turned him into a key figure in the law enforcement field.

The Bureau's fingerprint facilities had their origin in an offer made by the IACP in November 1921 to give the Justice Department the criminal identification files the association had been maintaining at its own expense in Washington since 1896. For its part, since 1909, the Justice Department had been keeping track of the prints of federal prisoners at its own Bureau of Criminal Identification at the Leavenworth, Kansas, penitentiary, where convicts did the work of filing and retrieving the prints.

As early as 1921, the Bureau asked the Justice Department to have the president authorize the Department of Justice to establish a consolidated Bureau of Criminal Identification in Washington. While the attorney general issued a departmental directive on October 23, 1923, establishing a fingerprint division in the Department of Justice, congressional approval was blocked by the opposition of the New York City police chief, who headed a law enforcement professional association that competed with the IACP. Congress finally provided an appropriation on July 1, 1924. Hoover took command of the Bureau just two months before the Bureau of Investigation officially took control of the two fingerprint collections.[28]

Hoover faced tremendous technical difficulties in getting his new facility into operation. He chose the former heads of the IACP collection and the Leavenworth collection to run the new division and had them select and train a staff of forty-seven in a leased building at 1800 Pennsylvania Avenue. The task ahead of these people was not only the consolidation of the two different sets of records, each organized according to different principles; they also had to catch up on the backlog of prints that had piled up during the year when the Identification Bureau was without appropriation. All this had to be done while at the same time cataloging the new prints that arrived daily and identifying the prints of suspects sent by cooperating local police forces around the country. The pride Hoover took in what his staff achieved was reflected in the uncharacteristically whimsical tone he adopted when he reported to the IACP that he had overcome "the difficulties caused by human frailty and the seemingly innate perversity of inanimate things."

> The beginning of things is always difficult and dangerous. I am not sure why this should be so. At the time when we are least able "to suffer the slings and arrows of outrageous fortune" we encounter them in greatest abundance and most trying form. The infant, both human and organizational, must endure and conquer if it hopes to survive.[29]

During the first five years of its operation, the Division of Identification had to rely for its existence on the attorney general's directive and on a line in the Justice Department's annual appropriation. (Not until June 1930 did Congress formally authorize the department to establish the Division of Identification and Information.) The insecurity of this situation led Hoover to seek publicity for the division even while he was avoiding it for the rest of the Bureau. He provided the *Washington Post* with a feature story about the new division on May 24, 1925, in which he carefully described the statutory authority and the technical need for the division (mindful of the recent fears over Bureau spying and expansion). He tied the new facility to the Republican administrations' theme of federal-local cooperation. "If [the Identification Division] succeeds," Hoover wrote in his *Post* story, "it must succeed largely because of the cooperation and vigorous support of the peace officers of the country for whose sole benefit it was created and exists." In a 1927 feature story, Hoover told a reporter that "the primary aim has been and it will so continue, to make the identification bureau a service agency and to see that it actually renders a positive and material assistance to peace officers throughout the country."[30] Hoover's transformation of the Bureau into a source of professional standards and scientific assistance for the law enforcement community during the twenties was, in fact, one of the most effective applications of the New Era principles to the problems of public administration.

Hoover's Bureau also became the nation's leading source of statistics about crime during these progressive years. On December 16, 1925, Hoover told the House Appropriations Committee that the country needed a system for assembling uniform crime statistics. In 1930, Congress finally gave the Bureau permission to begin collecting crime statistics, and in that year it issued the first of its *Uniform Crime Reports*. [31] The Bureau based its figures on the number of crimes known to the police—then and now a controversial way of measuring the extent of crime since, first, different police forces have different ways of organizing crime information, and second, the raw figures themselves reflect the tendency of citizens to report crimes to the police, which varies in different communities, and can also be manipulated by mayors and other public officials for the political purpose of showing the electorate falling (or rising) crime rates.

Hoover received one other important benefit from securing the *Uniform Crime Reports* for the Bureau: It gave him an excuse to put together a staff of researchers and writers that gave the Bureau a potential public relations capability. Stone's original guidelines had imposed a vow of silence on Hoover, although this was intended only to halt the Bureau's antiradical propaganda. At first, Hoover understood this as prohibiting all Bureau publicity, and, in 1924, he told Stone that he was turning down an invitation to address the annual convention of the International Association of Chiefs of Police in Montreal, saying that "I personally believe that the officials of the Bureau of Investigation should refrain as much as possible from any public appearance, as I believe that the work of the Bureau should be conducted quietly but effectively so that the results will be the criterion by which the Bureau shall be judged." Stone replied that Hoover was free to go to Montreal, but that he was "inclined to think . . . that your view with relation to publicity is the sound one."[32]

Within a year, Hoover found there was more slack in the reins than he had thought. In 1925, he did speak at the IACP convention, and that speech suggests he had hopes for the Bureau that he could not yet openly express. He told the chiefs that "the things that have been accomplished in the one brief year of our existence are but shadowy prophecies, sign-posts on the road of the future. . . . I assume the time will come when we will look back upon the then seemingly petty figures that represent the accomplishments of our first year with feelings of mingled pride and satisfaction, yet we will vaguely and smilingly recall our infantile hopes and fears in the light of having grown so great and traveled so far from such small beginnings."[33]

With the publication of the *Crime Reports,* Hoover may have sensed the coming end of his Bureau's obscurity. In the year the *Reports* began, Hoover was able to sharply increase his staff to a total of 655—400 of them agents, with about a 10 percent increase in budget. This was the first increase in the size of the Bureau since he had taken over. Because the only major change in the Bureau's responsibilities that year was the *Uniform Crime Reports,* it is likely that the increased staff was in the Research Unit of the Crime Records Division, which functioned throughout Hoover's career as his public relations office, supervising the Bureau's contacts with the media and with Congress and writing Hoover's speeches, articles, and book. Thus it may have been his institution of the *Reports* that gave Hoover the ability to capitalize on the publicity that came his way when the New Deal declared its war on crime in 1933 and sent Hoover and his G-Men into battle against the gangsters.

Because of the relatively relaxed atmosphere within the government service during the twenties, Hoover tolerated far more informality at the office than he would after the New Deal expansion. His niece Margaret used to visit him at his office on the third floor of the old Justice Department building at Vermont and "K" to see if he would have lunch with her, which he sometimes, but not often, would find the time to do. The White House used to get rid of obviously deranged visitors by sending them over to the Justice Department, and Hoover was sometimes called on to escort them from the building or, in severe cases, send them to the hospital.[34] Perhaps his father's illness may have given him the sensitivity to deal with such cases.

Margaret remembers Hoover's bringing home a briefcase full of work every evening during the twenties, and spending the hours before bed in his room working; her own room was next to his, and she could hear him rehearsing speeches late into the night. He had, she remembers, a stammer, not enough to have interfered with his debating, but annoying nonetheless, that he managed to overcome through practice.[35]

Hoover had put on weight during the twenties. Still tense and thin in 1924, he developed stomach problems that may have been an ulcer. He had to give up the tray of spicy condiments he kept on the dinner table, and had to drink a quart of acidophilus milk each day. His doctor told him to relax for an hour after dinner with a cigarette, and he persuaded Margaret to smoke with him. Though he soon gave it up, she smoked the rest of her life. Hoover evidently did learn to pace himself; under the Bureau's now less frantic regimen he filled out to the somewhat stocky figure of his later years, about 185 pounds distributed on a five-foot-ten-inch frame. Margaret remembers that it was after 1924 that the previously austere, intense Hoover began to stand out as a "sharp dresser." He and Baughman liked to wear white linen suits, and photos of Hoover with his top executives usually show him far more nattily dressed than his sober, business-suited colleagues. Invariably, he had a puff of a silk handkerchief in his breast pocket to match his tie.[36]

It was also during the twenties that Hoover started to collect antiques, particularly oriental ceramics, becoming a regular at C. G. Sloans auctions. He was later proud of two lighted curio cabinets in his home that were filled with jade and ivory figurines.[37]

Though Hoover liked to tease his niece (like everyone else who knew him well, she recalls many of his practical jokes), he also enjoyed taking her on long summer-evening walks to ice-cream parlors and movie theaters, and in the morning he would often have his driver drop her off at her job at the Library of Congress on his way to the Justice Department.[38] He even got her dates from among his fraternity brothers at Kappa Alpha. She remembers that he gave her a blanket assurance that they were all "gentlemen." In some cases, she recalls, he was mistaken.

Early in his career, Hoover was often confused with another John E. Hoover, an attorney in the Justice Department division that defended the United States in the Court of Claims; this Hoover had been in the department when J. Edgar arrived and he stayed until the thirties. Having two J. E. Hoovers got to be annoying when the other John E. Hoover applied for jobs and people assumed that it was J. Edgar who was trying to move out of the department. It was necessary, on occasion, for Hoover to inform his superiors that it was not he who was causing them to be pestered for references. In 1925, the Washington papers tried to turn the theft of a bicycle belonging to the son of John E. into a joke on J. Edgar and the Bureau, and Hoover pasted the story into his scrapbook.[39]

As a Washington native, Hoover took a personal interest in the Bureau's District of Columbia cases. The Bureau tended to be called when the district police were suspected of wrongdoing, and in 1929, Congressman Thomas Blanton asked Hoover to look into the disappearance of a Mrs. Helen Blalock, a palm-reader who had accused the police of brutality, and had been so intimidated that she fled for her life. Hoover's agents located her after a nationwide search and escorted her back to Washington where Hoover, accompanied by three of his agents and an entourage of reporters, met her at Union Station. Blanton told the press that he was "very much impressed with the efficient way our Department of Justice handled the Blalock matter. I want to commend very highly Mr. Hoover, the head of the Bureau of Investigation."[40]

Another local case led to Hoover's lifelong friendship with Rex Collier, the *Washington Star*'s Justice Department reporter. In September 1929, the police discovered the body of a nurse with a pajama cord tightly knotted around her neck. District detectives decided it was a case of suicide, but one of the policemen disagreed. He thought the woman had been murdered by her husband, and that there was a department cover-up. Hoover was called in to sort matters out after the officer's grand jury testimony led to the indictment of the husband and criticism of the police. The Bureau's investigation uncovered evidence that persuaded the grand jury to cancel the indictment and exonerate the district detectives.

The case was a sensational local story, but the Bureau agent in charge refused to cooperate with reporters and misled them about his progress in the case. Rex Collier was picked by the reporters as their representative, and he was sent to Hoover to complain about the Bureau's handling of the press. Collier told him that all Hoover had to do to avoid premature disclosures was to ask the reporters to hold their stories. Collier assured him that he could trust the reporters as long as he told them the truth. "Hoover investigated our charges," Collier said, "removed the inspector in charge and appointed another inspector who proved to be very cooperative. From then on my relations with Hoover and the Bureau grew into a long-time friendship."[41]

Hoover called Collier afterward to thank him for his advice in handling the press, and mentioned to him that he had recently been testifying before Congress. It had been apparent from one congressman's questions that he had the Bureau of Investigation confused with the Secret Service. Collier told him that this was because the Secret Service was well known and the Bureau was not; if Hoover gave some of his more interesting cases to the press the Bureau's name would begin to get around. The result was a feature story by Collier on the Osage Indian Case, one of the Bureau's great cases of the twenties and one of Hoover's favorites. Collier recalled that he published the story in the *Star* late in 1929 or in early 1930, and it was later syndicated in papers affiliated with the North American Syndicate.[42]

Hoover's Bureau did not completely halt political investigations during the twenties despite Stone's rules. Hoover did keep some of his antiradical cases open even after 1924. In 1925, he notified his superiors that he would continue to place in his files any information about radicals that he received from other agencies or in the course of other investigations, but that there would be no *specific* investigations for the purpose of acquiring intelligence on political dissidents. When Military Intelligence asked Hoover for information on radicals (the army maintained an elaborate domestic espionage network during the twenties, particularly in the unions, on the pretext of protecting potential defense production facilities and of being prepared to quell riots), Hoover replied that the Bureau had discontinued its own general surveillance of radical activities, but would continue to send the army any such information that it came across while engaged in normal criminal investigations.[43]

There were, however, many occasions during the twenties when

Hoover did not strictly confine his investigations to violations of federal law. The president constantly needs background information on individuals or groups to decide whether he should see them or reply to their letters. He also needs advance warning about situations that may touch on his role as constitutional or political leader, and his aides have to make sure he gets this information. One of J. Edgar Hoover's most important services to the White House (and one of his most important sources of power) was furnishing the president's assistants with this kind of information. The practice began in 1925 under Coolidge and continued for the rest of Hoover's career. Hoover began to anticipate these requests, and since his sources of information were superior to those of the White House, he would often be the first to bring news about a potential political problem to the attention of the president's top aides. Eventually, Hoover could justify investigating almost anything on the grounds that the president might ask him for information on the subject, and he had to be able to respond without delay.[44] For the most part, these investigations were innocuous, but they certainly did violate Stone's commandments. Political investigations had gotten the Bureau into trouble before, but there is no evidence that Hoover ever hesitated to do anything a president asked.

Early in Herbert Hoover's administration, White House aide Larry Richey began to ask Hoover to provide the White House with political intelligence. The sketchiness of the Bureau reports suggests a certain lack of enthusiasm for such assignments, although Hoover could not refuse White House requests. In November 1929, President Hoover learned that a self-styled patriotic group called the Sentinels of the Republic was lobbying against his new Child Health Commission. Richey asked J. Edgar to find out about the group, and on November 29 Hoover sent the aide the results of an investigation conducted by the Bureau's Chicago office. The report consisted merely of some of the Sentinels' publications—which showed the primitive state of the Bureau's political intelligence files at the time. Hoover's agents had had to begin this investigation by checking the phone book, the credit bureau, and the Library of Congress. "Under a suitable pretext," the director told Richey, agents visited the offices of the group, learning the names of the organization's officers and picking up some of the group's literature. Hoover closed his report by assuring Richey he would "do anything further [the White House] wishes in this matter."[45]

On December 11, 1929, Hoover reported to Richey on connections between the Foreign Policy Association and the American Civil Liberties Union. In 1930, another presidential aide asked Hoover for a "very discreet investigation" of Pittsburgh's American Citizens' Political Awakening Association. Again Hoover provided the White House with a list of the organization's officers and a report that it was shaking down Italian clubs for protection from the Prohibition laws. Hoover also investigated the NAACP and an Italian group called the Federation of Lictor—the latter was prompted by a telegram of support to the president from the group. When the president received an invitation to address the Moorish Science Temple in Chicago in 1931, the Bureau discovered that a black barber was the group's only member.[46]

A less innocent use of the Bureau took place in October 1931, when the White House learned that an editor of a financial newsletter was predicting specific bank failures to his subscribers; the White House felt this was contributing to the financial panic. The director sent the White House a report on the case and added that the editor had been "considerably upset over the visit of the agent. . . . It is obvious from his present attitude that he is thoroughly scared and I do not believe that he will resume the dissemination of any information concerning the banks or other financial institutions." Intimidating this citizen may not have been Hoover's primary intention when he had an agent visit the man, but it was certainly looked upon as a fortunate side effect.[47]

Hoover's Bureau had performed a more significant service for the White House in 1929 when the Navy League, a private pressure group founded in 1903, opposed the president's plans to participate in the 1930 naval conference. The president called for a congressional investigation of the League and asked the Bureau to gather information on the group. In 1931, the president and the League again came into conflict over a deep cut in the budget for military shipbuilding. The League published a pamphlet that attacked the president for betraying the country to the English and Hoover provided the president with information about the membership of the League and details on its activities. (One report raised the possibility of prosecuting the League for tax law violations.)[48] Neither the president nor the director ever had to defend the propriety of this investigation, even though it was certainly an instance of a case that seemed to the president to involve national security, but from the perspective of those being investigated was simply legitimate political dissent.

During the Coolidge and Hoover administrations, J. Edgar Hoover and the Bureau were under continuous pressure from private anti-Communist lobbies, particularly the National Civic Federation, to resume investigations of radicals. There is no reason to think that Hoover had had any change of heart regarding radicalism, but he kept his distance from these anti-Communist activists. He refused to do any Red hunting during the twenties because he realized that while neither Coolidge nor Hoover nor their secretaries of state were Bolshevik lovers, most of them, particularly Coolidge's secretary of state, Charles Evans Hughes, were defenders of civil liberties, even the civil liberties of radicals. As a private citizen, Hughes had tried to reverse the New York State legislature's refusal to seat its Socialist members; as for Herbert Hoover, not until after his loss to Roosevelt soured him did he become a hard-liner on domestic communism. J. Edgar Hoover probably would have been happy to join an attack on radicals if someone else with a strong political base had volunteered to lead it, but neither then nor after was he interested in leading an anti-Communist crusade all by himself.[49]

During the Coolidge and Hoover administrations, demands that the government move against communism were generally directed toward the White House, but sometimes the anti-Communists also appealed to the Justice Department. Some of these Red hunters had a vision of J. Edgar Hoover as a hero in chains ("padlocked" was the word they liked), desperate to get back into the antiradical business. There is no evidence, however, that Hoover gave the anti-Communists any encouragement, and along with the senior officials of the Justice Department, he did his best to discourage them.

Because of the Justice Department's withdrawal from the ideological wars during the twenties, some other department had to reassure the anti-Communist lobby that the government was not completely asleep while the Communists plotted. During the twenties, that role passed to the State Department, which acted as a conduit to the president for warnings about the Communist menace. (The State Department's Russian Division filled the gap left by the demise of the Bureau's General Intelligence Division of the twenties.)[50]

Secretary of State Hughes gave J. Edgar Hoover his last major antiradical assignment before he was appointed Bureau director. In January 1924 Hughes asked Hoover to prepare a memorandum "as to the communistic activities in the United States emanating from or directed by the Third International" for Hughes to use in his Senate testimony against diplomatic recognition for the Soviet Union. Hoover's report bulked to nearly 500 pages, and as assistant director of the Bureau he sat by Hughes's side during the secretary's testimony.[51]

Hoover's brief may have been the basis for Hughes's opposition to recognition because of the Soviet government's support of the subversive activities of the American Communist party. (There was disagreement among anti-Communists on the advisability of recognizing the Soviet Union. The right wanted to prosecute American Communists under the Logan Act, which made it illegal for unauthorized citizens to negotiate with foreign governments. But until the United States recognized the Soviet government, the law did not apply.)[52]

When J. Edgar Hoover assumed the directorship, he reassured the House Appropriations Committee that the report for the State Department had been exceptional, and did not mean the reorganized Bureau was still in the antiradical business.

> During the past few months we have limited our activities, necessarily, because of the scope of our authority and also because of the volume of the work, to investigation of radical matters only where there has been a violation of a Federal statute involved, and that is the policy we are following at present. We have many reports, practically hundreds a month, coming in to us advising us of an individual who is making communistic statements. However, there is no Federal law under which we can prosecute him at this time and there is no reason why we should waste our money in connection with that matter. The only reason we submitted that memorandum to the Secretary of State is that we have authority to submit to the Secretary of State, upon his request, information that he requires for administrative decisions.[53]

At the end of 1924, Hoover sent Stone a memo expressing his reluctance to take on any more anti-Communist assignments. He told the attorney general that the Bureau could still investigate Communists upon request from the State Department, but that this should be done without publicity and "on an entirely different line" than before.[54] He probably meant that no special Bureau division should be set up for antiradical investigations.

The National Civic Federation's Ralph Easley was the most persistent of the anti-Communists who beseeched White House aides to put the General Intelligence Division back into operation. Other antiradicals bombarded the White House with bizarre publications with hair-raising titles like *Subversive, Radical and Doubtful Societies Spread over America like a Gigantic Spider Web*. The AFL representative on the board of the National Civic Federation blamed the demise of the General Intelligence Division on the "pernicious . . . activity of the Civil Liberties Union" radicals who had succeeded in "securing the padlocking of the Bureau of Investigation." Because of the ACLU, he complained, "the Bureau was ordered to discharge all of its 'undercover men,' numbering about eighty. As a consequence, our national government is now without the direct knowledge of activities in these subversive movements."[55]

On April 26, 1927, Archibald E. Stevenson (of Lusk Committee fame) and Ralph Easley visited the Justice Department and met with J. Edgar Hoover and Assistant Attorney General Oscar R. Luhring to demand the Bureau once again be turned loose on Communists. Easley was told that "the Justice Department is taking no interest whatever in the activities of the Communists and other radicals in this country. It has not had a dollar to spend for that purpose." Stevenson suggested to Hoover and Luhring that by using "the constitutional requirement that the Federal Government shall guarantee a republican form of government to the several states, there may be found a way to correct this rotten situation. Think of it! 120,000,000 people without any protection whatever by the Federal Government, against the machinations of the radicals!"[56]

Stevenson and Easley recommended that the Justice Department simply add a line to its annual appropriation bill to cover investigations of radical threats to state governments, but they were told that this might derail the entire Justice Department appropriation, since any senator or congressman could object that the antiradical money was not covered by the general language of the appropriation or authorization, and then the bill would have to be sent back to committee. Easley and Stevenson next proposed that a separate antiradical bill be introduced, and they sent Hoover a draft early in 1928.[57] The Justice Department expressed no more than polite interest, and the idea died.

Easley and other anti-Communists kept up the pressure. In May 1930, Easley sent the president a fifty-two-page memo on a plan to establish anti-Communist bureaus in all of the forty-eight states, to be supported by private contributions until federal funding was available. Practically guaranteeing its rejection, as far as J. Edgar was concerned, was Easley's astounding suggestion that Gaston Means be hired to direct the operation.[58]

In 1930, J. Edgar Hoover was invited to testify before the Special House Committee, chaired by Hamilton Fish of New York, that was investigating Communist activities. Hoover provided the committee with an assortment of stories about Communist atrocities drawn from his pre-1924 briefs and investigations. His testimony provided ample proof that his fundamental attitudes about communism had not changed, but nevertheless, he resisted the committee's suggestion that the Bureau resume its general intelligence activities against radicals.

Instead, he argued that if Congress wanted the Bureau to work in this area, it should enact a new criminal statute similar to the peacetime sedition law Palmer had proposed in 1919.[59] The Bureau could then enforce it like any other law.

Hoover's appearance before the Fish Committee must have reminded him of more exciting times under Palmer. The press once again treated him as the boy wonder who had "made a strong impression. . . . Uncle Sam's boyish looking Sherlock Holmes reeled off facts and figures that carried deep conviction with the committee, who soon discovered it had before it a man who knows his onions." A friend sent this clipping to Hoover, who noted on the margin that his "summer attire was the only thing young and boyish about him."[60]

After listening to Hoover, the Fish Committee asked the Justice Department to draft a bill to authorize the Bureau to investigate Communist activities once more. Attorney General William Mitchell consulted with the director, and rejected the idea. Mitchell agreed with the congressmen that it looked as if the Communists were engaged in sabotage, but that if industrial sabotage was the real concern, both he and Hoover thought that the job should be given to the Labor Department, and that any new detective force needed for radical investigations should be housed in that department as well.[61] Nothing was going to lure J. Edgar Hoover into another Red hunt until he thought he had strong enough public and presidential support, and he knew he was not going to get it from Herbert Hoover.

Despite J. Edgar Hoover's attempts to avoid antiradical activities under Herbert Hoover, he could not completely avoid all involvement in the Hoover administration's seamiest episode of political repression: its effort to smear the Bonus Army Marchers of 1932 as violence-prone and Communist inspired. At the end of May 1932, the Bonus Army, 17,000 World War I veterans, had arrived in Washington and had set up a tent city to pressure Congress to pass the Patman Bonus Bill that would have authorized early payment of a veterans' bonus due in 1940. When the bill was defeated on June 17, about 2,000 of the marchers refused to leave their camp despite a government offer to pay their expenses. When the police failed to evict the veterans, the president ordered the army to clear the camps. On July 28, 1932, General Douglas MacArthur ignored the president's order to use only unarmed soldiers against the veterans; he disobeyed another to halt before entering the veterans' camp at the Anacostia Flats. Instead, in full dress uniform, MacArthur personally led a tear-gas and bayonet assault on the pathetic tent village of the marchers.

Since this occurred in July at the beginning of the presidential election campaign, the Bonus Army fiasco threw Herbert Hoover's aides into a panic. They called the heads of all federal intelligence agencies together on August 1 to plan ways of discrediting the arrested marchers. According to the minutes of the meeting, "Mr. Hoover reported for the United States Bureau of Investigation that it had made no investigation of any phase of the bonus marcher situation and therefore had no information available." Hoover agreed only to search the Bureau's fingerprint files to see if any of those arrested had prior criminal records. Since the Identification Division existed only to provide exactly that sort of information, this was the least Hoover could agree to do. Larry Richey asked Hoover to pursue other leads that might discredit the Bonus March, but Hoover provided only a hearsay report that the appearance of tanks may have kept the marchers from using their weapons against the soldiers.[62]

Since the administration was desperate for anything that would smear the marchers as Communists, a completely pliant director would have produced everything he could, yet Hoover provided only the minimum required. He gave the White House odds and ends of intelligence, but certainly he did not give them the comprehensive analysis that he would have submitted between 1919 and 1924, or later during the post-World War II Cold War. Obviously, he had decided that it was not worth the risk to help an administration soon to be out of power; one, moreover, that could not have protected him if he had gotten into any trouble for exceeding his authority. Hoover was always quick to sense political weakness and to distance himself from it. He was willing to take risks in pursuit of his objectives, but he had learned to do that only when guaranteed the support of powerful sponsors and public opinion.

Hoover seemed quite content with his secure and noncontroversial situation at the end of Herbert Hoover's administration. In 1932, he informed the attorney general that "the work of the Bureau of Investigation at this time is . . . of an open character not in any manner subject to criticism, and the operations of the Bureau of Investigation may be given the closest scrutiny at all times. . . . The conditions will materially differ were the Bureau to embark upon a policy of investigative activity into conditions which, from a federal standpoint, have not been declared illegal and in connection with which no prosecution might be instituted. The Department and the Bureau would undoubtedly be subject to charges in the matter of alleged secret and undesirable methods . . . as well as to allegations involving charges of the use of 'Agents Provocateur.' "[63]

It was during the late twenties that J. Edgar Hoover formed his personal attachment with the man who would be his inseparable companion for the rest of his life. This was Clyde Tolson, who joined the Bureau as a special agent on April 2, 1928.

For the first four years of Hoover's directorship, T. Frank Baughman, Hoover's friend from the Palmer raids, was still his closest associate—on and off the job. Hoover had given Baughman the rank of supervisor and had put him in charge of administering the headquarters staff. In terms of salary, Baughman ranked third in the Bureau from 1924 until 1928, behind Hoover and Assistant Director Harold Nathan. In 1928, Baughman received a raise that made him the second-highest paid man in the Bureau of Investigation.[64]

A year later, Baughman had started to slip. In 1928, Nathan once again outranked him, and each succeeding year Hoover promoted more headquarters staff ahead of his old friend. Hoover had lost interest in Baughman. (And, obviously, Baughman, who got married at about this time, had less time for Hoover.) Clyde Tolson had taken Baughman's place.

Tolson, five years younger than Hoover, was born in 1900. He came from Cedar Rapids, Iowa, where he attended business college before moving to Washington in 1918. His first job was clerking in the War Department, and by the end of the war he was a chief clerk for the Chief of Staff. In 1920, he became confidential secretary to the secretary of war. (Until the unification of the defense establishment after World War II, the secretary of war was the cabinet-rank civilian-head of the army.) Like the young Hoover, Tolson was an early achiever. At the age of twenty he was already supervising the secretary of war's office staff. Between 1920 and 1928, he worked for Secretaries of War Newton D. Baker, John W. Weeks, and Dwight F. Davis. At night he attended George Washington University Law School. He received his law degree in 1927 and was admitted to the District of Columbia bar on February 6, 1928.[65]

Hoover may or may not have known Tolson before he applied to the Bureau. In *The F.B.I. Story,* author Don Whitehead says Tolson had attracted Hoover's attention with his unusually frank application to the Bureau. Tolson had written that he planned to open a law practice in Cedar Rapids, so he was going to work for the Bureau only long enough to get some experience.[66] But since Hoover seldom received applications from people with Tolson's high-level administrative experience, and since Tolson had left a position of greater responsibility to join the Bureau in an entry-level position, it is likely that Tolson joined the Bureau with assurance from Hoover that he would get an early promotion.

There had been no lack of opportunities for the men to have met before. The Bureau was in regular contact with the War Department, so they could have met through the secretary of war's office. They were both members of the Military Intelligence Reserve; both were graduates of George Washington Law at a time when Hoover was active in alumni affairs (though they belonged to different fraternities— Hoover and many of his top aides belonged to Kappa Alpha, while Tolson was in Sigma Nu); and like Hoover and many of the Bureau's top officials, Tolson was a Mason.

Whatever the personal relationship between them at the beginning, Hoover took a personal interest in Tolson's career from the start. A month after Tolson joined the Bureau, Hoover sent him to the Boston office. (At this time new agent training was handled by the special agents in charge of the field offices.) Only four months later, in September 1928, Hoover ordered Tolson back to the Washington headquarters and put him in charge of the clerical staff with the title of chief clerk, which, though a low-ranking position, kept him in close contact with Hoover.[67]

Hoover had now decided he wanted Tolson to help him run the Bureau as his second-in-command, and so during the next year he moved Tolson rapidly through a series of positions to provide him with the paper experience necessary for his dossier: on July 31, 1929, he appointed Tolson special agent in charge of the Buffalo, New York, office and then, only a week later, he brought him back to Washington and promoted him to the rank of inspector at the Bureau headquarters. On August 16, 1930, just two years after Tolson entered the Bureau, Hoover made him his assistant director. (The promotion took formal effect on January 26, 1931.) Six months later, Hoover told a reporter from Tolson's home-town paper: "I hardly recall any similar case where a man has risen solely on merit with such rapidity."[68]

By July 1930, Hoover had reorganized the Bureau's headquarters staff into ten divisions. Hoover himself headed Division 1, which handled confidential investigations and personnel assignments, and Division 10, the Inspection and Training Division. Harold Nathan, who had been assistant director since 1925 (and in the Bureau since 1917), was in charge of investigations—Divisions 2, 3, 4, and 5, categorized by the type of crime involved. Tolson was assistant director in charge of personnel and administration, supervising Division 6, the National Division of Identification and Information; Division 7, the Office of the Chief Clerk; Division 8, Office of Files and Records; and Division 9, the personnel files.[69]

At first Tolson shared the rank of assistant director with Nathan; then, in 1936, Hoover officially recognized Tolson's unique status by changing his title to assistant to the director (later associate director).[70] For the rest of his career (he retired the day after Hoover died), Tolson was administrative chief of the Bureau, chairman of the Bureau's Executive Conference (a cabinet consisting of the assistant directors in charge of the different divisions), and Hoover's chief of staff.

Hoover was still living with his mother at Seward Square while Tolson was living in apartments in northwest Washington. For at least part of this time, Tolson shared bachelor quarters with Guy Hottel, the special agent in charge of the Washington field office, who often joined Hoover and Tolson on their vacations during the thirties and forties. Baughman worked for a while as Tolson's assistant, but this may have been a strain on both, and so Baughman was put in charge of the Bureau's firearms training program at Quantico, where he became a well-known and admired instructor for generations of agent-trainees.[71]

Hoover and Tolson now settled into the routine they would follow the rest of their lives. They rode to and from work together, ate lunches together, and vacationed together. In July 1930, for instance, they took a golfing holiday at the Summit resort in New Jersey. When Hoover traveled on official business, Tolson traveled with him. In May 1931, both nearly lost their lives when their plane caught fire and had to make an emergency landing at Aberdeen, Maryland.[72]

The relationship was so close, so enduring, and so affectionate that it took the place of marriage for both bachelors. Hoover called Tolson "Junior." Tolson sometimes called Hoover "Boss," sometimes "Eddie." He was the only person beside Baughman outside Hoover's family to use Hoover's childhood nickname of "Speed." In October 1930, he gave the director a photo of himself inscribed "To my best friend 'Speed' with Affectionate Regards, Clyde A. Tolson."[73]

Through the years, Hoover and Tolson were continually bedeviled by accusations of homosexuality. Hoover made it Bureau policy to track down every story and have his agents challenge the source to prove the allegation. Hoover had a hot temper, and the homosexual rumors could be counted on to unleash it. In the margin of one Bureau memorandum on a person spreading a report about him and Tolson, Hoover wrote, "I never heard of this obvious degenerate. Only one with a depraved mind could have such thoughts." When a Cleveland woman gossiped that Hoover was "queer" and kept a group of young boys for his pleasure, Tolson had the head of the Cleveland office visit her and make her tell her friends the rumor was not true. In the margin of another report on a rumor that Hoover was a "fairy" and Tolson was his "boy friend," Tolson wrote, "I am beginning to believe [censored] is nuts." Hoover wrote, "That is charitable. I think he is a despicable foul minded malicious rat." Two of Hoover's executives visited the person spreading this last rumor and told him "we did not purport to permit such statements to go unchallenged when they came to our attention and that if we heard such a statement, we would see to it the statement was not repeated; that anybody who said it would have to put up or shut up and we would take care of anyone who made such a statement."[74]

Whether the Hoover-Tolson relationship did include a sexual union is simply not known. An indication of the intimacy of the relationship is the collection of hundreds of candid photographs Hoover took of Tolson (who was strikingly handsome as a young man, as was Baughman) during their forty-two years together. Hoover did not expect these albums to survive his death, but they escaped the notice of Tolson and Hoover's secretary when they destroyed Hoover's personal effects in accordance with his wishes. These albums consist almost exclusively of photographs of Tolson in front of the varied backdrops of their vacation resorts. Although the photos convey a feeling of affection, when the two men appear together in a photo they are never seen touching one another, except in two group photos in which all present had their arms around each others' shoulders. On the other hand, Hoover took several photos of Tolson while he was sleeping, a situation in which many men might find it embarrassing to be photographed. Other photos show the two men in bathrobes or bare chested at the beach. The photos convey the sense of a caring, emotionally involved eye behind the lens, and whether it was a lover's eye or a close friend's, it was still qualitatively different from a business associate's.

Given Hoover's straitlaced Presbyterian upbringing and his almost fanatical conventionality, it is not inconceivable that Hoover's relationship with Tolson excluded the physically sexual dimension. Yet human drives being what they are, it is also possible that it was a fully sexual relationship. There is no compelling evidence for a definitive judgment in either direction. Weighing all known information, such a term as "spousal relationship" describes most fairly what is known about the bonds between the two men, bonds that grew stronger and more exclusive with the passing years.

A relationship as unusual as that between Hoover and Tolson was not publicly discussed and scrutinized by the press while they were living because they were the beneficiaries of a level of reticence about such matters that would seem positively Victorian just a few decades later. Only when a homosexual scandal broke into the open and forced a politician from office was it then discussed by the media, and then only under euphemisms like "family difficulties." Hoover was never abashed by his relationship with Tolson, and always insisted that if he was expected to attend a social affair, Tolson should also be invited. Throughout Hoover's life, official Washington simply accepted the situation at Hoover's own valuation: that he and Tolson were associates and friends. The prevailing attitude was that the actual nature of the relationship was no one else's business.

While Hoover and his tightly managed, streamlined Bureau of Investigation generally remained on the sidelines, crime was becoming a national obsession, particularly after the Wall Street Crash and the start of the depression. Crime is always dramatic, and the kind of crime that developed during Prohibition was very dramatic: vast bootlegging empires with their own wars, funerals, and peace treaties, and colorful crime bosses like Dutch Schultz in New York, Roger Touhy in Detroit, and, most sensational of all, the gorillalike king of the Chicago underworld, Al Capone.[75]

Al Capone was only the greatest of the many crime stories that took over the front pages after the Crash. The public's fascination with crime seemed to grow as its confidence in the government declined. When gangsters like Dutch Schultz announced plans to execute their rivals, and then followed through on their threats, they seemed to have their own set of laws, with the government a helpless bystander. The *New Haven* (Connecticut) *Register* said gangland outrages like the attempted murder of New York bootlegger Legs Diamond in October 1930 "fairly make the entire social fabric of the land tremble in anticipation of a possible extension of gang rule to wider and still wider areas of life."[76]

The fragmentary crime statistics of the period show that the crime level actually declined from 1918 until after World War II.[77] Neverthe-less, the incredible publicity given to a relatively small number of celebrity gangsters convinced the public that crime was on the rise. With the collapse of national morale because of the economic depression, that illusion became the conventional wisdom. The criminal came to symbolize all that was wrong with the country, and so he became the target of politicians seeking to repair the tattered image of authority.

Crime, particularly sensational crime, was coming to be seen at the end of Herbert Hoover's administration as a challenge to the authority of government and to the survival of conventional morality. There were few political leaders who were fully aware yet of the strength of the public demand that the national government respond to these local challenges, but the situation could not have escaped the notice of someone like J. Edgar Hoover, who instinctively resented any threat to authority. The country was suffering from a depression that was cultural as well as economic: a crisis of confidence in the standards and rules that had given order to life in better times.

At the end of the Hoover administration, the country was looking for a different kind of federal law enforcement than it was getting. Instead of getting credit for the considerable achievement of putting Capone in jail for income tax evasion, Herbert Hoover's beleaguered administration was ridiculed. As far as the press was concerned, Capone had been convicted of the wrong crime. The charges should have been murder, gambling, prostitution, and racketeering. The *Boston Globe* wrote that "it is ludicrous that this underworld gang leader has been led to the doors of the penitentiary at last only through prosecutions on income tax and liquor conspiracy charges."[78] The press was teaching the public to see crime as a test of the government's ability to meet violent challenges with violent force. The times demanded retributive, and not just procedural, justice.

The nation was looking to its national leaders for a response appropriate to the symbolism of crime, but the progressivism of Herbert Hoover (and of J. Edgar Hoover at this time) was incapable of meeting the new demand for direct federal action in local situations. Instead of action, President Hoover gave the country lectures about cooperation, states' rights, and constitutional limits on federal jurisdiction.

The case that exposed the depth of the public's new feeling of vulnerability around this time was the kidnapping of Charles Lindbergh's infant son on March 1, 1932, which was followed by a frustrating two-and-a-half-year search for the kidnapper. Lindbergh was the

American dream incarnate, and an attack on him was an assault on the dream itself. From the time of the first newsflash on the kidnapping until the switch was pulled on Bruno Richard Hauptmann at the Trenton, New Jersey, death house four years later, the nation treated the case as a national melodrama. Papers called it "a challenge to the whole order of the nation. . . . The truth must be faced that the army of desperate criminals which has been recruited in the last decade is winning its battle against society."[79] There was enough of this kind of hyperbole to make H. L. Mencken call it the "greatest story since the resurrection."

Pressure mounted on the president, but Herbert Hoover was not willing to have the Federal government go beyond providing technical and organizational assistance to local authorities—the formula he was attempting to apply to the economic collapse as well as law enforcement. On March 4, 1932, the president announced that he had authorized the postal inspector, the Secret Service, the Prohibition Unit, the Washington Metropolitan Police, and the Bureau of Investigation to join the investigation of the Lindbergh case if requested by local authorities. He designated J. Edgar Hoover coordinator of federal assistance.[80]

Finally, Hoover had been given the kind of job for which he had been preparing the Bureau during the past six years. He was to be given the chance to lead a federated national network of law enforcement agencies. What Herbert Hoover gave, however, he also took away. The president specified that the federal government was not taking responsibility for solving the crime; it was only assisting local authorities. Even that much would be contingent upon discovering a violation of a federal law. (There was still no federal kidnapping law, and Bureau agents did not have the authority to make arrests or carry guns.) The administration also stressed that it was not in favor of using the case as an excuse for extending federal authority in the area of law enforcement, although, given the state of public opinion, it would not actively oppose a federal kidnap bill (the "Lindbergh Law") then under congressional scrutiny.[81]

For the first time since 1924, a president had called on the Bureau to demonstrate concern at a time of public hysteria, and though Herbert Hoover's gesture was half-hearted and ineffective, the media responded with an enthusiasm that a more politically astute president would have interpreted as an invitation for more of the same. The *New York Times*'s story read like a Bureau of Investigation press handout, calling J. Edgar Hoover "one of the world's outstanding authorities on scientific crime detection." In a complete reversal of his antiheroic image of 1924, the *Times* described him as a "firm believer in Sherlockian methods of matching wits with the underworld."[82]

Despite the fact that few of its readers had heard of Hoover, the *Times* assured them that the Bureau had developed from "just another agency" into "one of the government's most formidable crusaders against crime" and claimed that "lawbreakers of high and low estate have come to have a wholesome respect for the Bureau." Even though the Capone case had been the work of Elmer Irey and the Internal Revenue Service, and the Bureau had contributed only an investigation that led to a contempt of court conviction, the *Times* claimed that Capone and other noted criminals had learned that "the bureau usually 'gets its man.' " (Hoover would not have corrected the paper's mistake; his later position was that Bureau involvement in a case automatically sealed the criminal's fate, so that whether or not the Bureau actually solved the crime, it deserved the credit.) According to the new publicity, the leader of this Bureau "plays a good average game on the links and collects old glassware and spinning wheels and never uses a railroad train when an air route is available."[83]

There were signs that the public was convinced that since crime had expanded into a nationwide system, law enforcement must also be nationalized. According to the *Camden* (New Jersey) *Courier Post*, "this crime shows that America needs a system of state 'Scotland Yards'—with a central organization at Washington." The *Philadelphia Record* urged that the police systems of all the states be unified into "one incorruptible central agency [that] can supervise our national battle against organized crime."[84]

The new interest in crime was quickly exploited by popular entertainment. This, too, showed that the public was interpreting crime as a challenge to the legitimacy of traditional authorities. First there was a cycle of money-making prison pictures in the thirties: *The Big House* (1930), *Convict's Code* (1930), *Ladies of the Big House* (1931), and *20,000 Years at Sing Sing* (1932), the last based on the reminiscences of a man Hoover later used as a symbol of excessive leniency toward criminals, the warden of Sing Sing, Lewis Lawes.[85]

A convict hero's suffering was too passive, however, and so the next wave of crime pictures featured gangster heroes modeled after celebrity criminals like Capone. The gangster movies killed off their criminals as the censors required, but as often as not gangsters died at the hands of rival gangsters. The police were almost nonentities. First there was *Little Caesar* (1930), starring Edward G. Robinson, then *Public Enemy* (1931) with James Cagney. These were so popular that more than fifty other gangster movies were made in 1931 that seemed to follow an amoral "crime without punishment" formula. There was no hero of the law charismatic and powerful enough to counterbalance the anarchic power of the criminal. The films showed an America in which the underworld had overpowered legitimate society, and exposed its protectors as incompetent, corrupt, and impotent.

Public expectations were creating a role for a new hero of the law, a role J. Edgar Hoover would assume once he had the necessary political backing. In the absence of effective federal leadership against crime, however, a grass-roots anticrime movement emerged between 1929 and 1933, a mass movement without a leader or a plan of action. Everyman became his own criminologist. There were calls for public hangings, floggings, and other panaceas. One fairly frequent suggestion was setting up an American Devil's Island for habitual offenders. Another was a more liberal application of the third degree. Some jurisdictions passed so-called public enemies laws (modeled on a law passed in 1931 in New York State) to permit jailing an individual "with a known record who consorts with known criminals and has no means of support." Other states copied New York's 1926 Baumes Law, which imposed a life sentence for a fourth felony conviction (the so-called three-time loser law). There was even a call for martial law from such a usually temperate figure as Warden Lawes of Sing Sing, who said that he "could stamp out racketeering in sixty days if he was a Mussolini." On August 24, 1931, a crowd of 20,000 attended an anticrime rally at Madison Square Garden in New York City. The American Legion was organizing and arming its members as police auxiliaries. Around the country, groups imitated Chicago's famous Secret Six, which had gotten the Treasury Department to send Eliot Ness and his "Untouchables" to Chicago.[86]

Even before the New Deal unveiled its crime program, the country had formed an idea of the kind of law enforcement it needed. The social forces that later coalesced into the myth of the G-Man had already been assembled: popular fascination with rituals of crime and punishment; an interpretation of crime as an attack on the nation and its values; a passion for vengeance against larger-than-life criminals; and a hunger for mass involvement in anticrime action. Above all, the crime hysteria of the pre-Roosevelt depression had convinced the country that only the federal government could cope with the crime problem now that it had come to be identified as a symbol of national decline.

What was needed was "a symbol of law and order who could

dish it out to the underworld exactly as they dished it out—only better. An individual who could toss the hot iron right back at them along with a smack on the jaw thrown in for good measure." But that was Chester Gould describing his new comic strip detective, Dick Tracy, in 1931. In a year it would be Hoover and his G-Men.[87]

CHAPTER 7

The New Deal FBI

Gee, but I'd like to be a G-Man
And go Bang! Bang! Bang! Bang!
Just like Dick Tracy, what a "he-man"
And go Bang! Bang! Bang! Bang!
I'd do as I please, act high-handed and regal
'Cause when you're a G-Man, there's nothing illegal.

I'd be known in all the best spots of New York
Like Twenty-One and Eighteen and The Stork.
To all the smartest nightclubs I would go
To find out all the things that a G-Man ought to know.

> From "When I Grow Up" ("The G-Man Song") by
> Harold Rome, *Pins and*
> *Needles,* 1937

THE FEDERAL BUREAU OF INVESTIGATION of the 1930s was one of the New Deal's truly spectacular political triumphs, and J. Edgar Hoover was one of Roosevelt's most valuable (and trusted) lieutenants. No "alphabet agency" of the New Deal captured the public imagination like Hoover's FBI. In a broad sense, Franklin D. Roosevelt was responding to the same crisis of confidence that produced the grassroots anticrime movement; he had to deal with the collapse of national morale as well as an economic collapse. While the other New Deal agencies struggled with the grim economic realities of the thirties, Hoover's Bureau grappled with the cultural depression—the public's belief that legitimate authority was confused, crumbling, and incompetent. On the surface, Hoover's great gangster cases of the early New Deal—Machine Gun Kelly, John Dillinger, Pretty Boy Floyd, and Baby Face Nelson—had no obvious relation to the fundamental crisis of the depression. But men and nations do not live by bread alone; they also need circuses. Hoover's FBI provided the circus.

The thirties saw the beginnings of the power Hoover wielded for the rest of his life. That power grew, first, from Hoover's amazing popularity during the decade as a celebrity and hero. The second source of power was secret, known at first only to a few in the very highest circles of government. This was the domestic intelligence apparatus Hoover assembled for Roosevelt as part of the president's covert preparation against the possibility of war, a secrecy made necessary because of the public's resistance to any attempt to make it realize the true danger of the international situation. Hoover was, in all these sensitive and confidential matters, Roosevelt's effective, loyal, and indispensable agent.

These factors combined to expand Hoover's power beyond anyone's expectations, certainly his own. His popularity protected him against the repugnance usually felt for the sneak and the snoop. Conversely, his access to secret and far-ranging sources of information lent authority to his increasingly sweeping pronouncements on political, social, and moral issues.

With the coming change to a Democratic administration, Hoover, as a holdover appointee, faced uncertain prospects in 1932. "The tenure of service of a police administrator," he wrote wistfully that year, "should be limited only by demonstrated inefficiency, the known greater efficiency of another man, or through the operation of those natural causes which will make it necessary that all of us 'some fine day' must cease active duty and prepare ourselves, if happily we have the time or inclination, for our journey into the 'great unknown.' " There were some European countries, he noted enviously, that kept the heads of the national police in office until "the Grim Reaper has made it necessary for a successor to be chosen."[1]

Roosevelt had designated as his new attorney general the same Senator Tom Walsh of Montana who had fought Hoover during the Red Scare and Teapot Dome. In early 1933, it was generally assumed that when Walsh took office he would fire Hoover, but on March 2 of that year, the senator had a heart attack on his way to the inaugura-

Hoover was born on January 1, 1895, in a white stucco house at 413 Seward Square, a residential neighborhood for civil servants, just behind the Capitol in Washington. The house next door later belonged to Hoover's brother, Dickerson, Jr.

Edgar's strong-willed mother, Annie Sheitlin Hoover, bore a remarkable resemblance to her son. His troubled father, Dickerson N. Hoover, was an engraver in the printshop of the Commerce Department's Coast and Geodetic Survey.

A nineteenth-century small-town American home, school, and church created J. Edgar Hoover. From them, and the segregated Washington of his youth, he learned the reverence for established authority that guided his long career. He became a Sunday School teacher at the Old First Presbyterian Church of Dr. Donald Campbell MacLeod (*top left*); at Washington's elite Central High School, he was valedictorian of the class of 1913, a champion debater, a captain of cadets (*right*), and took an active part in student social life (*bottom left*).

Joining the Justice Department in 1917, fresh out of George Washington University Law School, Hoover rose quickly. During the war, he registered interned aliens. This expertise enabled him to lead the nation's postwar drive to deport Communists. His formidable organizational skills led to his appointment as assistant director of the Bureau of Investigation in 1921 and then to the directorship in 1924.

Miller, News Picture Service; National Archives 65-H-133-2

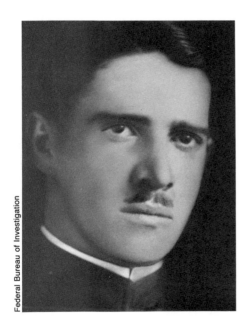

Federal Bureau of Investigation

National Archives 65-H-746

To 'Speed' with affectionate regards
9/11/44 *Clyde*

Hoover moved quickly to transform the Bureau from an old-line detective agency, politically controlled and staffed through patronage, into one characterized by professional law enforcement standards and scientific crime detection techniques, symbolized by Hoover's first innovation, the fingerprint collection of his Bureau of Identification (*above*). To prevent recurrence of scandal, he instituted a rigid system of control. He was aided by his closest associates during the twenties, his friend and aide T. Frank Baughman (*lower left*), who was recruited by Hoover in 1919, and then Clyde Tolson (*lower right*), who joined the FBI in 1928 and remained Hoover's intimate friend and associate director of the FBI for the rest of Hoover's life.

During the thirties, Hoover's success against notorious criminals like John Dillinger helped the Roosevelt administration restore confidence in the government. The New Deal war on crime made the Bureau, and agents like Melvin Purvis, famous.

Hoover served Roosevelt loyally as one of the most effective and trusted members of his adminstration. With Attorney General Homer Cummings, Senator Henry F. Ashurst of Arizona, and Assistant Attorney General Joseph B. Keenan (*left to right*), he watches President Roosevelt sign the 1934 package of crime bills.

Hoover and his companion and associate Tolson take a break during the filming in 1936 of a sequence of the FBI-endorsed *You Can't Get Away With It* (behind Hoover are moviemakers Bill Miller and Charles Ford). The popularity Hoover acquired during the thirties was a powerful factor in creating the independence from political control Hoover enjoyed for the rest of his career.

UPI/Bettmann Newsphotos

With Tolson always at his side, Hoover lived the life of a celebrity during the thirties, enjoying New York nightclubs (*above,* at a New Year's Eve party at the Stork Club), attending championship prize fights, and appearing in the gossip columns of friends like Ed Sullivan and Walter Winchell. Hoover and Tolson shared vacations at exclusive resorts in Miami Beach (*right*) and La Jolla as guests of wealthy friends.

AP/Wide World Photos

Roosevelt had Hoover secretly rebuild the Bureau's domestic intelligence facilities during the thirties. When the war came, the Bureau's counterespionage apparatus reassured the country that the problem of spying and subversion was under control, most dramatically by the FBI's capture of the Nazi saboteurs who landed on Long Island from a U-Boat. Hoover and Tolson enter the Supreme Court in 1942 to hear the conviction and death sentence of the saboteurs upheld by the high court.

tion and died.[2] Roosevelt had urgent need for an attorney general to provide him with a legal opinion on his authority to shut down the country's banking system. After conferring with Secretary of State–designate Cordell Hull, Roosevelt released the name of a stand-in nominee for attorney general: Homer Stillé Cummings.

Cummings was sixty-three and a Roosevelt loyalist of long standing from Connecticut.[3] The choice of Cummings was one of Roosevelt's luckiest strokes. Cummings's vigorous administration—he described his policy as "leadership rather than passive administration under old statutes and ready-made policies"—energized the whole Justice Department, and no division of the Department more than the Bureau of Investigation.

Neither Roosevelt nor Cummings came to Washington promising anything like a war on crime. The New Deal crime program developed naturally out of the approach to government signalled by Roosevelt's call for "action, and action now" in his inaugural address, and his militant appeal to the nation to "move as a trained and loyal army willing to sacrifice for the good of a common discipline."[4] Roosevelt had not promised any specific type of action against the depression, just action, action clothed in the rhetoric of war. Doctor New Deal's specialty was going to be psychology, his first concern the patient's mental health; the country was in for massive doses of public relations medicine.

As the New Deal unveiled its programs for combating the depression, something close to a war fever took hold of the cabinet. The Agriculture Department proclaimed a war on farm surpluses and rural poverty. The Civilian Conservation Corps was fighting youth unemployment and soil erosion. The National Recovery Administration, under Hugh Johnson, a retired cavalry general, held enlistment parades with American flags and Blue Eagle banners to kick off its drives. Inevitably, the lawyers and special agents at the Justice Department, Hoover among them, yearned for their own drum rolls and bugle calls.

The political theater of Roosevelt's hundred days may have had little immediate effect on the economic depression, but it had a great effect on the "cultural depression." National morale had revived, Leo Rosten wrote in 1935, because the president offered the country "a war for social justice . . . the panoply of a military campaign and a holy crusade . . . the altruism of a noble cause [and] the camaraderie of participation in mass activity."[5]

Homer Cummings entered the Justice Department armed only

with a firm commitment to the president's policies, and he judged a program by its contribution to social solidarity. The function of law, he said, was "to cement, and not to strain, the bonds of affection that exist between the people and the government they have erected." He thought "public indifference was, largely, the apathy of the disillusioned, resulting from the frequent failure of public authorities to supply . . . leadership."[6]

Cummings moved to make himself the leader of the anticrime movement by appearing before almost any citizens' group concerned with the crime problem—the International Association of Chiefs of Police (IACP), the American Legion, the Daughters of the American Revolution (DAR). Anticrime rallies before 1933 had been to protest the government's failure to act against crime. Cummings's presence made them demonstrations of support for the New Deal's as-yet-undefined anticrime program. By the late spring of 1933, his appeals for an "aroused public sentiment against racketeers" and his hints about a forthcoming "widespread war against gangsters and racketeers" had turned him into the most conspicuous figure in the anticrime movement.[7]

FDR was not in office two weeks before the White House began to call on Hoover for the same sort of informal information the director had furnished previous administrations. Though these first requests were harmless, they were still outside the strict bounds of Hoover's formal responsibilities, at least by Harlan Stone's guidelines. Yet Hoover's eager willingness to provide these services must have reassured Roosevelt that here was someone with whom he could work.[8]

Hoover also lobbied to make sure favorable endorsements of him reached the president. Hoover's old patron, Harlan Stone, got in touch with Roosevelt through Felix Frankfurter to inquire about Hoover's prospects; on April 22, FDR told Frankfurter "it is all right about Edgar Hoover. Homer Cummings agrees with me." Six weeks later, Roosevelt received a "Dear Franklin" letter from Francis P. Garvan, Hoover's boss during the Palmer days, now with the Chemical Foundation. "Do not let them lose you that boy, Hoover," Garvan wrote FDR. "I have advised him that he ought to get out and begin a permanent practice of law where he would make an undoubted success. But each day that you have relations with him or his bureau you will find him more necessary to your comfort and assurance. The more departments of investigation you can put under him, the more you will assure your administration against scandal."[9]

One of Homer Cummings's pet proposals during the spring of

1933 was to establish a "super police force" to lead his war on crime. His first plan was to merge existing federal forces, and on June 10, 1933, Roosevelt signed an Executive Order[10] that combined the Prohibition Bureau, the Bureau of Identification, and the Bureau of Investigation to create a new Division of Investigation within the Justice Department. The idea was to create painlessly and cheaply a federal anticrime force impressive enough to have a dramatic impact on public opinion by adding the Prohibition Bureau's 1,200 investigators to Hoover's 326 agents. Any merger, however, always raises the problem of deciding between the former leaders to select the head of the combined operation, and that was probably the reason why the order was dated to take effect two months later, on August 10.

The two-month delay gave Hoover time to argue against combining his Bureau with the ill-managed, ill-trained, and corrupt Prohibition unit. Hoover convinced Cummings that this would have "swamped us and undone all the work we had done to make the Bureau honest, sound, and efficient." Hoover evidently demonstrated his sincerity by offering to report to the new division head if Cummings kept the Bureau autonomous.[11]

The question of leadership was still unresolved on June 17, when a gun battle between Hoover's agents and gangsters in faraway Kansas City, Missouri, gave Cummings the pretext he needed to declare his war on crime. The Kansas City Massacre, as it came to be called, was a cornerstone of the FBI legend. Four Bureau of Investigation agents (together with an Oklahoma police chief and two local detectives) had been escorting an escaped convict to Leavenworth when they were ambushed by machine gun–wielding bandits in Kansas City's Union Station parking lot. The gang was led by Verne Miller and possibly included Charles "Pretty Boy" Floyd (although Floyd denied to his death that he was present). When the smoke cleared, Special Agent Raymond J. Caffrey and the three local police officers were dead; two of the other special agents were badly wounded. Their prisoner, escaped bank robber Frank "Jelly" Nash, was also dead. (The real purpose of the attack may have been to kill Nash to keep him from informing on his friends in the Midwest underworld.)

Cummings summoned reporters to his office and told them he "accepted the murder of a Department of Justice agent among the victims as a challenge to the government." He told them he had "ordered the entire government to work on the case." Editorialists, moviemakers, and civic leaders had come to interpret crime as a test of strength between organized society and the underworld. Now the country had an attorney general who used the same dramatic rhetoric: Verne Miller and his gang were no longer merely four individual criminals—they were the "army of crime." Special Agent Caffrey and the wounded agents represented, variously, the "government," "Justice," or even America itself. Killing Caffrey was the underworld's "declaration of war" against the United States.[12]

There are times when the right word at the right time can change the course of events. Cummings's snap description of the Kansas City Massacre as the start of the government's war on crime turned the sleepy backwater of the Justice Department into the hottest political property in Washington. General Hugh Johnson and the other New Deal chiefs had only vague and insubstantial targets (unemployment, poverty, farm failures) on which they could use only paper bullets. Homer Cummings could provide a show with real battles, real bullets, real heroes fighting real enemies with real guns.

Throughout July, news about Cummings's plans poured out of the Justice Department, and the attorney general frankly admitted that the "first purpose" of his campaign was its effect on public opinion. He was trying "to acquaint the public with the facts, to reinforce its demand for upholding the law."[13] Cummings's calls for federal leadership of the anticrime movement were now being echoed by sympathetic civic leaders, local politicians, and editorialists. On July 13, a *New York Times* columnist wrote that

> I favor a national police force for investigation and prosecution. The detectives of the United States will be like its soldiers. They will never know their next point of call. They will operate under centralized orders from Washington. They will have at their fingertips a complete international identification bureau. They will use radio, telegraph, telephone, photographs, fingerprints, Bertillon measurements—use, in fact, every science known to criminal detection."[14]

On July 30, Cummings was ready to unveil the new super police force. He finally revealed the June 10 merger of the three bureaus into the "new" Division of Investigation. However, instead of placing a new appointee over Hoover and Major E. V. Dalrymple, head of the Prohibition Bureau, Cummings fired Dalrymple and made Hoover director of the whole division, giving him John S. Hurley, the Prohibition Bureau's second-in-command, as his assistant. Hoover set up a separate Alcoholic Beverage Unit within the division to keep the "dry agents" out of his Bureau of Investigation. (With the repeal of Prohibition, this unit lost its reason for existence and almost all of the remaining dry agents [977 in all] were transferred back to the Treasury Department on May 10, 1934.)[15]

After all the talk of a super police force, a national police force, and a new crime bureau, this was something of a letdown. Discounting the sleight-of-hand with the doomed Prohibition Bureau and the Bureau of Identification (already part of Hoover's domain), Cummings had done nothing more than rename the old Bureau of Investigation the "Division of Investigation." (On July 1, 1935, the Division would finally be named the "Federal Bureau of Investigation.")

Hoover had by now enough friends and enemies in the media for the suspense over his reappointment to be a good story. In an unfriendly story in *Colliers,* Ray Tucker claimed that "President Roosevelt . . . may reorganize this miniature American Cheka, and Mr. Hoover may have been displaced by the time this article is published [the second week in August]." The article in *Colliers* offhandedly described Hoover as walking with a less than manly stride. This evidently amused some Washingtonians who knew about Hoover's friendship with Tolson, because a week later a Washington gossip columnist asked whether "anybody [had] noted that the Hoover stride has grown noticeably longer and more vigorous since Tucker charged him with 'walking with mincing steps.' "[16]

Hoover may have been helped to hold onto his job by an adulatory profile written by Courtney Ryley Cooper that appeared in the issue of *American Magazine* on the newsstands while Hoover's fate was being decided. Cooper called Hoover the mastermind of "the nucleus of America's first real national police force." Cooper said Hoover was "a complexity . . . a master detective who simply does not conform to any picture of the average crime chaser," a dreamer with a vision of "an amazing police force" that would always catch, always convict, its man. Hoover was indispensable to the organization, the genius who had hired and trained every employee and molded them all into a "championship outfit."[17]

During the spring of 1933, Cummings was tossing around such phrases as a "national police force" and an "American Scotland Yard" as he tried to envision the future of the Bureau of Investigation. He quickly realized, however, that a true nationalization of the country's police forces under federal control, given constitutional and budgetary realities, would have been impossible. Federal *leadership* of law enforcement, however, using Hoover's Bureau as an instrument, was a practical alternative. Instead of seeking new federal responsibilities, this policy would let the department concentrate on enforcing more vigorously and dramatically crimes already within its jurisdiction, notably kidnapping. (A federal antikidnapping statute, passed a few months after the Lindbergh tragedy in 1932, was already on the books.) Any expansion of federal jurisdiction would be carefully planned to keep it from placing impossible burdens on the Bureau's resources and to make sure it had potential for significant political impact. In a memo to Cummings opposing a complete federal takeover of national law enforcement, Hoover wrote that "it is perhaps not overlooked, but it is certainly under-emphasized, that the [crime] problem is a State one."[18]

Ever since taking command of the Bureau in 1924, Hoover had spoken in favor of a cooperative national law enforcement effort, with the Bureau providing local police with technical aid and coordination for their efforts. This complemented the attorney general's notion of selective federal intervention in crimes that promised the publicity he needed for his department. Once Cummings was committed to this notion, which was ambitious politically but modest logistically, Hoover was exactly the man he needed: hardworking; disciplined; in complete control of his small, tightly organized force; with an unblemished ten-year record of strictly obeying the orders of his attorney generals and of performing his duties quietly and discreetly.

Throughout the first two years of the New Deal, the public was far more interested in Attorney General Cummings than in J. Edgar Hoover and his crew of anonymous agents. Hoover was in the familiar role he had played under A. Mitchell Palmer, that of the expert organizer carrying out policies set by the politically imaginative Cummings. What captured the public's imagination was the sight of the federal government—represented by the attorney general—fighting it out with dangerous gangsters, the spectacle of the New Deal flexing its crime-fighting muscles in a demonstration of the new mood of confidence.

When Cummings began his anticrime drive, the public had no reason to expect much from the federal detectives. For more than a year, Hoover and his men (along with the rest of American law enforcement) had been chasing blind leads in the Lindbergh case. In July 1933, however, Hoover gave the attorney general a case that redeemed the federal government from its history of failure. This was the kidnapping of Oklahoma oilman Charles Urschel on July 23 by the Midwest bandit George "Machine Gun" Kelly and his wife, Kathryn.

The Urschel case was a landmark in the Bureau's official history for two reasons. First, it was a classic example of the kind of crime that could be solved only by a tightly coordinated nationwide force of investigators backed by scientific facilities able to analyze any evidence that might be uncovered. As such, it was the first of Hoover's many demonstrations that he had trained the FBI to put science to work for law enforcement. Second, it was also one of Hoover's first exercises in controlling the publicity about a case so as to turn it into part of the emerging legend of the FBI—in this instance as the "case in which we got our name," the case that turned FBI agents into "G-men."

The Urschel case was not only a demonstration of the Bureau's skill in solving a crime; it also demonstrated how Hoover and his publicists could extract from the many clues they used to solve a case only the ones showing the superiority of the FBI's scientific methods, discarding any that hinted chance or luck had any bearing on the FBI's success. The Bureau was able to pursue two parallel sets of clues. On July 31, Kelly got his $200,000 ransom from the Urschel family and released his victim. The next morning the FBI got Urschel's story and fitted together the clues as if they were pieces of a jigsaw puzzle. Urschel had been blindfolded, but he could hear noises that told him he was on a farm. He could hear planes passing twice a day, and he tricked his captors into telling him the time, so he had an idea of the planes' schedule. He also remembered the peculiar mineral taste of the water, the time of day when there was a rainstorm, and many other details. In combination, these clues helped the FBI draw a map that led them directly to where Urschel had been held. On August 10, the FBI raided the farm, arrested one of the kidnappers, Harvey Bailey, and picked up the trail of the others, Albert Bates and the Kellys.[19]

While the Bureau was running down these clues, it had another set of leads. Just before the Kellys kidnapped Urschel, Kathryn Kelly had gone to Fort Worth in an attempt to get two detectives to help her kidnap a wealthy Texas banker. The detectives had refused and had gone to the FBI with their strange tale. Based on this, the Kellys were the Bureau's prime suspects as soon as Urschel was kidnapped. Kathryn Kelly compounded her mistake by contacting the Fort Worth detectives again to find out if anyone suspected her and her husband. The detectives again went to the FBI, so the Bureau put the Kellys' Fort Worth home under surveillance. It did not take long for this investigation to focus attention on Kathryn's mother's farm outside Fort Worth.[20]

The Bureau had been able to solve the case two ways: one based on clever reasoning, the other on luck and Kathryn Kelly's blunders. Hoover turned the first into the official version of the Machine Gun Kelly story.[21] In the same way, he made sure the official stories about John Dillinger, Pretty Boy Floyd, and Baby Face Nelson all led to the same inexorable conclusion: Hoover had turned crime fighting into a science, and had turned the FBI itself into the ultimate weapon against crime.

While Cummings held the public's attention focused on the patriotic significance of the campaign against the gangsters, the Bureau brought the Urschel case to a spectacular conclusion. On September 26, it located Kelly in Memphis, Tennessee, and a squad of special agents and Memphis detectives (Bureau agents did not have the authority to make arrests on their own until 1934) raided the farm. As they rushed into the living room, Kelly poked his head out of the bedroom. When he saw the detectives' arsenal (shotguns, machine guns, and tear gas) he dropped his pistol and gave up without a fight. According to the story later put out by the Bureau, when Kelly spotted the Bureau agents he panicked and shouted "Don't shoot, G-Men, don't shoot." That, according to the story Hoover would tell and retell, was where the FBI got its nickname. (The "G-men" angle turns up for the first time in feature stories written by Rex Collier in July 1934.) According to the national press accounts of the arrest, when the officers broke into his room, Kelly merely "grinned sheepishly, hesitated a moment, and then the gun slipped from his hand to the floor. 'Okay, boys, I've been waiting for you all night.' "[22]

The Kelly case had a wealth of colorful human interest angles that would have made it a fabulous news story at any time. In 1933, it got even more publicity because Homer Cummings and the Justice Department had turned it into *political* melodrama. The department had put itself to the test by saying that "if this government cannot protect its citizens, then we had frankly better turn it over to the Kellys, the Bates, the Baileys, and the others of the underworld and pay tribute to them through taxes."[23]

Every few weeks for the rest of the year, Cummings announced another innovation in his war on crime. When the Flag Association held the final rally of its anticrime campaign, for example, Cummings announced that he was establishing a special prison for celebrity prisoners: Alcatraz, a former army prison in San Francisco Bay. Among the first inmates, he said, would be Machine Gun Kelly and Harvey Bailey; he hinted Al Capone would soon join them. Cummings had judged the public mood perfectly. Alcatraz, whatever its merits as a prison, was an immediate public relations success, instant folklore, the new symbol of the ultimate penalty short of death.[24]

The greatest case in FBI history was its hunt for John Dillinger during the spring and summer of 1934. The Dillinger case was also Hoover's greatest achievement in shaping a complex, unstructured news event into an incontrovertible FBI triumph. Initially, however, it was Homer Cummings who orchestrated the case.

Dillinger's crime spree began in May 1933 and lasted just over a year. During that short time, he captured the public imagination as no criminal had since Jesse James. Conveniently for Cummings (and Hoover), Dillinger began just as Cummings was organizing his anticrime drive, and the manhunt came to a climax just when the administration was trying to move its anticrime legislation through Congress. Cummings was able to label the Dillinger manhunt a test of the federal government's resolve, and to turn Dillinger's death into one of the greatest political triumphs of the 1930s.

John Dillinger, thirty years old in 1933, had been in jail since 1924 for robbing an Indiana grocery. As soon as he got out of jail on May 22, 1933, he began robbing banks, stores, even police stations, a trail that stretched from Florida to Wisconsin, Indiana to Arizona. He escaped from prison twice. The second escape was one of the classic stories in the history of American crime.

On January 25, 1934, Dillinger was arrested in Tucson, Arizona, and extradited to Crown Point, Indiana, to stand trial for murder. In Crown Point, photographers got the sheriff and the prosecutor to pose with Dillinger, arms around each others' shoulders, the law officers grinning with satisfaction, Dillinger with a sardonic smirk as though he were enjoying the thought of what was in store for his captors. On the night of March 3, Dillinger produced a wooden pistol carved from a broken washboard, disarmed the guards, stole their weapons, and left in Sheriff Lillian Holley's car. When he crossed the Illinois state line he violated the 1919 Dyer Act against interstate auto theft, and that brought the Bureau of Investigation officially into the case.

Cummings pointed to Dillinger's escape in his attempt to convince Congress to adopt the Twelve Point Anticrime Program he outlined on March 20. The underworld, he said, had "more men under arms than the army and navy of the United States," and the government needed reinforcements.[25] Cummings's proposals would expand federal

jurisdiction to include interstate racketeering, thefts from banks belonging to the Federal Reserve System, and the murder of federal
officers. They also strengthened the Lindbergh law and increased the
power of federal prosecutors. Later, he introduced additional measures
to give FBI agents the right to carry weapons and to make arrests
on their own authority.

Meanwhile, Dillinger was giving the Bureau a run of bad luck.
On March 31, two of Hoover's agents had him trapped in St. Paul,
Minnesota, but they let him escape through an unguarded rear door
(they did, however, wound him in the leg). Another fiasco quickly
followed. On April 22, Special Agent in Charge Melvin Purvis, the
chief of Hoover's Chicago field office, got a tip that the Dillinger
gang was hiding out at a northern Wisconsin resort called Little Bohemia. Purvis chartered a plane and set off with a squad of agents,
while another squad (under Inspector Samuel Cowley) flew in from
St. Paul with reinforcements. Hoover summoned newsmen to his office
and told them he had Dillinger trapped and this time he couldn't get
away.[26]

The raid was a disaster. Watchdogs began barking when they heard
the agents blundering through the woods. FBI agents and gangsters
fired blindly at each other, and Dillinger and his gang slipped out
an unguarded rear door—again. A hotel guest was killed in the cross-
fire, and a new and particularly murderous member of the gang, Baby
Face Nelson, ran into two agents and killed one of them. In Washington, there was talk of demoting Hoover; a petition from Wisconsin
called for Purvis's dismissal "at least until Dillinger is caught or
killed."[27]

The affair at Little Bohemia, as Melvin Purvis called it in his
memoirs, made law enforcement—specifically Hoover, Purvis, and the
Bureau of Investigation—look ridiculous, but it was just what Cummings needed to get his crime bills passed. Roosevelt himself entered
the fray and demanded that Congressman Hatton Sumners, chairman
of the House Judiciary Committee, send the House a favorable recommendation on Cummings's crime bills. Sumners said that he would
set aside his belief that the bills violated states' rights because "a
wrath like that which kindled the frontier when the vigilantes cleaned
out the gunmen is sweeping America" and that "these laws will smash
the criminal gangs and make another Dillinger impossible." Cummings
chimed in with demands for another 200 agents (to bring the total
force to 600), armored cars, and planes.[28]

On May 19, Roosevelt signed the first six of Cummings's crime bills as Hoover and Cummings stood at his side. The president called on the public to join in the war on the underworld: "Law enforcement and gangster extermination cannot be made completely effective so long as a substantial part of the public looks with tolerance upon known criminals . . . or applauds efforts to romanticize crime. Federal men are constantly facing machine gun fire in the pursuit of gangsters."[29]

Meanwhile, the country had gone Dillinger happy. He was being spotted everywhere, even overseas, and front-page cartoons poked fun at the Justice Department. *Time* magazine illustrated a rollicking story on the Dillinger hunt with a board game called "Dillinger Land": Skulls marked the places where lawmen or outlaws had died. A dotted line traced the reported trail of the outlaw, and question marks fanned out from his last sure sighting at Little Bohemia.[30]

Police everywhere were smarting under the abuse. The Indiana State Police issued a shoot-on-sight order. In Washington, Assistant Attorney General Joseph B. Keenan swore "I don't know where or when we will get Dillinger, but we will get him. And you can say for me that I hope we will get him under such circumstances that the government won't have to stand the expense of a trial." Hoover told Inspector Sam Cowley to "Stay on Dillinger. Go everywhere the trail takes you. Take everyone who ever was remotely connected with the gang. . . . Take him alive if you can but protect yourself." Cummings told the press his orders were to "shoot to kill. Then count to ten."[31]

On Saturday, July 21, Melvin Purvis got the famous tip from Anna Sage, the "Woman in Red." Sage, an East Chicago brothel-keeper who was facing deportation, had agreed to inform on Dillinger for the reward money and for a promise of help with the Immigration Bureau. She told Purvis that she and another woman would be going to the movies with Dillinger the next day. Purvis told his men that "If . . . we locate him and he makes his escape it will be a disgrace to our Bureau."[32]

This time Dillinger did not escape. While Hoover paced back and forth in his library at 413 Seward Square, the phone ringing every few minutes with the latest developments from Chicago, a detachment of special agents surrounded the lobby of the Biograph movie theater and the sidewalk out front. At 10:30 the movie was over. Melvin Purvis walked up behind Dillinger and ordered him to surrender. Dillinger started to run, digging into his pocket for his pistol. The agents opened fire and the FBI's most famous gangster was dead.[33]

Within minutes the news spread across Chicago and the country that Dillinger had been killed. Crowds rushed to the theater to gawk at the pools of blood (some dipped their handkerchiefs for souvenirs). The city morgue was thrown open for citizens to view the corpse of the man editorials had labeled the "arch-criminal of the age." Purvis's men had killed the most notorious criminal in American history.[34]

Hoover's challenge over the succeeding months was to make sure the agents on the scene at the Biograph, particularly Melvin Purvis, did not monopolize the credit that he felt belonged to the entire Bureau. He had to discover a way to convince the public that the case had been solved by a systematic application of the Bureau's scientific crime-fighting methods, and not simply by means of the lucky tip from the Woman in Red.

The national press was already ballyhooing the killing of Dillinger as the turning point in the war on crime. "Mr. Dillinger now knows," an editor wrote, "that no individual, no matter how clever and ruthless he may be, can wage war successfully on a hundred and twenty-three million people." One enterprising reporter rushed around the inquest sniffing pistols. He decided that Sam Cowley was Dillinger's killer, that Cowley was the man with "the deepest notch on his gun in the world." To most of the world, however, there was only one possible choice for the role of hero, and that was "Little Mel" Purvis, hailed from coast to coast as "the man who got Dillinger."[35]

In Washington, it was Cummings who held center stage. The *Washington Star*'s story hailed him as the "superpoliceman for [the] nation." Cummings provided the press with the department's official reaction to Dillinger's death: "In the removal of Dillinger, let a somber warning be spread among all the denizens, big and little, of the underworld. Let it be noted that the Federal Army of Justice is upraised in protection of the law. Dillinger's capture is not the end. It is only a fresh beginning."[36]

In all the excitement about Dillinger, Purvis, and Cummings, Hoover and the rest of the Bureau were almost forgotten. To refocus attention back on the Bureau, Hoover quickly began working with his friend Rex Collier to put out his own version of the Dillinger story, one in which the entire Bureau was the collective hero. Hoover and Collier claimed that the key break was not Anna Sage's tip, but the theft of the car belonging to the sheriff of the Crown Point jail: *That* was the federal offense that gave the Bureau jurisdiction. Based on the premise that the Bureau *always* got its man, from the moment it entered the case, Dillinger was doomed. Hoover's scientific investigators had been waiting impatiently, Collier wrote, for Dillinger "to knock the chip off their shoulders by violating some federal law."[37] Once the Bureau moved in, the outcome was certain; as Hoover liked to say, "before science all must fall."

As Hoover and Collier told the story, all inconvenient details— the fiasco at Little Bohemia, Anna Sage's tip, the controversial bargain between her and Purvis (a bargain repudiated by Hoover and the government)—were all irrelevant. The Bureau's scientific method was so infallible that if Dillinger had not been caught one way, he would have been caught another.

By dint of constant restatement, Hoover finally managed to turn his treatment of the Dillinger case into the definitive version, and the classic victory in the FBI's war against crime. Even thirty years after FBI agents killed Dillinger at Chicago's Biograph Theater, one of Hoover's top assistants was still saying the reason for the FBI's popularity was that "we did the job. We got the Dillingers." Hoover turned the anteroom of his office into a Dillinger museum, reminiscent of his collection of Palmer-raid trophies in 1920. A visitor in 1937 said that the prize exhibit was

> a startling white plaster facsimile of John Dillinger's death mask. It stares empty-eyed from under the glass of an exhibit case. . . . Grouped about the mask are souvenirs of the memorable night when the spectacular outlaw was cornered and shot down. . . . There are the straw hat he was wearing, a wrinkled snapshot of a girl which was fished from his trousers pocket, and the silver rimmed glasses he was wearing to heighten his disguise, one of the lenses snapped by a bullet. There is a La Corona-Belvedere cigar he was carrying in his shirt pocket that summer night, still banded and wrapped in cellophane.[38]

Hoover also learned two public relations lessons from his experience massaging the Dillinger case into the proper shape. The first was that the press will turn whoever it thinks is in charge of a case into its hero—so Hoover let it be understood throughout the Bureau that *he* was to be described as being in personal command of every important case. The second was that reporters would base their stories on the interpretation given by the first high-ranking official who managed to get his statement to the press—so Hoover made sure that he was ready with immediate press releases whenever a big story broke.

Hoover made sure nobody and nothing got between him and the cameras when the Lindbergh case was solved in late September, even though credit should have gone to the Treasury agents who placed gold certificates in the ransom money passed to the kidnapper. That had led to the break in the case on September 15, 1934, when a Bronx gas station attendant wondered why a driver had paid for his gas with a ten-dollar gold certificate. (Those bills were all supposed to have been turned in to banks in April 1933, when the country went off the gold standard.) The attendant noted the car's license number, and it belonged to Bruno Richard Hauptmann.

Hoover rushed to New York so he could stand beside New York City Police Commissioner John F. O'Ryan (along with Norman Schwartzkopf of the New Jersey State Police) during the announcement of the Hauptmann arrest. He was also able to pose for photographs shaking hands with Special Agent T. H. Sisk and the other two agents on the New York Lindbergh squad headed by Inspector John Lyons of the New York City Police. The *Washington Star*'s caption with this picture was that Hoover and his men were the "Justice Board of Strategy in Lindbergh Case." Rex Collier's story credited the "Sherlocks of [the] Justice Department" with trapping Hauptmann, and said that Hoover had supervised the interrogation. "The coolest customer I've ever seen," was Hoover's analysis of Hauptmann's character.[39]

The Bureau of Investigation, of all the law agencies involved in the case, had done perhaps the least, but in the long run, after a year of incessant publicity like those Washington-based stories by Rex Collier, the public decided that the Lindbergh case was one more triumph for the Justice Department.

Hoover was able to take advantage of the depression public's hunger for involvement in these great national melodramas. The Justice Department, with its crime war publicity, gave Americans everywhere a way of vicariously taking part in these great crime pageants. If the Justice Department got credit for a case, the whole country could congratulate itself on another victory over crime. Under these circumstances, no facts could withstand the public's will to believe in the Justice Department, the country, and itself.

In the months immediately following Dillinger's death, Purvis won even more glory for himself and the Justice Department. With Dillinger out of the way, newspapers designated Pretty Boy Floyd the new Public Enemy Number One (for his supposed part in the 1933 Kansas City Massacre). Purvis took personal charge of the case, tracked Floyd down, and killed him.

The national press ran pictures of Purvis flanked by Hoover and Assistant to the Attorney General William Stanley over the caption

"And Again Melvin Purvis Triumphs." Once again Hoover did his best to edge into the action; he told Rex Collier that Floyd had offered to make a deal with him, trading surrender for immunity. He had rejected the offer, Hoover said, because "he killed one of our men and he must take the consequences. Moreover we don't deal with gangsters." The Washington press picked up this story, but around the country Purvis was still the hero, and his statements and pictures filled the front pages.[40]

Purvis next set out after the new Public Enemy Number One, Baby Face Nelson. As the FBI closed in, Nelson killed Special Agent Herman Hollis and mortally wounded Sam Cowley, who now headed a roving public enemy squad. Purvis rushed to Cowley's deathbed and got an identification of Nelson as the killer; he then told reporters he had taken "an oath in Cowley's blood" to avenge him. IF IT'S THE LAST THING I DO, I'LL GET BABY FACE NELSON was the headline that appeared across the country.[41]

In Washington, Cummings and Hoover announced that they had issued a "shoot-on-sight order" for Nelson, but a few hours later they received word that Nelson's body had been found, dead of wounds from the gunfight with Hollis and Cowley. Cummings was "almost stuttering" when he announced, "It's 'Baby Face' Nelson. Our men got him. Our men got him."[42]

For Homer Cummings, the significance of these public enemy cases was their contribution to the Justice Department's campaign to create political support for the entire program of the New Deal. On the West Coast, however, Hollywood was seeing something else, and more glamorous, in Cummings's war on crime. The entertainment industry saw in the public enemies cases the raw material for classic adventure stories. While Homer Cummings readied plans for a gathering of the entire law enforcement community in Washington, at the end of 1934, to celebrate the achievements of the past two years and to plan for the future, Warner Bros. was starting work on the first of the G-man films that would turn Hoover and the FBI into heroes.[43]

Cummings's Attorney General's Conference on Crime met in Washington from December 10 to 13 with over 600 delegates. This was intended to turn his anticrime campaign into a permanent, nationally coordinated law enforcement alliance.[44] Instead, the conference was Cummings's final opportunity to appear before the public as the leader of the anticrime movement before Hollywood made Hoover the new national symbol of law enforcement.

Cummings imagined that the conference would begin a new age

in American law enforcement. Behind the leadership furnished by his department, a nationwide federation of professional law enforcement agencies would take shape, all dedicated toward advancing the same enlightened policies, all working to enlist the public in support of the law. The Justice Department would set national standards and provide professional training through its criminal divisions—the Division of Investigation, the Bureau of Prisons—and other agencies that he was planning. These would train police officers and support research on crime prevention, especially prevention of juvenile delinquency. Hoover's Division of Investigation was to play a vital part in this, but not the only part, or even the major part.

The crime conference, however, did not mark the beginning of a new era in law enforcement. It was in reality the beginning of the end of the anticrime movement of the thirties. Over the next few years, the reputation of Hoover and the Bureau of Investigation would so outstrip that of the rest of the department that it put Cummings and his bold proposals into the political shade. Instead of Cummings's dream of a comprehensive national law enforcement policy, the country would have the myth of the G-man.

Hoover had a solid reputation at the end of 1934, but he was not, in the precise sense of the term, a popular figure.[45] There was no popular interest in his personality, his ideas, his values. His political influence was nothing that could have concerned Roosevelt, Cummings, or the assistant attorney generals who directed the department's criminal investigations. But then, in 1935, he suddenly became a major celebrity, a media star.

Hoover had little say in the process that effected this transformation. Neither he nor his fast-assembling group of publicists were at first able to control the Bureau's new public image, which in many ways conflicted with Hoover's ideas about what the Bureau should represent. Nor was this glorification of the FBI planned or intended by Attorney General Cummings, whose law enforcement movement was an early casualty of the media's fascination with the FBI. Hoover's apotheosis was the work of the entertainment industry, specifically Hollywood's 1935 cycle of G-man movies.[46]

When the first G-man pictures arrived at the theaters in April 1935, Hoover's own publicists had been working on the FBI story for almost a year. Courtney Ryley Cooper, a flamboyant free-lance reporter from Kansas City, was the man most responsible for the

Bureau's new image. Cooper specialized in crime stories, and, early in 1933, *American Magazine* sent him to the Bureau to see if he could find something there. He came up with twenty-four stories about the Bureau, all but one published in *American Magazine*. He wrote three books on the FBI (one of them ghostwritten for Hoover) and four movies (again, with Hoover as the author of record).[47]

The stories Cooper wrote about Hoover's FBI gave the Bureau something more valuable than mere publicity. Cooper was clever and ambitious, and he quickly saw that there was more than one story packed away in the FBI files. He also saw, however, that if he simply wrote up the cases that Hoover and Tolson gave him, they would all be nothing more than versions of the same cops and robbers cliché. He needed something that would link the cases together, a "big story," that would make each incident part of an ongoing saga with a beginning, a middle, and, not an end, but a future. He would accomplish this by turning each case into an illustration of a specific Bureau technique or into a demonstration of the progress Hoover had made toward his goal of a reformed law enforcement profession. In this light, the Bureau provided enough material to last a lifetime.

Cooper's *American Magazine* features on the FBI, surrounded by formula adventures by Rafael Sabatini, Max Brand, Rex Stout, and Agatha Christie, established a standard approach to Bureau material that might be called the "FBI formula." Once perfected, the Bureau used this formula as a blueprint for its own publicity that projected an image for the Bureau in which the FBI's cases, techniques, and organization were all tied together in one tightly integrated package.[48]

Cooper's first story, "Getting the Jump on Crime," had a photo of a studious Hoover working at his desk. The essay began with a short description of a kidnapping in North Carolina and ended with an account of the nationwide manhunt for a fugitive killer. Each case was linked to all the others by a chain of information and command that connected the agents in the field to their commander in Washington, "the master detective," J. Edgar Hoover.

Cooper's FBI was a crime-fighting machine whose effectiveness, which verged on omnipotence, was completely the result of J. Edgar Hoover's leadership: his care in selecting and training his agents, his skill in leading them, the technical facilities he had assembled to interpret the evidence they collected. The feats of agent derring-do, the miracles of crime lab wizardry, the criminal convictions—Cooper showed that they proved the genius of the master detective behind the scenes who pulled all the wires, shuffled his agents' assignments, barked orders over the telephone, and flashed signals over the teletype.

Cooper made Hoover's agents conform to the image of the action detective of popular fiction, but with a crucial difference. Fictional detectives were lone wolves who solved their cases on their own; Hoover's agents were members of a team, and it was the organization that made them unstoppable. In Cooper's FBI formula, it was always J. Edgar Hoover and the entire FBI organization, never the individual agent, who got credit for the Bureau's successes.[49]

Cooper's "big story," the one that tied all the pieces together, was that Hoover's FBI was working to turn the country's fragmented, disorganized law enforcement into a cohesive, professional system. In Cooper's saga, every FBI case was a test of strength between crime and a newly invigorated criminal justice system guided by the spirit and intelligence of J. Edgar Hoover. The special agent, therefore, was a new type of American hero. Larger than life, he was "not an individual. Every officer of the Bureau of Investigation represented the full power of American Justice in 'getting his man.' "[50]

Some of Cooper's stories, like "Crime Trap,"[51] the second in the *American Magazine* series, listed Hoover as the author even though Cooper did the writing. Whether or not the stories were signed by Hoover, they had the Cooper trademark: They were fast-paced, irreverent, filled with slangy inside stuff about the underworld, gangsters, and gun molls who were "good lays"; they had a kind of "tough-guy" crime-writing style that was off-limits to Hoover's more tightly edited later writers.

Early in 1935, a revised version of Cooper's *American Magazine* articles appeared in hardcover as *Ten Thousand Public Enemies,*[52] the first and the most important book ever written about Hoover and the FBI. Cooper had by now perfected his FBI formula and used it to weave together everything he knew about the Bureau. The book had a coherent, fast-paced story with a vast cast of villains; the plot drew the reader into the action of the federal government's war on crime; and, of course, it had a hero: J. Edgar Hoover. *Ten Thousand Public Enemies* was a portrait of the FBI as a modern, scientific, irresistible crime detection machine, a disciplined army of expert scientific investigators gathering evidence for evaluation by the most advanced crime laboratories in the world, a law-enforcement agency led by Hoover, "the most feared man the underworld has ever known."

Cooper began the story of Hoover's FBI by presenting an iconoclastic view of the nature of American crime. Cooper's thesis was that

"organized crime, as imagined by the average person, with a super-criminal at its head, and underlings taking orders, is largely a myth.
. . . [T]he American citizen seems to possess a childlike faith in the theory that all crime is run by a guiding genius, and that if the brains of a plot be put in prison, then the problem of law enforcement is solved. The view is idiotic." The truth, Cooper claimed, was that crime "thrives because it has a foundation . . . composed of the fences, the bond salesmen, the doctors, the lawyers, the merchants, the automobile salesmen, the women confederates, the hideout owners, and a hundred and one other forms of a supporting background which lives on crime while crime thrives upon it."[53]

The theory that front-page criminals (Dillinger, et al.) could not exist without the support of a local criminal underworld had important implications for Hoover and the FBI. Instead of famous criminals reflecting on the competence of federal law enforcement (the FBI), Cooper was able to argue that big-time crime was the fault of the local police. It was because of inadequate local police forces that the Dillingers existed, not because there was a national crime organization as imagined by Hollywood and the pulp detective magazines.

The "army of crime," according to Cooper, was a grass-roots organization, and so the responsibility for fighting it also had to be at the grass-roots level. (This was an argument that helped Hoover avoid unwanted organized crime jurisdiction throughout his career.) The answer to the crime problem was not a national police force, but better local law enforcement.

Cooper had provided a justification for exactly the course Hoover had charted for the Bureau since the twenties. The Bureau, Cooper wrote, should maintain facilities that were beyond the capabilities of any local force, such as fingerprint files and crime laboratories. The FBI should offer statistical services to help local police understand their own problems in the context of national conditions and should direct nationwide searches once a criminal escaped local jurisdiction. But most of all, Hoover's Bureau should hold itself up as an example and an inspiration for the entire American law enforcement community.

Cooper's vision of the FBI's mission meant that for the Bureau to accomplish its task of professionalizing American law enforcement, it had to publicize itself, its procedures, and its goals. Cooper's thesis meant that the real significance of every FBI case was the contribution it could make toward persuading the public (and the police) to adopt the Bureau as the model for law enforcement: to learn its methods, accept its help, and follow its leadership. Cooper's ultimate weapon against crime was the image of the FBI itself as an incorruptible, irresistible, scientific organization of master detectives.

Neither Cooper nor Hoover ever proposed that the FBI itself should try to rid the country of crime. Their plan was that it provide the leadership for such a drive, which meant the FBI was doing its job only when it was in the news. Cooper's vision of the FBI's law enforcement role encouraged the Bureau to publicize its cases and to churn out books, movies, and radio and television shows about itself. To do its job the FBI had to chase headlines.[54]

While Hoover was careful, for obvious reasons, to reassure Cummings that he and the Bureau were loyal subordinates and knew their place,[55] Hollywood had no need to worry about stepping on bureaucratic toes. In 1935, when the movie industry turned the FBI and the gangster cases into popular entertainment, they took the formula that Hoover and Cooper had developed and radically altered it to suit the conventions and stereotypes of the adventure story. The result was the G-man formula, popular culture's own adaptation of Cooper's FBI formula.

Hollywood produced its 1935 "G-man cycle" of FBI pictures under circumstances that focused far more attention on these films than they deserved according to their merits as popular entertainment. The G-man movies were the last gangster pictures produced before violent crime films were outlawed under censorship regulations the industry adopted at the end of 1934. During 1935, the only gangsters on the screen were public enemies being gunned down by movie G-men, and at the end of the year not even FBI movies could feature armed gangsters. In movie history, the birth of the G-man marked the end of the gangster era.

Late in 1934, public pressure against movie sex and violence had forced the film industry to promise to abide by the Motion Picture Code drawn up in 1930, which had until then been largely ignored. The general intent of the code was to eliminate "harmful" film content; the specific target of the regulations was the violent crime film, the gangster movie. Nevertheless, the Production Code voted one last exemption from the antigangster rules so the studios could make a new kind of crime film "in the public interest" from a "new angle, namely Government activity in fighting crime." Through this temporary (until September 1935) exemption poured a whole cycle of movies glorifying Hoover's FBI: *Public Enemy's Wife; Public Hero Number One; Whipsaw; Mary Burns, Fugitive; Let 'Em Have It;* and *Show*

Them No Mercy. The most important of these was the film that turned Hoover and his Bureau into American legends, Warner Bros.'s *G-Men,* with James Cagney as the lead.[56]

G-Men rewrote history by giving its FBI director not only Hoover's historical role, but Homer Cummings's as well. In *G-Men* it was the FBI director, speaking for the entire nation, who appealed to Congress for the crime bills that Cummings had actually requested. Hollywood took the anticrime drive from Cummings, the Justice Department, and the New Deal, detached it from its political context, and gave it to the FBI. Hollywood's FBI was not part of the Justice Department. The G-men belonged to the nation as the grass-roots anticrime movement's own anticrime army.

G-Men redefined the FBI agent as the latest incarnation of a century-old stereotype in popular entertainment: the action detective hero who customarily works outside the cumbersome institutions of the government and the law. For Hollywood, the relationship between the FBI and the rest of the government was an annoying complication that obscured the Bureau's heroics and the public's hopes and fears. After Cagney's *G-Men,* the popular image of the FBI changed from a conventional government agency within the normal chain of command, carrying out policies determined by constitutional superiors, to a direct expression of the public's wrath against its enemies. The movie G-men and their director got their mandate, not from the attorney general, but from the nation itself, represented by an extraordinary session of Congress.

At the beginning of 1935, Homer Cummings was the undisputed head of American law enforcement, symbol of the New Deal's crackdown on crime. A year later he was in eclipse. J. Edgar Hoover was "Public Hero Number One," the national symbol of law and order. The rest of the Justice Department was in the FBI's shadow. In the popular view, the FBI was now an agency that stood apart from the rest of the government. Hollywood had made the Bureau a symbol of nonpolitical, militant national authority. Popular entertainment, with its enormous influence on public opinion, helped make J. Edgar Hoover and his FBI into an independent force on the national scene. In the future, anyone dealing with Hoover would have to deal with these new perceptions.

There was little Hoover could do at the beginning of the G-man craze to make the entertainment industry follow the FBI formula in its

adventure stories. Nevertheless, he regarded popular culture's glorification of the FBI with mixed emotions and worked hard, once he acquired the necessary leverage, to keep popular entertainment's FBI
in line with the image he was promoting for the Bureau.

For Hoover, the point of the FBI's cases was that they proved
he and the Bureau deserved to lead American law enforcement by
virtue of the professional training, careful organization, and scientific
methods he had instituted since taking over. His view was "there is
no magic in efficient law enforcement, no Sherlock Holmes theorizing
or fictional deduction, but . . . before science all things must fall,
including the ramparts of criminality."[57]

G-man entertainment did make a few gestures in the direction
of scientific crime fighting (dusting for fingerprints, plaster casts of
tire tracks), and it also celebrated the FBI's cases as part of a patriotic
war on crime. But beyond that the movie G-man was simply the
old free-wheeling action detective hero decked out in a new costume—
a three-piece suit. That was exactly the old-fashioned detective stereotype Hoover had tried to replace with the image of a professional,
scientifically oriented, investigative *organization.* "No single man in
the Federal Bureau of Investigation brought about any one of these
captures [of the public enemies]," Hoover told a youth group in 1936.
"It is truly a 'we' organization and not an 'I' organization."[58]

Hoover enjoyed the celebrity status he received because of the
G-man publicity, and he welcomed the opportunity fame gave him
to air his views on subjects that were no longer confined narrowly
to professional law enforcement. Nevertheless, his first reaction to
the movie industry's misinterpretation of the Bureau was to try to
counteract it by sponsoring his own carefully supervised FBI entertainment.

At this stage, it was out of the question for Hoover to think about
an official FBI movie. Instead, he tried to create an official FBI presence
in media that did not demand quite as much investment.

As early as 1935, Hoover was on the alert for chances to work
with cooperative publicists to promote the right popular image of
the FBI. His first opportunity came in July 1935, when he was visited
by Phillips H. Lord, the enormously successful producer, director,
and star of "Seth Parker," a radio program of New England music
and humor that had run every Sunday night on NBC since 1929.[59]
Lord had a new program called "Radio Crimebusters," and he had
an idea for a different format. He wanted to change the policemen
heroes of the show into FBI agents, and he wanted to base plots on
cases from the Bureau's files. Hoover liked the idea.

When Lord turned in his first script, Hoover was disgusted and told him it "just wouldn't do. . . . Our men don't act that way." He made Lord team up with Rex Collier and drew up a contract that gave Hoover, operating through Collier, complete control over the program. The show, which premiered on July 20, 1935, was called "G-Men." It ran until October 12, thirteen episodes in all. The first show was the Dillinger case, followed by the Osage Indian Case, Machine Gun Kelly, the Ma Barker Gang, Pretty Boy Floyd, and other famous kidnappings and robberies.[60]

Under Hoover's guidance, "G-Men" diverged even further from the usual action format until, by the final episode, it had turned into a static description of G-men at work in the crime labs. Hoover had replaced almost all action with careful analysis of clues and scientific examination of evidence. From the very first show, each episode was used as an opportunity to show how the FBI had turned teamwork and science into an awesome weapon against crime. Scenes were even invented just for this purpose: to prove that Dillinger knew he was doomed once the G-men got on his trail, "G-Men" has him going to a plastic surgeon who tells him he might die from the operation. "What's the difference?" says the bad man. "Ain't the G-Men hot on me?—I can't sleep.—They're everywhere.—Might's well croak now, if I can't get them off my trail."[61]

To eliminate the embarrassment of Anna Sage's tip, Hoover had Collier and Lord invent a solution that wrote her out of the case. Instead, agents identify Dillinger's ex-convict girlfriends through fingerprints left in one of his hideouts. This lets the Bureau put out an alert for a man in the company of "two blonds." The girls lead the agents to another abandoned hideout, and when they search the room they find movie stubs. These give them the idea of staking out the neighborhood movie theaters. There is also a pause for more scientific criminology: The agents listen to a medical lecture on the changes they can expect in Dillinger's appearance as a result of his plastic surgery.

By the time the show gets to the ambush at the Biograph, Collier and Lord have brought the FBI and Dillinger together without the "Woman in Red," without any luck, without any FBI foul-ups—and without any help from the local police. The radio G-men have caught Dillinger the way he should have been caught: by an inexorable, step-by-step application of FBI science and organization.

The problem with the show as entertainment was that Hoover's formula eliminated all the suspense, excitement, and personal heroism on which adventure stories depend. Despite the official endorsement, the show lasted only thirteen weeks at a time when the Bureau was enjoying its greatest popularity. According to Lord's daughter, the problem was a clash of personalities between two strong-willed individuals. For Lord, the FBI was merely a gimmick to add to the stock formula of crime and punishment he was a master at manipulating. Hoover's trips into the lab, the digressions about scientific crime fighting, slowed the action. As soon as he could, Lord cut himself loose from Hoover's control and turned "G-Men" into the classic adventure show "Gangbusters," with its violent action, frantic chases, and famous "coming on like gangbusters" intro: sirens howling in the night, then gunshots, then the sounds of prison (marching feet and clanking cell doors), and excited cries of: "Calling the Police. Calling the G-Men. Calling all Americans to war on the underworld."[62] That was the FBI of popular culture, it was not J. Edgar Hoover's.

Despite the Lord fiasco, Hoover went on to sponsor a "realistic" comic strip in 1936, which suffered the same fate as the radio show. Hoover started the comic strip when one of his favorite crime comics, "Secret Agent X-9,"[63] turned its private detective hero into an FBI agent—without Hoover's approval. After starting as a playboy private eye (served, like the Green Hornet, by an Oriental valet), X-9 became an FBI agent in 1936, working for a "Director" who was an exact double for Hoover: the same stocky build, the same natty three-piece suit with a puff of handkerchief in the pocket, the same wavy black hair. But Secret Agent X-9 was not an organization man, and his FBI was not a "we" organization. X-9 was a one-man Bureau of Investigation; the rest of the Bureau, even the director, were only a supporting cast. X-9 chose his own cases, analyzed his own clues, and dreamed up his own plans.

To counter this heresy, Hoover sponsored "War on Crime" (written, once again, by Rex Collier), which appeared on May 18, 1936, in forty-five papers across the country. It displayed a heroic portrait of J. Edgar Hoover over the caption, "Directing this round-up of kidnappers, extortionists, bandits and other predatory criminals is a keen-eyed, broad-shouldered lawyer, John Edgar Hoover, Federal Bureau of Investigation." Above Hoover's skull, as though emanating from his brain, floated the two classic images of the G-man: a white-garbed scientist peering through a microscope, and a stereotypical square-jawed special agent with his characteristic fedora.[64]

In "War on Crime" Hoover went a long way toward turning the FBI story into popular mythology, but he could not go far enough. He could not give his comic the one essential ingredient it needed to be successful—a real hero—without abandoning the "accurate" image he was promoting of the FBI as an organization of team players. There seemed to be no way Hoover could give popular culture a G-man hero without discarding the image of the Bureau as a team, as a "we" organization.

Unless, that is, *he* became that hero.

Late in 1936, the newspapers dropped "War on Crime," but the pulp magazines, popular ten-cent adventure monthlies, picked up the FBI. The first of the FBI pulps was *G-Men*, which began in October 1935 (and lasted eighteen years, until 1953). In December, another G-man pulp appeared, this one called *The Feds*. Before long, nearly every adventure pulp had FBI stories and crime-fighter tips from the Bureau, together with celebrity profiles of the director.

Each issue of *G-Men* had a "Public Enemies" comic, a "Famous Cases of J. Edgar Hoover" feature, and one of Hoover's speeches, taken from the public domain and passed off as an exclusive for the magazine. There was even a "G-Men Club," which pledged its members to

> Uphold the law and aid in its enforcement whenever possible. You must agree to back the Government Men in all their activities—and disseminate public opinion opposed to the gangster and the racketeer.
>
> Members of the G-MEN CLUB are expected to learn all they can about Department of Justice Activities and spread this knowledge on to others—discouraging crime by emphasizing the modern, scientific, sure-fire methods of today's manhunters.[65]

G-Men's main attraction was its FBI adventure novel, featuring the magazine's own G-man hero, Dan Fowler. Hoover made a customary appearance in these stories at the beginning, to send Fowler off on a mission to save the country from criminal conquest, and at the end, to pin another medal on Fowler, who idolized Hoover. The director's "crusading anger" reminded Fowler "of the righteous wrath of the prophets of old as they thundered out against the wickedness of Babylon and Gomorrah."[66]

G-Men's principal competition, *The Feds*, went even further in its buildup of Hoover as a national hero. Instead of Dan Fowler, "World's Greatest Man-Hunter," *The Feds* served up Hoover himself as "America's popular Public Hero No. 1" and "the world's leader in law enforcement circles." *The Feds*' version of the Dillinger story turned the case into a man-to-man battle between Hoover and the famous outlaw:

Here, as an example is John Dillinger. . . . His assets for a war against society are pistols and tommy guns, a dozen companions as vicious and reckless as himself, leadership of a sort, and an uncontrolled bitterness against humanity that expressed itself in the murder of helpless men.

Opposed to his petty arsenal is the weight of public opinion and the forces of government policing forces, headed by the Director of the Federal Bureau of Investigation, John Edgar Hoover.

Hoover is ten years older than Dillinger. He is a graduate of George Washington University and has practiced law before the Supreme Court. He is the keenest student of scientific criminology in the world.

To back up his knowledge and indefatigable efforts he has a highly trained personnel of six hundred agents scattered over the United States; a Bureau of Identification, technical laboratories, every asset that modern ingenuity can develop.

And John Dillinger, symbol of lawlessness, expects to best a foe like that![67]

Each issue of *The Feds* explained another phase of FBI work that "add[ed] to the prestige of John Edgar Hoover." This got the magazine a letter of thanks from Public Hero No. 1 himself, who was pleased by "such a comprehensive and true story of the activities of the Federal Bureau of Investigation. . . . It is one of the most comprehensive and intelligently written articles about the work of our Bureau which I have had the opportunity to read."[68]

Hoover's new image as the top G-man had to be backed up with some real action, and so in the mid-thirties he began to take to the field himself, elbowing aside his agents in some of the Bureau's biggest cases. In the 1920s, the law enforcement community had wanted Hoover to be a scientific manager. In the 1930s, a much larger audience wanted a detective hero, and so Hoover gave them the only man in the FBI who had the freedom of action demanded of an adventure hero: J. Edgar Hoover himself.

In the late thirties nobody, except a few incorrigible FBI-haters, thought it particularly strange to see a forty-year-old bureaucrat charging about the country waving a pistol and a pair of handcuffs. By fitting his image to the stereotype of the detective hero of popular culture, Hoover was giving the public what it expected of a detective hero: a G-man with the freedom from bureaucratic constraints of such action detectives as Secret Agent X-9 and Phillips H. Lord's Gangbusters.

The first, and most highly publicized, of the "Director's Cases" (as the Bureau promoted them) was Hoover's arrest of Alvin Karpis in 1936. Karpis was a member of the Ma Barker gang, and after FBI agents killed Ma Barker and her sons on January 16, 1936, Karpis was the last surviving big-name public enemy of the gangster era. With Dillinger, Floyd, Nelson, and the Barkers all dead, Karpis was Hoover's last chance to take on Public Enemy Number One face-to-face.

In November 1935, Karpis had robbed an Erie Railroad payroll. That made him front-page news, and Hoover passed the word throughout the Bureau that Karpis was "his" man. Hoover had his first chance to go after Karpis in March 1936 when he got word that the gangster was hiding in Hot Springs, Arkansas. Collecting his top assistants, including Tolson and publicity chief Louis B. Nichols, he chartered a plane to Arkansas; however, by the time he arrived, Karpis had fled, probably tipped off by local police.

On April 30, 1936, Hoover got a second chance. Again accompanied by Tolson and Nichols, Hoover took an overnight flight to New Orleans, where his agents had spotted the gangster. "I had told the boys how desperate he was," Hoover later wrote, "and had given them all a chance to back out if they wished to. Not one made a move. Then I told them they could put on bullet-proof vests if they wished to. Not one made a move."

As the G-men moved into position around Karpis's apartment, the gangster and a friend came out and got into their car. "I told the special agent who was driving to step on the gas," Hoover wrote,

> but just as we started a mounted policeman came gallumphing down the street on a big white horse, floppity-floppity-flop. We had to let him go by. He might not have understood what all the shooting was about and charged in on the wrong side. Then, as we started again, a child on a bicycle crossed our bow. We couldn't risk injuring the child, so we stopped again. Finally, we closed in on the gangsters and made the capture. At last, we had in our hands the most dangerous public enemy in the United States. "Put the cuffs on him, boys," I said.[69]

In a detail that inexplicably caught the public fancy, nobody had remembered to bring handcuffs, and so the G-men had to tie Karpis's hands with a necktie.

Hoover's critics claimed that he had gone after Karpis only because he had been taunted during the March 1936 Senate Appropriations Subcommittee Hearings by Senator Kenneth McKellar of Tennessee, who wanted to know why Hoover "wasn't out risking his neck" like the movie G-men. *Time* magazine said that Hoover had left the hearing room "boiling mad" and had passed the word in the Bureau that he was going to take charge of the Karpis arrest. The Bureau had its own explanation; it said that Karpis had personally challenged Hoover by threatening his life. "He sent word to Hoover that he intended to kill him, thereby avenging 'Ma' Barker's death. The threat was not an idle one to Hoover."[70]

The spectacle of the nation's leading lawman personally leading a raid against Public Enemy Number One produced such front-page headlines as HOOVER ORDERS STICK 'EM UP! Hoover told reporters that "the man who said he'd never be captured quit like the yellow rat he is and the rest of gangland is at heart. Why, we don't rank the yellow rats. It is you fellows who do that for us."[71] Kate Smith told her radio audience to send congratulations to Hoover, and thousands of letters poured into the Bureau.

Hoover went out into the field because his reputation as a detective hero now demanded that he prove his personal courage to the public and to his men. In some ways, Hoover's own cases were set-ups. He merely had to give the final orders in operations that had been brought one stroke shy of a successful conclusion—driving the golden spike, so to speak. Nevertheless, the situations were dangerous; they demanded bravery—but Hoover never lacked nerve. He had been put to the test in situations far more severe when he had to defend his antiradical programs against hostile federal judges and United States senators back in 1919 and 1920, when he was only twenty-five. Nobody who knew Hoover doubted his moral or physical courage.

Once Hoover had gotten a taste for this sort of thing it was hard to keep him in the office. On May 7, 1936, he flew to Toledo to lead a predawn raid on the hideout of Harry Campbell, another member of the Karpis-Barker gang. When newsmen asked Hoover if he had led the raid, he replied, "I did," but then modestly added that "it was a 'we' job, not an 'I' job." In December 1936, Hoover was finally able to get in on some shooting. While he was in New York on other business, his agents trapped a twenty-five-year-old bankrobber named Harry Brunette (and his wife) in an apartment on West 102nd Street. Hoover and Tolson rushed to the scene, where Hoover took command and ordered his men to open fire. The shooting lasted thirty-five minutes before a tear-gas bomb flushed out the Brunettes and set the building on fire. Hoover made the arrests himself, and the shoot-out earned him headlines—25 G-MEN LED BY HOOVER CAPTURE BANDIT ON WEST 102ND STREET—but also complaints. He had not informed the New York City police of his plans, and when they had arrived, attracted by the noise of the gunfire, he had sent them away to direct traffic. "The important thing," he insisted, "was not how or why Brunette was captured but that this embryo Karpis or Dillinger is in custody and that the taxpayers got what they paid for, the apprehension of criminals."[72]

Hoover's most spectacular display of personal heroics was his capture of Louis "Lepke" Buchalter, the head of the New York City protection racket that virtually ruled the garment industry, and of the nationwide mob execution service known as Murder, Incorporated. In 1937, Lepke went into hiding, which led to the so-called Big Heat, constant police harassment of the underworld to force Lepke's associates to turn him in. Finally, Lepke convinced himself that a deal had been worked out with the FBI to protect him from the New York State attorney general, Thomas Dewey, who had obtained an indictment of Lepke on charges carrying the death penalty. Lepke heard that federal charges would be limited to one narcotics offense carrying a ten-year sentence, but only if he surrendered to the FBI. The arrangement seemed plausible because Dewey was being promoted as a likely presidential opponent against FDR in 1940, and it was possible that Roosevelt was using Hoover to dim Dewey's reputation as the nation's leading racket buster.

The break came when columnist Walter Winchell broadcast an appeal to Lepke to turn himself in. Winchell got an anonymous call that Lepke would surrender, but to eliminate gunplay he wanted only Hoover and Winchell present. Winchell knew how to put together a good story. He called Hoover and arranged for him to be alone on Fifth Avenue and Twenty-eighth Street at 10:15 P.M. on August 24, 1939. When Winchell pulled up in his borrowed car exactly on schedule, Hoover got in and Winchell introduced him to the other passenger. "Mr. Hoover," Winchell said, "this is Lepke." "Glad to meet you," Lepke said hopefully.[73] Actually, Lepke was mistaken, and there had been no deal. The federal government convicted Lepke on the narcotics charge, then turned him over to Dewey, who convicted him of murder and electrocuted him in 1944.

An action hero is a celebrity, so Hoover's name began to appear regularly in the columns of reporters like Walter Winchell and Ed Sullivan. His diet, hobbies, and sports were all covered by the papers, and he learned to live like a star at the private cottages of rich friends in Florida and California. He did his drinking at the Stork Club and his vacationing at Palm Beach. Newspapers carried pictures of him fishing, playing tennis, hefting a machine gun, sitting at ringside at championship prizefights. He lost his appearance of nervous energy and his face gained an expression of solid self-confidence.

Hoover's celebrity status freed him to speak his mind openly and aggressively for the first time since Central High and Sunday school. He had started acting like a tough guy after 1935, and began talking like one. His speeches still stressed the Bureau's scientific expertise (he would never stop talking about that), and he still treated crime as a challenge to governmental authority, but he also began to emphasize an interpretation of crime as a threat to the moral order. More than merely a shift in rhetoric, this was an important indication of a change in his conception of his own leadership role.

Hoover and Cummings had earlier described Dillinger as a public enemy at war with the government and people of the United States. Now he began to use criminals as symbols of moral failure. In 1936, he told a youth group that

> John Dillinger was nothing but a beer-drinking plug-ugly, who bought his way from hideout to hideout, being brave only when he had a machine gun trained upon a victim and the victim at his mercy. When Dillinger finally was brought to bay, he was not a hero—he was not a Robin Hood, he was not a romantic motion picture figure but only a coward who did not know how to shoot, except from ambush.[74]

Pretty Boy Floyd now was "a skulking, disheveled, dirty, ill-clothed hobo and, as such, he was hunted down to his end, as a hoodlum, an ego-inflated rat."[75]

After 1935, Hoover's speeches almost always denounced the morals of lawbreakers. "These persons of the under-filth are not simply poor boys or moral invalids as the super-sentimentalist would have us believe," he told the DAR. "They are marauders who murder for a headline, rats crawling from their hide-outs to gnaw at the vitals of our civilization."[76] He told a young audience that

> There is no romance in crime and there is no romance in criminals. We have passed through an era in which ill-advised persons and sentimental sob-sisters have attempted to paint the desperate law violators of America as men and women of romance. They are the absolute opposite. They are rats, vermin, regurgitating their filth to despoil the clean picture of American manhood and womanhood. They sink deeper and deeper into a mire of viciousness which inevitably leads to filth in mind, filth in living, filth in morals and in bodily health. They travel steadily downward until at last they are no more than craven beasts.[77]

When his writers in the Crime Records Division did not give him the sort of hard-boiled rhetoric he wanted, Hoover berated them for their "namby-pamby" style. He did not hesitate to rip their speeches to shreds to make them sound the way he talked.

Hoover's emphasis now shifted from the criminal's acts to his intentions, from his overt violation of the law to the state of mind the violation indicates. Now it was the criminal's character, not the crime, that made him a public enemy, in some ways a reversion to Hoover's tendency of 1919–1920 to judge aliens by their beliefs and attitudes rather than their acts.

Hoover now demanded ostracism not just for criminals, but also for anyone who expressed any sympathy for criminals. In an echo of his attacks on the "parlor Bolsheviki" of the Red Scare days, he called on the public to "look upon all persons who designedly or otherwise help the criminal as being enemies to society." He was "proud to be termed a member of the so-called machine gun school of criminology," because "I shall be in a better position to face my fellow man with a clear conscience than members of the 'cream-puff school of criminology,' whose efforts daily turn loose upon us the robber, the burglar, the arsonist, the killer, and the sex degenerate."[78]

It is possible to detect in Hoover's shift in emphasis from a criminal's acts to his immoral values a movement out of the realm of conventional politics into what some have called antipolitics or status politics—the resentment felt by groups losing their once unquestioned social superiority. "True," Hoover told an audience in 1936, "they are dressed as we are dressed. They live as we live and often upon a better scale owing to the rich rewards of their so-called profession, but their standards of life are those of pigs in a wallow, their outlook that of vultures regurgitating their filth."[79]

The difference Hoover saw here was not so much between the law and lawlessness, as between respectability and indecency. "The law alone cannot keep people decent. It is an influence within themselves that makes their obedience to law voluntary. Crime multiplies not because people no longer respect law but because they no longer respect respectability." Crime, he said, "exists largely because of a lack of discipline." He defined "the criminal's code" as "I will take what I want when I want it."[80]

Hoover's role as scientific manager since 1924 had for a long time kept the moralist in him in check; now it burst forth to reveal the intense hatred of immorality that was also part of the progressive spirit. But while progressives, and Hoover himself even more than most, had earlier scapegoated the ethnic alien as the source of social disorder, now he denounced the moral alien, the law breaker, and not just as a criminal but as a sinner.

At last, Hoover was again able to speak out in defense of the morality of Seward Square and Old First Church, to insist that "social problems cannot be differentiated from moral problems. They are inseparable." Again he had a captive audience; again he had a text (his latest criminal case) to use as a basis for a sermon on the need to defend morality against the assaults of those who rejected the standards of respectability. In a 1940 speech, he called for "a return to the God of our fathers and most vigorous defense against the minions of godlessness and atheism, which are allied with the powers of destruction that today threaten America's future." He was sick "of the maunderings of fanatics and tuffet-heads, who believe that the way to educate the new youth is to allow the new youth to do anything it pleases. . . . We need a rebuilding of the foundations which made this Nation the greatest in all history, bulwarks formed of more staple materials than those of apathy, selfishness or indulgence."[81]

Hoover was no abstract thinker given to philosophical speculation, but his speeches of the late thirties on the causes of crime contained a summary of his basic principles of criminology. Crime, for Hoover, was not a product of social conditions or historical events; it was instead rooted in human nature: "We will have crime so long as the basic passions and instincts of human nature survive."[82] On another occasion, he explained that

> None of us can hope that lawlessness can be completely eradicated from the fabric of civilization. The warfare between crime and the forces of law and order has been the topic of narration and writing since prehistoric man learned to speak and write. Philosophies and religions center upon a basic theory concerning the struggle between the forces of good and evil.[83]

By the end of the thirties, Hoover saw criminal law as a branch of ethics, and that, in turn, as a part of natural law. His thinking had become fundamentally *antipolitical;* and crime was for him simply the principle of evil revealed in human form:

> Violation of the fundamental principles of sanitation and hygiene ultimately means incarceration or ostracism by reason of ill health. Violation of the laws of economics means virtual bondage. The infraction of the laws of morality, if not forfeiting health, will surely mar character and decency. Excepting nature's catastrophes, the great disasters of the past

50 years have all sprung from a failure to adhere to lawful authority. The World War was precipitated by a murder and economic gangsterism. The economic crash of 1929 followed a violation of basic economic laws.[84]

He rejected the criminal's political or historical context as having any relevance in understanding the nature of crime. He blamed the country's perilous situation in 1939 on a failure to study and understand eternal laws of nature.

Hunger, communism or the fear of foreign invasion . . . are but the consequences of lawlessness. . . . Hunger could not exist but through violation of economic laws and fundamental principles of social justice. Communism has as its basic principle the overthrow of the laws of our democratic social order, and it is rooted in the slimy wastes of lawlessness. In times like these we must of course be prepared against foreign invasions, but at the same time we must not forget that the basic cause leading to the decline of all civilizations in the past has been debauchery of law and order. . . . The major task of society today is to insure that law and order shall reign supreme.[85]

Hoover was not normally given to abstract speculation about fundamental questions of politics, but, in 1939, he attempted to define the difference between democracy and totalitarianism:

The pages of history are punctuated by the rise and fall of dictators. They are of three types. In the first instance, there are those who further their own selfish purposes and greed by operating behind a smoke screen of pseudo benevolence. Then there are the dictators of the gangster racketeering type who rule by might and even create ideologies to serve their own purposes and justify their own misdeeds. . . .

    The third type of dictator is the very antithesis of those which I have mentioned. It is the dictatorship of the people, for the people and by the people. In the United States we call it Democracy—the dictatorship of the collective conscience of our people. We could just as well call it Justice, for America stands for that.[86]

Hoover's definition of "Democracy" and "Justice" as the "dictatorship of the collective conscience" offers an extraordinary insight into his political ideas. Whether or not any of Hoover's ghostwriters were familiar with the background of the term "collective conscience" in the works of Emile Durkheim, Hoover could not have chosen an expression further removed from the historic American concept of constitutionalism. The phrase indicated an agreement with the right-thinking majority's impatience with constitutional limitations on its power. As age and influence heightened Hoover's sense of infallibility his Bureau would come to see itself as the moral, as well as legal, guardian of the nation, entitled to take whatever action it thought necessary to neutralize and destroy enemies of the moral order: in other words, it would act to enforce the "dictatorship of the collective conscience."

Roosevelt and J. Edgar Hoover would seem to be an ill-matched pair, and yet they worked together efficiently and effectively. In terms of background, personality, and temperament the two men had little in common: Roosevelt, the Harvard-educated patrician from upstate New York, his administration a magnet for the sort of liberals who instinctively detested (and were detested by) Hoover, married to a woman Hoover would have considered the very epitome of the "parlor pink"; Hoover with his passion for order and control, Roosevelt with his "technique of fuzzy delegation," his love of "freshness and vitality."[87]

Roosevelt liked Hoover, however. In 1940, when Attorney General Robert Jackson suggested to Roosevelt that he appoint Solicitor General Francis B. Biddle to take over the Justice Department after Jackson moved on to the Supreme Court, FDR's question was, "How does Francis get along with Hoover?" That same year, Biddle brought Hoover to the White House because an FBI agent had been caught tapping the phone of Harry Bridges of the Longshoremen's Union. "F.D.R. was delighted; and, with one of his great grins, intent on every word, slapped Hoover on the back when he had finished. 'By God, Edgar, that's the first time you've been caught with your pants down!' " To Biddle, this showed that "the two men liked and understood each other."[88]

Roosevelt's method of governing was actually suited to Hoover's temperament, despite their differences in managerial styles. Roosevelt wanted action, had promised the nation action, needed men who could provide action. And Hoover was a man of action. Give him an idea of what was needed, indicate the broad policy, and Hoover would fill in the details without any further guidance. In contrast to the generally improvisational New Deal style, Hoover's programs were not only comprehensive, they were readily expandable to meet future contingencies. That was how Hoover had operated under Palmer, and it was his method during the twenties, though on a miniature scale. Now Roosevelt let Hoover make the nation the laboratory for his theories of organization and leadership. Roosevelt gave Hoover an opportunity to do the work for which his whole prior career had prepared him, work that called forth all of his awesome drive and ambition. It is little wonder that Hoover responded to Roosevelt with gratitude and loyalty.

Roosevelt was by far the more worldly and tolerant of the two, but he, like Hoover, was capable of extreme cruelty and vindictiveness toward anyone he suspected of disloyalty toward himself or toward the nation. Roosevelt was able to make finer distinctions between dissent and disloyalty than Hoover, but neither man was overly concerned with the civil liberties of his enemies. To say this is simply to recognize that both men were deadly serious politicians, fully capable of almost any measure they thought necessary to maintain their hold on power.

There were also basic similarities between Roosevelt and Hoover in their general outlook on the world, although these are obscured by the conventional association of Roosevelt with political and economic liberalism and Hoover with conservatism. It would be more accurate to see Roosevelt as fundamentally uncommitted to any political or economic ideology, willing to adopt whatever strategy seemed most likely to produce national unity and survival. Likewise, Hoover was rarely concerned with economic ideology, though his imagination was not elastic enough to be able to visualize a situation in which national unity could survive a fundamental change in traditional social arrangements or moral values. Both men were instinctively on the alert for any threats to national security, and so both were far in advance of the public in recognizing the danger of the international situation of the thirties—Roosevelt because of his keen understanding of power politics (and insight into the intentions of Germany and Japan), Hoover because he was eternally suspicious of foreigners and radicals. Roosevelt expected war to come and knew he had to have a domestic security system in place when hostilities broke out, and in Hoover he had a man who knew how to install and run such a system.

Roosevelt's style of governing was also well suited to winning Hoover's loyalty. FDR liked to deal directly with the official who would be in operational charge of a policy, even if that meant keeping a cabinet member in the dark about activities in his own department. That was how Roosevelt dealt with the State Department, where Undersecretary of State Sumner Welles was closer to the president than Secretary of State Cordell Hull. With an attorney general of absolute loyalty like Homer Cummings there was no need for the conspiratorial manner in which Roosevelt often gave Hoover his assignments: the private meetings at the White House or on the presidential train, the special missions that cut the faithful and compliant Cummings out of the chain of command. With his shrewd insight into human nature, Roosevelt may have seen that these shows of confidence were a sure way of turning Hoover into his personal vassal. Francis Biddle, Roosevelt's attorney general from 1941 until 1945, learned from Harlan Stone that Hoover had a "complex character: if Hoover trusted you he would be absolutely loyal; if he did not, you had better look out."[89] Hoover did trust Roosevelt, and so he was absolutely, even excessively, loyal to the president.

It is not hard to imagine the Roosevelt charm turning Hoover into a loyal follower. But there was also much else in Hoover to appeal to such a connoisseur of personalities as Roosevelt. Hoover was an unusual type. Francis Biddle described how Hoover looked when he was on a case, his eyes "bright, his jaw set, excitement quivering around his nostrils."[90] Roosevelt, too, might have enjoyed that spectacle, he certainly found it interesting, perhaps even amusing.

The personal relationship between Hoover and Roosevelt erased any limit set by custom or law to the requests the president might make of the FBI director, or to the favors the director might do for the president. Hoover passed along political gossip about Roosevelt's friends and enemies, information about the plans of possible election opponents, and background material that might spare the president involvement in embarrassing situations. For his part, Roosevelt was not reluctant to ask Hoover to trace any piece of information he might need; he asked him to run down the source of unfriendly rumors or news stories and to fill him in on the background of citizens who wrote him letters or opposed his policies. Hoover's memos to Roosevelt were usually directed to Appointments Secretary Erwin "Pa" Watson or FDR's wartime advisor (and former relief director and Secretary of Commerce), Harry Hopkins. The range of Hoover's communications to Roosevelt was so wide that it is clear Hoover was willing to do anything the president asked, might ask, or, in Hoover's opinion, should have asked.

Hoover's relationships with Roosevelt's attorneys general were not uniformly good, but in no case were they impossible. He worked best of all with Cummings, who was an easy man to get along with. One reason Hoover had a comparatively free hand with the FBI after 1935 was that Cummings had to devote himself to the administration's attempt, through the "Court Packing" Bill, which Cummings drafted and which he unsuccessfully tried to move through Congress, to circumvent the Supreme Court's opposition to the New Deal's programs. The defeat of this bill on July 20, 1937, the worst blunder of Roosevelt's presidency, destroyed Cummings's political influence. Cummings stayed on for two more years as attorney general (he submitted his resignation in November 1938 to take effect in January 1939), but the defeat destroyed what was left (after Hollywood) of his painfully won position as the leader of American law enforcement, leaving a power vacuum for Hoover.[91]

After Cummings left, Hoover was closest to Francis Biddle, the attorney general from 1941 until 1945, and somewhat more distant from Frank Murphy (1939–1940) and Robert Jackson (1940–1941). Jackson, according to some reports, found Hoover a difficult person to work with, and, therefore, left him alone. Biddle drew Hoover into his confidence by including him in department planning sessions and by regularly meeting with him for lunch. It is likely that all three men, aware that Hoover's close relationship with the president had existed long before their own arrivals at the Justice Department, regarded Hoover more as the president's problem (if he was a problem) than theirs.[92]

Hoover did not neglect the management of the Bureau while he enjoyed his popular success and his political influence with the president. His major innovation during the thirties was the National Police Academy, which he started on July 26, 1935, with twenty-three police officers in the first class. The academy grew out of a joint recommendation by Hoover and Cummings at the December 1934 crime conference. This training school had the practical political effect of creating a strong constituency for Hoover and the FBI within local police leadership throughout the country, since an academy diploma was a powerful aid to a police officer's advancement.[93]

The National Police Academy was the capstone in the progressive national law enforcement edifice Hoover had planned in the twenties, and which Cummings had made Justice Department policy in 1933. The FBI would maintain a full range of scientific facilities for the use of local police forces, the National Police Academy would instruct local police in the use of those facilities, and the *FBI Law Enforcement Bulletin* would keep the police up to date in the latest Bureau-approved advances in scientific criminology. Meanwhile, the Bureau and Hoover would provide all of American law enforcement with a glamorous, wholly admirable image. When the idea of police training academies spread to local police forces a few years later, the Bureau worked to "dominate the training school situation" by sending speakers and specialists to participate in training sessions throughout the country.[94]

The size of the Bureau increased steadily throughout Roosevelt's administration: from 391 agents in 1933 to 898 in 1940—just before the enormous increase in war work throughout 1940 led to a doubling of the Bureau that year, and a redoubling the next year (to nearly 3,000 agents in 1942). The Bureau's wartime peak was almost 4,900 agents.[95]

Hoover's managerial style combined authoritarianism with collegiality. He controlled the FBI through an Executive Conference, at first consisting of his two assistant directors, Tolson and Nathan, and the heads of the divisions they supervised (who initially had the rank of inspector). Later, all the members of the conference were of assistant director rank or higher (Tolson, the assistant to the director, acted as chairman of the conference).

Hoover ruled these top officials with an iron hand. Field agents who felt oppressed by the Bureau's strict discipline had it easy compared to the constant scrutiny and abuse Hoover's executives had to endure from their perfectionist director. Hoover's demand that his executives accept responsibility for all errors committed by their divisions had them constantly apologizing, excusing, and explaining, and kept their personnel files filled with letters of censure. All policy proposals as well as the progress of all important cases were summarized in memoranda that were circulated throughout the conference and initialed by all members. Tolson would attach his own or the conference's policy recommendation, which would be either accepted or rejected by Hoover, who would also add his personal reactions to the memo in blue ink marginalia (only he used that color). Eventually, all members of the conference grew intimately familiar with Hoover's convictions, his attitudes, even his passing whimsies. His marginal comments often took the form of moral or patriotic exhortations, and gradually his subordinates adopted the same style, so that Hoover's moral earnestness became established as an expected corporate style.

What made life particularly difficult for these executives was Hoover's unrelenting scrutiny of the smallest detail of Bureau operations. All communications from the field were addressed "To the Director" so that they all passed across Hoover's desk. The same limitless energy Hoover devoted in 1919 and 1920 to producing a flood of paper was now devoted to scrutinizing the enormous paper flow of the Bureau. While Hoover's managers were expected to be able to comment on the largest policy decisions in the Bureau, they could also expect to have the smallest details of their operations reviewed by the director. For example, in November 1934, Hoover complained to Tolson that instructors at the training school for new agents were not emphasizing

> the necessity for strict discipline upon the part of all employees of the Bureau at all times. . . . I think it imperative, with the growing size of our Division, that strict discipline be maintained and that the new men particularly realize that we mean business, and that this is not a so-called college with the accouterments that generally go with college spirit.[96]

Despite their intimate friendship, Hoover did not hesitate to chew out Tolson when he felt it was deserved. He scolded Tolson because there had been two cases of athlete's foot in the employees' gym; he also charged the coaches with giving sedentary employees physical training that was too vigorous, and claimed the boxing matches were getting out of hand, that sooner or later there was going to be a serious injury. "I fully realize that all persons attending the instruction classes are advised that if the exercise is too vigorous they need not take the same, but there is a moral persuasion that exists in all such matters which we cannot overlook." Hoover even held Tolson responsible when the clock was slow in his official car, and when the windshield wipers failed to work.[97] Still, there is no sign that this ever affected the personal relationship between the two men. Until Tolson's health failed in the sixties, it seemed to be one of his functions to take care of "the Boss" on the job, and to accept abuse whenever the Boss was out of temper.

Hoover was a careful editor, and painstakingly reviewed and revised his speeches and the articles that were published under his name. He demanded that all copy that reached his desk be perfect; on one occasion he told Tolson that "I cannot take upon myself the duties of revamping [material for the *Law Enforcement Bulletin*]. It would be much easier for me to write it originally in the first place than to have the material sent to me and then expect me to go over it in detail and rearrange it." Anything having to do with the Bureau image received his special attention. He demanded to be notified whenever important persons appeared to take the headquarters tour, and he was furious whenever a VIP got away without a personal greeting and handshake. In 1935, a slip-up in this area (the wife of news broadcaster H. V. Kaltenborn had taken the headquarters tour without

Hoover finding out) had him complaining to Tolson that "it would be entirely possible for Mrs. Franklin Roosevelt to come down, casually join one of the tours, give her name, and be shown through, and the Director's office not even be informed that she had seen the bureau's work and activities."[98]

In November 1935, he berated all his top executives (Harold Nathan, Clyde Tolson, Hugh Clegg, John J. Edwards, and Edward A. Tamm), telling them, "I am getting somewhat weary and annoyed by the somewhat indifferent and nonchalant attitude taken by the Assistant Directors in handling their respective responsibilities. I am looking to a marked improvement in this condition."[99]

In 1935, the executives were censured for letting word of their deliberations leak out to the Bureau, leading personnel to anticipate the outcome before Hoover had made a final decision. He said that this embarrassed him; he warned that the lack of confidentiality also inhibited free discussion among the members of the Executive Conference.[100]

The inevitable effect of Hoover's terrorizing his aides was that he deprived himself of their independent judgment. Hoover himself complained about this, blasting the Executive Conference, in 1935, for acting as "rubber stamps" instead of "contributing ideas, suggestions and criticisms to the efficient and successful operation of the Bureau." He complained that he did not submit memos to them just to be checked for "typographical errors or for form, but the matter of policy is to be considered also." If that was all they were going to do, he told them, he could save on their $5,000 salaries by replacing them with $1,400 clerks. He then demanded that each member submit to him a memorandum stating any disagreement he might have with standing Bureau policies, admitting that "it seems rather silly to have to specifically request this kind of a statement from a presumably intelligent executive force."[101]

As a reward for coping with the high pressure demands at headquarters, Hoover brought his executives along when he went into the field on big cases in the late thirties. Afterward, he placed commendations for bravery in their files. After the Brunette arrest, he gave Tolson an official commendation: "[C]haracteristic of your reputation in the FBI, you performed all duties assigned to you on that occasion in a complete and efficient manner. You were subjected in the course of this raid to great physical danger, and you measured up to the high standard expected of all men of the Federal Bureau of Investigation."

Another arrest won Tolson a letter from Hoover that "the courage and fearlessness displayed by you were far beyond the ordinary call of duty."[102]

No one, aside from Hoover, was more responsible for the Bureau's public relations triumphs during the thirties, and its continued success over the years, than Hoover's number-three man and all-around troubleshooter, Louis B. Nichols, who joined the Bureau in July 1934 (two weeks before the Dillinger shooting) and retired in 1957 to take a $150,000 job as executive vice president and member of the board of directors of Schenley Industries (headed by longtime Hoover friend Lewis S. Rosenstiel). Nichols was in charge of Bureau public relations from the time he took over the Research Division on August 6, 1937, until he retired.[103]

A powerfully built man with an aggressive personality and a forceful, even bullying, manner, Nichols handled, in his phrase, the Bureau's "grief," which meant that he had to go toe-to-toe with the country's most powerful newsmen and politicians to protect the Bureau's interests. Within the Bureau's executive offices, however, Hoover's discipline reduced Nichols to a servile state. Nichols's file bulged with insulting letters of censure from Hoover, and his own memos to Hoover were filled with the most abject flattery of his boss. In 1935, while working as a writer in the Bureau's publicity office (the Crime Records Unit), Nichols wrote Hoover that "I would also like to suggest that all Agents be furnished with copies of the addresses you make from time to time. As I informed you last week, I consider your utterances on the occasion of the Police School Graduation one of the greatest experiences of my life. I sincerely believe if a copy of those remarks could be placed in the hands of every Agent in the field, the already deep felt pride in the Bureau would be increased." In 1937, Nichols arranged for Hoover to receive an honorary doctorate from his own school, Kalamazoo College, touting Hoover to the college president as "a man of destiny." When he did something wrong he would write groveling letters of apology to Hoover with such sentiments as "I regret my own shortcomings in the handling of the [deleted] case, there is no excuse and I can assure you that the matter of being stampeded by arraignments will not influence me again." His willingness to flatter Hoover with extravagant declarations of loyalty became the subject of Bureau folklore: One legend had him telling Hoover that if he had known beforehand about an uncomplimentary story in the *Washington Post*, he would have "gone over there and hurled myself bodily into the presses." Hoover is supposed to have commented, "Nick may not be very smart, but nobody can doubt his loyalty."[104]

Nichols was putting in thirty-five to forty hours of overtime each week, and this led to a physical and nervous collapse during the summer of 1936. Even while recuperating he protected Hoover's interests. A chance acquaintance told him that he had heard Hoover was jealous of any agent who got too much publicity. Nichols wrote Hoover that he had "promptly told [deleted] that this was nothing but a plain ordinary damned dirty lie, that you had no personal desire for publicity, and that every day you were besieged by newspaper reporters, and if you really did desire publicity you had ample opportunity to receive plenty of it."[105]

Bitter experience had taught Hoover that the greatest threat to his success, even survival, was his agents' potential for inefficiency, disobedience, or corruption—hence the complex administrative system he created with its reports, checks, cross checks, and constant inspections. In later years, agents wearily complained that headquarters acted as though they, and not the criminals, were the Bureau's real enemies. They were right. Lack of control over Bureau agents and their auxiliaries had led to the destruction of Hoover's antiradical program of the twenties. Corrupt agents like Gaston Means, and the inability of headquarters to control agents working for distant U.S. attorneys had destroyed the Bureau of Burns and Daugherty. As long as Hoover maintained absolute control over the Bureau, he felt he was safe, and so was his Bureau; as soon as he lost control they would both be in mortal danger.

The enormous public interest in the FBI in the late thirties posed a new challenge to Hoover's power over his men. Advertisers, the news media, and popular entertainment needed celebrities and heroes, and so his agents attracted offers of endorsements, publishing contracts, and roles in the movies and on radio. Hoover was aware that if his agents became famous, their public recognition might protect them from his discipline. The opportunity fame would give them to quit the Bureau and cash in on the Bureau's popularity would also weaken Hoover's authority, besides cheapening the Bureau's image. Finally, an all-star FBI threatened Hoover's doctrine that the Bureau's strength lay precisely in its teamwork, the interchangeability of its parts; that an FBI case was never an individual contest between a public enemy and an individual G-man, but was between a doomed, isolated, and degenerate rebel and the entire FBI, representing all of American law enforcement.

For all these reasons, Hoover gradually established a policy that prohibited individual agents from speaking in the name of the Bureau or, indeed, developing any sort of a public reputation. Moreover, any agent who left under less than the best of circumstances, or who conducted himself after leaving in a way that displeased Hoover, could count on being pursued by the wrath of the Bureau and having Hoover destroy his chances for a successful post-FBI career.

This was graphically illustrated when the most famous field agent in the Bureau's history, Melvin Purvis, was forced to resign from the Bureau. This was quite a fall from grace; only a year before the resignation, Hoover had written "Dear Melvin" that

> I wanted to write and repeat to you my expressions of pleasure and commendation which I tried to convey to you last night. The shooting and killing of John Dillinger by the Agents of your office under your admirable direction and planning are but another indication of your ability and capacity as a leader and an executive. I am particularly pleased, because it confirms the faith and confidence which I have always had in you. While the expressions of the public are most laudatory, you and I both know how fickle such may be, but I did want you to know that my appreciation of the success with which your efforts have met in this case is lasting and makes me most proud of you. . . . I was glad that the Division could "get" Dillinger and "get" him itself. This would not have been accomplished had it not been for your unlimited and never-ending intelligence, and I did want you to know how much I appreciate it.[106]

Shortly after the killing of Floyd, Hoover wrote him a similar letter of commendation, but during the hunt for Nelson, Hoover pulled Purvis off the case and the harassment began. Hoover sent inspectors to Chicago to look over Purvis's office, which they reported was in such bad shape that Purvis should be transferred to a smaller field office. They said he was "extremely temperamental, egotistical and . . . has been giving more time to his own personal interests and to his social activities than he had been giving to the office which he represents." He was accused of tolerating an agent in his office who "wears a so-called mustache consisting of about seven or eight hairs on his lip which are waxed and curled and give him an outlandish or clownish appearance."[107]

Hoover demanded Purvis respond to a report that there had been "a party during which you became intoxicated and brandished a gun threatening certain guests at the party." Purvis replied that the report was "an unmitigated and unadulterated lie." Hoover had Harold Nathan investigate the story, but it could not be substantiated.[108]

After many similar instances of harassment, Purvis finally resigned from the Bureau on July 10, 1935. There was great concern in the department about the public's reaction to the resignation. Cummings told Hoover to come up with a better official reaction than "No Comment," because that made it seem as if there had been a fight in the department. Hoover phoned Purvis to find out what reasons he was giving for leaving; he was reassured when Purvis said he had told reporters that he simply wanted to pursue business opportunities. Hoover put out a statement that "there was not the slightest basis for any impression of any lack of harmony or dissatisfaction upon his part or upon the part of the Bureau."[109]

At this point, Purvis had many attractive opportunities open to him; when he finally understood that Hoover had soured on him he had decided to accept some of them before interest in him cooled down. There were publishing offers and Hollywood studios that wanted him as a technical advisor and writer. Advertising agencies wanted him to sponsor products. (He appeared in ads for Dodge autos and Gillette razors.) As a lawyer, he could count on a good start in private practice anywhere in the country, particularly in Chicago. What he did not realize was how angry Hoover really was.

Purvis began his post-FBI career by writing a series of articles about the Bureau for *Redbook.* Hoover monitored these articles closely by getting advance copies from Bureau sources. Purvis subsequently turned them into a book, *American Agent,* [110] which was actually a highly favorable treatment of the Bureau but was described to Hoover by his aides as being "implicitly" critical of the FBI because it gave some credit to the local police and did not mention Hoover by name.

When Hoover learned that the Motion Picture Producers and Distributors of America (which handled censorship for the industry) was planning to hire Purvis, he told them he would "look with displeasure, as a personal matter," at their hiring the ex-agent; if the studios needed technical advisors, he would furnish agents to them "free of charge." He had the head of his Los Angeles FBI office keep an eye on Purvis's contacts with movie producers; whenever Purvis was close to landing a job, the Bureau would move in with offers of more authoritative (and free) help. When Santa Anita racetrack offered Purvis a security job, Tolson notified the track's management that if the track hired him, the Bureau would break off all contact with it, "inasmuch as he is persona non grata with the Bureau."[111]

Purvis eventually was hired in 1936 as announcer for a children's radio show called "Junior G-Men," which also had a club with badges, manuals, and other secret agent props. From there he moved to *Post Toasties* in 1937 to take over "Inspector Post's Junior Detective Corps," which was renamed "The Melvin Purvis Law and Order Patrol."[112]

Purvis's Junior G-Men Clubs infuriated Hoover, who wrote General Foods to insist they identify Purvis as an *ex*-agent of the FBI. The Bureau received many complaints in the thirties about children, and even some adults, who tried to use their Junior G-Man badges as authority for free-lance law enforcement. When the Michigan State Police arrested a Carl E. Neumann for carrying a concealed weapon, Neumann claimed he was an agent of the Department of Justice, and produced a Melvin Purvis badge as proof.[113]

Even before Purvis left the Department, Hoover had begun to rewrite history to replace Purvis with the martyred Sam Cowley as the hero of the gangster cases. On every possible occasion, Hoover and his aides repeated the Bureau party line that Cowley, the dead G-man hero, had really been the man who got Dillinger. An agent proudly wrote Hoover that he had given a speech in which he had charged Purvis with claiming "credit for handling [cases] actually in [the] charge of the late Inspector Sam Cowley." The agent told Hoover he had also instructed other agents to follow the same policy of "debunking" Purvis.[114]

During World War II, Hoover heard that Purvis, then in the War Crimes Section of the army's judge advocate general, "walks in the halo of having brought about Dillinger's death." Hoover noted on the margin, "I assume this myth will never be dispelled, and that due credit will never be given Sam Cowley." In 1948, Hoover spread the word that "whenever opportunity presents itself get over [the] truth—Purvis did not kill Dillinger and had very little to do in the case. Cowley was in charge and deserves the credit." Hoover referred to Purvis as "another case of one who was made by the Bureau and would never have been heard of but for his FBI connections."[115]

It did not take long for Bureau personnel to learn that they could ingratiate themselves with Hoover by providing him with derogatory reports on their former colleague. They told Hoover that Purvis was trying to organize a society of "dissatisfied men in the service" along with ex-agents; that Purvis was urging these heretics, according to

Hoover's informants, "through their political affiliations [to] oppose the Director." One agent wrote Hoover that Purvis was "something of a fool." Another wrote that he had heard people were "disgusted" with Purvis. Hoover even got a letter from an agent whose mother had written to him to say that Purvis was "undignified, even piffling."[116]

For the rest of his career, whenever Purvis was considered for an important job, one of Hoover's men would be sure to intervene with a damaging report. When the Senate Civil Service Committee wanted to hire Purvis to head its staff, an agent informed the head of the committee that Purvis was a "publicity seeker and in my opinion didn't have a gut in his body [and] . . . that in my opinion he would louse up any job he got into."[117]

Purvis knew, of course, that he was not Hoover's favorite ex-agent, but he never fully realized what was being done to him. He often tried to see Hoover in Washington (Hoover would send out word that he was "not available") and wrote him many friendly notes. At first Hoover kept up a pose of affability, but by the end would deliberately let the birth announcements of Purvis's children go unacknowledged.

Purvis killed himself in 1960, supposedly with the same pistol he carried at the Biograph. The last act of this pathetic drama brought out the cold inhumanity of Hoover's hatred toward anyone who had, in his estimate, threatened him or the Bureau. Hoover's lieutenants, after sounding the director out, recommended that no letter be sent to Purvis's widow and family. Hoover affixed his notation, "Right," to the bottom of the memo. After the funeral, Purvis's wife and children telegraphed Hoover, "We are honored that you ignored Melvin's death. Your jealousy hurt him very much, but until the end I think he loved you." Hoover's only reaction was to write in the margin of the telegram, "It was well we didn't write as she would no doubt have distorted it."[118]

Only absolute loyalty satisfied Hoover; the smallest slight was likely to be interpreted as treachery. This was true in his relationships with his subordinates, and it was also true during his domestic security investigations. He demanded that his subordinates demonstrate loyalty by enthusiastically attacking his enemies, and he refused to terminate inconclusive loyalty investigations by pointing out that even though it had not been proven that a subject was a Communist, neither had it been demonstrated that the person was anti-Communist.[119]

Hoover felt threatened by anything less than total control over his surroundings, and that extended even to control over the Bureau's history. His insistence that his top aides participate in the ceremonial degradation of disloyal outcasts like Purvis reveals this need for total uniformity of will and vision. Yet this obsessive need to control the minds and actions of his agents was probably a critical ingredient in Hoover's ability to run the Bureau as a tightly knit team made up of interchangeable agents handling cases according to standard, scientific procedures.

By refusing ever to forgive or forget anyone who crossed him, and by forcing his aides to help him persecute "enemy agents," Hoover was giving his subordinates a taste of what was in store if they ever gave him reason to turn on *them*. They knew that from the moment they were exiled, their former friends and colleagues would have to turn against them just as viciously as Hoover had made them turn against *their* former friends. Hoover seemed to identify so totally with the Bureau that life and lives outside it had no meaning. He could feel no sympathy for anyone who had not merged his life into the Bureau as completely as he. It is not likely he could have had as close a relationship with Tolson if Tolson had not committed himself unreservedly to the greater glory of the FBI, thus guaranteeing in advance that he would agree with Hoover on all matters great and small.

Since Hoover identified so completely with the Bureau, and since the Bureau was the only world that had any reality for him, he could sincerely consider his refusal to meet with a person to be a drastic punishment, a form of exile. That agents like Purvis also regarded the loss of Hoover's approval with such dread is a measure of the stubborn loyalty Hoover could inspire in his subordinates once they had experienced the solidarity and camaraderie of belonging to the Bureau. Hoover's subordinates certainly feared him, but many of them also loved him; the highest value of their professional lives was their loyalty to the FBI, and they knew that Hoover exceeded them all in the intensity of his devotion to the cause.

As war approached, Hoover's position in the government and with the public was almost unassailable. At the end of the thirties, Hoover and Roosevelt were secretly reviving the intelligence facilities dismantled by Harlan Stone. The Bureau was once again creating indexes of dangerous citizens and aliens, infiltrating political groups to gather general intelligence, and tapping phones, but by then Hoover had become such a reassuring symbol of security and stability to Americans that any protests were drowned out in the applause for Public Hero Number One.

CHAPTER 8

The FBI Front

Today, I am happy to report that our Axis undercover Enemies have been met and completely defeated. The much vaunted Axis Fifth Column in the Western Hemisphere has been uprooted and smashed. So far, there has not been a single act of successful enemy-directed sabotage in our nation. Espionage has been controlled.

J. Edgar Hoover, on "Victory,
F.O.B.," CBS Radio, October 7,
1944

SOON AFTER HIS INAUGURATION, Franklin D. Roosevelt began to call on Hoover for information on the activities of German-controlled Nazi groups in America. These requests led in the mid-thirties to the organization of a new domestic intelligence facility for the FBI, far more elaborate than anything Hoover had directed before the retrenchments of 1924. The first of these requests came in March 1933, when Secretary of State Cordell Hull asked the FBI to look into a threat against Hitler received by the German embassy, allowable under the section in the Bureau's appropriation that let it perform investigations for the secretary of state. A year later, March 9, 1934, Roosevelt ordered Hoover to gather evidence on "Nazi groups, with particular reference to the antiracial activities and any anti-American activities having any possible connection with official representatives of the German government in the United States."[1]

In August 1936, the international situation—the proxy war between

Russia and Germany in Spain, Japanese conquests in Korea, Italian annexation of Ethiopia—had grown so serious that Roosevelt felt he needed a regular source of comprehensive information on domestic subversion. He needed to know about any threat of violence from American Communists and Fascists; just as important, with the world situation as delicate as it was—he had just proclaimed neutrality in the Spanish civil war—he needed advance warning about any developments that could restrict his freedom of diplomatic maneuvering. He was particularly worried about agitation or propaganda campaigns that might mobilize public opinion against his foreign policy. On August 24, 1936, Hoover reported to FDR that the Communists had the capacity "at any time to paralyze the country in that they [could] stop all shipping in and out through the Bridges organization; stop the operation of industry through the Mining Union of Lewis; and stop publication of any newspapers of the country through the Newspaper Guild." Communists were also making efforts, he said, to infiltrate the federal bureaucracy, particularly the National Labor Relations Board.[2]

Roosevelt told Hoover he wanted systematic intelligence about "subversive activities in the United States, particularly Fascism and Communism . . . a broad picture of the general movement and its activities as may affect the economic and political life of the country as a whole." Roosevelt's request went far beyond anything that could be considered an investigation of violations of federal law, but Hoover told the president the Bureau could proceed under the clause in the FBI appropriation he had relied on during his previous investigations of the Nazis. Hoover informed FDR that the Bureau "might investigate any matters referred to it by the Department of State and that if the State Department should ask for us to conduct such an investigation we could do so under our present authority in the appropriation already granted."[3]

The next day (August 25), Roosevelt again summoned Hoover to the White House. With Cordell Hull present, FDR explained that Hoover needed a State Department request before he could make a general intelligence investigation. Hull turned to Hoover and reportedly said, "Go ahead and investigate the ————————."[4]

That August 25, 1936, directive provided Hoover with his basic authority for nearly forty years of domestic intelligence operations, and so Roosevelt's precise meaning, and Hull's understanding of what he was asking Hoover to do, had an important bearing on the future course of Hoover's career. For his part, there was no doubt in Hoover's mind that Roosevelt and Hull were authorizing him to investigate Communist and Fascist activities, as he wrote in a memo to an aide, "for intelligence purposes only, and not the type of investigation required in collecting evidence to be presented to a court."[5]

Roosevelt knew exactly what Hoover was doing since Hoover reported regularly to him about the Bureau's activities. Many of Hoover's reports to the president dealt with "subversion" defined so broadly that it included anything that might concern the president. Since FDR had every opportunity to correct any misunderstanding on Hoover's part, it must be concluded that Hoover's general intelligence work, including his surveillance of the left as well as the radical right, was precisely what Roosevelt intended.[6]

In a memorandum to Homer Cummings, Hoover said the purpose of his new General Intelligence Section was to "collect through investigative activity and other contact and to correlate for ready reference information dealing with various forms of activities of either a subversive or a so-called intelligence type." The Bureau had already compiled an index of 2,500 individuals "engaged in activities of Communism, Nazism and various forms of foreign espionage." Hoover recommended to Cummings and Roosevelt that the new general intelligence surveillance continue to be financed as a continuation of the request of the secretary of state without seeking any new authorization from Congress "in order to avoid criticism or objections which might be raised to such an expansion by either ill-informed persons or individuals having some ulterior motive."[7]

The subterfuge Hoover was recommending conformed to Roosevelt's general policy of not formally notifying Congress about the full extent of his defense preparations. These measures were secret only in the sense that they were not *officially* brought to the attention of the legislature. The rabid opposition of the isolationist bloc in Congress and the volatile state of public opinion made Roosevelt's desire for secrecy very understandable. Writing about Roosevelt's secret cooperation with the British, Robert Sherwood, in *Roosevelt and Hopkins,* made a point that applies equally to Roosevelt's secret use of the FBI to gather information on the activities of American Nazis and Communists:

> it is an ironic fact that in all probability no great damage would have been done had the details of these plans fallen into the hands of the Germans and the Japanese; whereas, had they fallen into the hands of the Congress and the press, American preparation might have been well

nigh wrecked and ruined as, indeed, it came perilously close to being when the House of Representatives voted on the extension of Selective Service."[8]

The organization of the FBI's new General Intelligence Section brought the president an ever-increasing amount of political intelligence. Much of this dealt with subversive activities, but a good deal simply reported on any political developments Hoover thought might be of interest to the president: the Communist party's plans for the 1936 elections, an American Youth Congress march on Washington, or demonstrations against unemployment planned by a Communist-supported group, the Workers Alliance.[9]

On February 16, 1938, the Nazis seized power in Austria, followed by unification with the Third Reich the next month. In the United States there was mounting anxiety about the possibility of becoming involved in another European war. Some demanded the country reaffirm its neutrality, others that the nation prepare to defend itself against enemies abroad and fifth columnists at home. The government was called upon to take action against a supposed spy threat, so the army, navy, and FBI announced (on orders from Roosevelt) that they were busy on "the greatest spy hunt ever" and that suspects were "undergoing a severe grilling" by the FBI.[10]

That was not enough to calm a mounting hysteria in some quarters. On May 9, the American Legion announced that it was setting up its own spy-hunting outfit, and on May 10, Congressman Martin Dies called on the House to organize a special committee to investigate foreign "isms." Dies's proposal led to the establishment of the House Un-American Activities Committee (HUAC) on May 26. The administration tried to block Dies and the Legion by having the Bureau announce on May 12 that it had completed a twelve-volume report on Nazi espionage activities. On June 20, the government used the FBI report to indict eighteen American Nazis, calling it "the greatest peacetime spy ring in history."[11]

As Hitler moved into Czechoslovakia on October 1, 1938, Hoover was expanding the Bureau's domestic intelligence network by sending a security specialist to each of his forty-five field offices, including the new field offices in Alaska, Hawaii, and Puerto Rico; he also set up new facilities for "specialized training in general intelligence work. There was now so much intelligence work going on in the government that the investigating agencies were getting in each other's way. On

June 26, 1939, Roosevelt issued a directive allocating intelligence responsibilities among the army, navy and FBI, giving Hoover responsibility for the Western hemisphere.[12]

All of these arrangements, in fact the very existence of the government's new domestic security apparatus, were still unknown to the public on September 1, 1939, when Germany invaded Poland, touching off a general war in Europe. The time had come for Roosevelt to unveil the government's new domestic intelligence establishment. Secrecy was no longer an advantage, since the public had begun to panic and needed to be reassured that the government was prepared for the emergency. When Hoover learned that the New York City Police Department had just formed a fifty-man sabotage squad (and had plans to increase it to 150), he sent an urgent message to the attorney general on September 6: a public message from the president was needed at once to keep the security situation from getting out of hand. Hoover asked FDR to direct all police agencies to turn over to the Bureau "any information obtained pertaining to espionage, counterespionage, sabotage, and neutrality regulations."[13] That same day, the president issued the statement Hoover had requested:

> The Attorney General has been requested by me to instruct the Federal Bureau of Investigation of the Department of Justice to take charge of investigative work in matters relating to espionage, sabotage, and violations of the neutrality regulations. . . .
> To this end I request all police officers, sheriffs, and other law enforcement officers in the United States promptly to turn over to the nearest representative of the Federal Bureau of Investigation any information obtained by them relating to espionage, sabotage, subversive activities and violations of the neutrality laws.[14]

On September 9, FDR proclaimed a state of emergency, and on November 30, 1939, when Hoover appeared before the House Appropriations Committee, the public learned the details of what Hoover and Roosevelt had been doing covertly since 1936. He told Congress about what he was now calling, once again, the "General Intelligence Division," citing the president's Proclamation of Emergency as specific authority for its operations. He revealed that the division had "compiled extensive indices of individuals, groups, and organizations engaged in . . . subversive activities, in espionage activities, or any activities that are possibly detrimental to the internal security of the United States." The General Intelligence Index contained the names of those "who may become potential enemies to our internal security, such as known espionage agents, known saboteurs, leading members of the Communist Party, and the bund."[15]

Hoover told the Appropriations Committee that Roosevelt's September 6 directive had charged the FBI with coordinating "all the matters of investigative work relating to espionage, sabotage, and violations of the neutrality regulations, and any other subversive activities." This included investigating propaganda "opposed to the American way of life" and agitators stirring up "class hatreds." In practice, this meant Hoover would have to examine all suspicious political groups to determine which deserved intensive surveillance. Even if there *was* no evidence that a group had been infiltrated by subversives, the Bureau would keep it under surveillance on the grounds that it might *become* a target for subversion. Nearly all liberal political groups thus came within Hoover's purview. One of the least justifiable investigations on grounds that a potential for infiltration existed was the Bureau's surveillance of the NAACP, which began in 1941 and lasted for the rest of Hoover's career.[16]

One of the most important of Hoover's domestic intelligence operations was the Custodial Detention Program, to select "dangerous" individuals for arrest in time of emergency. (This began in June 1940.) Hoover's superiors in the Justice Department insisted on direct control over such a politically explosive matter, however, and the department took over the administration of the program in April 1941.[17]

As World War II approached, nothing prevented Hoover from investigating any group or person in the country to determine whether the organization was infiltrated by subversives, or whether the individual's "liberty in this country in time of war or national emergency would constitute a menace to the public peace and safety of the United States Government."[18] This situation was so obvious that it could not have been overlooked by either Hoover's superiors in the Justice Department or Roosevelt. It is FDR, therefore, who has to bear the final responsibility for removing all effective restraints from Hoover's surveillance of the American political scene.

On June 14, 1940, Roosevelt wrote Hoover a "Dear Edgar" letter, to thank him "for the many interesting and valuable reports that you have made to me regarding the fast moving situations of the last few months. You have done and are doing a wonderful job, and I want you to know of my gratification and appreciation."[19]

Hoover was surprised and pleased. He replied that this was

one of the most inspiring messages which I have ever been privileged
to receive; and, indeed, I look upon it as rather a symbol of the principles
for which our nation stands. When the President of our country, bearing
the weight of untold burdens, takes the time to so express himself to
one of his Bureau heads, there is implanted in the hearts of the recipients
a renewed strength and vigor to carry on their tasks. In noting the vast
contrast between the Leader of our Nation and those of other less fortunate nations, I feel deeply thankful that we have at the head of our
Government one who possesses such sterling, sincere, and altogether human qualities.[20]

Hoover had been skating on thin ice since 1936 when he organized
his new division on the basis of an oral communication from the
president, but with no written confirmation. Many of the reports
Hoover furnished the president could not be covered by even the
most expansive definition of the word *subversive.* The FBI had become
a political police force operating at the beck and call of the president.
A misuse of appropriated funds might have been the least of the charges
against him had the political winds shifted and Roosevelt found it
necessary to disavow knowledge of what Hoover had been doing. The
torrent of flattery (with his unfortunate use of the word *Leader* in
an intended contrast of FDR with Hitler and Mussolini) let loose
by Roosevelt's short note may have reflected Hoover's relief at finally
having the president's written approval for actions which—as he well
knew from his grillings in 1920 and again in 1923—could be considered
improper, perhaps even criminal. With Roosevelt's letter in his files
he was off the hook.[21]

Hoover did not have to worry about protecting himself against
attacks during the thirties because his traditional critics left him pretty
much alone—at least compared to his running battles with liberals
during the Palmer days. A few heretics, including Jack Alexander
in the *New Yorker* and Kenneth Crawford in the *Nation,* cast a skeptical eye on Hoover's towering public relations image, but these few
unamplified voices were heard, largely, by the already convinced. The
two leading liberal weeklies, the *Nation* and the *New Republic,* raked
Hoover over the coals now and then on general principle, but until
his resumption of domestic surveillance became known late in 1939,
liberals had little to support their gut feeling that Hoover was up to
no good. Even his foes had to admit that the FBI's record on civil
liberties was far better than the neanderthal performance of the state

and local police. It was hard to argue that Hoover's professionalism did not represent an improvement over the status quo.[22]

After a decade of near immunity from criticism, in 1940 Hoover opened himself to violent attack from the left by raiding the headquarters of the American veterans of the Spanish civil war. The Justice Department had long been investigating the Detroit headquarters of the Abraham Lincoln Brigade for violating the federal statute against the unauthorized recruitment of Americans to fight in foreign wars. Throughout the course of the Spanish conflict, the department could not make up its mind whether to prosecute. Finally, on February 3, 1940, long after Franco's victory (the Spanish civil war ended on March 28, 1939), the department had the U.S. attorney in Detroit obtain conspiracy indictments, and early in the morning of February 6, the FBI rousted twelve of the Lincoln Brigade veterans from their beds and brought them to Detroit FBI field office for booking.[23]

The arrests were bound to outrage the left. The Abraham Lincoln Brigade was a pristine symbol of the Popular Front period—which lasted from 1935 until the Hitler-Stalin Pact on August 24, 1939—when the Soviet Union and international Communists were in the vanguard of the struggle against Hitler. The way the veterans were treated after their arrest made things even worse. After their booking at the field office, they were handcuffed, chained together, then, on their way to jail, paraded in front of photographers (reviving bitter memories of the Deer Island radicals twenty years before). The arrests brought the left, demoralized since the Hitler-Stalin Pact, back to life; denunciations rained down on Hoover and the Justice Department from the liberal and radical press. After a week of this, on February 16, the new attorney general, Robert Jackson, had the charges dismissed, saying that he could "see no good to come from reviving in America at this late date the animosities of the Spanish conflict so long as the struggle has ended and some degree of amnesty at least is being extended in Spain."[24]

In May, the department released a report by its Civil Rights Section, which stated that the charges against the Bureau had been exaggerated and that the most sensational abuse (chaining the prisoners together for the benefit of photographers) was the fault of the federal marshals, not the FBI. Jackson reported that the facts did not "justify any charge of misconduct against the Federal Bureau of Investigation" but the Bureau's critics called the report a "whitewash."[25]

The Lincoln Brigade fiasco caused liberals to take a closer look at what "G-Man Hoover" and Roosevelt had been up to on the antiradical front. What they discovered astounded them. In reviewing Hoover's testimony before the House the previous November, they found that he had told the congressmen about the revival of the General Intelligence Division, and two months after that, on January 5, 1940, he had told the Appropriations Committee about the index of persons to be taken into custody in an emergency.[26] Liberals now began to connect the "new" Hoover with the "old" Hoover of the Palmer-Daugherty years.

Hoover fought back by telling friendly politicians and reporters that the controversy was a Communist "smear" plot to destroy the FBI. Meanwhile, he was furnishing Roosevelt with reports on the Communist affiliations of the Bureau's critics. Roosevelt was very receptive to this sort of insinuation: at that time, which was during the period of the Hitler-Stalin Pact (from August 24, 1939, until June 22, 1941), he himself and his preparedness policies were under ferocious attack from the left, right, and center; like Hoover, he had come to question the fundamental sincerity of his critics: "If I should die tomorrow, I want you to know this," he told Secretary of the Treasury Henry Morgenthau, Jr., "I am convinced that Lindbergh is a Nazi." On March 16, 1940, FDR went out of his way to show his support for Hoover at a White House Press Club dinner. "Edgar," he called out in full sight and hearing of the assembled press, "what are they trying to do to you on the Hill?" Hoover replied, "I don't know, Mr. President." Roosevelt gave a "thumbs-down" gesture and announced, "That's for them."[27]

A year later, liberals got another jolt when they learned that the Bureau had been tapping phones. They had always suspected this; now they also learned that the Justice Department had authorized the practice when lawyers for Harry Bridges, head of the International Longshoremen's and Warehouseworker's Union, acquired evidence that the FBI had been tapping Bridges's phone to build their case to deport the Australian-born labor leader. Attorney General–designate Francis Biddle defended the Bureau's wiretapping policy at a press conference on October 9, 1941, during his confirmation hearings:

> the stand of the Department would be, as indeed it had been for some time, to authorize wiretapping in espionage, sabotage, and kidnaping cases, where the circumstances warranted. . . . As a matter of policy wiretapping would be used sparingly, and under express authorization of the Attorney General.[28]

On several occasions, Hoover changed policy on wiretapping to match the level of support he was receiving from his superiors. On

May 21, 1940, he had received a directive from Roosevelt he used ever after as his fundamental authority for telephone surveillance. Roosevelt had written that though he was in general agreement with the Supreme Court's 1939 prohibition on wiretapping (the *Nardone* decision), he was "convinced that the Supreme Court never intended any dictum . . . to apply to grave matters involving the defense of the nation." It was too late to take action after sabotage and assassinations had been committed, so Roosevelt "authorized and directed" Attorney General Jackson to use "listening devices" against "persons suspected of subversive activities against the Government of the United States, including suspected spies." He asked Jackson to limit these techniques to a minimum and to restrict them as far as possible to aliens.[29]

Hoover's shifts in his policy on wiretapping during the thirties (he began the decade prohibiting it as "unethical") leave the impression that he really did not care much about it, but he knew that others cared a great deal. He knew that a certain superstitious aura surrounded the popular image of the secret agent lurking in the basement or closet, surrounded by a tangle of wires, earphones strapped to his head, scribbling away at his notebook. For some people, government wiretapping was a symbol of all other government invasions of liberties. To others, it was a symbol of whether or not the government was willing to do all it could (and should) to protect the public against its enemies. In 1941, the president and Congress were primarily concerned with showing a frightened public that the government was using every method available to protect against threats that were, up to the moment of Pearl Harbor, thought more likely to come from spies, saboteurs, and fifth columnists than from external attack. Wiretapping was a symbol that security, not civil liberties, was the administration's greatest concern.[30]

If liberals had known what was going on behind the scenes they would have been even more worried. Between September 9, 1939, and Pearl Harbor, December 7, 1941, Hoover sent FDR some 1,039 numbered intelligence reports, and then another 1,600 during the war. FDR received an average of more than two reports a day from Hoover during this period, some only a page long, but others running on for hundreds. The greatest number of them dealt with Hoover's South American intelligence operations; the second largest category was his surveillance of domestic and foreign Communists.[31]

In some of his reports, Hoover tried to "educate" the White House about communism in the face of Roosevelt's lack of enthusiasm for suppressing the Party. One such effort consisted of a detailed history of the origins of the different factions in the Party; his informant, Hoover claimed, had a connection with the Party, that "lends weight and authority to his observations on the subject." According to Hoover's informant, "the American Communist Party was nothing but a network of Stalin's Agents and spies."[32]

Hoover also kept watching for anyone being proposed for government employment who might be tied to the Party. Each time Walter Reuther was considered for a government post, Hoover would circulate a letter that Reuther had sent his friends in the United States in 1934, when he and his brother were working in Russia; the letter ended with a call to "Carry on the fight for a Soviet America." In another memo Hoover flatly accused Reuther of being a Communist.[33]

Hoover's intelligence reports to FDR are a triumph of quantity over quality. Items of no possible consequence are mixed with astounding pieces of information, some false, some true. No one, not even a person with the incredible abilities of Roosevelt's indefatigable aide, Harry Hopkins, could have made any systematic use of the sheer volume of material Hoover sent to the White House every day. Hoover liked to claim that the FBI was strictly a fact-gathering organization, and drew no conclusions from its findings. The Bureau left all evaluation to its political superiors. While never really true, it was a defensible policy in criminal investigations. The essence of intelligence work, however, is sifting through the chaff for the grains of wheat. The bulging boxes of FBI reports show that Hoover never recognized the importance of interpreting the results of his investigations so they could serve some useful purpose.

Hoover, with his suspicion of anything that might threaten authority, may have thought the implications of facts he reported were self-evident. He may have believed that any suspicion at all about a person made him a threat to security, since the basis of security was confidence that orthodox ideas and values were universally accepted. To someone so committed to traditional values, denunciations of heresy, whether they had any basis in fact, had a ritual value as important as any real information they might convey, since they helped increase conformity and strengthen solidarity.

Little of the material Hoover gathered on Communists could be used to prosecute the Party. The Smith Act of June 28, 1940, gave the government a powerful weapon to use against radicals by making it illegal to advocate the overthrow of the government by force, or to organize or belong to a group that had such a goal. (This was essentially the law Hoover and Palmer had wanted in 1920.) There were only two prosecutions based on the Smith Act until after the war, however; the New Deal Justice Department did not approve of the law, and once the war began the Communists strongly supported the war effort.

In 1939, when Whittaker Chambers carried his reports of Communists in government to the State Department, he found the Roosevelt administration was not at all eager to unleash the unpredictable and probably uncontrollable passions of a hunt for Red spies. Neither did Hoover press energetically for action when he received the same reports from Chambers a few years later, or when he came across evidence that the Soviets were using American Communists for espionage. Hoover and his defenders later declared that he had been inhibited by the Roosevelt administration's refusal to heed his clear warnings about subversion. The truth is that Hoover and Roosevelt were in general agreement about the nature of the threat to domestic security. While Germany and Japan were the enemies, German and Japanese spies and their sympathizers were their main worry. As a result of his investigations of Martin Dies's mostly bogus charges of Communist influence in government, Hoover himself at this time was less than convinced the threat of Communist espionage was as great as claimed by the radical right. That changed after the war, when the Soviet Union succeeded Germany as the enemy, and then circumstances made it prudent for Hoover to distance himself from what the Republicans charged were the Red-tinged policies of the Roosevelt administration.[34]

On December 7, 1941, at 2:30 in the afternoon, FBI headquarters in Washington reached Hoover in New York and connected him to a phone line to Hawaii. He could hear the bombs exploding as the special agent in charge of his Honolulu office, Robert L. Shivers, described the Japanese attack. Hoover ordered Assistant to the Director Edward A. Tamm to set the Bureau's war contingency plans in motion, and rushed to the airport for a plane back to the capital.[35]

That night, before he went to bed, Hoover dictated two memos to the president. The first listed thirteen war measures he had that day put into effect. The Bureau had already prepared a list of 770 Japanese aliens who would require detention, and Hoover had ordered their arrests as soon as Roosevelt had signed the same "alien enemies" proclamation the youthful Hoover had learned to enforce twenty-four years before. (This was distinct from the notorious roundup of 110,000 Japanese-American *citizens* that Roosevelt ordered on February 19,

1942.)[36] Hoover also had halted travel and communications to Japan, and placed guards at Japanese government facilities. He then placed all Bureau offices on a twenty-four-hour alert and canceled all leaves.

The second memo, attached to the same cover letter, was a summary of a phone intercept of a December 5 conversation between a Japanese in Hawaii named Mori and a relative in Japan. The subject of that phone call was the weather conditions in Hawaii, the location of the American fleet at Pearl Harbor, and whether searchlights were in use at the airfields. Mori answered some of these questions directly, others with apparent non sequiturs. Finally, Mori was asked what kind of flowers were in bloom in Hawaii, and he answered, "hibiscus and poinsettia." Hoover pointed out to the president the possibility that some phrases, such as the references to flowers, may have been a code; he told FDR that "it is entirely possible that the information sought in this conversation with Japan might have been a prelude to the proposed bombing of the Hawaiian Islands today." On December 6, Hoover related, the FBI immediately made this information available to the Military Intelligence Division and the Office of Naval Intelligence in Honolulu.[37]

As word of the Japanese attack reached the nation's capital, a chill ran through the Washington intelligence establishment. An intelligence fiasco of catastrophic proportions had obviously occurred. Assistant Secretary of State Adolf A. Berle wrote in his diary that December 7 had been a bad day, but at least he was not the chief of naval intelligence.[38] Perhaps no one was at fault; perhaps everyone was at fault; the political survival of the administration decreed that *somebody* was going to have to take the blame. Nobody in the chain of command between Washington and Hawaii could have felt safe that day. Hoover was in that chain of command, and the Mori memo shows that he had already started to set up his defense.

On September 9, 1939, Roosevelt had publicly announced that the FBI was in "charge of investigative work in matters relating to espionage and violations of the neutrality regulations." A directive of June 24, 1940, had given Hoover primary responsibility for intelligence within the Western Hemisphere, except for the Canal Zone. But *not*, Hoover was relieved to be able to say, for Hawaii. In a series of follow-up memoranda, Hoover had delayed the FBI's acceptance of primary counterespionage responsibility in the Islands until he could expand the Bureau's presence there. So on December 7, security in the islands was a "joint operation" Hoover shared with the army and navy while "the Federal Bureau of Investigation continue[d] to extend its operations in this field."[39]

On December 12, Hoover erected another barricade between himself and blame for Pearl Harbor by relaying matters of which he had certain knowledge. Again he called attention to the Mori intercept and said that the Honolulu agent in charge had insisted to army and navy authorities that the flowers must refer to the Hawaiian Islands. "The Office of Naval Intelligence scoffed at the significance of the message," Hoover told the White House, "and did not refer it to anyone higher in the Navy. . . . The importance of this message to the Special Agent in Charge of the Honolulu FBI office is indicated by the fact that he called an officer from his home, seven miles away, to come to his office for a copy of the Dr. Mori conversation." Finally, the agent managed to put a copy of the transcript in the hands of the district naval intelligence officer at 6:00 P.M. Saturday night.[40]

Hoover then told Roosevelt that ten days before the attack, the military authorities in Hawaii had intercepted and decoded a message from Japan that "contained substantially the complete plans for the attack on Pearl Harbor as it was subsequently carried out." The message had also specified a code word that would be broadcast three times as a signal for the attack. Military authorities in Hawaii, Hoover reported, had been told about this message. On December 5, he said, the code word for the attack was intercepted, "which indicated that the attack was to be made on Saturday or Sunday, and this information was sent by Military radio to the Hawaiian Islands. . . . At this time," he concluded darkly, "it is impossible to determine whether there was a breakdown in the Military radio and a failure of the messages to reach their destination, or whether the messages were delivered but not acted on by the Military authorities."[41]

In a confused, misleading, and inaccurate way, Hoover was alluding to one of the most puzzling and hotly debated issues in the Pearl Harbor controversy: the so-called winds execute message. On November 26, the navy had intercepted and translated a message from Tokyo to the Japanese embassy in Washington that said if normal communications with Japan were cut off, the embassy should listen for one or more of three coded phrases about the weather that would be inserted into the normal short-wave news broadcasts. These words would be repeated five times at the beginning and again at the end of the broadcast as a safeguard against coincidence. Upon receipt, Japanese embassies were to destroy codebooks and secret documents.

The War and Navy departments alerted their communications units to listen for the execute message. Between December 5 and December 7, they received a number of false alarms (weather messages that were not repeated the correct number of times). After the attack on

Pearl Harbor there were rumors that a genuine "execute" *had* been received. This warning, according to the rumors, had not been passed to military authorities at Pearl Harbor or (accounts varied) had been disregarded.[42]

In 1946, the joint congressional commission that investigated the attack on Pearl Harbor concluded that "no genuine message, in execution of the code, and applying to the United States, was received in the War or Navy Department prior to December 7, 1941." Nor did that commission find that the original message, with or without the "execute," could be considered, by any stretch of the imagination, "substantially the complete plans for the attack on Pearl Harbor," as Hoover had reported to Roosevelt. Finally, the congressional committee found that "granting for purposes of discussion that a genuine execute message applying to the winds code was intercepted before December 7, it is concluded that such fact would have added nothing to what was already known concerning the critical character of our relations with the Empire of Japan."[43]

Hoover had passed along to the president a vague, obviously unsubstantiated, and probably false report. He provided no context, no sources; he offered no evaluation of the report's implications, meaning, or consequences. There would have been enormous controversy over the failure at Pearl Harbor with or without Hoover's memo, which had no discernible influence on Roosevelt; still, this was a reckless performance, especially since Hoover's report to Roosevelt was so obviously motivated by his vested interest in deflecting blame away from the Bureau and, incidentally, settling some old scores with bureaucratic rivals.

By the time Hoover had sent his December 12 message to the White House, Secretary of the Navy Frank Knox had already visited Pearl and was on his way back to Washington with his personal report on the general lack of preparedness before the attack. Republicans were muttering that Roosevelt had somehow tricked the country into war; rumors (of the sort Hoover had sent along) were now circulating that someone had deliberately kept warnings of an attack from the military command at Pearl. Partly to lay these paranoid rumors to rest, Roosevelt immediately appointed a board of inquiry headed by Supreme Court Justice Owen Roberts to fix responsibility for the disaster.

While the Roberts Commission was still in Hawaii, where it met from December 22 to January 10, and while Wake Island, Hong Kong, Shanghai, Guam, and Manila were all falling to the Japanese, an anonymous memo was circulating through the government. It called on the commission to look "into the adequacy of the FBI, the agency directed by the President and supposed by the public and Congress to deal with the fifth column in our territory."[44]

There was worse in store for Hoover. About December 29, a story by John O'Donnell in the *Washington Times-Herald* claimed that

> the nation's super Dick Tracy, FBI Director J. Edgar Hoover, is directly under the gun . . . [the] preliminary report . . . places the Pearl Harbor Fifth Column blame directly in Hoover's lap. Army and Navy intelligence are not primarily responsible for the detection of enemy civilians operating as Fifth Columnists. By order of the President, this has become Hoover's direct responsibility. Long-time Capitol Hill foes of FBI Chief Hoover have been whetting up their snickersnees, itching to take a crack at the detective hero as far back as the days of kidnappers and gangsters. Leaders are holding them back with the promise that the report of the Roberts Board of Inquiry will provide the ammunition for an all-out drive to oust Hoover from his seat of tremendous power.[45]

Hoover immediately put out a statement that the story was "without a scintilla of foundation," and that "jurisdiction over Hawaiian matters was vested principally in the naval authorities and not in the FBI." He had reason to be worried. The military commanders at Pearl, Admiral Husband B. Kimmel and General Walter C. Short (and their families) were receiving death threats; some editorials were recommending the firing squad for them, or the traditional revolver and a single bullet. With the Japanese (for all anyone knew) racing toward California, the public was in a mood for revenge; officials could visualize the president scanning the federal roster to see who he would throw to the wolves. Hoover could only wait and see if O'Donnell's story, obviously a trial balloon floated by his enemies, made him a candidate for public sacrifice.

Then, at one of the most difficult moments in Hoover's career, Roosevelt ordered press secretary Stephen Early to call Hoover and let him know on December 29 that he still had the president's confidence. By then Henry Stimson, Frank Knox, and the president had reached agreement that the blame for the disaster lay in Hawaii and not in Washington; the political reaction to Secretary of the Navy Knox's report blaming the Pearl Harbor authorities had convinced the White House that there was no need for anyone to take the blame except Kimmel and Short. Hoover was safe.

As soon as he put down the phone Hoover sent a handwritten note to Early:

You do not know how much I appreciate your call today and the message you gave me. Please thank the President for me. To think that with all his cares and responsibilities he could think of such a matter is just another evidence of his great heart and understanding. I am deeply touched.[46]

He filled the rest of the letter with a diatribe against O'Donnell, whom he compared to a mule, "without pride of ancestry or hope of posterity." The letter was an almost audible sigh of relief.

But if Hoover was out of the firing line, his mind would not let go of the idea that someone, somewhere, had been guilty of, in a favorite phrase of his, "nonfeasance or malfeasance." Unwilling to let the matter die, on January 5, 1942, Hoover sent the White House copies of documents the FBI had taken from the Japanese consulate in Honolulu on December 7. One described a code used by a spy in a beach house to signal the disposition of the American fleet to Japanese submarines. The second was a series of messages between Japanese Consul General Kita and Japanese Foreign Minister Togo informing Togo of arrivals and departures of warships at Pearl. The most sensational message, dated December 3, instructed Kita to "hold on your list of code words . . . right up until the last minute. When the break comes burn immediately and wire us to that effect." In *The F.B.I. Story*, Don Whitehead wrote that when Special Agent in Charge Robert Shivers saw the translations of these messages he blurted out, "My God, if we'd had these earlier!"[47]

In Hoover's earlier message to the White House on Pearl, he blamed everyone except the Bureau for what went wrong. Now he had someone specific in mind for the role of villain. Hoover had been feuding with the Federal Communications Commission (FCC) chairman, James L. Fly, since September 1939, because Fly had refused to let him tap wire messages between the United States and Tokyo, Berlin, Rome, and Moscow. Fly had also refused to give the FBI the FCC's file of fingerprints of radio and telegraph operators.[48]

The messages his agent had snatched from the Japanese at Honolulu gave Hoover a chance to get even. "It is perhaps significant to observe," Hoover's January 5 memo continued,

that several conferences have been had by representatives of the FBI with officials of the Federal Communications Commission regarding the coverage of international . . . messages. . . . However, the FCC insisted that this type of information could not be made available because of existing statutes. . . . Repeated efforts, and in fact entreaties, were made . . . but all of these requests were without success."[49]

Even if these messages had been decoded and handed over to Kimmel and Short in time it is unlikely they would have made any difference. These were commanders who had not been able to interpret correctly the far less cryptic "war warning" from Chief of Staff George C. Marshall and Chief of Naval Operations Harold R. Stark on November 27, in which they had informed Kimmel and Short that "Japanese future action [is] unpredictable but hostile action possible at any moment" and "you are directed to undertake such reconnaissance and other measures as you deem necessary" and "an aggressive move by Japan is expected within the next few days."[50] Short and Kimmel were sure that Japan's first move would be against American or British possessions in Southeast Asia, so they decided to protect their equipment against sabotage by local Japanese. They locked up their guns and ammunition, and bunched the ships and planes so they might be more easily guarded—unintentionally making them easier targets.

Ironically, Hoover himself was liable to the charge of having ignored a "clear" signal of the attack. In 1940, he met with Dusko Popov, a British and German double agent whom the British had code-named Tricycle (supposedly because he liked to go to bed with two women at once). Tricycle showed Hoover an espionage questionnaire given to him by the Germans. The most detailed portion of this document was a series of questions about military installations at Pearl Harbor.[51]

Popov later claimed he told Hoover that the questionnaire was "a serious warning indicating exactly where, when, how and by whom your country is going to be attacked." Instead of being properly impressed, Hoover, who had been prejudiced against Popov by reports about the spy's uninhibited life-style, threw him out of the office. This "irrational, ranting man," Popov charged, "was the person responsible for the disaster of Pearl Harbor."[52]

Whatever the questionnaire might have been, it was certainly not the "detailed plan of the Japanese air raid" Popov called it. After the war, Japanese intelligence officers denied the Germans were giving them intelligence assistance; the type of installations mentioned in the questionnaire suggests the Germans were collecting intelligence for their own sabotage operations.[53] If the questionnaire had been taken seriously, it might have even helped reinforce the Pearl Harbor commanders in their belief that the real danger was from saboteurs.

The Popov incident, the "winds execute" story, and the other Pearl Harbor "warnings"[54] all illustrate the signal-noise problem in evaluating intelligence reports. In *A Man Called Intrepid,* William Stevenson points out that at any given time, the intelligence signals foreshadowing a move by the enemy are part of the general uproar of information, some true, but much of it possibly false, including deception material deliberately planted by the enemy or (even more effectively) by the enemy's secret friends. In hindsight, it may seem that the true warnings should have stood out like beacons. A distant observer, looking back, is unaware of all the other distractions, some of them contradictory, that at the time seemed equally important.[55]

Popov's charge that Hoover was responsible for Pearl Harbor is preposterous, but in one small way Hoover *might* have helped contribute to the mind-set that led to Kimmel and Short's catastrophic error of judgment in reacting to the November 27 "war warning." Hoover had played a major role in the administration's strategy of responding to the public hysteria over spies and sabotage; instead of giving the public a reasonable appraisal of the extremely small danger of sabotage, the government magnified the problem so as to magnify the government's success in coping with it. For two years, the public had been hearing that sabotage was as dangerous a threat to the country as the possibility of direct enemy attack. When Kimmel and Short decided that the major threat to Pearl was sabotage, their conclusion paralleled the uninformed public opinion of the day, which Hoover and the FBI had no small part in molding.

Hoover also did his share to contribute to the babble of intelligence noise in the months preceding Pearl Harbor. On July 26, 1940, he reported that the Japanese thought their navy was the best in the world, and that in their opinion Pearl Harbor was of little value to the United States since the Japanese could blockade it so easily. Later that summer, he gave the White House information that German and Italian agents in South America had been "instructed to wait 'until [the] Japanese move.'" Hoover's informant advised him that "it was not certain as to just what 'move' in the order refers to; that, however, the order has been verified as having been issued." In September, FDR returned the favor, sending Hoover a letter Eleanor Roosevelt had gotten from "the American white wife of a Japanese" who warned of Nazi espionage in South America and said that "the Japanese are planning to strike at the Hawaiians and Philippines at the first available opportunity. Be on your guard."[56]

Throughout 1941, Hoover sent the White House many reports on Japanese war preparations; as relations deteriorated these reports became even more frequent. He told Roosevelt the Japanese had plans for evacuating their personnel from the United States on a ship due to arrive in San Francisco on November 1. He learned from an informant in the German embassy that in case of war (which the Germans expected President Roosevelt would launch against Japan), the Japanese would strike first at the Philippines, and that the real purpose of the current Japanese-American negotiations in Washington was to collect information on American war plans for the Germans. Hoover notified the White House that Japanese diplomats, particularly intelligence agents, were leaving the United States for South America; other Japanese personnel were inquiring about the earliest flights to Rio. On December 2, Hoover reported still more Japanese diplomats sailing out of the country from New York and San Francisco. On that date he also reported that for two days the Japanese consulate in San Francisco had been "destroying a tremendous amount of paper in the furnace of its building."[57]

Hoover simply passed these reports to the White House without any effort to evaluate them or provide a context for the president to use to interpret them. Some of Hoover's reports actually did point toward the possibility of a Japanese attack (somewhere, but definitely not at Pearl); then again, others seemed to argue against the possibility. In the aggregate, however, they were worse than useless: They were harmful because the mass of unevaluated information made the careful evaluation of any one item impossible. In that sense, Hoover indirectly contributed to the government's failure to correctly interpret the useful information it did receive.

Hoover's reaction to the Pearl Harbor attack also raises the possibility that his charges against Commissioner Fly might have masked some degree of bitterness toward Roosevelt himself. A Hoover-approved analysis that appears in *The F.B.I. Story* strongly suggests that if Fly had permitted the FBI to intercept those messages, the surprise attack would have been averted. Whitehead tends to place the sole responsibility on Fly; he explains "Hoover had White House assurances that . . . [a] proclamation [from Roosevelt overruling Fly and permitting the taps] would be signed and Department attorneys were working on a final draft giving the FBI this authority, when the Japanese attacked at Pearl Harbor."[58]

But another writer who knew Hoover, Ralph de Toledano (whose biography of Hoover came out the year Hoover died), suggests that Hoover harbored resentment toward Roosevelt for his slowness in overruling Fly. "Had the White House acted less lethargically in granting Hoover that authority," de Toledano writes, "Pearl Harbor might have been averted." De Toledano found that this was the general feeling of top officials at the FBI, including Louis Nichols, although de Toledano was not able to question Hoover. Even though Hoover and Roosevelt worked well together, de Toledano says, Hoover was "ambivalent" toward Roosevelt, particularly because of differences in their assessment of the seriousness of Communist infiltration of the government.[59]

Hoover's reaction to Pearl Harbor reveals important aspects of his personality: his instinct to search at once for scapegoats when confronted with a disaster, and his characteristic resentment toward those who refused to take seriously his warnings of danger; he would interpret their failure not as professional disagreement or human error but as a personal insult and an affront to his professional competence— and very nearly, as disloyalty.

World War II saw all the components of Hoover's Bureau operating smoothly and efficiently. Operationally, he directed intelligence in the United States and South America. Bureaucratically, he protected the FBI's turf from encroachment by competing intelligence agencies. Ideologically, he drew on his own growing (but unsystematic) apprehensions about a decline in national values to rally other conservatives against what he perceived as increasingly dangerous departures from the traditional American way of life. During the war, these goals complemented one another and contributed to the clear sense of direction that was obvious in all of Hoover's activities. After the war they increasingly came into conflict, and it became harder and harder for Hoover to identify his specific goals and to discover what strategy would best achieve them.

The day after Pearl Harbor, President Roosevelt put Hoover in charge of national news censorship. Hoover functioned as director of censorship for less than two weeks; on December 16, he turned the job over to Byron Price, news editor of the Associated Press. While Hoover never explained why he shed this job so quickly, there were several likely reasons. One is that Hoover's success in publicizing the Bureau depended on the network of alliances he had built up with favored and sympathetic newsmen; this would have been destroyed if he became their censor. Another reason might have been a realistic appraisal of his Bureau; censorship would require expert evaluations of the intent, significance, and effect of the release of information. To run an effective censorship office, Hoover would have needed the services of individuals of independent judgment, exactly the type he could not tolerate in the Bureau. Hoover knew where to draw the line when accepting responsibility, and he was always realistic in recognizing his limitations.[60]

Hoover also avoided becoming involved in the evacuation of Japanese aliens and Japanese-American citizens from the West Coast. He first learned of plans for this at a meeting in the office of Secretary of the Treasury Morgenthau on December 10, 1942. One of Morgenthau's agents on the West Coast had recommended a general roundup of Japanese in California; the Treasury Department wanted Hoover's opinion on whether this would be possible.[61]

Hoover told Morgenthau that Biddle would not approve any such "dragnet or roundup procedure." The FBI had prepared individual cases on the alien enemies it had arrested, and each arrest had been approved by the attorney general. He pointed out to Treasury that many of the Japanese they were talking about arresting were American citizens, and

> of course citizens of the United States were not being included in any arrests as the authority to make arrests was limited to alien enemies and unless there were specific actions upon which criminal complaints could be filed, [Biddle] had not approved the arresting of any citizens of the United States.[62]

Hoover's agents had acquired a complete picture of the Japanese spy system during a break-in at a Japanese consulate. He was sure that he could deal with disloyal Japanese aliens and citizens as individuals, and after Pearl Harbor the Justice Department had begun processing such cases. By early February 1942, two months after Pearl, Hoover, Naval Intelligence, and Military Intelligence all agreed that they had destroyed the Japanese espionage organization.[63]

The officer in charge of the Fourth Army on the West Coast, Lieutenant General John L. DeWitt, however, came down with a severe case of Pearl Harbor jitters. When Hoover heard of plans for a mass roundup of Japanese citizens, he told his SAC (special agent in charge) in San Francisco that "there is no law at the present permitting us to pick up citizens [so] I do not believe that they can put over any plan to clean people out of that area unless there is some very imminent prospect of attack. . . . I thought the army was getting a bit hysterical." DeWitt became even more hysterical when West Coast politicians and the national press, abetted by columnists both reputable (Walter Lippmann) and disreputable (Westbrook Pegler), began demanding a roundup of Japanese-American citizens as well as aliens.[64]

Faced with the opposition of the Justice Department to their depor-

tation plans, Secretary of War Stimson and Assistant Secretary John
J. McCloy appealed to Roosevelt, who gave the army carte blanche.
The War Department prepared a presidential order for an evacuation,
and on February 19, 1942, Roosevelt signed Executive Order 9066,
which declared the West Coast a military area, leading to the removal
of 120,000 Japanese to the Rocky Mountain states. Biddle theorized
that in this instance FDR was going to rely on the secretary of war
for advice, and no one else, "not even J. Edgar Hoover, whose judgment as to the appropriateness of defense measures he greatly respected. The military might be wrong. But they were fighting the
war."[65]

Hoover revealed his opinion of the relocation of Japanese-Americans in a massive, two-volume report (480 pages) on conditions in
the Relocation Camps he prepared in 1943. He stated that it was

> extremely unfortunate that the Government, the War Relocation Author-
> ity, and the public, did, in the past, seize upon what they first believed
> to be a simple determining factor of loyalty. There actually can be only
> one efficient method of processing the Japanese for loyalty, which consists
> of individual, not mass, consideration.[66]

Prudence and principle both compelled Hoover to keep the Bureau
out of the internment operation. The FBI's small size meant it would
have had to rely on the army for operational support, and so, without
control of the operation, the Bureau would share the blame later,
when the inevitable reaction against the roundup set in. Hoover had
learned that much from the Bureau's alliance with the American Protective League and the local police in 1919 and 1920. From that time
on, he had avoided, as far as possible, joint operations in which he
was not clearly in charge.[67]

Second, Hoover spoke out so often, and so consistently, against
such dragnets that there is no reason to doubt that he was generally
opposed to them—though the Red raids and the Smith Act trials
after World War II show that in certain circumstances he could enthusiastically support wide-scale arrests based on a criterion of guilt by
association. With the significant exception of his hostility towards
blacks, however, he did not stigmatize groups by ethnic origin but
by their beliefs. There is nothing to suggest in his report on the relocation camps that he objected to penalizing citizens as well as aliens
for disloyalty, but he wanted to know if the individuals really were
disloyal before he punished them. He would therefore reject any system
of punishment that applied equally to the loyal and the disloyal simply
because of their race; for Hoover the distinction between loyalty and

disloyalty was too important to be subordinated to any other test or standard.

Hoover was proud of his war against the German intelligence in South America; he was always disappointed that "the story of a great piece of work" had never been told.[68] Getting the American public interested in South America has defeated greater public relations talents than Hoover's, however. Despite his best efforts, he never managed to convince the White House or the public that his South American operation—based on the June 24, 1940, presidential directive that gave the FBI intelligence responsibilities for the Western Hemisphere—was anything but a sideshow.

There is actually an uncharacteristic lack of conviction in Hoover's memos on his Latin American operations; it is doubtful that even he believed his FBI was really suited to mucking about in heathen countries where only mad dogs and G-men wore neckties and spit-shined shoes. But if Hoover's South American adventures were less than a public relations triumph, his reputation as a home-front spy-smasher and sabotage hunter rivaled his fame as a peacetime gang-buster.

Hoover began planning his Special Intelligence Service, or SIS, for South America in May 1940, a month before Roosevelt formally apportioned intelligence responsibilities between the FBI and Naval and Military Intelligence, giving South America to the FBI.[69] Within a few months of the directive Hoover began sending agents to Central and South America, some as undercover agents, other as legal attachés to embassies or liaison officers with South American police forces.

The FBI's objective was to provide Washington with information on Axis activities in South America and to destroy enemy intelligence and propaganda networks there. There actually was a great potential for trouble in the South American republics and colonies. There were 360,000 Germans in Brazil, 194,000 in Argentina, and 129,000 in Chile, many of them in well-organized Nazi-controlled nationalist groups. There was an enormous colony of 280,000 Japanese in Brazil, and another 60,000 in Peru. The Germans had a continentwide radio propaganda network, great influence in South American governments (particularly Argentina and Chile), and enormous commercial interests that provided the Wehrmacht with strategic raw materials. (Responsibility for denying the Germans these materials rested primarily with Nelson Rockefeller's Office of the Coordinator of Inter-American Affairs.)

Hoover never had more than 360 agents at any one time in South America. Nevertheless, his SIS identified 887 Axis agents in Latin America, leading to arrests of 389 and convictions of 105. The Bureau located 281 propaganda agents and obtained sixty arrests. Thirty saboteurs and 222 smugglers were identified. The Bureau managed to have 7,064 enemy aliens relocated, 2,172 interned, and 5,893 deported. SIS investigations led to the capture of thirty radio transmitters by local police and the shutting down of twenty-four radio stations. Four SIS agents lost their lives in this effort.[70] The Bureau's major achievement was probably its exposure of the Nazi activities of the officials of several South American governments, especially Chile and Argentina. FBI operations helped limit these countries' support for Germany and led, in the case of Chile, to a break in its relations with the Axis.

Hoover achieved this record with a small expenditure of resources through his characteristic strategy of using the FBI as the catalyst for unifying and directing the counterespionage efforts of local South American authorities. His principal tactic was to bring South American security officials to Washington to study FBI methods at the National Police Academy. By the end of the war he had an FBI-trained network of local security officers in place throughout the continent.

Judging by the number and scope of the Bureau's reports on South America, Hoover had borrowed another technique of his war on crime. He evidently committed a large detachment of the Bureau's writers and publicists to the battle to convince relevant audiences in the White House that the South American theater was of vital importance to the war effort. The bulk of the 2,600 numbered intelligence reports Hoover sent to Roosevelt dealt with South America. Most of these concerned specific political developments that had strategic ramifications; early in the war he produced a set of bound volumes, one for each country, on enemy influence and activities. Many of the reports, though, and some of the bulkiest, were intended primarily to sell the SIS to the president: for example, a March 21, 1942, report on *United States Dependency on South America*.[71] (One can imagine Hoover's frustration that his rivals in Military and Naval Intelligence did not have to issue propaganda about the importance of *their* theaters.)

One of Hoover's advertisements for the SIS was an April 1942 volume, *Axis Aspirations Through South America*. This argued that, potentially at least, South America was more important than the European or Asian theaters, since America and Canada "could not be successfully invaded from the present bases in Europe or Asia. . . .

There is evidence that the Axis powers would use South America . . . as a base from which to attack our country." Hoover suggested that if the Axis could gain control of a Latin American republic without having to launch an invasion, then an attack on North America, seemingly impossible, would suddenly become a real danger. Hoover had to admit that there was little chance of this happening since all the countries of South America except Chile and Argentina had already broken with the Axis (Chile would follow in January 1943, but Argentina would hold out almost until the end of the war). The enemy's most immediate aim, therefore, was to deny the United States use of South American raw materials, and to destroy Latin American solidarity by stirring up wars between neighboring countries which might lead to the overthrow of existing governments and the establishment of regimes more sympathetic to the Axis. This scenario, Hoover said, was *not* farfetched, because the entire region was swarming with enemy intelligence agents, saboteurs, and propagandists.[72]

The result of Hoover's wartime experience in Latin America may have been to temper his enthusiasm for expanding FBI operations overseas. Although late in the war he proposed using the FBI's "legal attachés" at American embassies as the nucleus of the postwar intelligence system, he did not fight as hard as might have been expected for his plan. The reason may have been the puny reward (in terms of prestige and power) he had received from his South American operations compared to his efforts and expectations. Certainly he did not get the publicity he thought he deserved; but Americans do not get famous in South America—they get rich.

Hoover's primary goal during the war was to prevent the kind of mass hysteria that had blighted the home front during World War I. That was the constant theme of all the Bureau's wartime publicity, which would begin by telling the audience that Roosevelt had given the FBI a monopoly over "all investigative work in matters involving espionage, sabotage, subversive activities, and violations of our neutrality regulations"; the message would then be to urge the public to "leave it to the FBI": "if you know of any un-American activities, report them to the FBI and then say nothing more."[73]

In his anticrime publicity during the thirties, Hoover had turned his cases into arguments for adopting the FBI as a model for all law enforcement. In a similar way, he used publicity about the Bureau's triumphs over Nazi saboteurs and Japanese spies to prove that the country was so well protected that there was no need for public concern. "The untold story back of the FBI's antisabotage and antiespionage precautions," Don Whitehead wrote in *The FBI Story,*

> was that Hoover had two primary motives in initiating them: first, there must not be any enemy espionage and sabotage such as there had been in World War I; and second, there must not be permitted to develop any vigilante system of wartime law enforcement. The records of the FBI reveal Hoover's motives to be that simple.[74]

Hoover began his campaign to publicize the Bureau's counterspy activities with an article written "with" Courtney Ryley Cooper that appeared in the January 1940 issue of *American Magazine.* "The citizen should consider his particular task to be fulfilled when he reports his suspicions to the nearest F.B.I. office," was the message. A cartoon showed Uncle Sam raising a giant boot, labeled "The F.B.I.," to crush the "Spy Menace" snake. A flashlight beam that lit the way was "Public Cooperation."[75]

The same message was carried to movie audiences in *The F.B.I. Front,* a Bureau-assisted "March of Time" documentary released in 1942. The purpose of the film, according to the producers, was to "calm the ambitions of any amateur sleuth who fancies himself an adequate substitute for the trained, scientific, and, above all, humane agents of the F.B.I."[76]

Hoover persuaded the public to "leave it to the FBI" by "mystifying" counterespionage to show that it was so complex, so technical, even so boring that no layman should get involved, or even want to get involved. "The well-brought-up spy never works alone," wrote Frederick L. Collins in 1943 in his Bureau-endorsed book, *The FBI in Peace and War,*

> He is part of a system that operates not only on a coast-to-coast hookup, but on a continent-to-continent one. It is 1,000 to 1 that the man an amateur might catch by his unguided efforts is not the boss of that system. To blot him out accomplishes little. On the other hand, it may be fatal to any hopes of destroying the system itself and capturing its boss men if we arrest the private in the ranks or even alarm him.[77]

Hoover had several reasons for opposing free-lance spy hunting. It usurped a function of the government which could lead to a decline in the government's prestige and hence his own. As a progressive, Hoover thought direct mass action of any kind was inefficient. Finally, from his bitter experience after World War I, he knew civilian spy hunters would inevitably commit abuses of civil liberties, and these would someday come back to haunt him and discredit his Bureau; he would not repeat his old mistakes. And so he would say, in speech after speech, that "the trailing of the spy or the saboteur is a job for men of experience. This is not a task for the amateur sleuth, and certainly there is no place here for roving vigilantes."[78]

That was also the message of the popular entertainment Hoover sponsored during the war. In 1944 he had Nichols work with Louis De Rochement on a movie account of the Bureau's wartime cases. This was *The House on 92nd Street,* which came out early in 1945, the second in the three classic FBI movies (along with *G-Men* and *The FBI Story*). *The House on 92nd Street* was filmed in an earnestly journalistic, pseudo-documentary style with the by-now-obligatory fingerprint file and crime laboratory scenes, and it made counterespionage work seem dauntingly complicated. So did Hoover's *This Is Your FBI,* which premiered on April 6, 1945, and, with its memorable "Love for Three Oranges" theme, ran for almost nine years. Its slogan, intoned by veteran movie G-Man Frank Lovejoy, suggested that to "your F.B.I. you look for national security . . . and to the Equitable Society for financial security. These two great institutions are dedicated to the protection of you, . . . your home and your country." It would be hard to imagine a more deglamorized view of law enforcement or counterespionage than Hoover served up in *This Is Your FBI.* "In this country," Lovejoy would conclude each week, "espionage is under control." *That* was Hoover's message during World War II.[79]

Hoover would not have been able to sell the public on this proposition if plants and military bases had started to blow up right after Pearl Harbor. One major act of sabotage, and he could have forgotten about the "leave it to the FBI slogan." But there were no proven incidents of sabotage (out of 19,649 investigated reports). German efforts to land saboteurs by submarine (eight landed in 1942, two more in 1944) were turned into publicity triumphs for Hoover's G-men, who captured them before they could do any damage. Between 1938 and 1945, FBI investigations resulted in ninety-one spying convictions, most of the arrests coming in the first few months after Pearl Harbor.[80] By any measure, German and Japanese undercover operations were a miserable failure. By that standard, the FBI's performance was a brilliant success.

As he had done in South America, Hoover adapted his concept of an FBI-coordinated law enforcement movement to wartime conditions on the home front. The greatly expanded FBI (from 1,596 agents in fiscal 1941 to 4,886 in 1944) stayed in charge of counterespionage

and espionage investigations, but even these numbers were inadequate
for the Bureau to supervise security throughout the defense industry
and to maintain watch over subversive activities across the country.
Hoover's solution was to rely on cooperation with local police and
with carefully selected civilian groups to maintain adequate security.

Three large-scale outreach programs were the foundation of his
coordinated domestic security network. The most important was his
ties to local police, which he put on a wartime footing with his "FBI
Law Enforcement Officers Mobilization Plan for National Defense."
This sent FBI executives into the field for quarterly training sessions
with police executives. By 1942, 73,164 police officers had participated
in these conferences.[81]

The second component maintained security in the defense industry.
Hoover established a network of informants in defense plants whose
job it was to bring reports of sabotage to the attention of the FBI.
By July 1942, Hoover had created a network of 20,718 informants
in nearly 4,000 industrial plants.[82]

Late in 1940, Hoover organized the third part of his security network. This was his American Legion Contact Program. Its immediate purpose was to head off the Legion's plan to organize its own
counterespionage force in 1940, with its own badges, manuals, and
credentials (in effect, a reincarnation of the World War I APL). Hoover
was also worried by the growing enthusiasm within the Legion for
the House Un-American Activities Committee's antiradical investigations chaired by Congressman Martin Dies, since Dies was attacking
the Bureau as well as Roosevelt for being soft on Communists. By
October 1943, the Bureau had recruited about 60,000 Legion members
into this program[83] who could be relied on to vouch for FBI claims
that the security problem was under control.

FBI publicity was also an integral part of Hoover's wartime program, since an efficient mobilization of the country depended on the
public's confidence that the home front was secure. By the time Hoover
helped Frederick L. Collins write his 1943 tribute to the Bureau, *The
FBI in Peace and War,* the G-man myth had worn such deep grooves
into the national consciousness that all Collins had to do was mention
Dillinger, Floyd, or Barker to produce reverberations of the whole
heroic legend in the reader's imagination. *Peace and War* served up
a synopsis of the FBI's post–*Ten Thousand Public Enemies* cases,
and paid dutiful tribute to the FBI's science and teamwork, but Collins
structured the book around a portrait of Hoover as an all-powerful
protector of the nation—and of the national faith. Hoover was such

an important symbol of security in wartime popular culture that even the comics used him in their adventures. He was "J. Arthur Grover," whose FBI laboratories produced the serum that turned a 4-F weakling into Captain America; he was also the boss of "The Shield" (known as "the G-Man Extraordinary"), and the Washington contact for the Justice Society of America.[84]

During the war, FBI publicity (and public interest) focused on Hoover as the public symbol of the protection provided by an invisible Bureau. The country's self-protective need to believe in the power and intelligence of its wartime leaders produced an image of Hoover cast in even more heroic dimensions than before. In *The FBI in Peace and War*, Collins claimed Hoover's "greatest asset is that aloneness. . . . This spiritual isolation, this utter irrelation to the petty, scheming, wire-pulling, job-grabbing world around him, . . . is the man's outstanding quality [and] has increased immeasurably the prestige of the Bureau and the respect with which it is universally regarded." Collins's Hoover was a superman, but also an everyman: "Get him out for dinner when he has time for it—which is seldom enough these days—and he is the gayest companion imaginable."[85]

For a man of Hoover's moralistic temperament, it was impossible to separate protection of the nation's security from defense of its moral values. He made it part of his leadership role to speak out on the goals of the war effort, and so he often restated his basic beliefs in terms of the wartime emergency.[86] Audiences expected a law and order harangue from Hoover, and he would not disappoint them. They also expected him to say something about the war, and again, he would not fail, so now his speeches would shower insults on Hitler as well as Dillinger.

In Hoover's wartime speeches his bureaucratic and organizational responsibilities were often pretexts for speaking out on more urgent concerns. He would argue that the FBI was doing everything necessary to maintain home front security, so there was no need for the public to get involved in spy hunting. That established, he would then assert that there was a fundamental moral connection between crime during peace and the problems of domestic subversion and foreign attacks during wartime. Before Pearl Harbor, he said, there was "a distinct connection between the professional destructionist [a term he sometimes used for "radical," evidently related in his mind to "anarchist"] and the professional criminal. Both . . . [were] in a state of revolt against the American way." The link was that "our national apathy toward the subject of crime represents a condition which in fact is an incubator for the things which are anti-American."[87]

The criminal and the revolutionary both attacked the property rights of law-abiding citizens: "If you lose [your possessions] . . . it makes little difference whether they are taken by an ordinary murderer or an international pirate masquerading as a self-appointed savior of a country whose language he can barely speak." The Bureau's success against the public enemies of the thirties made him wonder, in one speech,

> what might have been the effect today had steps been taken to curb the crazy antics of the Austrian paper hanger twenty years ago. True, he was the product of his times—but so were Capone, Buchalter, Karpis, Dillinger, Touhy, and a host of other gangsters who almost seized control of whole communities. Through prompt and decisive action they no longer menace society, and the same might be said of Hitler and his gangster associates had other peoples faced the truth and then acted with certainty.[88]

Hoover's wartime theme was that the nation was in danger because "we have allowed ourselves to become soft and compromising, making concessions to wrong when interference with our personal indulgences and pleasures would have been the price to be paid to further the principles of Democracy."[89] (In Hoover's rhetoric, "we" did not mean Hoover and it did not mean his respectable audience; it meant an unregenerate "them," like the infidels who had stayed away from his Sunday school classes.)

Since the causes of crime, subversion, and aggression were all moral in nature, Hoover's solution was also moral:

> We must clean up democracy at home while watching for threats to it from abroad. If every home awakened to its responsibility overnight there would be a renaissance of that virile, indomitable spirit which is only found in free and God-fearing peoples. . . . What we need is a return to God, more individually a return to the practice of religion. That is, without doubt, the greatest need in America today.

During the anticrime campaign of the thirties, Hoover and Cummings had used law enforcement to spur a revival of national morale; now Hoover's goal seemed to be a moral revival.[90]

Since Hoover was a moralist, he rejected any theory of behavior that disregarded the personal morality of the gangster, the subversive, and the aggressor. His books and speeches of the late thirties had turned the crimes of Dillinger, Karpis, and Ma Barker into blasphemies against traditional values. Now he added "the Communist and the Bundsman" to that list of public enemies. "They represent," he said, "more than a mere political party. They espouse a way of life, a fanatical worship of materialism, destruction, and the blacking out of decency. They stand for the overthrow of democratic institutions, social, governmental and religious, even while their lying leaders in our midst seek to delude us with a mumbo-jumbo of high-sounding phrases."[91]

Hoover's own life and experience had always furnished him with material for his speeches, which were often filled with autobiographical references. His more optimistic hopes for the American future were really a romanticized memory of his own boyhood, as when he told a Rutgers graduating class that

> it has long been held that the basic institutions of America are the home, the school and the church. At no period in our national life have they meant more than they mean today. The early formation of character is the responsibility of the parents in the home. Here the groundwork is laid. Where the home fails, a grave handicap is placed upon the school and the church. The work of home and school must be supplemented by the work of the church. From each comes a vital and essential contribution to the character of the future citizen.[92]

His bleaker vision of what was in store for the country after the war drew on his more recent personal experiences. When Hoover said that "the home . . . is imperiled" he might have had his own situation in mind. In 1938 Hoover's mother had died after suffering from cancer. By all accounts the stronger of his parents and, according to his nieces, a woman who exerted a powerful authority over Hoover, her death may have left him with an irrational, but understandable, sense of being cut adrift from any source of authority in his own life, and he may have projected this loss on the nation at large. "There is a depression of sympathetic and constructive leadership on the part of adult America. All too frequently we have adopted a 'do nothing' attitude. We have been inclined to let things drift and expect youth to escape the evil consequences."[93]

He must have reflected during the war on the contrast between his life in his childhood home, which had lasted until he was forty-three, and then his solitary condition, which he could foresee would be permanent. There was personal significance in his lament that, "regrettably, the home is not the same potent factor it once was. There has been a woeful deterioration because we adults have failed, not the home as an institution."[94]

He finally left Seward Square, which was turning predominantly black, and moved into a detached, suburban-style house in Northwest Washington, the same area of town where Tolson lived. All of Hoover's living family had now left Washington; he was at home alone except for the dogs he and his mother had loved. (Hoover's first dog belonged to his mother, who had named it Spee Dee Bozo, perhaps after Speed, Hoover's own nickname; after that Hoover had a succession of cairns, usually two at a time, one of whom was always named G-Boy.)[95]

With his mother gone, Hoover's friendship with Tolson was his only close relationship, except for casual friendships with businessmen and politicians. The friction at the office that had sometimes made Hoover annoyed with Tolson was by now smoothed away, and Louis Nichols had taken Tolson's place as Hoover's punching bag, accumulating dozens of censures for real or imagined failings. Hoover's notations on Tolson's letters after the thirties were sometimes joking but always affectionate. Hoover scrawled "This is a fine spirit" at the bottom of Tolson's memo in 1940 volunteering to go to London to serve as liaison with British intelligence.[96] When he gave Tolson his "Ten Year Service," he wrote

> Words are mere man-given symbols for thoughts and feelings, and they are grossly insufficient to express the thoughts in my mind and the feelings in my heart that I have for you. . . . No one knows better than I the invaluable assistance you have been to the Bureau and to me personally as its Director. You have indeed been a true friend as well as a loyal associate. . . . I hope I will always have you beside me.[97]

Now a confirmed bachelor, Hoover seems to have spent time pondering what he had missed in not having had a son, and reflections on the nature of the father–son relationship regularly appear in his speeches, few of which, during the war, lack at least a passing reference to sons left without fathers because of war, death, or abandonment. Perhaps his own sense of loss from his father's withdrawal into mental illness and his mother's recent death made him tell a radio audience that sons deprived of a father's love "long for a word of understanding, a smile of sympathy, a little companionship. They grope in bewilderment for an answer, and they quite naturally become antagonistic and morose." His situation as a bachelor made him envy and romanticize a father's experience guiding his son's development: "Fathers often fail to realize that their greatest possible contribution to the betterment of the world is the proper rearing of their sons. . . . Real companionship between father and son pays dividends of inestimable value to both."[98]

Youths, he said, would follow leaders. If their fathers would not lead them, then they would look outside their homes. "The emergence of a Hitler illustrate[s] that people must follow some leader, no matter how base he is, no matter how clearly an opportunist he is. America, then, must be fully awake to her responsibility in developing and maintaining a leadership of the highest quality." Hoover blamed the failure of leadership, which mirrored a general weakening of authority in society, on "that school of thought which holds to the theory that youth should be self-directed [and which] contributes to the future bankruptcy of the land." If parents failed to exercise authority, their children might be influenced by criminals, but that was not the worst that could happen to them or the nation. The worst would be that American society, weakened by the decline of authority, would be left vulnerable to the "Communist virus." Communists were "reaching out to extend their insidious influence into the field of youth training."[99]

In Hoover's mind there was a clear connection between the exercise of authority by a strong father that prevented crime, and a similar exercise of leadership within the nation to deter subversion and aggression. "The generation that has gone before you failed miserably in its duty to the future," he told a class of university graduates, "we became soft. Pacifism swept the land. We foolishly helped our enemies to become strong." In 1944 he said that "adults have failed to keep faith with youth."[100]

Hoover even seems to have imagined himself leading a national effort to make up for the failures of modern fathers to fulfill their traditional role. "Ignorance on the part of too many fathers," he argued, "accounts for their sons' lack of an essential sense of good citizenship."[101]

> What efforts are being made to marshal the fathers who remain at home to make up in part for the fathers and big brothers who have gone to war? . . . I dare say that virile leadership in every community in the land would attract enthusiastic volunteers once a program was arranged and recruits were told what to do.[102]

In 1943, at the invitation of former President Hoover, he became a member of the national board of directors of the Boys Clubs of America. Perhaps this was a vicarious and typically bureaucratic way of satisfying the longing for a son that was reflected in an article he wrote for *Parents Magazine,* "The Man I Want My Son to Be."[103]

The dream of having a son seems to have stirred Hoover's imagination. He recoiled, however, from the idea of a wife. In 1939, a Washington women's page reporter asked him why he was a bachelor. The story ran under the title "J. Edgar Hoover Wants an Old Fashioned Girl."

"Every time I find a girl I'd like to marry, she is already married to someone else. I go out to dinner parties, not necessarily large formal ones, but small ones in private homes of my friends, and I will meet a girl and think, 'Now there is a girl for me.' And what happens? She is either the hostess, or the wife of someone else. Someone always beats me to the girl."

But why hasn't the glamour man ever married? Questioned on this all-important subject, Mr. Hoover said: "Well, there are a number of contributing factors. Of course there has been my job, which has been confining from a romantic standpoint. It has to be done thoroughly, and by thoroughly, I mean that I have to be ready to leave here for any part of the United States at any time. What wife would stand that? Then there was my mother. Not that she did not want me to marry. It was not that. I made a home for her and took care of her until she died two years ago. The other children in the family were married, and I stayed with mother. So, you see, mother and the job were contributing factors, as well as the missing girl. . . . The girls men take out to make whoopee with are not the girls they want as the mother of their children. I am not criticizing the so-called glamour girls. They are attractive in their way, but they do not appear to me to be real or sincere, and they do not measure up to my idea of what a girl should be. I have always held girls and women on a pedestal. They are something men should look up to, to honor and to worship. If men would remember this and keep them there, married life would be better. I have had that idea about women all my life. And here is something that I will confess. . . . If I ever marry and the girl fails me, ceases to love me, and our marriage is dissolved, it would ruin me. I couldn't take it and I would not be responsible for my actions. There, now you see, how much I think of marriage and of finding the right girl."[104]

In Hoover's imaginative world males were figuratively sons and females were mothers. In a figurative way, the broad intent of his own efforts to provide national leadership was to make his fellow citizens and his FBI colleagues as dutiful to national authority as he had been to the most important authority figure in his own life, Annie Hoover.

In his wartime speeches a pessimistic moralism increasingly supplanted the progressive vision, and this was particularly noticeable in his warnings about the decline of the home as the basic institution of authority in society. During the war a new idea had joined his reflections on the country's future, a suspicion that he and the nation were being robbed of something precious, the old-fashioned home. "The American home," he told a 1942 audience, "is not what it once was and it is time that every adult paused to take stock of himself." He told a law school graduating class that "the home, in many ways, is imperiled. When the home is destroyed, everything in our civilization crashes to its doom. . . . Every day it is my task to review the histories of scores who obey only the laws of their own choosing. Always the one thing that stands out is a lack of moral responsibility and any feeling of religious conviction." Blame for this lay with "the literature of writers who decry religion and argue that distance from God makes for happiness." Along with the home, the other basic institutions of society were in a state of decline. Religion was under attack, so "while we fight for religious freedom, we must also fight the license sought by the atheist and those who ridicule, scoff and belittle others who would seek spiritual strength." The school, too, was being weakened by progressive educators who peddled "an insidious and unsound educational quackery that would rule out all the principles of discipline and control which, if carried to its illogical conclusion, would produce a generation of iconoclastic morons and criminals."[105]

The rhetoric of most American leaders during the war understandably swelled with pride over the nation's prodigies of production and triumphs of arms. The country had always understood its history as a success story, but even without that predisposition, most Americans could hardly see World War II in its final stages as anything except a national triumph. As the end approached, however, Hoover seems to have seen a future filled with danger, failure and defeat.

Hoover nurtured his relationship with President Roosevelt by sending him odd bits of intelligence in the hope that they might amuse or divert him. Like any high official, Hoover was interested in keeping a stream of paper crossing the president's desk to remind him he was still on the job. Humorous notes or items of personal interest had the best chance of surviving the president's gatekeepers. Shortly after Pearl, Hoover sent the president a pair of carved Brazil nuts picked up by an SIS contact in Brazil, one "purporting" to be Roosevelt, the other Vargas of Brazil, and he reported that a South American government had just arrested an American because he was a Republican, on the assumption that "any political party which is out of office in the United States must necessarily be an enemy of the United States Government."[106]

Hoover's best effort along these lines was in 1943, when he told FDR that an Arkansas newspaper editor with whom he was acquainted was heading a drive to place a plaque on a trackside telegraph pole that Roosevelt's dog had used during a presidential train trip to Mexico. He enclosed a clipping from his friend's paper, which reassured readers that despite a recent flood, "the pole still stands, on as dry land as it was the day the Cocker Spaniel and his handler jumped off the president's special car."[107]

Of more significance were the reports he furnished Roosevelt on members of the president's staff. During Harry Hopkins's January 1941 visit to England as Roosevelt's personal representative, Hoover was able to report back to the president that the British were impressed with Hopkins's combination of a "very charming but almost shy personality with a very vigorous and dynamic mentality." Roosevelt was reported as being delighted "to know that the G-Men were checking up on his personal representatives.[108] (Hoover's memo was addressed to Erwin Watson, but he may have calculated that his report would be shown to Hopkins, his key contact at the White House, a man worth cultivating.)

The most significant of these confidential investigations was Hoover's report on Roosevelt's personal representative in the State Department, Undersecretary of State Sumner Welles. In September 1940, while returning to Washington from Alabama after Senator William Bankhead's funeral, Welles got drunk and made a homosexual pass at a Pullman porter. The porter filed a complaint with the railroad, and one of Welles's enemies, William Bullitt, former ambassador to France, eventually heard the story; for the next three years he used it as a weapon to drive Welles from the State Department.

When rumors about Welles reached the president, he had Hoover investigate to get the facts. Hoover reported that the story was true, and that Bullitt had told a leading enemy of FDR's, Burton Wheeler. In 1942, Secretary of State Cordell Hull, who cordially hated Welles and resented his close collaboration with the president (and, perhaps, Welles's greater ability and experience as a diplomat), also got the story from Bullitt and went to Hoover to see if it was true. Hoover was no friend of Welles, but he refused to tell Hull anything without permission from the president. Hull went to the Senate with his story, and Owen Brewster of Maine interviewed Hoover on April 27, 1943, asking to see the report. Again Hoover refused.

Hoover's comments on the case to Biddle are interesting, because he singled out a lack of self-control as the explanation for homosexual behavior. He discussed the matter with Attorney General Francis Biddle, saying that Welles's behavior puzzled him because there was no *pattern* of homosexual behavior, only incidents that were committed while Welles was so drunk that he could not remember them afterward. Biddle advised the president that the incident had festered far too long, and he should let Welles go before the situation got completely out of control. Finally, facing the threat of a Senate investigation and fearing that Bullitt had leaked the story to the Roosevelt-hating Patterson-McCormick chain of papers, Welles submitted his resignation on September 25, 1943.[109]

Hoover's success in ingratiating himself with Franklin Roosevelt did not do him any good with the First Lady. She complained to FDR that Hoover was spending too much time persecuting Communists and not enough on chasing Nazis, and Hoover would respond with statistics (which Roosevelt would pass along to her) proving she was wrong. She denounced the FBI's treatment of the Abraham Lincoln Brigade veterans to her husband, saying that "we are developing a Gestapo in this country and it frightens me."[110]

Hoover learned about Eleanor Roosevelt's hostility through a source that made the reports particularly credible and damning. One of Eleanor's friends, Josephine Truslow Adams, was a Communist, and she would pass along her exaggerated and sometimes entirely fanciful recollections of Eleanor's remarks to other Communists, and some of these were informers who reported them to Hoover.[111]

Hoover's belief that he had a deadly enemy in Eleanor may have been the reason he kept an explosive dossier on her among his Official and Confidential files. This was a report to Hoover from an FBI agent that the army's Counter-Intelligence Corps (CIC) claimed to have planted a microphone in a Chicago hotel room through which they secured evidence that Mrs. Roosevelt and her friend (and later biographer) Joseph Lash had "engaged in sexual intercourse during their stay in the hotel room." The source of the story was the head of the army's Military Intelligence Division, John Bissell, who said that the previous MID chief had told him that the tapes had been played for Roosevelt, who then had a "terrific fight" with Mrs. Roosevelt in front of Hopkins and Watson. Supposedly the president had been so furious he had disbanded the CIC and ordered its members sent to the Pacific "for action against the Japs until they were killed."[112]

The only sure facts in this case are that the CIC did bug Eleanor Roosevelt's Chicago hotel room, that she learned of it and complained, and that Roosevelt disbanded the CIC. Nothing else about Hoover's O & C file report rings true. If a patrician like Roosevelt were going to have a "terrific fight" with his wife, he would not have it in front of the servants—that is, in front of Hopkins and Watson. Hoover did believe Eleanor and Lash were having an affair, but several factors make it doubtful. There was the difference in their ages (Lash was thirty-three years at the time, Eleanor fifty-eight), and Eleanor Roosevelt's loyalty to a young friend of hers with whom Lash *was* in love. The most likely explanation is that the story had been improved upon several times in the retelling by army secret agents who suspected the New Deal of being infiltrated by Communists and who hated Roosevelt for abolishing their unit and ruining their careers. The incriminating tapes were probably of a meeting between Lash and his girlfriend, and there probably was no "terrific fight." The preposterous account of the orders to the Pacific sounds like the general run of ravings from Roosevelt-haters during the war years.[113]

The Eleanor Roosevelt file is the kind of material on prominent figures that Hoover kept in his "secret files." (His Official and Confidential files survived his death; his Personal and Confidential files were almost all destroyed by Tolson and his secretary, Helen Gandy.) Hoover claimed that he sequestered this material to keep it out of the hands of agents and clerks who might spread rumors. Others have said that these were Hoover's "blackmail files," and that Hoover kept this material separate from the central files both to protect himself (since he had no business gathering it, and had used illegal techniques to acquire it) and to have it handy when he wanted to use it.[114]

During Hoover's lifetime the news media would not print scandalous information about the private lives of public figures, but it was widely suspected, and in some quarters known, that Hoover *did* leak damaging information to news media, to government agencies and committees, and to employers. His targets were individuals he suspected of disloyalty or of insufficient zeal in combating disloyalty and, because he regarded opposition to him or the Bureau as subversive in itself, Bureau critics. It is probably true, as was generally suspected, that one of the reasons Hoover had so few critics was fear of his confidential files. On the other hand, Hoover's open attacks on his enemies would have been enough to deter all but the most committed opponents of the Bureau; critics knew that once they had crossed Hoover they would never have any respite from his assaults. Fear of Hoover's files may even have been a convenient excuse to avoid confrontations with him when the real reason was a fear of encountering such a fierce polemicist in open debate.

During the war, Hoover jealously guarded his intelligence territory against any encroachments by rival agencies. He had occasional problems with the ONI and MID, but the president's June 24, 1940 directive giving him jurisdiction over the home front put him in an unassailable position to repel their invasions of his investigative preserves. His major difficulties were caused by foreign intelligence services operating in the United States, and by friction with William Donovan's Office of Strategic Services (OSS), whose establishment was one of the major bureaucratic defeats of Hoover's career.[115]

Early in 1941, foreign intelligence was streaming into the White House from thirteen different agencies. Roosevelt was faced with an urgent need to establish some sense of order. The possibility that Roosevelt would appoint an intelligence "czar" alarmed Hoover and the chiefs of the two military intelligence services; they told Roosevelt that they were working effectively as a committee of equals and would prefer not to have a supervisor. Nevertheless, in the early summer of 1941, a single director of intelligence was a real possibility, and Roosevelt had several candidates in mind: his lifelong friend, New York socialite Vincent Astor (husband of the long-lived philanthropist, Brooke Astor); Mayor Fiorello La Guardia, who was director of civilian defense and so had an interest in propaganda and intelligence; and, of course, Roosevelt's eventual choice, former Assistant Attorney General William J. Donovan, the World War I hero (Congressional Medal of Honor, leader of the "Fighting Sixty-Ninth," featured in the movie of the same name). Roosevelt had sent Donovan, then an influential New York lawyer, overseas as his personal emissary to survey the international situation and to collect ideas on how to solve the intelligence problem. Donovan's plan called for a new organization that would take charge of all overseas intelligence, collect it, interpret it, conduct covert operations and supervise foreign propaganda.[116]

Most presidents try to have a variety of information sources to avoid having their policy choices limited by any one subordinate's particular priorities and perceptions. Roosevelt had already responded to the world emergency by setting up what amounted to two new personal intelligence services. One was the Bureau of the Budget, which he moved from the Treasury into the White House in February 1940; the other was a secret intelligence gathering force under newsman John Franklin Carter, who operated under the cover of Adolf Berle's office in the State Department. FDR did not share the bureaucrat's enthusiasm for clarifying and rationalizing the organizational structure of the intelligence establishment. From where he sat, the more competition between intelligence services the better.[117]

During the late spring and early summer of 1941, Roosevelt was still trying to make up his mind who to put in charge of foreign intelligence (he appointed Donovan the coordinator of information on June 18, but did not announce the decision until July 15). As he had in 1933, once again Hoover had to sweat out the possibility that he would have to report to a new boss. This seemed especially likely when Roosevelt put Vincent Astor in charge of liaison with British Intelligence,[118] seemingly grooming him for the job of overall intelligence chief.

On July 3, 1941, while Hoover was away in Atlantic City, New Jersey, the special agent in charge of his New York office, T. J. Donegan, called headquarters in Washington. He reported that Astor had broken off the weekly intelligence conference he chaired and had ordered Donegan to locate Kermit Roosevelt, Teddy's son and FDR's cousin, who had recently arrived in New York from London and was to check into New York Hospital for treatment of alcoholism and other ailments. He had not reported to the hospital, and when last seen was in the company of a German masseuse.[119]

Assistant to the Director Edward Tamm told Donegan to begin a very discreet investigation, but when Hoover learned what was going on he ordered the investigation halted at once, fearing the repercussions if it were discovered that the FBI was looking for a member of the president's family. Astor was furious and threatened to have Donegan and Hoover fired. Donegan complained to his director that "I do not have to subject myself to being treated in this manner and I also feel that you would not expect me to be so treated."[120] Hoover's well-known policy was to treat any attack on one of his men by an outsider as an attack on himself. When Hoover heard how Astor had treated Donegan he was outraged. He also realized that Astor, as far as Hoover knew still a competitor for the top intelligence job, had put himself in an untenable position.

The White House now ordered the FBI to look for Kermit, but Hoover ordered Astor be told, as was later reported back to him, that "you were so damned mad that you were considering resigning tonight; that for 18 years you had run the Bureau honorably and efficiently and that you did not like his comments at all; that you did not propose to take them from anyone and that you had authorized me to tell him that as far as the Directorship of the FBI was concerned that he, Donovan, the Attorney General could have it any time they wanted it." This had the desired effect of putting Astor into a panic as he realized what FDR's reaction would be if Hoover actually did quit. He begged the FBI to arrange a phone call to Hoover, saying nervously that "it is nonsense about him resigning his job."[121]

On July 5, Hoover fired off a letter to the White House complaining about Astor's "very arrogant and overbearing manner," and called Astor to tell him the episode had made him feel "this job doesn't mean so much to me anyway. . . . [I]t's a terrible headache and if anybody wants it . . . they can have it merely for the asking because I am not very keen about it anyway."[122]

Astor tried to paper over the problem by saying it showed "the need for a large coordinator." Hoover replied, "Now I don't know anything about the Colonel Donovan situation and I, of course, care less. But the point . . . is if they want Colonel Donovan to come in or if they want you to come in. . . ." Hoover didn't care.[123]

Astor was now apologizing frantically, protesting to Hoover "I'm terribly fond of you. . . . If I've hurt your feelings I do apologize very humbly." The call ended with Astor babbling about his fervent desire to see Hoover, while Hoover replied blandly, "That's all right, indeed."[124]

The advantage Hoover had gained over Astor must have reassured him that Astor was not a serious rival, but it had no effect on FDR's decision to make Donovan coordinator of information. A year later, on July 11, 1942, Donovan's organization was reorganized as the OSS and was attached to the Joint Chiefs of Staff. Perhaps the most important reason Roosevelt chose Donovan over Hoover was simply Donovan himself—that is, the difference between the education, experience, and outlook of the two men. Donovan was a man of enormous international experience; he and Winston Churchill knew and admired each other, and he had firsthand knowledge of world affairs acquired during a lifetime of travel. His magnetic personality, his amazingly large circle of friends, supporters, and allies in America, and his professional stature had opened the way for him to meet and discuss world problems with the leaders of government and industry everywhere. And then there was the narrow, provincial Hoover, who never crossed either ocean in his life (in fact, never ventured outside the United States except for a Caribbean vacation in the thirties).

Since the president had been receiving Hoover's brand of intelligence reports for a year, he must have been impressed by Donovan's proposal for establishing within his office a Board of Analysts to analyze and interpret intelligence findings. By mid-October 1941, Donovan had over a hundred experts working for his Research and Analysis Unit producing studies for the board. This was in sharp contrast to the unevaluated gossip Hoover persisted in forwarding to the White House throughout his career. Hoover's stock insistence that the FBI would simply furnish facts, and leave the interpretation and conclusions to others, which handicapped him in doing effective intelligence work, may thus have kept him from expanding his intelligence operations beyond Latin America during the war.[125]

The in-house "experts" Hoover relied on for his "analysis" were expert primarily in anticipating the preferences of their all-powerful director. To expand his capability beyond fact-gathering would have demanded the presence of individuals with intellectual independence, something he would not tolerate in his subordinates. This was the hidden penalty Hoover paid for the tight discipline he kept over his employees. He was deprived of any advice uncontaminated by expectations of his likely reaction to it. Hoover never solved this problem, a perennial dilemma for all military-style organizations.

But limited as he was, Hoover would have had a hard time topping some of the analytic efforts of Donovan's experts. They issued a fifty-seven-page memorandum forecasting peace in Asia as long as Russia was not defeated. This was completed on December 3, four days before Pearl Harbor. Early in 1942, Donovan said that great numbers of Nazi saboteurs were ready to enter the United States, where they were to be greeted by legions of Nazi fifth columnists.[126]

Once Donovan's organization was established, Hoover could only grit his teeth and make sure he blocked Donovan's periodic attempts to expand his operations within the United States, which was operationally off-limits to the OSS. When he learned that Donovan had sent an operative into Mexico, he roused Sumner Welles to protest that the "Donovan organization be dissolved."[127]

Hoover got another chance to discredit Donovan in October 1942, and he made the most of it. The British had discovered that the Spaniards kept the cipher books for their maritime codes in the embassy safe, so if they could get into the embassy they could keep current with the latest changes in the codes. In July, this assignment was turned over to Donovan, who gave it to Donald Downes, the same agent who had aroused Hoover's wrath in Mexico. On the night of July 29, 1942, he sent three operatives into the embassy to photograph the code books. The operation proved enormously productive, and was repeated in August and September.[128]

In October, disaster, in the form of Hoover, struck. While the OSS men were inside the embassy, the FBI pulled up with sirens shrieking and lights flashing, and the OSS agents had to flee. Downes called Hoover's behavior "near treason" and said that "I don't believe any single event in his [Donovan's] career ever enraged him more."[129]

Hoover's war with Donovan was not just professional rivalry. OSS agents were authorized to use violent and illegal covert methods overseas, and it would have been disastrous (as well as contrary to law) to allow them to begin using them in the United States, particularly in the face of express prohibitions in Donovan's enabling charter that prevented the OSS from operating on American soil. Experience had taught Hoover that the FBI, as the most visible federal investigative agency, was usually blamed whenever federal agents were discovered in dubious activities. (In the past, Hoover had been blamed for the misdeeds of the Secret Service, the postal inspectors, and Military and Naval Intelligence.) There was, therefore, the usual mixture of selfishness and principle in Hoover's lifelong fight with the OSS— and later the CIA (Central Intelligence Agency)—to keep them from operating within the United States.

In 1943 it was American policy to do everything possible to placate Stalin because it was not yet possible to comply with his demands for a second front. Donovan came up with the idea of a liaison arrangement between the OSS and the Russian secret police, the NKVD, that would not only coordinate their operations in German territory, but extend to an exchange of missions in the two capitals. Donovan submitted his proposal for OSS-NKVD cooperation to the Joint Chiefs of Staff, and on February 10, 1943, a subcommittee of the Joint Chiefs determined that the "military advantages . . . from such reciprocal exchange . . . of missions appear to outweigh the disadvantages" and recommended that the Joint Chiefs approve the plan.[130]

But now Hoover had gotten wind of the idea, perhaps through his sources in Military Intelligence, and he dashed off a protest against the plan to the White House. Hoover's memo gave Roosevelt second thoughts, and he notified Admiral William D. Leahy, chairman of the Joint Chiefs, about Hoover's protests, and told him to "take this up" with the JCS. Hoover followed up his advantage with another memo to Attorney General Biddle in which he charged the NKVD with trying to "obtain highly confidential information concerning War Department secrets" (an oblique reference to the Manhattan Project); he warned that an NKVD mission in the U.S. would "be a serious threat to the internal security of the country." Now Biddle was alarmed, and he forwarded *this* warning to FDR, who again let Leahy know that he was worried.[131]

The Joint Chiefs were thoroughly alarmed by Hoover's warnings and the president's agitation. Although a majority of the Chiefs still favored Donovan's proposal, they decided that so many political ramifications had developed that Leahy should have a private meeting with the president to request guidance. Nearly a month went by; then, on March 15, the Joint Chiefs received word that Roosevelt had decided to kill the plan.[132]

OSS historian Bradley Smith writes that "Hopkins, Biddle, and Roosevelt surely acted as they did because they feared that Hoover would let the conservative press loose on the administration if they went through with the deal. The 'domestic political situation' that stopped the president from approving the exchange was not distrust of the Soviet secret police but apprehension about what Hoover and his conservative friends might do. That may make the presidential decision partially ideological, but if so, the ideology was less a fear of communists than of anticommunists."[133]

This would be only one of many times Hoover's influence with the political right would be a consideration in the formation of government policy. There were, however, other reasons, besides Hoover's opposition, to be skeptical about the wisdom of Donovan's plan. Letting the Stalinist secret police set up a base in Washington (which may have seemed a mere trifle to military chiefs eyeing the main prize of access to Soviet knowledge about the Germans) really was a reckless idea. Had the president agreed to the Donovan arrangement, it would not have taken any signal from Hoover for the Roosevelt-haters to recognize a chance to skin the president alive.

In December 1944, Hoover had to fight off another attempt by Donovan to help a foreign intelligence service get established in Washington. Hoover sent a memo to Biddle in which he argued against Donovan's plan to permit the French to operate in the United States. He wrote that

it is incontestable that even under the best of circumstances and when dealing with the friendliest and most stable of allies that intelligence organizations of foreign powers must not be permitted to become established on American soil and should be discouraged wherever possible from taking root any place in this Hemisphere.[134]

Hoover had ideological reasons for refusing to permit foreign intelligence agencies to operate in the United States. He also had a bureaucratic motive. Foreign intelligence agencies would cooperate closely with the American intelligence agency that had arranged for their installation in the United States, and which were, besides, operating in their home territories. Practically speaking, the foreign intelligence networks in the United States would have given the OSS a way of evading the restriction on its activities in the United States by, in effect, using their foreign colleagues to gather information and mount covert operations within the United States. Hoover was ferocious in defending his turf against any potential threat, no matter how far-fetched. On one occasion, Francis Biddle's assistant attorney general, James Rowe, advised the attorney general to observe Hoover and imitate him to defend the Justice Department against encroachments from other agencies. He said that "Hoover, a realist, keeps the army on the run and they respect him for it."[135]

Donovan's many run-ins with Hoover during the war made him automatically suspect the FBI director when press leaks sabotaged Donovan's proposals for a smooth postwar transformation of the OSS into what is now the CIA, perhaps with himself as its director. He may have been right.

On November 18, 1944, Donovan proposed to Roosevelt that a new foreign intelligence agency be established. Its director, assisted by an advisory board of the Secretaries of State, War, and the Navy, would report directly to the president. Donovan's plan ran into opposition from the army, navy, and FBI. Hoover submitted his own proposal, which called for reversion to the FBI's prewar system of cooperation with the army and navy, supplemented by an expanded network of FBI "legal attachés" at American embassies and a new evaluation and analysis section within the State Department.[136]

All these plans collapsed when someone leaked Donovan's plan to Walter Trohan, Washington correspondent of the rabidly anti-Roosevelt *Chicago Tribune,* on February 9, 1945. The McCormick-Patterson chain of papers—the *Washington Times-Herald, New York Daily News* and, of course, the *Tribune*—charged that the "New Deal plans to spy on [the] world and home folks" and that Roosevelt had a "super gestapo agency . . . under consideration." All of the New

Deal's enemies jumped into the fray, making preposterous charges
that Donovan's plan was "another New Deal move right along the
Hitler line." Donovan's supporters fought back, but for all practical
purposes the Trohan leak destroyed Donovan's hopes for a future in
postwar intelligence. Donovan protested to Roosevelt that this was
not "a mere leak but a deliberate plan to sabotage" any reorganization
of intelligence. He was sure that Hoover was responsible, and, despite
any conclusive evidence, historians have tended to agree with him.[137]

Hoover ended the war as the undisputed chief of domestic intelligence, with an even chance in the still unsettled race to control postwar foreign intelligence. For twelve years he had enjoyed a close
working relationship with a president who trusted him and whom he
trusted in return.

That left Hoover vulnerable when Roosevelt died, because the
secrecy that surrounded Hoover's restoration of the FBI's domestic
intelligence apparatus during the thirties kept Hoover and Roosevelt
from openly seeking legislative authority for the Bureau's new intelligence operations. Hoover had to rely instead on a series of informal
understandings, personal directives, and legal subterfuges to conceal
the fact that he had abandoned Harlan Stone's restriction of the Bureau
to investigations of federal crimes. Hoover's lack of clear and unassailable legal basis for operations that eventually consumed the major portion of the Bureau's resources made him violently defensive whenever
the Bureau's authority for its secret operations was questioned. Hoover
was forced to rely on vague presidential directives that he interpreted
according to their spirit as elastic and comprehensive, but that were
later dissected according to their letter as narrow and restrictive. For
a man who hated ambiguity as much as Hoover, this created a lifelong
sense of grievance at being forced to operate in a grey area of dubious
legality.

Now his fate was in the hands of a new president, a man whose
only dealings with Hoover had been to criticize the Pearl Harbor
investigation for absolving Hoover of any blame for failure by the
FBI.[138] Harry Truman did not know how to win Hoover's trust and
affection. He never knew what a valuable political ally Hoover could
have been—but he would learn he could not have chosen a more
deadly enemy.

CHAPTER 9

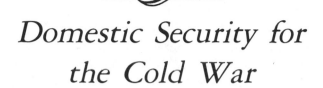

Domestic Security for the Cold War

[I never implied] that President Truman was disloyal or pro-Communist. He was blind to the Communist menace and used very bad judgment.

Hoover, after his
testimony against Truman
before the Senate Internal
Security Subcommittee,
1953[1]

ONLY SOMEONE WHOSE MEMORY was filled with the echoes of the past would have reacted as Hoover did when the cold war began. Stalin was on the move in Europe, civil wars were breaking out in Greece and China, and Truman, who was remobilizing the military, was too distracted to evaluate the domestic consequences of the world crisis. But Hoover had lived through all this before.

Once again, bolshevism was spreading from Russia. Once again, American radicals and their friends were giving support to Moscow. To Hoover it seemed a rerun of 1919. Once again, there would be pressure for a drive to suppress the American defenders of Communist revolution. But this time Hoover would not make the mistakes that had defeated his first assault on the Communist party in 1920 and had nearly destroyed his career.

J. Edgar Hoover was fifty years old in 1945. He had been dealing with the pressures of mobilization and demobilization for twenty-eight

275

years; he had been the nation's chief domestic intelligence officer since 1936 when he and Roosevelt had reestablished the political surveillance system. He had been involved in war scares so often that his responses were almost routine.

Knowing the demands that war inevitably would place on the country's internal security forces, particularly the FBI, Hoover could anticipate what he would have to do to calm the public hysteria that always accompanied international crises. He might not know whether the future would bring war or peace, but like an experienced general, he knew that in his position he had to prepare for action, and to stockpile ammunition, tourniquets, and stretchers.

Based on the "war signals" he had been receiving throughout 1945 and 1946, Hoover was convinced the country was at best facing a protracted period of tension, at worst armed conflict or a Pearl Harbor–type surprise attack. Hoover knew that, as the international situation grew more frightening, the public would look to Washington for reassurance that the home front was safe from spies, saboteurs, and subversives, and he knew the FBI would be expected to provide the proof. If there were another surprise attack, he would have to show that he had reported every possible indication he had received. If war actually broke out, there would once again be irresistible demands for a roundup of aliens and citizens suspected of disloyalty, and he knew he would be expected to direct the operation.

Roosevelt's death on April 12, 1945, left Hoover without the absolute assurance of White House support on which he had relied for the past twelve years. Roosevelt and Hoover had been collaborators in any number of sensitive and dangerous operations; Hoover had erected a domestic security system relying largely on informal oral directives from a president he trusted implicitly. Most of all, Hoover had long depended on Roosevelt's capacity to project a sense of unquestioned authority to provide him with the buttress of security and stability that his own personality had always demanded.

But now, instead of Roosevelt, who had proven time and again that he would support and defend him, Hoover had Harry S Truman, a man who had criticized Hoover's preparations for Pearl Harbor and had rejected the conclusions of the Roberts Commission, which had absolved the FBI of blame. Truman took office surrounded by aides whose liberal views made them Hoover's natural enemies, and Truman himself made it clear that he regarded Hoover and the FBI as enemies of civil liberties. Truman had also made Hoover uneasy when he fired Attorney General Francis Biddle on June 30, 1945, and replaced him with Tom C. Clark. Although Biddle had blocked almost all of Hoover's recommendations for prosecutions under the sedition laws, Hoover felt he knew where he stood with him. When Hoover had gotten into trouble (as he had by wiretapping Harry Bridges), Biddle had protected him. Clark, however, who had been chosen to placate the Texas congressional delegation, gave Hoover the feeling he made his prosecutorial decisions on the basis of partisan political pressures, and so Hoover felt far less secure. Despite the outward friendliness he showed Clark when, as a Supreme Court justice, Clark joined the decision that upheld Hoover's Smith Act case against the leadership of the Communist party, Hoover did not think of him as a man of principle. For his part, according to one Justice Department insider, Clark was "intimidated by Hoover." Truman and Clark's arrival made Hoover feel that in these perilous postwar times he was on his own. He would have to cement his alliances with the conservative anti-communists in Congress and throughout the country who were his natural patrons and clients.[2]

Hoover watched over the events of 1945, 1946, and 1947 that would unleash the cold war—the breakdown of the London Foreign Ministers' Conference (September 1945); Stalin's February 1945 speech on permanent rivalry between communism and capitalism; Winston Churchill's Iron Curtain speech at Fulton, Missouri (March 5, 1946); American aid to Greek anti-Communist forces in March 1947; the creation of the Marshall Plan in June 1947; and George Kennan's enunciation of the policy of containment in his July 1947 "Mr. X" essay in *Foreign Affairs*—as a professional who would have to deal with the impact of these policies on domestic security and as a lifelong anti-Communist who associated communism with everything that threatened his own basic values. Hoover's performance during the Truman administration can be understood only by recalling the two sides of Hoover's public role: the domestic security professional who was acutely aware of the hazards of neglecting any sign of danger, and the moralist who was always prone to turn his operations into dramatizations of right and wrong, particularly when the conflict involved Hoover's historical enemy, communism.

Hoover had never relaxed his suspicions of communism and the American Communist, a "corruptionist who now uses the tricks of the confidence man until his forces are sufficiently strong to rise with arms in revolt." Nevertheless, a rational assessment of world events was just as important as his predisposition against communists in determining his actions in 1919 and again after World War II. Hoover's campaign against communism under Palmer was sparked by alarm over the spread of bolshevism in Europe in 1918 and 1919 and subsided when the Red tide receded. It was a reaction to the real (though, to a less inflamed imagination, remote) possibility of a domestic uprising aided by foreign support. Likewise, the domestic security controversies of the Truman administration grew out of popular alarm over the truly tense atmosphere in Europe and Asia after World War II. Hoover was not alone in responding to the fear that this time, as well, there was the danger of a foreign attack aided and abetted by domestic sabotage, espionage, and subversion.[3]

In 1919, it had been the Communists' own predictions of impending armed conflict that convinced Hoover that world revolution was at hand. After World War II, Hoover's extensive taps on the phones of American Communists and Soviet representatives produced similar predictions of imminent Communist triumph; there seemed to be evidence that the country was on the verge of a climactic confrontation between capitalism and communism. Early in 1946, Hoover began reporting to the White House that American Communist officials were discussing the Soviet Union's "firm belief" that in "a few short years" Communists would be in control of every country in Europe. In 1947 he told the president that the Communists were developing plans for sabotage and slow-downs in defense plants in the expectation of a war between the United States and the U.S.S.R.[4]

Since Hoover tended to attach great importance to anything he heard from Communist or ex-Communist sources, he was disturbed when a French Communist official close to Stalin, Jacques Duclos, denounced Earl Browder, chairman of the American Communist party, for his wartime policy of collaboration with capitalism. In July, Browder was replaced by the thoroughgoing Stalinist, William Foster. At the same time, the Party resumed its old name, dropping the wartime alias of the "Communist Political Association." There also followed an immediate reversal of the Popular Front program of cooperation with the United States government and an increase in Communist propaganda and agitation. Hoover sent the White House urgent warnings about this new militancy among the American Communists. (One of Hoover's memos reported that a "generally reliable" source had said that Browder's removal meant that Stalin had been deposed, and that V. M. Molotov was now probably in charge.)[5]

Behind Hoover's warnings about coming hostilities may be detected what might be called a Pearl Harbor syndrome: a determination that in case of enemy attack he would have documentary proof that he had not been caught napping. Since the movements of Japanese diplomats might have been a warning of Pearl Harbor, if anyone had interpreted them properly, Hoover now kept the White House informed of the travel plans of Soviet diplomats and their families.[6] However, Hoover continued to follow his "no evaluation" policy, still believing that his duty was simply to pass along every signal of danger he received—it was his superiors' responsibility to separate the signals from the noise. Hoover's repeated warnings about the likelihood of war might be viewed as a cynical effort to protect himself, but it was more than that. Hoover's whole career proves that he was a serious person who did not indulge in useless exercises. He took the threat of war with the Soviet Union seriously enough to make its possibility the basis of FBI planning for the rest of the Truman administration.

Over the years Hoover had developed a characteristic leadership style. He generally would search for ways to organize his activities into a comprehensive program that demonstrated the Bureau's professional competence. This would involve creating alliances with other agencies in pursuit of his objectives, rallying public support for them, and shaping his entire program so that it drove home a moral lesson to the nation. The post–World War II anti-Communist mobilization was no exception. It was a total response to the international and domestic crisis in which all aspects of the Bureau's operations—the loyalty program within the government, the legal and covert attack on the Communist party, and the espionage cases against Hiss, the Rosenbergs, and others—were not only preparations for new military conflict, but also a resumption of Hoover's old crusade to reinforce the traditional values of Seward Square. By committing himself to ritual battle again against his old antagonist, the American radical, he would once more heap the sins of modern society on the Communist, proclaim him an un-American traitor and drive him and his obscene values out of the American community.

The first of the postwar spy cases broke on June 6, 1945. John Stewart Service, a State Department China expert, was arrested for passing hundreds of classified State Department documents to *Amerasia,* a left-wing diplomatic journal. The "espionage" here could have been considered an extreme instance of the "document leaks" that support the mainstream news industry except for the fact that the editor of the journal, Philip Jaffe, was a radical. After an FBI investigation, the Justice Department charged Service, Jaffe, and four others with espionage; it then infuriated Hoover by settling the case on reduced charges because the department felt its case had been weakened by the actions of the FBI and OSS in searching the magazine's offices without a warrant. In 1950, there were two inquiries into sensational charges (unproven then, but given new support in a 1986 study) that the Justice Department had fixed the case (one by a Senate panel under Millard Tydings, and another by a New York grand jury).[7] The Justice Department's inept handling of the *Amerasia* case made Hoover suspect a lack of real seriousness in the administration's attitude toward a serious national problem, the unfolding evidence of widespread Communist espionage.

Late in 1945, Hoover began to feel frustrated at his inability to make the White House pay attention to his warnings about suspected Communists in government, particularly in the case of Harry Dexter White. White, the assistant secretary of the treasury, had been Henry Morgenthau's right-hand man since 1934, and in June 1946, he was appointed by Truman to the International Monetary Fund (IMF) despite warnings that he was a spy. Three of Hoover's sources had named White as a member of a Soviet espionage ring: Whittaker Chambers (interviewed in depth by the Bureau on May 10, 1945); Igor Gouzenko, a Russian code clerk at the Soviet embassy in Canada who defected in September 1946 (questioned by the FBI in October of that year); and, most importantly, the "blond spy queen" Elizabeth Bentley. From 1938 until 1945, Bentley had acted as a spy courier for her lover, Jacob Golos, one of the top operatives in Soviet espionage in the United States, and she told her story to the Bureau on November 7, 1945. Her revelations provided the background for Hoover's investigations not only of Harry Dexter White, but of Alger Hiss, William Remington, Cedric Belfrage, and dozens of other notable cases of the late forties. Hoover disseminated Bentley's description of Soviet espionage activities throughout the government in memos in which he concealed her identity under the code name Gregory.[8]

On November 8, 1945, Hoover sent Truman (through the president's military aide, General Harry Vaughan) his first report on Harry Dexter White, stating that White was a member of a Communist espionage ring. On December 4, he followed this with a seventy-one-page memo (dated November 27) on all of Bentley's revelations, specifically her charges against White. Still another memo on the case, dated February 1, was delivered to the White House on February 4. On

October 21, 1946, Hoover sent the White House an updated account of Bentley's testimony.[9]

By disregarding these warnings, and appointing White to a post in the IMF, Truman gave the Republicans ammunition to charge him with incompetence (the most charitable interpretation) or else a sinister willingness to tolerate Communists in government. Hoover himself seems to have wavered between these two positions. The warnings, however clear they seemed in retrospect (for example, in 1953, when Hoover gave a detailed account of them to the Senate Internal Security Subcommittee), were obscured at the time by the usual high ratio of noise to signal. Truman knew that nearly every member of the New Deal administration had been accused of being a Communist; he knew that Hoover had carried many of these charges to the White House. Why should the Harry Dexter White case be any different? Had the public been less hysterical, and, thus, not so ready to believe the worst, Truman could even have defended himself by showing some of Hoover's more farfetched and alarmist war warnings to the press.

Ironically, Hoover had earlier anesthetized even himself with his warnings of subversives in the government. A few years before, in 1942, he had not followed up on Chambers's accusations against Hiss and others when he first learned of them. Even Hoover, sympathetic though he was to the motives and goals of the Red hunters of the depression and World War II years, recognized that many of them were irresponsible and dangerous. Martin Dies, for example, had charged that top administrators in the Office of Price Administration, the FCC, and thirty-five officials in the Board of Economic Warfare were, if not Communists, then simply "irresponsible, unrepresentative, radical and crackpot." Dies even accused one of being a nudist. Of the 1,124 names Dies sent to Francis Biddle in October 1941, Hoover's investigation had discovered grounds for dismissing only two, and disciplining one. Hoover knew that Elizabeth Dilling's *Red Network* (a notorious 1934 compilation of rumors about undercover Communists) had listed social worker Jane Addams, Wilson's Secretary of War Newton Baker, Senator William Borah of Idaho, Mrs. Justice Brandeis, Ambassador William Bullitt, Eleanor Roosevelt, Secretary of the Interior Harold Ickes, and Mayor Fiorello Laguardia. "Lists" of communists were so common and generally so worthless, that not even Hoover paid them much attention.[10]

The FBI had statutory authority to enforce the Espionage Acts and the Hatch Act, so it was Hoover's duty to be on the lookout for spies. His interest increased in 1945 when he began to get multiple reports from independent sources naming the same government employees as underground Communists. But the reason Hoover became so insistent in warning the administration about spies and subversives immediately after the war was his awareness that international tensions almost always were accompanied by a spy scare, and to survive it he would have to produce spectacular spy cases to prove the situation was under control. But now Hoover's warnings about Communist infiltration of the government had to compete with ten years of very similar warnings from the extreme right as well as the mass of unevaluated rumors he himself continuously sent to the White House so he would not be open to charges that he had ignored the one rumor in a hundred that turned out to be true.

On May 29, 1946, Hoover sent the White House an extreme example of such unverified reports. This stated that a "source believed to be reliable" had said there was an enormous Soviet espionage ring in Washington" that was trying to obtain information about atomic energy, and he listed the people involved, all "noted for their pro-Soviet leanings": Under Secretary of State Dean Acheson, Acheson's Assistant, Herbert Marks, former Assistant Secretary of War John J. McCloy, Assistant Secretary of War Howard C. Peterson, Secretary of Commerce Henry A. Wallace, Paul Appleby and George Schwartzwalder, both of the Bureau of the Budget, Edward U. Condon of the Bureau of Standards, and Alger Hiss, Abe Feller, and James R. Newman, all connected with the United Nations and serving in various branches of the government. Hoover called special attention to Hiss, Appleby, Condon, Schwartzwalder, and McCloy. Condon, according to Hoover's source, was "nothing more or less than an espionage agent in disguise." Hoover's informant also claimed that Senator Brian McMahon's investigation of the Atomic Energy Commission (AEC) was going to give these spies a chance to pick up an enormous haul of atomic secrets. In another memo, Hoover had even accused McMahon's secretary of being a Communist. The Bureau had learned "through various sources" of the "pro-Russian" political views of Acheson, Peterson, and Wallace, so "it is not beyond the realm of conjecture that they would fit into a scheme as set out above." He reminded the White House that Hiss "has been reported to this Bureau as a former member of the Communist underground organization."[11]

Searching for spies and persuading the government to act against them were only part of Hoover's internal security activities in early 1946.

Another was to have plans ready in case he was called upon, in an outbreak of hostilities or of public hysteria, to arrest enemy sympathizers. This cold war "Custodial Detention Program" entailed such elaborate preparations, and posed such enormous legal and political risks, that it affected almost everything Hoover did in domestic intelligence during the Truman administration. In fact, making the complicated legal, logistical, and political arrangements necessary in order to be able to round up suspects is the thread that connects the seemingly unrelated parts of Hoover's wide-ranging domestic security operations during the cold war. Taken out of the historical context, Hoover's custodial detention programs appear bizarre as well as ominous. But against the background of the post–World War II war scare, his expectation that he might soon be forced to make such arrests to defuse scares and war hysteria is perhaps no less disturbing, but hardly irrational. As head of the FBI, it was expected that Hoover would have detailed detention plans ready for instantaneous execution in the event of an attack by the Soviet Union. Such a situation, where detainees would have to be chosen by ideology rather than nationality, would have presented the FBI with problems of unprecedented complexity.[12] Unlike earlier instances of internment, the Alien Enemy Proclamation would have been useless (most of the suspects would be citizens) and a roundup of Eastern European ethnic groups would have been preposterous: These were among the most anti-Soviet groups in the country.

Planning a detention program, and compiling lists of those to be arrested based on their beliefs and associations, was a major part of the Bureau's intelligence work during the 1940s and 1950s. Hoover's Palmer raids had been derailed, and Palmer's reputation destroyed, because not every detail of the dragnets had been worked out ahead of time. Hoover's memory of that disaster fully explains his meticulousness in planning his cold war detention programs. In March 1946, Hoover advised Attorney General Clark that he was going to "intensify [the Bureau's] investigation of Communist Party activities and Soviet espionage cases" to produce a complete list of "all members of the Communist party and any others who would be dangerous in the event of a break in diplomatic relations with the Soviet Union, or any other serious crisis involving the United States and the U.S.S.R." Since in any emergency large numbers of those detained would be American citizens, he requested that the department survey available legislation to see what additional authority should be sought from Congress.[13]

Friction between Hoover and the administration over the Custodial

Detention Program, as well as the White House's resistance to his reports on Communist infiltration of the government, convinced Hoover he could not count on Truman or Clark for the support he would need in an emergency. When he recalled how attacks from such liberals and civil libertarians as Louis Post, Judge George Anderson, Tom Walsh, and others had nearly destroyed him during the Palmer days, he decided that he and the Bureau had no alternative but to treat the Truman administration as a potential enemy and to seek new political alliances.

Hoover's 1919–1920 experience had also made him thoroughly aware of how important public support was to the success of any massive internal security campaign, which would inevitably provoke enormous opposition and be subjected to legal challenge. In February 1946, Hoover approved a recommendation from his Executive Conference that "an effort should be made now to prepare educational material which can be released through available channels so that in the event of an emergency we will have an informed public opinion." The goal was to undercut the "flood of propaganda" that would be unleashed "in the event of extensive arrests of Communists."[14]

Eventually, shaping public opinion to support FBI action against communism became a coordinated effort by the Crime Records Division, the Bureau's top executives, and the field SACs. Field agents were trained to work with the local media to develop anti-Communist public opinion, and Hoover's own speeches took on a more pronounced "cultural orientation" even when addressing such groups as HUAC on the operational side of exposing Communists. To gain public support for the Bureau's position on communism, its presence in popular entertainment once again reached the levels of the mid-thirties. The focus was now on the newest G-man hero, the undercover informant, on the radio, movie screen, and, soon, television. This new G-man was seen infiltrating the Communist party, surreptitiously passing evidence to his superiors in the Bureau, and, finally, confronting the Party as a witness in congressional hearings or in the courtroom.[15]

In June 1946, the Republican National Committee announced that the theme of its fall election campaign would be the choice between "Communism and Republicanism." Democrats were now frightened, so in July, a subcommittee of the House Civil Service Committee charged that there was immediate need for a commission to create a "complete and unified" program to root out government employees "whose primary loyalty is to governments other than our own." For the next few months, Congress busied itself passing laws to give existing

departments the power to dismiss disloyal employees, and to provide
new agencies (for example, the AEC) with this authority. The Chamber
of Commerce joined the battle against Communists in government
with a highly publicized report in October, compiled with FBI assistance, claiming that Communists and fellow travelers had penetrated
the government, especially the State Department, and, more to the
point, the labor unions. The chamber called for a drive to expel "subversives" from any positions from which they could influence public opinion, direct government policy, or control the economy. The day before
the November election, Republican Congressman Joseph Martin
claimed that the choice was between "chaos, confusion, bankruptcy,
state socialism or communism, and the preservation of the American
way of life." The Communist issue was infecting all of American
politics. A Washington Republican argued that "if someone insists
there is discrimination against Negroes in this country, or that there
is inequality of wealth, there is every reason to believe that person
is a communist."[16]

The Republicans' Red-baiting campaign gave them control of the
House and Senate for the first time in more than a decade. Truman
belatedly realized that his enemies had captured the most explosive
political issue of the day, and that they were not going to give up a
winning strategy. On November 25, in a desperate effort to capture
the initiative in the internal security controversy, he accepted the recommendation of the House subcommittee and appointed a Temporary
Commission on Employee Loyalty to report on ways of dealing with
this problem; the commission was chaired by Hoover's nominee,
A. Devitt Vanech.[17]

Hoover submitted his views to the Temporary Commission in a
memo on January 3. He warned that "subversive or disloyal persons"
in the government were a threat to security; they might commit espionage, influence government policies to suit the interests of a foreign
power, clothe enemy propaganda with the cloak of "official sanction,"
or recruit other individuals to serve a subversive conspiracy. He recommended that a Loyalty Review Board be established with the power
to "approve or overrule" departmental decisions regarding loyalty of
employees, and that the FBI should have the continuing responsibility
of investigating subversion among incumbent employees. Despite demands by civil libertarians to allow accused employees to confront
their accusers, he also insisted that the FBI be allowed to keep its
sources and files confidential.[18]

The Temporary Commission adopted many of Hoover's ideas (the

Loyalty Board, for one), but he was nonetheless profoundly dissatisfied with the commission's report of February 20, which reflected Truman's conviction that there was no real loyalty problem—only a loyalty *issue*. In Hoover's eyes, the commission's proposals were only a cosmetic improvement on the existing loyalty programs. Despite "the [admitted] inadequacy of existing loyalty procedures," Hoover complained, the new program would not "materially change existing conditions." Truman ignored these objections when he issued his administration's Loyalty Program, Executive Order 9835 of March 22, 1947. The Truman program limited FBI investigations to incumbent employees, handed the investigation of new employees and those on temporary duty to the Civil Service Commission, left the decision on firing employees with unfavorable reports up to the heads of agencies, and gave departments discretion on whether to call on the FBI for its services. Coming after his failure to persuade the administration to act against White and other suspected spies and his friction with the Justice Department over the Custodial Detention Program, Truman's Loyalty Program convinced Hoover that Truman and Clark were simply not serious in their response to the espionage and subversion crisis.[19]

Hoover signaled his break with the Truman administration in a spectacular appearance before the rabidly anti–New Deal and anti–Truman House Un-American Activities Committee (HUAC) on March 26, 1947; this served notice that he had renounced his historic allegiance to the executive and was joining forces with Congress in the battle over the loyalty issue. Only a week before Truman had issued his Loyalty Program, the new Republican chairman of HUAC, J. Parnell Thomas, had invited Hoover to appear before the committee to "submit any recommendations or proposals touching upon any aspects of Communism." As he had always done when invited to appear before any congressional committee except the House and Senate Appropriations committees, Hoover declined. He told Attorney General Clark he did not wish to testify, and that he had heard from Thomas that the real purpose of the hearing was "a full dress denunciation of Communism." He added that his appearance would result in a disclosure of Bureau techniques and a drying up of sources. In a private briefing, Thomas, via Louis Nichols, had alerted Hoover to HUAC's intentions, which were even more partisan than usual. Thomas told Nichols that HUAC knew "the Director had been under wraps for years, that the Administration favored Communists." Hoover could use the committee, Thomas added, as a "sounding board . . . a grand opportunity" to "say anything he wanted to say."[20]

Once he saw Truman's Loyalty Program, Hoover suddenly changed his mind about appearing. He ordered his aides to arrange an immediate appointment for him with the committee, and to draw up a statement on communism for his testimony.[21]

Hoover had decided that Truman's Loyalty Program was not strong enough to deflect congressional charges that the administration was incapable of dealing with the security issue. His experience told him that, for the country at large, and the FBI in particular, this would be the most important issue in American politics. Like everyone else in the country (except Truman), Hoover probably saw the Republican victory in the 1946 congressional elections as a sure sign that the Republicans were going to win the presidency in 1948. Political expediency dictated that he move over to the winning side.

But Hoover's defection was not simply expediency. Hoover was also a moralist. In his opinion, Truman was defending evil when he sided with those accused of disloyalty, rather than their accusers. In Hoover's mind, by trying to force the FBI to share its statutory responsibility under the Hatch Act to investigate government subversion with the less-qualified Civil Service Commission, Truman was also weakening national security.

Hoover realized the audacity and the risk of abandoning his traditional power base within the executive branch of government. He asked a friend to accompany him when he went to testify, saying "this is a big day for me. . . . I'm going to make my first public statement on Communism before the House Un-American Activities Committee." The friend reported that Hoover afterward "felt very good about the speech and the reaction to it."[22]

Hoover's HUAC testimony resurrected and updated the brief against the Communist party he had presented in 1919 and 1920. He used the Communists' own boasts and predictions of success to provide an interpretive context of motive and intent for the recent history of American communism. Attorney General Biddle's finding in the Harry Bridges deportation case gave him the precise formulation of his thesis, which was that the Communist party "believes in, advises, advocates, and teaches the overthrow by force and violence of the Government of the United States." Despite the recent changes in Party line, he said, the "American Communist, like the leopard, cannot change his spots . . . the one cardinal rule . . . [is] that the support of Soviet Russia is the duty of Communists of all nations." To refute Communist denials of violent intent, he employed the technique of interpreting Communist peace offerings as threats concealed in "Aesopian language" (a phrase borrowed from Lenin's pre-1917 writings that referred to speech that concealed its real meaning). Since Communists were masters of deceit, experts like himself were needed to explain the true conspiratorial import of the Party's deceptively idealistic slogans.[23]

He painted the congressmen a picture of a Communist party of some 74,000 members, with ten sympathizers for each, who knew "it is a fight to the finish and that their backs are against the wall." Moreover, he said, "the size of the Party is relatively unimportant because of the enthusiasm and iron-clad discipline under which they operate." He gave the congressmen one of his favorite statistics: "In this connection, it might be of interest to observe that in 1917 when the Communists overthrew the Russian government there was one Communist for every 2,277 persons in Russia. In the United States today there is one Communist for every 1,814 persons in the country."

The heart of Hoover's testimony was his endorsement of HUAC's crusade to keep "Communists and sympathizers out of government services," which was necessary because government agencies had failed to take the Bureau's warnings seriously. Out of the 6,193 cases the Bureau had investigated under the Hatch Act, he said, there had been only 101 firings, twenty-one resignations, and seventy-five cases of administrative action. He told HUAC about one employee of the Federal Security Agency who had been retained even after the Bureau submitted a fifty-seven-page report on his Communist party activities. Then, after he had voluntarily left the government, he had turned up on the National Committee of the Communist Party. It was a Party requirement, Hoover added, that to be eligible for the position of committeeman, an individual had to have been a party member for at least four years.

This kind of nonfeasance had made his own and HUAC's anti-Communist drives necessary. "I do fear," he said, "for the liberal and progressive who has been hoodwinked and duped into joining hands with the Communists . . . [for the] school boards and parents [who] tolerate conditions whereby Communists and fellow travelers under the guise of academic freedom can teach our youth a way of life that eventually will destroy the sanctity of the home, that undermines faith in God, that causes them to scorn respect for constituted authority and sabotage our revered Constitution." The Communist party, he said, was a "Fifth Column if there ever was one. It is far better organized than were the Nazis in occupied countries prior to their capitulation. . . . There is no doubt as to where a real Communist's loyalty rests. Their allegiance is to Russia, not the United States."

Hoover told HUAC its mission was to rally the public against communism, exposing Communists to public wrath wherever they might be found. "I feel that once public opinion is thoroughly aroused as it is today, the fight against Communism is well on its way. Victory will be assured once Communists are identified and exposed, because the public will take the first step of quarantining them so they can do no harm. Communism, in reality, is not a political party. It is a way of life—an evil and malignant way of life. It reveals a condition akin to disease that spreads like an epidemic and like an epidemic a quarantine is necessary to keep it from infecting the Nation."

Anticipating an attack from liberal Democrats for openly siding with such an implacable enemy of the Roosevelt and Truman administrations as HUAC, Hoover struck first by claiming that "anyone who opposes the American Communist is at once branded as a 'disrupter,' a 'Fascist,' a 'Red baiter,' or a 'Hitlerite,' and becomes the object of a systematic campaign of character assassination." He told HUAC that he and they would have to expect such attacks because "the basic tactics of the Communist Party are deceit and trickery."

Hoover's appearance before the committee announced his alliance with the antiadministration Red hunters. In joining forces with HUAC, Hoover achieved formal recognition as the senior partner, the leading power of the anti-Communist right. For his part, he endorsed HUAC's strategy against subversives: destroying them by means of "prescriptive publicity." Both the FBI and the committee, Hoover told the congressmen, aimed at the same goal, "protection of the internal security of the nation," but the methods were different: While the FBI had to produce evidence acceptable in a court of law, HUAC's "greatest contribution" was "the public disclosure of the forces that menace America—Communist and Fascist. . . . This Committee renders a distinct service when it publicly reveals the diabolic machinations of sinister figures engaged in un-American activities."

Hoover's HUAC appearance was a virtuoso performance: a tirade against the indifference of liberals to the Communist threat, an advertisement of his own and the Bureau's preparedness, and an appeal to the public to approve and support the new anti-Communist drive. Behind all this was Hoover's cherished vision of the FBI as a progressive, professional agency, specially equipped to lead a national movement, a force with a special responsibility to provide national leadership.

Hoover saw himself as a national leader, and to him a national leader turned public events into moral lessons, and used controversy to increase public support for the central values of society. "The best antidote to Communism," he said, "is vigorous, intelligent, old-fashioned Americanism with eternal vigilance," and that was what, in this emergency, he was going to provide.

HUAC's enthusiastic response to Hoover's testimony (members hailed it as "the most masterful and conclusive statement of your career on the subject of this very definite menace") encouraged him to escalate his rebellion against the administration and the president. When Harry B. Mitchell, head of the Civil Service Commission, tried to perform his duties under Truman's Loyalty Program, Hoover threatened to pull the FBI out from all loyalty work unless the commission left *all* investigations to the Bureau. He wrote Clark that he was willing to give the Civil Service Commission

> the full, complete, entire and exclusive responsibility for conducting all investigations of Government employees about whose loyalty there is any question whatsoever. I want you to know that this Bureau is perfectly willing to withdraw from this field of investigation rather than to engage in a tug of war with the Civil Service Commission over the investigative jurisdiction of subversive employees of the Federal government.[24]

Hoover had previously reserved his imperious manner for subordinates and equals. Now he no longer bothered to conceal his arrogance and insubordination from his superior, the attorney general of the United States. Clark knew, and Truman knew, that the administration needed Hoover. But, with his new allies, Hoover no longer needed the administration. That meant it was more important than ever for Hoover to strengthen his relationships with the conservatives throughout the government, economy, and society. This was his power base now that he had cast himself loose from the administration.

Truman made one final attempt to defeat Hoover's monopoly over the loyalty program by trying to let the Civil Service Commission conduct investigations of at least the new employees, but he quickly learned that this was a futile gesture, easily circumvented by Hoover's friends in Congress. According to aide George Elsey, Truman was at this point "very strongly anti-FBI," and wanted to "hold [the] FBI down, [being] afraid of [a] 'Gestapo'." But he also recognized the brutal political strength of Hoover's alliance with HUAC and resigned himself to the fact that Congress would not tolerate anything that seemed to hobble the FBI, lamenting that "J. Edgar will in all probability get this backward-looking Congress to give him all he wants. It's dangerous." As Truman had foreseen, instead of giving the Civil Service Commission $16 million and the FBI $8.7 million as the administration had originally proposed, Congress provided the FBI with $7.4 million and the Civil Service Commission only $3 million. This effectively turned the program over to the FBI.[25]

Truman had grievously wounded Hoover's professional pride by refusing to act on his warnings about subversion. Since Hoover firmly believed that he knew more about security than anyone else, and since he felt this superiority was obvious to anyone not blinded by an ulterior motive, he could not accept the sincerity of any who opposed him in this area.

After March 1947, Hoover maintained formally correct relations with the White House, but there were no more friendly chitchats like those he had shared with FDR, and even with Truman prior to 1947. (After the Republican victory in the November 1946 elections, Hoover had sent Truman an essay on "the Penalty of Leadership," which Hoover felt expressed some "good homespun philosophy" from which the president might "get some consolation.") Hoover did continue to furnish Truman with political intelligence that would help him against his rivals within the Democratic party, but he gave him no help against the Republicans.[26]

Truman and his aides recognized that they had made a dangerous enemy in Hoover, but they failed to understand the nature of his bitterness against the administration. Truman said, "Hoover was concerned with his own future: If he thought the Democrats would win the election in November, he would [do what Truman wanted] but if he thought the Republicans would win he would probably answer all questions [about a politically sensitive spy case involving William Remington]." The White House was unable to grasp the depth of the resentment which had surfaced in Hoover and his supporters, resentment that made them attack anyone who stood against the anti-Communist drive. The administration even made a pathetic attempt to have Hoover denounce "the meddling of the House Un-American Activities Committee and how they dried up sources of information which would have been accessible in the prosecution of spies and communists," but Hoover made sure that his aides issued no statements that could be interpreted as being "critical of the Committee."[27]

Once Hoover had broken with the administration over the loyalty issue, the popular press looked to him for authoritative official statements on the Communist menace. Truman could still use the presidency to define the foreign threat, but he lost the ability to control the domestic security agenda. When *Newsweek* ran a feature on "Communism and Its Influence in America" it therefore turned to Hoover, "the one responsible Federal official most directly concerned with Communism and Communists." Hoover told *Newsweek's* readers that "we effectively protected ourselves against spies and saboteurs during the late world war without sacrificing the civil rights of a single citizen. We can protect ourselves against the infiltration of Communists by the same defensive, democratic means in the American way." He really had in mind something different than the sort of professional counterespionage work by the Bureau he had promoted as the answer to Nazi spies. Now he meant the use of publicity to expose Communist infiltration. He hailed the work of HUAC, saying that when the committee

> fulfills its obligation of public disclosure of facts it is worthy of the support of loyal, patriotic Americans. This committee has for its purpose the exposure of un-American forces and as such its files contain voluminous information which, when used with discretion, provide an excellent source of information. The FBI, unlike this committee, must of necessity keep the contents of its files confidential.[28]

The "slogan in the fight against Communism," he wrote, should be "uncover, expose and spotlight their activities. Once this is done, the American people will do the rest—quarantine them from effectively weakening our country." But the Communists were not the only menace: there were also "Communist sympathizers," "fellow travelers," and "Communist stooges." It did not matter whether they were "innocent, gullible, or willful . . . because they further the cause of Communism and weaken our American democracy." Against them all, Hoover said, the best defense was "our own American way of life."

J. Edgar Hoover's most important domestic security case during the Truman years—the 1948–1949 Smith Act prosecution of the national leadership of the Party—had its origins in his preparations for an emergency custodial detention program. When the Justice Department rejected Hoover's request for new legislation to authorize detention of dangerous citizens during hostilities (which the Justice Department thought was politically impossible), Hoover endorsed a Bureau recommendation that the department prosecute test cases under the Smith Act to obtain a judicial precedent. Then, in an emergency, the FBI could arrest Communists as

> substantive violators [of the Smith Act]. This in turn has an important bearing on the Bureau's position should there be no legislative or adminis-

trative authority available at the time of the outbreak of hostilities which would permit the immediate apprehension of both aliens and citizens of the dangerous category.[29]

Gil Green, one of the Smith Act defendants, later pointed out that the Bureau's strategy "was predicated on the inevitability of war, for [the above memo] did not say 'should' hostilities break out but *'at the time'* they do." From Green's point of view, this choice of words had sinister connotations, but a more likely interpretation is that Hoover and his aides were acting on the sincere belief that there was a real likelihood in the near future of war between the United States and the Soviet Union.[30]

Like the great gangster cases of the thirties, Hoover also saw the Smith Act cases as a chance for the FBI to mobilize public support for a new FBI-led crusade, this time an anti-Communist movement with the FBI in its traditional role: the Bureau would supply research for the rest of the movement (through informants, wiretaps, and surveillance), maintain technical facilities (its files), and provide professional training and advice which would include training conferences, speeches by Hoover and his staff, FBI publications on communism, and staff assistance to HUAC, the Senate Internal Security Subcommittee, and other anti-Communist investigators. Hoover differed from more politically opportunistic anti-Communist conservatives in that he saw anticommunism as a comprehensive cooperative movement, cast in the mold of his anticrime drive of the thirties. Moreover, all his anti-Communist activities had an internal consistency because they were all connected by his institutional need to have ready a workable plan for the custodial detention of Communists and their sympathizers for the war emergency he expected would soon occur.

Hoover's preparations for the Smith Act prosecution of the Communist party retraced the path he had followed as the young director of Palmer's Radical Division in 1919. During 1946 and 1947, Hoover compiled a historical study of the American Communist party, aimed at demonstrating its legal vulnerability under the 1940 Smith Act; he then submitted the massive "brief," which bulked to 1,350 pages with 546 exhibits, to the internal security section of the Justice Department. Hoover's purpose in 1919 had been to convince the secretary of labor to deport alien Communists; now he had the more difficult task of persuading a hostile Justice Department to seek a grand jury indictment against American citizens, and then to persuade a jury to find them guilty. He did have the advantage, this time, of having a federal law on the books almost identical to the peacetime sedition law he and Palmer had wanted in 1920. In broad design, Hoover was replaying the 1919–1920 assault on the American Communists, but he was avoiding this time the mistakes that had defeated him before.[31]

In February 1948, shortly after Hoover urged Attorney General Clark to seek prosecution of the Party leadership to "obtain . . . judicial recognition of the aims and purposes of the Communist party," HUAC demanded that Clark explain why he had not begun any Smith Act prosecutions. The committee had been holding up its own inquiry so as not to interfere with a New York federal grand jury looking into subversion. To keep HUAC satisfied, Clark would have to show them some results in New York. On June 29, the New York grand jury indicted the twelve members of the Communist National Board for conspiring to organize the Party in 1945, when the Party had dropped the pretense of being the Communist Political Association and reorganized as a Stalinist party. The timing of Clark's decision to prosecute was so obviously political that it outraged Hoover's sense of professionalism: In an effort to avoid splitting the Democratic party over the issue of anticommunism, Clark had the indictments sealed until July 20 to delay announcement until after the Democratic party convention. (This was a futile effort; former Vice President Henry Wallace and Senator Glenn Taylor of Idaho and their Communist backers bolted the Democratic party and ran against Truman on the Progressive ticket.) Thus it was not until it suited the administration's political purposes that Hoover was allowed to arrest five of the Party's top leadership at its New York headquarters on July 20; the remaining seven were arrested over the next two weeks.[32]

The Justice Department's decision to restrict prosecution initially to the twelve members of the Communist National Board disappointed Hoover, who had wanted to arrest all fifty-five members of the National Committee before it had time to hide its records, thus leaving only the roundup of the rank and file for the beginning of hostilities. In an internal memo, Hoover complained that the arrest of only a dozen Communists proved that the administration was "insincere" in its anticommunism. The timing of the arrests, he said, was designed as "a political move . . . timed to break just before the convening of the Wallace-for-President convention in Philadelphia today." Hoover went on to say that

it had been hoped that the Grand Jury investigation would be carried out in much the same way as the investigation of the Industrial Workers of the World [IWW] in 1917 during World War I. The IWW case was inaugurated by a simultaneous national move against every IWW headquarters throughout the United States. All national and local leaders of the IWW were indicted and over one hundred sentenced to long prison terms. As a result of this joint national action the IWW was crushed and has never revived. Similar action at this time would have been as effective against the Communist Party and its subsidiary organizations.

Hoover added that he himself had been "in an executive position in the federal service at that time and had an important part in the IWW prosecution and thus . . . [knew] from experience that a local prosecution is not effective against a national organization if those in charge of the prosecution sincerely desire to suppress conspiratorial activities of the sort engaged in by the Communist Party."[33]

Practically speaking, however, the Smith Act trial of the "Eleven" at New York's Foley Square Federal Courthouse (William Z. Foster's case had to be separated from the others because of bad health) was probably even more devastating to the Party than the larger roundup Hoover had wanted. The government astounded the Communists and disrupted their defense by producing one of their most trusted colleagues as a prosecution witness. This was Herbert Philbrick, a middle-level official of the Party who had been an FBI informant since 1940. The Party was staggered by the sensational disclosure that the FBI had penetrated its inner circles, and that its most tightly guarded secrets were in the hands of the government. Following Philbrick to the witness stand was another FBI informer, Angela Calomaris, who had stayed active in the Party until just before her testimony. In later Smith Act trials, Philbrick and Calomaris would be joined by another government witness, John Lautner, who had set up much of the Party's underground in the United States. Lautner defected to the FBI when the Party accused him—falsely—of being a double agent and then expelled him in January 1950.

The testimony of Philbrick and Calomaris disoriented and demoralized the Party's leadership. It made them suspect each other as FBI informers. The FBI encouraged this paranoia in the Party by placing "snitch jackets" on members of the Party—that is, planting false evidence that individual Communists were working for the Bureau, a disruptive technique that dated at least back to 1920 and the attempted "frame-up" of Louis Fraina, one of the founders of the American Communist Party. (Fraina was cleared of charges that he was a Bureau double agent at a famous Party "trial." His accuser probably *was* working for the Bureau.)[34]

The government devoted most of its efforts at the Foley Square trial (which lasted from January 17 to October 14, 1949) to proving the guilt of the Communist party. For this, it relied on quotations from Communist classics going back to the *Manifesto.* Since it was not immediately obvious how this venerable material pertained to the overthrow of the American government in 1949, the prosecution supplied ex-Communists as expert witnesses, the most important being Louis Francis Budenz, former managing editor of the *Daily Worker,* who had left the Party in 1945.

Federal Judge Harold Medina allowed Budenz incredible latitude to show that, regardless of what the actual words in the Communist classics seemed to say, American Communists understood them to mean that "the Communist party of the United States is basically committed to the overthrow of the Government of the United States as set up by the Constitution of the United States." Medina allowed Budenz to interpret the seditious ideas and beliefs behind the sometimes innocent-sounding words of not only the defendants, but Marx, Engels, Lenin, and Stalin as well. Budenz informed the jury that denials of violent intent by Communists, or any documents they produced to refute their bloody-mindedness, should be rejected as "window dressing asserted for protective purposes."

Hoover congratulated Judge Medina after the jury found all eleven defendants guilty; Medina also sentenced their lawyers to jail terms for contempt for their disorderly conduct during the trial, an action that made it difficult, in some cases impossible, for later Smith Act defendants to secure legal counsel. All the defendants except a heavily decorated war veteran received the maximum five-year sentence permitted for conspiracy under the new federal code (he received three years). Unfortunately for their chances, the defendants had the handicap of appealing their convictions during the early days of the Korean war. This certainly had an effect on the reception given their appeals by the United States Court of Appeals and the Supreme Court, both of which turned them down. Seven of the Communist leaders reported to prison, the other four fled to try to continue their Party activities underground.

Over the next few months, Hoover was able to round up the remaining members of the Communist party hierarchy to stand trial, the so-called second echelon trials. In the end, 126 Communist leaders were indicted and ninety-three convicted. Only ten were acquitted; the remainder died before trial, were excused for bad health, or had their trials end in hung juries. The Smith Act drive finally slowed in 1954, when Hoover complained that by unmasking his informants, the trials were reducing "the highly essential intelligence coverage which this Bureau must maintain in the internal security field."[35] He therefore urged the Justice Department to prosecute only the most important leaders; he recommended careful consideration before a trial as to whether the greater benefit would result from prosecution or from continuing to maintain the informants in place.

On August 5, 1948, just two weeks after the arrests of the Smith Act defendants, Harry Truman made a blunder that turned the loyalty issue into a political free-for-all between the administration and its enemies in the FBI and Congress. On that day, former State Department official Alger Hiss was appearing before HUAC to answer charges brought by Whittaker Chambers. Truman's gaffe was to endorse a reporter's characterization of "the Capitol Hill spy scare" as a "red herring to divert the public's attention from inflation." This was a direct challenge to HUAC and to Hoover, because by now Hoover had become one of Whittaker Chambers's most important sponsors.

Initially, Hoover, like Truman, had been unable to take the charges against Hiss seriously. The FBI had first investigated Hiss when his name appeared on the list that the Dies Committee gave Roosevelt in 1941. When Chambers told the FBI, in May 1942, that Alger Hiss and his brother Donald were undercover Communists while they were in the Agriculture Department, Hoover rejected the resulting eight-page memo as "either history, hypothesis or deduction." Hoover's dismissal of Chambers's charges might have been a simple error, or it might have been because of Hoover's pique against Dies personally, which may have made him less than enthusiastic about helping Dies prove his cases. The episode also demonstrated Roosevelt's way of handling the nuisance of Red hunters like Hoover and Dies, which was to pit them against one another.[36]

Then, on May 10, 1945, in a markedly changed international climate and with a new president in the White House, Chambers had his second interview with the FBI. Now Hoover did take the twenty-two-page report on the interview seriously, and began leaking its contents to his allies in the anti-Communist movement. In October 1945, Hoover got corroborating information from Elizabeth Bentley and from the Canadian Royal Mounted Police interrogation of the Soviet defector, Igor Gouzenko—and, on the basis of these new suspicions, got permission from Clark to place a tap on Hiss's phone. Secretary of State Dean Acheson interviewed Hoover about the Gouzenko revelations, but Hoover, while confidentially telling Acheson about the charges against Hiss, said that "he did not feel it was the time to make any accusations as he lacked direct proof."[37]

Hoover sent his first warning about Hiss to Truman on November

27, 1945, a memo on "Soviet Espionage in the United States," based on the Elizabeth Bentley interviews. In March 1946, he advised the State Department to ease Hiss out informally since bringing charges against him would have unmasked Hoover's confidential sources and would have "alert[ed] him and ruin[ed] an important investigation." Hoover proposed that key people in Congress should be told of the allegations against Hiss, so that Congress could be portrayed as the source of the charges to conceal the FBI's role in the investigation. For the remainder of 1946, Hoover continued to send reports on Hiss to Truman, Secretary of State James F. Byrnes, and Attorney General Clark. By the end of the year, Hiss's advancement in the State Department was blocked on Byrnes's orders, and Hiss had learned of the probe into his loyalty. This may have been why he left the department on December 10 (or perhaps the offer to head the Carnegie Endowment was irresistible). In any case, Hiss moved to the Endowment post on February 1, 1947.[38]

The "red herring" confrontation between Alger Hiss and Whittaker Chambers finally became public on August 3, 1948, when Chambers, now a writer and editor for *Time* magazine, appeared before HUAC. He repeated his accusations that Hiss had been part of an underground Communist party group of government employees headed by Harold Ware, son of the Communist party's famous "Mother" Ella Reeve Bloor. Hiss was by far the most important government official yet accused of being a Communist: Reporters' ears perked up when Chambers reminded them that Hiss had organized both the Dumbarton Oaks conference to plan the United Nations, and the inaugural meeting of the United Nations at San Francisco. Moreover, Hiss had been with Roosevelt at Yalta, already a red flag to the Republicans. Chambers claimed that the "purpose of the [Hiss-Ware] group at that time was not primarily espionage. Its original purpose was the Communist infiltration of the American government. But espionage was certainly one of its eventual objectives."[39]

Chambers's account of his activities as an espionage agent for the Soviet Union during the mid-thirties provided powerful support for Bentley's account of the Communist underground, which Hoover had already endorsed. The time Hoover spent investigating Chambers in 1947 had convinced him that Chambers's account, like Bentley's, was true. The information they furnished became the basis of Hoover's portrait of the Communist underground. This meant that he had a great personal and organizational investment in the credibility of such witnesses as Chambers, and an equally great investment in having their charges taken seriously by government officials and the public. Truman's "red herring" characterization was therefore a reflection on the integrity of the anti-Communist investigators, and so a swipe at Hoover himself.

Hiss's August 5 refutation of Chambers's charges was so convincing and effective that it seemed the Communists-in-government investigation had been destroyed and that Truman's was going to be the final verdict on the spy hunt. Hiss even denied that he had ever known Chambers at all. One member of HUAC moaned, "We've been had! We're ruined!"[40] Richard Nixon, in a moment that was the real beginning of his rise to national power, saw a way to salvage something. "Although the committee could not determine who was lying on the issue of whether or not Hiss was a Communist, we could at least determine which was lying on the issue of whether or not Chambers knew Hiss." Nixon's insight eventually led to the charge of perjury on which Hiss was eventually indicted, tried, and convicted: on one count of having lied when he said he had not known Chambers, and (the statute of limitations having expired on the more serious charge of espionage) on a second of having falsely denied turning over classified documents to Chambers (among them the notorious "pumpkin papers" Chambers briefly hid in his garden).

Hoover threw all his resources into the effort to prove the perjury cases against Hiss, but was bothered and often frustrated by being a step or two behind Nixon and his energetic HUAC investigators. Hoover had 300 agents working on the case before the trial started on May 31, 1949. Once it began, he pored over the transcripts for blots on the Bureau's record. When the government prosecutor's opening remarks mentioned that Bureau agents had been unable to find Hiss's typewriter, Hoover had his aides search the prosecutor's files to see if there was any reason to consider the prosecutor, Thomas Murphy, "unfriendly toward the Bureau."[41]

On July 7, 1949, the first Hiss trial in New York ended in a hung jury (8–4 for conviction). Richard Nixon called for a probe of Judge Samuel H. Kaufman's fitness for the bench. (This kind of harassment may well have affected the attitude of the other Judge Kaufman, Irving Kaufman, who was the Rosenbergs' judge a year later.) A few weeks earlier, taking no chances that he might have antagonized Hoover, Nixon offered a House resolution commending the Director for his twenty-five years at the head of the FBI.[42]

The second trial began on November 17, 1949, with a new judge, Henry W. Goddard, a new defense team headed by Claude B. Cross, and a new prosecution strategy, one that stressed the material evidence of the documents and the typewriters and not Chambers's credibility. (Hiss's first lawyer, Lloyd Paul Stryker, felt that he could have gotten hung juries "forever" in this case, but that trying for an acquittal was an error.) On January 21, Hiss was found guilty on both counts of perjury.[43]

Finally, after all these years, Hoover had the politically unanswerable proof he had needed in 1919 that the Communist enemy was capable of treason, and had in fact committed treason. At last, one of the anticommunist right's endless and amorphous charges about treachery in government had been proven. It was no longer possible to dismiss theories about treason in high places as paranoid drivel, because the case against Hiss had been, in light of his background, reputation, and achievement, the most improbable of all. The Hiss conviction gave the other charges of disloyalty circulated by HUAC and, soon, Senator Joseph McCarthy of Wisconsin their "essential touch of credibility[,] . . . revolutionized public opinion" on the issue of communism and made it difficult for anyone ever again to talk about red herrings. The Hiss case had the effect of placing the burden of proof on the accused, instead of the accuser. "Without the . . . case, the six-year controversy that followed might have been a much tamer affair." In sum, the Hiss case was "a disaster for American liberalism."[44]

Truman had bet the prestige of his presidency that the spy scare was a hoax, and he had lost, thereby ceding to Hoover the job of defending internal security, which should have been his by right of office. Truman's inability to master the politics of this issue created a power vacuum in Washington that a host of ambitious politicians— notably Nixon and McCarthy—hastened to fill. As he had with Palmer, Hoover supported them from his fortified and partially concealed position within the FBI, letting HUAC and McCarthy gather much of the credit as well as the abuse.

Despite the advantages of letting others do the Bureau's political fighting, Hoover was by now too jealous of his own and the Bureau's reputation to be completely happy at being overlooked when the credit for a success like the Hiss case was being passed out. In one memo he complained that "we have missed the boat in many ways. *We* . . . didn't bring out the Hiss-Chambers connection. Furthermore we have been totally dead for months in our public relations when there were opportunities to get in some 'punches.' We are paying for it now. I hate to say 'I told you so' but I have for months been seeing this coming but could get no response." In a note to Clyde Tolson and Louis Nichols he said, "I am getting concerned about our public relations situation. We seem to be 'going to seed.' . . . [In the field of government loyalty investigations] the FBI which does the real work has been unusually silent. During the Hiss-Chambers case we have not made any effort thru our contacts to protect our position. All of this quiescence on part of FBI in all its fields results in public and Congress losing interest in us. By the time we wake up it may be too late to regain our prestige."[45]

Richard Nixon, who had gained the most from the Hiss case, may have become worried that Hoover felt slighted, and so he again paid Hoover an extraordinary tribute on the floor of the House. On January 26, 1950, Nixon presented his report on the Hiss trial. He insisted on sharing credit for the success of the case with the FBI, and he pointedly excluded mention of Truman's Justice Department; he blamed the department for having "failed or refused to institute an investigation which would lead to prosecution and conviction of those involved." The Hiss case meant, according to Nixon, that "we must give complete and unqualified support to the FBI and J. Edgar Hoover, its chief. Mr. Hoover recognized the Communist threat long before other top officials recognized its existence. The FBI in this trial did an amazingly effective job of running down trails over 10 years old and in developing the evidence which made the prosecution successful." The final lesson of the Hiss case was that the public should defend Hoover and the Bureau against anyone who would compromise their independence. "When the National Lawyers Guild or any similar organization is successful in obtaining an investigation of the FBI and access to its records," said Nixon, "a fatal blow will have been struck against the protective security forces of this nation."[46]

Hoover's most sensational spy case of the cold war, Julius and Ethel Rosenberg's conviction for passing atom bomb secrets for the Soviets, was played out in the midst of a classic wartime spy scare, when the wrath of the home front was unleashed against traitors believed responsible for the dangers facing the troops overseas. From the time of the Rosenbergs' arrests—Julius on July 17, 1950; Ethel, his wife, on August 11 of the same year—through the trial—which began on March 6, 1951—to their conviction on March 29 and the imposition of the death penalty on April 5, American troops were fighting in Korea, first falling back before the North Korean invasion of June

25, 1950, then advancing to the borders of Communist China, then retreating before the combined forces of Communist China and North Korea. At the same time, the U.S. faced the danger (some said the opportunity) of war with Stalin's Soviet Union, which had possessed the atom bomb since September 1949 (provided them, so it was believed, by Western traitors).

Hoover's anti–Communist allies were now even more willing than he to equate communism with treason and to blame disasters overseas on traitors at home. Judge Irving R. Kaufman imposed the death penalty on the Rosenbergs with the explanation that "this country is engaged in a life and death struggle with a completely different system. This struggle is not only manifested externally between these two forces but this case indicates quite clearly that it also involved the employment by the enemy of secret as well as overt outspoken forces among our own people. All our great democratic institutions are, therefore, directly involved in this great conflict." Evidently Kaufman saw the Rosenbergs' execution as a way to signal that the legal system was enlisted in this battle. The Rosenbergs' crime was "worse than murder," and their role "in putting into the hands of the Russians the A-bomb, years before our best scientists predicted Russia would perfect the bomb, had already caused, in my opinion, the Communist aggression in Korea, with the resultant casualties exceeding 50,000 and who knows but that millions more of innocent people may pay the price of your treason."[47]

Hoover was far more circumspect in expanding on the ultimate effect of the Rosenbergs' crime, although he had no doubts about Julius Rosenberg's guilt—that had been too strongly established by the testimony of David Greenglass and by overwhelming circumstantial evidence. Hoover's reluctance to go as far as many other anti–Communists in trumpeting the case's significance is worth noting because of the enormous credit he got for solving it. Judge Kaufman praised him publicly at the conclusion of the trial, saying, "Great tribute is due to the FBI and Mr. Hoover for the splendid job they have done in this case."

The reason for Hoover's uncharacteristic modesty was that he knew that the secrets Rosenberg had gotten from his brother-in-law, David Greenglass, and passed to the Soviets were not "the" secrets of the atom bomb, as Kaufman believed. Moreover, the execution of the Rosenbergs, while certainly supported by Hoover (though with important, though temporary, reservations), really represented a *failure* of strategy on Hoover's part. This failure, however, was successfully concealed from the public until long after Hoover's death.[48]

When Hoover called the theft of the atom bomb secrets the "Crime of the Century," he was not referring to the Rosenbergs but to Klaus Fuchs, the German-born English scientist who gave Harry Gold atomic secrets from the Los Alamos laboratory. The investigation that uncovered the Fuchs-Gold espionage operation was one of Hoover's proudest accomplishments. It was FBI codebreakers in the U.S. who discovered the evidence that led British counterintelligence to Klaus Fuchs. His confession on January 24, 1950, provided the Bureau with a description of "Raymond," the American courier to whom he had turned over information on the construction of the bomb. After a complex and ingenious investigation, the kind Hoover loved to describe as proof of the Bureau's mastery of scientific investigative methods, the FBI tracked down "Raymond," Harry Gold, whose confession to the Bureau on May 22, 1950, revealed that there had been a second spy at Los Alamos. This was David Greenglass, who implicated his brother-in-law, Julius Rosenberg, as the person who had recruited him to join the spy network, and to whom he had passed his crude sketches of the atom bomb. There the trail ended, because Julius refused to talk and denied all of Gold's and Greenglass's allegations.

The prosecutorial system often, even usually, results in the last member of a conspiracy who confesses, or the member who does not confess, suffering the maximum punishment, while his co-conspirators who cooperate with the government escape with lighter penalties, though equally guilty. The unfairness is enormously magnified by the death penalty. Harry Gold testified against the Rosenberg conspirators (for the most part, his testimony implicated Greenglass; he had no direct contact with Rosenberg). His role in the spy network was comparable to that of Rosenberg, and the secrets he had gotten from Fuchs far more important than those Rosenberg had gotten from Greenglass. Yet he got a thirty-year sentence for the same offense that cost Rosenberg and his wife their lives on June 19, 1953. (Greenglass got fifteen years.) Rosenberg's real crime, and the one for which he paid with his life and his wife's, was his refusal to provide the FBI with the information Hoover needed to prosecute the other members of his spy ring. Some of these people were already known to the FBI, and their houses were under surveillance on the day of the execution in case Rosenberg cracked and gave the Bureau the evidence it needed to arrest them.[49]

The indictment of Ethel Rosenberg was essentially a prosecutorial ploy. Hoover had been the first to suggest indicting her, telling Attorney General J. Howard McGrath that "there is no question . . . if Julius Rosenberg would furnish details of his extensive espionage activities it would be possible to proceed against other individuals . . . proceedings against his wife might serve as a lever in this matter." Hoover had reached a dead end in his investigation of the Rosenberg spy ring, and needed information that could only come from Rosenberg. Ethel's indictment, trial, and death were all part of a failed plan to force information out of Rosenberg. Thus, the Rosenberg case was no great triumph in Hoover's mind, and although he put the best public face on, he left it to others to magnify the case as an anti-Communist triumph. He himself was not inclined to overestimate the importance of what the Rosenbergs had given the Russians. A year before the execution, Hoover wrote his agents that it had not been "solely through the operations of the Rosenberg espionage network in this country" that the Soviets had gotten the bomb; he told them that the Russians had been "working on atomic energy projects during this period and had undoubtedly developed certain phases . . . independently of any data received through espionage." In his own account of the case, Hoover said flatly that it was "as a result of the arrangements made . . . by Harry Gold and Dr. Fuchs [that] Soviet Russia was to obtain secrets of the atom bomb."[50]

The failure of his plan to pressure Rosenberg into talking by bringing his wife to trial was why Hoover was shocked to learn Judge Kaufman was determined to execute Ethel as well as Julius. He also had a difficult time reconciling himself to the execution of a woman, a mother of two small children. Kaufman had sent prosecutor Irving Saypol to Washington to obtain Hoover's thoughts on the sentences; Kaufman was disturbed to learn Hoover would not support the recommendation of a death penalty for Ethel, but he was undeterred by Hoover's warning that the public would be revolted by the execution of a wife and mother. Hoover also sent a memo to the attorney general calling attention to the fate of the two children who would be orphaned if the execution was carried out. In their examination of the case, Ronald Radosh and Joyce Milton note that Hoover was the only public official to ask that the children be taken into consideration. Kaufman, however, was determined that his sentence make the strongest possible statement against espionage, and so he followed his own inclinations.[51]

Hoover eventually reconciled himself to Mrs. Rosenberg's execution, but only through what seems to have been willful self-deception about her qualities as a mother. To a plea from *her* mother that she confess her guilt for the sake of the children Ethel had replied, "Don't mention the children. Children are born every day of the week." To

Hoover this revealed Ethel to be an unnatural woman without a normal mother's heart.[52] That let Hoover work himself up to the same revulsion he had once felt for Ma Barker, who had been not only a criminal but a blasphemy against the memory of his idolized mother and the institution of motherhood.

Hoover published his personal account of the atom spy case in the May 1951 issue of *Reader's Digest,* written, presumably, immediately after the Rosenbergs were found guilty. He focused exclusively on Fuchs and Gold; the Rosenbergs were not mentioned at all. "In all the history of the FBI," he wrote, "there never was a more important problem than this one, never another case where we felt under such pressure." He turned the case into another demonstration of scientific detective work, more proof that only the FBI possessed the scope, skills, and experience to protect the country from spies so clever, dangers so great. A Hoover crime story always had a point: but where Kaufman had interpreted spying as a crime against the state (in effect, treason), Hoover underlined the moral meaning of the case. It was, he said, a "staggering revelation of how a foreign power, espousing a doctrine of hate, frightfulness and slavery, can unfasten the loyalties of free men and women and turn them into traitors. . . . In them we see the tragic horror of communism: it blights the moral strength of man, leaving him only a puppet to be manipulated at will." The moral rather than the political evil of communism was what most appalled Hoover, so crimes committed by Communists were most meaningful as external signs of this invisible blight. Thus any contact at all with communism, even on the level of theory, was dangerous, potentially contagious, as the case of Harry Gold proved: at last, Hoover wrote, Gold came "to see that Communism had robbed him of the conscience of a free American, completely paralyzing his power of moral resistance. No spiritual force was left within him to stay his deeds of treason."[53]

Throughout his career, once Hoover decided he could not trust someone, that person was marked for life. If he was subsequently unfriendly to the Bureau, that validated Hoover's judgment. If he was friendly, it proved his insincerity. This was how Hoover viewed Truman after 1947. Administration ineptitude, most notably the legal blunders that permitted the exposure of raw FBI files during the 1949 trial of Justice Department employee Judith Coplon for stealing government documents for the Russians, greatly embarrassed Hoover and the FBI, and confirmed him in his disdain for Truman. Even so, the president's political plight became so desperate in his second administration that several times he sought Hoover's help. In August 1950, Truman's aide Stephen Spingarn made an unsuccessful attempt to persuade Hoover to endorse the administration's security policies and to oppose HUAC's attacks on the administration's handling of the loyalty problem, but Hoover, of course, declined. Late in 1951, during the heat of the "mess in Washington" scandals, Truman frantically searched for an impartial and respected official to head a commission on government corruption. He approached Judge Thomas Murphy, who had prosecuted Alger Hiss; he asked former Roosevelt counsel Samuel Rosenman and Senator Wayne Morse of Oregon. According to reports, he even offered the job to Hoover, who turned him down.[54]

Hoover's success leading the government drive against Communists effectively discredited the Justice Department; it gave him what amounted to a veto over Truman's replacement for the feckless and embattled J. Howard McGrath as attorney general. Hoover was able to block Justin Miller's appointment as McGrath's successor. He had disliked Miller since the thirties when Miller handled press relations for Homer Cummings, which put him in de facto competition with Hoover's own public relations operations. In 1952, during the confirmation hearings on James McGranery, who was eventually named to replace McGrath, a senator phoned Assistant Director Louis Nichols and told him that there was a rumor that McGranery "had it in" for Hoover, and that if this were true, McGranery would not be confirmed. Nichols responded that the Bureau was not enthusiastic about McGranery, but was inclined to accept him as the best of a bad lot (the alternatives were Miller, Charles Murphy, or Clark Clifford).[55]

The political reality was that, after 1947, actually Truman had no weapons to use against Hoover. The president had gotten himself into a situation where any criticism of the director would only confirm the rumor that the administration was hampering the FBI's drive against domestic Communists. The president was pathetically reduced to taking private satisfaction when an old friend wrote what Hoover would have called a "brief" against the FBI. This was Max Lowenthal's *Federal Bureau of Investigation,* which appeared in the fall of 1950 to the consternation of Truman's aides, who feared that the president would be blamed for Lowenthal's attack on one of the public's most admired heroes.[56]

Truman could do little more than enjoy Lowenthal's assault privately, however. Hoover's prestige by late 1950 was so much greater than Truman's, that the president felt compelled to deny he had even read the book when questioned about it at a press conference.

Hoover's counterattack on Lowenthal was so violent as to recall the battles he waged against critics of the Palmer raids. Lowenthal posed much the same potential danger to Hoover as Louis Post and the 1920 *Lawyers' Report:* Hoover's anti-Communist drive, and, for that matter, Hoover's career, would be jeopardized if the public's attention could be shifted from the purpose of the Bureau's operations, the destruction of unpopular groups and ideas, to the abuses of individual rights that occurred almost inevitably in any such proceedings. Hoover had learned from his experiences over the years how important it was to discredit such critics, so he made it Bureau policy to denounce criticism, and the critics themselves, whenever the FBI came under attack.

Lowenthal came under fire from Hoover's defenders even before his book was published. On September 1, 1950, Congressman George Dondero made a speech on the floor of the House in which he, in effect, called Lowenthal a traitor for trying to destroy the FBI, an institution that "stands four-square for the American way of life." Dondero called Lowenthal a man who "lusts and thrives on obscurity" who had managed to install his "pawns" throughout the government so "they can spy more effectively." Lowenthal was "not unknown at the White House." Dondero predicted that "when he is caught the revelation will be a bigger shock to this nation than the exposé of Benedict Arnold. It must be done. The Nation can take it. But it cannot win the war of survival with Russia if this man is allowed to continue his clever, diabolical scheme to undermine our national security." His imagination inflamed by materials supplied him by Louis Nichols, Dondero claimed Lowenthal all but controlled the government, and that "there are few men in official Washington today who have dared to stand up against him." He demanded that "every person still in the Government who has had a Lowenthal endorsement, should be identified and their loyalty determined."[57]

HUAC investigators called on Lowenthal's publisher, William Sloan; they visited Lowenthal at his home and subpoenaed him to appear before the committee. They even approached Lowenthal's attorney, former Senator Burton Wheeler, and suggested that he not represent Lowenthal at the hearing on September 15, 1950. HUAC then timed the release of Lowenthal's testimony (during which Lowenthal skillfully rebutted all allegations against his loyalty) so it appeared the day before the publication date of his book. The Society of Former Special Agents reprinted an article from the *Reader's Digest*—"Why I No Longer Fear the FBI"—written by the ACLU's Morris Ernst, an unlikely, but longtime, ally of Hoover's, and distributed it as an answer to Lowenthal. The head of the Society sent a copy to Truman.[58]

The book in question was hardly the literary lynching that Hoover and his friends claimed. A compilation of clips from the *Congressional Record* and the press, it certainly could not have been mistaken for the hymn of praise Hoover thought was his due. Lowenthal's lawyer-like style made the book read like a legal brief for an adversarial proceeding; in that sense it was one-sided and demanded a rejoinder in the same spirit. What it got, though, was a barrage of personal and professional abuse. The Bureau's reaction was out of all proportion to the offense and seemed intended to intimidate any other prospective critics who might think of blaspheming against Hoover. Perhaps it had that effect: It was fourteen years before another critical book on the Bureau, Fred J. Cook's *FBI Nobody Knows,* appeared.[59]

The break between Hoover and Truman was a symptom of a greater split in American political culture during the early years of the cold war. The internal security issue was an emotional magnet that attracted vast numbers of Americans who, like Hoover, were profoundly disturbed by trends in society that they associated with the New Deal and with Roosevelt. One of the New Deal's greatest successes during the depression was the creation of a strong sense of community, but it was an extremely promiscuous and expansive form of community that let many previously excluded groups feel a part of the national family.

This was unsettling, even outrageous, to old-stock Americans, like the Hoovers of Seward Square, who had traditionally defined themselves through invidious comparison to outsiders: ethnics, Jews, Communists, criminals, the poor, the immoral rich. To them, the New Deal's indiscriminate sense of community was un-American, and, in comparison to the old patterns of status and exclusion, it was.

Not until it was too late did Truman and his advisors recognize the seriousness of the internal security issue—that it had become a test of loyalty to the conservatives' idea of traditional Americanism. By Truman's standards, when conservative anti-Communists infused politics with their moralism, they moved outside the permissible bounds of political behavior. However, by failing to take seriously the ostensible concerns of the anti-Communist right—subversives in government—Truman seemed to show lack of respect for their values, and for the millions of traditional Americans who identified with those values.

The motives of Hoover and the anti-Communist right were so baffling as to seem irrational to Truman. A measure of Truman's bewilderment was his embrace of an analogy between contemporary anticommunism and historical outbreaks of "witch-hunting" in order to explain the cold war scare. He actually commissioned a study that surveyed the "hysteria and witch-hunting" of the Salem witch trials, the Alien and Sedition acts, the anti-Masonic movement (Truman was very proud of being a Mason), the Know-Nothings, the Ku Klux Klan, the Palmer raids, Huey Long, and Father Coughlin. When Joseph McCarthy inflamed public opinion with his Lincoln Day speech in Wheeling, West Virginia ("I have here in my hand . . ."), Truman distributed the study to House Speaker Sam Rayburn, the Voice of America, the Democratic National Committee, important congressmen, and liberal organizations across the country. He even enclosed copies of the study in his personal correspondence and often referred to it in his off-the-cuff speeches as his own explanation of what was happening. Truman thought that any fair-minded person would see that the similarities between those earlier outbursts of intolerance and the current one discredited the Red hunt and exposed it as a bout of national insanity.[60]

During the Truman administration, liberals tried to explain the emotional motivation of right-wing figures like Hoover through such dismissive theories as Theodore Adorno's *Authoritarian Personality*, Richard Hofstadter's "pseudo-conservativism" (a phrase borrowed from Adorno), and the notion of "status politics" (Hofstadter, Daniel Bell, and Seymour Martin Lipset). But by contemptuously rejecting the moral concerns buried within the conservative anticommunism of Hoover's supporters, by treating their ideas as unworthy of serious discussion ("projective rationalizations arising from status aspirations and other personal motives"), liberals were dismissing the traditionalists' sense of emotional loss, which stemmed from the decline of home, church, and school; their resentment at the collapse of traditional values; and their feeling of being displaced by irreverent and incomprehensible intruders who undermined decent and familiar standards. These were becoming the most explosive issues in American politics.[61]

While theories that stressed the irrational components of cold war anticommunism might have seemed plausible within liberal circles, they were completely unconvincing to the public at large as they ran up against the inconvenient facts of the guilty verdicts against Alger Hiss, William Remington, and the Rosenbergs. Let those verdicts stand, and the field belonged to the cold warriors. Liberals could protest endlessly against red herrings, witch-hunts, and status politics, but all Hoover and his allies had to do was to point to the Smith Act Eleven, Alger Hiss, and the Rosenbergs to prove that the specter of communism was real.

While liberals dismissed Hoover and his allies as "pseudo-conservatives," Hoover worked out his own theory of "pseudo-liberalism." He defined this as the tolerant attitude toward communism that masked a tolerant, perhaps even enthusiastic attitude toward other violations of respectability and traditional standards that produced social breakdown. Once the lines were drawn between "pseudo-conservatives" and "pseudo-liberals" (to use their characterizations of each other), the FBI's great anti-Communist cases of the Truman administration became tests of strength between opposing ways of life.

In Hoover's great cases during this period, liberalism stood indicted for having failed to perform the most elementary function of government: to provide for the common defense. Thus discredited, liberalism also had to bear Hoover's indictment as an abandonment of traditional American values. For Hoover, the Communist cases demonstrated anew that the battle between Americanism and un-Americanism was a struggle for the soul of the nation. Thus he could say that the Harry Dexter White case was more

> than the charges against one man. This situation has a background of some 35 years of infiltration of an alien way of life into what we have been proud to call our Constitutional Republic. Our American way of life, which has flourished under our Republic and has nurtured the blessings of a democracy, has been brought into conflict with the godless forces of communism.[62]

During the Truman administration, Hoover had accomplished what he had tried—and failed—to do during the Palmer raids. This time he was armed with the prestige acquired over his long career, together with the peacetime sedition law he had lacked in 1920, a series of spectacular loyalty cases, and an international emergency that produced a need and a demand for action against the disloyal. He had set out on a course of action that would eventually, by the mid-fifties, crush the American Communist party as a viable political organization.

Hoover had always related current controversies to ultimate moral concerns, whether he was denouncing Emma Goldman, Ma Barker, or Ethel Rosenberg. The coming of the cold war burned out his preoccupation with lesser forms of moral degeneration to focus on the survival of the traditional American way of life. In 1947, he had told a conference of Methodist ministers that he had "never doubted that secularism . . . is the basic cause of crime, and crime is a manifestation of secularism." Now he proclaimed that Communism was the final, apocalyptic form of secularism:

> [T]he danger of Communism in America lies not in the fact that it is a political philosophy but in the awesome fact that it is a materialistic religion, inflaming in its adherents a destructive fanaticism. Communism is secularism on the march. It is a moral foe of Christianity. Either it will survive or Christianity will triumph because in this land of ours the two cannot live side by side.[63]

In truth, for Hoover, *communism* was the real crime of the century.

The internal security issue that shook and eventually destroyed the Truman administration was a symptom of a fundamental reordering of the American political consciousness. The search for spies, the hunt for disloyal government officials, the extirpation of the Communist party in the courts of law during the early years of the cold war were all part of a struggle to redefine the limits of political respectability. And J. Edgar Hoover's official position naturally placed him at the center of the loyalty, spy, and Communist cases. His skill at representing legal cases as moral dramas also put him at the center of the battle to define the limits of political orthodoxy. He had at last been able to place the authority of the government behind his drive to make the values of Seward Square the official morality of the nation.

CHAPTER 10

The Eisenhower Presidency

[The Communist party is] well on its way to achieving its current objective, which is to make you believe that it is shattered, ineffective and dying. . . . When it has fully achieved this first objective . . . it will then proceed inflexibly toward its final goal.

J. Edgar Hoover, 1958[1]

J. EDGAR HOOVER'S POWER had increased mightily during the Truman administration, but battling with a president was not natural or congenial to him. He was by temperament an insider, most comfortable as the lieutenant of a powerful leader he could trust and respect, one who trusted and respected him. Eisenhower was such a man. Moreover, Eisenhower let Hoover know that he wanted him to play an important role in the administration. Seven years of Truman's mutterings about "Gestapos" and "witch-hunts" and "red herrings" had wounded Hoover. Not only was the lack of personal respect from the president humiliating, but Truman's distrust was a reflection on Hoover's credentials as the country's foremost expert on domestic communism, and Hoover felt he had earned the right not to have his authority in that area questioned by anyone. With Eisenhower in the White House, Hoover was once again working for a president who, like Roosevelt, solicited his opinions, took his advice, and acted on his recommendations. Truman's appointees as attorney general did not seem to have consistent law-enforcement principles, particularly by contrast to Roosevelt's. But with Brownell and Rogers, Hoover could again feel he was working for men who *were* serious.[2]

Eisenhower's first attorney general, Herbert Brownell, recalled the J. Edgar Hoover who worked for him as a man at the peak of his powers. According to William Rogers, who succeeded Brownell, Hoover often said that the eight years of the Eisenhower administration were "the best and happiest years he ever had." Eisenhower felt, as Hoover did, that priority had to be given to security in any conflict with civil liberties, and naturally shared Hoover's disdain for Truman and his administration. Eisenhower came to Washington in full agreement with Hoover on the urgency of firing security risks, who were, of course, also attractive targets as emblems of twenty years of treason. After seven years of Truman's contemptuous treatment, here was a great man—Eisenhower—who was solicitous, almost deferential to Hoover. Later, when Hoover remembered the presidents he had served, Eisenhower was the only one he called both "a great man" and "a great President."[3]

Being welcomed back into the councils of the White House gave Hoover complete control over everything that affected him professionally and personally. He had mortally wounded the Communist party with the Smith Act and espionage case prosecutions. During his battles with the Truman administration, he had cemented his alliances with congressional conservatives, so his budget was now as sacrosanct as his files. His "educational" campaign to prepare the public for custodial detention of Communists had made him and the Bureau symbols of cold war Americanism. Now the new administration's deference to him in law enforcement and internal security gave him the final assurance he needed that he was safe from all political challenge.

The search for total order and perfect security that had guided Hoover in his professional career was also now a marked feature of his personal life. Anything that might introduce unpredictability was banished from his comfortable and increasingly luxurious routine. The New York City nightclubbing, the jaunts to national parks, the personal descents into the field to take part in important cases were now things of the past. His daily, weekly—even yearly—schedule took on rigid patterns, and any deviation, no matter how slight, could rouse him to fury.

Each morning he was picked up at his home at Thirtieth Place by his black chauffeur, James Crawford, whom he had made a special agent in 1943. Crawford had been driving for him since 1935, as well as handling the outdoor chores around Hoover's house. Then

they picked up Tolson at his home nearby and continued on to downtown Washington. In good weather, Crawford let the two off near
the White House so they could walk the last seven blocks to FBI
headquarters at the Justice Department on Pennsylvania between
Ninth and Tenth.

The personnel in Hoover's office had not changed for decades.
The office staff was supervised by Helen Gandy, his secretary since
before he became director. His door was guarded by another black
special agent, Sam Noisette, and his messenger was still another black
agent, Worthington Smith; all were fixtures since the early thirties.

Lunch with Tolson, at Harvey's Restaurant on Connecticut Avenue, was another daily routine. The owner of Harvey's was a close
friend of Hoover's, and for twenty years he picked up the bill for
meals. There was even a special table reserved for Hoover and Tolson,
near the cashier's cage, where they could be protected from unwanted
visitors—their backs to the wall, empty tables on each side, a serving
cart separating them from other diners. Hoover had to watch his
weight and usually ordered the same lunch every day: grapefruit, cot-
tage cheese, black coffee.

During the course of a week, Hoover and Tolson ate dinner at
each other's house, a third evening with one of Hoover's neighbors.
The other evenings they had Crawford drive them to Harvey's, where
they often met old friends. And since Hoover did not like to be seen
drinking in public, one of Tolson's tasks was to keep the drinks hidden
under his napkin.[4]

Hoover still kept long hours in the office, working until the early
evening, often appearing on Saturdays and Sundays. Before dark and
on the weekends, he enjoyed working in his garden, supervising Crawford on the lawn and the roses. The house and property had to be
in perfect condition, and Crawford had to give immediate attention
to areas of chipped paint or fallen leaves. The black live-in maid,
Annie Fields, prepared what meals Hoover ate at home and kept
the house, by now filled with a fantastic array of bric-a-brac (gifts,
mementos, and the small Oriental art objects he collected), in perfect
order. Hoover did not like to have strangers work at the house, so
when outsiders had to be brought in for repairs, Crawford or Fields
had to watch them and report back to Hoover on the work. He also
wanted reports from them on how the day had gone for his two dogs.
He was more fond of them now than ever.

His social life involved the same unchanging group of friends,
men of his own generation, with only a few new additions after the

forties. Nearly every weekend in Washington he went to the racetrack with Tolson and George Allen, head of the Reconstruction Finance Corporation under Truman and now a prosperous Washington lawyer and lobbyist. He accumulated enough losing ticket stubs to paper a folding dressing screen for his bedroom.

Hoover's year revolved around two prolonged vacations with Tolson. He spent Christmas and New Year's in Miami at the Gulf Stream Hotel, owned by the family of G. David Schine, the McCarthy staffer who was the focus of the Army-McCarthy hearings. Washington cronies like Allen joined him there, and William Rogers and Richard Nixon would visit when they were vacationing at Key Biscayne.

Even more important to him was his yearly summer visit to the Del Charro Hotel in La Jolla, California, where he and Tolson were guests of the owner, Texas oil man Clint Murchison. (Hoover refused to admit that he was ever off duty, or that either the Miami or La Jolla trips were vacations; his subordinates had to go along with the fiction that the Florida trip was an inspection of the Miami field office, the California trip a prolonged medical check-up at the Scripps Clinic.) When Murchison built his hotel, he put up a bungalow in back especially for Hoover and Tolson. (There were also cottages for Murchison and fellow oil billionaire Sid Richardson.) In the morning, Hoover and Tolson would meet their Texas and Hollywood friends—Murchison, Richardson, the Billy Byers, Wofford Cain, Buddy Fogelson, Greer Garson, Don Harrington, Robert Thompson, Bing Crosby, Phil Harris—and then spend the day at the Del Mar track (operated by a Richardson and Murchison foundation), where Hoover and Tolson would watch the races from the Directors' Room. The California trip also included a few days in Beverly Hills as guests of Dorothy Lamour and her husband.

Hoover's passion for order and control extended to the most minute details of his vacation arrangements: Mark Felt, Tolson's top aide in the seventies, once had to handle the logistics of the La Jolla trip. He remembers that "Hoover insisted on the same seats in the plane, the same rooms in the same hotels, the same restaurants, the same haberdasher, and the same pleasure ride." Every detail had to be precisely scheduled by the local field office: For example, the luggage had to arrive in their rooms exactly three minutes after they arrived.[5]

For a man of fifty-eight (in 1953), Hoover's health was good, but his weight had risen to 200 pounds—and that was something else he now brought under control. He lost some 33 pounds through diet and exercise and decided that his agents should do the same. Achieving their "desirable" weight according to the Metropolitan Life height/ weight chart—to Hoover, the lower figure was the "allowable" one— became an inflexible requirement within the Bureau, and an excess pound could hold up raises and promotions.[6]

The chief interests of his youth—education, religion, youth work— he now continued by sitting on the boards of such institutions as George Washington University, the National Presbyterian Church, and the Boys Clubs of America. Whereas before he had participated directly, now he managed and controlled the participation of others. In this way he continued to feel he had a role in the life of the community while insulating himself from the unpredictability and irritations of firsthand contact with the objects of his benevolence.[7]

Hoover's sense of order and security during the fifties rested on the national consensus, which he had helped build, that nothing was more important than domestic security, and that the Communist party was the most dangerous threat to that security. Having defeated the party, he had absolute confidence in his ability to deal with his responsibilities—as long as they continued to center on the Communist party. If he knew anything, he knew American communism and how to control it. But the self-confidence he had acquired from this success gave him a personal reason to resent calls that the FBI take on new federal law enforcement responsibilities, since they introduced an element of uncertainty into his tightly organized routine. He knew domestic security; in other areas, his preeminence was not so unassailable. As long as the country continued to believe its most dangerous threat came from communism, his position was secure.

Even before the inauguration, Eisenhower made sure Hoover felt he was an insider again. "There had come to my ears," Eisenhower later explained,

> a story to the effect that J. Edgar Hoover . . . had been out of favor in Washington. Such was my respect for him that I invited him to a meeting, my only purpose being to assure him that I wanted him in government as long as I might be there and that in the performance of his duties he would have the complete support of my office.[8]

Eisenhower's practice was to ask for Hoover's advice whenever government policy touched on internal security, whether or not he intended to follow Hoover's suggestions. Eisenhower's self-conscious air of naiveté flattered Hoover and contrasted sharply with the tendency of Truman and his aides (particularly Stephen Spingarn) to think they knew more than Hoover about internal security problems. Eisenhower had to eliminate the popular impression that the executive branch was congenitally soft on communism, and having Hoover as a visible supporter was the most effective way of doing it.[9]

Eisenhower managed his office through a strict staff system, so Hoover did not have the same informal lines of communication as he had enjoyed under Roosevelt, but he did enjoy an excellent working relationship with Herbert Brownell, and a close friendship with William Rogers, who was Brownell's deputy attorney general and then attorney general himself after 1957. Rogers was Hoover's principal liaison with the administration, and though the two men had not met before 1953, they hit it off immediately. Within a short time, Hoover was closer to Rogers professionally and socially than he had been to any previous superior in the Justice Department. Rogers drew Hoover into the social life of the department and the administration, entertained Hoover at his home (where Hoover joined the family in songs around the piano), and was Hoover's guest at Thirtieth Place. Rogers made Hoover a part of the Justice Department's policy-making elite; he had Hoover "participate all the time" and included him in the twice-a-week department lunches "with all the people, the top assistants . . . [where] we ironed out our problems."[10]

Rogers got the administration and Hoover off to a good start by letting him know that the FBI's loyalty reports, which the Truman administration had often disregarded, now had the force of law. He went so far as to notify Hoover that during the first year of the administration, the attorney general had refused to endorse thirty-three persons for presidential appointment solely on the basis of their FBI reports. "There could be no more convincing proof of the value of the FBI investigations," he told Hoover.[11]

Early in 1953, Eisenhower scrapped Truman's Loyalty Program; in its place, he set up a system of security officers in each department of the executive branch. Employees undergoing investigation were suspended pending the resolution of any charges, and the burden of proof was effectively shifted to the employee. Through a change in the grounds for dismissal, an employee now had to prove that his employment was "clearly consistent with the interests of national security," and that he was "reliable, trustworthy, of good conduct and character, and of complete and unswerving loyalty to the United States." No longer did it have to be proven that a person was disloyal, only that he was a "security risk." Dismissed employees had the dubious consolation of not being automatically branded Communists; they might also be drunks, homosexuals, mental cases, or dope addicts.[12]

The State Department, the favorite target of congressional suspicion, was the target of the Eisenhower administration's most ruthless drive against "security risks." Secretary of State John Foster Dulles hired ex-FBI agent Scott McLeod as department security officer, and McLeod put together a security staff of fellow former agents. Before long, McLeod announced he had fired 500 State Department employees without hearings. In October 1953, Eisenhower claimed 1,456 "subversives" had been dismissed, although most of these had been let go for reasons other than disloyalty. However, under the new "security risk" classification, the former director of atom bomb research at Los Alamos, J. Robert Oppenheimer, and State Department China experts John Carter Vincent and John Paton Davies, whose continued government employment had fueled the ire of the radical right, were ruled security risks, although in no case was there proof of disloyalty.[13]

The new administration's loyalty program was not enough by itself to quiet congressional loyalty investigators. With the dazzling example of Richard Nixon's career before them, senators and congressmen who aspired to national visibility wanted to uncover their own spy rings. When the new Congress organized under Republican leadership, there were three committees ready to investigate the executive branch: the House Un-American Activities Committee (HUAC), now chaired by ex-FBI agent Congressman Harold Velde of Illinois; the Senate Judiciary Committee's Internal Security Subcommittee, chaired by Senator William Jenner of Indiana; and Senator Joseph McCarthy's Permanent Investigations Subcommittee of the Committee on Government Operations (whose chief investigator was first ex-agent Don Surine and later Frank Carr, former head of the Bureau's New York field office).

Hiring an ex-FBI agent to run a security program had become the best way of demonstrating a serious approach to the issue. This gave Hoover additional influence throughout the government, because the ex-agents were no use to their employers unless they preserved their access to FBI reports by staying on good terms with the director. Hoover had become not only the country's leading Communist hunter, he was also the leading trainer of other Communist hunters.

The administration's alliance with Hoover, and its willingness to follow the director's lead in domestic security, were important parts of its long-range strategy to neutralize the congressional investigators who had so bedeviled the Truman administration. Eisenhower's plan for controlling the loyalty issue was not denouncing or disavowing rabid congressional anti-Communists such as McCarthy, but using the FBI to give them "sensational competition."[14]

Hoover's appearance before HUAC in 1947 had signaled his break with Truman; now, in 1953, he made another sensational appearance before Congress, even more unmistakably partisan than before, to signal his loyalty to the new administration. The issue was the Truman administration's handling of the Harry Dexter White espionage case.

In November 1953, Attorney General Brownell, perhaps stung by the recent Democratic victories in the off-year elections, and certainly feeling the pressure of Senator McCarthy's charges of espionage at the army electronics research laboratories at Fort Monmouth, New Jersey, decided to make an issue of the difference between the Eisenhower security program and the Truman administration's cavalier attitude toward spy cases ("red herrings"). After clearing his plans with the president, Brownell charged that Truman had promoted Assistant Secretary of the Treasury Harry Dexter White to "a more important position" as executive director of the International Monetary Fund despite Hoover's reports about White's "spying activities for the Soviet Government."[15]

The Democratic party exploded in indignation, particularly when the new Republican chairman of HUAC, Harold Velde, followed up on Brownell's charges by subpoenaing the former president. Truman rejected the subpoena on the grounds of the separation of powers, but went on national television to deny Brownell's story. He claimed that he *had* seen Hoover's report on White, but too late to stop the Senate from confirming the nomination. Truman went further and said he had promoted White only because he had an understanding with Hoover that this would help the FBI with its investigation.[16]

This left Truman open to a devastating counterattack. On November 17, Brownell and Hoover appeared before Senator Jenner's subcommittee. Hoover later let it be understood that Brownell had ordered him to appear, but Brownell clearly remembers that Hoover "volunteered." Hoover put the nasty little political brawl in the context of the "conflict with the godless forces of communism [who] . . . distort, conceal, misrepresent, and lie to gain their point. Deceit is their very essence. . . . [T]o a Communist there are no morals except those which further the world revolution directed by Moscow."[17]

Hoover denied there had been any arrangement between him and

Truman; he claimed White's promotion had even hampered his investigation. He also contradicted Truman's statement that White had been surrounded with persons of proven loyalty, noting that one of White's close IMF associates was later removed as a security risk in December 1952. Although Hoover later denied that he had impugned Truman's loyalty, clearly he had done just that.

The Eisenhower administration had convinced Hoover of its sincerity, and now Hoover was going to be as useful to Eisenhower as he had been to Roosevelt, and for much the same reason. Roosevelt and Eisenhower showed Hoover they shared his values and respected him. They gave him important and satisfying assignments, and backed him when he needed support. Truman and his liberal backers were consigned to the hated category of "pseudo-liberals," anti–anti-Communists whose toleration for Communists made Communist subversion possible. Drew Pearson reported that the Washington consensus was that Hoover had "been waiting a long time" to get even with the former president. "He hated Truman and almost everyone around him."[18] Once Hoover decided someone deserved his loyalty, he gave it without reservation, and so Eisenhower's enemies became Hoover's enemies.

The Eisenhower administration's struggles with Senator Joseph McCarthy gave Hoover another chance to prove his loyalty, even though Hoover and McCarthy had a close friendship that dated back to 1946, when McCarthy first arrived in the Senate. The first investigator McCarthy had hired was a ten-year FBI veteran, Donald Surine, whom Hoover had recommended and who acted as a liaison between Hoover and McCarthy. When McCarthy took over the chair of the Investigations Subcommittee in 1953, his staff was stocked with other ex-FBI agents, and his chief counsel was Roy Cohn, who had developed a close working relationship with Assistant to the Director Louis Nichols during his tour in the Justice Department as a special assistant. When McCarthy fired veteran Red-lister J. B. Matthews as his staff director, after Matthews's charges that the Protestant ministry was Communist-infiltrated, he hired yet another ex-FBI agent, Frank Carr. Later, McCarthy took on another former agent, Jim Juliana, as chief investigator.[19]

Through Nichols, Hoover made information from the FBI files available to McCarthy and his staff (probably in the form of "reports" based on the files, and not the "raw" files themselves). This was done very confidentially. Hoover was already sensitive to charges that he had divulged files to congressional committees, especially since much of the FBI's intelligence had been obtained by wiretapping. Even by the indulgent Justice Department theory that the circulation of wiretap information within the department was not "divulging," giving the information to Congress would have been a prima facie violation of the law. Although Hoover did give information from his files to friendly reporters and congressmen, he and the Justice Department made a careful semantic distinction when they said that the "files" were strictly confidential. It probably was true that Hoover, except for a very few occasions when directly ordered to do so by the president, never let outsiders see FBI "raw" files. However, information derived from the files was clearly the lifeblood of the Washington anti-Communist establishment.[20]

Hoover and McCarthy were not only ideological allies, they were close socially. They often went to the track together, and Hoover and Tolson were frequent dinner guests at the home of McCarthy and his assistant, later his wife, Jean Kerr.[21] In August 1953, McCarthy stayed at the same La Jolla hotel as Hoover and Tolson during their summer vacation. On that occasion, Hoover told a reporter for the *San Diego Evening Tribune* that

> McCarthy is a former Marine. He was an amateur boxer. He's Irish. Combine those, and you're going to have a vigorous individual, who is not going to be pushed around. . . . The investigating committees do a valuable job. They have subpoena rights without which some vital investigations could not be accomplished. . . . I view him as a friend and believe he so views me.
>
> Certainly, he is a controversial man. He is earnest and he is honest. He has enemies. Whenever you attack subversives of any kind, Communists, Fascists, even the Ku Klux Klan, you are going to be the victim of the most extremely vicious criticism that can be made.[22]

McCarthy was a useful ally to Hoover, who could use the senator to expose suspects against whom there was not enough evidence for prosecution, or whose prosecution would expose valuable FBI sources. But since the Hoover-McCarthy alliance was struck up during the Truman administration, there was a potential for conflict once Eisenhower was elected. McCarthy's attacks on the Truman administration had not bothered Hoover, because he had disassociated himself from its Loyalty Program; but under Eisenhower, an attack on the government's competence in domestic security was now an indirect attack on Hoover and the Bureau.

Despite the claims of friendship, Hoover had to make a choice between McCarthy and Eisenhower, and at a time when McCarthy needed him most, Hoover threw his support to the president. Hoover's cooperation with HUAC proved he had no qualms about the methods McCarthy was using against his suspects; HUAC and McCarthy were seen as useful complements to the FBI in Hoover's anti-Communist campaign. However, Eisenhower had made the presidency the legitimate symbol of national authority once again, and as such, Hoover would not support attacks on it, even when the attacks were in the name of anticommunism. To Hoover, one of the evils of communism was its attack on lawful authority, so anticommunism, to be authentic, had to defend that authority, not attack it.

The Army-McCarthy hearings that began on April 22, 1954, developed out of McCarthy's earlier investigation of subversion at the Signal Corps research center at Fort Monmouth, New Jersey, and his subsequent charges that the army had blocked his efforts. The hearings became a national sensation, carried on all three television networks. On the ninth day of the hearings, when it was apparent that McCarthy was losing ground, he tried to gain the offensive by claiming he had a "carbon copy" of a "personal and confidential" letter from J. Edgar Hoover to the army warning of thirty-four security risks at Fort Monmouth.

The army's chief counsel, Boston attorney Joseph Welch, objected to the introduction of a letter as evidence without an affidavit from Hoover that he had actually written it. Hoover replied that McCarthy's letter had not actually come from the Bureau, although a memorandum from the Bureau *had* been sent to the army the same day as the "purported" letter, and that much of the information and language in the letter was identical to that in the fifteen-page memorandum. Welch was then able to get the devastating admission from McCarthy's staff that the letter was in fact "a carbon copy of precisely nothing."[23]

Hoover's reply was carefully calibrated in its implications. Instead of focusing on what was accurate in McCarthy's statement (that the contents were a faithful summary of the FBI memo), Hoover's reply called attention to what was fraudulent about the letter—its format. Hoover's reply left the impression that McCarthy had tried to foist a forged document off on the Senate, and that he had conspired with disloyal employees to obtain classified information without proper authorization.

The controversy over the letter unnerved McCarthy and he tried to excuse his possession of it by publicly congratulating the officials who had been passing him documents despite presidential directives. "As far as I am concerned," he said, "I would like to notify those 2 million employees that I feel it is their *duty* to give us any information they have." Eisenhower now felt McCarthy, by advocating "a wholesale subversion of public service," had finally so discredited himself that he could at long last be safely attacked. By casting the influence of the presidency into the battle against McCarthy, Eisenhower gave the essential encouragement to the coalition that ultimately brought McCarthy down by censuring him.

As in his 1947 HUAC appearance, Hoover had certainly weighed the balance of power between the executive and the Congress and adjusted his alliances so that when the battle was over, the FBI would emerge stronger than before. But while Hoover was always determined to win, winning was never his only concern. Eisenhower and McCarthy both stood for patriotic values, but as long as Eisenhower adhered to Hoover's vision of a secure, anti-Communist America, the president, as the supreme authority, deserved support, and Hoover would loyally defend him. McCarthy's failure to acknowledge this authority, and his willingness to encourage conflict and divisiveness, cost him Hoover's support.

One of the many irreconcilable conflicts between Hoover and American liberals was over civil rights. To its supporters, the civil rights movement was a clear case of justice, but to Hoover it was above all a challenge to established authority—the authority of the police, the government, and, in many cases, the FBI—so it aroused the same anxiety and alarm in him as any other kind of rebellion. On a more personal level, it posed a challenge to the privileged style of life he had created for himself, because much of his comfort depended on personal services rendered to him by blacks.

Hoover had surrounded himself with blacks in menial service positions—James Crawford, Sam Noisette, and Worthington Smith. He depended on them so completely that, during the war, he made them special agents to keep them from being drafted. He had another black driver attached to the Miami field office to be available during Hoover's winter vacation and one more in California to drive him while he was at La Jolla. These five men were the only black agents in the FBI until the early sixties. Together with Hoover's live-in maid, Annie Fields, the key people servicing and maintaining Hoover's private existence were all black.[24]

Hoover demanded constant service from these attendants. Crawford was required to be on duty from the time Hoover awoke until he returned from dinner in the evening. According to his wife's bitter recollections, Crawford worked fifteen hours a day, seven days a week—holidays included! When Hoover went to the office on Saturdays and Sundays, Crawford, Smith, and Noisette all had to be there ready for service. Whenever Annie Fields was away from Hoover's house, Crawford was expected to be her replacement.[25]

Hoover seems to have had the old-fashioned Southern attitude that a white man should not ask another white man for personal service. He may still have venerated the Seward Square standards that measured gentility by the presence of black "help." In the Seward Square of his youth and early adulthood, the only blacks in the neighborhood *were* the help. The situation was the same in Northwest Washington, where he now lived, a bastion of white flight; it was segregated by restrictive covenants, and middle-class status there was a matter of race as much as income.

Then, too, Hoover grew up at a time when respectability in Washington meant the exclusion of blacks. Black membership in an elite institution was a contradiction in terms. Every group he had belonged to as a boy had defined its elite status by its exclusion of blacks, and the FBI was nothing if not elite. During the fifties, Hoover's agents believed that he had taken a stand that there would never be a black agent (that is, a *real* agent) as long as he was director; he was able to maintain that policy until the Kennedy administration demanded that he recruit blacks. When Hoover did offer token compliance, he always maintained that he would not lower Bureau standards—meaning that any standards blacks could meet were too low for him.

There was yet another reason Hoover was inclined to be hostile to blacks. From his earliest days with the Radical Division, Hoover had been concerned with black civil rights organizations almost exclusively in terms of their potential as targets for Communist infiltration. His condescending attitude toward black intelligence and judgment made him inclined to see these organizations as easy prey for the skilled propagandists and agitators of the Communist party. The more effective the black organizations were, therefore, the more tempting they were to the Communists. In short, from Hoover's perspective the country would be better off without an organized black civil rights movement—and, by implication, without effective black leadership.[26] As long as it existed, Hoover saw only the potential for disloyalty, and whatever information he received seemed to confirm his belief in the insincerity and illegitimacy of black protest.

Hoover's memos to Eisenhower about the black movement presented the black movement in this prejudicial fashion. Early in 1953, he gave the president a study entitled "The Communist Party and the Negro," although he had to report that despite the Party's having devoted an "inordinate" amount of its time to recruiting Negro members, its efforts had been a failure." In 1956, Hoover furnished the White House with a detailed report on the national conference of the NAACP that was held in Washington from March 4 to March 6. He repeated his previous finding that the NAACP was anti-Communist and free of Communist domination, but he focused almost exclusively on the Party's efforts to infiltrate and influence it. His reports on Communist activities at the conference were so detailed, the conference seemed hardly distinguishable from a Communist cell meeting.[27]

Eisenhower shared Hoover's lack of enthusiasm for civil rights and his paternalistic attitude toward blacks. Neither man tried to justify prejudice or racial injustice, but both understood the Southern point of view on race and sympathized with it—Hoover influenced by his birth in Washington, Eisenhower by his service in a segregated army and his many Southern friends. Both identified instinctively with the racial elite of the country, and, in 1954, that elite was exclusively white. More importantly, both were well aware that their political lives depended upon staying within the consensus of public opinion, and that their authority was based on the fact that they upheld the same moral convictions as the majority of Americans. In 1954, that majority, while it may have been opposed to racial injustice in principle, was unprepared for any drastic changes to accommodate new racial standards. Eisenhower was a man without any profound convictions about racial equality, but with a keen political sense that told him how explosive this issue was; his most fervent wish was that the conflict over desegregation could be postponed until it was the responsibility of his successor.

In that spirit, Eisenhower made anxious inquiries to Brownell about whether the attorney general could avoid speaking out against segregation when he appeared before the Supreme Court in the *Brown* school desegregation case. Brownell, who knew how to deal with Eisenhower, replied that it was his duty to be prepared to answer all questions put to him by the Court. The word *duty* "settled the matter as far as Eisenhower was concerned." The Court did ask Brownell his opinion, and he answered that he thought "segregation in the public schools was unconstitutional." Eisenhower refused to say publicly whether he approved or disapproved of the decision, only that it was the law and he would abide by it.[28]

Brownell himself, though unsympathetic to civil liberties in loyalty matters, was strongly committed to federal protection of civil rights. He supported federal antidiscrimination cases in the courts even though he was never strongly backed by Eisenhower. Brownell's efforts to have the Justice Department support the civil rights movement were also undercut by Hoover's unconcealed opposition to the department's civil rights initiatives. When Hoover had to justify his reluctance to take an aggressive stance against civil rights violations, he would point to the difficulty, indeed impossibility, of getting Southern juries to convict whites for crimes committed against blacks. He felt it was useless to put the Bureau's energies into futile pursuits that might distract from the fight against internal subversion. The insurmountable problem, he said, was "local prejudice," which made it "most difficult to obtain convictions even under the most favorable conditions and with clear-cut evidence."[29]

Hoover had twenty-five years of experience with the failure of Southern prosecutors to prosecute and Southern juries to convict. Ever since Frank Murphy established the Civil Rights Section of the Justice Department in 1939, Hoover had seen nearly all his civil rights investigations fail because of the Southern code against convicting whites for crimes against blacks, or because his superiors in Washington abandoned him when the political heat was on. (In 1947, he reported that out of 1,570 investigations, there had been only twenty-seven convictions in twenty years.) By the late forties, Hoover's discouragement in this area was so profound that he tried to avoid civil rights cases whenever he could. By the fifties, this had become fixed Bureau policy.[30]

Hoover's resistance to pressure that he accelerate civil rights enforcement involved him in a vicious cycle of controversy with civil rights leaders. They would criticize FBI inaction, and then he would respond as he did to all criticism of the Bureau, by attacking their motives for saying anything against an organization so important to national security. By the fifties, Hoover's experience with the civil rights movement had largely been one of bitter conflicts with its leaders over their criticism of his performance, so he was programmed to react with hostility whenever a civil rights leader crossed his sights.

Hoover's resentment of his critics was just as bitter when he found that their charges were true. He might correct the situation quietly, but for public consumption he would still deny the charges and attack those who made them. In 1955, Adam Clayton Powell, the black congressman from Harlem, charged that Southern blacks were reluctant to seek aid from the FBI in the South because the majority of the agents there were Southerners with racist attitudes. The FBI Executive Council made a study of the actual situation, and happily reported to Hoover that 37.4 percent of the agents in the South were Northern-born. Hoover surprised his aides by replying that "the percentage of Southern Agents assigned to such cases is entirely too high and must be more equalized," and so, in 1956, the Bureau hurriedly trained Northern agents for transfer to the South. A year later, the percentage of Northerners in Southern offices had risen to 68 percent. But for Hoover, truth, when it came to criticism of the FBI, was no justification.[31]

Civil rights cases also created morale problems among Hoover's agents, who resented having to conduct unpopular investigations with little chance of success, particularly when the suspects were often the same local police officers with whom they had to conduct daily business. The agents sometimes apologized by explaining that the whole thing was a political charade that had to be performed for the benefit of the Justice Department. Hoover had to lecture his agents to give civil rights investigations their "most meticulous attention." He told them, "I am well aware of the problems which Civil Rights cases frequently create with regard to relations with the police and the public. If the Bureau is to avoid criticism from all sides in the Civil Rights field, the challenge made by these problems must be met by judicious and careful handling of each case." In 1952, Hoover told his agents that he had heard a friendly chief of police remark that "the FBI has the unhappy duty of investigating Civil Rights violations. They don't like it but they are good policemen and they carry out their orders." He commented that he was "very much concerned over the fact that some of our personnel have apparently expressed themselves to the effect that the FBI does not favor Civil Rights investigations. I want it clearly understood that all Bureau personnel should be most careful not to indicate any views or expressions of opinion regarding any matters over which this Bureau has investigative jurisdiction."[32]

Once school segregation was outlawed—by the May 17, 1954, *Brown* vs. *Board of Education* decision—Hoover had to fight to keep his agents from lending moral support to the South's "massive resistance" to the law. His personal racial preferences as a native of old Washington and his progressive commitment to professional standards were now in sharp conflict; he insisted that his agents, at the very least, support the national standards as set by the Supreme Court. He warned them that "recently allegations have been made by individuals representing organizations that Bureau Agents have expressed

themselves as being opposed to integration of races in public schools."
He said he had not been able to substantiate these charges, but that
"the matter of racial segregation in public schools has been reviewed
and passed on by the Supreme Court of the United States. There is
no occasion for any agent . . . to express his views on this question.
. . . The expression of personal opinions by Agents cannot be disassociated from their official status."[33]

After the *Brown* decision, Southern states concocted a variety of
political and legal stratagems to block enforcement of the new standards while impatient civil rights organizations challenged Southern
resistance. In December 1955, Rosa Parks's refusal to give her seat
in a segregated city bus to a white passenger sparked the Montgomery
bus boycott that moved Martin Luther King, Jr., into national promi-
nence and eventually produced a Supreme Court decision declaring
such ordinances unconstitutional. On March 14, 1956, Eisenhower
was faced with a manifesto of some one hundred Southern members
of Congress pledging themselves to oppose desegregation by every
legal means. Eisenhower looked upon both sides as extremists and
trouble-makers. In an appeal to Billy Graham to help cool tempers,
he said that he was a "champion of real, as opposed to spurious progress" and so would "remain a moderate in this regard."[34]

After decades of seeing FBI investigations rejected by white Southern juries who upheld the code of white supremacy, Hoover instinctively sidestepped cases like the Emmett Till murder in 1955. Till, a
black youth from Chicago, was kidnapped and murdered in Money,
Mississippi, for wolf-whistling at a white girl. Hoover told a national
radio audience that

> We had no right to investigate because there was no violation of federal
> law. Three days later, we received word that the body of the boy had
> been found in the Tallahatchie River. . . . The Department ruled that
> there was, on the facts, no violation of federal civil rights statutes, and,
> accordingly, the FBI was to conduct no investigation.[35]

Hoover's explanation seemed less than convincing. Because of his
success in turning the FBI into a symbol of justice, the public had
come to expect the dispatch of FBI agents as an indication of the
concern of the Federal government. Refusal to send the FBI into a
case was therefore interpreted to mean Washington was not taking
a situation seriously. The country knew instinctively, and the informed
more specifically, that Hoover had always found a federal angle to
justify FBI involvement when it suited him (an interstate car theft

angle in the Dillinger case, a white slave law violation in the Klan investigation of the twenties, fraud in the Marcus Garvey case). On the legalities, Hoover was right; on the basis of practical experience, he was right; as a political leader, he was beginning to misjudge his public.

The Till murder and the inability of local or federal justice to deal with it infuriated Attorney General Brownell, who was now convinced that new civil rights laws were needed, that the courts had so restricted the application of these from the Reconstruction era that they were unenforceable, particularly in the context of local prejudices. Brownell wanted to make sure the president and the cabinet knew how bad the situation was in the South; he also wanted them to be under no illusions about the resistance they could expect if the administration sought the new legislation from Congress he was going to recommend, so he had Hoover survey Southern racial attitudes and report to the cabinet on his findings.[36]

Hoover made his report, "Racial Tension and Civil Rights," on March 9, 1956. While he intended it to be an objective report on the racial attitudes of Southerners, it also revealed his own feelings. His briefing was hardly an enthusiastic defense of civil rights, but neither was it, as has been charged, "bigoted and narrow-minded." For the most part, it was just what Brownell had ordered: an impartial account of the attitudes of segregationists and civil rights activists that were likely to lead to violence.[37]

Racial tension, Hoover told the cabinet, had mounted "almost daily" since the Brown decision of May 17, 1954. "In many areas reason has given way to emotion. When such a situation exists, the potential for serious outbreaks of violence is ever present and can be triggered by incidents which in a calmer period would go unnoticed." Underlying the resistance to racial change he detected two cultural traditions, a "States Rights" backlash against federal power (a "resurgence of Jeffersonian principles") and "a clash of culture when the protection of racial purity is a rule of life ingrained deeply as the basic truth." Drawing upon his familiarity with Southern attitudes, as well as the reports of his agents, he talked about the paternalistic spirit of white Southern culture, "a carryover from the days of slavery," that accepted in principle the need for greater opportunities for blacks but denied that school integration was the proper way to obtain it. Behind the white Southern fear of integration, he said, "stalks the specter of racial intermarriage."

He pointed out that the "master and servant relationship in the

South is still the rule," creating sharp differences in cultural attitudes which led whites to have a contemptuous attitude toward blacks "regardless of the unfairness of judgments." He gave the cabinet examples of the emotional conflicts desegregation had created in Southern communities: interracial gyms and lavatory facilities frightened Southern parents on the grounds that "colored parents are not as careful in looking after the health and cleanliness of their children." He also made a delicate allusion to a difference in "morals" in which "the benefit of matrimony and recourse to divorce [among blacks] give way to convenience and consequent illegitimacy." Southerners felt that the higher crime rate among blacks would result in "greater opportunities of interracial strife" if the "racial bars" were let down. Finally, "the claim is made that Southern Negroes are usually below the intellectual level of white children. The further claim is made that it would take a generation to bring the races to a parity."

Hoover took care not to indicate to the cabinet that he agreed with such attitudes. As a matter of fact, his account of them showed a considerable effort to distance himself from what were, in fact, his own leanings. In the context of his report, he was simply reporting on these attitudes as fundamental obstacles to integration whether one agreed with them or not.

Still, some hostility toward civil rights did seep through despite his best intentions. Hoover's description of the Montgomery, Alabama, bus boycott focused on the fact that its organizers had broken a local ordinance barring interference with businesses. He described black efforts to "rock the boat" in Montgomery without mentioning the white provocations, thus portraying black protest as willful disruption and an insubordinate challenge to authority, rather than as a response to long-standing injustices.

Hoover branded the violent white resistance to the desegregation of the University of Alabama in February 1956 "disgraceful," but he also smeared the effort to integrate the school by mentioning that the NAACP had withdrawn its suit to have one of two young black women enrolled "on the claim that she was a hussy, i.e., had [a] baby 6 months after marriage." He also mentioned without comment the university's expulsion of the only woman to be admitted on the grounds that she had made false charges against the university, nor did he comment on this subterfuge of the school administration.

His discussion of the Communist party's interest in civil rights left the impression that every civil rights incident advanced the Communist goals of recruiting "Negroes into its ranks and [using] . . .

the Negro as a rallying point to further its aim of weakening the United States." The NAACP's scheduled March on Washington (for March 1956) was said to be in line with Communist plans, and to be spearheaded by Communists.

Hoover told the cabinet that "one of the most encouraging developments" in racial matters was the improved attitude of Southern police toward civil rights, and said that the Bureau was helping by running special training schools on civil rights enforcement for Southern police forces. Nevertheless, he complained that, when investigating "atrocious acts of violence" in the South, "the difficulties which our Agents face at times are almost indescribable. The Negroes are afraid to talk and in case after case we have had to wait until nightfall to go see them if we hoped to secure any information. In other instances we are greeted by open antagonism on the part of some local authorities."

He concluded with a distribution of blame so balanced between whites and blacks as to justify nothing except strict neutrality by the federal government.

> The question of civil rights is interrelated with racial prejudices; charged with highly emotional surges. The law-abiding people of the South neither approve nor condone acts of brutality and the lawless taking of human lives. On the other hand, historic traditions and customs are part of a heritage with which they will not part without a struggle. Militant resources of both those who stand for and against segregation have been mobilized, and impulsive precipitated action could unleash acts of violence. The mounting tension can be met only with understanding and a realization of the motivating forces. Delicate situations are aggravated by some overzealous but ill-advised leaders of the NAACP and by the Communist Party, which seeks to use incidents to further the so-called class struggle.

Hoover's briefing certainly did not make Eisenhower any more enthusiastic about Brownell's plans for civil rights legislation, which he reluctantly approved only because of his high regard for his attorney general. Hoover had confirmed Eisenhower's worries about the potential for trouble if civil rights agitation increased, and the president was worried by Hoover's warning about the danger of the Communist party "doing its best to twist this movement for its own purposes" and trying to "drive a wedge between the administration and its friends in the South."

After Hoover's presentation, Brownell proposed legislation that would establish a Civil Rights Commission to study voting rights violations, upgrade the Civil Rights Section of the Justice Department to

a division under its own assistant attorney general, establish a set of
new voting rights laws, and give the attorney general new authority
to seek civil injunctions to secure voting rights. Eisenhower adopted
Brownell's suggestion and submitted the program to Congress in 1956,
where it was passed by the House but expired in Senate committee.
The next September, after major efforts on its behalf by Eisenhower
and Senate Majority Leader Lyndon Johnson, the Civil Rights Act
of 1957 was signed into law. According to Brownell, Hoover supported
this legislation and spoke in its favor to congressmen.[38]

The Civil Rights Act of 1957 did raise the status of Frank Murphy's
old Civil Rights Section to a division with its own assistant attorney
general, but Brownell's resignation in October 1957 left civil rights
without an advocate in the cabinet. And so, despite the new division,
civil rights again sank to a low departmental priority. In 1959, the
Civil Rights Commission that had been established under the 1957
Act reported that the record of the new division was no better than
it had been when it was merely a section.[39]

Despite the passage of the new Civil Rights Act and the increased
mobilization of the civil rights movement, Hoover still believed that
neither public consensus nor political support was strong enough to
outweigh the risks if the Bureau pursued civil rights violations more
aggressively in the South. Throughout his career, even when he agreed
with the action that was urged on him (as, for instance, when anti-
Communists urged him to move against the Communist party between
1924 and 1933), Hoover was always unwilling to take a vulnerable
advance position where he could not count on overwhelming political
and public backing. Besides his personal attitudes, therefore, every
consideration that had any weight argued against action in this field.
It would take irresistible pressure, including unmistakable presidential
leadership, to get him to change this policy. This would not occur
until the Johnson administration.[40]

Besides civil rights, another unwanted issue the fifties placed on
Hoover's agenda was organized crime. Once again, he rejected suggestions that he modify his exclusive emphasis on domestic security. Hoover looked upon demands that the Bureau make a new commitment
to organized crime investigations as an implicit challenge to his authority and competence, because he had been on record for years denying
that organized crime even existed. This stand put him in an embarrassing position when, on November 14, 1957, New York State Police
Sergeant Edgar L. Croswell discovered a conference of more than

sixty Mafia dons in the upstate New York town of Apalachin. In the ensuing uproar, the question was asked why Hoover, with his secret sources of information, had not known about the Mafia while it grew to the extent revealed by the Apalachin conference. Hoover's critics pulled out the statements he had made over the years in which he denied the existence of any such national crime syndicate, thus making him out to be either a fool or deliberately obtuse. (There was even some muttering about corrupt bargains between Hoover and organized crime to keep out of each others' bailiwicks.)[41]

Once again, the explanation lay in the "ancient echoes" of Hoover's experience. Since 1933, when Courtney Ryley Cooper's first articles appeared in *American Magazine,* Hoover had consistently rejected the notion that organized crime existed. The Hoover-Cooper theory, it will be recalled, was that nationally prominent crime figures existed only because local law enforcement failures nurtured "the roots of crime" that produced celebrity criminals. Therefore, when the FBI killed a Dillinger, it was because local authorities had been unable to deal with the criminal before he finally did something that came under federal jurisdiction, and not because the overall situation was a federal responsibility. The national crime problem, according to Hoover's formulation, was a local one; the FBI could help by giving the local police technical assistance and by furnishing them with a model of professionalism. Even in the 1950s, he was still deriding the notion of a national crime syndicate as "baloney."

Hoover was also reluctant to recognize the existence of organized crime because any effective campaign against it would require a "task force" strategy using personnel drawn from all available branches of government. Under those circumstances it would be impossible for him to preserve the FBI's autonomy or to have complete control over the operations of his agents. And if Hoover's experience over the years had taught him anything, it was that he had to have absolute and exclusive control over all Bureau activities; it was essential to his survival. Preserving (and expanding) FBI independence of action, even at the cost of limiting the Bureau's growth and responsibilities, was an absolute for Hoover.[42]

Attorney General Rogers, who tried to engage the Justice Department in organized crime prosecutions, conceded that Hoover had to be dragged "kicking and screaming" into organized crime investigations. Rogers said that

Mr. Hoover was opposed to it the way we went into it. As I say, he had a feeling that the lawyers in the Department should let the FBI know what it was they wanted investigated and the FBI would investigate it. Now that as a premise is sound, a perfectly sound proposition, but in order to make an attack on organized crime at the national level, you had to go beyond that. You had to have coordination of people in the Alcohol Tax, in Customs, the Treasury, et cetera, so you had to have a major national cooperative effort. And in order to do that we had to discuss it with the FBI, work out our plans, and so forth. Now at that time, as happens so often in government, there were some differences, but those differences never became serious, as far as I was concerned, with the FBI or with Edgar Hoover.[43]

The state of the law regarding wiretaps and bugs was another reason Hoover was determined to maintain the FBI's independence from any outside agencies when investigating organized crime. Since the Bureau would most likely have to use wiretaps and bugs if it wanted to get results, and since these illegal techniques posed a danger were they to become known, Hoover was particularly insistent that he have complete control over investigations that utilized them. Even though he was dealing with a new America in the late 1950s, Hoover's frame of reference for judging the relative risk of his operations was still his disastrous experience during the Red Scare raids of 1919 and 1920 when uncontrolled cooperation with local police and civilian volunteers had destroyed his antiradical campaign and exposed him to the humiliation of a congressional investigation. In *The Investigators,* James Q. Wilson observed that

Hoover knew instinctively what every natural executive knows: having a monopoly position on even a small piece of turf is better than having a competitive position on a large one. Just as Hoover resisted the Nisei evacuation and the Huston plan because they required collaboration, so also he opposed allowing FBI agents to serve as members of Justice Department "strike forces" sent to cities to root out political corruption and attack organized crime.[44]

This needs correction in only one detail. Hoover did not "instinctively" know the need for autonomy. He had won that knowledge through hard and painful experience.

Hoover's unwillingness to investigate organized crime when it became a national issue perplexed many of his supporters because it was so obviously destructive to his own reputation and that of the Bureau. As with civil rights, Hoover's behavior is less puzzling when it is understood in light of his long memory and his struggle not to repeat the mistakes of the past.

In 1957, the Senate Rackets Committee under John McClellan

of Arkansas (with John F. Kennedy a member and Robert F. Kennedy committee counsel) revived the perennial idea of a federal national crime commission; the Justice Department responded by setting up a Special Group on Organized Crime. Instead of cooperating, however, Hoover reacted to this affront by instituting an FBI "Top Hoodlum Program," which required every field office to draw up a list of the ten most important underworld figures to target for intensive surveillance. Despite the accomplishments of the Organized Crime Group, Hoover told his enraptured supporters on the House Appropriations Committee that the Group was engaged only in "nest feathering publicity" and "speculative ventures." His opposition doomed the Special Group, which died after two years. In 1959, there were 400 agents in the New York office assigned to investigating Communists; only four were assigned to organized crime.[45]

By the end of the decade, the FBI had come to seem so backward and out of touch with the organized crime situation that Hoover had to work hard to keep the usually docile International Association of Chiefs of Police from calling for a federal central clearinghouse on organized crime; that would have set up another rival to the FBI's leadership. By 1960, however, the pressure for anti–organized crime action had grown so great that finally Hoover caved in; he accepted the evidence presented to him by his aides, notably William C. Sullivan of the Domestic Intelligence Division, that something along the lines of organized crime *did* exist.[46]

Hoover began using microphones in criminal (nonsecurity) investigations in an attempt to make up for lost time in expanding his knowledge of organized crime. In mid-1959, the Chicago field office requested permission to plant a bug at a mob meeting place on Chicago's North Michigan Avenue. In a radical departure from his past policies, Hoover gave his approval, basing his action on a memorandum from Brownell that granted him permission to plant microphones in cases of "internal security and the national safety." This was later taken by many to mean that Hoover had exceeded his authority, but Brownell later explained that he intended "national safety" to include federal crimes. The Chicago microphone surveillance was enormously productive and, in 1960, provided the Bureau with a complete list of the names of the members of the Mafia's "national commission."[47]

Hoover's resistance to FBI involvement in the fields of civil rights and organized crime was rooted in bureaucratic considerations, per-

sonal attitudes, hard-won experience—but most deeply in the view
of the world he had developed during his formative years in government
in the twenties and thirties. He had gained his first professional success
and then his national reputation because he responded skillfully to
an increasingly unified national consciousness that demanded federal
leadership against local situations that were newly perceived as national
problems. He was a progressive not only in his scientific approach
to public problems, but—even more generally—in his innovative
responses to new conditions. But as he grew older, instead of capitalizing on new challenges, Hoover tried to deny their existence, at least
as problems fit for federal attention. While he successfully applied
innovative methods in the twenties and thirties, fear of losing the
security he had won for himself by employing them made him resist
grappling with problems that might demand new approaches.

Hoover had turned the FBI into a symbol of federal leadership,
but it was a species of leadership—developed under Herbert Hoover
and expanded by Franklin D. Roosevelt—that sought to lead the country by mobilizing local communities and local elites, leaving intact
the local authority structures that ruled in the South, in the unions,
and in the cities. The pressure during the fifties for federal civil rights
enforcement and for federal drives against organized crime demanded
an expansion of federal leadership that went far beyond the role Hoover
had created the FBI to fill. Hoover's FBI had been able to act as a
symbol of high ideals and patriotic sentiments only because it stayed
aloof from involvement in the kinds of local problems that the federal
government was now being called upon to address. Neither organized
crime nor organized segregation could be fought by working *through*
local power structures, since they were maintained *by* those structures.
By demanding action in these new areas, the FBI's critics were really
asking Hoover to undercut and overthrow the elites with whom he
had been in alliance all his life.

Though reluctant to move on civil rights and organized crime, Hoover
redoubled his efforts in domestic security. He bombarded Eisenhower
with a staggering quantity of memos about the Party, generally addressed to the Special Assistant for National Security Affairs, an office
first filled by Robert Cutler and then by Dillon Anderson and Gordon
Gray. When Eisenhower took office, the latest of Hoover's massive
"briefs" on the American Communist party—"The Role of the Communist Party USA in Soviet Intelligence"[48]—was awaiting him.

There was also a weekly FBI "Current Intelligence Summary,"

largely a digest of rhetoric emanating from the Communist party and front groups, together with advance warning about Party activities (no bomb plots, just fund-raising campaigns, marches, petition drives) that Hoover had received from his informants and wiretaps ("reliable informants"). Hoover also produced an annual analysis of the "Communist Party Line" and summaries of "Communist Party Activities." Throughout the fifties, despite the total collapse of American communism, Hoover never slackened in his efforts to persuade the president and the public that, all appearances to the contrary, the threat from communism was greater than ever.[49]

While the Justice Department's Smith Act prosecution of the "second echelon" Communist officials was battering away at the Party's leadership (forty-two indictments between 1953 and 1956), some of the international tensions that had given rise to the cold war Red Scare were easing. After the death of Stalin and the Korean War armistice (both in 1953), the Russians evacuated their troops from Austria (in May 1955) and Eisenhower met with the leaders of Britain, France, and the Soviet Union in Geneva (in July 1955). After 1956, the government abandoned the detention camps set up under the Internal Security Act of 1950. Hoover's reaction to all this was to complain about "growing public complacency toward the threat of subversion."[50]

The Smith Act itself, one of the cornerstones of Hoover's anti–Communist drive, was one of the casualties of the relaxation of tensions at home and abroad. On October 17, 1955, the Supreme Court granted a writ of certiorari, agreeing to review the *Yates* case, a Smith Act conviction in all appearances identical to *Dennis,* the 1951 decision that had upheld the Smith Act conviction of the Foley Square Eleven. Such an action could only mean that the Court was considering changing its mind about the constitutionality of the Smith Act. The department notified the Bureau on March 15, 1956, that future Smith Act cases must include evidence of "an actual plan for a violent revolution" before the department would try to prosecute them.[51]

While the *Yates* decision—which effectively reversed *Dennis* by requiring proof of incitement to revolutionary action, not merely incitement to revolutionary belief—was not rendered until 1957, the Justice Department's restrictions on new Smith Act prosecutions disrupted Hoover's domestic security program.[52] The Smith Act, in conjunction with the Custodial Detention Program, had given direction and focus to the FBI's surveillance against the Party, as well as a gauge for evaluating the usefulness of the Bureau's operations and the intelligence it was gathering.

The demise of the Smith Act as a viable prosecutorial weapon was a blow to the FBI more because of its function as an operational compass than because of its worth as a legal weapon. More than a year before the department's directive, the FBI had stopped regular use of the Smith Act. Almost all of the Bureau's Smith Act cases had been launched immediately after the Supreme Court upheld the convictions of the Foley Square Eleven in its 1951 *Dennis* decision, and Hoover had stopped new prosecutions after November 1954 because of the "valuable informants" he was losing when they testified at the trials. The government sought no further Smith Act prosecutions until the 1956 election campaign, when the administration polished up its anti-Communist credentials with ten additional indictments. Thus, by 1956, the Bureau was making use of the Smith Act only as a pretext to justify its continued investigation of the Party.[53]

Nevertheless, the Smith Act was still important enough for the Supreme Court's decision to draw a worried reaction from Hoover. He sent a memo to cabinet members and other top officials on the "Reaction of Communist Party, USA, to Recent Supreme Court Decisions." He complained that the "Party as a whole is jubilant over these decisions." He quoted one Communist, who said, "[T]his decision will mark a rejuvenation of the Party in America. We've lost some members in the last few years but now we're on our way again. The people are sick and tired of witch-hunts." Hoover quoted another Communist who said it was good to have an "extreme leftist" on the Court, but Hoover refrained from identifying which of the nine was meant.[54]

Despite Hoover's worries, at the end of 1955 the Party was leaderless, directionless, reduced to 22,000 members, and staggering "toward its climactic crisis [of 1956] as a cripple." Then came news of Khrushchev's speech on the crimes of Stalin given at the 20th Congress of the Soviet Communist Party in February 1956 (obtained and published by the State Department), followed by authoritative accounts of Soviet anti-Semitism. In June 1956, Communist authorities in Poznan, Poland, killed more than a hundred protesters and wounded hundreds more, and finally, in October, Soviet tanks rolled into Hungary and crushed the last illusions of the American Communists. The Party was, for all practical purposes, finished. Nevertheless, in 1956, Hoover summoned his domestic intelligence agents to a conference to decide on a new strategy against the Party, now that they no longer had the Smith Act. The growing demoralization of the American Communist party pointed Hoover toward a momentous change in his approach to domestic intelligence. Sensing a historic opportunity to administer the coup de grâce to the bewildered remnants of the Party, he and his aides decided to use their informants to actively stir up dissension by asking embarrassing questions about Hungary, and by stimulating discussions about Khrushchev's speech and Soviet anti-Semitism.

The plan that emerged from the Bureau's field conferences in 1956 was formally known as its COINTELPRO (Counter Intelligence Program), an aggressive campaign to destroy the Party by circulating disruptive rumors about the Party and individual members, and by employing other "dirty tricks" to destroy the Party's ability to function.

William C. Sullivan, the assistant to the director in charge of the expansion of COINTELPRO during the sixties, described the program as the application of wartime counterintelligence methods to domestic groups: "No holds were barred. . . . We have used [these techniques] against Soviet agents. They have used [them] against us. . . . [The same methods were] brought home against any organization against which we were targeted."[55]

COINTELPRO was greatly expanded during the sixties, but during the Eisenhower administration the sole operation of this type was COINTELPRO–CPUSA, directed against the American Communist party. This was the longest-lived of the programs (1956 to 1971) and accounted for more than half—1,388 out of 2,370—of all the Bureau's reported COINTELPRO actions. (There is good reason to believe, however, that the reported incidents were only a small fraction of the actual number of COINTELPRO operations.)[56]

The goal of COINTELPRO was initially described as "keeping the pot boiling" within the Party by raising such questions at Party meetings as the invasion of Hungary and Soviet anti-Semitism. The Bureau soon saw that the technique offered the opportunity "to direct our disruptive tactics toward a specific goal," thus manipulating the Party in desired directions. Soon, FBI informants were becoming so influential in Party feuds that Hoover and his top aides seriously contemplated having the Bureau support particular factions in struggles to control the Party. (Hoover decided the safest course was to maintain a "middle of the road" position in such Party fights to avoid backing a losing faction and thus having the Bureau's informants expelled from the Party.)[57]

Some of Bureau's COINTELPRO techniques might be defended, such as having informants in the Party raise the issue of Khrushchev's denunciation of Stalin during Party meetings. Some were more offensive: Upon learning that a Party official was a homosexual, the FBI arranged to have him arrested in order to "embarrass the party." Other techniques were pointlessly cruel, such as provoking the neighbors' complaints that resulted in the ouster of a Communist mother as a Cub Scout den leader. One of the most effective—and most ruthless—was to put a "snitch jacket" on a Party member by framing a loyal Party member as an FBI informant to discredit him with his comrades. The Bureau also made anonymous phone calls to keep the Party from renting meeting halls, and it sent anonymous reprints of anti-Communist publications to Party members. The only restraint on the Bureau's ingenuity in devising ways of disrupting the Party was fear of getting caught.[58]

The shock of world events in 1956 might have been too great for the American Communist party to survive even without the added punishment inflicted by COINTELPRO, but from the Bureau's perspective the program was an enormous success. At the end of the year, the Party was a ghost of its former self with a membership down to between 4,000 and 6,000, many of whom were FBI informants. By December 1957, the paid-up membership sank to a low of 3,474. American Communists had gone the way of the buffalo; now Hoover and his domestic security agents had to worry about suffering the same fate as the buffalo hunters.[59]

As a legal basis for COINTELPRO, Hoover relied on a somewhat strained interpretation of the Communist Control Act of 1954. Never ruled upon by the Supreme Court, that law stated that the Communist party was "not entitled to any of the rights, privileges, and immunities attendant upon legal bodies created under the jurisdiction of the laws of the United States." The Party was to be considered outlawed as a matter of policy, although Party membership was not made a crime (so that the Party would not have an excuse to refuse to register under the McCarran Internal Security Act of 1950, which required the Party to disclose its officers and membership rolls to the Subversive Activities Control Board). The *organization* could therefore be considered fair game, even though *individual* Communists supposedly still had some rights.[60]

While his superiors, careful readers of official documents, and, of course, the Communists themselves, were well aware of COINTELPRO, Hoover recognized how controversial the program would be if it ever became general knowledge. For this reason, all COINTELPRO operations had to be approved by Bureau headquarters in Washington. The lowest level at which they could be approved was by the assistant director in charge of Domestic Intelligence, but most were passed on by Hoover personally.[61]

While COINTELPRO was legal, proper, and successful by Hoover's standards, it involved the government in the same kind of behavior that was supposedly the reason for denying the Communist party legitimacy as a political movement. Sidney Hook, a leading intellectual supporter of the anti-Communist drive, argued that a political conspiracy (specifically the Communist conspiracy) was outside the bounds of constitutionally protected political activity because it sought

> to attain its ends not by normal political or educational processes but by playing outside the rules of the game. Because it undermines the conditions which are required in order that doctrines may freely compete for acceptance, because where successful it ruthlessly destroys all heretics and dissenters, a conspiracy cannot be tolerated without self-stultification in a liberal society.[62]

COINTELPRO made Hoover's FBI more of a conspiracy than the Bureau's "subversive" Communist target, since the Party was, for the most part, operating unapologetically and openly. Worse, the success of COINTELPRO would encourage the Bureau to expand those techniques to other targets when the political climate so dictated, as it would during the late sixties.

In March 1960, a COMINFIL (Communist Infiltration) component was added to COINTELPRO–CPUSA. Previous COMINFIL operations had been to *discover* Communist infiltration; the new one was aimed at *preventing* Communist infiltration of mass organizations. The standard COMINFIL technique was to release information about Communist participants in marches and rallies without, of course, admitting the FBI source. The intent and often the effect was to discredit the organizations sponsoring the event, the event itself, and, inevitably, the goals of the event. This expansion of COINTELPRO (like the COINTELPROs developed during the fifties) represented a drastic intrusion by a police force into the American political process. Previous Bureau behavior of this kind had been isolated and infrequent. Now it was systematized and given official approval.[63]

While the COMINFIL program gave Hoover a pretext for keeping groups such as the NAACP under surveillance despite the lack of any evidence of illegal activities, he seemed at times impatient with his self-imposed restrictions on COINTELPRO that limited its use to Communist-infiltrated organizations. The Bureau justified regular surveillance of the Black Muslims by a need to determine whether the group should be cited on the attorney general's list of subversive organizations whose members were barred from government employment, and whether it met the new requirements for prosecution under the Smith Act. Hoover complained that the Justice Department attorneys who evaluated FBI reports "always come up with more reasons for no positive action and none for [a] constructive approach." Hoover prodded his agents by asking, "Is there no action [the] Dept. can take against the NOI [Nation of Islam]?" He sent examples of the group's rabid rhetoric to the Justice Department to support his suggestion that it be cited on the attorney general's list. Nevertheless, during the Eisenhower administration, Hoover did not expand COINTELPRO's targets beyond the Communist party.[64]

COINTELPRO–CPUSA was Hoover's pragmatic response to new circumstances in the mid-fifties that included the withdrawal of the Smith Act as a linchpin for the Bureau's anti-Communist activities and the outlaw status of the Party under the Communist Control Act. It was, finally, an ingenious strategy to exploit the demoralized state of the American Communist party in 1956. But if COINTELPRO was a rational and successful effort in 1956 to capitalize on a unique moment in the history of the Communist movement, it is less easy to understand Hoover's motive for not only maintaining the program after 1956, but even expanding it. It seemed so clear to Brownell, for one, that the Party had been crushed for good, that he retired to Wall Street at the end of 1957 with the satisfaction of having accomplished his two goals as attorney general: destroying the Communist party and passing the first civil rights laws since Reconstruction.[65]

But Hoover had thought he had destroyed the Party once before; the Palmer raids, the raid on the Bridgman convention, and the state sedition trials of the Communist leaders had reduced its membership to about 5,000 in the early twenties. The Party had been as weak then as it was in 1957, and yet it had rebounded to a strength of 80,000 during World War II. So while some looked at the Party in 1956 and saw only its collapse, Hoover saw only the low point of a recurrent cycle of increase and decline during which the country must not be lulled into dismantling its antiradical facilities as it had done in 1924.

Throughout Eisenhower's presidency, Hoover used his prestige to counter any indications that the government might be abandoning the basic assumptions of the cold war. Even though the Party appeared to be on its last legs, Hoover cautioned Eisenhower that this was no time to relax the pressure:

> The Communists now [seek] . . . to divert public attention by now claiming allegiance to the United States and purporting to sever their ties

with the Soviet Union. They will fool no one by this tactic. Nor will they trick this country into relaxing its vigilance. So long as Communist dictatorships threaten the peace of the world, the Communists and their agents will remain a serious threat to our internal security. It is only by continuing to expose their tactics and activities that we shall prevent the resurgence of this international conspiracy in the United States.[66]

As the world situation changed and the American Communist party collapsed, the threat to national security from a Communist fifth column became less credible. Hoover shifted the focus of his anti-Communist campaign from the Party's efforts to overthrow American institutions to its supposed responsibility for subversion of American values. He charged that the Party was trying to "drive a wedge between the American people and the American way of life" and he decried the tendency "to ignore the anti-American statements that are preserved in communist archives." He now claimed his expertise gave him authority to separate the "authentic" from the "subversive" in American reform movements.[67]

For Hoover, the specter of communism was more than the shadow of the real-life Communist. Communism was merely "the latest form of the eternal rebellion against authority," a tendency rooted in the fallen nature of man. There would never be a moment when the serious anti-Communist could beat his sword into a plowshare or his files into papier-mâché. Anticommunism had a positive value as a defense of American values whether or not there still were any Communists. To Hoover, the Communist, or even his memory, was as essential a part of the moral lessons he taught the nation as was the absent sinner when, as a boy, he taught his Sunday school at the Old First Church at the foot of Capitol Hill.

Hoover had always had the confidence of his opinions, and now his success and power made him seek a more effective forum from which to deliver moral instruction to the public. At the same time the Bureau was developing COINTELPRO to "neutralize" the Party, Hoover's Domestic Intelligence Division was starting work on a study of communism aimed at the mass market. The book that finally emerged after many revisions, *Masters of Deceit,* was Hoover's primer for Americans, an instruction in the "stern reality" of the world.

The initial draft of the book was produced in the Research and Analysis Section of the Domestic Intelligence Division under the supervision of its chief, William C. Sullivan. Even though *Masters of Deceit* (like Hoover's earlier book, *Persons in Hiding*), was ghostwritten, it was as much a reflection of his ideas and feelings as if he had written it himself. His style of thought and expression so permeated the Bureau that the FBI's writers had institutionalized a style indistinguishable from Hoover's characteristic patterns of speech and thought. Moreover, Hoover's editing was vigorous and rigorous; nothing got out of the Bureau unless his assistants were absolutely sure it would meet with his approval. All his aides, and Louis Nichols in particular, bore scars from his wrath when the Director discovered "J. Edgar Hoover" had said or written something that did not suit him.[68]

Masters of Deceit was published in 1958 by Henry Holt, a publishing firm owned by Clint Murchison, the Texas oilman who put Hoover and Tolson up each summer at his hotel in La Jolla. To judge by the financial arrangements for the book, Hoover had reached the point where he regarded the Bureau as an extension of himself. Even though the book was written on government time by government employees, Hoover and his associates split the money among themselves. *Masters of Deceit* sold 250,000 copies in hardback, 2 million in paper (twenty-nine printings by 1970). Proceeds were divided evenly among Hoover, Tolson, Louis Nichols, *This Week* magazine editor William I. Nichols, and the FBI Recreation Fund.[69]

The book's actual writers made nothing, which certainly bothered their boss, William C. Sullivan, who later said, "We used to joke at the bureau, '*Masters of Deceit*, written by the Master of Deceit who never even read it.'" The last paragraph of the book (before the appendices) may have been a veiled indication of how his bullpen of writers felt about their work. After Stalin's death, Khrushchev ridiculed him for ordering a book written by the Party Central Committee to be published as "written by Comrade Stalin and approved by a commission of the Central Committee." "As you see," *Masters* quoted Khrushchev, "a surprising metamorphosis changed the work created by a group into a book written by Stalin. It is not necessary to state how and why this metamorphosis takes place."[70] This sounds like a muffled protest from Hoover's anonymous ghostwriters.

Masters of Deceit assembled all of Hoover's arguments for continuing the anti-Communist crusade no matter how weak the American Communist party might appear. There were the old statistics that despite the American Communist party's infirm state, proportionately, there were more Communists (counting their sympathizers) in the U.S. than there were in Russia on the eve of the revolution. If the Party still seemed too small to worry about, Hoover turned that into another reason for keeping it under surveillance: "[T]he present menace

of the Communist Party in the United States grows in direct ratio
to the rising feeling that it is a small, dissident element and need
not be feared." Finally, Hoover used his ultimate argument. The size
of the Party in the United States was irrelevant as long as Moscow
was running the international movement: "Night after night, week
after week, these men and women are plotting against America, working out smears, seeking to discredit free government, and planning
for revolution. They form the base of a gigantic pyramid of treason,
stretching from the little gray house with green shutters to the towers
of the Kremlin."

In 1919, Hoover linked American Communists to the revolution
sweeping Europe; in 1950, to the theft of the atom secrets and the
infiltration of the government. But in 1958, it was harder and harder
to connect the theoretical threat of revolution to current events, or
to exploit any lively public conviction that an American Communist
uprising was an immediate possibility. *Masters of Deceit* came out
just as the Party itself was visibly crushed into the dust and during
a general relaxation of the most extreme cold war tensions. Since
the newspapers were no longer providing Hoover with the headlines
he needed to dramatize the danger of communism, the solution was
to look to popular mythology and sentimental entertainment for hor-
rific images. Enrolling a young man (Eric) in the Party, for example,
took on the character of a pact with the devil: "In the presence of
an eighteen-year-old girl [the obligatory Black Mass virgin?] and a
dark-haired stooped old man [the Black Man?] Eric signed his application for party membership." Again, "At the age of sixteen, as he
later said, Lenin ceased to believe in God. It is reported that he tore
the cross from his neck, threw this sacred relic to the ground, and
spat upon it."

Other imagery was drawn from horror movies: "The CPUSA is
a freak [that] has grown into a powerful monster endangering us all"
and "the W. E. B. DuBois clubs are new blood for the vampire of
international communism." The reader was told that "Communism
is cannibalistic. Its servants are periodically offered as sacrifices on
the communist altar." He learned that communism changed "a child
of God into a soulless social cog." (Perhaps this was a recollection
of the science fiction film of the fifties, *Invasion of the Body Snatch-
ers*, that had an "alien life form" ["alien way of life"] transforming
Americans into zombies without human feelings or free will.) *Masters
of Deceit* turned the Communist into a Frankenstein's monster who
"doesn't just grow; he must be created."

During the forties, Hoover had used crime as proof that there was a failure of leadership in America, that parents, ministers, youth leaders, and teachers were not providing young Americans with a sense of community, so they turned instead to criminal companions for the security they should have gotten from home, school, and church. In *Masters of Deceit,* Hoover used communism to convince Americans that their survival depended upon "a rekindled American faith, based on our priceless heritage of freedom, justice, and the religious spirit." Without totally abandoning the thesis that the Communist fifth column, supported by the Soviets, could overthrow the U.S. government, Hoover now claimed that the real danger was the "destruction of the American way of life" through the spread of "a communist mentality representing a systematic, purposive, and conscious attempt to destroy Western civilization and roll history back to the age of barbaric cruelty and despotism, all in the name of progress." Although the Communists might be only "a few men and women," through "thought control" their spiritual "infection" had spread "to most phases of American life."

Since communism was a false religion, the only defense against it was a return to true religion. "The very essence of our faith in democracy and our fellow man is rooted in a belief in a Supreme Being." The religious underpinnings of Americanism, he said, consisted of a belief in the dignity of the individual, in mutual responsibility, in the concept of life as having a meaning that transcends political systems, in a sense of stewardship, and in an intrinsic morality rooted in the nature of things.

> To meet this challenge no hesitant, indifferent, half-apologetic acts on our own part can suffice. Out of the deep roots of religion flows something warm and good, the affirmation of love and justice; here is the source of strength for our land if we are to remain free.

Hoover's reversion to type as the earnest Christian soldier defending church, school, and home was nowhere more evident than in the 1959 film version of Don Whitehead's authorized history of the Bureau, *The FBI Story.* The movie showed the Bureau itself as an idealized version of Hoover's home at Seward Square, a substitute for the family he had never been able to create for himself as an adult.

Whitehead was a two-time winner of the Pulitzer Prize and chief of the *New York Herald Tribune*'s Washington Bureau. He began *The FBI Story* in 1955 with the close cooperation of Louis Nichols and the Crime Records Division.[71] The book appeared in 1956, stayed on the best-seller lists for thirty-eight weeks, and was serialized in

170 papers. Like *Masters of Deceit,* it was conceived during the period when the Bureau's anti-Communist program was undergoing the upheaval that led to COINTELPRO and the decision to supplement conventional surveillance with new measures that included a public relations drive to keep the public aroused against the Party.

Most of *The FBI Story* is a readable, engaging history of the Bureau filled with anecdotes, human interest and many previously unknown facts about the Bureau, particularly its undercover work. But Whitehead ended his story by claiming that the FBI's real significance in American history was not in the crimes it solved and the laws it upheld, but in the values it expressed:

> The history of the FBI, in reality, is the story of America itself and the struggle for an ideal. . . . In the whole struggle, the FBI represents the people's effort to achieve government by law. . . . And the FBI in the future will be as strong or as weak as the people demand it to be. No more. No less.[72]

The transformation of the FBI into a microcosm of traditional America was carried to its logical conclusion in the Warner Bros. film version. The movie turned the book into something the *Saturday Review* called "One G-Man's Family." The drama came less from the gunfights with gangsters than from the conflict between its FBI hero and his wife (James Stewart and Vera Miles) as Stewart's FBI career disrupted, time and again, their domestic happiness.

Hoover's admirers who went to see *The FBI Story* expecting something like the old G-man movies would have been puzzled by Warner Bros.'s new breed of family-oriented G-men. The *New York Times* complained the show was more concerned with "the joys and sorrows of the American home and the bliss of domestic security than the historic details of crime." The program seemed to treat the Bureau's great cases as "occupational hazards" that were sandwiched between such domestic obligations as getting the kids off to school and sitting down to a bowl of breakfast food.

> The F.B.I. agent is presented as a pillar of the American home, as much as—or even more than—a pillar of law enforcement and protection against Communist spies. . . . "This country's growing and crime will grow with it," one of the eager beavers says. . . . It sounds like a slogan: "Be a G-Man and Give Your Family Complete Security."[73]

Hoover had turned the FBI into a substitute family, and now Hollywood had given him a dramatization of his fantasy, which made his first viewing of the film an emotional experience for him (and a nerve-racking one for his associates and for Mervyn LeRoy, the director). As LeRoy recalled, "I was never so nervous in my whole life . . . and for this reason, they didn't laugh in the right places . . . including Mr. Hoover and Mr. Tolson and [Cartha] Deke De-Loach and everybody that were in there. [But then] . . . Edgar stood up and he motioned for me to come over to him and he put his arms around me and he said, 'Mervyn, that's one of the greatest jobs I've ever seen,' and they all started to applaud. I guess they were all waiting to see how he liked it. . . . Because you're doing a man's life. . . . Well, it was a beautiful story, it was the story of the FBI."[74]

This decade of triumph ended, however, with some disturbing signs that the anti-Communist consensus Hoover had worked so hard and so successfully to create was beginning to crumble around the edges. In May 1960, two months before the Democrats met in Los Angeles to nominate John F. Kennedy for the presidency, Hoover was startled by a riotous student protest in San Francisco against Hoover's historic ally, the House Un-American Activities Committee.

This explosion was several years in the making. Opposition had been mounting to HUAC as a symbol of how anticommunism had become a steamroller flattening political dissent. For the two years before the San Francisco riots, Hoover had tried to shore up HUAC's prestige by letting FBI informants still in the Party testify before the committee. Their appearances contributed little new information but did impart new drama to the old HUAC roadshow. In 1954 and 1955, Hoover had been unwilling to let even the Justice Department have his Communist informants for Smith Act prosecutions. Now he was so concerned about HUAC's survival that he was willing to offer his most precious resource. In return, HUAC members used the hearings to defend and glorify the FBI: "Where in God's name would our nation be," asked one committee member, "if the F.B.I. wasn't able to get patriotic American citizens to go into these organizations in which Communists, crooks, cheats and traitors infiltrate? You should be ashamed of yourself for attacking the F.B.I." HUAC and Hoover were, wrote historian Walter Goodman, like "a pair of mischievously indiscreet lovers."[75]

The new wave of attacks on HUAC had begun in May 1958 when industrialist Cyrus S. Eaton denounced HUAC and went on to charge that there were hardly any Communists left in the country "except in the minds of those on the payroll of the F.B.I." Three days later, the anti-Communist movement was able to marshal a thousand HUAC supporters at New York City's Hunter College to defend the committee against Eaton. In 1959, HUAC stirred up another storm of protest when it sent the names of suspected Communist teachers in California to local school boards, costing some their jobs. California Congressman James Roosevelt offered a House resolution to abolish HUAC and turn its functions over to the Judiciary Committee. Harry Truman joined the attack by calling HUAC the "most un-American thing in the country today." In April 1960, Roosevelt made his most scathing attack yet on the committee. He called it "sanctimoniously cruel" and an "agency for the destruction of human dignity and Constitutional rights."[76]

Hoover defended HUAC because he strongly felt it rendered an essential, even irreplaceable, service to the anti-Communist cause. By using information from FBI files to denounce members of organizations suspected of Communist influence, HUAC warned Americans away from any group Hoover suspected of having Communist links. If the committee were to lose its credibility, the Bureau would have to perform these risky and improper tasks itself, because this "educational" underpinning of the anti-Communist drive was essential to the Bureau's success and Hoover's own security.

The San Francisco demonstrations against HUAC on May 12, 1960, shocked Hoover to such an extent that he had his researchers produce a study ("Communist Target—Youth; Communist Infiltration and Agitation Tactics") that argued the demonstrations were the greatest "communist coup" in twenty-five years. The committee itself weighed in with "Operation Abolition," a forty-five-minute film, narrated by committee staffer Fulton Lewis III, attacking the demonstrators. Hundreds of copies were circulated around the country, sometimes with HUAC witnesses—such as John Lautner—along to run the projector, answer questions, and make sure no one missed the point. "Looking at the riots and chaos Communists have created in other countries," Hoover said, "many Americans point to the strength of our nation and say 'It can't happen here.' The Communist success in San Francisco in May 1960 proves it can happen here."[77]

There *were* Communists at San Francisco. Also present was Frank Wilkinson, the field representative of the National Committee to Abolish the House Un-American Activities Committee, who was the target of a ferocious FBI attack for his work against the committee. By focusing exclusively on the Communist presence at San Francisco, however, Hoover blinded himself to the emergence of a different kind of radicalism and protest politics, a new generation of political activists that was unlike anything Hoover had seen before. Walter Goodman wrote that the protesters' "discontent was formless and pervasive. They saw after eight years of Dwight Eisenhower what the young have often seen, their destinies in the hands of old, cautious, unimaginative, unfeeling men, and they needed to break out. The campus at Berkeley became a testing place of this remarkably non-ideological, even anti-ideological movement."[78]

Before the San Francisco demonstrations, Hoover had patiently preached to the older generation of Americans, blaming them for the moral or political deviations of the young, warning parents that unless they kept their children tied to the apron strings of traditional values, they would be led astray by the Pied Piper of communism. Now in 1960, John F. Kennedy, a man twenty-three years Hoover's junior, was running for president, and Americans still younger seemed to be losing faith in the ritual repudiation of communism whenever and wherever anti-Communist professionals like HUAC or himself proclaimed its presence.

Hoover had always thought of himself as in sympathy with the young. In the thirties, he had been their hero. Now he was having difficulty understanding them or their values; he was even uncertain as to whether they had values at all compatible with his. Within the Bureau he became zealous in banishing anything that reminded him of the emerging youth culture and youthful rebellion: long hair, casual dress, informal manners.

Hoover's major public appearance in 1960 was his speech to the American Legion Convention in Miami, Florida, on October 18. In his speeches, Hoover had always cut a wide swath through crime, communism, religion, and patriotism, but rarely had he been as sweeping in his denunciation of the modern world. He seemed to see himself and his generation coming under attack from a new breed of aliens, "pseudo-liberal" internationalists for whom "patriotism has become a dirty word, and belief in God old-fashioned, if not 'ridiculous.'" Hoover was the head of one of the most powerful agencies in the government, was politically invulnerable, and was speaking before a collection of prosperous and secure Americans; nevertheless, he seemed almost frightened and sounded the alarm to his audience of patriots to rally before it was too late: "You and your organization have proved yourselves to be loyal Americans, and yet you have been the victims of vituperation, lies and vulgar accusations which are the only weapons of the coward and the guilty." He railed against the young, holding them to be willfully susceptible to Communist blandishments:

The diabolical influence of communism on youth was manifested in the
. . . communist-inspired riots in San Francisco, where students were
duped into disgraceful demonstrations against a Congressional committee.

These students were stooges of a sinister technique stimulated by clever
communist propagandists who remained quietly concealed in the background. . . . The never-ending struggle of the communists to capture
the minds and loyalties of American youth goes on incessantly. . . .
Glowing reports have been submitted by these adept and devious communist leaders concerning the pliability and receptiveness of their audiences.
. . . Alarming, too, is the ease with which some major educational institutions have been duped, under the much-abused term of "academic freedom," into permitting underhanded attacks to be made on democratic
institutions and officials of government by instructors responsible for the
higher education of our young people.

Perhaps the recent ineffectiveness of HUAC as an anti-Communist
forum made him uncomfortable; he complained that he was being
forced to fight his enemies under unfair conditions because "America
must adhere to the laws of God and man. As a result, our fight is
doubly difficult because of the Communists' reckless disregard of the
code of morality."

For the first time, however, Hoover's charges of Communist infiltration were being resisted by part of the political mainstream. There
had always been some who opposed him and the Bureau, but they
had been outside the political consensus. Now Hoover was coming
under attack by a new force in American society—politically active
youth—one that was not, like the old left, self-alienated from mainstream politics. There were many young Americans to whom Hoover
was not the hero of the Dillinger days, but rather "a symbol and
tool of the Establishment, a deadening hand extended from Washington
to quash the impulses of dissent wherever they might spring up."[79]

Perhaps in recognition of his inability to understand the values
of the new generation, Hoover abandoned his efforts to have the FBI
take a leadership role against juvenile delinquency. Official FBI entertainment during the forties and fifties, such as radio's "This Is Your
FBI," had shown agents spending as much time trying to rehabilitate
youthful offenders as chasing spies. But Hoover's idea of youth work
meant using school and church to strengthen the family bonds that
would inculcate middle-class morality. The solid family life of the
Hardestys of *The FBI Story* or of Hoover's respectably middle-class
agents was in itself a weapon against crime. The youth culture's rejection of middle-class decorum as an ideal left Hoover without any
solution to the crime problem compatible with his personal beliefs,

since middle-class respectability was the core of his defense against the spread of lawlessness.[80]

Hoover had husbanded his power and prestige during the fifties by strictly limiting his responsibilities to domestic security, his area of greatest expertise. While his reputation reached its zenith during the Eisenhower years, his success came at the cost of avoiding involvement in some of the most pressing issues of the day.

Hoover began the decade secure in an America he loved and understood. He ended it with a sense of trepidation: He was affluent, comfortable, completely secure, pampered in every way by an FBI he had trained to give him every imaginable personal service, but now new forces, young and strange, were growing up around him and threatening that security.

A strangely mixed metaphor Hoover used in 1960 may have sprung from his growing cultural disorientation. "The Trojan snake of communism," he told the Legion, "has discarded its disguise for brute force and slaughter. Communism, shed of all its false smiles, is on its bloody march again." At a time when the country was turning to a new leadership, one bold enough to confront the country's historic injustices, Hoover insisted the times were too dangerous to disturb the existing order. "We are at war with the Communists," he said as the Eisenhower era grew to a close, "and the sooner each red-blooded American realizes that the better and safer we will be!"

Hoover had created such a comfortable and secure life for himself within the Bureau and in the protected enclaves of his wealthy friends, that the new America that had grown up outside the FBI seemed unruly, strange, and contemptuous toward decent standards. As racial protest and cultural turmoil increased at the end of the decade, the contrast between the middle-class decency Hoover had preserved within the FBI and the rest of America became dramatically clear. As he reached the age of sixty-five in 1960, the idea of retiring into such a society seemed fearsome and abhorrent. The America he had known at Seward Square no longer existed except, figuratively, within the FBI.

CHAPTER 11

Kennedy Justice

"They call him 'Bobby'!"
Hoover to an aide

THE THREE MEN Hoover hated "most in the world," he once said, were Martin Luther King, Jr., Quinn Tamm (the independent-minded director of the International Association of Chiefs of Police) . . . and Robert Kennedy. Conflict was probably inevitable between J. Edgar Hoover and Robert Kennedy: the master of bureaucratic survival (the "ultimate bureaucrat," Victor Navasky called him) versus the action-oriented "maximum Attorney General." But there was more here than professional friction. Their hostility went beyond differences in policy—and beyond personality conflicts. There was something in Robert Kennedy that threatened Hoover, and threatened the values he stood for.[1]

Hoover was sixty-six years old in 1961 when John F. Kennedy announced in his inaugural that "the torch has been passed to a new generation of Americans, born in this century." Hoover was not of Kennedy's "new" generation of Americans, he was not of this century, and he had no intention of passing on the torch; by law, he did not have to retire until his seventieth birthday, January 1, 1965. For all Kennedy's brave words about New Frontiers, without forbearance from the right wing that idolized Hoover, the new president was not going to be able to govern the country. The day after the election, Kennedy decided to ask Hoover to stay.[2]

353

Kennedy's election and his appointment of his brother Robert as attorney general called attention to how old Hoover had grown in the job he had held for thirty-six years. John F. Kennedy was the first chief executive younger than Hoover, and he was much younger—twenty-three years younger, born the year Hoover had entered the Justice Department, 1917. Truman had been eleven years older than Hoover, Eisenhower five years older. The men Kennedy brought into his cabinet were also younger than any Hoover had dealt with before: The average age was forty-seven, ten years younger than the members of Eisenhower's cabinet. Attorney General Robert Kennedy, the Kennedy with whom he was going to have to deal, was thirty years younger than Hoover. For a while, until RFK heard about it, guides on the FBI headquarters tour used to point out that the attorney general was born the year after Hoover took over the Bureau.[3]

Given the difference in their ages, it might have been normal for Hoover to feel the natural resentment age has toward youth. But in 1961, youth was itself a politically significant fact. JFK called his program the *New* Frontier; his complaints against Eisenhower had often boiled down to the charge that Eisenhower was old, his administration was old. Kennedy offered an image of energy and youth, and his campaign helped politicize the split between youth and age, the much-debated generation-gap. Youthfulness, and one's relation to it, was emerging as a sign of the gulf that was opening, while hardly anyone noticed, between the traditionalists and modernists in American society.

Hoover was by far the most visible, as well as the oldest, of the holdovers from the Eisenhower administration, and so he stood in contrast to the Kennedys as a symbol of the generation they were pushing aside. Hoover gave the media an irresistible foil to the Kennedys. Norman Mailer dramatized the "agreeable" image of the young president by tearing into Hoover's "lack of personality." Hoover was, he said, an unheroic leader: "a man who embodies his time but is not superior to it—he is historically faceless." The FBI "has at present a leader, but not a hero. So it is faceless in history. And because it is faceless it is insidious, plague-like, an evil force"; by contrast, Kennedy had a face, "the face of a potential hero."[4] Given the Bureau's well-honed alertness for "smears" it is unlikely that Mailer's swipe was not brought to Hoover's attention. In any case, Hoover could have read the same idea in dozens of forms, all resolving to the same perception: the Kennedys were young and dynamic; Hoover was antediluvian and rooted in ancient prejudices. This would have been galling even for a man of modest and retiring ego, and Hoover was no such person.

What upset Hoover most about the president's choice for attorney general were the traits that characterized RFK as young, mannerisms that may have made him a symbol of the youthful irreverence that had frightened Hoover during the San Francisco demonstrations against HUAC in the spring of 1960. Hoover complained to his aides that Bobby tossed darts into a dartboard while they talked, and some of the darts missed the board and hit the woodwork—"pure desecration, desecration of public property." Hoover called the incident "the most deplorably undignified conduct [he and Tolson] . . . had ever witnessed on the part of a Cabinet member." He objected to Kennedy's bringing the family dog to the office; Hoover was just as attached to *his* dogs, but there was a regulation against animals in Federal buildings. Hoover's reaction to seeing the attorney general visiting the FBI area of the Justice Department in his shirt-sleeves was to warn his men to have their jackets on at all times, perhaps as a rebuke to Kennedy for his informality: "Our employees should always be busy; engage in no horse play; and be properly attired. No one knows when and where A.G. may appear."[5]

The Kennedy years were a prelude to the post-1965 counterculture that emerged later as part of the antiwar movement. "Youth culture" was the phrase during the Kennedy years, its climax, perhaps, the appearance of the Beatles on American television on February 9, 1964. The primary mark of the times was not so much rebellion as relaxation of discipline: the court decision that allowed the printing of Henry Miller's *Tropic of Cancer,* the irreverent outbreak of Pop Art in 1962, Ken Kesey's *One Flew Over the Cuckoo's Nest,* the 1962 decision outlawing school prayer.

The more relaxed and informal spirit of the times made Hoover's retrograde policies on grooming—short hair, dark suits, hats—seem a slap at the Kennedys and the youth culture. Agents were censured for wearing sport coats, needing haircuts, or having unshined shoes. An agent entering training in November 1961 said, "Me . . . in a hat? I thought. Never. Back at home they'd have laughed me off the beach. Only old men wear hats, and nobody wants to be an old man so nobody wears one. But in a few months I'd be Special Agent Norman Ollestad of the F.B.I. . . . And I'd have to have a hat. All F.B.I. men wear hats, everybody knows that."[6]

Robert Kennedy drew the same kind of intense personal loyalty from his followers that Hoover had long inspired in his agents, had always insisted on, and now, in his late years, may have doubted his ability to command. The stories Kennedy's associates tell about their years with him stress their loyalty to him and his to them, proudly measured by the overwhelming demands he made of them, and the willingness, even the joy, with which they responded—this at a time when Hoover was enforcing overtime quotas on his men and then using the statistics as a measure of their devotion.

The stories about Hoover that circulated throughout the Bureau around 1960 centered on his demand that his men furnish demonstrations of personal loyalty. There was a plaque in every FBI office:

"Loyalty"

If you work for a man, in heaven's name work for him; speak well of him and stand by the institution he represents.

Remember—an ounce of loyalty is worth a pound of cleverness.

If you must growl, condemn, and eternally find fault, why—resign your position and when you are on the outside, damn to your heart's content—but as long as you are part of the institution do not condemn it; if you do, the first high wind that comes along will blow you away, and probably you will never know why.

ELBERT HUBBARD

An agent was told that "if the Director does not receive adulatory letters from the agents he takes this as an indication of apathy towards the Bureau and a sign of disloyalty and lack of dedication." It was important to send such letters "on the occasion of [the director's] birthday, the anniversary of his assuming the Directorship and on the occasion of his Appropriations message to the Congress." Hoover's response to Bob Kennedy seemed to challenge Hoover to produce a like reaction from his own men, and so he tried to demonstrate to himself, to his men, and to the Kennedys that his quota of charisma had not declined.[7]

Both Hoover and Robert Kennedy aspired to be the leaders of young, active, tough men, but it was Kennedy who could stagger through fifty-mile hikes while, according to one of Hoover's top aides, Hoover received daily vitamin injections in the office (in view of the medical malpractice of the day, those vitamin potions may have been laced with amphetamines). There were ideological, bureaucratic, and political reasons for the clash between the two men, but there was also the age-old struggle between the young bull and the old bull for dominance over the herd, a battle in which time, as Hoover was only too well aware, was on the side of the younger.

Hoover knew his reappointment was unpopular with the president's aides, and he learned through the grapevine that Robert Kennedy was in the habit of saying "Just wait" whenever the topic of getting rid of him came up. As the president's brother, the attorney general was not only Hoover's superior in the bureaucratic hierarchy, but he behaved like his superior in fact as well, far more than any previous attorney general. The disparity in their ages made the trappings of rank on which Kennedy insisted—for example, a direct line to a phone on Hoover's desk, a buzzer to summon Hoover to his office—seem deliberate slights and personal affronts to Hoover. While both men tried at first to keep their relations civil, someone who knew them both said that "Hoover had his catalogue of complaints, and one must conclude he grew to resent Bob very much."[8]

Hoover's dislike for Robert Kennedy had in it more than a touch of contempt. RFK and his brother, though they had won the 1960 election, simply did not have the political strength to back up the demands for submission and obedience that they were making on Hoover. The fact that John Kennedy had retained Hoover was a sign of his political weakness. Out of 68 million votes cast in 1960, Kennedy was elected with a margin of fewer than 120,000. Counting votes for minor party candidates, he won with less than a majority. Reappointing Hoover was an important gesture to reassure the conservatives who had voted against him that the new administration had not totally abandoned the familiar ways of the past. "It was important," Robert Kennedy said, "as far as we were concerned, that [Hoover] remained happy and that he remain in his position because he was a symbol and the President had won by such a narrow margin and it was a hell of an investigative body and he got a lot of things done and it was much better for what we wanted to do in the South, what we wanted to do in organized crime, if we had him on our side."[9]

The more personal link between the Kennedys and Hoover was Ambassador Joseph P. Kennedy, Jack and Bob's father, an old friend of the director's. An extremely conservative Democrat, the elder Kennedy had kept up a long and friendly correspondence with Hoover, making sure to include many flattering references to the Bureau and its director. Joseph Kennedy had been a friend and admirer of Joseph McCarthy, often entertaining him at Hyannis Port; in fact, Joe Kennedy had asked McCarthy to take Robert Kennedy onto his staff in 1953 when McCarthy took over the Permanent Investigations Subcommittee of the Committee on Government Operations. McCarthy hired RFK as assistant counsel to the Subcommittee's chief counsel, Roy Cohn, whom Bob Kennedy came to detest. Kennedy left the Subcommittee staff in July 1953, and then returned in January 1954 as minority counsel for the Democratic senators, which made him Cohn's (and McCarthy's) antagonist. There soon was conflict between Kennedy and Cohn. During McCarthy's investigation of the Signal Corps center at Fort Monmouth, New Jersey, Kennedy became convinced that Cohn and the FBI had misrepresented the evidence that linked a black woman who worked as a Signal Corps teletype operator to the Communist party. According to Cohn, Kennedy stormed into the Bureau and demanded that Louis Nichols let him see the files in question. He was turned down, and Hoover wrote "the attitude of Kennedy in this matter clearly shows need for absolute circumspection in any conversation with him." Cohn later said that Hoover had at this time formed an impression of RFK as "an arrogant whipper-snapper."[10]

When the Democrats captured control of Congress in 1954, Kennedy stayed on as chief counsel of the investigative Subcommittee which, under Chairman John McClellan, turned to investigating organized crime though Kennedy himself also kept probing for Communists. Outsiders might have thought that Kennedy's experience on the McClellan Subcommittee would have recommended him to Hoover, but because of Hoover's customary hostility toward rivals in the field of law enforcement, coupled with his refusal (at that time) to admit the existence of the organized crime network that Kennedy and McClellan had uncovered, the Senate investigative work made Robert Kennedy even less popular with the director. (Courtney Evans had been the Bureau's liaison with the committee; after the 1960 election, Hoover made Evans his liaison with the Justice Department and the Kennedys, and set up a new Bureau division for him to head, the Special Investigations Division, with a responsibility for organized crime.)

After JFK won the election, Joseph Kennedy intervened to insist that Jack appoint Bob attorney general. In a surprising gesture, RFK visited Hoover in the Justice Department to get his advice on whether to take the job. Hoover urged Kennedy to do so, probably because he believed that if plans had gone far enough for his opinion to be asked, he could not afford to put up any barriers. Kennedy himself told an aide he did not think Hoover meant it.[11]

In Robert Kennedy, then, Hoover saw a man who was attempting to wield authority far in excess of what could be justified by the administration's political strength. And based on confidential sources, in John Kennedy Hoover saw a man who lacked sexual self-discipline, which Hoover interpreted as weakness of character. Although Hoover had initiated a polite correspondence once Kennedy had started his political career (and Kennedy reciprocated just as politely), the director was also privy to one of the most carefully concealed secrets in Kennedy's past. (The *most* carefully concealed, and the most explosive, was Kennedy's health—Addison's disease, severe allergies, and crippling back pain that had him dependent on pain-relieving drugs during his first months in the White House.) During World War II, while an ensign in Naval Intelligence, Kennedy had an affair with a much-married and much-traveled woman named Inga Arvad (a one-time Miss Denmark who later married movie cowboy Tim McCoy). Arvad, who had spent time in Nazi Germany, where she had met Goering and Hitler, was suspected (falsely) of being a German agent, and so Hoover bugged her room at the Fort Sumter Hotel in Charleston, South Carolina, where she stayed with Kennedy. Soon afterward, Kennedy was shipped to the Pacific for his encounter with the Japanese on PT-109. (There are those who feel that Hoover had something to do with breaking up the affair; others feel that Ambassador Kennedy had again stepped in. However, at the time, nothing was more likely in the normal course of events than sea duty for a naval officer.) Hoover, to whom self-control was everything, had in his files tapes of the youthful John F. Kennedy in bed, discussing government and military matters with a woman under suspicion as an enemy agent. It may have been this that initially caused Hoover to form his low estimation of the president's leadership qualities.[12]

Circumstances soon confirmed Hoover's sense of the Kennedys' inadequacies. Only three months after the inauguration came the Bay of Pigs catastrophe. For Hoover, nothing could have defined the difference more between the competence of Eisenhower's experienced veterans and Kennedy's youthful and untried amateurs. The disaster also confirmed Hoover's lifelong distrust of the OSS/CIA, and reinforced his disposition never to gamble his job on cooperation with the intelligence agency.

Worse was to follow. After the Bay of Pigs disaster, the CIA redoubled its efforts (begun in 1960 under Eisenhower) to have Castro assassinated. Whether or not the Kennedys personally approved of these plans (the evidence is unclear), the special commission on Cuba set up by the president and chaired by the attorney general kept unrelenting pressure on the CIA to "get rid of Castro and the Castro regime." In 1960, the CIA had recruited Chicago underworld figures John Rosselli and Sam Giancana in a scheme to assassinate Castro. The CIA theorized that the mob would be interested in eliminating

Castro so as to recover its prerevolutionary control of the Havana vice rackets. Whether the mob ever tried to do anything in exchange for its CIA money is unclear; there were indications the Mafia turned the operation into a scam to fleece the CIA. In April 1962, however, the Agency decided to revive the mob connection and began supplying John Rosselli with murder weapons, including guns and poison pills.[13]

Meanwhile, Hoover had learned the president was involved in another sexual liaison, one with more serious implications than the Inga Arvad affair. This was Judith Campbell (later Judith Campbell Exner), a twenty-five-year-old divorcee introduced to him by Frank Sinatra. In 1961 and 1962, she made regular visits to the White House, and often spoke to Kennedy by phone. Hoover had become increasingly concerned that the underworld was trying to exploit its connections with Sinatra and his friends to gain access to the president. Now he learned that Campbell was the mistress, not only of Kennedy, but of mobsters Sam Giancana and John Rosselli. On March 22, 1962, Hoover visited Kennedy to spell out the danger of sharing a woman with the Mafia. The last Kennedy-Campbell phone call was a few hours after Hoover's meeting, and afterward Kennedy also avoided the company of Frank Sinatra.[14]

Whether or not Hoover knew about the CIA-Rosselli-Giancana assassination plots during the March 22 meeting, he soon learned that Kennedy had been unwittingly skirting with a scandal that would have linked the presidency to the underworld and to some of the CIA's most unsavory and irresponsible machinations. On April 10, Hoover briefed Robert Kennedy about the CIA-Mafia connection. Kennedy's reaction (he demanded a briefing from the CIA and then forbade them to proceed with any such plans without his approval) seems to suggest that he had *not* known what the CIA was doing.

When RFK reported back to Hoover on his discussions with the CIA and the action he had taken, Hoover told him that "the 'gutter gossip' was that the reason nothing had been done against Giancana was because of Giancana's close relationship with Frank Sinatra, who, in turn, claimed to be a close friend of the Kennedy family." Regardless of whether Hoover's motive in saying this was to rub salt in Kennedy's wounds or to protect the attorney general and the president from embarrassment, that meeting must have been difficult for Robert Kennedy. Although this warning would be acted upon, the Kennedys tended to dismiss others from Hoover (such as unfounded rumors he had heard about Kennedy breach-of-promise suits and other love affairs) as attempts by Hoover to let them know he was on the job. The fact is that Hoover *was* on the job.[15]

During the sixties, the Bureau tried to indoctrinate its agents in what can be seen as anti–New Frontier attitudes. Trainees were told "they have more Communists in the Harvard Yard than you can shake a stick at." They heard that Adlai Stevenson's supporters were "Communists, Communist sympathizers and pseudo-intellectual radicals." They learned "how easily 'eggheads' like Stevenson have been duped by the Communists." An instructor labeled the NAACP a "Communist front group [that] . . . has been instigating fictitious complaints against police officers in Civil Rights cases in an effort to embarrass law enforcement." Other instructors charged that the ACLU was a Communist front organization, and that leading papers were "enemies of the Bureau and frequently attack the Director and the Bureau because of our security program." The new agents were told that "the Director is very much in sympathy" with the movement for impeaching Earl Warren, "and that the Director feels that this country would be a lot better off without Communist sympathizers on the Court." Agents were also indoctrinated in the attitude that the Justice Department was an enemy and could not be trusted. Instructors informed new agents that "the Director has learned from the bitter experiences of the Roosevelt and Truman administrations when the Justice and State Departments were infiltrated with Communists that the Bureau must be free of the control of any Department or executive in Government so that the Bureau can fulfill its responsibilities."[16]

Throughout Hoover's directorship, the FBI had embodied the American values of science and progress, patriotism and security, and popular justice. Now, in the sixties, Hoover's FBI was deliberately distancing itself from the cultural aspirations of much of the nation. This gap was starting to seem preposterous to some of the public and even to some agents. Hoover's refusal to alter the FBI's grooming habits, his insistence on regulations that included Bureau approval of the marriage plans of agents (and the investigation of their fiancees), and rules against married agents' attending nightclubs without their wives indicated a determination to insulate the Bureau from the general liberalization of American social conventions. For the first time, both critics and defenders of the Bureau began to notice how far apart were the FBI's norms and those of the world outside. Hoover and

the Bureau were not the only ones alienated by all of the changes
sweeping American culture, of course. An angry radical right flour-
ished in the sixties that included H. L. Hunt, Fred Schwarz's Christian
Anti-Communist Crusade, and the insubordinate General Edwin A.
Walker, among many others, and for them the Kennedy administration
was coming to represent the changes they feared and detested. Hoover's
alienation from the New Frontier made him more than ever the idol
of the right wing. Out of favor with the administration and its constituency, he symbolized the values still held by older members of middle
America, by Southern whites, rich conservative Texans, and traditionalists frightened of change.[17]

But there were other factors eroding Bureau morale. In the late
fifties and sixties, a career in the FBI was becoming less of a plum
for a young lawyer. The Bureau still paid well—much better than
the Secret Service, better than Justice Department lawyers of equivalent
seniority, and one grade above the pay for Ph.D.s in the CIA (all
testimony to Hoover's clout with Congress)—but the opportunities
in private practice were even greater. The chief financial attraction
of the Bureau was actually its retirement program, considered the
most generous in government. Agents could retire with one-third pay
after twenty years, two-thirds after thirty years. The result was again
to reinforce the absolute conformity of agents and their obedience
to any whim of Hoover's, so as not to jeopardize their pensions, since
Hoover still could dismiss agents without appeal. (The Bureau was
exempt from Civil Service Regulations, though veterans could appeal
to a grievance board outside the Bureau.)[18]

The closed, highly disciplined Bureau, permeated with Hoover's
inflexible presence, ran counter to the expectations and habits of most
college graduates in the sixties. The Bureau began to have trouble
recruiting new agents. In the fall of 1960, there were three occasions
when new agents' classes had to be postponed for lack of applicants.
Without broadcasting the fact, the Bureau began to look to nonlawyers
as agents. At the beginning of the sixties, sixty-one out of 349 agent
recruits were from the Bureau's clerical workers, many of whom had
gone to work for the Bureau direct from high school and so were
presold and preindoctrinated in the Bureau's ways, called by its critics
"Bureau-think." This inbreeding, with its consequent suspicion of outsiders, was one reason why some critics charged that the Bureau had
become a "secret society."[19]

It was around this time that veteran executives who had been
part of the Bureau as it grew under Hoover began to retire; the most

important example was the departure of Louis B. Nichols, who retired in 1959 to take a lucrative executive position with Schenley Distillers. In the opinion of many in the media, Nichols was the man most responsible for the Bureau's public relations success over the years. He had handled the Bureau's "grief" from the mid-thirties until his retirement, at which time he was one of the two assistants to the director with special responsibility for the Crime Records Division, the Bureau's publicity office.[20]

Nichols was replaced by Cartha DeLoach, who was smooth and facile where Nichols had been overbearing and intimidating. Nichols had many faults, including an inability to organize his routine, which kept his file full of exasperated censures from Hoover. He was, however, straightforward and blunt, and would either answer a query or simply refuse to provide information without equivocation. Nor was his loyalty ever in question: He was Hoover's man every hour of his life, one of two friends and associates who named sons after Hoover (the other was an old friend from the Bureau of 1919, George Ruch.)[21]

As the Bureau diverged from the rest of the Justice Department, Hoover's aides had to try to negotiate the Bureau's relations with the department while defending themselves against Hoover's suspicions that any dealings with it indicated disloyalty to himself. Assistant Director Courtney Evans, as Hoover's liaison to the department and the White House, had the impossible task of explaining Hoover to RFK and vice versa, and keeping them both happy. Deputy Attorney General Nicholas Katzenbach said that the only way Evans could do this was to "explain something to Bobby one way and explain something to Hoover another way. And I don't think anybody could have done the job in any other way."[22]

Hoover's age was now working to isolate him from all but the oldest political figures in Washington, and these tended to be conservative congressmen and senators from the one-party South. At the same time, his in-fighting with the Kennedys demanded greater energy and concentration, so he had to cut back on volunteer work, such as his service on the Board of the Presbyterian National Center. To complete a general constriction of his social life, aging began to take its physical toll on both him and those close to him: In 1962, he had surgery (probably a prostatectomy); the following year, Tolson had major heart surgery, followed by a series of strokes over the next few years. His older friends began to die off, and this all resulted in a greater withdrawal into the Bureau and the protection it afforded him against the passage of time.[23]

Hoover's fight against the forces of change caused him to continue to let opportunities for law enforcement leadership slip away. While the country was undergoing a drastic increase in crime—in reality the first real crime wave of Hoover's career—Hoover continued to fulminate against the "beastly punks" who were coddled by "muddle-headed sentimentalists." It was left to President Kennedy, who established the President's Committee on Juvenile Delinquency and Youth Crime in May 1961, with brother Bob as chairman, to try to do something about the surge in crime.

The New Frontier's approach to the crime problem was, predictably, far from the law enforcement philosophy promoted by Hoover over the years. Robert Kennedy and the director of the president's crime committee, David Hackett (an old prep school friend), were impressed by the "opportunity theory" of Lloyd Ohlin and Richard A. Cloward. In their study, entitled *Delinquency and Opportunity* (1960), Ohlin and Cloward explained crime as the result of social barriers that blocked the middle-class aspirations of the poor. Hackett and RFK were convinced that delinquency was a "cover word" for poverty, and that, in turn, was a cover word for racial discrimination. The Juvenile Delinquency Act of September 1961 was based on Ohlin and Cloward's theories, and Ohlin was made head of the Office of Juvenile Delinquency that was established under the act.[24]

The Kennedy administration was searching for innovative ways to grapple with the causes of crime: causes which the New Frontiersmen saw in the removal of terroristic social controls over the black community, the culture of poverty itself, and, perhaps, improved reporting of crime (one of Hoover's earliest innovations), particularly within the black community where crimes against blacks had often been ignored. They refused to follow Hoover in blaming crime on the moral failings of the poor; they tended to see it as a misguided but understandable attempt by the poor (often the nonwhite poor) to gain entry into the middle class, or at least to gain the material possessions enjoyed by the middle class. To Hoover, though, crime was an assault against the middle class and its values, and its punishment was an essential defense of that way of life.

Hoover and the Kennedys simply saw the world differently, conditioned by different experiences and different expectations. To Hoover, the values of the middle class defined the moral bounds on behavior, and so the solution to crime was to indoctrinate the young in the life style of the middle class: home, school, and church. From the perspective of the Kennedys' aristocratic family background and cosmopolitan experience, the middle class's own racial prejudices and status distinctions produced the deprivations that led to crime. For Hoover, and millions like him, the Ohlin-Cloward theory—providing social services for the poor instead of stepping up the repression— was an assault on the respectability and dignity of the middle class. Hoover had always seen middle-class morality as the normal condition from which juvenile delinquents slipped or regressed. Robert Kennedy and his aides in the Justice Department had discovered an underclass, largely black, that had never had any contact with the middle-class values Hoover defended (except to see them as alien and meaningless). By the 1960s, Hoover's ideas were so far removed from the activist philosophy of the Kennedy Justice Department that the notion of having the FBI play its earlier role in formulating national crime prevention policy was probably unimaginable to both Hoover and the Kennedys.[25]

Ever since the Apalachin embarrassment in 1957 and Attorney General William Rogers's short-lived Special Group against organized crime, Hoover had been trying to build up the Bureau's store of information on the mobs without compromising the FBI's autonomy by joining interagency anticrime strike forces. When Robert Kennedy came to the Justice Department, with his reputation as an expert on organized crime, he had every intention of setting up a National Crime Commission to combat organized crime. But faced with Hoover's adamant opposition to any such venture, he had to abandon the proposal. Without Hoover's support, it would have been politically and practically futile.

Because of Hoover's lack of enthusiasm for such investigations, Kennedy had to rely on the department's Organized Crime and Racketeering Section of the Criminal Division (under Edwyn Silberling) rather than the FBI to coordinate information. He also went outside the Bureau to organize a team of twenty lawyers to press the investigation of Jimmy Hoffa and the Teamsters (this was the so-called Get-Hoffa squad under former FBI man Walter Sheridan).[26]

By the end of 1961, however, Hoover had abandoned his opposition and had made organized crime an FBI priority, with Courtney Evans's Special Investigations Division spearheading the effort. Hoover's explanation of his change of heart was that until the September 1961 anti-racket laws (steered through Congress by Robert Kennedy), "the FBI had very little jurisdiction in the field of organized crime." Arthur

Schlesinger calls this excuse a "transparent fraud," but Hoover *was* pointing toward the real reason for the change in policy. True, Hoover could have found the jurisdiction before had he wanted to, but until September 1961, he could not be sure of the overwhelming public and political support he needed in this sensitive and often unrewarding (in the statistical sense dear to Hoover) area. Kennedy's success in getting the new crime laws passed meant that Hoover now had a mandate, not just from the politically weak administration, but from the people he had to please, his supporters in Congress.[27]

Hoover's enlistment in the fight against organized crime created even more opportunities for conflict between him and Kennedy. After New York Mafioso Joseph Valachi had told his story to the FBI, Kennedy's aides carefully probed the Bureau to ascertain whether Hoover objected to Valachi's testifying before the McClellan Committee. The Bureau gave the impression that it approved. Just before Valachi's testimony in September 1963, evidently worried that the public was going to learn a phrase from Valachi that it had not yet heard from the Bureau, Hoover tried to slip a reference to "La Cosa Nostra" into a bylined article in the *Reader's Digest.* Kennedy's press secretary, Edwin Guthman, killed the article, and Hoover retaliated with an editorial in the *FBI Law Enforcement Bulletin,* which said Valachi's testimony served "in a larger sense to magnify the enormous task which lies ahead." The media interpreted Hoover's word *magnify* to mean that the Justice Department and the McClellan Committee had made the FBI's job more difficult. Though within the department the Bureau claimed "magnify" meant "call attention to," Hoover refused to provide a public clarification.[28]

The Bureau's increased reliance on illegal microphone surveillance made Hoover nervous; he knew that if he got caught he could not count on Kennedy's support. Bugs that involved trespass *were* illegal, and if he formally requested authority from RFK to use them he might very well be turned down. He therefore found another way to "share" the responsibility with the attorney general: He made sure that on several carefully documented occasions (two meetings between FBI agents and the attorney general in Chicago and New York), Kennedy was exposed to the fruits of the illegal bugs. On both occasions tapes were played of conversations between organized crime figures. Hoover later claimed that it was "inconceivable" for Kennedy to claim he did not know that the tapes were from microphone surveillances and produced a dozen affidavits from agents at those sessions to support his position. However, Edwin Guthman, who was also present at the meetings, said that "the clear impression we received was that the FBI had obtained the recordings from local law enforcement sources." It was left to the unlucky Courtney Evans to try to sort things out; it is possible that both Kennedy and Hoover thought they were right, and that Evans, at the time, allowed each of them to form whatever impression best suited their respective purposes. Hoover certainly never asked Kennedy to authorize bugging in so many words, and when FBI bugging came to Kennedy's official attention (in a May 1963 investigation of a skimming operation at Las Vegas casinos), he gave orders through Katzenbach that it be stopped. He later claimed, convincingly, that this was the only time he ever knew that the FBI was using illegal electronic surveillance.[29]

Despite all the rancor, the fact still remains that Kennedy succeeded in getting Hoover finally to commit the Bureau wholeheartedly to organized crime investigations. Robert Kennedy counted it as one of his accomplishments that "for the first time the FBI changed their whole concept of crime in the United States."[30]

When Robert Kennedy took over the Justice Department, the FBI was not only all-white (with the exception of Hoover's servants); it was defiantly all-white. Some agents would parody Kennedy: "Boys, if you don't work with vigah, you'll be replaced by a niggah," referring to the flood of blacks they could expect if they didn't expose the civil rights movement as a Communist front. But others were beginning to realize that these sentiments were out of step with the times. One agent recalls that some of the racist remarks he heard in training had "rung a hollow note," but another reported that the Bureau at the beginning of the sixties was characterized by strong "anti-Negro prejudices." He estimated that "in about 90% of the situations in which Bureau personnel referred to Negroes, the word "nigger" was used and always in a very derogatory manner."[31]

Hoover was infuriated by Robert Kennedy's pressuring him to hire black agents. To Kennedy's incessant questioning as to how many he had, Hoover finally responded there were five. What he did not say was that they were all employed in various forms of personal work for him. Afterward, Hoover said Kennedy "wanted me to lower our qualifications and to hire more Negro agents. . . . I said, 'Bobby, that's not going to be done as long as I'm Director of this Bureau.' " Nevertheless, Hoover gave in slightly and agreed to double the number of black agents—to a grand total of ten—by the end of 1962.[32]

Hoover's disputes with Robert Kennedy over civil rights began in 1961 when Kennedy had to protect the Freedom Riders against violent mobs that were trying to block the attempts of these students, both black and white, to desegregate interstate buses and bus depots in the South. On May 4, 1961, Bob had to send 600 United States marshals to Montgomery, Alabama, to protect them. That fall, 3,000 soldiers had to be dispatched to Oxford, Mississippi, to force James Meredith's admittance into Ole Miss. In 1963, Alabama erupted: The National Guard had to be federalized to make Governor George Wallace obey court orders to admit blacks to the University of Alabama, and in September of that year, four girls died in the bombing of a black church in Birmingham.

In response to demands that the FBI take an aggressive part in the Justice Department's effort to protect the demonstrators, Hoover insisted that the FBI was strictly an investigative agency, and not a police force with peace-keeping responsibilities. His position was that the Bureau could only investigate crimes after they had been committed. The sight of FBI agents standing by taking notes and pictures for use in future investigations while demonstrators and even federal officers (marshals and Justice Department personnel) were undergoing violent attack infuriated Kennedy's aides. But the attorney general realized that the director could not be budged from this policy. His strategy for dealing with Hoover, in Victor Navasky's judgment, was to "avoid confrontation over anything but great issues of policy."[33]

Hoover was also reluctant to involve the Bureau in protecting the rights of blacks to vote under the Civil Rights Acts of 1957 and 1960. To force the Bureau to assist them in their work, the Civil Rights Division under Burke Marshall and John Doar devised what they called a "box memorandum" for the Bureau, an instruction list so detailed and so specific that it coerced the Bureau into providing the information required by the department for its legal cases. In general, however, while John F. Kennedy was president, Hoover responded only grudgingly to department pressure for more aggressive civil rights enforcement, performing only what would be necessary to avoid the appearance of outright insubordination. Kennedy and his aides, to preserve what little cooperation they were getting from him, let Hoover deal with them on his own terms.

The Kennedy administration cannot escape all blame itself for the Bureau's flawed performance in civil rights. John F. Kennedy's leadership in this area was not as forceful as might have been expected, based on his campaign rhetoric, in which he had talked about ending housing discrimination "with a stroke of the pen"; it was not until November 1962 that he issued the executive order he had promised. He also resisted making the dramatic moral gestures the civil rights movement demanded, because he needed the support of Southerners to pass his education bill and other legislation; he believed, with justification, these would benefit blacks more tangibly than any proclamation.

Events would prove that only a commitment of prestige by a politically powerful president would make J. Edgar Hoover endanger his conservative and Southern constituency by abandoning his policy of studied neutrality between black and white activists. President Kennedy did not have the political strength that would let him make that total commitment, and so in asking the FBI to take the lead in the Southern civil rights struggle, the administration was asking it to help overthrow a caste system, to fight a civil war. For Hoover to risk that, he needed far more political backing than Kennedy could give him. The administration was simply not strong enough politically for Hoover to take any risks on its behalf, even if he had wanted to.[34]

It had been J. Edgar Hoover who had coordinated the campaign, between 1919 and 1923, that broke Marcus Garvey and destroyed his black nationalist movement. In the 1960s, Hoover presided over a campaign to destroy Martin Luther King, Jr. The two episodes differ in circumstance, motive, and method, but Hoover's reaction was the same. Two black men had appeared on the American scene with extraordinary abilities for organizing the black masses to demand their rights, and both times, though for different reasons, Hoover came to the conclusion that they were dangerous, and had to be destroyed— Garvey he jailed and deported; King he was still trying to break when James Earl Ray shot King in 1968 in Memphis, Tennessee.

King had first come to national attention as a leader of the Montgomery, Alabama, bus boycott in December 1955. The FBI took formal notice of him in September 1958, when it learned that he had been introduced to Benjamin Davis, a black Communist party leader. When King figured prominently in the Freedom Rider campaign in May 1961, Hoover ordered an investigation. As Hoover reported to Attorney General Robert Kennedy on January 8, 1962, in the course of this investigation the Bureau learned that one of King's most trusted advisors had been identified in the early fifties as a key financial backer and advisor to the Communist party. This was Stanley Levison, a New York attorney whose friendship with King over the next seven years would be Hoover's pretext for the merciless persecution of King by the Bureau that continued even after King's assassination.[35]

Until Levison turned up as King's advisor, the FBI was under the impression that he had left the Party by the end of 1955. The Bureau had even tried unsuccessfully to recruit him as an informant in February 1960. The King link made the Bureau reevaluate its position and decide Levison must have been a "sleeper" (a passive undercover Communist) whose purpose was to manipulate the civil rights movement by controlling King. From 1961 on, the Bureau subjected Levison to almost continuous surveillance, including wiretaps, bugs, burglaries, and shadowing. It never discovered the slightest hint that Levison was other than what he represented himself to be, an ardent supporter of the civil rights movement and of King as the most effective leader of the movement. Nevertheless, in all his many reports to the White House, to the attorney general, and to Congress, and in the FBI's leaks to the media, Hoover never qualified the Bureau's allegations that Levison was a Communist as being inferences based on circumstantial evidence. Hoover and the Bureau treated Levison's identity as an active Communist agent as an unquestionable fact that justified all their other attacks on King.

The attorney general, the president, and their aides had no difficulty recognizing the dangerous position into which they had been placed by Hoover's January 8 note about Levison and King. Once Hoover had officially notified them that Martin Luther King, Jr., to whom they were tightly tied in the public mind, was associating with Communists, they were in the same position as Harry Truman when he received Hoover's warnings about Harry Dexter White. If they ignored Hoover's reports, they might some time in the future face the same kind of pillorying as Truman when Hoover and Herbert Brownell had denounced the former president in 1953.[36]

Robert Kennedy's immediate response to Hoover's warning was to assume that the FBI was right, but that King did not realize Levison's Communist ties. Therefore, he had one of his aides, John Seigenthaler, alert King but without specifying the name of the supposed Communist associate. Another aide, White House Special Assistant for Civil Rights Harris Wofford, acting on his own, delivered a warning to King, this time mentioning Levison by name. Deputy Attorney General Byron White, more observant of the chain of command, asked the FBI whether King should be told about Levison. Hoover replied that to do so would "definitely endanger our informant and the national security." In a note for internal Bureau consumption, Hoover added that "King is no good anyway. Under no circumstances should our informant be endangered."[37]

The Bureau learned in February 1962 that King's Southern Christian Leadership Conference (SCLC) had hired Jack O'Dell on Levison's recommendation for its New York office. The FBI believed that O'Dell, like Levison, was a member of the Communist Party National Committee. This made the Bureau even more sure that Levison was a Communist agent, and late in March, after getting Robert Kennedy's approval, the Bureau placed a tap on Levison's phone. Hoover already had a microphone in place in Levison's office on his own authority, as was then department practice, and on May 11, 1962, King's name was added to the Bureau's Emergency Detention list as someone to be arrested at an outbreak of hostilities. On the basis of the Levison-O'Dell connection, the Bureau, on October 23, 1962, was able to justify a full-scale investigation of the SCLC for the purpose of determining the extent of Communist infiltration (COMINFIL). This made it possible for the Bureau to seek authorization for wiretap and microphone surveillance of King's office at the SCLC.

The Bureau's surveillance of King took on additional intensity on November 18, 1962, when he was quoted as saying he agreed with a report of the Southern Regional Council that "there is a considerable amount of distrust among Albany [Georgia] Negroes for local members of the Federal Bureau of Investigation. . . . FBI men appear to Albany Negroes as vaguely-interested observers of injustice, who diffidently write down complaints and do no more." King said that "one of the great problems we face with the FBI in the South is that the agents are white Southerners who have been influenced by the mores of the community. To maintain their status, they have to be friendly with the local police and people who are promoting segregation." King thought the Bureau ought to staff its field offices in the South with more Northerners.[38]

Any attack on the Bureau infuriated Hoover, but particularly this one, since, in 1955, Hoover had responded to similar charges by doing exactly what King advocated. And so when Hoover inquired into the actual situation in Albany, he was not so surprised to learn that four out of the five agents were from the North. (The Bureau did not take official note of the unabashed racism of the fifth and "dominant" agent, who was a Southerner.) DeLoach was assigned the task of bringing the facts to King's attention, or "straightening him out," as the Bureau liked to say when going after its critics.[39]

When DeLoach called King in Atlanta, however, he was out, so a message was left for King to return the call. Notoriously inattentive to such matters, King never got back to DeLoach, who took this as a willful affront to himself and the Bureau, an admission that King had made his charges in bad faith. He notified his superior, Assistant to the Director John Mohr, that King "obviously does not desire to be given the truth. The fact that he is a vicious liar is amply demonstrated in the fact he constantly associates with and takes instructions from Stanley Levison who is a hidden member of the Communist Party." From this point on, Hoover treated King as a personal enemy as well as a Communist.[40]

In June 1963, the Kennedy administration was pressing Congress for a new civil rights law, and so it could not afford a scandal of this nature. Robert Kennedy and Burke Marshall again urged King to end his relationship with Levison. On June 22, the president himself took King out into the Rose Garden; comparing the situation to the Profumo sex scandal that was wrecking British Prime Minister Harold Macmillan's government, he said that if King did not break with Levison, the Kennedy administration, King, and the civil rights movement might all be destroyed. Meanwhile, the Bureau was leaking stories about the SCLC-King-O'Dell relationship to Southern papers that were always interested in anything that smeared the civil rights movement.

The rumors about King's Communist connections were now becoming a factor in the politics of civil rights. Governors George Wallace of Alabama and Ross Barnett of Mississippi testified at hearings on the civil rights bill that King was a Communist and that the whole movement was Communist-controlled. Rumors about King's Communist involvement also terrified liberal members of Congress, who begged the administration for guidance and reassurance about whether it was safe to support King. The Kennedys put together a carefully crafted reply denying that King was a Communist or Communist-controlled, but accompanied this with an oral briefing that set forth the Levison connection.

Robert Kennedy was now so concerned about the accusations that on July 16, 1963, he gave serious consideration to the possibility of wiretapping King's home phone. He changed his mind when the administration finally got a promise from King, on July 23, that he would break with Levison and O'Dell. When Hoover reported to them that King had not lived up to his pledge, Robert Kennedy gave Hoover permission, on October 10, 1963, to place taps on the phones in King's Atlanta home and SCLC office. These taps, and the microphones the

After his long, secure partnership with FDR, Hoover quickly lost confidence in Harry Truman (*above* with Attorney General J. Howard McGrath) and his ability to provide effective leadership to deal with the issue of Communists in government. He allied himself with the House Un-American Activities Committee, making a sensational appearance before HUAC in 1947 (*left*), turning the Communist issue into a brutal assault on the Truman administration.

Hoover emerged as a senior member of the anti-Communist right, first by aiding Richard Nixon (*above*) in his successful investigation of Alger Hiss in 1948; then by effectively investigating the Rosenberg atom spy case and aiding the prosecution of the leadership of the Communist party; finally, by backing Senator Joseph McCarthy, a close personal friend (*left*, with Hoover, Tolson, and a fellow guest, at the El Charro Hotel).

Eisenhower and Attorney General Brownell quickly won Hoover's loyalty and made him an important part of their administration. Hoover responded by aligning FBI policies with theirs, demonstrating his loyalty by appearing before the Senate Internal Security Subcommittee in 1953 to attack Harry Truman's handling of the Harry Dexter White espionage case, and by breaking with Joseph McCarthy when he began attacking the army and the administration.

Hoover and the Kennedys distrusted each other from the start, and Hoover allied himself with the conservatives who saw the Kennedy administration as a symbol of the social change they hated and feared. It was only under Lyndon Baines Johnson, a friend of some twenty years, that Hoover finally began to aggressively enforce civil rights laws in the South.

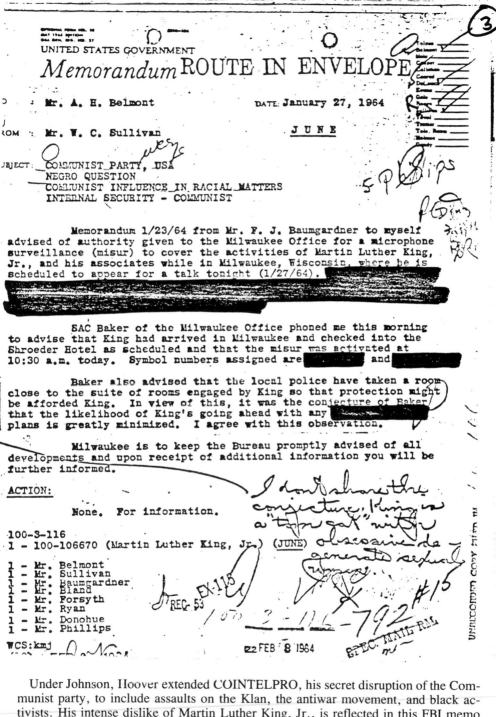

OPTIONAL FORM NO. 10

UNITED STATES GOVERNMENT

Memorandum ROUTE IN ENVELOPE ③

TO : Mr. A. H. Belmont   DATE: January 27, 1964

FROM : Mr. W. C. Sullivan   J U N E

SUBJECT: COMMUNIST PARTY, USA
NEGRO QUESTION
COMMUNIST INFLUENCE IN RACIAL MATTERS
INTERNAL SECURITY - COMMUNIST

        Memorandum 1/23/64 from Mr. F. J. Baumgardner to myself
advised of authority given to the Milwaukee Office for a microphone
surveillance (misur) to cover the activities of Martin Luther King,
Jr., and his associates while in Milwaukee, Wisconsin, where he is
scheduled to appear for a talk tonight (1/27/64).

        SAC Baker of the Milwaukee Office phoned me this morning
to advise that King had arrived in Milwaukee and checked into the
Shroeder Hotel as scheduled and that the misur was activated at
10:30 a.m. today. Symbol numbers assigned are ████████ and ████

        Baker also advised that the local police have taken a room
close to the suite of rooms engaged by King so that protection might
be afforded King. In view of this, it was the conjecture of Baker
that the likelihood of King's going ahead with any ████████
plans is greatly minimized. I agree with this observation.

        Milwaukee is to keep the Bureau promptly advised of all
developments and upon receipt of additional information you will be
further informed.

ACTION:

        None. For information.

100-3-116
1 - 100-106670 (Martin Luther King, Jr.) (JUNE)

1 - Mr. Belmont
1 - Mr. Sullivan
1 - Mr. Baumgardner
1 - Mr. Bland
1 - Mr. Forsyth
1 - Mr. Ryan
1 - Mr. Donohue
1 - Mr. Phillips

WCS:kmj   22 FEB 8 1964

[handwritten] I don't share the conjecture. King is a 'top cat' with obsessive degenerate sexual urges.

    Under Johnson, Hoover extended COINTELPRO, his secret disruption of the Communist party, to include assaults on the Klan, the antiwar movement, and black activists. His intense dislike of Martin Luther King, Jr., is reflected in this FBI memo discussing a proposed microphone surveillance of King's hotel room. Hoover's handwritten comments urge his agents to keep their eyes on King, calling him "a 'tom cat' with obsessive degenerate sexual urges."

Although Richard Nixon saw Hoover as a valuable political ally, he and his aides were impatient with Hoover's increasing reluctance to authorize illegal and sensitive surveillance techniques. Though Nixon had been Hoover's friend since 1947, some of the most dangerous threats to Hoover's control of the FBI were instigated by Nixon's White House. When White House aide John Ehrlichman visited Hoover's home, crammed with souvenirs of the past, it confirmed his view of Hoover as a relic who had survived beyond his time.

A serene Hoover, shortly before his death. He had survived all attempts by the Nixon White House to weaken his autonomy and the independence of his Bureau.

Death came in the early morning of May 2, 1972. Hoover's body lay in state in the Rotunda of the Capitol. His funeral procession wound down Pennsylvania Avenue through the official Washington where he had lived his entire life, past the White House and the Justice Department, past the still uncompleted FBI headquarters that now bears his name, and past the site of his by-then-vanished boyhood home. His grave is in the old congressional cemetery near Seward Square, a few yards from that of Clyde Tolson, who died on April 14, 1975.

Bureau began installing in King's hotel rooms in December 1963, were soon producing a mass of incriminating evidence—incriminating not in the sense that it furnished any support for the Communist-control theory, but that it gave Hoover intimate knowledge about sexual activities of King's that were hard to reconcile with his role as religious leader and moral spokesman. These revelations would lead Hoover to sanction even more aggressive attacks on King during the Johnson administration.

For Hoover, the implications of the King case were clear. The Kennedys had not broken with King, and they had not exposed him. While they had not left themselves as vulnerable as Truman had in the Harry Dexter White case, they still had in Hoover's eyes shown themselves the type of "pseudo-liberals" whose regard for the rights of Communists had time and again frustrated his anti-Communist campaigns. Another recent episode may have led Hoover to the same conclusion. In 1962, as an act of Christmas clemency, the Kennedys had released Junius Scales, who was the only Communist convicted under the membership provisions of the Smith Act. (The Foley Square Eleven and the others had been convicted of *advocating* the overthrow of the government.) The release outraged Hoover: Even though Scales had broken with the Party, he had refused to name any of his fellow Communists. "Naming names" was Hoover's price for certifying the rehabilitation of ex-Communists, and the Scales precedent, he feared, would make it impossible to insist on that test in the future. "Naming names" had long been part of anti–Communist orthodoxy, and so the Kennedys had damaged the cause. Hoover had always felt that the Communist's protectors were as dangerous as the Communist himself. Before, this conviction had pitted him against the Truman administration. Now it gave him one more reason to hate the Kennedys.

Hoover began his career providing A. Mitchell Palmer with the research, the analysis, and the strategy for the 1919–1920 antiradical drive. In the 1960s, Hoover found *himself* relying on an ambitious, younger aide for knowledge of developments in the radical movement, plans to combat it, and analyses of his agents' reports. This was William C. Sullivan, who had entered the Bureau in 1941 at the age of twenty-nine. From 1961, when Hoover promoted Sullivan to head the Bureau's Domestic Intelligence Division, until 1971, when he left the Bureau under fire, Sullivan was Hoover's window into radical America.[41]

Sullivan, who as head of the Research Section of the Domestic

Intelligence Division prepared the monograph that served as the plan for COINTELPRO against the Communist party in 1956, was responsible for the extension of that program to the Socialist Workers party in 1961, the Ku Klux Klan in 1964, the Black Nationalists in 1967, and, finally, in 1968, the New Left. William Sullivan was the FBI official most responsible for the Bureau's shift after 1963 from a strategy that stressed preparations for an "internal security emergency" (primarily utilizing the Emergency Detention Act of 1950) to one that aimed at combating domestic unrest.

By the 1960s, the tight discipline Hoover maintained over his subordinates and his insistence on absolute loyalty and conformity made it unlikely that an independent thinker would reach the top ranks. In William Sullivan, however, Hoover thought he had chosen and trained a man whose judgments he could rely on, a man of integrity and intelligence who could chart the Bureau's course through the shifting currents of American radical politics. Hoover was profoundly mistaken, however, and what he took for initiative and independence in Sullivan was in reality a surpassing ability to flatter Hoover by catering to his prejudices. Near the end of his life Hoover finally admitted that "the greatest mistake I ever made was to promote Sullivan."[42]

William C. Sullivan was not a typical FBI executive. An exception to the rule drilled into FBI personnel that an "agent never volunteers information," Sullivan was opinionated and willing to share his ideas with an unusual range of acquaintances: professors, writers, reporters, and intellectuals. He even looked different from the conventional G-man. Unlike the smooth organization men who staffed Hoover's executive conferences, Sullivan was a short Irishman who reminded one writer of a "James Cagney type with a New England accent thrown in." He had an unpredictable personality: He was personally sloppy, typed his own memos, full of errors, and picked up the nickname "Crazy Billy" from his colleagues. There were important officials who could not abide him, including Tolson and DeLoach, but many others would not stand for a word against him even after he left the Bureau— among them Courtney Evans and John Mohr.

Like Hoover, Sullivan had a talent for turning laws and programs to purposes unforeseen by their creators. As Hoover had made use of the deportation statutes to cripple American radicalism, Sullivan adapted the techniques developed against Nazi and Soviet agents during World War II and the early cold war and used them to fight domestic radicals. While coordinating COINTELPRO–CPUSA in

Washington, Sullivan became the greatest expert on communism the Bureau ever produced—except for Hoover himself, of course. The Bureau's blanket surveillance of the Party put Sullivan in a position to analyze every meeting, every phone call, every conversation of the Party leadership. He probably knew more about American communism than the Communists themselves.[43]

Hoover seems to have seen a younger version of himself in Sullivan. He encouraged Sullivan to develop anti-Communist tactics so innovative as to recall Hoover's own creative period, four decades earlier. Like the young Hoover, Sullivan understood the value of research and looked for novel ways to use the fruits of that research against his enemies. Sullivan was willing to get out of his office and talk to independent scholars and Communist intellectuals. He built up contacts among academicians, and during the early sixties even gave a series of lectures at the Harvard Graduate School of Business Administration. He collected a personal library of 3,000 volumes on communism, which he lent to his colleagues. In all this he was almost unique; the only other man in the FBI who had ever investigated Communist thought and history so thoroughly had been Hoover himself.

In no other subordinate did Hoover ever tolerate Sullivan's sort of independence. Sullivan seemed to cast a spell over Hoover; some FBI colleagues saw a father-son bond between them. One small indication was Hoover's use of a familiar form of address with Sullivan. Hoover's practice was to call his agents "Mister." When they reached the executive level he dropped the "Mister" and called them by their last name. But Tolson he called Clyde; Louis Nichols was Nick. After Nichols left the Bureau in 1959, the only man Hoover ever again called by a nickname or first name was Bill Sullivan.[44]

On August 23, 1963, at the height of his investigation of the Martin Luther King–Stanley Levison–Jack O'Dell relationship, Sullivan gave Hoover a sixty-seven-page brief on the Communist party's efforts to infiltrate the civil rights movement. Sullivan's report concluded, "There has been an obvious failure of the Communist Party of the United States to appreciably infiltrate, influence, or control large numbers of American Negroes in this country." The report did contain the careful qualification that "time alone will tell" whether future efforts by the Party to exploit blacks would be as unsuccessful as those in the past. Nevertheless, Sullivan's meaning was plainly that Communist infiltration of the civil rights movement need be of no further concern to the Bureau or the country.[45]

Hoover was baffled. Sullivan's latest memo not only contradicted the steady stream of reports he had been sending the director about the Communist influence on Martin Luther King, Jr., but everything the Bureau had been saying about communism and civil rights for decades. Hoover fired the report back to Sullivan with the handwritten comment that "this memo reminds me vividly of those I received when Castro took over Cuba. You contended then that Castro and his cohorts were not communists and not influenced by communists. Time alone proved you wrong. I for one can't ignore the memos re [deletion, presumably Levison and O'Dell] as having only an infinitesimal effect on the efforts to exploit the American Negro by the Communists."[46]

Hoover's rejection of his memo threw Sullivan into a state of panic. His own account of this controversy is self-serving and has to be weighed carefully; Sullivan told his story after he left the Bureau in 1971 and had broken with Hoover. There is no reason, though, to doubt his statement that the August 23 report precipitated a crisis: "This [memorandum] set me at odds with Hoover. . . . A few months went by before he would speak to me. Everything was conducted by exchange of written communications. It was evident that we had to change our ways or we would all be out on the street."[47]

In the weeks immediately following Sullivan's August 23 memo, whenever Domestic Intelligence sent Hoover a report on King and Levison (or, for that matter, any report on Communist activities), Hoover would ridicule it with comments like "just infinitesimal!" (on a report on Communist plans for taking part in the August 28 March on Washington) or "I assume CP functionary claims are all frivolous" (on a report on Communist plans to hold follow-up rallies after the march to advance "the cause of socialism in the United States"). Sullivan was caught in a trap of his own making: He had programmed his division to produce an unending flow of reports on Communist activities that hardly made sense in light of his August 23 brief. Conversely, the August 23 brief was refuted by the division's own reports on continuing Communist machinations.[48]

According to Sullivan, the men of the Domestic Intelligence Division were in an uproar. They thought they would all be transferred out of Washington; selling their homes and uprooting their families would ruin them financially. They wanted another memo written to the director to "get us out of this trouble we were in."[49]

Instead of holding to what he felt was an accurate assessment of the declining fortunes of the American Communists, Sullivan wrote a memo to Hoover on August 30 that retracted everything he had said on August 23, and tried to smooth the dispute with flattery:

The director is correct. We were completely wrong about believing the evidence was not sufficient to determine some years ago that Fidel Castro was not a communist or under communist influence. On investigating and writing about communism and the American Negro, we had better remember this and profit by the lesson it should teach us.

Personally, I believe in the light of King's powerful demagogic speech yesterday [the "I have a dream" speech] he stands head and shoulders above all other Negro leaders put together when it comes to influencing great masses of Negroes. We must mark him now, if we have not done so before, as the most dangerous Negro of the future in this nation from the standpoint of communism, the Negro, and national security.

It may be unrealistic to limit ourselves as we have been doing to legalistic proofs or definitely conclusive evidence that would stand up in testimony in court or before Congressional Committees that the Communist Party, USA, does wield substantial influence over Negroes which one day could become decisive.

We greatly regret that the memorandum did not measure up to what the director has a right to expect from our analysis.[50]

On September 16, 1963, Sullivan followed this memo with a recommendation of "increased coverage of communist influence on the Negro." He now proposed something new: "We are stressing the urgent need for imaginative and aggressive tactics to be utilized through our Counterintelligence Program—these designed to neutralize or disrupt the Party's activities in the Negro field." Stripped of terms of art, Sullivan was proposing unleashing the COINTELPRO techniques on Martin Luther King, Jr.[51]

Hoover reacted to this dizzying shift by challenging Sullivan once more to back up the August 23 report. He rejected Sullivan's latest reversal of position and his recommendation of intensified efforts against the Party:

No, I can't understand how you can so agilely switch your thinking and evaluation. Just a few weeks ago you contended that the Communist influence in the racial movement was ineffective and infinitesimal. This—notwithstanding many memos of specific instances of infiltration. Now you want to load down the Field with more coverage in spite of your recent memo depreciating CP influence in racial movement. I don't intend to waste time and money until you can make up your minds what the situation really is.[52]

After he left the Bureau, Sullivan tried to justify his vacillations by arguing that he was acting under duress when he altered his convictions and "engage[d] in a lot of nonsense." He argued that Hoover's objections to his memos were not sincere, that Hoover was deviously maneuvering his subordinates into providing him with the conclusions he wanted. Hoover, Sullivan later held, was challenging him to "come back and say, 'Mr. Hoover, you are right, we are wrong. There is communist infiltration of the American Negro. We think we should go ahead and carry on an intensified program against it.' He knew, when he wrote this, he knew precisely what kind of reply he was going to get."[53]

Sullivan's explanation is hardly convincing. In those days before the Freedom of Information Act, Hoover could not have imagined that these memos would be read by anyone except himself, Sullivan, and a few other high-ranking Bureau executives, so he had no reason to be coy. If Hoover had wanted a different conclusion from Sullivan, there was nothing to stop him from simply telling Sullivan to give him one. What must have bothered Hoover was that Sullivan was asking him, on the basis of one sixty-three-page brief, to reverse a consistent position of forty years' standing, one that was supported by millions of words of testimony and hundreds of thousands of pages of research. Hoover, not Sullivan, was going to have to go before Congress, the attorney general, and the president to explain the Bureau's new position on the domestic Communist threat. Unless he was absolutely certain and had supporting evidence, he was not going to expose himself to the uproar that would follow an announcement by J. Edgar Hoover that the country could relax because the Communist menace had disappeared.

Moreover, Hoover was a lawyer. Sullivan was not. Hoover was used to the technique of firming up a position by throwing objections at its supporters to see how they defended it. He had been doing that all his life. It is very likely he was doing so again: month after month Sullivan had been giving him reports on the danger of Communist influence over the civil rights movement and particularly over the most important black leader, Martin Luther King, Jr.; now Sullivan sent him a policy analysis that represented a reversal of Sullivan's current position. Naturally Hoover challenged Sullivan for more evidence.

Only by assuming that Hoover was serious in his challenge to Sullivan to support his position can sense be made out of a note Hoover wrote Tolson during Sullivan's vacillations: "I have certainly been misled by previous memos which clearly showed communist penetration of the racial movement. The attached is contradictory of all that. We are wasting manpower and money investigating CP effort in racial matter if the attached is correct."[54]

Rather than trying to maneuver Sullivan into furnishing him with dishonest evaluations of Communist influence in the civil rights movement, as Sullivan claimed, Hoover seems to have been trying to discover the actual situation. Throughout his career, Hoover had always made sure he had the facts on his side when he sallied forth into political controversy. The Bureau's position had always been that the Communists were continually attempting, but failing, to gain influence over American blacks; that position had provided the context within which Hoover had interpreted connections between civil rights and communism whenever they were discovered. But at this critical moment in the history of the civil rights movement, when it was essential that he be acquainted with the truth, Hoover was let down by Sullivan, who readily admitted later that he knew he was being dishonest: "Here again we had to engage in a lot of nonsense which we ourselves really did not believe in. We either had to do this or we would be finished."[55] But Hoover's whole career shows that he was a serious person. He did not want nonsense; he wanted the facts.

After he retracted his August 23 memorandum, Sullivan tried to prove the sincerity of his latest set of convictions. He became the moving force behind the Bureau's aggressive campaign to discredit King within the government, to disrupt and neutralize his movement, and to destroy him professionally and personally.[56] For the rest of his FBI career, Sullivan seemed to try to redeem himself for his brief show of independence by becoming ever more extreme in his attacks against protesters and dissenters.

Sullivan's dishonesty, of course, does not excuse Hoover. He had created a system in which, finally, advancement came to opportunists who had learned persuasive ways of giving back to Hoover his own prejudices and opinions disguised as independent, objective, corroborative thinking.

On October 15, 1963, the Intelligence Division gave Hoover a fuller statement of its revised position on Communist influence in the civil rights movement. This was a monograph by Sullivan called "Communism and the Negro Movement—a Current Analysis." In an effort to distance himself from his August 23 memo, Sullivan was so extreme in his treatment of Martin Luther King that Sullivan's superior, Assistant to the Director Alan Belmont, characterized the October 15 memo as a "personal attack" on the civil rights leader that he predicted would "startle" Robert Kennedy "in view of his past association with King." Nevertheless, Belmont said, "we will be carrying out our responsibility by disseminating [it] outside the

Bureau." Hoover approved its distribution, writing in the margin, "We must do our duty" and "I am glad you recognize at last there is such influence." The October 15 report did, in fact, anger Robert Kennedy, especially when he heard that the Pentagon was using it to justify its own opposition to civil rights. He ordered Hoover to retrieve all copies.[57]

That attempted smear of King was just one of many in the brutal assault on King that Sullivan (with Hoover's approval) would direct until King's death in 1968. The King affair revealed the extent to which Hoover's iron discipline had turned the Bureau into an echo chamber resounding with his passions and phobias. The assistants on whom he depended for information about the world fed him reports designed to anticipate and reinforce his increasingly rigid fixations and obsessions. This was partly because Hoover was increasingly loath to accept information that challenged his priorities and the policy of his Bureau. It was also partly the result of the structure of the Bureau. Everything depended on Hoover, and his subordinates were too intimidated to correct his misconceptions; and for that, Hoover had only himself to blame.

Sullivan's abasing himself before Hoover was not unusual within the Bureau: It was the norm. Agents seemed to be both proud and embarrassed about stories that showed how completely Hoover dominated them. The system of discipline that Hoover had developed in the 1920s to protect himself from the errors of his agents now was proving incapable of producing agents who could protect him from his own mistakes.

The tall tales agents told about life in the Bureau largely revolved around their absolute subjugation to Hoover's whims. One classic story had Hoover announce that an agent had been killed in a gunfight. Actually, he was only wounded, but since the director could never be wrong, his buddies drew straws to see who would go to the hospital to finish him off. Another legend claimed that Hoover's driver once got into an accident while turning left. Forever after, the rule for his chauffeur was, "No left turns!" Because Hoover used the margins of memos for his comments, he became irritated whenever the typist failed to leave enough room. Once, when the margins got too narrow, he scrawled "Watch the borders!" His puzzled lieutenants put the Bureau offices near Mexico and Canada on alert. Hoover was supposed to have objected to the appearance of a new agent and whispered to an assistant director, "One of them is a pinhead. Get rid of him." The aide checked the hats of the group and, to be safe, fired the owners of the three smallest.[58]

A pair of young agents who entered the Bureau in 1960 gave remarkably consistent descriptions of an organization in absolute thrall to the arbitrary will of one man. As part of their training, new agents were indoctrinated in an idealized legend of Hoover's life, and how "he built this Bureau from the ground up." A lecturer told the trainees that "the Director chose the path of sacrifice, and electing to forgo private wealth and what to lesser men are the pleasures of life, he dedicated himself instead to the creation of the organization we are proud to serve today. Against all odds, our Director stuck doggedly to his purpose; today he remains the guiding light of the F.B.I.—in spite of liberal-leftist moves for his ouster." Despite the fact that "our Director has served thirteen attorney generals, has assisted seven presidents . . . he still works longer hours than any of us, every day of the year . . . yes, boys, J. Edgar Hoover is an inspiration to us all. Indeed, it has been said, and truly—'the sunshine of his presence lights our lives.' "[59]

The culmination of the new agents' indoctrination was a meeting with Hoover, and there were days of rehearsals for the great moment. "Everything you say and do must be positive," the recruits were told. "If you look away from the Director's face like you just did with me you'll be fired! Just like that. If there's a quiver in your voice or you wipe your mouth or pick at your nose . . . the Director doesn't miss things like that. They're signs of weakness! Another thing—don't let me catch you standing around in the corridors with your hands in your pockets"—the instructor stuttered—"d-deviates do that. P-playing with themselves. You know . . . p-pocket p-pool."[60]

As part of their military-style preparation for meeting Hoover, the recruits studied his height (5' 9"), and his weight—which varied between 168 and 200 (190 in 1961). They were given three "approved" greetings: "Good morning, Mister Hoover," "Pleased to meet you," or "How do you do?" Deviations from these formulas, said the instructors, might be dangerous, but these three "have been tested hundreds of times and nothing ever happened."

They were told not to scuff their feet on the carpet, and not to look down, because "occasionally, our Director enjoys standing on a little box when he greets people in his office. Of course, it's just a small one, only six inches high. Pretend you never even notice it! Not long ago we had a new agent who for some reason just couldn't keep his eyes off it. He was fired." They had to carry handkerchiefs, because the director was supposed not to like moist handshakes.

A trainee would remember his introduction to Hoover the rest of his life. "The face was impossible, like papier-mâché, and much older than any of the photographs revealed, but there was strength in those hard eyes and in his hand as we exchanged a firm Bureau handshake that would have made our administrator proud."

In January 1962, a disgruntled ex-agent, Jack Levine, sent a thirty-eight-page memo to Herbert J. Miller, the assistant attorney general in charge of the Criminal Division of the Justice Department, complaining about Hoover's management of the Bureau. Levine's complaints ranged over topics like anti-Semitism, racial prejudice, and right-wing proselytizing, but almost all concerned Hoover's unlimited power over the lives and careers of agents.[61]

Like other agents, Levine recounted many of the folktales that illustrated the power of Hoover's prejudices in the administration of the Bureau. There were stories about a supervisor fired because he had hired a clerk with pimples, another criticized for buying *Playboy* "because the Director looks upon those who read such magazines as moral degenerates." Levine himself was advised to resign because a whiskey bottle was found in an apartment where he was rooming. These "unreasonable perfectionist attitudes of the Bureau and the futility in protesting or offering constructive criticism," he said, made agents afraid to bring problems to the attention of headquarters, so headquarters was denied the information needed to administer the FBI intelligently.

One reason for the demoralization of the Bureau, Levine thought, was Hoover's practice of enforcing regulations by means of disciplinary transfers. Levine pointed out the severe economic consequences for the agents of this policy, which may have been an important factor in turning the Bureau into an organization of yes-men. When Hoover established his system of discipline, agents rented their homes or lived in rooming houses or hotels. In the years after World War II, however, America had become a nation of homeowners, and agents owned homes, too. Now an administrative transfer—orders to report immediately to a post that was likely to be on the other side of the continent—was a catastrophe that could cost an agent thousands of dollars from a forced sale. Agents were willing to do almost anything to avoid the director's wrath if it meant that kind of punishment.

Levine also thought that the strict rules and regulations had become so onerous, and the demands for performance so great, that the only recourse for many agents was to evade rules, falsify records, and otherwise compromise their integrity. The result was moral rot pervading the Bureau, caused, ironically, by the very system Hoover had installed to prevent dishonest and unprofessional behavior. Levine offered as an extreme example the system of "voluntary" overtime combined with demands that the Bureau show an improvement in this area each year. At the time Levine wrote, the quota had reached the incredible average of three and a half hours per day per agent. Widespread cheating was necessary to achieve this, and since everyone was doing it, administrative chaos resulted, which allowed many to evade all supervision. Levine also reported that pressure for convictions led to unreported use of illegal microphone surveillance, wiretaps, and mail openings.

William C. Sullivan's decision to swallow his principles and misrepresent his convictions about the danger of communism in America in 1963 had drastic consequences for American society. The ease with which he abandoned his convictions on that critical matter may have been conditioned by countless smaller compromises he had had to make over the years to survive in Hoover's FBI. Hoover's system of leadership was turning his men into liars, and so, eventually, he had to rely on liars for advice.

On November 22, 1963, Robert Kennedy was holding a luncheon meeting at Hickory Hill, his home in McLean, Virginia: the topic was organized crime. Back at the Justice Department, Angie Novello, his secretary, was too overcome by the news from Dallas to be able to call her boss. Hoover placed the call for her. Kennedy later remembered that the director said, " 'I have news for you. The President's been shot.' Or, 'I have news for you' and I might have said, 'What?' and he said, 'The President's been shot.' And—well, I don't know what I said—probably 'oh' or something—and I don't know whether he then—I asked him or got into whether it was serious, and I think he said, 'I think it's serious.' He said, 'I'll call you back . . . when I find out more.' I don't remember anything more of that conversation." When Hoover called back, Kennedy recalled that "he was not a very warm or sympathetic figure"; Hoover did not seem upset. "Not quite as excited as if he was reporting the fact that he found a Communist on the faculty of Howard University."[62]

In such circumstances, a failure to unmistakably express comfort and compassion will make a deep impression. Hoover's lack of emotion, whether deliberate or not, was gradually interpreted by RFK and his friends as calculated heartlessness. It is far more likely, however, that Hoover had other things on his mind, because once again, there had been an enormous failure of American intelligence. Hoover was untouched by the Bay of Pigs fiasco, but that had cost Allen Dulles his job, and Dulles was a man who had been in government even longer than Hoover: He had entered government service in 1916. Now, as after Pearl Harbor, there was no telling where the blame would fall, and Hoover had to learn whether he could be held to account.

As soon as word of the assassination reached Washington, Hoover put together a preliminary report that he gave to Lyndon Johnson the next day. From the very beginning of the investigation, everyone involved—Hoover, the FBI, the CIA, and then the Warren Commission—was under pressure to issue a report that would convince the public that Oswald was the lone assassin. In a phone conversation with Johnson aide Walter Jenkins, Hoover said, "The thing I am most concerned about, and so is Mr. Katzenbach, is having something issued so we can convince the public that Oswald is the real assassin." Katzenbach was even more specific: "Speculation about Oswald's motivation ought to be cut off, and we should have some basis for rebutting thought that this was a Communist conspiracy or (as the Iron Curtain press is saying) a right-wing conspiracy to blame it on the Communists." On December 9, 1963, soon after the commission was named, Katzenbach wrote each member asking them to issue a press release stating that the FBI report said Oswald was the lone assassin.[63]

Behind this rush to provide documentation for this lone assassin position was fear, on the part of the White House, of public reaction if any of the circumstantial evidence linking Castro to the assassination were to become known. This is not to say that anyone was convinced that Castro was definitely responsible, but there was so much seeming plausibility to the chain of events connecting Havana to Dallas that the White House feared uncontrollable demands for revenge against the Cuban leader. Because of the agreement that had ended the Cuban missile crisis of October 1962 (the United States guaranteed it would not attack Cuba if the Russians removed their missiles), a renewed conflict with Cuba would certainly have created a new confrontation with the Soviet Union, whose outcome could not be foreseen.

As far as Hoover knew, the CIA plots to assassinate Castro had been halted in 1962. This was, however, not the case. The CIA had a highly placed contact in the Castro government, Rolando Cubela, code-named AMLASH, with whom it continued throughout 1963 to plot the demise of the Cuban leader. On September 7, Castro gave an unusual interview to an Associated Press reporter in which he stated that he knew about planned attempts on his life, and said, "We are prepared to fight and answer in kind. United States leaders should think that if they are aiding terrorist plans to eliminate Cuban leaders, they themselves will not be safe." On September 12, 1963, the Coordinating Committee for Cuban Affairs, which was in charge of the assassination plots, agreed that Castro might retaliate in some way. Nevertheless, on the very day President Kennedy was assassinated—in fact, while the killing was taking place—a CIA case officer in Washington was telling AMLASH he would be given a gun and other assassination weapons to use against Castro. "As AMLASH and the case officer broke up their meeting, they were told the President had been assassinated."[64]

Hoover pushed his agents hard to complete their investigation quickly because the House, the Senate, and the State of Texas were all planning their own studies. The FBI report was delivered to Johnson on December 5. According to William Sullivan, Hoover tried to head off any other inquiry into the assassination by leaking an advance copy of the report to the press. Johnson, however, knew that even Hoover's prestige was not high enough to allow him to declare the matter settled on the basis of the FBI's conclusion. To mollify Hoover, Johnson told him that he had wanted to "get by" on just the FBI report, but because of all the rumors, he had to have a high-level committee evaluate it. Hoover regarded the Warren Commission as a potential adversary, its very existence a threat, and so the Bureau's main concern during the investigation it conducted for the Warren Commission was to protect its own reputation and avoid criticism.[65]

The assassination of John F. Kennedy seemed to place Hoover in the role he had so often played in the past: reassuring the public that the government had a dangerous situation under control. But while Hoover's agents conducted the Warren Commission's investigation, the result of his own investigation of the Bureau's handling of the Oswald case was a blow to his confidence in the abilities of the FBI.

The Bureau had first opened its Oswald security file on October 31, 1959, when it learned that Oswald had defected to the Soviet Union. The FBI's investigation at that time concluded that even though Oswald's experience in the U.S. Marines had placed him in proximity to U-2 operations in Japan, no important security leak was involved.

Hoover did suggest to the State Department, though, that Oswald's identity might be used by the Russians to slip an impostor back into the United States.

In June 1962, after his return from Russia, Oswald was interviewed by the FBI. His case was closed on August 20, 1962, after a second interview, even though the field agents in Fort Worth, Texas, found him hostile and evasive, and there were many suspicious circumstances that might have been followed up. The Bureau's position was that Oswald's marriage to Marina in Russia, which certainly had to be approved by the authorities, would have been unlikely if they were going to use him as an agent. The Secret Service, on the other hand, thought that letting Oswald have a Russian wife might have been envisioned by the Soviets as giving them a future hold over him.

In September 1962, shortly before the October missile crisis, the Bureau learned that Oswald had subscribed to a Communist paper, *The Worker,* which contradicted his statements that he was disenchanted with communism. When combined with one or more other suspicious activities, that subscription would have been enough to qualify Oswald for the Emergency Detention list under the rules then in effect, but the agents neglected to follow through.[66]

Special Agent James Hosty of the Dallas field office, who had been assigned the Marina Oswald file, finally noticed Oswald's *Worker* subscription and recommended reopening the case. Approval was given on March 26, 1963. In April, the New York office learned that Oswald had joined the Fair Play for Cuba Committee and had been passing out pro-Castro material in Dallas. This information was not reported to Dallas until the end of June, and was not sent to Washington until September.

In August, Oswald moved to New Orleans, which was at that time a hot-bed of anti-Castro activity. On August 1, 1963, in fact, the FBI seized a ton of dynamite and other weapons that anti-Castroites had stockpiled near New Orleans. While he was in New Orleans, Oswald tried to join one anti-Castro group on August 7, and was then arrested when he was spotted passing out pro-Castro material by a member of the group he had tried to join, who scuffled with him. Evidently, Oswald, whether he was acting on his own or under instructions, had been trying to infiltrate the group. On this occasion, Oswald requested another interview with the FBI; again he misrepresented his politics and political activities. Later that month, Oswald took part in a radio debate during which he defended Castro and called himself a Marxist.

The most obvious danger signal missed by the Bureau was in September, when Oswald left New Orleans and went to Mexico City, where he met with a diplomat at the Soviet embassy who was also an officer in the KGB. The Bureau even believed the diplomat belonged to a KGB unit responsible for assassination and sabotage assignments. Oswald also attempted to meet Cuban officials in Mexico City to get permission for a trip to Havana. The report on Oswald's activities in Mexico City was on a desk in Washington on November 22.[67]

In early November, the Dallas office learned that Oswald had returned to Dallas and was working at the Texas Book depository. Agent Hosty interviewed Oswald's wife, who seemed afraid. Two weeks before the assassination, Oswald visited the Bureau's Dallas office and left a note for Hosty that threatened to blow up the FBI and the Dallas Police Department if Hosty did not stop bothering Marina. Two days after the assassination, Hosty later reported, he destroyed the note on orders from his supervisor.

The Bureau's initial internal investigation after the assassination convinced Hoover that the FBI's handling of the case was so deficient that the only way to minimize criticism, since the Bureau could probably not escape it completely, was to fix all blame on Lee Harvey Oswald as a lone assassin, unaided by any conspiracy that might have (1) tied the killing to prior CIA plots or (2) raised the question of why the FBI was unaware of a widespread plot.

Everyone concerned with the investigation had reason for keeping it focused exclusively on Oswald. For this reason, Hoover assigned the work for the Warren Commission to his Criminal Investigations Division, rather than the Intelligence Division that had handled the Oswald security file. Despite the Bureau's awareness of the CIA involvement in assassination attempts, the FBI did not investigate possible Cuban government involvement, and there were no interviews of Cuban informants. In July 1964 (two months before the release of the Warren Report), when FBI headquarters finally learned of the AMLASH plot, the agents conducting the investigation for the Warren Commission were not informed.

The results of the FBI's internal investigation, ordered while the Warren Commission investigation was still under way, contained a devastating analysis of FBI deficiencies: "Oswald should have been on the Security Index; his wife should have been interviewed before the assassination, and investigation intensified—not held in abeyance— after Oswald contacted Soviet Embassy in Mexico." Hoover's immediate reaction was to punish everyone connected to the Oswald file.

The Inspection Division warned him that such disciplinary action might prove embarrassing. The Warren Commission might subpoena agents who would then have to say that they had been punished for their handling of the case; their punishment would surely be interpreted as an admission by the FBI that its handling of the case had been deficient. Hoover refused to delay, saying, "In any event such gross incompetency cannot be overlooked nor administrative action postponed." Even after DeLoach wrote a long memo warning against the public relations danger of admitting the Bureau was in the wrong by punishing FBI personnel, Hoover wrote, "I do not concur," and, on December 10, sent out seventeen censures (including one to William C. Sullivan) for "shortcomings in connection with the investigation of Oswald prior to the assassination."[68]

Hoover was particularly outraged that Oswald had not been on the list of individuals considered dangerous enough to be picked up in wartime. When every FBI official who studied the case came back with the conclusion that under the prevailing criteria, Oswald had not qualified for the list, Hoover replied, "They were worse than mistaken. Certainly no one in full possession of all his faculties can claim Oswald didn't fall within this criteria."

When the Warren Report was released on September 24, 1964, Hoover ordered a thorough review of what it said about the Bureau. "Chapter 8 tears us to pieces," he said. He was informed that "the Commission has now set forth in a very damning manner some of the same glaring weaknesses for which we previously disciplined our personnel such as lack of vigorous investigation after we had established that Oswald visited the Soviet Embassy in Mexico." He was also told that some of the agents' testimony makes the Bureau "look ridiculous and taints its public image." (An agent had referred to the Dallas police station as resembling "Yankee Stadium during the World Series games," which the Inspection Division called "editorializing and flamboyant.")[69]

Hoover's fury against the offending agents boiled over again because the Warren Commission report revealed to the public some of the Bureau's failings that he had already uncovered. The Inspection Division urged more disciplinary action. Hoover informed his executives that the personnel who did not include Oswald on the Security Index "could not have been more stupid . . . and now that the Bureau has been debunked publicly I intend to take additional administrative action." Four days after the release of the report, eight of the original seventeen agents were again punished. Belmont warned Tolson again that this was a mistake because it would be interpreted as admitting, "See, the Commission is right, Mr. Hoover has taken strong action against personnel involved in this case and thus admits that the Bureau was in error." Hoover replied, "We were wrong. The administrative action approved by me will stand." Then he made an astonishing statement: "I do not intend to palliate actions which have resulted in forever destroying the Bureau as the top level investigative organization."[70]

As always when criticized by outsiders, Hoover ferociously defended the Bureau against the Warren report even while he was saying, within the walls of the Bureau, that "there is no question in my mind but that we failed in carrying through some of the most salient aspects of the Oswald investigation. It ought to be a lesson to all, but I doubt if some even realize it now." He ordered a rebuttal of the Warren Commission for the few mild criticisms it made of the Bureau, and he insisted that the FBI counterattack start at once. His aides suggested releasing to the press the Bureau's criticism of the Warren Commission several days before sending the commission a copy, so that the Commission's eventual reply would have less impact. Hoover agreed, saying the Bureau did not owe the Commission any courtesy, and that if the Bureau did not strike back hard, "we might as well lay down and let anybody and everybody kick us around and not defend nor retaliate."[71]

Hoover's shock at the poor performance of the FBI revealed by the assassination did not seem to be shared by his top executives, who treated the matter strictly as a public relations problem. A month after the report was released, DeLoach reported to the Executive Conference that the Bureau had been damaged by the Warren Commission, but that the damage could be overcome with a combination of expanded press relations and investigative achievement; they should adopt Hoover's maxim, DeLoach said, that "nothing is more devastating to a smear than an offensive of real outstanding accomplishments." Hoover himself, who took the episode to heart (it was "his Bureau" that had done this to him) was not so sure: He said sadly that "the FBI will never live down this smear which could have been so easily avoided if there had been proper supervision and initiative."[72]

There was another FBI failure relating to the assassination that Hoover never spoke of and never admitted. Throughout the three years of Kennedy's presidency, Hoover knew of the massive amount of hate mail the president received, much of it violent and filled with sexual slander. Hoover should have been warning the president that he stood in constant danger of attack. Though the country had not yet begun the decade of assassinations that Jack Kennedy's death inaugurated, the director of the Bureau that had been designed as the chief executive's main arm of defense against crime should have been more alert to the threat to the president's safety that these slanders represented. Perhaps Hoover was less vigilant because he, too, disliked the Kennedys. But not even Robert Kennedy had fully appreciated the amount of hatred that had been focused on his brother by 1963: "the Teamsters, the gangsters, the pro-Castro Cubans, the anti-Castro Cubans, the racists, the right-wing fanatics, the lonely deluded nuts mumbling to themselves in the night." Hoover's greatest failure under Kennedy may have been his blindness to the implications of the rabid opposition the president was attracting, and from this followed his failure to provide the White House with pointed commentary and intelligence on the magnitude of the threat to Kennedy.[73]

Hoover's recognition of the FBI's vulnerability because of its handling of the Oswald security file may have affected the way he conducted his affairs under Kennedy successor. Hoover knew and liked Lyndon Johnson, vastly preferring him to the Kennedys. Now he had one more reason for making clear his loyalty to Johnson: It was obvious to Hoover that his only safety lay in complete and absolute subservience to Lyndon Baines Johnson, who was going to make the final decision as to whether any heads would roll.

Hoover's aversion to Kennedy, Kennedy's men, and the values of the New Frontier made him seek refuge against the tumultuous, changing world outside the Bureau. His few ventures away from the Bureau were to the protected environs of exclusive hotels in Florida and Southern California, and the homes of his rich Texas and Hollywood friends. He had dropped all social contact with surviving relatives, even with his niece, Dickinson's daughter, who worked in the fugitive section of the Bureau, and with Lillian's son, his nephew Fred, an FBI agent who retired in 1952. (Fred's son, Fred Robinette III, became an agent in 1968.) His only personal relationship continued to be with Tolson, and Tolson's health was disintegrating markedly after his 1963 heart surgery. Tolson now looked weak, painfully thin, and much older than Hoover, even though he was five years his junior.

The Bureau was Hoover's home now; it had absorbed the essence of the Victorian-era Seward Square. The Seward Square of the sixties, a black neighborhood that was cloaked with fear after sundown, must have seemed an abandoned (and somewhat embarrassing) husk, part of the disordered society that was lapping at the edges of the safe haven Hoover had created for himself within the FBI. Since May 1960, there had been a plan to merge several Methodist churches into one that would be housed in a new building to be constructed on the site of Hoover's old home. In February 1963, when construction was about to begin, a New Jersey woman told the FBI that she was ready to head a citizens' committee to preserve 413 Seward Square if Hoover approved, and Capitol Hill neighborhood organizations rounded up endorsements from groups claiming to represent 12 million Americans. But like the Central High alumni at the time the school had passed into black hands, Hoover preferred to let his past vanish rather than have it preserved in the declassed possession of blacks. He passed along word that he did not want to take part in this movement and ordered that "any further efforts in this regard be discouraged."[74] The church built on the site in 1966 has a stained-glass window dedicated to Hoover with the motto "Statesmanship Through the Christian Virtues."

After the assassination, Hoover's barely suppressed resentment of RFK surfaced, now fueled by his need to prove his absolute loyalty to Lyndon Johnson. The story was circulated that when Kennedy tried to use the direct phone to Hoover's desk, Hoover let it ring until it stopped, then said, "Put that damn thing back on Miss Gandy's desk where it belongs." Hoover thought that Courtney Evans was too close to Kennedy, so he replaced Evans as liaison to the department and the White House with Cartha DeLoach, who had gotten to know Johnson when he was the Bureau's congressional liaison; DeLoach was, moreover, a Southerner (from Georgia).[75]

Robert Kennedy made gracious overtures to Hoover in an attempt to at least preserve civilities. In December, Kennedy gave his staff, including Hoover, engraved cuff links as a souvenir of their years together, and Hoover, to give him credit, responded with a handwritten note of thanks for "a constant reminder of a friendship I shall always treasure." It is doubtful, however, that Ethel Kennedy's attempt to loosen Hoover up when the cuff links were given out did her husband any good. She teased him, "Don't you think Chief Parker [of the Los Angeles Police Force, whom Hoover detested] is a wonderful man? Don't you think that if you ever retired, he'd be the man to replace you?" According to a witness, "Hoover reddened slightly and replied meekly, 'Yes, Ethel.' " In May 1964, Kennedy made another peace overture: Congratulating Hoover on his fortieth anniversary as director, he wrote, "In the past few months I have not had the pleasure of associating with you as closely as formerly. I regret this but would not want this occasion to pass without congratulating you on this milestone and wishing you well in the future."[76] (Hoover replied that "Time flies by very fast indeed when a person is engaged in the type of work he enjoys doing.") Kennedy thought, wrongly, that things were on the mend and told his press secretary, "I am glad we wrote him."

While cultivating Johnson, Hoover let it be known, with an air of satisfaction, that "I didn't speak to Bobby Kennedy the last six months he was in office." (He left in September 1964 to run for the Senate in New York.) And Kennedy, when he learned that Hoover had begun to deal directly with the White House without notifying him, sadly told an aide, "Those people don't work for us anymore."[77]

Robert Kennedy's friends bitterly resented what they interpreted as Hoover's lack of compassion for Bob and his haste to ingratiate himself with Johnson (but, with Johnson hating and fearing Kennedy as he did, even if Hoover had not disliked Kennedy, Johnson would have insisted on Hoover's help against him). In fact, the feelings of Kennedy's friends were so intense on the subject of Johnson that some considered Special Assistant for National Security Affairs McGeorge Bundy a traitor for staying on under LBJ. It was easy for Hoover to exploit Johnson's fear of a Kennedy plot to overthrow him in 1964. He knew that any speculations he passed on to the White House in that regard would get a ready hearing from Johnson, who was eager to believe the worst of Robert Kennedy.

It had been a foregone conclusion, under President Kennedy, that Hoover would have had to leave when he reached the mandatory retirement age on New Year's Day, 1965. The assassination had changed everything. It had carried one of Hoover's oldest and closest friends into power at the White House, a president who craved the kind of loyal service only Hoover knew how to give. As 1964 began, Hoover had every reason to hope that Kennedy's end meant that his own had been indefinitely postponed.

CHAPTER 12

LBJ's FBI

I'd rather have him inside the tent pissing out than outside pissing in.

LBJ's perhaps apocryphal explanation of why he kept Hoover as FBI Director.[1]

WHEN LYNDON JOHNSON took over the presidency he was surrounded by Kennedy loyalists. Some of them resented Johnson for taking command so quickly. Others harbored grudges over slights, real or imagined, to the prerogatives of the Kennedy family. All of them felt that fate and Johnson had snatched the power they had won in 1960, and which should have been theirs till at least 1968. It did not matter that Johnson paid regular tribute to the memory of the lost leader, or that Johnson turned his legislative program into a memorial to the dead president; there was still resentment of Johnson as a usurper—in the minds of some, a particularly loutish and graceless usurper. And always, Johnson was conscious of the hovering figure of the slain president's brother Robert, the one person in politics Johnson most hated and feared, stationed where he could do the most damage, in the government's most strategic domestic office, that of attorney general.

In November 1963, Johnson desperately needed men whose loyalty he could count on, men who would, in a famous LBJism, kiss his ass in Macy's window on the hottest day of the year, and swear it

smelled like a rose. Lyndon Johnson knew J. Edgar Hoover, knew
him well, had known him as a friend and a neighbor for some twenty
years. Johnson never quite put Hoover to the Macy's window test,
but he did get many tokens of loyalty and praise from him. After a
televised tour of the LBJ hill country, Hoover told Johnson the program "was excellent and more particularly brought out your humble-
ness and your down to earth characteristics"; Hoover described a
televised news conference as "terrific. The soundness and sincerity
of your answers were masterful. I only wish our Washington Senators
Baseball Team had an outfielder as capable in fielding some of the
hot ones you handled. They were certainly loaded but you handled
them like a Mickey Mantle." More importantly, by defending Johnson
and attacking his enemies, Hoover proved that he was a man Johnson
could trust.[2]

Hoover's warm relationship with Johnson had begun nearly twenty
years earlier, in 1945, when Lyndon and Lady Bird bought their first
house in Washington. It was on Thirtieth Place in the northwest section
of Washington, a suburban block of detached, two-story houses in
varied architectural styles, separated only by carefully tended lawns
and shrubbery, the same block to which Hoover had moved in 1939.
The neighborhood children got to know Hoover and he got to know
the Johnson girls. Later in his life, Hoover used to tell stories of his
years as Johnson's neighbor: When Johnson was in the Senate and
"we were neighbors," he said, Johnson "had a little dog he called
Little Beagle Johnson. Every few days he would come over in the
evening and say, 'Edgar, Little Beagle Johnson's gone again. Let's
go find him' and we would go off looking all over the neighborhood."[3]

Johnson's last attorney general, Ramsey Clark, felt that the nearly
two decades they spent as neighbors "almost disqualified" Johnson
from being able to properly supervise Hoover. "The Johnson daughters
felt he was a rich uncle or something. Not that they'd see him that
much, but in the old days he'd occasionally come over for breakfast
on Sunday." For LBJ, who was "young enough to have grown up
in the Dillinger days and he liked that sort of thing," Hoover was
still America's Number One G-man.[4]

For his part, Hoover admired Johnson. Some of his best friends
were Texans like Clint Murchison and Sid Richardson, and he said
of Johnson, "You can't box him in. He will do as he pleases, whether
right or wrong as far as security is concerned. Texans don't like to
be told what to do. This is characteristic of Texans. They are a separate
breed of man. I admire the intelligence and fearlessness of a man of
that kind."[5]

Hoover's presence in Johnson's administration was reassuring to those people most upset by Johnson's Great Society and civil rights policies. When LBJ decided to keep Hoover as director, he received hundreds of letters congratulating him on his decision; some even recommended that he consider Hoover for higher office: secretary general of the United Nations, for example. One writer thought Johnson should split the recently resigned Arthur Goldberg's Supreme Court seat between Hoover and Tolson and make them co-justices. Conservative columnist Russell Kirk wanted Hoover as attorney general. There were many Americans who simply relied on Hoover and they would accept no substitute. In December 1964, Art Buchwald took a harmless dig at Hoover by claiming he was a "mythical person first thought up by the Reader's Digest." One of Johnson's Texas friends wrote LBJ that he knew many people who believed the story, and he asked for an affidavit that he could show to "certain people in Dallas" to prove Hoover was "a real live individual." Hoover's supporters might not have been all that sophisticated, but they were fiercely and humorlessly loyal.[6]

With the prestige and political backing Hoover had throughout the country, his presence would help prove that civil rights was not a Communist plot (or, at least, not only a Communist plot); only with Hoover at its head could the FBI serve effectively as a signal of the government's disgust with racial violence in the South. Given the FBI's past resistance to active civil rights enforcement, it was also felt that only Hoover's unquestioned authority over the Bureau could ensure that Field agents would actually comply with a drastic shift in the Bureau's civil rights policy.

Hoover was also useful to Johnson when the law-and-order backlash to racial demonstrations and ghetto riots made crime as important as Vietnam as a political issue. In 1966, Johnson was able to draw on Hoover's prestige to give some credibility to his anticrime program, and as a gesture of the administration's concern about the crime issue, LBJ proposed to Congress a sixfold increase in enrollment at the FBI's National Academy to facilitate the training of local police officers.

A friendship with Lyndon Johnson was rarely conducted on a basis of equality. Johnson was domineering, even cruel in his dealings with his closest associates, sending them through wild mood swings of depression and exaltation as he lavished or withheld affection. In contrast, the Hoover-Johnson arrangement was more like a genuine friendship than the typical quasi-sado-masochistic relationships Johnson had with his other associates. LBJ at times was exasperated by some of Hoover's mannerisms (he complained that Hoover spoke so fast he couldn't understand him), but he also called Hoover regularly for wide-ranging discussions on the issues of the day; Johnson simply liked to talk to an old friend who sympathized with his problems. (Johnson's diary lists some sixty phone conversations with Hoover during his administration.)[7]

While Johnson treated Hoover with great respect, both of them knew Hoover was vulnerable because of the Bureau's questionable performance in the Oswald security case, which had put it in an adversarial relationship with the Warren Commission. Hoover was even more vulnerable because of his age. He would reach the mandatory retirement age of seventy on January 1, 1965. Once Johnson decided that having Hoover would help him consolidate his power, however, he made the waiver of mandatory retirement as painless as possible. The normal procedure was for the overage official to retire and then be rehired as an annuitant, meaning he had to be rehired every year. (This is what Hoover did for Tolson in 1970.) By using the mechanism of a waiver, Johnson ensured that it would take a positive act by any future president to get rid of Hoover; had Hoover been an annuitant, his superior—the attorney general—would have had to recommend to the president a new reappointment each year. At the time Johnson made the waiver, Robert Kennedy was the attorney general. Since no one knew the future, the assumption was that it would have been Kennedy who would have had to recommend Hoover's reappointment. (As it happened, Kennedy left the Justice Department in September 1964.)[8]

The ceremony Johnson staged in the White House Rose Garden to announce the waiver of retirement was both graceful and gracious.

> J. Edgar Hoover is a hero to millions of decent citizens, and an anathema to evil men. No other American, now or in our past, has served the cause of justice so faithfully and so well. . . .
>
> J. Edgar Hoover has served the government since 1917—he has served nine Presidents, and this Sunday, he celebrates his fortieth year as Director of the FBI. Under his guiding hand, the FBI has become the greatest investigation body in history. . . .
>
> Edgar, the law says that you must retire next January when you reach your seventieth birthday, and I know you wouldn't want to break the law.
>
> But the nation cannot afford to lose you. Therefore, by virtue of and pursuant to the authority vested in the President, I have today signed an Executive Order exempting you from compulsory retirement for an indefinite period of time.[9]

One of the most effective ways Hoover could reciprocate and thus demonstrate his loyalty to Johnson was to attack Robert Kennedy. Until Robert Kennedy's death, Hoover kept up a running feud with him, which must surely have been gratifying to Johnson. The most sensational was a 1966 row over whether RFK had authorized the FBI's use of microphones (involving illegal trespasses) in organized crime investigations while he was attorney general. News commentator Robert Spivack said "There is little doubt that J. Edgar Hoover has severely damaged the image of Sen. Robert F. Kennedy, particularly among young people to whose idealism Kennedy has appealed. By portraying him as party to what is essentially the dirty business of snooping, Hoover is saying that Kennedy is no innocent, but a hard and ruthless young man on the make." Congressman Wayne Hays of Ohio got in touch with Johnson to let him know how much he had enjoyed the rhubarb, and suggested that "you should fire J. Edgar Hoover on the strength of Bobby Kennedy's statements and answer the backlash by pointing at Kennedy. . . . This is your best bet for getting rid of both men."[10]

Immediately after John Kennedy's assassination, Hoover started to bypass Robert Kennedy and deal directly with the White House. Robert Kennedy had earlier felt that even though it was difficult, it was "not too bad" working with Hoover; in April 1964, however, he told an interviewer Hoover was "dangerous" and was "rather a psycho." He thought the FBI was "a very dangerous organization . . . and I think he's . . . senile and rather frightening." A sign of Hoover's hostility was his removal of Courtney Evans as White House liaison, replacing him with an old friend of Johnson's, Cartha De-Loach, head of the Crime Records Division, who had known Johnson since the Senate days. DeLoach achieved an extraordinary degree of intimacy with Johnson. Hoover tolerated this, although there were rumors that he was jealous of DeLoach's rapport with LBJ. Hoover knew Johnson's personality, his incessant demands on his subordinates' time and his need for constant reassurance of their loyalty, and so the director was grateful for the buffer DeLoach provided between himself and the president. DeLoach was apprehensive that Hoover *would* become jealous, however, and he begged Johnson to check with Hoover before asking personal favors of him.[11]

One reason DeLoach was so useful to Johnson was that he was a figure of political significance in his own right; he had inherited the extensive network of media contacts developed by Louis Nichols, and he had gone beyond Nichols in cultivating an even broader spectrum of Bureau supporters. DeLoach could offer Johnson media advice as well as provide access to the press for manipulating public opinion through selective leaks. DeLoach's role as a power in the American Legion also made him a useful ally for the White House. The Bureau had always been concerned about the Legion's tendency to run amuck hunting for spies and subversives. In 1953 Hoover had given DeLoach responsibility for straightening out the Legion; to do this, DeLoach gained control of the Americanism Committee of the Legion, which let him orchestrate the Legion's political platform, leading a reporter to call the Legion's annual conventions "FBI productions." As the Vietnam War escalated, DeLoach encouraged the Legion to back Johnson's war policy, and brought delegations from the Legion to the White House as a show of support at critical moments.[12]

Because of the extraordinary rapport between them, there was no service Hoover would refuse Johnson, no matter how far removed it might be from his law enforcement or domestic intelligence responsibilities. Not since the FDR-Hoover relationship was there anything approaching the political use the Johnson administration made of the FBI.

During the 1964 Democratic convention in Atlantic City, New Jersey, Hoover sent a team of agents under DeLoach to collect information on the political opposition (chiefly the Mississippi Freedom Democrats' challenge to the regular [Jim Crow] Mississippi delegation) and to monitor the possibility of a convention stampede to nominate Robert Kennedy for vice president against Johnson's wishes. The Bureau sent Johnson's aides a stream of political intelligence. This was done, of course, without Kennedy's knowledge, and since Kennedy was still attorney general at the time, Hoover's loyalty to Johnson had put him in the position of spying on his immediate superior. DeLoach later wrote presidential aide Bill Moyers, "I'm certainly glad that we were able to come through with vital tidbits from time to time which were of assistance to you and Walter [Jenkins]." The tidbits consisted of forty-four pages of memoranda gained from wiretaps on the Student Non-Violent Coordinating Committee (SNCC) and Congress of Racial Equality (CORE) headquarters, and telephone messages on "minute to minute developments." The Bureau team also worked to create difficulties for demonstrators against Johnson. Johnson later congratulated Hoover on the intelligence the Bureau had furnished during the convention, calling it "one of the finest [jobs] the President had ever seen."[13]

Johnson used the Bureau for other political tasks. He had DeLoach supervise the sensitive investigation of Walter Jenkins after Jenkins's arrest on charges of making a homosexual approach in a YMCA restroom in October 1964. At the outset, before it was clear that the situation could not be contained, the White House had DeLoach explore ways of controlling the damage without destroying Jenkins, one of Johnson's most trusted and valued aides. Other services included a background check on members of Barry Goldwater's campaign staff. During the 1968 campaign, Johnson suspected the Republicans of plotting with the South Vietnamese to delay negotiations in Paris until after the elections, and so Hoover looked into alleged contacts between Spiro Agnew and China lobby member Anna Chennault, but was unable to give Johnson the evidence he wanted.[14]

Hoover also provided LBJ with foreign intelligence. It is possible that Johnson did not trust the CIA after the Bay of Pigs operation and the Kennedy assassination. In any case, following the 1964 invasion he ordered Hoover to establish an FBI intelligence post in the Dominican Republic and he thought enough of the FBI's performance in that country to ask Hoover to recommend possible candidates for appointment as U.S. ambassador there.[15]

The relationship between Hoover and Johnson was so close that it encouraged both men to use the Bureau in all these ways, which would have been impossible if they had felt constrained to observe any of the formalities of normal Justice Department protocol. The confidence bred in Hoover by his friendship with LBJ made him defiant and contemptuous toward his Justice Department superiors, and reinforced him in his belief that the Bureau should be subject only to his will as he acted for the president in the best interest of the nation.

Lyndon Johnson inherited a Justice Department that was making enormous efforts to reorient American law enforcement toward the understanding and prevention of crime instead of just denouncing and repressing it. In 1963, Robert Kennedy's Committee on Poverty and the Federal Administration of Federal Criminal Justice (chaired by Francis A. Allen) recommended that a recognition of crime's roots in the culture of poverty be made the basis of federal law enforcement and proposed a new Office of Criminal Justice to implement the shift in philosophy. In 1964, the new Criminal Justice Act established that office under the direction of the deputy attorney general, Nicholas Katzenbach. The Office of Criminal Justice, said Robert Kennedy, would "deal with social problems that affect the criminal process, such as narcotics, or juvenile delinquency, or the right of privacy.

We want it to be a voice inside the Department and a forum outside the Department." Another Kennedy-sponsored program that implicitly challenged Hoover's law enforcement leadership was the Community Relations Service, set up under the Civil Rights Act of 1964, directed by Roger W. Wilkins; its goal was to deal with disorders through negotiation and compromise rather than force. By the time Johnson became president, therefore, the Justice Department was speaking with two voices, Hoover's and Robert Kennedy's, each offering diametrically opposed philosophies of law enforcement, each aspiring to a position of leadership in the law enforcement community.[16]

The Office of Criminal Justice was a liberal source of law enforcement ideas that challenged Hoover's "machine gun" school of criminology; it also provided an institutional alternative to the FBI as the symbol of federal law enforcement leadership. When Katzenbach became attorney general in September 1964, his deputy, Ramsey Clark, became head of the Office of Criminal Justice. Clark thus became the department's and the country's leading advocate of fighting crime by combating poverty. And that made Clark and the Warren Court (which had just affirmed the right to free counsel in the *Gideon* decision) the chief targets of Hoover's attacks on permissiveness in law enforcement.

As the Justice Department responded to national concern about crime with new and ambitious programs of federal assistance to local law enforcement, Hoover's typical reluctance to share authority meant that the FBI took no part in the new initiatives; a diminishment of the Bureau's impact on law enforcement inevitably ensued as rivals, like the Law Enforcement Assistance Administration, increased in importance. The FBI had no role in such major federal anticrime initiatives as the District of Columbia Crime Bill of 1967 or the major crime legislation to come out of the Johnson administration, the June 1968 Omnibus Crime Control and Safe Streets Act. Nor did the FBI provide leadership in the Justice Department efforts against juvenile delinquency or crimes against small business.[17]

The sixties' long hot summers of riots in urban ghettos, with their cries of "Burn, Baby, Burn," made law and order a torrid political issue. The public was therefore intensely interested in the battle between Hoover and the Justice Department—between the attorney general's program of combating crime through an attack on poverty, and J. Edgar Hoover's denunciation of permissiveness as the cause of crime. Against public demands for stern measures against criminals—meaning black urban criminals—the Justice Department argued accurately but, as it turned out, unconvincingly that crime statistics were unreliable, that homicide rates were down, and that the crime the public most feared, black violence against whites, was one of the rarest types of crime. Hoover's argument was more persuasive because he told the public what it wanted to believe: that it was within the power of the government to curb crime by getting tough, and that Supreme Court–mandated and Justice Department–encouraged permissiveness was the reason for the crime wave.[18]

Hoover found the Kennedy-Johnson Justice Department and Attorney General Ramsey Clark perfect symbols of what was wrong with law enforcement, especially after Clark stated, at the National Conference on Crime Control in March 1967, that there was no crime wave. (Clark was badly misquoted: He did not deny crime was increasing; he simply quarreled with the image of a wave on the basis that it implied rising and falling rates. He said that the rates simply kept rising.) Hoover's view of crime was in sharp contrast to Clark's. He saw "at all levels of our society . . . a pervasive contempt for law and order. . . . The soaring crime rate, widespread, open defiance of constituted authority, threaten, if unchecked, to plunge our Nation into the abyss of violence and anarchy." The split between the attorney general and the director reflected the enormous political gulf in the country between those who were trying to understand crime and disorder as symptoms of structural injustices in American society, and others who saw them only as attacks on society that had to be repelled by repression and punishment.[19]

One of the important clashes between Hoover and the Johnson attorney generals was over the response to urban riots: Hoover wanted to use covert methods to combat them; the Justice Department wanted negotiation and open contacts with protesters. Hoover treated the rioters and their leaders as subversives out to overthrow the government and destroy society; the Justice Department saw them as the products of unjust social conditions and believed that the most effective response would be political reform and social change. The FBI set up undercover programs to harass and disrupt protest movements, and drew up lists of targets for covert action—such as its Rabble Rouser and Agitator indexes; the Justice Department set up the Community Relations Service.[20]

The president tried to please both Hoover and his attorney generals, Katzenbach and Clark. Johnson agreed with the Justice Department's philosophy of fighting crime by fighting poverty, which was an intrinsic part of his Great Society program. But faced with widespread revolt against the social welfare approach, he could not afford to antagonize the law-and-order masses for whom Hoover was spokesman and symbol.

Paradoxically, Hoover's isolation within the Justice Department made him willing to comply with the department's pressure to curtail such intrusive techniques as electronic surveillance. On March 30, 1965, Attorney General Katzenbach ordered Hoover to seek his approval for all wiretaps and microphone surveillances, and required that his approval be obtained again to continue them beyond six months. At the same time, there was evidence that congressional support for the use of sensitive techniques was eroding. Early in 1965, Senator Edward C. Long of Missouri began an investigation of government invasions of privacy. Congress was showing nervous but unmistakable signs of finally wanting to assert its long-dormant control over the Bureau. In 1966, Hoover would have to work hard to defeat Eugene McCarthy's attempt to give the CIA oversight committee authority over the FBI, and the 1968 Crime Bill would provide that FBI directors after Hoover would have to be appointed by the president and approved by the Senate. Perhaps sensing the approach of these measures, Hoover knew the time had come to eliminate techniques that would only become more risky in the future. On September 14, 1965, Hoover notified Katzenbach that he was severely restricting the use of many sensitive techniques, and was eliminating the use of microphone surveillance (bugs). About this time Hoover, also ended trash covers (searches of trash), mail covers (records of addressees and recipients of mail), and break-ins.[21]

In restricting electronic surveillance, Hoover made such an about-face that he went almost as far as Ramsey Clark, who was absolutely opposed to such techniques except in instances of national security, and who refused to use the legal procedure for court-authorized wiretapping that was later provided by the 1968 Crime Control Act. Hoover's motive was not to please his superiors; it was that he knew if he were caught, none of them would give him the unwavering support he had once gotten from such men as Biddle and Brownell. Nor, in this instance, could he count on the support of his patron in the White House. Lyndon Johnson was also opposed to wiretapping, and on July 1, 1965, he had issued an executive order prohibiting the practice by federal agencies except in cases of national security, and ordered all agencies to review their policies with regard to bugs.

Hoover was more willing than many in the Bureau to give up these surreptitious techniques, because he had always seen them as more symbolic than essential. If the public demanded them as evidence of a commitment to serious law enforcement or counterespionage, he was ready to oblige. If the public recoiled from them as signs of an oppressive government, he was also ready to oblige. During the Long investigation, Hoover wrote: "I don't see what all the excitement is about. I would have no hesitance in discontinuing all techniques—technical coverage [i.e., wiretapping], microphones, trash covers, mail covers, etc. While it might handicap us I doubt they are as valuable as some believe and none warrant FBI being used to justify them."[22]

Ironically, Hoover's high prestige in Congress and with the public regularly contributed another type of threat to his autonomy. The FBI's reputation disposed Congress to demonstrate its concern over law enforcement issues by turning difficult jobs over to the Bureau despite Hoover's protests. For example, Congress wanted to merge the Drug Enforcement Agency into the FBI, an echo of the attempt in 1933 to merge the Bureau with the Prohibition unit. Hoover had never wanted to have anything to do with drugs because of the temptations they placed in the way of his agents. The sheer size of the DEA would also have swamped the Bureau and created a force too large for even Hoover to maintain tight one-man control. In 1964, he said, "I am against, and have been for years, the growth of the FBI. I think we are entirely too big today, bigger than we should be. I would have liked to see the FBI remain small; but that has been impossible because Congress has yearly enacted legislation expanding the investigative jurisdiction of the Bureau." Hoover was determined to keep the FBI completely under his control, and he would make any strategic sacrifice necessary to accomplish this.[23]

In resisting the Johnson administration's law enforcement program, Hoover was instinctively placing himself on the popular side of the debate over law and order. Lyndon Johnson's law enforcement policies were very much imposed from the top down. Unlike the successful war on crime waged by Roosevelt and Homer Cummings, the Johnson administration was responding to pressure from the intellectual elite (legal scholars and social scientists) in drafting its law enforcement reforms, and not to grass-roots pressure. For a brief period in 1964, the prestige of the administration (of Johnson himself, and Robert Kennedy) could persuade Congress and the public to support their progressive and innovative ideas on crime prevention, but as urban disorders became widespread, and Johnson's popularity continued to be eroded by the Vietnam War, the public reverted to its customary view of law enforcement as a moral drama that should culminate in the physical extirpation of despised symbols of immorality. The FBI had its roots in this ritual drama, and it had prospered in the past by providing law-and-order rituals to satisfy the demand created by the mass media. It was natural, then, for Hoover to reject the Justice Department's theory of law enforcement, which was so at odds with the ideas that had made the Bureau great. And when the public looked for an alternative to Ramsey Clark, it saw J. Edgar Hoover, who had never changed his ideas, whose words and attitudes were as familiar as old gumshoes.

According to Hoover's analysis, there were two principal causes of the breakdown of order in the sixties: the preaching of civil disobedience, and the lax enforcement of the law ("turnstile justice"). He rejected, of course, any defense of civil disobedience; whatever its goals, to him it was willful defiance of the law, the ultimate attack against society. "Freedom cannot long survive," he told the Michigan Bar Association, "where defiance and contempt are tolerated or condoned. That is why our country can ill-afford the binge of so-called 'civil disobedience' which has erupted on the streets of major cities and across the campuses of many colleges and universities." Combine civil disobedience and permissiveness, and the result was New York City, Hoover's horrible example of the ruin awaiting the rest of the country if the nation did not mend its ways: "New York City is really a jungle of crime. It is no longer safe to ride on subways. Police dogs ride the trains to protect passengers from being assaulted and attacked." He advised "anyone in New York City not to walk through Central Park at night or in Manhattan."[24]

For Hoover, the answer to crime was not to be found in innovation but in a return to tradition: "The laws of Moses must remain the guideline not only for those who engage in the practice of law, but for our entire body of civil and criminal codes. They must continue to dominate the atmosphere of the United States. They must remain our National Creed."[25]

To Hoover the Justice Department's war on the social and economic roots of crime obscured its essentially moral basis. While the Justice Department linked poverty and crime, Hoover continued to see the rise in crime, and the overall decline in morality, as a failure of discipline. "Poverty is not the sole factor contributing to crime," Hoover complained, "but sociologists emphasize the role of poverty and are always asking for large sums of money for programs

which will not strengthen the community's defenses against crime."
Publicize the names of youthful offenders, he demanded. "Focus attention on youth, take away the 'hero' glamour and have parents appear
in court where they can face the humiliation which is due them when
the facts of inadequate home life and lack of discipline are revealed."[26]

Hoover's denunciations of society's declining respect for authority,
particularly police authority, made him a natural spokesman for the
police community in the sixties as it came to feel itself an embattled,
betrayed minority of "New Centurions" protecting a soft, ungrateful
public. Hoover's doctrine of police professionalism had always stressed
freedom from political control. In the context of the sixties that meant
freedom for the police to meet urban and racial disorders with strict
law-and-order tactics, unfettered by the political considerations of
those who might want to negotiate with demonstrators as citizens
(and voters) with legitimate grievances rather than as criminals deserv-
ing only arrest and punishment. He was one of those who interpreted
Supreme Court decisions protecting the rights of the accused like the
1964 *Escobedo* decision (which invalidated a confession when the accused was denied access to his lawyer) and the *Miranda* decision in
1966 (which required police to inform a suspect of his constitutional
rights) as attacks on the police.[27]

It was up to law enforcement, Hoover said, to restore national
discipline. "One of the greatest challenges we in law enforcement have
to face today is public indifference toward crime, corruption, and other
vices which enter into human life." He told another audience that
"there is no doubt in my mind—and history proves—that the best
interests of America lie in a law-abiding, decent and orderly society.
We cannot live with lawlessness, unbridled vulgarity, obscenity, pro-
fane blasphemy, perversion and public desecration of every sacred
symbol. To react to them with less than the full resources at our
command would be intolerable. I firmly believe it is time for us to
get on with the perpetuation of self-evident truths, which, with divine
guidance, have served our nation so well over the years past."[28]

Hoover had always suspected the country's loyalty to traditional
values was broad but shallow, and that it was only because of wills
as strong as his own that order and respectability were maintained
in an American society infiltrated by aliens uncommitted to traditional
Christian, middle-class values. The sixties confirmed his worst suspicions. His harangues against the symbols and agents of moral decline—
black activists, antiwar demonstrators, and hippies—found echo
throughout mainstream America. His outspoken attacks on the new,

the different, the rebellious—on whatever subverted unity and order—
made him an iconic figure, fiercely defended, fiercely attacked, a symbol
of popular resentment of the collapse of the racial status quo and of
the creed of God, country, and family. He was seen as old-fashioned,
and he knew it. "I trust you will give consideration to my remarks,"
he said, "and not dismiss them as typical of the traditional age-old
lament about the moral climate of one's native land. We are courting
disaster if we do not soon take some positive action against the growing
moral deterioration in this land. It is a grievous trend which is being
steadily reflected in the attitude of contempt which many of our people
have for the values which made this Nation great."[29]

Hoover countered the Justice Department's sociological approach
to crime with his own program: professional standards and scientific
methods. Expanding the Quantico National Police Academy was his
contribution to improving the standards of law enforcement (although
he withheld these facilities from police forces headed by enemies like
Los Angeles's William Parker). He bragged to Supreme Court Justice
Tom Clark that his Academy would be the West Point of law enforcement, that he was sending the faculty of eight men to graduate schools
around the country for their master's degrees, and that "we will have
the top faculty in this field." He boasted about the Bureau's new
technology, and especially the National Crime Information Center
Computer that went into operation in January 1967.[30]

Behind Hoover's covert war against dissent during the sixties was
his rage against moral decline and those he regarded as its symbols
and agents—black activists and antiwar demonstrators—and his frustration that traditional values were no longer being upheld by national
leaders. He liked to quote Herbert Hoover: "We may commit suicide
from within by complaisance with evil, or by public tolerance of scandalous behavior, or by cynical acceptance of dishonor. These evils
have defeated nations many times in the past."[31]

He saw protesters as "arrogant, demanding legions of irresponsible
youths" who had infiltrated "the ranks of other groups—particularly
among certain one-time civil rights organizations whose leadership
has grown increasingly contemptuous of the United States and vitriolic
in opposition to our country's courageous defense of freedom in Vietnam. These hucksters of misunderstanding and discord do not truly
represent the noble cause of civil rights which has been served so
genuinely and unselfishly by patriotic men and women from many

areas of our national life." He held Martin Luther King, Jr., personally responsible for the "idea that you can violate a law if it is wrong," and said that though he rarely complimented Harry Truman, he applauded him for calling King a damned fool.[32]

As the war and protests against the war grew ever more unmanageable in the late sixties, Hoover's angry outbursts against protesters and rebels suited the mood of the White House. In 1964, Johnson had proclaimed call for a war against poverty, a "domestic enemy which threatens the strength of the nation," but in 1968 he had switched to a call for a war on crime, and he signed a draconian new crime law for the District of Columbia and a new package of national crime control legislation. Eric Goldman, an historian who served as an aide to Johnson, wrote that by the "Summer and Fall of 1966 the domestic reformer of the Great Society days had become a war chief . . . the ebullient leader given to moments of testiness and rage was now, day after day, bitter, truculent, peevish—and suspicious of the fundamental good sense and integrity of anyone who did not endorse the Vietnam War. This Lyndon Johnson was not only depressing; at times he could be downright frightening."[33]

While the mood was turning sour within the White House, the public was forming a final, lasting image of the ancient and frustrated Hoover as he lashed out at the decade's strange and outrageous young protesters; he became a furious scold who turned himself into the voice of middle America's backlash against racial and antiwar protest, against rising crime, and against the constitutional scruples that kept the police from applying the simple and direct and nostalgically remembered machine-gun justice of the Bureau's glory days.

Lyndon Johnson's greatest achievement as president was to break the back of legally tolerated terrorism against blacks in the South. Johnson used all of his prodigious political skills to put the government and the nation behind a program of vitalized enforcement of new and existing civil rights laws, and Hoover's FBI played a vital and valiant role in this cause. Hoover directed massive investigations of racial violence in the South and he forestalled more violence by disrupting and eventually destroying the South's network of murderous Klans.

Hoover's energetic performance under Johnson contrasts sharply with his reluctance to act under Truman, Eisenhower, and Kennedy. Nevertheless, while the change in the Bureau's civil rights policies during the Johnson administration was dramatic, it should not be supposed that it represented a new attitude toward civil rights on Hoover's part. The factors that produced Hoover's attack on the Klan had little to do with any change of heart regarding racial equality or the proper place of blacks in American society.

Justice Department officials in the Civil Rights Division agree that somehow Lyndon Johnson had finally managed to persuade J. Edgar Hoover to order the FBI to enforce civil rights laws in the South in an aggressive and effective fashion. John Doar, who led the Civil Rights Division's prosecutions of civil rights cases in the South, said that originally "the Bureau was ill-prepared for its predicament," but that in 1964, "when a deep-seated change came upon America, a change brought about by many individuals, groups and forces, the Bureau changed as well." Ramsey Clark gives credit to Johnson himself for turning Hoover around. "I think Mr. Johnson showed that he could do more with Mr. Hoover than anybody who'd ever tried. Getting Mr. Hoover to go down to Jackson, Mississippi, to open that FBI office was quite a feat. I wouldn't have bet much on being able to talk him into doing it, but he did."[34]

The most important reason for this change was presidential leadership and determination. Johnson created a role for Hoover in the same kind of moral and political dramas that Roosevelt and Cummings had staged in the thirties; LBJ even followed the same script. First he selected particularly atrocious crimes to interpret as attacks on society, then he drafted new laws to arm the FBI in a crusade against the rebels; finally he dispatched the FBI to destroy those who had defied the authority of the national government.

No previous president had ever had Johnson's clear, total, and passionate commitment to civil rights. Hoover had always made it his policy to avoid fruitless investigations if he felt he would be abandoned by his superiors—especially in investigations of white terror against blacks in the South. Now, shielded by the president's aggressive stance, he was willing to enter this treacherous and controversial area.

The Johnson administration's war against the Klan followed a pattern almost identical to Homer Cummings's classic response to the Kansas City Massacre in 1933. The date was June 22, 1964. Three young civil rights workers—Michael Schwerner, James Chaney, and Andrew Goodman—disappeared near Philadelphia, Mississippi, two days after the Senate passed the civil rights bill that Lyndon Johnson had described as part of John F. Kennedy's legacy. Attorney General Robert Kennedy ordered Hoover to treat the disappearance as a kidnapping and to dispatch his agents to the scene. The next day, agents from New Orleans arrived in Philadelphia (there was no FBI field office in the state of Mississippi; the Bureau was represented only by "resident agents": one- or two-man offices functioning principally as liaisons with local police). That day, Johnson also dispatched a fact-finding team, led by former CIA director Allen Dulles, to Mississippi. Before leaving, Dulles conferred with Hoover and Kennedy; once there, he interviewed the governor of Mississippi, Paul Johnson, and the head of the Mississippi Highway Patrol. He returned to Washington with a recommendation that the FBI significantly increase its presence in the state. It was during this crisis that President Johnson signed the new civil rights law (July 2), which banned racial, religious, and sex discrimination in employment practices and accommodations; it empowered the attorney general to initiate private suits to force deseg-regation, terminated federal funding of discriminatory state or local agencies, and extended the life of the Civil Rights Commission.

On July 19, Hoover himself flew to Jackson, Mississippi, to open the new FBI office there, and to announce he was sending 153 agents into the state, a dramatic signal that the FBI was now fully committed to the war against racial terror. Following through on the new initia-tive, in July 1964, the FBI held a national law enforcement conference on civil rights. That same month, headquarters sent its field agents outlines of civil rights lectures for them to use when speaking before law enforcement and civic groups.[35]

Johnson made sure Hoover knew how much he appreciated this effort by sending him a letter of congratulations (drafted by DeLoach) commending him for

> the tremendous success of your trip to Mississippi. I find a great solace to lean on an old friend, such as you, in handling such delicate assignments of great importance to our country. Obviously you left behind you in Mississippi a feeling of good will and a renewed determination among local authorities to prevent outbreaks of lawlessness and terrorism. You may rest assured that I will be calling upon you from time to time in the future to handle additional assignments.[36]

When another racial murder shocked the country the next March, Johnson again used Hoover and the Bureau to dramatize the govern-ment's determination to combat terror and to mobilize Congress for more civil rights legislation. This was the murder of Mrs. Viola Liuzzo, a white volunteer assisting Martin Luther King's protest march from Selma to Montgomery. The murder occurred at the end of a month of violent racial confrontations in Alabama. On March 7, 1965, Sheriff

Jim Clark of Selma, Alabama, had led club-wielding state troopers in a tear-gas attack on civil rights marchers. On March 15, President Johnson went before a joint session of Congress to introduce the Voting Rights Act of 1965, ending his speech with his historic quotation of Martin Luther King, Jr.'s "We Shall Overcome." On March 21, Martin Luther King, Jr., and Ralph Bunche led their four-day march from Selma, Alabama, to Montgomery, where King gave a speech in the old Confederate capital on March 25. That night, a group of Ku Klux Klan members shot and killed Mrs. Liuzzo, who was driving marchers from Montgomery back to Selma. Within eight hours the Bureau had solved the crime. (One of the four Klansmen who killed Mrs. Liuzzo was an FBI informer.) President Johnson went on national television, with Hoover standing by his side, to announce that "our honored public servant" had captured the murderers. "I cannot express myself too strongly in praising Mr. Hoover and the men of the FBI for their prompt and expeditious performance in handling this investigation. It is in keeping with the dedicated approach that this organization has shown throughout the turbulent era of civil rights controversies." Johnson promised new legislation and renewed efforts to crush the Klan. He told the nation, "We will not be intimidated by the terrorists of the Ku Klux Klan any more than we will be intimidated by the terrorists in North Vietnam." Despite the triumph of this moment, the presence of FBI informer Gary Thomas Rowe in the murder car provoked a sharp controversy about the duty of an informer to prevent crime as well as report on it.[37]

Hoover's private comments to Johnson that same evening, however, show that he was as suspicious as ever about the civil rights movement. When LBJ asked Hoover's advice about calling Liuzzo's husband to offer his condolences, Hoover told him to have an assistant "call this man and, if the man behaves himself, the President could consider talking to him later. I stated the man himself doesn't have too good a background and the woman had indications of needle marks in her arms where she had been taking dope; that she was sitting very close to the Negro in the car; that it had the appearance of a necking party."[38]

Johnson's March 26 speech may have been his most effective act in turning the public against the Klan and racist terror. It would not have been as effective if he had not had Hoover by his side: not only because of the FBI's reputation for solving difficult cases (fully justified in this instance), but because of Hoover's own immense prestige as a symbol of law enforcement. Johnson was using the FBI for the purpose for which Theodore Roosevelt had created it, to show presidential outrage over a great moral issue and to dramatize the importance of new legislation, in this case the Voting Rights Act, signed on August 6.

For Hoover it was not the issue of racial equality that presented a moral issue in the Liuzzo case or in the murders in Philadelphia, Mississippi, the year before; it was the challenge Klan violence posed to legitimate authority, his own and that of the federal government. Hoover had always hated the Klan; in fighting it he was not so much protecting black rights as putting down a white revolt against the law and against the authority of the national government. As an old Washingtonian with a Southern orientation Hoover would also despise the Klan as a blot on the honor of the white race: The Klansmen, Hoover said, were "a group of sadistic, vicious white trash. . . . [y]ou can almost smell them where they live."[39]

As for Hoover's attitude toward black rights, they had not changed and were still paternalistic at best, mean-spiritedly racist at worst. "The colored people," he told an audience of newspaper editors in 1965, "are quite ignorant, mostly uneducated, and I doubt if they would seek an education if they had an opportunity. Many who have the right to register very seldom do register. They can proceed in due time to gain the acceptance which is necessary and rights equal to those of the white citizens of their community." He mocked the solicitude for black dignity in the new guidelines for police behavior, which he blamed on the Supreme Court: The court has "gone into the field where police officers must address them in courteous language, particularly in the case of Negroes as instead of saying 'boy, come here,' they want to be addressed as 'Mr.' "[40]

Because Hoover could not see the civil rights struggle as a moral issue, he insisted on steering a course between black protest and white backlash. He claimed that "the Federal Bureau of Investigation has been the target of both extremes in the civil rights issue and I believe this shows the FBI has followed the proper course in its handling of this most delicate issue." He denounced attempts to use the FBI to protect demonstrators: "The FBI will continue to . . . stay within the bounds of its authorized jurisdiction regardless of pressure groups which seek to use the FBI to attain their own selfish aims to the detriment of our people as a whole."[41]

To Hoover, the real significance of a black civil rights organization was still the opportunity it offered for Communist penetration and control. Even when defending the patriotism of the civil rights movement, he reminded his audience that it was suspect because the Communists wanted to dominate it so badly: "Let me emphasize that the American civil rights movement is not, and has never been, dominated by the communists—because the overwhelming majority of civil rights leaders in this country, both Negro and white, have recognized and rejected communism as a menace to the freedoms of all. But there are notable exceptions—dangerous opportunists and morally corrupt charlatans who would form an alliance with any organization, regardless of its nature, to advance their own power and prestige." Since Hoover did not specify whom he had in mind, he raised doubts about all black leaders with his vague accusations.[42]

John Doar was right in praising the Bureau's new commitment after 1964: "All of these events—the buildup of violence in Mississippi, the resurgence of the Klan, the disappearance of Schwerner, Chaney and Goodman, the competition from Sheridan's unit [Walter Sheridan led a team of nine lawyers from the Department's Criminal Division to investigate terrorism], Mr. Dulles' trip to Mississippi, the additional manpower of the new Jackson office, and Mr. Hoover's personal visit—combined to produce a magnificent change in the Bureau's performance in Mississippi." The change, however, was less than met the eye, and as for his fundamental attitudes about social change, Hoover's beliefs were the same as before.[43]

The Bureau was able to move so fast in the Viola Liuzzo case in 1965 because, as part of the upheaval that sent Hoover to Jackson, the FBI had begun to combat the Klan in a new way.

Hoover's attack on the Ku Klux Klan was the first in a series of new departures that by the end of the Johnson administration would have the FBI, in the words of a Senate committee, taking "the law into its own hands, conducting a sophisticated vigilante operation against domestic enemies," not only against Communists and Klansmen, but also against black radicals and antiwar activists. What the FBI did to combat the Klan was to go beyond investigating its members' violations of federal laws; it engaged in a program of covert operations to disrupt, discredit, and destroy the organization itself.[44]

This shift in Hoover's tactics began in June 1964, when a team of Justice Department lawyers Attorney General Robert Kennedy had sent south to study the problem of the Klan recommended using against the Klan the same techniques that had been so successful against the Communist party. Kennedy liked the idea and wrote Johnson: "Consideration should be given by the Federal Bureau of Investigation to new measures. . . . The techniques followed in the use of specially trained special assignment agents in the infiltration of Communist groups should be of value. If you approve, it might be desirable to take up with the Bureau the possibility of developing a similar effort to meet this problem."[45]

In late July 1964, the Bureau moved responsibility for the Klan and other "hate groups" from the General Investigative Division to William C. Sullivan's Domestic Intelligence Division (where it had been prior to 1958). Within a year, the Bureau had 2,000 informants in the Klan, which meant that 20 percent of the total membership was working for the Bureau. FBI informants had positions in seven of fourteen Klan groups, headed one state Klan, and even created a splinter Klan group under FBI direction. In short order, Sullivan's division was providing the Justice Department with complete intelligence on the Klan for use in the legal battle against white terror.

But Sullivan went far beyond mere intelligence gathering. He recommended to Hoover that the Bureau create a "White Hate" COINTELPRO. On September 2, 1964, Hoover sent a directive to the field announcing this new counterintelligence program for the "Disruption of Hate Groups":

> The purpose of this program is to expose, disrupt and otherwise neutralize the activities of the various Klans and hate organizations, their leadership and adherents. . . . The devious maneuvers and duplicity of these groups must be exposed . . . through the cooperation of reliable news media sources. . . . We must frustrate the effort of the groups to consolidate their forces or to recruit new or youthful adherents. . . . no opportunity should be missed to capitalize upon organizational and personal conflicts of their leadership.[46]

Hoover had precedents for the counterintelligence program against the Klan (COINTELPRO–White Hate Groups). Most obvious, of course, was the COINTELPRO that the Domestic Intelligence Division had directed against the Communist party since 1956 and the Socialist Workers party since 1961. For the first time, however, the Bureau's counterintelligence techniques of harassment and disruption were being directed against groups that did not have, even tangentially or theoretically, contact with foreign intelligence or an international revolutionary movement.

Another precedent for the new COINTELPRO, and one perhaps more relevant in its strictly domestic orientation, was Hoover's long-standing policy of launching counterattacks against his critics (Martin Luther King, Jr., would be one example). Since Hoover interpreted criticism as conspiracies designed to disrupt and neutralize the FBI ("smear campaigns," he called them), he responded in kind, using his media contacts and assets to expose and discredit the critics before they could achieve their supposedly subversive purposes.

There were powerful reasons why Hoover decided to adopt a counterintelligence approach to the Klan rather than relying on law enforcement. His experience in bringing civil rights cases before white juries in the South had been profoundly discouraging, and his greatest success in this area had come in the late twenties when he had used morals charges to discredit the head of the Klan—ample justification to believe that the indirect approach promised greater success than the direct.

Hoover's rapport with Johnson, and his antagonism toward the Justice Department, also made him prefer operations he could conduct in total independence from the department. Since the COINTELPRO operations did not have to produce criminal cases for the government to prosecute, Hoover could avoid cooperation with or interference by the department. COINTELPRO could also proceed without requiring the assistance of Southern law enforcement officers, and so the Bureau could avoid antagonizing those contacts that were so valuable in ordinary criminal investigations.

Since the Klan was violence-prone—indeed its only purpose was violence—disrupting it could be justified as a program to prevent violence that did not stifle rights of expression or assembly. Attorney General Nicholas Katzenbach, who approved of the program, explained that "the central point . . . is that some Klan members in those states, using the Klan as a vehicle, were engaged in repeated acts of criminal violence. It had nothing to do with preaching a social point of view: it had to do with proven acts of violence. The investigation by the FBI was hard, tough, and outstandingly successful. . . . I authorized them. In the same circumstances I would do so again today." Therefore Katzenbach could say, "To equate such efforts with surveillance or harassment of persons exercising constitutionally guaranteed rights is, in my view, unmitigated nonsense." The anti-Klan operation of the 1960s clearly reminded Hoover of his first campaign against the Klan in the twenties, in which his exposure of the immoral private lives of Klan leaders, through White Slave law prosecutions, had caused "red faces and the decline of the Klan."[47]

Nevertheless, the COINTELPRO–White Hate started the Bureau down a slippery path unmarked by any of the clear guidelines given it in the past by Hoover's preoccupation with the Communist party. There were those within the Bureau who traced the FBI's later difficulties to this "substantial enlargement" of the domestic Intelligence Division's responsibilities. For the first time, an American government agency was formally engaged in fighting crime, and by the due process of law, but by methods characteristic of the shadowy world of spies and counterspies.

Hoover was entering an area where he did not have clear legislative or presidential direction. Previously, he had always been forced to channel his powerful sense of outrage against his enemies through the legal process by capturing them and bringing them to trial. Now he was able to act on his feelings directly, without the discipline and restraint of legal procedures. Hoover and the Bureau were acting in an area where only their own sense of right and wrong provided direction for Bureau operations.

Hoover began the new COINTELPRO by asking his field agents to send him their suggestions for specific operations and warned that the existence of the program was not to be revealed to anyone outside the Bureau. Agents were to concentrate their efforts on the violence-prone "action groups" who used "strong-arm" tactics, and the special agents in charge (SACs) were to give these assignments to agents who had interest, initiative, and imagination. "If an enthusiastic approach is made to this new endeavor," Hoover promised, "there is no reason why the results achieved under this program will not equal or surpass our achievements in similar-type programs directed against subversives." The COINTELPRO–White Hate operations that emerged disrupted Klan meetings, sowed dissension within local Klans, circulated rumors (both true and false) about the morals of Klan leaders, supplied material on Klan activities and membership to the media, and overwhelmed Klansmen with "overt" surveillance, round-the-clock coverage by groups of agents for the purpose of irritating and inconveniencing the target.[48]

Already, and even before 1964, COINTELPRO-type techniques were being used in the Bureau's continuing program of harassment against Martin Luther King, Jr. This was being done under the provisions of the original COINTELPRO–CPUSA. On the pretext that King, still in contact with O'Dell and Levison, was Communist-controlled, and so a legitimate target for counterintelligence techniques, William Sullivan had received Hoover's approval to use "imaginative and ag-

gressive tactics" against King "to be utilized through our Counterintelligence Program—these designed to attempt to neutralize or disrupt
the party's activities in the negro field." On December 23, 1963, Sullivan chaired a nine-hour brainstorming conference in Washington that
proposed twenty-one different operations against King. He reported
to Hoover that the conference had discussed methods of gathering
"information concerning King's personal activities . . . in order that
we may consider using this information at an opportune time in a
counterintelligence move to discredit him." An April letter from
Hoover to his SACs used these very words to instruct agents not only
to continue their efforts against King, but also to consider using
their media contacts against him.[49]

Sullivan and Hoover were now working in tandem. Sullivan, frantic
to prove his reliability, had programmed the machinery of the Domestic Intelligence Division to supply Hoover with information about
three types of activities sure to infuriate the director: criticism of
Hoover and the FBI, contacts with Communists (still Levison and
O'Dell), and sexual behavior unbecoming a minister and married man.
Hoover's frustration at his lack of success in using this material to
persuade the administration, the civil rights movement, or the media
to destroy King made him all the more grateful to the one man who
would take direct action: William C. Sullivan himself. Not only was
Sullivan ingratiating himself with Hoover when he harassed King;
he was also giving Hoover the best possible proof that he, Sullivan,
believed in the truth and significance of the material the Domestic
Intelligence Division was producing. The conspiracy against King was
a glue creating an unhealthy bond between Hoover and Sullivan.

A week after Sullivan's December conference, *Time* magazine
named King its Man of the Year for 1963. Hoover was outraged:
"They had to dig deep in the garbage to come up with this one."
Sullivan had the answer: The Bureau would groom a successor to
King. Once the Bureau had managed to persuade the country that
King was "a fraud, demagogue and moral scoundrel," Sullivan wrote
Hoover, "confusion will reign, particularly among the Negro people."
Therefore, the Bureau should build up another black leader (they
chose New York attorney Samuel R. Pierce, Jr.) to take King's place.
Hoover approved, and added, "I am glad to see that 'light' has finally,
though dismally delayed, come to the Domestic Intelligence Division.
I struggled for months to get over the fact that the communists were
taking over the racial movement, but our experts here couldn't or
wouldn't see it." Sullivan knew it was not enough merely to agree

with Hoover. His actions had to prove he really believed what he was saying.[50]

Throughout 1964, Hoover and Sullivan urged their agents to exploit every opportunity to discredit King and the SCLC. Since the pretext for the operation against King was his contact with Communists, the Bureau tried to strengthen its case by redefining "Communist": "[I]t should be interpreted in its broadest sense as including persons not only adhering to the principles of the CPUSA itself, but also to such splinter and offshoot groups as the Socialist Workers Party, Progressive Labor and the like." Sullivan's Domestic Intelligence Division set up a special unit in the Internal Security section to handle "the over-all problem of communist penetration within the racial movement," based on Hoover's theory that the proper approach to the civil rights movement was to watch it as a target for Communist subversion.[51]

Microphone surveillance of King's hotel rooms produced what the Bureau called "entertainment," sounds of King partying, drinking, and engaging in sexual relations. Now Hoover had another reason for hating King: "King is a 'tom cat,' " he told his aides, "with obsessive degenerate sexual urges." One tape had King in a hilarious mood describing the sexual accomplishments of his friends, mixing sexual and religious allusions, and telling a joke about the sex life of John F. Kennedy that involved Mrs. Kennedy and the presidential funeral. Convinced that this would persuade President Johnson and Attorney General Robert Kennedy that King was "one of the most reprehensible . . . individuals on the American scene today," Hoover gave copies of the report to Kennedy and the president.[52]

In March 1964, the conflict between Hoover and King finally reached the public when Hoover's January testimony before the House Appropriations Committee was released. The press reported that Hoover had told the committee, chaired by Congressman Howard Smith of Virginia, a segregationist, that "Communist influence does exist in the Negro movement." King, concerned that Hoover's remarks provided support for "the salacious claims of southern racists and the extreme right-wing elements," challenged the Bureau to come forward with hard evidence. King also said, "I think it was very unfortunate that such a great man as Mr. Hoover allowed himself to aid and abet the racists and the rightists in our nation by alleging that you have Communist infiltration in the movement."[53]

The Bureau's campaign to destroy King's reputation continued throughout 1964. Derogatory reports on King went to the White

House, to universities planning to award King honorary degrees, and to religious organizations. When King received an appointment to meet with the pope, the Bureau contacted New York's Cardinal Spellman (a close ally of Hoover's) to see if he could "ensure that the Pope is not placed in an embarrassing position through any contact with King." When the pope met with King anyway, Hoover found the meeting "astounding," and said, "I am amazed that the Pope gave an audience to such a [censored]."[54]

Despite Hoover's efforts, King's prestige mounted in this country and abroad. Hoover thought the information he had collected should have been enough to destroy a dozen Kings, and yet he could not persuade anyone in power to use it. When King was chosen for the Nobel Peace Prize on October 14, 1964, the Bureau gave briefings on King to Ralph Bunche, Adlai Stevenson, Vice President Hubert Humphrey, Nelson Rockefeller, and the American ambassadors to England and Sweden—anyone who might come into contact with him. Hoover sent Humphrey a copy of the Bureau's catalog of smears ("Martin Luther King, Jr.: His Personal Conduct") along with a personal letter. The Nobel Prize seemed to drive Hoover into a frenzy. He wrote on one memo that King should have gotten the "top alley cat" prize instead.

Hoover had always been able to find influential allies to spearhead his attacks on his enemies. Now the establishment had too much invested in King as a symbol of nonviolent social change to indulge Hoover, whose frustration at his inability to destroy King swelled out of all proportion to King's real or supposed offenses. The civil rights leader came to represent all the cultural changes that had enraged Hoover during the sixties, and his failure to "neutralize" King reminded him of his inability to halt the nation's apostasy from the values of Seward Square. Frustrated beyond endurance, Hoover finally made his own public attack on King.

The venue was a rare press conference held on November 18, 1964, for a group of women reporters led by veteran journalist Sarah McLendon, at which Hoover recited all his complaints against King. He was particularly bitter about King's charge that the Bureau was insensitive to blacks because of its large proportion of Southern-born agents in the South, while he said actually 70 percent were Northerners. He capped his diatribe with the highly quotable claim that King was "the most notorious liar" and "one of the lowest characters in the country." Hoover's public relations advisor, Assistant to the Director Cartha DeLoach, seated next to Hoover, sensed a disaster in the making. He immediately passed a note to Hoover asking him to take the "liar" remark off the record. Hoover ignored the request. DeLoach passed him another note, and this one too was ignored. Finally, after a third note, Hoover told the reporters, "DeLoach tells me I should keep these statements concerning King off the record but that's none of his business. I made it for the record and you can use it for the record."[55]

DeLoach believed the King press conference marked the beginning of the end of Hoover's unassailable public image, although the panic Hoover's blast touched off within the civil rights movement seemed proof of the director's political strength. From another perspective, however, the incident was a measure of the weakness of his old anti-Communist right-wing coalition. Where before Hoover would have been able to galvanize congressional committees and departmental security officers to take action against King, now he could only let loose his charges in the hope that they would be heard by alienated bands of right-wing radicals in the hinterlands, for whom Hoover's word was still gospel. Within the government and the national media, Hoover's lack of decorum and gracelessness did more to discredit him than to taint King. He had been able to appeal directly to the most powerful institutions in American society during the fifties, but now more and more, he was having to seek allies who were not part of the American mainstream.[56]

Hoover's "notorious liar" attack made headlines across the country. King released a statement suggesting that Hoover had "faltered under the awesome burden, complexities and responsibilities of his office." He wrote Hoover that "I was appalled and surprised at your reported statement maligning my integrity. What motivated such an irresponsible accusation is a mystery to me," and he demanded a meeting.[57]

Hoover's advisors counseled him against seeing King, and at first he agreed with them, saying, "O.K. But I can't understand why we are unable to get the true facts before the public. We can't even get our accomplishments published. We are never taking the aggressive but [the] . . . lies [by King] remain unanswered." William Sullivan took this outburst as a command to retaliate, and he made a composite tape of King's sexual activities, and composed a letter to accompany it:[58]

King, look into your heart. You know, you are a complete fraud and a greater liability to all of us Negroes. White people in this country have enough frauds of their own but I am sure they don't have one at this time that is any where near your equal. You are no clergyman and you know it. I repeat that you are a colossal fraud and an evil, vicious one at that. . . .

King, like all frauds your end is approaching. You could have been our greatest leader. . . . But you are done. Your honorary degrees, your Nobel Prize (what a grim farce) and other awards will not save you. King, I repeat you are done. . . .

The American public, the church organizations that have been helping—Protestants, Catholics and Jews will know you for what you are— an evil beast. So will others who have backed you. You are done.

King, there is only one thing left for you to do. You know what it is. You have just 34 days in which to do (this exact number has been selected for a specific reason, it has definite practical significance). You are done. There is but one way out for you. You better take it before your filthy fraudulent self is bared to the nation."[59]

Sullivan gave the tapes and the note to a trusted agent who carried them to Miami and put them in the mail to King. When the package arrived in Atlanta, however, it was set aside and not opened until January 5, after King returned from Sweden and the Nobel Prize ceremony.

Meanwhile, according to Nicholas Katzenbach, the FBI was going about Washington offering to play the tapes for government officials and reporters. It so disturbed *Newsweek*'s Ben Bradlee that he told Burke Marshall and Katzenbach about it, and they flew to Texas to tell the president what Hoover was up to. Johnson seems to have interpreted all this as a political brawl between an old friend, Hoover, and a political ally of a Johnson enemy (King and Robert Kennedy were forever linked in the public mind). Far from putting a stop to Hoover's activities, Johnson passed word to him to be careful, that Bradlee could not be trusted.[60]

King was aware of what the FBI was doing; when Hoover spoke darkly about "moral laxness" in the civil rights movement in a speech on November 24 at Chicago's Loyola University, King released a statement that he wanted to meet Hoover to end the fight in order to "get on with the larger job of civil rights and law enforcement."

This time Hoover agreed to see King, and on December 1, 1964, they met in Hoover's Washington offices together with DeLoach and King's SCLC associates, Ralph Abernathy, Andrew Young, and Walter Fauntroy. The two sides disagreed afterward on what had transpired at the meeting: DeLoach claimed King spent the fifty-five minutes of the meeting effusively praising the director and retracting any criticism of the Bureau, while Andrew Young recalled the meeting as a brief and formal exchange of greetings followed by a fifty-five-minute monologue by Hoover on the accomplishments of the FBI. According to Young, Hoover was "disarming" and congratulated King on winning the Nobel Prize. For his part, Hoover bragged that he had lectured to King, and claimed that "I never addressed him as Reverend or Doctor." After the meeting the public aspect of the controversy died down, and Andrew Young said the arrest of the murderers of the three civil rights workers in Philadelphia, Mississippi, reassured King and his aides that the FBI really was enforcing the law against terror.[61]

After his meeting with Hoover, King traveled to Stockholm to receive his Nobel Prize. It was not until January 5, 1965, after he returned, that he and his aides finally listened to Sullivan's tape. They had no doubts that the tape and the note came from the FBI, especially since none of their other enemies had the technical ability to produce them. Some of King's friends thought the Bureau had been trying to blackmail King into declining the Nobel Prize. Others thought the purpose was to goad King's wife into divorcing him. A third theory was that the plan was to put the thought of suicide in King's mind. Whatever the idea had been, Hoover's FBI was using the dirty tricks it had perfected against the Communist party and the Ku Klux Klan against King. Unable to persuade the government or the public of the danger posed by King, and made bold by his close relationship with Johnson, Hoover was dispensing with any of the formal legal justifications he had always insisted on before committing the FBI to action. The first COINTELPROs had maintained a tenuous hold on legal jurisdiction by assuming the outlaw status of the Communist party and Socialist Workers Party and the intrinsic violence of the Klan. Now he was taking it upon himself to identify and "neutralize" threats to the American way of life.

Hoover's battle with Martin Luther King, Jr., while somewhat embarrassing to Johnson, probably did not do LBJ much political harm. Polls showed that most Americans backed Hoover against King (50 percent backed Hoover, 16 percent King in February 1965). Bearing in mind that King's backers had no alternative except to support Johnson, Hoover's rhetoric, inflammatory as it was, might actually have helped Johnson by reassuring conservative whites alienated by the civil rights movement. By another measure, however, as reflected in letters to the White House on the affair, public opinion ran against Hoover, 518 to 234.[62]

When Martin Luther King, Jr., was assassinated on April 14, 1968,

the manhunt for his killer provided a strange incident in which Hoover
managed to show his disdain for both King and Robert Kennedy.
At first, Hoover resisted having the Bureau get involved on grounds
that it was not a federal offense, but he was overruled by Ramsey
Clark. Despite his initial reluctance, the hunt became one of the biggest
in Bureau history, with 3,075 agents on the case. The FBI finally
located the murderer, James Earl Ray, in London on the day of Robert
Kennedy's funeral (Kennedy had been killed on June 5, 1968). The
announcement of the arrest was delayed several hours so it would
come out during the funeral service. DeLoach told Ramsey Clark
he had tried to hold up the announcement, but that it had not been
possible. When Clark learned the Bureau announcement had been
typed hours before the funeral, he dismissed DeLoach as his liaison.
Clark said that he was never able to understand why the Bureau
had gone through this charade: "I mean, it's too bizarre for me to
understand, but for some reason they decided they'd remind everybody
the FBI was still on the job about that time of day and they did."
Hoover was actually reminding the one man who counted, Lyndon
Johnson, that he was on the job, and that the FBI had supported
Johnson to the end and beyond in his rivalry with Robert Kennedy.[63]

Hoover's next step outside the law was to apply the disruptive tactics
of COINTELPRO to an attack on black radicalism. The decision to
launch a counterintelligence attack on the "black nationalist" movement came after two years of requests from Johnson for action against
black rioters. Ever since the first black ghetto riots in the summer
of 1964, Lyndon Johnson had been pressing Hoover for intelligence
on urban disorders so he could plan his responses and acquire proof
that the riots were of course, the result of a plot, hopefully directed
by Communists. Johnson's aim of course, was to use this information
to discredit the rioters.

As each summer's riots grew progressively worse after those of
1964 (Watts in August 1965, followed by those in Newark, Chicago,
Cleveland, Brooklyn, Omaha, Baltimore, San Francisco, and Jackson-
ville, and then the cataclysmic Detroit riots of July 1967), Johnson
grew more importunate in his pleas for information and help from
the Bureau. Hoover was under intense pressure to produce large quanti-
ties of up-to-the-minute intelligence, and the FBI had to develop an
extensive intelligence network in order to give advance warning to
both national and local officials.

While Hoover denounced the rioters and their leaders, and talked

about the Communist role in the riots, he never went as far as those
who saw the riots as part of a centrally controlled plot with some
mastermind in charge. After the first group of riots (Harlem, Brooklyn, Newark, Chicago, Philadelphia), Hoover reported to Johnson that
there was no systematic planning or organization behind them; but
in some cases, he said, there were people involved with a history of
Communist affiliation.[64]

Hoover was never able to find the conspiracy that LBJ wanted.
Nevertheless, as Hoover's reports became more voluminous, they contributed to Johnson's sense that he was besieged in hostile territory,
with black guerrillas controlling the cities. Hoover's description of
his visit to the White House on July 25, 1967, during the Detroit
riots, shows the sense of anxiety that enveloped the capital. As the
night wore on, Hoover remembered, "tickers came in indicating that
riots had broken out in Pontiac, Michigan; in Michigan City; in Flint,
Michigan; in Cambridge, Maryland; in Philadelphia; in Rochester;
and in Harlem, New York City, among the Puerto Ricans. The President stated that he had been of the opinion that there was a concerted
action and a pattern about all of these riots and he wanted me to
have prepared immediately a memorandum for him giving evidence
in depth as to the riots which have occurred and as to any evidence
which would indicate that there has been concerted action to bring
about these riots. . . ."

Hoover could give the president little assurance that an investigation would provide any proof of conspiracy:

> I told the President . . . there has not been any concerted action in
> the riots which have occurred. . . . Practically all of the riots have been
> triggered by some individual incident in the various communities, such
> as the arrest of a Negro for violation of some law, and immediately
> following such an arrest, the riot would break out. . . . So far as we
> have been able to ascertain, there had been no outsiders come into the
> various communities at the beginning to initiate these riots, but it was
> a fact that after the riot was in full force, persons from another jurisdiction
> came into the communities to participate in the riots. In so far as the
> communists were concerned, we had no information indicating that the
> communists initiated the riots, but they, of course, joined in after they
> had once started.[65]

What Hoover *could* do was to provide Johnson with a cast of
villains on whom to focus national resentment. The best case could
be made against H. Rap Brown of the Student Non-Violent Coordinating Committee (SNCC), whom the FBI arrested on charges of instigating a riot in Cambridge, Maryland. Hoover could also serve up more

rhetoric against King, charging him with encouraging disrespect for the law. When Hoover testified before the Kerner Commission in late July 1967, he told DeLoach he was unhappy with the "superficial generalities" the Bureau's writers had given him about the riots. He wanted "more vicious" quotes, "really tough ones," and he wanted a quote by King "about riots in Chicago; that it was something healthy and desirable to have hate come to the surface; that things like that would tie him down."[66]

The riots of 1967 and Johnson's pleas for help persuaded Hoover and Sullivan that the time had come for the Bureau to expand its operations against the black power movement. In September 1967, Attorney General Ramsey Clark told Hoover to "use the maximum resources, investigative and intelligence, to collect and report all facts bearing upon the question as whether there has been or is a scheme or conspiracy by any group of whatever size, effectiveness or affiliation, to plan, promote, or aggravate riot activity." Hoover responded in October of that year with a program for "the development of ghetto-type racial informants." Over the next year the Bureau developed a network of over 4,000 contacts in its Ghetto Informant Program, which supplied the Bureau and the White House with a steady stream of information about activities and sentiments in America's black communities.[67]

Hoover did not limit his response to the racial disorders of the late sixties to intelligence-gathering. The harassment of King since 1963 provided Sullivan and Hoover with an organizational base from which to expand COINTELPRO into the civil rights movement. In mid-1967, the Domestic Intelligence Division had one COIN-TELPRO (within the CPUSA rubric) harassing King, the nation's foremost black leader (under the pretext of his links to Communists), while it had another COINTELPRO (White Hate) attacking the Klan without having to prove any communist connection. It was therefore a small step to create a COINTELPRO specifically aimed at the radical arm of the civil rights movement. Sullivan had proven to Hoover that he could orchestrate these campaigns without getting caught, and he could point to real accomplishments in the COINTELPROs against the Communists and the Klan, and the attacks on King, which, if they had not noticeably hurt the leader, had certainly not helped him either. They had gratified Hoover without embarrassing him.[68]

White America was now scared out of its wits by urban riots and the rhetoric of Black Power—Stokely Carmichael: "It's time we stand up and take over. Take over. Move on over or we'll move on over you"; and H. Rap Brown: "Violence is as American as apple pie!" The FBI was accustomed to playing an active role in times of crisis, and this was to be no exception. However, instead of the high profile FBI campaigns of the past, on August 25, 1967, Hoover approved Sullivan's proposal for a COINTELPRO directed against "black nationalist, hate-type organizations."

Hoover's announcement of the new COINTELPRO adopted the form and even the very words of his authorization for the Klan COINTELPRO. The field was advised to "ensure the targeted group is disrupted, ridiculed, or discredited through the publicity and not merely publicized. Consideration should be given to techniques to preclude violence-prone or rabble-rouser leaders of these hate groups from spreading their philosophy publicly or through various mass communication media." Hoover's instructions made it clear that the goal was to discredit, not prosecute, black militants. He told his agents that "many individuals currently active in black nationalist organizations have backgrounds of immorality, subversive activity, and criminal records," so he ordered them to collect such information whenever possible for use in counterintelligence operations. Soon the Bureau's harassment of King and the Southern Christian Leadership Conference was shifted to the new program—SCLC from the outset, King in February 1968.[69]

In the spring of 1968, Hoover announced to his agents that "for maximum effectiveness . . . and to prevent wasted effort," he was setting "long-range goals" for the Black Nationalist COINTELPRO.

1. Prevent the coalition of militant black nationalist groups. In unity there is strength; a truism that is no less valid for all its triteness. An effective coalition of black nationalist groups might be the first step toward a real "Mau Mau" in America, the beginning of a true black revolution.
2. Prevent the rise of a "messiah" who could unify and electrify the militant black nationalist movement. Malcolm X might have been such a "messiah"; he is the martyr of this movement today. Martin Luther King, Stokely Carmichael, and Elijah Muhammed [sic] all aspire to this position. Elijah Muhammed is less of a threat because of his age. King could be a very real contender . . . should he abandon his supposed "obedience" to "white liberal doctrines." Carmichael has the necessary charisma to be a real threat in this way.

Besides preventing violence, Hoover told his agents that COINTELPRO operations should "prevent militant black nationalist groups and leaders from gaining respectability," and to prevent the long-range growth of black nationalist organizations, especially among black youth.[70]

The Bureau launched 360 disruptive operations under the rubric of COINTELPRO–Black Nationalist Hate Groups: rumors to the media about Elijah Muhammad's sexual conduct, alerting the IRS to possible tax fraud by black organizations, and planting stories that portrayed the 1968 Poor People's March on Washington as dominated by violence-prone radicals. In November 1968, COINTELPRO–Black Hate concentrated its attention on the Black Panther party, a black radical organization led by Bobby Seale, Fred Hampton, and Eldridge Cleaver that had adopted some of the trappings of the counterinsurgency Green Berets. The Bureau deliberately tried to incite confrontations between this group and its militant rivals within the black radical movement. It has been impossible to prove conclusively that the Bureau was responsible for specific acts of violence, but a Senate investigative committee concluded that "the chief investigative branch of the Federal Government, which was charged by law with investigating crimes and preventing criminal conduct, itself engaged in lawless tactics and responded to deep-seated social problems by fomenting violence and unrest."[71]

By the end of Lyndon Johnson's administration, the Bureau was carrying on a highly publicized war against the Ku Klux Klan and a clandestine war against black radicalism. In the course of expanding COINTELPRO, Hoover had become increasingly willing to overlook the legal sanctions required for his actions. In the past, Hoover had been able to wage his wars in the open, supported by grass-roots approval and powerful political allies. He had been able to build his defense of the values of Seward Square around the arrest and prosecution of outcasts provably guilty of criminal (or deportable) offenses. Now there was no longer a clear consensus on the unassailability of the middle-class values Hoover had always upheld. The cement of anticommunism no longer held together the coalition of his allies (like HUAC and the SIS) who had fought his fights for him in the past. Now he could no longer count on the support of the Justice Department when he stumped for repression of anyone brash enough to challenge the status quo.

Once Hoover had embarked on this secret course, it would be difficult for him to reverse direction. Having encouraged Sullivan to make counterintelligence the basis of Bureau policy, Hoover and Sullivan were now both implicated, and for either to retreat might have raised doubts about the other's loyalty and reliability, and so Hoover's fall from grace had begun to gather momentum.

The final stage in Hoover's expansion of counterintelligence techniques was his covert war against the New Left. In launching this COINTEL-PRO, Hoover finally abandoned the guideline that had provided direction to his antisubversive campaigns since 1919: that to qualify for the full attentions of the FBI there had to be some connection, no matter how tenuous, between the American target and the international revolutionary movement. Hoover continued to study the Old Left's attempts to forge an alliance with the New Left (perhaps he hoped as much as the Old Communists that the effort would succeed; it would have made his job so much easier), but he admitted that what he was now attacking was "a new style in conspiracy—conspiracy that is extremely subtle and devious and hence difficult to understand . . . a conspiracy reflected by questionable moods and attitudes, by unrestrained individualism, by nonconformism in dress and speech, even by obscene language, rather than by formal membership in specific organizations."[72]

Beginning with the Bay of Tonkin Resolution on August 4, 1964, the bombing of North Vietnam in February 1965, and the dispatch of the first combat troops to Vietnam on March 3, 1965, the opposition to Lyndon Johnson's Asian policy swelled into a vast antiwar movement. To the president it seemed the chief obstacle to winning the war. To Hoover the peace movement was another arrogant assault on America's ideals and dignity by that wrong-thinking and immoral segment of youth whose growth he had been watching nervously since 1960. From the first peace demonstrations in early 1965, Hoover worked to provide Johnson with advance information on antiwar demonstrations, to discredit the antiwar movement as Communist-inspired and anti-American, and, secretly, to disrupt it as he had the Klan and the Black Power movement.

On April 27, 1965, presidential advisor McGeorge Bundy asked Hoover for any information he might have on the Communist role in the antiwar demonstrations. The next day, the director met with Johnson at the White House. Johnson told Hoover

> that he was quite concerned over the anti-Vietnam situation that has developed in this country and he appreciated particularly the material that we sent him yesterday containing clippings from various columnists in the country who had attributed the agitation in this country to the

communists as there was no doubt in his mind but that they were behind the disturbances that have already occurred. [The CIA had] stated that their intelligence showed that the Chinese and North Vietnamese believe that by intensifying the agitation in this country, particularly on the college campus levels, it would so confuse and divide the Americans that our troops in South Vietnam would have to be withdrawn in order to preserve order here and it would enable North Vietnam to move in at once.[73]

Hoover realized that he could not possibly provide Johnson with proof that a foreign conspiracy was responsible for the antiwar movement any more than he had been able to show a conspiracy as the cause of the ghetto riots. He would do what he could, however, and what he could do was give Johnson the Students for a Democratic Society as a scapegoat. When he returned to the Bureau, Hoover ordered his aides to prepare a memo for Johnson

> containing what we know about the Students for a Democratic Society. While I realize we may not be able to technically state that it is an actual communist organization, certainly we do know there are communists in it. . . . What I want to get to the President is the background with emphasis upon the communist influence therein so that he will know exactly what the picture is. . . . I believe we should intensify through all field offices the instructions to endeavor to penetrate the Students for a Democratic Society so that we will have proper informant coverage similar to what we have in the Ku Klux Klan and the Communist Party itself."[74]

The Students for a Democratic Society, or SDS, would be the surrogate for the Communist party in Hoover's attack on the antiwar radical movement. He could not prove that SDS was allied to international communism; the best he could do was endlessly quote one statement by Communist party leader Gus Hall to the effect that the SDS was an organization that the Party had "going for us." (Hoover made it his policy never to mention SDS without the Gus Hall tag line.) The rapid growth of SDS (from 10,000 in October 1965 to 80,000 in November 1968) and its militant rhetoric made it a provocative target for Hoover's attacks on the antiwar movement. By coincidence, it was just about the size the Communist party had been when Hoover attacked it in 1919 and 1947.[75]

Hoover despised SDS's political beliefs, of course, but he also disliked that "its members dress in beatnik style," which he interpreted as a gesture of contempt for authority. The New Left, Hoover told parents, had "unloosed disrespect for the law, contempt for our institutions of free government, and disdain for spiritual and moral values." It was a "new-style subversion that is erupting in civil disobedience and encouraging young people to mock the law. If the infection continues to spread, the foundations of our republic will be seriously jeopardized." He called the DuBois Club, a Communist-backed campus front, "new blood for the vampire of international communism," and said that it worked "together with other so-called 'New Left' organizations such as the Students for a Democratic Society . . . in furtherance of the aims and objectives of the Communist Party throughout the nation."[76]

Hoover's barrage of FBI reports about the Communist role in the antiwar movement reinforced President Johnson's tendency to reject antiwar protest as Communist-inspired. Although a later Senate committee thought it was "impossible to measure the larger impact on the fortunes of the nation from this distorted perception at the very highest policymaking level," there is some independent testimony on the effect of Hoover's reports. Inside the White House, according to Eric Goldman, Johnson "extolled the FBI and the CIA: they kept him informed about what was 'really going on.' It was the Russians who stirred up the whole agitation for a suspension of the bombing of North Vietnam. . . . The Russians were in constant touch with anti-war senators—and he named names. . . . 'The Russians think up things for the senators to say. I often know before they do what their speeches are going to say.' "[77]

Hoover's relentless warnings about Communist influence in the peace movement—in January 1966 he said the Party had an "ever-increasing role in generating opposition to the United States position in Vietnam"—were certainly intended to raise doubts in the public mind about the patriotism of the antiwar protesters. In his 1967 appearance before the House Appropriations Committee, Hoover said that "I do not believe that everybody who is opposed to the foreign policy in Vietnam is necessarily a Communist. That, of course, would be ridiculous as a charge, but there are many gullible people who are against the policy in Vietnam as a result of the propaganda put out by some college professors who are naive and some students lacking in maturity and objectivity who are constantly agitating and carrying on demonstrations in some of our largest universities."[78]

Because Hoover was not able to provide Johnson with proof that the demonstrations were Communist-dominated and foreign-backed, LBJ ordered the CIA to search for alien influence in the antiwar movement. In 1966, the FBI and the CIA negotiated an informal agreement to share the fruits of each other's investigations. The CIA search for the foreign link was called Operation Chaos and lasted from 1966 until 1974. Two years later, in 1968, the army formally established a domestic intelligence section for the same purpose.[79]

Besides keeping his eye on the student protesters, Hoover was asked by Johnson, in March 1966, to "constantly keep abreast" of contacts between foreign officials and "Senators and Congressmen and any citizen of a prominent nature." In 1967, Hoover provided the White House with information on speeches by seven antiwar senators. Also responding to pressure from LBJ, Ramsey Clark, in December 1967, set up an Interdivisional Information Unit, headed by Cartha DeLoach, to coordinate the flood of information on the antiwar movement. Later renamed the Interdivisional Intelligence Unit, in 1971 this was reorganized as the Intelligence Evaluation Committee with Hoover in charge.[80]

Until 1968, Hoover's surveillance of the antiwar movement was to provide the government with advance warning of demonstrations. This in itself was intrusive and chilling, but after 1968 Hoover went on the offensive as an active participant in an effort to disrupt and discredit opposition to the war.

As the number of campus demonstrations increased (400 in the 1966–1967 school year, 3,400 in 1967–1968), the Bureau intensified its surveillance. The takeover of Columbia University in the spring of 1968 by SDS-led antiwar students provoked Sullivan and Hoover to take more serious action against campus radicalism. In part, this was a response to pressure on the Bureau from above. An FBI official who had a role in formulating the COINTELPRO–New Left said the program was a response to "a tremendous amount of pressure from the White House" to do something about the "overall problem" of the "thousands of bombings, the arsons, the disruption, the disorder. Our academic communities were being totally disrupted, and I think that a vast majority of American people were subjecting the representatives of Congress and . . . the White House staff and other people in Government to a great deal of pressure, as to why these things were taking place and why something wasn't being done."[81]

The Bureau retained an institutional memory of how Communist cells had developed on college campuses in the thirties, and of the struggle to remove Party members from government posts in the forties. Sullivan's top deputy said, "I did not want to see a repetition of that sort of circumstances come about." As it had in 1919 and 1947, the Bureau was also hoping that Congress, perhaps in response to Bureau reports, would arm the FBI with "new types of legislation" it could use against the radical movement.[82]

The most important reason for the COINTELPRO against the New Left was Hoover's personal outrage at the campus rebellion against authority: the authority of the president, of college deans, and, not incidentally, his own. In urging Hoover to create a COINTELPRO against the New Left, the Domestic Intelligence Division told him that "the New Left has on many occasions viciously and scurrilously attacked the Director and the Bureau in an attempt to hamper our investigation of it and to drive us off the college campuses."[83]

Hoover justified the Bureau's newest COINTELPRO to his agents simply as a defense of the social order not limited to the enforcement of specific statutes. "The most recent outbreak of violence on college campuses represents a direct challenge to law and order and a substantial threat to the stability of society in general," he wrote his men. "The Bureau has an urgent and pressing responsibility to keep the intelligence community informed of plans of new left groups and student activists to engage in acts of lawlessness."[84]

The Bureau's definition of its new target was broad and all-inclusive: The New Left was "a subversive force" dedicated to destroying "our traditional values." It had "no definable ideology," but had "strong Marxist, existentialist, nihilist and anarchist overtones." The vagueness of this definition, according to the Senate committee that investigated COINTELPRO, resulted in targeting almost every antiwar group, and spread to students demonstrating against anything.[85]

Hoover's campaign against the New Left stripped away any pretext of seeking to prosecute crimes or prevent violence. Its purpose was, purely and simply, to combat those political opinions that the director found obnoxious by discrediting the people who held them. A directive dated May 23, 1968, informed SACs that the purposes of the new COINTELPRO were to "counter wide-spread charges of police brutality that invariably arise following student-police encounters"; to collect evidence on the "scurrilous and depraved nature of many of the characters, activities, habits, and living conditions representative of New left adherents"; to "show the value of college administrators and school officials taking a firm stand"; and to expose "whether and to what extent faculty members rendered aid and encouragement" to the antiwar movement. "Every avenue of possible embarrassment must be vigorously and enthusiastically explored. It cannot be expected that information of this type will be easily obtained, and an imaginative approach by your personnel is imperative to its success." In July he suggested that anonymous letters about students' behavior be sent to parents, neighbors, and employers, and that agents should also send to parents articles from student newspapers showing the "depravity" of the New Left ("use of narcotics and free sex").[86]

Between 1968 and 1971 (when the COINTELPROs were terminated), there were 291 COINTELPRO operations directed against the New Left, the majority of them aimed at keeping individuals from speaking out against the war; others manufactured disinformation to disrupt antiwar organizations and demonstrators. As the Bureau departed from the emergency detention law as rationale for its lists of "dangerous" individuals, the lists the Bureau used to classify targets for covert action became so large the numbers got out of hand. First there was the Rabble Rouser Index in August 1967, then the Agitator Index, then, in January 1968, the Key Activist Index. All were justified as modifications of the old Security Index. There was even a Key Activist photo album for ready reference.[87]

The Bureau's operations against the New Left were ingenious and imaginative, though ultimately futile and not a little pathetic: A field office drafted and sent a complaint (with a fictitious signature) to *Life* magazine about a favorable review it published of Paul Krassner's *Realist* magazine, stating that the periodical was obscene and the editor a "nut." Students for a Democratic Society was the target of rumors that it was racist; in so doing, the Bureau hoped to stir up conflicts between SDS and black nationalist organizations. The Bureau tried to discredit Antioch College, whose students were notably militant, by attempting to prove Antioch's graduates were poorly prepared for professional careers. (The idea was dropped when the Bureau's study showed Antioch's alumni actually did quite well.) Agents sent a copy of *Screw* magazine (with a cover letter from "a concerned student") to a member of the New Jersey State Senate's Education Committee, complaining that it had been sold at Rutgers by " 'hippie' types in unkempt clothes, with wild beards [and] shoulder length hair." Agents spread reports of communal living in the New Left, and distributed scurrilous verses about radicals' affection "for grass and Jewish ass."[88]

The COINTELPRO–New Left permitted Hoover to strike out at those things he had opposed since his earliest days. He was just as offended by the personalities, actions, and beliefs of black radicals and the New Left as he had been by the alien Communists of 1919 or the Communist party of the cold war years. Yet he had no legal weapons to use against them as he had before. In 1919, he had used the quasi-legal machinery of the deportation acts to disrupt the radical movement—and it had worked. Then, in 1964, he had—with the encouragement of his superiors—used extra-legal techniques of harassment to disrupt the Klan. Now he had a president he admired and respected pleading with him for help against the black activists and antiwar protesters who were tearing his administration apart. Under other circumstances, Hoover might simply have redoubled his efforts to sway public opinion by speaking and writing, but William Sullivan, whose secret techniques had been so successful against the Party or the Klan, gave him a more satisfying way of expressing his outrage against the sixties' assaults on traditional values.[89]

Hoover's final COINTELPRO had committed the FBI to battle with the vast rebellion of draft-age America who were against a war that, by 1968, had sent a million Americans into combat on the other side of the globe. There is something quixotic in the spectacle of the seventy-three-year-old Hoover (in 1968), with 6,590 agents at his command, trying to turn back a grass-roots movement that at its peak could collect crowds of hundreds of thousands. Only confidence bred of Hoover's earlier successes against the Old Left and the Klan, fanned to a fever pitch by William Sullivan's enthusiasm, could have encouraged him to embark on such a venture, so reckless, so irresponsible, and finally, so hopeless.

Hoover probably never felt as much affection for anyone outside his family (excepting always Tolson) as he did for Lyndon Johnson. The most consistent element in Hoover's actions during the late sixties was his loyalty to the president. When Johnson withdrew from the 1968 presidential campaign on March 31, 1968, out of a sense of the overwhelming failure of his political leadership (and out of a perverse desire to punish the nation that had withheld its love from him), Hoover wrote him:

My Dear Mr. President:

I wanted to send you this personal note to let you know of the deep feeling of sorrow which overcame me last night when I heard you announce your decision to retire from office next January. No one can question that you and your family deserve the opportunity to spend more time together and to enjoy some of the pleasures which have been denied during a brilliant career of public service.

Nonetheless, the Nation can ill-afford to lose so devoted and gifted a leader. The personal sadness which I feel is intensified not only by our long years of association and personal friendship, but also by my knowledge of the tremendous loss your retirement will be to the people of the United States.[90]

During the bleak last year of Johnson's administration, Hoover seemed to be working hard to keep up his own morale and that of his superiors. He told Ramsey Clark he did "not favor the view that the country is depraved and all that. . . . I think we have a great block of fine people in this country; that there may be some depraved citizens, but it is not a depraved society." He complained of the tendency "to debunk our Patriots in history. . . . It was that sort of thing that I thought drove President Johnson from running for a second term." Perhaps he was thinking at that moment of the scourging he himself had been getting from the press.[91]

At Ramsey Clark's urging, Hoover wrote an editorial for the August 1968 issue of *FBI Law Enforcement Bulletin* in which he repeated that "America is NOT a sick society. . . . Too much attention is given to various dissident elements . . . [that] are complaining about conditions which they helped to create. Now, they want our whole society to plead guilty to mass ineptness." To Hoover, the protesters were not part of the real America, "the hard-working, tax-paying, law-abiding people of this country. . . . It is wrong to malign and accuse this vast group every time a crisis develops."[92]

Tolson's declining health was now a professional as well as a personal hardship for Hoover. Strokes in 1966 and 1967 kept Tolson from walking or reading except with great difficulty. His customary position a pace behind Hoover when they walked to work together now stretched to fifteen or twenty feet—Hoover said he sometimes speeded up on purpose, to force Tolson to exert himself more.

Tolson's poor health meant that Hoover was no longer protected by his friend's caution and meticulous attention to detail (Tolson's detractors called it negativism). Tolson had been the one who made sure the Bureau's executives did not "free wheel," always a mortal sin in Hoover's Bureau. It is doubtful that Sullivan would have been allowed the latitude he enjoyed in the sixties if Tolson had been his old watchful self. To some extent, Tolson had been the inside man in the FBI, freeing Hoover to concentrate on the Bureau's external affairs. As Tolson weakened, Hoover had to handle both jobs. Given the scope of the Bureau's operations at this time, that might have been too much for any man, even Hoover in his prime. Now that the director was in his seventies, it *was* too much for him, and his performance in public became more erratic and his discipline over Sullivan looser and less consistent.

Tolson's illnesses made Hoover protective, even to the point of forcing on his acquaintances and superiors a recognition of their close relationship. Hoover had his top aides lobby to have Tolson awarded the same President's Distinguished Federal Civilian Service Medal that Hoover had gotten in 1958 (the first year it was given). Such exposure embarrassed Tolson, but Hoover was determined that his friend receive recognition for the forty years he had devoted to Hoover and the Bureau. Hoover's aides put together an elaborate presentation for Tolson's nomination in January 1963, but the Justice Department did not submit it to the White House. Shortly after Kennedy resigned as attorney general, Hoover tried again. Tolson told him, "I would appreciate it if this were not sent forward," but Hoover ignored him. With DeLoach lobbying at the White House and the Civil Service Commission (which actually managed the awards), Tolson was among the winners for 1965—but he was in the hospital and could not attend the presentation ceremony.[93]

If the FBI was less and less in control of events, and Hoover in less control of the FBI, there was at least one area in which he could maintain total control. This was the fictional FBI that appeared every Sunday night on ABC, starring Efrem Zimbalist, Jr., as the roving trouble-shooter Inspector Erskine. The show premiered in September 1965 and ran for nine years. A highly rated show for most of its run, it did not seriously decline in the ratings until after Hoover's death. At its peak it was watched by 40 million Americans every week, with millions more overseas in countries from Canada to Singapore.

Hoover profited from the show: his condition for permitting ABC to make the program was that ABC (whose president, James Hagerty, Eisenhower's former press secretary, was an old friend) had to buy the television rights of *Masters of Deceit* for $75,000. Before signing, Hoover checked with Johnson, who decided to approve because of the precedent established by the very favorable tax ruling Eisenhower had gotten for the profits on his memoirs. Hoover also got $500 for each episode, which in April 1966 he signed over to the FBI Recreation Fund.

Hoover watched over television's FBI as closely as he did the real Bureau. There was an agent in Hollywood to oversee the filming of the program, and Hoover and Tolson supervised the scripts at every stage of their development. Hoover never appeared as a character in the show, but Erskine's office was supposed to be next door to the director's, and Hoover did make an appearance to announce the beginning of each new season.

Hoover did not review the scripts simply for accuracy; he was on the lookout for any detail that might conflict with his ideal vision of America and the FBI. When television violence became an issue, Zimbalist recalls, Hoover put out a rule that "there would be no more deaths—immortality. We didn't kill anybody, I think, the last three or four years." DeLoach remembered that whenever there was a complaint about the show, Hoover ordered him to kill the program; this happened seven times, and each time DeLoach had to write a memo defending it. But the action was not as important to Hoover as its re-creation of the FBI of his dreams: unfailingly polite, white, male, middle-class agents to whom the FBI was family, men protecting a public that responded with gratitude and respect.[94]

The real Bureau grew from about 6,000 to almost 7,000 in the Johnson years, but Hoover's age was creating a distance between him and his top assistants. DeLoach, who was closest to him during the Johnson years, was only forty-eight when Johnson left office; Hoover was seventy-three. The result, according to Ramsey Clark, was that Hoover was now "a very lonely man. It was sad in a way. He had no close friends. His social contacts were just incredibly limited." His only confidant, Tolson, did little to keep him in contact with society.[95]

By the end of Johnson's administration, Hoover's Bureau was engaged in an undercover and covert war against radical America, a war that went far beyond combating violence; as it blocked dissidents from speaking, turned them against one another, and used rumor and slander to discredit them and their causes, the Bureau attempted to restrict the political choices available to Americans. It even fomented conflict between such armed and volatile black extremist groups as the Black Panthers and the Blackstone Rangers, thus promoting, instead of preventing, violence. Hoover fanned the flames of the law-and-order backlash against black power and the antiwar movement. That put him in a politically contradictory position: though loyal to Lyndon Johnson, his law-and-order rhetoric helped LBJ's opposition by persuading the public that the Justice Department and the Supreme Court were responsible for the increase in crime and urban disorder.

Hoover's secret COINTELPRO attacks on the rights of Americans were so dangerous that had they become a model for a comprehensive, coordinated assault by all domestic security agencies, federal and local, the results on political freedom would have been catastrophic. Measured by Hoover's previous wars against radicalism, however, his efforts in the sixties were puny indeed. Even though the country was at war in Vietnam, there was neither the international crisis nor the home front panic essential to the earlier drives. Because he could not document to his own satisfaction the proof of foreign backing for black radicalism and antiwar protest that LBJ wanted, Hoover was unable, even unwilling—no matter how much the protesters and rioters infuriated him, and no matter how much he wished them punished—to take the unrest of the sixties as seriously as the threats of the past.

Shifts in legal and public opinion made it more dangerous for the Bureau to continue many intelligence-gathering methods of the past; this also made Hoover more cautious about committing himself publicly and irretrievably to a major assault on the sixties' radicalism. This public caution was a factor in his covert recklessness. Hoover resented the Supreme Court decisions that protected the rights of privacy, and he opposed the Justice Department's efforts to combat crime through social reform, but in the sixties he also adjusted himself to the times by quietly curtailing many of the Bureau's more intrusive techniques.

The sixties were a time of conflict between new national standards and old, locally based customs governing race relations, law and order, and private morality. The legal revolution that sparked this conflict was, in many ways, a top-down change, imposed by the Supreme Court and by political activists appealing to a sympathetic federal court system. It was not supported by any deep consensus across the nation, so there was outrage and resistance on the part of those who had an investment, emotional or material, in local traditions.

Hoover was not alone in being unable to chart a straight course through the mid and late sixties. Lyndon Johnson's administration, dominated by an uncontrollable war that finally placed 500,000 troops in combat halfway around the world, was no better able to comprehend foreign or domestic events. Johnson's war policies attempted to apply superpower strategy and the bipolar lessons of Munich and Korea to a world caught up in the antiimperialist flames of nationalism; Johnson's liberal toleration of pluralism and protest clashed with his conviction that opposition to a president's foreign policy bordered on treason. Hoover habitually reacted to the challenge of the present with the responses of the past, but even a man as adaptable as Johnson could not free himself from crippling old myths when confronted with the realities that forced themselves on the White House and Capitol during the Vietnam years.

Neither Johnson nor Hoover had any doubt that they were right, but both were politically astute enough to know that the divided country did not offer them the consensus necessary for a total national mobilization against the Communists in Southeast Asia, or against the black and antiwar protesters at home. Both resorted to halfway, incremental measures that encouraged the resistance they were so eager to crush. Therefore, Hoover did not feel confident enough in his political or public support to use all the techniques at his disposal to give full expression to his outrage against dissidents, just as Johnson was too unsure of his domestic support (and of the response of the Communist bloc) to use all the military force at his command.

If Hoover had limited his response to Johnson's calls for help to the gathering of intelligence about antiwar demonstrations, he would have remained on fairly solid legal ground, and his long record of achievements would not have been so eclipsed in history by the evils of COINTELPRO. Clearly, Hoover had an obligation, particularly when ordered by the president, to provide what information was needed at a time when troops were regularly being dispatched to quell uprisings. But when Hoover elected to play a secret but active role in the political and social turmoil of the time, when he furtively disrupted and destroyed political organizations, he had embarked on a conspiracy to decide by force those issues that in a free country must be resolved politically. The Bureau's efforts were finally ineffectual and even self-defeating because they further radicalized the opposition to the war and increased black alienation from white society. But ineffectual though they were, Hoover's COINTELPROs still represented tentative steps toward a government that sought to maintain its power through secret manipulation of the political process, instead of through the consent of the governed.

CHAPTER 13

Nixon and Hoover

Dick, you will come to depend on Edgar. He is a pillar of strength in a city of weak men. You will rely on him time and time again to maintain security. He's the only one you can put your complete trust in.[1]

Lyndon Johnson to Richard Nixon,
December 12, 1968

NIXON CAME INTO THE White House with great expectations of Hoover. After all, Hoover had helped Nixon make the "biggest play" of his career, the Alger Hiss case. (Nixon was forever counseling his aides to read the Hiss chapter in *Six Crises* and to apply its lessons to their current scam.) With a disastrous war on his hands, much of the country in revolt against it, and many in the government opposed to his foreign and domestic policies, Nixon faced brutal problems as he set himself up to govern the country. He was counting on Hoover to once again help him make some "big plays."

Before the inauguration, Hoover visited Nixon at his headquarters at New York's Hotel Pierre. The president-elect told him, "Edgar, you are one of the few people who is to have direct access to me at all times. I've talked to [John] Mitchell about it and he understands." In view of their long relationship, this was no more than the director thought he had a right to expect.[2]

Hoover had been there at the beginning of Richard Milhous Nix-

on's national career, one of the first to spot Nixon's potential when
he was a young member of HUAC. There had been times during
the Hiss case when Hoover was unsure whether the energetic and
able Nixon might be in competition with Hoover and the Bureau,
but his fulsome tribute to Hoover at the end of the case formalized
an historic alliance that made Nixon a national figure, and institutionalized Hoover as guarantor of national security with his own political
base. Their alliance had been a vital part of their success.[3]

Nixon guessed that he and Hoover had probably attended more
than a hundred of the same social events over the years. Hoover remembered those occasions with pleasure, particularly afternoons with Nixon
at Griffith Stadium watching the Senators (where he was always impressed by Nixon's knowledge of the game). Hoover and the Nixons
ate dinner at each other's homes, and Nixon would sometimes stop
on the way to his own vacation place in Key Biscayne to visit Hoover
in Miami. While Nixon was out of political office, Hoover had Nichols
or DeLoach pass whatever information Nixon wanted, particularly
on communism, to Nixon's secretary, Rose Mary Woods. Nixon's domestic counsel, John Ehrlichman, said that, for Nixon, "Hoover was
more than a source of information—he was a political advisor to whom
Nixon listened." Nixon thought he benefited politically from his close
association with Hoover because it protected his right flank from conservative attack.[4]

Hoover and Nixon in 1969 were battered veterans of two decades
of political wars. For them the world was a battlefield filled with
active or potential enemies, "pseudo-liberals" and "jackals of the
press."[5] Nixon came to the presidency deeply scarred by his close
loss to Kennedy in 1960 and the disastrous defeat for the California
governorship in 1962. He had learned he could never relax against
his political enemies, no matter how secure his position seemed. He
could never assume an election was won until the votes were counted,
and, based on his experience in Texas and Illinois in 1960, not even
then. To his mind, he was a victim forced forever to defend himself
against unrelenting and unscrupulous enemies.

The paradox of the Nixon presidency for Hoover was that despite
a close personal relationship that dated back to 1947, never did people
in the White House try harder to bend him to their will. Nixon's
aides viewed Hoover with a dispassionate, even cynical gaze. They
were not interested in—in fact, they were hardly aware of—Hoover's
past triumphs. Confident of their own powers, they were not intimidated by the years of experience that had gone into Hoover's formidable

reputation. Press a few buttons, clip on a few American flag lapel pins, and they could do the same thing for a new man. They wanted to know what Hoover could do for them now, and they were not impressed; they wanted to know what he could do to them, and they were not afraid. Theodore White said that Nixon's men understood the present and the future, but they did not understand the past. When they visited Hoover at his home or office, the display of relics from the Dillinger days did not work their magic; they simply labeled Hoover as old-fashioned, an archaic remnant of an irrelevant era.[6]

Since John Ehrlichman was Hoover's contact with the White House at the beginning (in early 1970, after Ehrlichman was promoted from counsel to the president to assistant for domestic affairs, the FBI-liaison role was given to the new counsel, John Dean), he received all of Hoover's reports. "In general," he said, "the FBI investigative work I saw was of poor quality. The Bureau dealt excessively in rumor, gossip and conjecture; sometimes a report was based on 'a confidential source'—the Bureau euphemism for wiretapping or bugging. Even then the information was often hearsay. . . . When FBI work was particularly bad I sent it back to Hoover, but the rework was seldom an improvement." Ehrlichman soon found that he could get better results by hiring an ex–New York City policeman with good contacts at the NYPD intelligence unit (Jack Caulfield, who later figured in the Watergate hearings).[7]

Ehrlichman's attitude toward the director at their first meeting was cool and contemptuous: "The Director of the Federal Bureau of Investigation was 74 years old when I first met him, briefly, at the Hotel Pierre in New York during the late-1968 transition. His appearance surprised me. His big head rested on beefy, rounded shoulders, apparently without benefit of neck. He was florid and fat-faced, ears flat against his head, eyes protruding. He looked unwell to me."[8]

When Ehrlichman visited Hoover's office he was simply amused by the trophies, pictures, flags, and awards that crowded the room; he was scornful of what he called the "Wizard of Oz" route Hoover had constructed for his visitors to walk before they were ushered into his presence. For Ehrlichman, Hoover was an old bore: "The Director had strong and definite views on a great many subjects and I was massively exposed to all of them: Black Panthers, domestic Communism, the Congress, the FBI budget, Hubert Humphrey and his supporters, Russia, Bureau training, Bureau procedures and morale, the Kennedys, the need for more FBI agents abroad, and much more." When Ehrlichman complained to Nixon about having to listen to all of this, Nixon sympathized: "I know, but it's necessary, John. It's necessary."[9]

In September 1969, Nixon made the extraordinary gesture of visiting Hoover for dinner. Ehrlichman and Attorney General John Mitchell, who accompanied Nixon, were surprised the president had accepted since he rarely accepted social invitations, even from cabinet officers.

Seen through Ehrlichman's eyes, Hoover's efforts to please his guests were ridiculous, even pitiful. Hoover greeted them at the door. Drinks were served by a tall black agent, Sam Noisette, wearing a steward's jacket, whom Ehrlichman remembered having seen earlier tending the door at Hoover's office. The living room, a hall of memories for Hoover, seemed "dingy, almost seedy" to Ehrlichman. Hoover's neighbors were in awe of the hundreds of pictures of Hoover with the great and famous that covered every inch of the walls; the Bureau even kept diagrams so they could all be put back in the same place after the walls were painted. Ehrlichman was scornful. What he noticed was how old they were: "Most of them had been there for years and were brown and faded." He condescendingly noted that some of them showed Hoover with "old-time movie actresses whose names I couldn't recall." He estimated there were 400 or 500 pictures in the living room so close their frames were touching.[10]

"When the President was settled, Hoover's longtime friend and housemate, Clyde Tolson, looking pale and pasty, came down the narrow hall stairs and shambled into the living room. Tolson was introduced to each of us, chatted briefly, but then excused himself. When he was gone, Hoover told us, at length and in detail, about the deteriorating state of Tolson's health." (Despite the innuendo here, Tolson was not living with Hoover. He had just gotten out of the hospital, and Hoover put him up for about four weeks.) The dinner was prepared by Hoover's maid and served by the agent. There were steaks flown in from Clint Murchison's ranch and chili from Chasen's in Los Angeles.[11]

During dinner Hoover brought up business. He complained about problems he was having infiltrating the construction crews building the new Russian embassy. Nixon said he would look into it and take care of the "little shits" at the State Department. When Hoover told them about bag jobs and other derring-do by the FBI, Ehrlichman thought his purpose was to get their reactions to these illegal activities. "Later, in thinking back to that dinner, I realized that Hoover had every right to believe that both his superiors, Nixon and Mitchell, approved of FBI bugging, taps, and bag jobs. He told us about FBI operations against domestic radicals and foreigners, and our reactions were enthusiastic and positive."[12]

Hoover was proud of his house, and was sure that it made a good impression on visitors. Friends and neighbors were impressed with the care he and James Crawford, his driver/handyman, lavished on it. All Ehrlichman noticed was that the dining room was "small" and "crowded," the way to the basement recreation room passed down the "narrowest of stairs." Ehrlichman found more to ridicule in the recreation room. Near the door was a bar, and the wall behind it was papered with the coy sort of nude pin-ups one saw in the old *Esquire.* Even the lampshade was covered with nudes. "The effect of this display was to engender disbelief—it seemed totally contrived. That impression was reinforced when Hoover deliberately called our attention to his naughty gallery, as if it were something he wanted us to know about J. Edgar Hoover."[13]

Nixon and Mitchell had made an important gesture in visiting Hoover, one that acknowledged Hoover's prestige as so great that when the president associated with him, the president was the gainer. But this was wasted on Ehrlichman, who would be more important to Hoover during the Nixon administration than either Nixon or Mitchell. As far as Ehrlichman was concerned, Hoover was an old fool to be humored as long as necessary, and to be gotten rid of as soon as possible.

Despite their warm friendship, Nixon's attitude toward Hoover reflected a pattern some have detected in his attitude toward other older men, particularly Eisenhower (but also De Gaulle). Nixon revered them, he thirsted for their approval, he admired their capacity to command allegiance and respect (including his own), but he was also impatient with their plodding ways, their caution, their refusal to take advantage of opportunities. Nixon's impatience with Hoover, and none of his reverence, rubbed off on Chief of Staff H. R. Haldeman, Domestic Counsel John Ehrlichman, and their "Beaver Patrol" of young aides. Never one to refuse the requests of politically sympathetic presidents, Hoover now repeatedly had to ward off White House requests for actions he considered imprudent and dangerous. He quickly learned he could not trust Nixon's staff, and since Nixon was so insulated by them, Hoover had to be wary of any orders he received from the White House. When he refused to comply with some of the administration's most urgent domestic security directives, the staff turned against him.[14]

Some of Nixon's men later blamed Watergate and the subsequent ruin of the Nixon administration on Hoover, even though the director died six weeks before the June 17, 1972, burglary. Their theory was that Nixon and his aides had to set up the White House "Plumbers" in 1971 to stop news leaks because Hoover was not up to the job. Since Hoover blocked the administration's plans to reorganize the official domestic intelligence network, the White House had to organize its own team of investigators, and that created an opening for G. Gordon Liddy, who went on to sell John Mitchell and the Committee to Re-Elect the President (CREEP) on the plan to bug the offices of the Democratic National Committee. If Hoover had been a better team player, they believed, the Nixon administration would never have recruited men with a penchant for "black bag jobs" and Water-buggery.[15]

Leaks and demonstrations and ways to deal with them would be Hoover's and Nixon's most pressing mutual concerns. No leader can afford to have his plans disclosed to his opponents or the public before he is ready to make them known. No leader wants to face unruly, violent, and, in an age of media-dominated politics, irresistibly photogenic crowds filled with his enemies. In December 1968, Johnson told Nixon, "The leaks can kill you. . . . If it hadn't been for Edgar Hoover I couldn't have carried out my responsibilities as Commander in Chief. Period." For Nixon, even more than Johnson, leaks and demonstrations were mortal threats to his ability to govern the country, and he would need Hoover to help him deal with them. Having to wage a massive, undeclared war in Asia, while simultaneously trying to negotiate with the North Vietnamese, made both Johnson and Nixon depend on secrecy to mask their moves. They had to keep the enemy from knowing about their negotiating positions and to keep the antiwar opposition from mobilizing to frustrate their war strategy. For this, Nixon, like his predecessor, would look to Hoover for solutions.[16]

Nixon also resented and feared mass political violence. "Nixon's mind," wrote Theodore White, "which seeks control and order above all, had long been scarred by mobs—he had met them first in 1952, when the stories of his 'secret fund' had run a gauntlet of provocations at his rallies across the country. He had been physically endangered by mobs jeering, spitting and rock throwing on his trip to Venezuela which he reports in his *Six Crises*. He had a visceral hatred of street wildness. And though the street wildness of 1968 was directed against

Hubert Humphrey, it aroused in Nixon's mind a responding, clinical anger that long outlasted the campaign." To Nixon, amassing information on demonstrators and outmaneuvering them was not merely a political necessity, it was also an emotional instinct of physical self-preservation, reawakened by the chanting mobs of protesters who pelted his inaugural parade with rocks and smoke bombs.[17]

Nixon had discovered, however, that he could turn the threat posed by demonstrations into an opportunity to rally *his* supporters. Essentially, he turned his aggressive campaign technique of personal attacks on his opponents into a principle of government: Now the "nameless few" were the antiwar demonstrators, and he made their appearance and behavior, not their cause, the issue that most concerned the public. That meant he needed detailed intelligence on what was happening in the antiwar movement, and when it was going to happen.[18]

In his speech accepting the Republican nomination on August 8, 1968, Nixon made Ramsey Clark an issue of the campaign: "If we are to restore order and respect for law and this country, there's one place we're going to begin: we're going to have a new Attorney General of the United States." He pledged to his "forgotten Americans" that he would appoint "tough law and order justices to the Supreme Court," and he promised to take personal charge of a war against disorder, bragging that "I am an expert in this field."[19]

Then, not long after his inauguration, Nixon began to be tormented by news leaks about his confidential plans for the war. Johnson had told him that he had been at first "frustrated, then angered, and, finally, nearly obsessed by the need to stop them." Nixon soon learned that Johnson's concerns were justified, and he was soon as obsessed and frustrated by leaks as his predecessor. During the first five months of his term, Nixon said, he had twenty-one serious leaks, forty-five in all during the first year.[20]

To solve this problem, Nixon turned to Hoover. He learned from Hoover there were three ways of combating leaks: background checks, physical surveillance, or wire taps. Nixon claims that Hoover told him tapping was the "only" effective way to track down the leakers, and that he had been given such assignments by every president since Roosevelt. Nixon then set up a procedure by which Henry Kissinger would give Hoover the names of individuals who were suspected of divulging the information. "I authorized Hoover to take the necessary steps—including wiretapping—to investigate the leaks and find the leakers."[21]

On March 17, 1969, Nixon had started bombing North Vietnamese forces in Cambodia. Secrecy was all-important not only to avoid protests in this country; Prince Sihanouk of Cambodia had approved the bombings, but because of his country's neutrality he would have to denounce them if they should become known. On May 9, 1969, the *New York Times* carried a front-page story by reporter William Beecher on the bombing and on Sihanouk's failure to protest. Nixon and Kissinger believed their strategy had been sabotaged by dissidents in the government, presumably on Kissinger's staff at the National Security Council. Nixon believed the Cambodian bombing had saved American lives, and was putting pressure on the North Vietnamese to negotiate. "The *Times* leak threatened everything."[22]

The morning the story appeared, Kissinger phoned Hoover and told him to "make a major effort to find out where [the leak] came from" and to handle the matter discreetly "so no stories will get out." Nixon wanted "maximum secrecy" for the project because he felt that it would damage morale for the White House staff to discover it was being tapped; he also feared disclosure of the wiretapping would make it a "potent issue" for the antiwar movement. Seventeen wiretaps were installed as part of the investigation, which included four newsmen (Marvin Kalb of CBS, Henry Brandon of the *London Times,* Hedrick Smith of the *New York Times,* and Beecher) and thirteen members of the White House, State, and Defense Department staffs. Hoover thought the leaker was Morton Halperin of the NSC. Hoover's report to Kissinger described a "definite Kennedy philosophy" among many of the members of his staff, and concluded that a large proportion of the Systems Analysis Agency personnel in the Pentagon were McNamara people. Hoover was sure that the culprit was one of these "so-called arrogant Harvard-type Kennedy men," but the identity of the leaker was never definitely proven. The real source may have been eyewitness accounts by an English reporter who had flown over Cambodia and seen the bomb craters. His account had already appeared in the English press.[23]

Hoover had the clearest of presidential authority for his investigation of the Cambodia bombing leak. Moreover, the law as currently interpreted by Attorney General John Mitchell was that the president had a constitutional right to order wiretaps in national security cases without a warrant (in 1972 the Supreme Court's *Keith* decision would reject this doctrine except in cases involving a foreign power). Nevertheless, Hoover was not willing to simply act as the president's agent, as he had so often in the past. Though he ordered an immediate wiretap on Halperin as the most likely suspect, three days later he requested and received written authorizations from Mitchell for that and all the remaining taps.[24]

Besides making sure that he had written authorization for the Kissinger wiretaps, Hoover had them segregated from the rest of the Bureau's operations. He gave the job to William Sullivan as a personal assignment, ordered that no duplicates of the logs be kept, and kept the logs and all other records out of the regular FBI files (at first in his own office and later in Sullivan's). The reports on the taps were not indexed and filed, and so the names of persons overheard were not entered in the department's ELSUR (electronic surveillance) index, which was used by the department to determine if any of its cases had been contaminated by accidentally overhearing defendants in unrelated wiretaps. (Sullivan claimed that this procedure was requested by General Alexander Haig, Kissinger's aide, who was the liaison between Kissinger and the FBI on this matter. Haig denied this, and said that he simply stressed the need for confidentiality.) This procedure served the White House's interest as well as Hoover's: If knowledge of the taps were kept out of the FBI files, they could be shielded by executive privilege if an inquiry were ever made.[25]

Hoover did not consider the Kissinger taps an FBI operation; he saw them as a White House project in which the Bureau merely provided a technical service. Even then they made him nervous. Soon after installing the taps, Hoover went to Attorney General John Mitchell in a state of great concern and asked him to intervene with the White House to get the seventeen taps removed. At the White House, Mitchell talked with Haig or Kissinger and they agreed the taps were "a dangerous game" that might be "explosive," but the taps remained in place.[26]

Hoover's increasing reluctance to implicate the Bureau in the White House's progressively reckless attempts to stop the leaking of sensitive information was reflected in his response to an order from Nixon to put syndicated columnist Joseph Kraft under surveillance. In June 1969, Nixon had Haldeman ask the FBI to tap Kraft's home after Kraft had written that Nixon's recent peace proposals were unlikely to succeed. Nixon suspected Kraft was being influenced by the administration's enemies, perhaps even by the North Vietnamese. This time Hoover refused, so Nixon had Haldeman use his own private investigator, Jack Caulfield, the former New York City detective, to install the tap. Nixon *was* able to persuade Hoover to have Kraft followed when he went to Paris to meet with North Vietnamese officials; again, Hoover had William Sullivan do the job personally. (Sullivan used French police to tap Kraft's hotel room. Evidently Hoover felt this shifted blame sufficiently away from the Bureau.) In November 1969, probably in response to a White House request, Hoover asked Mitchell for authorization to tap Kraft's home in Washington, but the authorization was never signed and the tap never installed.[27]

It was clear to Hoover that in the inflamed atmosphere of 1969 nothing would be more disastrous than discovery of a tap on a newsman or an opposition politician. It must have puzzled Hoover that Nixon did not see this danger, or that he did not care. On the other hand, Hoover's caution became increasingly irritating to White House aides who, driven by Nixon to attack the problem of leaks, were doing so without concern for legalities or the risk of exposure. Their recklessness increased Hoover's determination not to let the FBI become officially involved.

As the crisis over the war deepened during 1970, relations between Hoover and the Nixon White House grew worse. From Washington's perspective, the country seemed to be ready to revolt. During the year, there were 3,000 bombings and 50,000 bomb threats, including the famous Greenwich Village bomb factory on New York's West 11th Street. There were explosions and fires at the University of Wisconsin and Harvard. Black and white radicals were protesting the murder trial of Black Panther leader Bobby Seale in New Haven. The army was looking over contingency plans for occupying New Haven to block a threatened march by students to free Seale.

When Nixon ordered the invasion of Cambodia on April 30, campuses across the country erupted. On May 4, National Guardsmen on the campus of Kent State University in Ohio fired into a crowd of students and killed four (nine others were wounded). The week following Kent State, 400 colleges were shut down in protest. Nixon responded by blasting "these bums . . . blowing up campuses . . . burning books." Early on the morning of May 9, a distraught Nixon wandered out to the Capitol Mall to argue policy with student protesters camping near the Lincoln Memorial.[28]

Hoover had always seen it as part of the role of a national leader to harangue the nation on the sins of its youth. Since 1968 he had secretly been doing more than that. His COINTELPRO–New Left had been disrupting student protests through tactics designed to hold young radicals up to scorn and to spur parents and teachers to take action against them. In his rhetoric against the protesters, Hoover was even more violent than Nixon. He characterized the new student radical as "new . . . different . . . a paradox because he is difficult to judge by the normal standards of civilized life. At heart, he's a revolutionist, an anarchist, a nihilist. His main reason for being is to destroy, blindly and indiscriminately, to tear down and provoke chaos. . . . They conceive of themselves as the catalyst of destruction—bringing to death a society they so bitterly hate."[29]

But despite this rabid rhetoric, Hoover undercut the urgency of his warning by admitting the situation would become really dangerous only if "the Old Left can—exploiting the factionalism of the New Left—recruit sizeable numbers of these alienated students with their feelings of hostility toward America and the democratic process." In that case, "this nation indeed faces a bleak future." In his heart Hoover shared the Old Left's contempt for the New Left as a "vulgarized, superficial version of the historic doctrines of Marx." He said it was "no wonder Old Left observers are often aghast at the ideological concoctions of these young militants!" The New Left, Hoover said, was a mélange of "Old Leftism" (Soviet communism, Maoism, Trotskyism), some unusual new ingredients (Castroism, anarchism, Che Guevaraism, Third Worldism, student powerism, and mysticisms), and "dashes of drugs, astrology and hippies." Unlike the old Communists, who devoted themselves to study of the Marxist classics for guidance, the New Left "has not developed a workable ideology or intellectual programs which relate thought to action, enabling it to know where it is going or even what it wants. It is almost like a maddened, half-blind pugilist who compensates for his lack of vision by striking out indiscriminately in all directions." Hoover seemed to agree with the Old Left that the New Left's worship of "impulsive action now" constituted the Marxist heresy of "adventurism."[30]

Hoover's response to domestic unrest in the seventies was petulant but, compared to his past crusades, almost purely rhetorical. In discussions with White House aides he railed against the broken windows and red paint splattered on the Justice Department walls by the May 1970 protesters, he cheered on the construction workers who chased antiwar demonstrators up Broadway in New York, and he shed no tears for the students shot at Kent State ("the students invited and got what they deserved"). But when the Nixon administration tried to draw Hoover into a comprehensive plan of action against the antiwar movement, he dug in his heels and refused. There was a wide gap between Hoover's private feelings (fully in sympathy with the president) and his professional judgment (which told him that massive intelligence operations conducted against a movement supported by so many Americans, using techniques no longer tolerated by the courts or much of the public, would be a disaster for the president, for the FBI, and, not incidentally, for himself should they become known.)[31]

Hoover was absolutely convinced that the day of the high-handed surveillance techniques the Bureau had once used was long past. As he explained to Richard Helms of the CIA, "There is widespread concern by the American people regarding the possible misuse of this type coverage. Moreover, various legal considerations must be borne in mind, including the impact such coverage may have on our numerous prosecutive responsibilities. The FBI's effectiveness has always depended in large measure on our capacity to retain the full confidence of the American people. The use of any investigative techniques which infringe on traditional rights of privacy must therefore be scrutinized most carefully."[32]

In May 1970 the strain of trying to wage war and conduct secret diplomacy while the nation was in turmoil pushed Nixon to find ways of dealing with an "epidemic of unprecedented domestic terrorism." Faced with what he called as a "new phenomenon of highly organized and highly skilled revolutionaries dedicated to the violent destruction of our democratic system," his administration proposed a reorganization of the federal intelligence community as an answer. This was to push Hoover closer to a break with a president than at any time since the tense days of 1947 during the Truman administration.[33]

Nixon and his intelligence advisors were frustrated by Hoover's termination of black bag jobs and mail openings, his limitations on wiretaps and microphone surveillances, and his restrictions on the recruitment of campus informants (they now had to be twenty-one years old). They were resentful that earlier presidents had had the benefit of these sources and techniques; now, facing far more critical domestic situations, they were having to fly blind. Hoover had even ended regular liaison with the CIA because it would not give him the name of an FBI agent who had talked to the Agency without his permission. Criticism of this feud with the CIA caused Hoover to end liaison with all other external agencies except the White House. Hoover also informed all intelligence services he would not authorize any more electronic surveillance for them on his own as he had in the past, but would refer the requests to the attorney general for his approval. That effectively halted FBI assistance to other intelligence agencies since none would go on record requesting permission for illegal acts.[34]

It seemed to Nixon that Hoover had become frightened by "the temper of the times [that] was turning against him." Nixon thought that Hoover was "determined not to give anyone ammunition in his last years to damage him or his organization. He had always been rigidly territorial when it came to the functions and prerogatives of the FBI. He totally distrusted the other intelligence agencies—especially the CIA—and, whenever possible, resisted attempts to work in concert with them. He was sensibly reluctant to go out on a limb for anyone, lest he find himself suddenly alone." Nixon's comments suggest that some of the administration's rage against its enemies was now being directed against Hoover, whose caution seemed all that was protecting the antiwar movement from the righteous wrath of the president's men.[35]

On June 5, 1970, Nixon called the directors of his intelligence agencies to the White House—Hoover, Richard Helms of the CIA, General Donald V. Bennett of the Defense Department, and Admiral Noel Gayler of the National Security Agency—and gave them a dressing down. He told them they were disorganized, inefficient, and unproductive. He wanted them to reorganize themselves into a single, streamlined unit that could keep him informed on domestic unrest. Hoover was to be chairman; the staff was to be directed by the White House's Tom Charles Huston, who had been in charge of the administration's campaign to mobilize the Internal Revenue Service against its enemies. Huston had also had the responsibility of collecting information about foreign involvement in campus disturbances, and in the course of this work had formed an alliance with the FBI's assistant director in charge of Domestic Intelligence, William C. Sullivan.[36]

Ostensibly, the goal was to improve intelligence on the antiwar movement, particularly in its more violent manifestations—the SDS, and the Panthers. The problem, Nixon told the group, was that the American people, "perhaps as a reaction to the excesses of the McCarthy era, are unwilling to admit the possibility that 'their children' could wish to destroy their country." He also dropped a hint of another reason for wanting to intensify intelligence gathering: "We must develop a plan which will enable us to curtail the illegal activities of those who are determined to destroy our society." This may have meant that the administration was already looking past the stage of intelligence-gathering to using the new intelligence to disrupt the antiwar movement. What was very clear to all present at the June 5 meeting was the president's dissatisfaction with their current efforts. General Bennett said that "the President chewed our butts."[37]

There was a dizzying complex of bureaucratic maneuvers hidden behind the convening of this summit conference of American intelligence. The Nixon administration was convinced it needed a new weapon against domestic radicals and the antiwar movement. And there was general agreement that Hoover had become overly timid in the measures he was willing to use. Beyond that, there were a variety of bureaucratic and personal ambitions. The other intelligence agencies were eager to have restrictions relaxed on the use of sensitive intelligence-gathering techniques and to once again be able to call on the FBI to assume the risk of these techniques on their behalf. Tom Charles Huston himself aspired to a role in domestic intelligence equivalent to Henry Kissinger's in foreign affairs, and the reorganization he was going to propose, if adopted, would give it to him. But, probably, the most important intrigue was the Iago-like maneuvering of William C. Sullivan, Hoover's own assistant director. At the beginning of the Huston plan negotiations, Sullivan was one of ten assistant directors at headquarters; at the end, he emerged as Cartha DeLoach's successor as assistant to the director, effectively the number-two man in the Bureau because of Tolson's declining capacities.

Because he was in charge of the Domestic Intelligence Division, and was the FBI executive most concerned with changes in the organization of domestic intelligence, Sullivan had become close to Huston; he had also cemented a close relationship with Robert Mardian, the assistant attorney general in charge of the Justice Department's Internal Security Division. Both Sullivan and Mardian had their offices in the Federal Triangle Building a block away from the main Justice Department building, and they often discussed their dissatisfaction with Hoover's performance in domestic intelligence. Sullivan believed that Hoover's curtailment of sensitive techniques had effectively put the Domestic Intelligence Division, which he headed, out of business.[38]

Three days after Nixon's tongue-lashing, the heads of the intelligence agencies reassembled to set the staff (headed by Sullivan, and drawn from the staffs of the participating agencies) to work. In his opening remarks as chairman, Hoover stated that "the president wants a historical study made of intelligence operations in the United States and the present security problems of the country." There followed a heavy silence until Huston said, "I didn't hear the President say that we should prepare a historical document. . . . I understand President Nixon to say that he was dissatisfied with present-day problems in the security and intelligence fields. Further, the President wants to know to what extent they are being solved and what we can do to elevate the quality of our intelligence operations." Sullivan, who was present, said, "You could hear a pin drop." After a few moments of silence, Admiral Gayler agreed, "Yes, Mr. Hoover, that was also my understanding." According to Sullivan, "The silence continued as Hoover became crimson. . . . That meeting increased Hoover's hatred of Huston."[39]

Hoover had proposed a "historical study" because he thought the current unrest had to be understood in the context of previous radicalism, its rise and fall, and the risks and benefits the past disclosed of the measures that might be taken against it. His view was not given even the politeness of a hearing. "We're not talking about the dead past," Huston said, "we're talking about the living present." But for Hoover the past was very much alive. One of Hoover's aides said that Hoover "was still carrying that badge of criticism for the Palmer raids. And he remembered it."[40]

Over the next two weeks the staff hammered out a proposal that recommended a permanent interagency committee on intelligence. It would "evaluate intelligence, coordinate operations, prepare ongoing threat assessments on domestic protest, and develop new policies." Huston and Sullivan both thought this was the most important part of the plan, which also listed a series of options for the president regarding surveillance techniques (mail opening, burglaries, electronic surveillance, and the use of on-campus informants). The options ranged from removing all restrictions, to keeping them under the present (Hoover-inspired) limitations. If the president went in the direction indicated by Sullivan and Huston, there would be a new secret organization, with Huston as the authoritative White House director in charge of domestic intelligence.

When Hoover saw the draft of the proposal, shortly before the final staff meeting on June 23, he said he would not sign it unless it was redrafted to remove the most extreme options (removal of restrictions) and the recommendation for the interagency committee. Sullivan said Hoover told him he was no longer willing to "accept the sole responsibility." If someone "higher than myself" approved a surveillance, "then I will carry out their decision. . . . But I'm not going to accept the responsibility myself anymore, even though I've done it for many years." Sullivan suggested that rather than forcing the other agencies to rewrite a report they had already approved, Hoover should attach his objections as footnotes, which is what he did.[41]

The final draft, basically drawn up by Sullivan, began with a survey of the radical situation. It focused on the antiwar movement (the

SDS) and the black radical movement (the Black Panther Party), and downplayed the Communist threat. It then turned to a list of specific proposals for changes to counteract the radical threat.[42]

Hoover's footnotes in effect disassociated him from every one of the plan's recommendations. Electronic surveillance: "The FBI does not wish to change its present procedure of selective coverage on major internal security threats as it believes this coverage is adequate at this time. The FBI would not oppose other agencies seeking authority of the Attorney General for coverage required by them and thereafter instituting such coverage themselves." Mail coverage: "The FBI is opposed to implementing any covert mail coverage because it is clearly illegal and is likely that, if done, information would leak out of the Post Office to the press and serious damage would be done to the intelligence community." Surreptitious entry: "The FBI is opposed to surreptitious entry." And so on down the list of techniques: "The FBI is opposed to removing any present controls and restrictions relating to the development of campus sources. To do so would severely jeopardize its investigations and could result in leaks to the press which would be damaging and which could result in charges that investigative agencies are interfering with academic freedom." Military undercover agents in domestic intelligence: "This would be in violation of the Delimitations Agreement."

The most important recommendation, by far, was for a supervisory body to coordinate intelligence operations. The report claimed there was no "correlation of operational activities in the domestic field," which might have been a veiled reference to disruptive counterintelligence operations along the lines of COINTELPRO. The proposed intelligence committee, with members representing the various agencies, would have a head appointed by the president to "coordinate intelligence originating with this committee in the same manner as Dr. Henry Kissinger, Assistant to the President, coordinates foreign intelligence on behalf of the President." Hoover again was unequivocally opposed. All he would do was make an innocuous offer to prepare "periodic domestic intelligence estimates," which would have been little more than the reports he submitted each year to the House Appropriations Committee.

The other agencies got their first sight of Hoover's footnotes on June 23. The signing ceremony was scheduled for June 25, so they had no time to react. When the representatives of the NSA and the Pentagon called Huston to protest they were, calmed by Huston assurances that the proposal would go through despite Hoover's objections.

Neither Huston nor Sullivan seemed too concerned, one participant remembered. But when the intelligence chiefs met to sign the report on June 25, Hoover insisted that they sit through his reading of the entire forty-three-page report. As he finished each page he would ask: "Does anyone have any comment on page one?" Then he would repeat the same question to each member. Each time he came to Huston, he would get his name wrong. "Any comments, Mr. Hoffman? Any comments, Mr. Hutchinson?" and so on. Hoover's memory was sharp as a tack, and this was no sudden bout of forgetfulness. He was determined to humiliate this twenty-nine-year-old who had been sent to crack the whip over the old men of American intelligence. At one point during Hoover's jibes at Huston, Sullivan remembers, "I saw Dick Helms, who was sitting on Hoover's right, lean back in his chair and wink behind the director's back at Tom Huston." After a while Gayler and Bennett began quarreling over Hoover's footnotes. Helms restored order; Hoover finished a hurried reading; and the four chiefs signed the document.[43]

Huston was furious, but he still thought he would get his way and end up as the domestic Henry Kissinger, with Hoover reduced to carrying out his orders. Huston sent his own recommendations to the president along with the report, urging Nixon to adopt all of the most extreme options. His cover letter to Haldeman blasted Hoover: "The only stumbling block was Mr. Hoover. He attempted at the first meeting to divert the committee from operational problems and redirect its mandate to the preparation of another analysis of existing intelligence"; he finally "refused to go along with a single conclusion drawn or support a single recommendation made. . . . As you will note from the report, his objections are generally inconsistent and frivolous—most express concern about possible embarrassment to the intelligence community (i.e., Hoover) from public disclosure of clandestine operations."[44]

Huston insisted that "of all the individuals involved in the preparation and consideration of this report, only Mr. Hoover is satisfied with existing procedures." Moreover, Huston assured the White House that Hoover was not supported even by his own men, that "those individuals within the F.B.I. who have day-to-day responsibilities for domestic intelligence operations privately disagree with Mr. Hoover and believe that it is imperative that changes in operating procedures be initiated at once." He urged the president to ignore Hoover's objections, and to bring him around with a "stroking session" and an "autographed photo" of the whole group. "Having seen the President in action with Mr. Hoover, I am confident that he can handle this situation in such a way that we can get what we want without putting Edgar's nose out of joint."

On July 14, Nixon approved almost all of the Huston plan. He discounted Hoover's objections, feeling that Hoover had not been able to surmount "his natural resistance" to working with the CIA. Nixon also thought Hoover feared going on record as approving the plan because the other agencies might then use this against him by leaking the information that Hoover was once again up to his old illegal intelligence-gathering tricks. The point of the whole exercise was to get the intelligence community moving against radicals while keeping the president legally uninvolved, so Nixon had Haldeman pass word to Huston that Huston himself should sign the order to implement the plan.[45]

The absence of the presidential signature on the report presaged its doom. The army intelligence chiefs said, "They passed that one down about as low as it could go," and concluded President Nixon and Haldeman " 'didn't have the guts' to sign it themselves. To the other heads of intelligence, the use of Huston as a possible scapegoat indicated 'what a hot potato it was.' "[46]

When Hoover saw the memo from Huston announcing the president's approval of the most extreme recommendations of the plan, with Hoover as chairman of the committee and with Huston as the "personal representative to the President for domestic intelligence," he rebelled. He saw he was being asked to take enormous risks by having to authorize the illegal acts of other agencies. "This ad hoc committee is going out of business just as soon as the report is finished," he said. "Then when we start to put these programs into effect, where am I going to go to get backup? Where am I going to get approval? That puts the whole thing on my shoulders."[47]

Taking Cartha DeLoach with him, Hoover rushed to Mitchell's office to warn that the new procedures were too dangerous and that they put the president in the position of having approved, though indirectly, illegal activities. Mitchell, who had been completely bypassed in the planning, was surprised when he saw the plan, and told Hoover to "sit tight" until he had seen the president. Hoover had put Nixon and Mitchell on notice that though they might load him down with all the authority they wanted, if he thought anything might endanger him or the Bureau, he would demand they sign off on it. Since avoiding presidential complicity was at the heart of the plan, such a demand was enough to render it useless.[48]

Mitchell went to the president with Hoover's warnings and said that he agreed with the director. Nixon realized, as he wrote later, that "if Hoover had decided not to cooperate it would matter little what I had decided or approved. Even if I issued a direct order to him, while he would undoubtedly carry it out, he would soon see to it that I had cause to reverse myself. There was even the remote possibility that he would resign in protest." On July 28, before the planned August 1 date of implementation, Nixon withdrew his approval and all copies of the plan were rounded up, not to be revealed to the public until John Dean's testimony during Watergate.[49]

Huston tried to salvage his work by furnishing the White House with a point-by-point rebuttal of the objections Hoover had raised to the plan. Of Hoover's claim that his present efforts were adequate Huston said, "The answer is bullshit!" To Hoover's objection that the risks were too great and the plan was going to get the president into trouble, Huston said, "The Director of the FBI is paid to take risks where the security of the country is at stake." Huston ridiculed Hoover's fears of leaks, saying the leaks could be avoided and were being avoided. He was particularly caustic about Hoover's insistence on getting the attorney general's approval before employing any illegal techniques: "I would tell Hoover that he has been instructed to do them by the President and he is to do them on that authority. He needn't look for a scapegoat. He has his authority from the President and he doesn't need a written memo from the AG. To maintain security, we should avoid written communications in this area.

"There is this final point . . . what Hoover is doing here is putting himself above the President."

But it was all in vain. The plan was dead.[50]

Obviously Hoover thought the Huston plan was dangerous and would not work, and these were powerful reasons for not becoming involved in it. His rejection clearly revealed once again the caution that had always been part of his temperament. Hoover had learned over the years that in the normal alternation of political fortunes his victims might someday be his prosecutors. It did not pay to get the Bureau too blatantly involved in political battles. First Eugene McCarthy's candidacy, and then Robert Kennedy's, proved that the protest movement had become part of mainstream politics, far too large to be *openly* attacked as subversive. Today's protesters might very well be in power tomorrow.

But Hoover's rejection of the Huston plan also has to be viewed in the light of what he *was* willing to do to the radicals of the late sixties and early seventies as long as he had total and sole control over the operations. The fact is that he *was* harassing the antiwar movement, he *was* battling black militants, and he was directing his Black Nationalist and New Left COINTELPROs against precisely the organizations Huston wanted to target in his plan.

If anything, Hoover's dirty war against black radicals had gotten even dirtier under Nixon. His efforts to "expose" Martin Luther King, Jr., had not slackened even though King had been dead for a year. He furnished ammunition to conservatives to attack King's memory, and he tried to block efforts to honor the slain leader. Meanwhile, the Black Panther party had become the primary target of the COIN-TELPRO–Black Nationalist Hate Groups. The "Panther Directives" intensified the Bureau's disruptive activities against the BPP and led to some of the most dangerous COINTELPRO operations ever launched against any group.[51]

While the Bureau's own anti-Panther operations were nonviolent, some of them encouraged violence on the part of others. For example, in its attempt to destroy the 3,000-member Black Panther party, the Bureau, from 1969 until 1971, encouraged local police to mount operations against the Panthers. In Chicago on December 4, 1969, police raided a house used by the Black Panthers and killed Illinois Panther chairman Fred Hampton and Peoria chairman Mark Clark. Hampton's bodyguard was an FBI informant who had given the Bureau the tips and the diagram of the house which were used in the raid.[52]

Hoover targeted not only the Panthers for disruptive operations, but those he perceived as the 1970s version of the "parlor pinks" of 1919. These were the celebrities who entertained and supported the Panthers' cause. Early in 1970, Hoover visited Nixon to crow that he was going to accuse Leonard Bernstein and Peter Duchin of actively supporting the Panthers. In the course of the attack on the Panthers' Hollywood supporters, the Bureau caught an unstable young screen actress, Jean Seberg, in its net. The results were tragic.

Seberg had gotten interested in black radicalism while in Paris pursuing her film career. She had a lover, a North African, who was friendly with the Black Panthers in Los Angeles, and through him Seberg got to know Panther leader Bobby Seale. She became a supporter and financial contributor to the Panthers, and thus a subject of interest to Hoover and the Bureau.[53]

In April 1970, when Seberg was in the fourth month of pregnancy, the Bureau sought a way to make her an object lesson to any other parlor pinks who might be thinking of supporting the Panthers. According to one former FBI agent who worked in Los Angeles at the time, a culture of racism had so permeated the Bureau and its field offices that the agents seethed with hatred toward the Panthers and the white women who associated with them. "In the view of the Bureau," this agent reported, "Jean was giving aid and comfort to the enemy, the BPP. . . . The giving of her white body to a black man was an unbearable thought for many of the white agents. An agent, whose name I will not mention, for obvious reasons, was overheard to say, a few days after I arrived in Los Angeles from New York, 'I wonder how she'd like to gobble my dick while I shove my .38 up that black bastard's ass.' "[54]

Agent Richard Wallace Held telegraphed Washington:

> Bureau permission is requested to publicize the pregnancy of Jean Seberg, well-known white movie actress, . . . by advising Hollywood Gossip-Columnists in the Los Angeles area of the situation. It is felt the possible publication of "Seberg's plight" could cause her embarrassment and serve to cheapen her image with the general public. It is proposed the following letter from a fictitious person be sent to local columnists:
> I was just thinking about you and remembered I still owe you a favor. So—I was in Paris last week and ran into Jean Seberg, who was heavy with baby. I thought she and Romain [Romain Gary, Seberg's estranged husband] had gotten together again, but she confided that the child belonged to [deleted] of the Black Panthers, one [deleted]. The dear girl is getting around.[55]

Washington gave its approval, ordering a two-month delay so as not to compromise a phone tap the Bureau was maintaining on the Panther headquarters in Los Angeles and until the pregnancy was obvious. On May 19, 1970, gossip columnist Joyce Haber published an item about the Seberg pregnancy in the *Los Angeles Times.* The story did not use Seberg's name, but gave enough details to make her identity obvious. Haber did not get the tip directly from the FBI, but it is likely that, in a roundabout way, the Bureau was the original source, and in Washington Hoover was circulating a memorandum on Seberg's support of the Panthers to Ehrlichman, Mitchell, and Kleindienst.[56]

Other papers began to print stories referring to the possibility that Seberg was carrying a black baby, and shortly before the baby was due she tried to kill herself with an overdose of sleeping pills. Then *Newsweek* printed the story, and in the shock, the baby was born prematurely and died two days later. Seberg never recovered from the loss of the baby and the merciless press harassment. In 1976, Jean Seberg was notified by the Justice Department that she had been the target of this COINTELPRO. That knowledge completed her emotional destruction, and three years later she succeeded in taking her own life; her ex-husband, who had tried to help her through the crisis by claiming he was the dead baby's father, killed himself not long afterward.

Seberg was a celebrity, so her passion and death became a part of the gossip history of Hollywood. The COINTELPRO attack on her was no different from hundreds of other documented attacks on obscure radicals and their friends, stories that were never told because the victims were not glamorous, not famous, and, in many of the worst cases, not white.

A campaign as vicious and lawless as the one against Seberg proves there was nothing Hoover would not do to destroy black radicalism. After his destruction of Marcus Garvey and his attempt to destroy King, that fact hardly needs more proof. Why, then, did he hang back when Sullivan and Huston dangled the opportunity to direct a united federal intelligence drive against the Panthers and other black militants?[57]

The answer is that secrecy was so essential to the Black Panther COINTELPRO that expansion was out of the question. What the Bureau was doing was so improper, so likely to generate sympathy for the Panthers, so certain to damage, maybe even destroy, Hoover and the Bureau if it were exposed, that it was far too dangerous for anyone not under the Bureau's strict discipline to be involved in the operation or to know about it. Moreover, even within the Bureau, the number of agents and operations involved had to be kept small enough so that Hoover could supervise every step of every case. To bring other agencies into contact with FBI operations against the Panthers would have made exposure almost a certainty. Paradoxically, then, the very impropriety of what Hoover was doing kept him from being able to expand his operations or to cooperate with other agencies if he were to keep the lid on. Hoover was taking risks by authorizing even his small and contained operation against the Panthers, but his control over the Bureau was so absolute, insubordination so rare, that the danger must have seemed minimal to him.

The second principal target of the Huston Plan was to be the Students for a Democratic Society, and of course this was also the main target of Hoover's COINTELPRO–New Left. As with the Black

Panther COINTELPRO, the SDS operation could not then be expanded without unacceptable risk to Hoover and the FBI. Hoover's aides recall that Sullivan was forever pressing Hoover to expand the COINTELPRO–New Left, but that Hoover consistently resisted. Mark Felt remembers that Sullivan "wanted to conduct an investigation of every member" and that "this got to be a big hassle inside the FBI." John Mohr also states that "Sullivan wanted to investigate everybody" within the SDS, but that Hoover restricted opening files to only a small number of Weathermen.[58]

If the Black Panther and New Left operations are compared to Hoover's great drives against the Communists in 1919 and 1947, and against the gangsters of the thirties, another difference emerges. While all of those drives had their undercover aspects, some of which would not comfortably stand the light of day, secrecy was not really their essence. Their secret components were merely part of very highly publicized campaigns in pursuit of goals supported by the overwhelming majority of the public, the legal establishment, and the government elite. If the secret operations were exposed, as they sometimes were, they would not, and did not, greatly damage the Bureau because there was really no secret about what in general the Bureau was doing. A term such as "confidential" should be used to distinguish those covert operations that could be exposed without mortal danger to the Bureau (because they were sanctioned by higher authority and supported by the public) from those that were truly "secret" they were so improper as to jeopardize the Bureau's very survival if they became known.

The COINTELPRO operations of the late sixties and seventies were "secret" and so were exceptions to Hoover's overall conduct as director of the FBI. They underscore the fact that for all Hoover's efforts to cling to legal justifications in his confidential operations (recall the use of the Smith Act, the Communist Control Act, and the Internal Security Act to buttress the covert war against the CPUSA, and President Johnson's approval of the infiltration of the Klan), his personal antipathy to the unrest of the sixties was so great that he was willing to cast aside restraints he had abided by all his life.

He had always been willing, of course, to use any effective method to destroy blacks who had the ability to rally the black masses. His racial prejudice on this score tended to overwhelm his commitment to legalism whenever he was confronted by what he was wont to call a potential black "Messiah," whether it was Marcus Garvey, Martin Luther King, Jr., or the Black Panthers.

Likewise, COINTELPRO–New Left derived more from Hoover's

somewhat pathetic self-image as a foster parent to America's youth, acting *in loco parentis* at a time of parental abdication of responsibility. While many of the operations against the New Left sought to prevent meetings and block airing of radical beliefs, others were naive efforts to bring the young radicals back under parental or college discipline by exposing behavior that would shame parents and college administrations into taking action against their wayward charges.[59]

The circumscribed, self-contained quality of Hoover's late COIN-TELPROs also distinguishes them from his earlier efforts. The hallmark of Hoover's great drives of 1919 and 1947 had been their comprehensive, expansive quality. Sullivan was thirsting to similarly expand the COINTELPROs in the late sixties and seventies. But to Hoover, the idea was impossibly dangerous. He would never permit himself to be caught up in someone else's crusade, particularly one that was in advance of, rather than in response to, public demands for action.

Hoover's refusal to give up the hunt for reds can also be understood as a defense against getting caught up in a disastrous drive against non-Communist radicals whose American roots were not at issue. Sullivan ridiculed Hoover's continued concern with the Old Left: he said there were only 2,800 members left in the Communist party, only half of them active. The only people who thought there were any connections at all between the Old and New Lefts, said Sullivan, were "Gus Hall and J. Edgar Hoover" and "I have my doubts about Gus Hall." But Sullivan was not complaining about Hoover's militancy against communism. He was fighting to be unleashed against the New Left without worrying about whether or not there were links between antiwar protest and the Communist party. Hoover was not willing to risk *that* unless he could be covered by the panoply of legal weapons that had been developed to fight the Communist party. To do this (weakened though those laws had been by court decision and congressional repeal) Hoover would have to find evidence of infiltration of the New Left and the Panthers by the Old Left. Hoover kept insisting the connection might develop, and he kept the Domestic Intelligence Division looking for it. Hoover's experience had taught him that unless the Bureau could point to that Communist connection, it would be disastrous to expand his attacks on radicals.[60]

Hoover's opposition to the Huston plan derived from his lifelong approach to domestic intelligence. He always saw the real threat to the country as a radical uprising aided by the Soviet Union. This meant the American Communist party aided by international communism. In the past, he made his most aggressive (and therefore most risky) assaults on radicalism during periods of superpower tension, but now, in the 1960s and 1970, Nixon was promoting detente with Russia and unveiling his opening to China. For Hoover, specific surveillance techniques were always subordinated to larger operational, bureaucratic, and political ends. Specifically, he was always primarily concerned with being ready for war hysteria in times of world crisis, with preparing the American people for the necessary roundups, and with defending traditional American values against the attacks he associated with communism.

He was not willing to engage in the sensitive and dangerous operations urged on him by the Nixon administration unless he could fit them into a comprehensive plan developed in response to a true international crisis. He was not willing to move unless he could count on the massive, overwhelming support of the American people.

In the short run, the Nixon administration was simply interested in smearing and destroying antiwar dissenters; in the long run, it wanted to use attacks on dissenters to turn the "silent majority" into the basis of a lasting Republican coalition. But for Hoover, a domestic intelligence system was a permanent bulwark against foreign espionage and the long-term threat of a resurgent international Communist movement, and for the protection of the home front in case of war. It was not simply a tool to be used in domestic politics. Hoover had learned during the twenties how easily the FBI could be destroyed if it were misused, and he was not going to do anything that might ruin his life's work.

The demise of Huston's plan was the end of his White House career (a fortunate fall: it kept him from an involvement in Watergate), but William Sullivan rose out of the ashes of the fiasco as the FBI strongman. It is, in fact, possible to see the Huston affair as a power play by Sullivan, one in which he benefited no matter what happened to Huston and the plan. It was Sullivan who pushed Huston to urge the most extreme recommendations of his proposal on the president; it was Sullivan who reassured Huston that Hoover's objections could be discounted. To Hoover, Sullivan represented himself as guardian of the Bureau's interests against the reckless plans of others. In memos to Hoover, Sullivan disassociated himself from the plan and said he had serious reservations about it. Whatever the outcome, Sullivan would benefit. What actually happened was that DeLoach, who had earlier announced his intention to resign from the Bureau to join Pepsico, finally left in July 1970. Hoover then elevated Sullivan to the rank vacated by DeLoach, assistant to the director, the number-three position behind Tolson and Hoover.[61]

Both DeLoach and Mohr warned Hoover against appointing Sullivan, but he told Mohr that "he could think of nobody with the Bureau who was more loyal than Sullivan." (Hoover told Sullivan that he had not chosen Mohr because Tolson, under whom Mohr worked, had told him Mohr drank.) It may have been, however, that Hoover saw that Sullivan was angling for Hoover's downfall and the top spot, but that he was worried about Sullivan's influence with the administration and hoped to placate them and Sullivan. Never had Hoover had as rebellious a subordinate as Sullivan, but rarely had he had one as talented and capable of leadership. Sullivan's promotion to be Hoover's top assistant in July 1970 meant that Hoover was supporting Sullivan's eventual candidacy for the directorship if he would only mend his ways and bide his time. That Hoover was willing to take such a gamble says much about his respect for Sullivan's abilities; it also suggests Hoover's opinion, perhaps, of the leadership abilities of his other safe, loyal, and predictable executives, who were passed over by him when he chose the man who would lead the Bureau when he was gone.[62]

Hoover's power to conduct secret operations like the COINTELPROs against the Panthers and the SDS depended on the absolute freedom he had won from any inquiry into the internal operations of the Bureau. Not since the 1920 investigation of the Palmer raids had the in-house memos and private business of the Bureau been exposed to public gaze. Except for a remarkably few breeches of security—the Coplon case for example—Hoover had been able to pick and choose what the public would learn about the Bureau. He had never suffered the indignity of having an outside, unsympathetic investigator look into what he had been doing, what the Bureau had become, and what it looked like from the inside. And it had been that luxury of freedom that let him indulge himself with such abuses of power as his persecution of King, the late COINTELPROs, and his harassment of Bureau critics.

On March 8, 1971, that changed forever. That night a group calling itself the Citizens' Commission to Investigate the FBI broke into the FBI field office at Media, Pennsylvania. The burglars were never caught. The Bureau was convinced the theft was the work of supporters of the Catholic East Coast Conspiracy to Save Lives, in retaliation for the recent indictment of its leaders on the grounds of conspiring to blow up the capital's power system and to kidnap Henry Kissinger.

Ironically, the Bureau had expected something like the Media burglary, and had recently begun to equip its offices with new security systems, but the Media office had not yet transferred its sensitive files to the new safe. On the morning of March 9, agents reporting for work discovered that their files dealing with domestic security were missing. The Bureau realized it had to brace itself for an uproar when and if the documents stolen from the files were made public.

That was not long in coming. On March 22, Senator George Mc-Govern and Congressman Parren Mitchell of Maryland received photocopies of the files, but both refused to have anything to do with the stolen materials, and they turned the documents over to the Bureau. At the end of the month, however, an eighty-two-page extract of the documents was published by the New Left journal *WIN*. [63]

The documents showed a wide spectrum of FBI domestic surveillance activities. They revealed a wiretap on the Philadelphia office of the Black Panthers. There was a file on all the colleges in the Philadelphia area, as well as a collection of files on the SDS and others in the New Left movement. The Bureau had been getting reports on demonstrations from the Philadelphia police, and there was a memo from the registrar at Swarthmore College giving information on Congressman Henry Reuss's daughter, who was active in the antiwar movement. The files also revealed surveillance of the Jewish Defense League, the Ku Klux Klan, and the National Black Economic Development Conference. [64]

Hoover's aide Mark Felt called the raid "the turning point in the FBI image" because release of the files helped the New Left show some justification for its "paranoid fear of the FBI, which it hysterically equated with the Soviet secret police." This view of the Bureau, according to Felt, "seeped into the press and found growing expression among the more bewitched and bothered opinion makers." Felt thought that "at an earlier time the Media documents leaked to the press would have been accepted for what they were, but given the distemper of the times, the disclosures were turned into a weapon with which to cripple the effectiveness of the FBI and law enforcement generally." [65]

Hoover reacted furiously. He kept some of the Bureau's top investigators working on the case for months, and he closed 100 out of 536 Resident Agencies because they were too vulnerable to attack. It is possible the Bureau could have ridden out the storm over the Media documents without making fundamental changes except for the fact that one of the documents bore the caption COINTELPRO–New Left. (It recommended interviewing students in order to "enhance the paranoia endemic in these circles and . . . further serve to get the point across there is an FBI agent behind every mailbox.") Not for another year was the hint of the COINTELPRO caption picked up, but nevertheless, COINTELPRO was now compromised. (On March 20, 1972, NBC correspondent Carl Stern demanded documents dealing with COINTELPRO–New Left under the Freedom of Information Act. Denied his request, Stern sued, and on December 6, 1973, received the documents.)[66]

Bureau secrecy was under attack on other fronts. On April 24, Congressman Hale Boggs accused Hoover of tapping congressional phones and infiltrating college campuses and asked Mitchell to fire the director: "When the FBI adopts the tactics of the Soviet Union and Hitler's Gestapo, it's time for the Director no longer to be the Director." Hoover called Mitchell to say there had not been a congressional wiretap since 1924, and that the FBI was so careful about not shadowing congressmen, even inadvertently, that when a subject being trailed entered the grounds of the Capitol, the surveillance was dropped. Hoover went into a frenzy calling congressional leaders to assure them that the charges were untrue. Deputy Attorney General Kleindienst wanted to know if by any chance some employee had been guilty without Hoover knowing. Hoover replied, "I did not believe so, although you can't ever tell as we used to have so few employees and now have about 20,000 today, but I seriously doubt it because it would have had to be done by the Washington Field Office and that is under pretty close contact and control here at headquarters because of its location." He complained that when he had his usual lunch at the Mayflower he had been besieged by reporters.[67]

Adding to Hoover's worries was a proposal in the perenially critical *Nation* magazine on February 8, 1971, for an investigation of the Bureau. By April a committee had been formed by such Hoover enemies as Norman Dorsen, Burke Marshall, Roger Wilkins, and others, to organize a conference for this purpose. (The conference was held at Princeton on October 29 and 30, 1971, and the results published in 1973 as *Investigating the FBI*.) In a lengthy letter declining the committee's invitation to send an FBI representative to the conference, Hoover accused it of prejudging the FBI. He complained that in bringing charges against him, he hoped that critics would remember how difficult it was for public officials to sue for slander. "The result is that in so many cases of criticism my only recourse is that of taking some personal pleasure in knowing that the critics have abundantly proven, in the reams and volumes that they have published, that one of their principal charges—that I am beyond criticism—is totally false."[68]

While the secrecy surrounding COINTELPRO had not yet been pierced, the handwriting was on the wall. No longer could Hoover be sure that knowledge of these operations could be contained within the Bureau. It was time for damage control. On April 28, 1971, Hoover formally terminated all the COINTELPROs that had been the foundation of the Bureau's domestic security operations since 1956. The Domestic Intelligence Division's new chief, Charles Brennan, told Hoover that "although successful over the years, it is felt they should now be discontinued for security reasons because of their sensitivity." Hoover allowed for counterintelligence operations in "exceptional instances," but demanded that requests be submitted on an individual basis. Termination of the formal COINTELPROs did not totally eliminate *all* counterintelligence operations, and investigators were later able to find individual cases after April 1971. Nevertheless, Hoover's action had deprived the Domestic Intelligence Division of the major part of its operations. That also meant Hoover had cut deeply into the source of William Sullivan's power.[69]

Meanwhile, Hoover's attempt within the Bureau to ensure Sullivan's loyalty by making him his heir-apparent was proving to be a failure. There was a new irritant now, a speech Sullivan made before newspaper officials in Williamsburg, Virginia, in October 1970, in which he was widely reported as downgrading the danger of communism. In the question period after the speech Sullivan said that the Communist party had been greatly contained through the years and that he did not feel its current threat was serious. It was headline news when a high FBI official gave voice to heresies like that. Mark Felt said that "Hoover was furious. For years he had emphasized that the CPUSA was 'an integral part of the international Communist conspiracy.' It was, moreover, Hoover's very defensible contention that the CPUSA, however circumscribed by the FBI, was still giving secret aid and comfort to the New Left and to its terrorist off-shoots."[70]

Sullivan also quarreled with Hoover over Hoover's leak to the House Appropriations Committee on November 19, 1970, about the supposed plans by the East Coast Conspiracy to Save Lives to "blow up the underground electrical conduits and steam pipes serving the Washington, D.C., area in order to disrupt Federal Government operations" and to kidnap an unnamed White House staff member (Henry Kissinger). "If successful, the plotters [Catholic priests Philip and Daniel Berrigan] would demand an end to U.S. bombing operations in Southeast Asia." Eight days later, on November 27, Hoover gave the same testimony to the Senate Appropriations Subcommittee in closed session, but this time the word leaked out and was the principal news story over the Thanksgiving weekend. The Bureau rushed to secure indictments against the Berrigans and their associates and arrested them on January 12, 1971.[71]

The Berrigan case was a disaster for Hoover, who had to face charges that he had prejudged defendants in a complicated case, and that an incomplete investigation had been rushed by him to a half-baked conclusion in order to salvage his reputation. (The trial took place from February to April 1972 and resulted in acquittals on the conspiracy charges, but guilty verdicts against Philip Berrigan and Sister Elizabeth McAlister for smuggling letters into the Lewisburg, Pennsylvania, Federal Prison. Ramsey Clark was one of the lawyers for the defense.) Hoover blamed Sullivan, who had briefed him on the Berrigan case, even though Sullivan said he had warned Hoover not to use the information: "I don't think we'll even have a case against them, and they could have a case against us."[72]

The bad publicity left Hoover so despondent that Attorney General Kleindienst called to console him. "I wanted him to know and the President to know," Hoover told Kleindienst, that "if at any time my presence embarrasses the Administration, I am willing to step aside. The Attorney General said they could expect that from me, but the thing is going to subside and we will just go on and carry the business as we should. I said that is what I intend to do but I wanted him and the President to know [that] at any time it is felt I may be a burden or handicap to the re-election, I would be glad to step aside. The Attorney General said I was a good American."[73]

Hoover's clashes with Sullivan reached a climax during the summer of 1971, during the frantic investigation of Daniel Ellsberg for leaking the "Pentagon Papers" (a Robert McNamara-commissioned study of the steps by which the United States had become involved in Vietnam) to the New York Times on June 13, 1971. The White House ordered a full-scale investigation to see how many other people were involved. Nixon called the Pentagon Papers "the most massive leak of classified documents in American history" and said he desperately needed to know "what more did Ellsberg have, and what else did he plan to do?"[74]

As agents fanned out to interview everyone who knew Ellsberg to gather information on Ellsberg's motives, the Domestic Intelligence Division, which was handling the case, asked Hoover if it could interview Ellsberg's father-in-law, New York toy manufacturer Louis Marx.

It so happened that Hoover and Marx were good friends (Marx gave Hoover a shipment of toys to distribute each Christmas), so Hoover specifically told Charles Brennan, head of Domestic Intelligence, not to interview Marx. Brennan misread Hoover's "NO H" as "H OK" and permitted the interview to take place. When Hoover learned about the mistake, he was furious and ordered Brennan demoted and transferred. Brennan was Sullivan's protégé, and Sullivan went over Hoover's head to the White House and got Mitchell to order Hoover to cancel Brennan's punishment. That confirmed suspicions already brewing in the Bureau that Sullivan was disloyal.[75]

On June 7, 1971, just before the Pentagon Papers leak, Sullivan had suddenly begun quarreling with Hoover and the other executives over a recent Executive Conference decision to expand the number of FBI agents attached to American embassies in foreign capitals (the so-called "legal attachés"). After initially going along with the majority of the Executive Conference in support of Hoover's proposal, Sullivan reversed himself on June 16 with a blistering attack on the "lack of objectivity, originality and independent thinking" among Hoover's executives. He charged that because of "racial conflict, student and academic revolution, and possible increase in unemployment, this country is heading into ever more troubled waters and the Bureau had better be fully prepared. . . . This cannot be done if we spread ourselves too thin." Puzzled by Sullivan's attack on a policy he had supported a few days before, Hoover had one of his aides analyze Sullivan's memo. The conclusion was "there has to be something wrong for him to do such an abrupt about face at this time . . . [it seems] more definite . . . that he is more on the side of CIA, State Department and Military Intelligence Agencies, than the FBI."[76]

The FBI quickly determined that Ellsberg alone was responsible, but the White House was not satisfied. Nixon felt that he had made his concern about Ellsberg clear to Hoover, and yet still Hoover was "dragging his feet." He also thought Hoover was afraid that a full-scale FBI investigation would turn Ellsberg into a martyr. Mitchell told Nixon that Hoover was going easy on Ellsberg because of his friendship with Ellsberg's father-in-law. Nixon guessed that a final reason for Hoover's refusal to cooperate was his long-standing dislike for "sharing his territory" with the other agencies that were also investigating Ellsberg.[77]

It was the White House's dissatisfaction with Hoover's performance in the Ellsberg case that caused Nixon to set up his own team of investigators to search out leaks in the government. This began on

July 17, 1971, when Ehrlichman put Egil 'Bud' Krogh, a lawyer on the staff of the Domestic Council staff, in charge of stopping the leaks. David Young, a lawyer from the Kissinger staff, Howard Hunt, formerly of the CIA, and G. Gordon Liddy, a former FBI man, were on Krogh's team. Since they were supposed to stop leaks, David Young put up a sign calling the group "Plumbers." Liddy later became the brains behind the plot to bug the Watergate offices of the Democratic National Committee. Hunt was arrested when a check from him was found on one of the Watergate burglars.[78]

There is no doubt that the reason for the Plumbers was Nixon's frustration with Hoover. "I wanted someone to light a fire under the FBI in its investigation of Ellsberg, and to keep the departments and agencies active in pursuit of leakers. If a conspiracy existed, I wanted to know, and I wanted the full resources of the government brought to bear in order to find out. If the FBI was not going to pursue the case, then we would have to do it ourselves. . . . I wanted a good political operative who could sift through the Pentagon papers . . . I wanted ammunition against the antiwar critics. Soon the Plumbers were doing the kinds of things Hoover refused."[79]

Sullivan's attacks on the legal attaché program, his insubordination over Brennan, and his private dealings with the White House finally convinced Hoover that Sullivan could no longer be trusted. On July 1, 1971, Hoover called Assistant Director Mark Felt, head of the Inspection Division, into his office and informed him that he was being promoted to a newly created number-three position as Tolson's assistant with the title deputy associate director and that this was being done specifically to bring Sullivan under control and to establish tight discipline over Brennan's Domestic Intelligence Division. Felt remembers that during the meeting "I saw something I had never seen before: the Director looked tired." Hoover told him, "I need someone who can control Sullivan. I think you know he has been getting out of hand." (Felt said that an important factor was Tolson's deterioration. It was Tolson's traditional role to ride herd on head-strong employees, but although Tolson was mentally sharp he had no stamina, and could not keep up with Sullivan.)[80]

Sullivan was not without defenses. He had an ally in Kissinger's aide, General Alexander Haig, a close friend and once a neighbor. Felt says Sullivan had other friends in the White House, and "spent half his time there." His most important asset was his close relationship with the assistant attorney general for Internal Security, Robert Mardian. In fact, Hoover was so suspicious of Sullivan's relationship with Mardian, that on June 2 he had ordered FBI executives to have no contacts with outsiders unless the FBI legal counsel was present.[81]

Once Hoover promoted Felt, Sullivan realized he was doomed, and he concocted a last-ditch strategy to bring Hoover down. He went to Mardian and told him that he was in trouble, that he thought he was going to be fired, and that it would be dangerous to leave the reports of the seventeen Kissinger wiretaps with Hoover. Sullivan knew those wiretap reports were hot, because on July 1, as part of its preparations for the Ellsberg trial, the Justice Department had filed an inquiry to search the ELSUR index to see if Ellsberg had been overheard in any wiretaps. Ellsberg did not appear in the ELSUR, but Sullivan knew that this was only because the Kissinger wiretaps had not been indexed in the ELSUR, and Ellsberg *had* "walked-in" on those taps. On July 12, 1971, Mardian flew to San Clemente to report to Nixon that Sullivan had told him Hoover might, in Nixon's words, "use the seventeen wiretaps we placed on administration aides and reporters in 1969 as blackmail leverage in order to retain his position in the Bureau." Nixon said he had long heard rumors that Hoover had held onto his job so long because of "subtle" blackmail of presidents, but he had not believed them. Nixon also did not believe Hoover would ever disclose anything affecting national security. Nevertheless, Nixon ordered Mardian to get the wiretap reports from Sullivan. Nixon said "that was the last I heard of any supposed threat from Hoover. I never said anything to him about it."[82]

Sullivan hoped turning the reports of the Kissinger-ordered wiretaps over to the White House had proved his loyalty to the administration. The next step was to act in such an insubordinate and challenging way that Hoover would have no choice but to fire him, which would confront the administration with a choice between Sullivan, who had proven himself an administration loyalist, and Hoover, who had been defying the Nixon administration almost from the start. On August 28, Sullivan wrote Hoover a letter (with a copy to Mitchell) in which he accused Hoover of running the Bureau contrary to the president's best interests, and listed many of his personal grievances.

Hoover visited Mitchell and got permission to fire Sullivan. He called DeLoach at Pepsico, evidently to get the support of Donald Kendall, Pepsico's president, a friend of Nixon's. He even got Mardian lined up on his side. Sullivan had clearly misread the administration's support of him. On September 3, 1971, Hoover ordered Sullivan to "submit your application for retirement after taking the annual leave to which you are entitled." Sullivan at first resisted but took his vacation when he saw that Hoover had already put Alex Rosen in his place as assistant to the director. While he was away, on September 9, the purge continued as Sullivan's protégé Charles Brennan was removed from his post and shunted off into a meaningless position watching over the Ellsberg investigation. Felt says that Hoover appreciated the "poetic justice of this" because Brennan had held onto his job after the mix-up over the Louis Marx interview only because the White House had said that he was vital to the Ellsberg case. At Hoover's first meeting with Brennan's replacement "the entire time was spent in emphasis on the restraints and curbs which had to be applied to the operations of the Domestic Intelligence Division."[83]

Sullivan returned from his enforced vacation in the last week of September, evidently hoping somehow to stay in the Bureau, but he found the locks on his door changed, Rosen in his office, and a search in progress for the missing Kissinger tapes. On October 6 he finally gave up and applied for resignation. When he cleaned out his personal effects, he left behind his autographed picture of J. Edgar Hoover. Felt remembers that he seemed "edgy" because he was not permitted to get into his file cabinets, which was where the only copy of the Bureau's notorious December 1964 letter to Martin Luther King, Jr., was later found. When Sullivan was ready to leave, Felt accused him of being a Judas, and Sullivan challenged him to a fight. "He was like a little banty rooster, and I think he really would have fought me had I accepted his challenge, although I am half again his height."[84]

When Felt went to report that Sullivan was gone, Hoover shook his head and said, "The greatest mistake I ever made was to promote Sullivan!" Then he turned and stared out the window so long that Felt thought he had forgotten he was there. Felt excused himself, and left Hoover alone with his thoughts.[85]

Hoover's battle with Sullivan concerned not simply power, but the FBI's future. Hoover was curtailing all of the secret activities that had been championed by Sullivan over the past decade, while Sullivan, urged on by the administration, wanted to expand them. Hoover's political sense told him the Bureau was going to have to operate far more openly than ever in the past. Like it or not, the public and the Congress were going to be looking over the FBI's shoulder from now on. If the Bureau was to preserve its historic relationship of trust with the public, it was going to have to conduct itself in a manner open to inspection; this was what Sullivan had found impossible to accept.

Sullivan's strategy, insofar as it was intended to provoke the administration to fire Hoover, nearly worked. Several times during 1971 when Hoover came under attack, Nixon had to defend the director and deny he had any intention of removing him. At one press conference he said, "I am not going to discuss the situation with regard to Hoover's tenure in office when the matter has not been raised with me, either by me or with me." He even said that criticism of Hoover was only making him "dig in."[86]

By fall 1971, Nixon had changed his mind. Ehrlichman, who led the assault on Hoover in the White House councils, said, "Hoover seemed to me like an old boxer who had taken too many punches. He had stayed in the fight past his time, feebly counterpunching. But he had lost his judgment and vigor. He had become an embarrassment." Ehrlichman sent Nixon what the president thought was a "brilliantly argued memorandum written . . . by G. Gordon Liddy, a member of the White House staff and a former FBI agent. The memorandum analyzed in detail the complex situation presented by Hoover's long tenure as Director and concluded with a strong recommendation that he should resign." The Sullivan revolt made Nixon think that the Bureau's morale was sagging and what "had once been Hoover's source of strength—his discipline and his pride—were now seen as temperament and ego." He also recalled Sullivan's charges that "Hoover was trapped in outdated notions of the communist threat and was not moving with flexibility against the new violence-prone radicals." Arguing against firing Hoover was Mitchell, who said that it might involve a public confrontation and pointed out that despite all the criticism, "Hoover still had very substantial support in the county and in Congress. To millions of Americans J. Edgar Hoover was still a folk hero."[87]

Nixon later said he made the decision to remove Hoover only with great reluctance. He thought that Hoover was being attacked by the same old coalition of enemies who hated him as "a symbol of beliefs and values that they opposed, particularly his crusade against domestic communism and subversion, his strong stand for tougher anticrime legislation, and his opposition to legal and judicial permissiveness." Nixon did not want to desert Hoover while he was under attack, but he told Mitchell that "Edgar isn't even aware that . . . he is thinking too much of himself and not enough about the cause he wants to serve." Nixon also wanted to get his own appointee in place so that if he lost the election, the Democrats would not be able to appoint someone who would harass Nixon and the Republicans.[88]

The decision to fire Hoover was made around October 1971. Nixon always had problems asking people face-to-face for their resignations, and he called in Ehrlichman to help him prepare for the ordeal. Ehrlichman suggested an artful way of slipping in the knife, and then Hoover was invited to the White House for a breakfast meeting with the president.[89]

When Hoover appeared for his scheduled execution, Nixon found him as "alert, articulate and decisive" as he had ever seen him. It seemed as if Hoover was acting especially energetic to demonstrate that his mental and physical faculties were still vigorous. After consoling him about the Princeton Conference that was investigating the FBI, Nixon pointed out "as gently and subtly as I could" that the attacks were only going to get worse in the future. He told Hoover it would be tragic if he had to leave while under attack instead of with the chorus of tribute and gratitude Nixon said he could arrange at that time. But Hoover was having none of it. He made a strong statement of loyalty to Nixon, saying, "More than anything else, I want to see you re-elected in 1972. If you feel that my staying on as head of the Bureau hurts your chances for re-election, just let me know. As far as these present attacks are concerned and the ones that are planned for the future, they don't make any difference to me. I think you know that the tougher the attacks get, the tougher I get." On the other hand, he made it clear to Nixon that he was not going to submit his resignation. If Nixon wanted his resignation, he would have to ask for it.

Nixon appreciated the irony of the situation—he had done the same thing to Eisenhower in 1952 when there was pressure for Nixon to resign from the Republican ticket when it was discovered he had a private "slush fund" from wealthy contributors to defray his expenses. Faced with the necessity of taking the initiative himself, Nixon says, "I decided not to do so." His "personal feeling" was one factor, but "equally important" was his judgment that asking for Hoover's resignation "would raise more political problems than it would solve."[90]

Nixon's aides were waiting impatiently to find out what had happened, but Haldeman told Ehrlichman, "Don't ask. He doesn't want to talk about it." Ehrlichman "was to forget that the Nixon-Hoover breakfast had ever taken place." In fact, Ehrlichman later discovered that Hoover had walked out of the meeting not only with his job intact, but with a new commitment from Nixon for a 20 percent increase in his overseas contingent of legal attachés. Later Nixon called the meeting "a total strike-out" and indicated that he had been surprised by Hoover's stubbornness since Mitchell had led him to believe that Hoover was ready to leave.[91]

At the end of 1971, Hoover had successfully withstood challenges to his position from within and without the Bureau. With Mark Felt as his right-hand man, he had once again established firm control over the FBI. He had ended the COINTELPRO operations that posed the greatest danger to himself and the Bureau, and he had resisted all efforts to draw the FBI into reckless new ventures. There were still occasional neighborly phone calls from Nixon, but Hoover had placed his relationships with the White House on a correct and formal basis.

The White House made a final attempt to enlist Hoover in one more of its schemes, but now Hoover's defenses were up. In March 1972, the White House, under intense pressure because of a scandal involving an alleged payoff from ITT to fix an antitrust case, tried to use the FBI laboratory to discredit a key piece of evidence. This was a memo from ITT lobbyist Dita Beard to her employers bragging that Mitchell had told her the case could be settled for a $400,000 contribution to the Republican party to support the 1972 Republican national convention. Columnist Jack Anderson had gotten hold of the memo and published it on February 19, and the scandal looked as if it could damage the president's reelection.

The White House strategy was to attack Anderson on the memo. It got Beard to swear that the memo was a forgery, and then sent John Dean to Hoover to ask him to test it to prove it was a fake. Hoover was initially cordial, especially when Dean explained that Attorney General-designate Richard Kleindienst (he called Hoover "Mr. Hoover" and Hoover called him "Kleindienst") was being attacked by the "jackal" Jack Anderson. (According to Dean, Hoover called Anderson "the lowest form of human being to walk the earth. He's a muckraker who lies, steals and . . . he'll go lower than dog

shit for a story.") Dean returned to the White House confident that
Hoover was on their side. Hoover even offered to send over his "files"
on Jack Anderson.[92]

As soon as the FBI lab tests were completed, Hoover called Dean,
told him to see Felt and hung up abruptly. Felt let Dean see the
report before Hoover signed it, and Dean "read the letter with dismay.
. . . In FBI jargon, Hoover was saying the Dita Beard memo was
legitimate."[93]

Dean was furious and first tried to persuade Felt and then Hoover
to modify the FBI report to say that it was not in conflict with the
ITT findings. "Call Dean right back," Hoover told Felt, "and tell
him I said for him to go jump in the lake! I want to cooperate when
I can, but this request is completely improper!" Dean tried again on
February 24 to get the Bureau to change the report. This time he
demanded Hoover let the ITT expert talk to the head of the FBI
lab. Felt said to Hoover, "I doubt very much that our Lab is going
to change its position." Hoover laughed and said, "No, I don't think
so either." When Felt called Dean to tell him that the Bureau stood
by the report, Dean did not return his call. Felt said, "I am glad
that the FBI was able to resist White House pressure to take part
in a cover up which in some ways was a prelude to Watergate."[94]

The White House did not tell ITT about the FBI report, and
urged them to release their expert's findings that the Beard memo
was a forgery. On March 23, Hoover humiliated the Republican senators who backed Beard on the strength of the ITT report when he
released the FBI lab report. Once again the White House was furious
with Hoover, and there was talk again of kicking him upstairs as
"director emeritus." Colson urged Nixon to fire the director, but the
administration's public opinion polls still showed that Hoover was
too popular to touch.[95]

When Nixon saw the FBI's report and was told that Hoover would
not alter it, Charles Colson said he had never seen him so angry.
Nixon wrote a note to "his friend Edgar" asking him to cooperate,
and had Ehrlichman carry it to Hoover to "turn him around." That
didn't work either. Nixon mused sadly, "I don't understand Edgar
sometimes."[96]

Hoover was now approaching his forty-eighth anniversary as FBI director; he had been in the Justice Department almost fifty-five years.
It had been on May 10, 1924, that Harlan Stone had called him into

his office in a long-vanished Justice Department building and put him in charge of the old scandal-ridden Bureau of Billy Burns and Gaston Means and Harry Daugherty.

Of the men who had started with him in the Justice Department, almost all were dead: Gregory, Flynn, Burke, Garvan; on September 8, 1971, Baughman had died, and Hoover had traveled to Florida for the funeral. Tolson was feeble, infirm, hardly able to get to the office. Ancient and seemingly eternal, John Lord O'Brian lived on, still defending civil liberties against Hoover as a director of the Fund for the Republic. Some of the memories, too, were growing dim. The names of Emma Goldman and Alexander Berkman, of Dillinger and Floyd and Nelson, of Hiss and the Rosenbergs, of Hoover himself, were part of American legend, but who could still remember what those great battles had meant to the country when Hoover and the Bureau were going into combat armed with bullets, files, and microphones?

The old Seward Square home was gone, Seward Square itself widened, cut clear of greenery, a part of the city to be avoided at night. The Old First Church was gone, Brent School, the Old Central High, the building that replaced it now in possession of the blacks who had not been able to enter the doors of any of the institutions that had formed Hoover's youth. The George Washington University Law School where he had studied nights after days spent working at the Library of Congress had moved to a new campus. The Justice Department buildings where Hoover had directed the Red Scare raids had vanished long ago.

And yet those long-vanished institutions still lived on in him, still steeled his resolve in ways inexplicable to his young aides and rivals. More than half a century before, he had absorbed a concept of leadership from Central High, from Dr. Donald Campbell MacLeod, from such politicians as Theodore Roosevelt and Woodrow Wilson: the belief that a leader had an obligation to preach to the community, to uphold the values that ought to be, but were not, the rules of society. A leader had the duty of shoring up all the other institutions of social authority—school, church, and family—as well as the law and government, to support the very principle of authority and defend it against all challenges. He had absorbed a faith in science and a commitment to professionalism during the progressive twenties, which he turned into an absolute drive to free law enforcement from political interference and control.

He had made many compromises during his long career. His abso-

lute self-confidence and unshakable courage rested on his allegiance
to a formalistic notion of the law, to an ideal of apolitical professionalism in law enforcement, and to a scholarly approach to problems of
loyalty and subversion; yet in the course of his life he had departed
at one time or another from every one of these principles. His personal
code was corroded by the flaws of the American society of his youth,
when racial prejudice and exclusion had been the basic fact of Washington society; these were still the rule in the FBI despite a few token
blacks. The America he had known had always been ready to abandon
justice and fair play when confronted by black challenges to white
supremacy, and Hoover reverted to this bias when blacks were not
politely content with their lot. The America of his youth had not
hesitated to use lawless means to repress radicals and aliens, Hoover
continued to use them when more respectable means failed.

This peculiar blend of patriotism and prejudice, of bureaucratic
cunning and homespun morality, of professional pride and absolute
personal devotion to his Bureau, produced in Hoover a kind of bravery
rare at any time, but particularly in the Washington of Richard Nixon.
Twice during his career Hoover had the courage to battle the president
of the United States in the president's own personal arena of national
security, and twice he had prevailed. When he defeated Truman, he
had been in his prime. As an old man, weaker, less vigorous, he still
had the energy and will to put down a revolt by the most powerful
rival ever to emerge out of the ranks of the FBI; he still had the
courage to defy the power of the White House when he thought
its policy would destroy the Bureau. He could look forward to his
fifty-fifth anniversary knowing he had kept his Bureau clear of the
intrigues of the Nixon White House, and he was still leading it according to his own design and standards. He was still his own man,
and in 1972, there were very few in Washington who could say as
much.

On May Day 1972, Hoover's black agent-chauffeur, Tom Moton, arrived at 4936 Thirtieth Place at about 7:45 A.M. For the past three
months Moton had been Hoover's driver, ever since Moton's brother-
in-law, Hoover's longtime driver James Crawford, had retired. For
years Hoover had left the house at 7:30 but recently the time had
gotten somewhat later. Now he often did not leave until 8:30. When
Tolson was well enough to go to work they would stop by his house
to pick him up. This day Tolson stayed home, and Moton and Hoover

drove directly to the Justice Department at Tenth and Pennsylvania. Moton drove Hoover into the Justice Department courtyard and dropped him off at a door near the elevator that went almost directly to his office. Hoover arrived in his office at three minutes past nine.[97]

Hoover put in a full day of work on May 1. Several times he conferred with Deputy Associate Director Mark Felt, who either came to his office or talked to him over the intercom. As usual, Hoover asked Felt for a summary of the day's news events as well as routine questions about the stream of office paperwork. The job of briefing Hoover about these details had once been Tolson's, but Felt had taken over this and most of Tolson's other duties. Felt remembers that Hoover was "alert, forceful, typically aggressive, and, so far as I could tell, completely normal in very respect."

Congress had designated May 1 "Law Day," and the Bureau that day released a law proclamation to the law enforcement community. It was an attack on the protesters who had been the targets of the recently ended COINTELPRO operations, denouncing the

> extremists of all stripes in our society [who] ceaselessly attempt to discredit the rule of law as being biased and oppressive. They have no conception of—or purposely choose to ignore—its role and history. It is not surprising that these divisive elements concentrate their abuse on the law enforcement officer. Above all, he stands firmly in the path of mindless actions that would reduce our government of laws to mob rule or the whims of lawless men. . . . The process of change in a democracy requires discipline and responsibility that will not unleash unrestrained forces that would rip the fabric of our freedoms. That fabric derives its strength through the warp and woof of laws that orderly guide the process of change by defining our individual and corporate duties. Changes in our society would otherwise simply result from those who could impose their will on others without regard for the validity of their arguments or the rights of those who do not share their views.

As usual, Hoover remained at his desk all day and left the office shortly before six, the signal that the executive staff could leave for the day.[98]

Moton was waiting for him in the courtyard. He drove Hoover to Tolson's house, where the two men had dinner together. At 10:15 Moton drove him home. As usual, Hoover let his two Cairn terriers, G-Boy and Cindy, run in the backyard, then brought them in. Before going to bed he called James Crawford, who still did yard work for him; a nursery had delivered some new rose bushes and he wanted Crawford to meet him in the morning to decide where they should

go. At last he went to bed; another May Day had passed without
the Revolution he had predicted for a May Day in 1920, fifty-two
years before. He had been twenty-five years old then; now he was
seventy-seven.

Next morning, Annie Fields, his housekeeper, cooked his invariable
breakfast of toast, soft-boiled eggs, and coffee—the eggs to share with
his dogs. It was the same breakfast Annie Hoover used to make for
him when he had started work at the Justice Department. The eggs
were ready for him at 7:30, but Hoover did not appear. A few minutes
later Tom Moton pulled up in Hoover's limousine. Still no Hoover.
At about 8:00 James Crawford arrived to get his instructions about
the roses. Still no Hoover. The three black servants conferred nervously, then Annie went up stairs and knocked on his door. No answer.
She pushed it open. Hoover was lying on the floor in his pajamas.
She panicked and ran downstairs. Crawford came up and felt Hoover's
hand. He was dead.

Their first call was to Tolson, and Moton was dispatched to get
him. Then Annie called the Bureau. The headquarters nurse notified
Hoover's private physician, who pronounced Hoover dead at the scene;
his initial opinion, confirmed later, was that the cause of death was
a heart attack. (The official verdict of the Coroner's Office examiner,
Dr. James L. Luke, was hypertensive cardiovascular activity; the immediate cause was probably a heart attack.) At 9:45 A.M. Assistant to
the Director John Mohr walked up to Deputy Associate Director
Mark Felt and said, simply, "He is dead." Felt did not comprehend
at first. He was sure that Mohr meant Tolson. Then it sank in. The
only leader they had ever known was gone. J. Edgar Hoover was
dead.[99]

"It is hard to assess my exact feelings," Mark Felt said. "I felt
no sense of personal loss, because my relationship with Hoover had
been restricted to the office. Hoover had once fraternized on a limited
basis with some of his top officials, but during his later years, Tolson
was the only Bureau official who had any social contact with the
Director." Cartha DeLoach, from his executive offices at Pepsico, wrote
his longtime "friendly" media contact, Walter Trohan of the *Chicago
Tribune,* that while he "respected him, I never loved him as a true
friend," and said that Hoover had to bear the blame for the Bureau's
later disarray because "he refused to groom a successor and would
not tolerate mention of such a matter."[100]

Tolson was now nominally acting director, in charge of the Bureau.
Actually he was dazed, bewildered, and helpless. Almost crippled,

he had to be led through the events of the next few days like a child. John Mohr and Helen Gandy had to handle the funeral arrangements. Their first thought was for a Masonic funeral, but then President Nixon took over and decreed a state funeral with military honors. That put the army in charge, and the funeral was conducted like a military operation, with maps, diagrams, and step-by-step procedures dictated by army ceremonialists.[101]

Congressmen rushed to get their tributes placed in the *Congressional Record* for reprint back home. Eventually there would be a 328-page, black-silk-bound book that collected their speeches, the proceedings at the funeral, and newspaper editorials from around the country. Senator James B. Allen of Alabama introduced a resolution to name the uncompleted new FBI headquarters after Hoover. Despite objections that the building was a monstrosity, the resolution was seconded and referred to committee.[102]

Congressman Don Clausen of California paid tribute to the Hoover of the thirties: "As a boy he was my hero and as a man, he remained my hero. And he always will be. A G-Man, when I was a boy, was a man who gave me something to trust, something to cling to, as I sought assurances of security, something I could believe in. . . . J. Edgar Hoover was truly a Christian soldier for peace in America. . . . His name will linger on forever in the hearts and minds of all Americans privileged to live in his time and under his protective shield of service. . . . May the good Lord look kindly upon this man, my hero."[103]

Most newspapers did little more than recycle their old clippings of Hoover's achievements, but some tried to take a fresh look at the familiar record. The Southern papers did the best; his style of leadership was still admired in that part of the country. Elsewhere he was simply a national fixture, someone to love or hate. One Southern paper said that "Mr. Hoover could not really have survived his long years in office by sheer power alone. Even the weakest of presidents would have forced his ouster. Instead, what was recognized in him was the deepest devotion to the welfare of his country, his undying love for its capabilities, and his peculiar genius for detecting threats to democratic government." Another saw Hoover's power as coming from his extraordinary rapport with the public: "The FBI Director has come possibly closer than any other public figure to speaking out for the average man and woman in America—the great mass of people sometimes referred to as a 'silent majority.' He was plain and blunt about the things he saw as dangers to national security and to the protection of the American home. He attacked the complacency which is an invitation to the triumph of evil. He stood four-square for law obedience as the safeguard of lives and safety."[104]

Vice President Spiro Agnew said that Hoover's detractors "disliked him for the qualities that endeared him to all other Americans, his total dedication to principle and his complete incorruptibility."[105]

On the evening of May 2 there was an open casket wake at Joseph Gaylor's Funeral Home at Wisconsin and Harrison, not far from Thirtieth Place. Some agents were surprised when they saw the man who had controlled their lives. One said, "He looked like a wispy, gray-haired, tired little man. There, in the coffin, all the power and the color had been taken away." One of Hoover's nieces said, "He looked very good . . . but smaller than I remembered. I guess death does that to you."[106]

On May 4, by House Concurrent Resolution 600, Hoover's body lay in state in the Rotunda of the Capitol on the catafalque built for Lincoln. Hoover's coffin was only the twenty-second to rest on it, the first time for a civil servant. Before him there had been only presidents, exceptional members of Congress, two unknown soldiers, and a general. Mohr had bought a casket that weighed over a thousand pounds; it was so heavy that two of the military pallbearers injured themselves struggling up the Capitol steps. Led by the FBI Executive Conference as honorary pallbearers, much of official Washington listened as Chief Justice Warren Burger delivered the eulogy. He called Hoover "a man who epitomized the American dream of patriotism, dedication to duty, and successful attainments." Some in the audience may have doubted the accuracy of Burger's prediction that "his role, in perspective, will be seen as that of a man trained as a lawyer who always tried to strike the difficult and delicate balance of efficiency in enforcement of laws but within the law and within constitutional limitations."

After the service, Attorney General Kleindienst appointed L. Patrick Gray acting director. Gray was the assistant attorney general for the Civil Division of the Justice Department, and had been nominated for deputy attorney general when Kleindienst took over from Mitchell. (Nixon's plan was to avoid a confirmation hearing on Gray, required under the 1968 Crime Control Act, until after the November election by waiting until then to actually nominate him as director.) Half an hour later Tolson telephoned Felt and asked him to draft his resignation from the Bureau and have Tolson's secretary sign it. Gray had expected the resignation and had Felt draft an acceptance.[107]

Hoover's body spent the night of May 3 in the Rotunda. On May 4 it was driven to Hoover's church, the National Presbyterian Church (now Center) on Nebraska Avenue in far northwest Washington beyond the Naval Observatory. This was the successor church to the Old First of Hoover's youth. The pastor was Edward L. R. Elson, chaplain of the Senate. The funeral was structured as a television appearance for the president, who would deliver the eulogy. Seated in the first row were President and Mrs. Nixon, the FBI Executive Conference, Gray and his wife, and Attorney General Kleindienst. Behind them sat Vice President Agnew and other dignitaries.

Elson read a selection of scriptural texts. A friend of Hoover's, Elson admired the man and had brought him onto the board of trustees of the church. He chose these texts for his eulogy as his tributes to Hoover's career, but they might have set some minds to wondering what future investigations of Hoover's career might turn up. Some of Elson's biblical passages were conventional (II Timothy: "I have fought a good fight, I have finished my course, I have kept the faith"; and I Corinthians: "For now we see through a glass, darkly; but then face to face"). Others were more pertinent, almost ironic in their relevance. One touched on a leader's absolute power and almost seemed drawn from the tall tales agents told of Hoover's ego (the 46th Psalm: "the heathen raged, the kingdoms were moved; he uttered his voice, the earth melted. . . . Come, behold the works of the Lord, what desolations he hath made in the earth. . . . Be still, and know that I am god; I will be exalted among the heathen"). Another accurately gauged the moral fervor of Hoover's lifelong pursuit of criminals and Communists (Ephesians 6: "For we wrestle not against flesh and blood, but against principalities, against powers, against the rulers of the darkness of this world, against spiritual wickedness in high places").

Nixon's funeral eulogy, four weeks before the initial Watergate burglary, the beginning of the disasters that would bring him down, was for the most part a predictable attempt to wrap Hoover's glory around the administration. Nevertheless, Nixon did show insight into the multi-faceted role Hoover had played so long on the American scene. After dutifully paying tribute to Hoover's "long life [that] brimmed over with magnificent achievement and dedicated service to this country which he loved so well" (he called him "one of the giants"), Nixon said that Hoover "became a living legend while still a young man and he lived up to his legend as the decades passed"— almost the exact same words Tom Charles Huston used when complaining of Hoover's refusal to cooperate with plans to expand domestic intelligence. He observed that "the greatness of Edgar Hoover will remain inseparable from the greatness of the organization he created and gave his whole life to building, the Federal Bureau of Investigation. He made the FBI the finest law enforcement agency on earth, the invincible and incorruptible defender of every American's precious right to be free from fear." Yet Nixon also recognized that it was not simply for his achievement that Hoover was honored so much and so long, but for the opportunity he gave Americans to pay tribute to values and traditions largely discarded as inconvenient or irrelevant in a mass society. "America has revered this man not only as the Director of an institution, but as an institution in his own right. For nearly half a century, nearly one-fourth of the whole history of this Republic, J. Edgar Hoover has exerted a great influence for good in our national life." America knew who he was, and he never changed: "While eight Presidents came and went, while other leaders of morals and manners and opinion rose and fell, the Director stayed at his post."

Then Nixon took advantage of the opportunity to get in a last swipe at his (and Hoover's) enemies: "When such a towering figure— a man who has dominated his field so completely for so many years— finally passes from the scene, there is sometimes a tendency to say, 'Well, this is the end of an era.' " Nixon vowed to carry on Hoover's fight. "The good [that] J. Edgar Hoover has done will not die. The profound principles of respect for law, order and justice will come to govern our national life more completely than ever before. Because the trend of permissiveness in this country, a trend which Edgar Hoover fought against all of his life, a trend which has dangerously eroded our national heritage as a law-abiding people, is now being reversed. The American people today are tired of disorder, disruption, and disrespect for law. America wants to come back to the law as a way of life, and as we do come back to the law, the memory of this great man, who never left the law as a way of life, will be accorded even more honor than it commands today."

After the service a convoy of ten cars formed with a motorcycle escort; then began the long procession from the church for a last drive across the width of the city to Congressional Cemetery. "As we left the church grounds and turned onto Nebraska Avenue," Felt remembered, "there was an amazing sight. As far as the eye could see, there were solid lines of uniformed police officers on each side of the avenue. Many were from the Washington Metropolitan Police Department but others had come from surrounding areas. It was an unforgettable scene and I later learned it had been arranged by the military authorities." The procession led past the Mayflower Hotel, where Hoover had so often held court at lunch with Tolson, then passed a few blocks from the site of the old Justice Department at Vermont and K, two blocks from the site of the Old George Washington University Law School, then past the White House, down Pennsylvania Avenue, past the still uncompleted new FBI building that would bear his name, past the Justice Department, then turned from Pennsylvania to Constitution at the site of the Old First Church. Then circling by the Capitol and back to Pennsylvania, it passed through Seward Square, past the Methodist Church that stood on the site of the old house at 413—Seward Square now beaten, unkempt, nearly treeless, the old cobblestones asphalted. Finally the cars turned left on Potomac and into the Congressional Cemetery, where a newly dug grave waited next to his father, his mother, and the sister, Sadie Marguerite, who had died seventeen months before J. Edgar was born. Black neighborhood children, drawn by the commotion, clambered over tombstones for a view. Elson threw a ritual handful of dirt onto the casket. The military escort folded the flag and handed it to Tolson, who was "bewildered and enfeebled, blinking in the bright spring sunshine." Then the crowd turned to their cars. The cemetery workers waited until they were alone to lower the casket, while children swooped down to take the flowers from the unguarded baskets. The J. Edgar Hoover story had come to an end.[108]

EPILOGUE

Freedom of Information

WHEN HOOVER DIED ON May 2, 1972, the Bureau he built died
with him. The organization survived, of course, but the aura that
had surrounded and protected it was gone. With the death of the
director, the FBI lost its power to command obedience and fear. It
no longer displayed a firm conviction of what the nation should be
and the evils it needed protection from. Battered by criticism during
the Watergate period, it retreated to a value-neutral, noncommittal
stance on the great issues of the day; no more than the Internal Revenue
Service or the Commerce Department would it strive to capture the
imagination of the public and express the values and aspirations of
the nation.

Within months after Hoover's death the Bureau was in disarray.
During Acting Director L. Patrick Gray's confirmation hearings it
became clear that John Dean and the Nixon administration had exploited him in order to stay informed of the FBI's progress in the
Watergate investigation. Gray was forced to ask the president to withdraw his nomination as permanent director. Then, while still acting
director, Gray had to resign in disgrace on April 27, 1973, when he
admitted destroying State Department cables White House Plumber
Howard Hunt had altered to implicate President Kennedy in the assassination of South Vietnam's President Diem.

Worse was to follow. In December 1973 and March 1974, documents exposing COINTELPRO were released to NBC reporter Carl
Stern, the result of his Freedom of Information Act lawsuit. In 1975,
the Bureau had to disgorge the entire record of its covert operations

486

against the Socialist Workers Party. Public pressure forced Attorney General Saxbe to conduct an in-house investigation of COINTELPRO; then, in 1975 and 1976, the Bureau had to make full disclosure of that program and its other illegal activities during the hearings of the House and Senate Select Committees on Intelligence (chaired by Congressman Otis Pike and Senator Frank Church). When the Senate Select Committee's voluminous report was released on April 28, 1976 (conservatives had managed to suppress the House Committee's report on January 29, 1976), the broad record of the Hoover FBI's secret activities was opened. It showed, said the Senate Select Committee, a "pattern of reckless disregard of activities that threatened our constitutional system." In the course of this public flogging it seemed fitting that even television's "The FBI" lost its public audience and went off the air in September 1974, after nine years of prime time programs.

With Hoover gone, the fear that had once intimidated critics also vanished. Now able to scrutinize the FBI's files through the Freedom of Information Act (which was strengthened in November 1974), Hoover's former enemies played a game of "Match the Dossier." Some, like Congressman Robert F. Drinan, crowed when they found their dissent had been considered so dangerous as to warrant Hoover's attention. Others were crushed to find they had been ignored. Detractors ridiculed the Bureau for wasting its time on triviality, though many skeptics were surprised and not a little disappointed to find that the release of such dossiers as those on Hiss and the Rosenbergs vindicated the integrity of Hoover's major investigations.

Finally, six years after Hoover's death, the government sought a posthumous legal condemnation of Hoover's secret power. On April 10, 1978, the Carter administration indicted three former officials of the FBI for authorizing burglaries of the relatives and friends of fugitive members of the radical Weather Underground. Charged were Acting Director L. Patrick Gray, Acting Associate Director Mark Felt, and Assistant Director Edward S. Miller. (Immediately after Hoover's death the Bureau, under intense pressure from the White House to locate the Weather Underground fugitives, had revived the "black bag jobs" Hoover had banned in July 1966. The burglaries named in the indictments took place from May 1972 until May 1973.) Though Gray's case was eventually dropped, Felt and Miller were convicted in November 1980 and a month later given fines of $5,000 and $3,500, less significant as punishments than as guidelines for future Bureau executives. Of course, the real defendant was the ghost of J. Edgar Hoover.

Had Hoover lived, he would certainly have tried to block the

House and Senate investigations and stem the flood of FOIA requests. Perhaps in the changed climate of Watergate even he, with his bureaucratic skills, his savagery toward his enemies, his prestige with the public and in Congress, and his influence within the Justice Department, would not have been able to stop the investigations completely. After Watergate, the whole government was in disrepute, and as the most aggressive and best known federal agency, the FBI had to absorb a large share of the punishment. Hoover's liberal opposition was finally enjoying revenge for the repression it had suffered; the public was in the mood to see the government punished for Watergate and the pathetic end of the Vietnam adventure.

The common assumption that secrecy was the sole basis of Hoover's power cannot survive an objective appraisal of his career. His success was based first on a proven record of his ability to perform important, difficult, and sensitive tasks at the highest level of government. These often involved matters that had to be kept confidential for reasons of state; at other times they had to be kept secret because they were, plainly, illegal and improper. Nevertheless, the critical achievements of Hoover's career, those that made him indispensable, were not secret at all. Even if not fully exposed to public gaze, they were widely known within the government itself on a need-to-know basis, and the larger part of Hoover's activities *were* conducted in full view of the entire nation: reorganizing the Bureau along progressive and scientific lines in the twenties, spearheading a dramatic and convincing display of government power during the gangster days of the early New Deal, demonstrating to the public during World War II that it was adequately protected against Nazi espionage and sabotage, reassuring a tense and nervous nation that it was safe from Communist subversion during the great surges of international Communist expansion that followed the two world wars, and, finally, during the mid-sixties, signaling the end of the nation's patience with white terror against blacks. Nor was it ever any secret that Hoover was using all available means to gather information about the Communist party; the government and most of the nation applauded the result of this surveillance, which was nothing less than the destruction of American communism.

Hoover's career would not have been possible without his extraordinary powers of sustained effort and dogged concentration. The men who worked for him were never in doubt that he knew what he was doing and what *they* were doing, and that he cared intensely about everything that touched his Bureau. That intensity burned away opposition and forged permanent loyalties with allies who had never encountered such determination. His faith in himself and his Bureau, combined with his uncanny leadership abilities, let Hoover dominate and motivate strong, ambitious men in a field rife with opportunities for corruption and for political advancement at the expense of the organization. Despite all obstacles, he was able to build one of the best disciplined and proudest agencies in American history. His techniques for running the Bureau—keeping it subject to his will by ingenious networks of rules, regulations, reports, and inspections; and creating an independent power base in the government and the public that was almost irresistible—required intelligence, dedication, sacrifice, and a sophisticated sense of public relations. The men who knew more of the truth about Hoover than anyone else, the agents and top officials of the FBI, were permanently loyal to him with very rare exceptions, proud to have been part of his FBI, and grateful for the opportunities Hoover had given them. Behind the skillfully constructed image of the director there was a real man who was able to convince congenitally suspicious and cynical law enforcement officers that he meant what he said, believed what he taught, and stood ready to act on his beliefs, ably, energetically, and, if necessary, ruthlessly. His agents amused themselves with stories about Hoover's whims and caprices, but they also carried with them the conviction that they belonged to a special elite because J. Edgar Hoover had taken them into his FBI. Every FBI office had a picture of Hoover and his favorite tract on loyalty on its wall, and, while he was alive, the FBI's loyalty to J. Edgar Hoover was the vital principle of one of the most efficient organizations the country has ever known.

Hoover's prestige within the government was nourished by his standing with the public, popularity so great that an attack on him was treated as an attack on values venerated by much of the nation. The beliefs Hoover absorbed from Seward Square, from Central High, and from the Old First Church were the bedrock convictions of middle-class America, and he never contemplated changing them or departing from them. His faith in those traditions appealed to the millions of Americans who were alarmed at moral relativism and the ambiguity produced by rapid social change in twentieth-century America.

Hoover's conviction that the values he had absorbed in his early life were true and applicable in all situations gave him unshakable confidence in his professional and political judgment. He was certain that the personal ambitions, patriotism, and Christian beliefs venerated by Seward Square were the permanent core of Americanism. He had no doubt that any action in accord with his instincts would be in the best interests of the Bureau and the nation. The confidence Hoover had in his own judgment is evident at every stage of his long career. It gave him the assurance to act in a coherent and sure manner during times of crisis and emergency when confidence and decisiveness are desperately needed, so he could offer his superiors comprehensive programs capable of almost infinite expansion. He was always able to convince those who fought with him and against him that he knew precisely what he wanted and how to get it.

Hoover absorbed from his Washington boyhood at the turn of the century a concept of leadership thoroughly familiar in years gone by, but strange and unexpected in the last half of the twentieth century. A public figure then was expected to be a moral guide and spokesman as well as an effective administrator. He was looked to for generalized moral encouragement and exhortation in all matters, public and private. Almost by default, Hoover was, by mid-career, one of the last surviving examples of the old-fashioned style of leadership that could be counted on to give ritual affirmation to an unchanging moral code. Hoover vigorously represented throughout his life that population of traditional Americans, largely middle-class, Protestant, and Anglo-Saxon, who were frightened by the changes they felt were depriving them of their privileged position in an ever more pluralistic society.

Exceptional leadership depends on a unique resonance between the man and his times. A leader exists in what André Malraux called a "non-rational framework." He has to have "something of the sorcerer in him" to produce the enthusiasm and discipline that makes great achievements possible. There is no doubt that Hoover possessed that touch. He acquired it from his entire background and biography, from his home, his school, his church, from his eager response to the great crises of his times, and from his early grasp of the new and exciting ideas of scientific law enforcement and progressive management.

Hoover's greatest successes grew out of his aggressive response to demands for action at times of national emergency. It may be argued how real those dangers were, but there is no question that the public alarm was real. The public was frightened by the spread of communism across Europe and the organization of the Comintern in 1919; by the economic paralysis of the thirties with its parallel collapse of national pride and confidence; by the fear of Nazi spies in the late thirties and during the war; and, finally, by the outbreak of tensions and the perceived likelihood of a third world war in 1947. The country was anxious and Hoover reassured it, and for that he won the permanent gratitude of the nation.

Hoover gained power because he instinctively knew that in times of panic the public's call for action must be answered, and he was able to discover creative and convincing ways to demonstrate that the government had the situation in hand. He worked on the assumption that in critical circumstances the question was not whether there would be drastic action, but who would direct it, federal authorities or self-appointed guardians like the Texas anti-Communists in 1954 who tried to impose the death penalty on members of the Communist party. Throughout his career, Hoover warned that vigilante action was the real alternative to the FBI in times of crisis. One need not excuse the inexcusable in Hoover's career to recognize that the danger of grass-roots violence is very real in a democratic society and that preventing it demands energetic government initiatives.

The very qualities that made for Hoover's success and popularity encouraged his assaults on political freedom. Those actions, open as well as secret, will permanently stain his record in American history, and during his lifetime they made him as much hated by the left as he was loved by the right. Hoover's instinct for action, his ability to organize effective and comprehensive operations, and his impatience with ambiguous situations made him willing to adopt extralegal means when legal weapons failed him in the battle against those he saw as the nation's enemies—whether the legal doors were closed by Court decisions (as in the Communist party COINTELPRO), or by local prejudices (the Klan COINTELPRO), or by the absence of political consensus (the Black Nationalist and New Left COINTELPROs).

In an age struggling to tolerate cultural diversity and individual freedom, Hoover was bound to offend almost as many as he pleased when he preached the old verities. Many of his cherished values and traditions were weapons the old elites used to maintain their social privileges; their rejection was part of the self-affirmation of groups struggling to emerge from second-class citizenship; during times of debate over national policy, his traditional values were powerful defenses of the status quo and supports for the prerogatives of authority. Hoover's role as moral spokesman, which made him so secure against efforts to remove him, also made him a prominent target for attacks by those who felt oppressed by the structure and values of American society.

Hoover's historic legacy is profoundly ambiguous. He achieved his life's goal by destroying American communism, and was a powerful support for traditional values; however, those values supported racial and other injustices, and his covert attacks on personal and public enemies violated principles of constitutional limits on government power. But in a paradoxical way, when they were finally revealed, his transgressions made the nation more conscious than ever of the importance of insisting, even in times of emergency, that the government obey the law and conduct itself in a manner open to independent scrutiny.

His most unassailable achievement was creating one of the great institutions in American government. The FBI since Hoover has been trying to return to the original progressive vision that Hoover formulated during the 1920s under Harlan Stone. For a decade it has been striving to embody what was permanently valuable in Hoover's dream of professional, scientific law enforcement.

Hoover's real significance in American life was of a kind fated to perish with him. That was the day-to-day, year-to-year leadership he furnished the Bureau, the law enforcement profession, and the nation. That sustained record of national leadership stemmed from personal qualities of a charismatic nature incapable of being transmitted to any bureaucracy, even one as self-consciously molded in Hoover's image as the FBI.

A political system, a nation, cannot survive unless those who are frightened and endangered by change feel that their interests are being represented and protected. The government must adapt to shifting circumstances, but at the same time it must stand as a bulwark against disorder and a pillar of stability and continuity. For much of the century, for millions of Americans, J. Edgar Hoover was that bulwark and pillar. As long as they saw Hoover standing guard they could believe that the familiar community ruled by age-old traditions, the America they could recognize as the country they knew and loved, still endured.

But he himself endured too long. It was the tragedy of the man and of the nation that in the end Hoover's great qualities of leadership and his unrivaled organizational abilities no longer served the vital needs of the nation—they were devoted instead to protecting Hoover's own interests and those of his FBI. Hoover ended his life embittered and isolated, his Bureau a monument to his past—and to his memories of an America that hardly existed outside its walls.

Notes

Abbreviations

AG	Attorney General
CCP	Calvin Coolidge Papers (microfilm)
DDEL	Dwight D. Eisenhower Presidential Library, Abilene, Kansas
DJ	Department of Justice
FDRL	Franklin D. Roosevelt Presidential Library, Hyde Park, New York
FOIA	Freedom of Information Act
HHL	Herbert Hoover Presidential Library, West Branch, Iowa
HSTL	Harry S. Truman Presidential Library, Independence, Missouri
JEHF	Hoover Memorabilia Collection of the J. Edgar Hoover Foundation, presently held at the J. Edgar Hoover Library, Freedoms Foundation, Valley Forge, Pennsylvania
JFKL	John F. Kennedy Presidential Library, Boston, Massachusetts
LBJL	Lyndon B. Johnson Presidential Library, Austin, Texas
NA	National Archives, Washington, DC
O&C	Official and Confidential
OCPA	Office of Congressional and Public Affairs, FBI
OF	Official File
OH	Oral History
RG	Record Group
SANSA	Special Assistant for National Security Affairs
WGHP	Warren G. Harding Papers (microfilm)
WHCF	White House Central Files
WWP	Woodrow Wilson Papers (microfilm)

Short Forms for Government Reports

Attorney General A. Mitchell Palmer on Charges	U.S. House, Committee on Rules, *Attorney General A. Mitchell Palmer on Charges Made*

	Against Department of Justice by Louis F. Post and Others, 65th Cong., 2nd sess., June 1, 1920
Investigation Activities of the Department of Justice	U.S. Senate, Investigation Activities of the Department of Justice, Letter from the Attorney General, Transmitting in Response to a Senate Resolution of October 17, 1919, a Report on the Activities of the Bureau of Investigation of the Department of Justice against Persons Advising Anarchy, Sedition, and the Forcible Overthrow of the Government, 66th Cong., 1st sess., Nov. 15, 1919
Senate Select Committee, Final Report, Book III	U.S. Senate, Select Committee to Study Governmental Operations with Respect to Intelligence Activities, Final Report, Supplementary Detailed Staff Reports on Intelligence Activities and the Rights of Americans, Book III, 94th Cong., 2nd sess., Report No. 94–755, Serial 13133–5
Senate Select Committee, Final Report, Book V, Assassination of JFK	U.S. Senate, Select Committee to Study Governmental Operations with Respect to Intelligence Activities, Final Report, The Investigation of the Assassination of President John F. Kennedy: Performance of the Intelligence Agencies, Book V, 94th Cong., 2nd sess., Report No. 94–755, Serial 13133–5
Senate Select Committee, Hearings, Vol. 2, Huston Plan	U.S. Senate, Select Committee to Study Governmental Operations with Respect to Intelligence Activities, Hearings, Huston Plan, Vol. 2, 94th Cong., 1st sess., Sept. 23, 24, 25, 1975
Senate Select Committee, Hearings, Vol. 6, FBI	U.S. Senate, Select Committee to Study Government Operations with Respect to Intelligence Activities, Hearings, Vol. 6, FBI, 94th Cong., 1st sess.

Chapter 1:   The Hoovers of Seward Square
(pp. 5–35)

1. Hoover's home at 413 and his brother's at 411 were demolished to make room for the Capitol Hill Methodist Church, which has a stained-glass window dedicated to Hoover. A replica of the window is in the Hoover Memorabilia Collection, JEHF.

2. Photograph in Hoover Memorabilia Collection, JEHF; phone interview, Margaret Hoover Fennell, Jan. 30, 1985.

3. The genealogy is a small unpaginated memo pad in box 53 of Hoover Memorabilia Collection, JEHF, henceforth referred to as Genealogy. The church (still standing), then known as the Metropolitan Presbyterian Church, is now the Capitol Hill Presbyterian Church.

4. Hester O'Neill, "J. Edgar Hoover's School Days (Part 3)," *American Boy and Open Road,* July 1954, p. 34; Ovid Demaris, *The Director: An Oral Biography of J. Edgar Hoover* (New York: Harpers Magazine Press, 1975), p. 3; Ralph de Toledano, *J. Edgar Hoover: The Man in His Time* (New Rochelle, N.Y.: Arlington House, 1973), pp. 36, 39.

5. Rev. John Chester, D.D., *Discourse Delivered at the Funeral Services of Mrs. Anna Hitz in the Metropolitan Presbyterian Church of Washington, D.C., on March 8, 1883* (Washington, D.C.: R. Beresford, 1883); Edward L. R. Elson, *The J. Edgar Hoover You Ought to Know, by his pastor* (n.c.: The General Commission on Chaplains, 1950; reprinted from *The Chaplain*), p. 4; O'Neill, "School Days (Part 3)," p. 8; de Toledano, *J. Edgar Hoover,* p. 42.

6. *Genealogy,* JEHF.

7. C. Vann Woodward, *The Strange Career of Jim Crow* (New York, 1955); Constance McLaughlin Green, *Washington: Capital City, 1879–1950* (Princeton: Princeton University Press, 1963), p. 326.

8. Green, *Washington: Capital City,* p. 139.

9. Ibid., pp. 216–217.

10. Interview in the *Washington Post* on the occasion of the 1934 Morro Castle disaster; de Toledano, *J. Edgar Hoover,* p. 37.

11. Photograph in Hoover Memorabilia Collection, JEHF. For a discussion of the growth of Washington during Hoover's childhood, see Green, *Washington: Capital City,* pp. 132–146.

12. Letter, Dickerson N. Hoover to Hoover, Apr. 19, 1904, JEHF.

13. Ibid., n.d.

14. Letter, Annie M. Hoover to Hoover, Oct. 6, 1906 [?], JEHF.

15. Ibid., Sept. 9, 1912.

16. Phone interview, Margaret Hoover Fennell, Jan. 30, 1985.

17. Hoover kept small pocket diaries for 1908, 1909, and 1910, and these are in the Hoover Memorabilia Collection, JEHF, hereafter referred to as *Diary. Diary,* Sept. 11, 1910.

18. O'Neill, "School Days (Part 3)," p. 8; *Diary,* Jan. 12, 1908, and Feb. 15, 1909; phone interview, Margaret Hoover Fennell, Jan. 30, 1985.

19. Elson, *The J. Edgar Hoover You Ought to Know,* p. 4.

20. *Diary,* Dec. 27, 1907, and Jan. 8, 1909; phone interview, Margaret Hoover Fennell, Jan. 29, 1985; *Genealogy.*

21. Demaris, *The Director,* p. 7; letters, Annie M. Hoover to Hoover, Sept. 9, 19, 16, 1912; phone interview, Margaret Hoover Fennell, Jan. 26, 1985.

22. *Diary,* Jan. 8, 1909; Apr. 18, 1909.

23. *Diary,* Feb. 14, 15, 16, 1909; Jan. 9, 1910; June 23, 1910; Sept. 11, 1910; and *Genealogy.*

24. Phone interview, Edward L. R. Elson, Jan. 16, 1985.

25. Elson, *The J. Edgar Hoover You Ought to Know,* p. 4.

26. *Washington Star,* Sept. 19, 1909, part 2, p. 5; Sept. 26, 1909, part 5, p. 1.

27. *Diary,* Sept. 19, 1910.

28. Robert W. Lynn and Elliott Wright, *The Big Little School: Two Hundred Years of the Sunday School* (New York: Harper, 1971), pp. 15, 14.

29. Ibid., pp. 17, 33.

30. Ibid., pp. 25, 82.

31. Henry Seidel Canby, *An American Memoir* (Boston: Houghton Mifflin, 1947), p. 68, quoted in Lynn and Wright, *The Big Little School,* p. 80.

32. H. Wayne Morgan, "Toward National Unity," *The Gilded Age,* (Syracuse, N.Y.: Syracuse University Press, 1970), p. 2, quoted in Lynn and Wright, *The Big Little School,* p. 58.

33. Lynn and Wright, *The Big Little School,* p. 83; phone interview, Ervin N. Chapman, historian of the National Presbyterian Center, Washington, D.C., Jan. 28, 1985.

34. Lynn and Wright, *The Big Little School,* p. 59.

35. Phone interview, Edward L. R. Elson, Jan. 16, 1985; Lynn and Wright, *The Big Little School,* pp. 40, 48, 49. Probably the most famous of all the Sunday school songs was from Anna and Susan Warner's *Say and Seal,* a popular novel of 1860:

> *Jesus loves me, this I know,/For the Bible tells me so;*
> *Little ones to him belong,/They are weak but he is strong.*
>
> *Jesus loves me—he who died,/Heaven's gate to open wide;*
> *He will wash away my sin,/Let his little child come in.*

The song "Shall We Gather at the River" was first sung in 1865 at a great Sunday school parade in Brooklyn. These slow and sentimental songs had given way by the turn of the century to more martial songs appropriate to the age of the Rough Riders and John Philip Sousa (who grew up in Hoover's Capitol Hill neighborhood):

> *Hear the tramp, tramp, tramp of the Sunday-School Brigade,*
> *Whether rain or shine we are always on parade;*
> *By our Savior led, in the sunshine of His love,*
> *We are marching on to the land of joy above.*
>
> *Hear the tramp, tramp, tramp of the Sunday-School Brigade,*
> *We would win that crown which will never, never fade;*
> *We will trust our King, wheresoever be the way,*
> *We will follow Him to the realm of endless day.*

Other militaristic Sunday school songs had titles like "We Are in the Saviour's Army," "I Am a Little Soldier," and "Hold the Fort." Another type of song that would have been popular in Hoover's Sunday school was the so-called sunbeam song. These portrayed children as "sunbeams" shining in their parents' lives (Lynn and Wright, *The Big Little School* passim).

36. Lynn and Wright, *The Big Little School,* p. 48.

37. Edward L. R. Elson, "J. Edgar Hoover—Churchman," quoted in Lynn and Wright, *The Big Little School,* p. 97.

38. Dickerson Jr. became inspector general of the service, and was a fairly prominent figure in Washington during the late twenties and thirties. He died in 1944. Five issues of Hoover's *Weekly Review* survive in the Hoover Memorabilia Collection, JEHF.

39. Lynn and Wright, *The Big Little School,* p. 54. The complete lyrics are:

I am a little Hindoo girl,/Of Jesus never heard;
Oh, pity me, dear Christian child,/Oh send to me His word.

Oh, pity me, for I have cried/So great I cannot tell,
And say if truly there's a heaven,/Where such as I can dwell.

40. Memo to author on JEH attendance at Brent, District of Columbia School Attendance Office; *Report* of the Board of Education, 1908; *Washington Star,* Dec. 22, 1968, has the story of the destruction of his school to make way for a newer building; *Genealogy;* phone interview, Margaret Hoover Fennell, Jan. 30, 1985.

41. Phone interview, Richard Hurlbert, District of Columbia School Board historian, Jan. 13, 1985.

42. *Report* of the Board of Education, District of Columbia, 1908, p. 35; phone interview, Richard Hurlbert, Jan. 13, 1985.

43. For an example of how Hoover worked within a received system, see his brief on the death penalty in the small *Debate Memorandum Book,* n.d., in the Hoover Memorabilia Collection, JEHF. The brief is analyzed later.

44. *Diary,* Jan. 19, 21, 1908; Apr. 8, 1908; Jan. 4, 1909; July 28, 29, 30, 1909.

45. "I and Albert Beck worked in garden from 1.15 o'clock to 2.30 o'clock." *Diary,* Feb. 2, 1908; Apr. 9, 1908.

46. de Toledano, *J. Edgar Hoover,* pp. 8, 37.

47. *Diary,* Feb. 18, 1909.

48. *Diary,* Jan. 21, 1908; Jan. 3, 5, 1909; Aug. 28, 1909; July 31, 1910; and letter from Annie M. Hoover to Hoover, Sept. 16, 1912, JEHF.

49. *Diary,* Aug. 29, 30, 1909; Aug. 1, 24, 1910.

50. "Went to Theater," *Diary,* Feb. 18, 1909, and Sept. 30, 1909; "Went to Chase's Theater in the evening," *Diary,* Aug. 25, 1910; letter from Dickerson Hoover, Sr., to Hoover, Sept. 8, 1912, JEHF; letter from Annie M. Hoover to Hoover, Sept. 16, 1912, JEHF.

51. *Diary* Aug. 1, 8, 9, 10, 19, 20, 21, 22, 1910.

52. O'Neill, "School Days (Part 3)," p. 34.

53. *Here's to Old Central* (Washington, D.C.: Alumni Association of Central High, 1967) pp. 18–19.

54. O'Neill, "School Days (Part 3)," p. 35.

55. *Central High Alumni Record,* Feb. 1941; Lawrence J. Heller, quoted in the *Washington Star,* May 7, 1962.

56. One of the school's legends involved an early graduation ceremony. According to the alumni association's history of the school, in the middle of the guest speaker's remarks "came an interruption from the outside alley! The colored slop collector was collecting his hog garbage and yelling 'Slops! Slops!' in a very loud voice. The windows of course were open, and the General [the graduation speaker] called out to inform the man that it was his turn to speak. All the boys giggled. The General said, "One at a time, my friend.' Then he turned to the class. 'That man is a magician! he is a Negro man, sir' (necromancer). The boys laughed outwardly but groaned inwardly" (*Centennial History of Central High School* [Washington, D.C.: Alumni Association of Central High School, 1976], p. 2).

Another episode preserved in school history involved the death in 1888 of the school's first principal, run down by a black man on horseback. As the newspapers described the incident, the principal was on a bicycle, while the man on horseback had evidently lost control of his mount; however, the school legend emphasized the racial stereotype by specifying that the death was caused by a "drunken" negro (*Here's to Old Central,* p. 8; *Centennial History,* p. 16).

57. Phone interview, Richard Hurlbert, Jan. 13, 1985.

58. *Centennial History,* p. 90.

59. *Diary,* Sept. 29, 1909.

60. *Diary,* Jan. 18, 1910; *Centennial History,* p. 90.

61. Hester O'Neill, "J. Edgar Hoover's Schooldays (Part 4)," *American Boy and Open Road* (Sept. 1954), p. 22.

62. Ibid., p. 23.

63. *Debate Memorandum Book,* JEHF.

64. *Diary,* Sept. 27, 1909.

65. Interview, Walton Shipley, Central High School historian, Dec. 17, 1984.

66. *Diary,* Jan. 7, 1910; *Central High Review,* Feb. 11, 1913, quoted by O'Neill, "School Days, Part 3," p. 35.

67. *Centennial History,* p. 93.

68. A program listing Hoover's parents is in the Hoover Memorabilia Collection, JEHF. See also *Centennial History,* p. 92; O'Neill, "School Days, Part 4," p. 22.

69. *Centennial History,* p. 92.

70. O'Neill, "School Days, Part 4," p. 23.

71. John Higham, *Strangers in the Land: Patterns of American Nativism, 1860–1925* (New York: Atheneum, 1973), pp. 110, 159.

72. Robert T. Handy, *A Christian America: Protestant Hopes and Historical Realities* (New York: Oxford University Press, 1984), pp. 74, 78–79, 89; Higham, *Strangers in the Land,* pp. 62, 77–86.

73. William Preston, Jr., *Aliens and Dissenters* (Cambridge, Mass.: Harvard University Press, 1963), p. 25.

74. Ibid., p. 26.

75. Higham, *Strangers in the Land,* pp. 55, 138, 200.

76. Walter Lippmann, *A Preface to Politics* (New York: Kennerly, 1913), pp. 200, 301.

Chapter 2: The Alien Enemy Bureau
(*pp. 36–55*)

1. It was Hitz who persuaded Wilson to support Brandeis for membership in the Cosmos Club over anti-Semitic opposition (E. Digby Baltzell, *The Protestant Establishment: Aristocracy and Caste in America* [New York: Vintage, 1964], p. 187).

2. Elmer Louis Kayser, *Bricks Without Straw: The Evolution of George Washington University* (New York: Appleton-Century-Croft, 1970), p 218; interview, Hugh Y. Bernard, GWU Law School historian, Jan. 22, 1985.

3. For a comparative analysis of the careers of all three, see Eugene Lewis, *Public Entrepreneurship: Toward a Theory of Bureaucratic Political Power* (Bloomington, Ind.: Indiana University Press, 1984).

4. Interview, Hugh Y. Bernard, Jan. 22, 1985.

5. Hester O'Neill, "Thirty Years on the Job," *American Boy and Open Road* (May 1954), p. 32; notebooks in Hoover Memorabilia Collection, JEHF; interview, Hugh Y. Bernard, Jan. 22, 1985. See also newspaper clipping dated Apr. 2, 1921 (no source) in the Hoover Memorabilia Collection, RG 65, NA, which lists Hoover hosting, as president of Kappa Alpha, a reception for the president of George Washington University.

6. The GWU yearbooks for 1916 and 1917 list all graduates with their honors, and no honors are listed after Hoover's name.

7. Ovid Demaris, *The Director: An Oral Biography of J. Edgar Hoover* (New York: Harpers Magazine Press, 1975), p. 8; "Acceptance of Resignation," Apr. 6, 1917, in Hoover Memorabilia Collection, JEHF.

8. *AG Report 1917,* p. 70. See also Burton to Mulcahy, Oct. 2, 1939, Department of Justice Public Affairs (FBI General Correspondence), Aug.–Sept. 1939, RG 60, NA.

9. Stanley Coben, *A. Mitchell Palmer, Politician* (New York: Columbia University Press, 1963), p. 116. See also Hoover Personnel File, FBI 67–561, FOIA Reading Room, FBI; Kidd to Appointment Clerk, July 20, 1917, Justice Department, Office of Chief Clerk, RG 60, NA.

10. *DJ Register, 1918,* p. 24.

11. John Lord O'Brian, "New Encroachments on Individual Freedom," p. 94, and Charles A. Horsky, "Remarks," p. 3, in *Buffalo Law Review, John Lord O'Brian Commemorative Issue,* (Buffalo, N.Y.: University of Buffalo, N.Y. 1974) (hereafter referred to as *Law Review*).

12. Quoted by John G. Laylin in "Memorable International Cases and Friendships with John Lord O'Brian," *Law Review,* p. 40. In later years, O'Brian, a courageous civil libertarian (and a director of the Fund for the Republic, which the Hoover-backed House Un-American Activities Committee attacked in the fifties), was somewhat embarrassed about his role in "recruiting" Hoover for the Justice Department. It was something, he said, that he would "prefer to whisper in dark corners." Quoted by Horsky, *Law Review,* p. 4.

13. Memo, O'Brian to Gregory, Dec. 14, 1917, DJ File 190470, Gregory Papers, Box 2735, RG 60, NA.

14. *AG Report 1917,* p. 413.

15. Homer S. Cummings and Carl McFarland, *Federal Justice: Chapters in the History of Justice and the Federal Executive* (New York: Da Capo, 1970; originally published in 1937), p. 488.

16. Joan M. Jensen, *The Price of Vigilance* (Chicago: Rand McNally, 1968), p. 15.

17. Ibid., p. 16.

18. For a history of the APL and its relationship to the Justice Department, see Jensen, *The Price of Vigilance.*

19. John Higham, *Strangers in the Land: Patterns of American Nativism, 1860–1925* (New York: Atheneum, 1973), p. 102.

20. Jensen, *Price of Vigilance,* p. 27.

21. Ibid., pp. 26, 27.

22. Ibid., p. 29.

23. Cummings and McFarland, *Federal Justice,* p. 414. Jensen, *Price of Vigilance,* p. 107. John Lord O'Brian, "New Encroachments on Individual Freedom" 66 *Harv. L. Rev.* I(1952), quoted in *Law Review,* p. 92.

24. O'Brian to Attorney General, Oct. 7, 1918, DJ File 190470, Gregory Papers, Box 2735, RG 60, NA. Warren had drafted and guided through Congress the Trading with the Enemy Act that became law on October 6, 1917. This established the office of the Alien Property Custodian filled by future Attorney General A. Mitchell Palmer. He also directed the prosecution of the IWW leaders in Chicago (Cummings and McFarland, *Federal Justice,* p. 423; Jensen, *Price of Vigilance,* p. 107). O'Brian to Gregory, "I have already expressed my opinion to you that such legislation is not only unconstitutional but embodies the worst possible policy." Apr. 18, 1918, JD File 189083, RG 60, NA, quoted in Jensen, *Price of Vigilance,* pp. 106–107, 121.

25. *AG Report 1917,* p. 56; Jensen, *Price of Vigilance,* p. 161.

26. *AG Report 1917,* p. 57.

27. Ibid., p. 58.

28. Ibid., p. 67, 70, 71.

29. Ibid., pp. 57–59, 74.

30. *AG Report 1918,* pp. 9, 28.

31. Gregory to O'Brian, Dec. 5, 1917, DJ File 190470, Gregory papers, Box 2735, RG 60, NA. O'Brian's arrival in the Department was Oct. 1, 1917.

32. O'Brian to Gregory, Dec. 14, 1917, DJ File 190470, Gregory Papers, Box 2735, RG 60, NA.

33. Hoover to O'Brian, Dec. 17, 1917, DJ File 9–16–12–1384, RG 60, NA.

34. Hoover to O'Brian, Dec. 28, 1917, File 9–16–9–414, DJ Control Files, Classified Subject Files, Correspondence, RG 60, NA.

35. Hoover to O'Brian, Dec. 28, 1917, File 9–16–12–1549, and Hoover to O'Brian, Dec. 28, 1917, File 9–16–12–1726, DJ Control Files, Classified Subject Files, Correspondence, RG 60, NA.

36. Hoover to O'Brian, Dec. 18, 1917, File 9–16–12–1400, DJ Control Files, Classified Subject Files, Correspondence, RG 60, NA.

37. Hoover to O'Brian, Dec. 29, 1917, File 9–16–12–1689, DJ Control Files, Classified Subject Files, Correspondence, RG 60, NA.

38. See Hoover to O'Brian, July 3, 1918, File 9–16–19–51–269 Section 2, DJ Control Files, Classified Subject Files, Correspondence, RG 60, NA.

39. See O'Brian to Sprague, Aug. 15, 1918, File 9–16–19–51–290 (drafted by JEH), the handwritten calculations following that letter, File 9–16–19–51–291, and the reply, Sprague to O'Brian, Aug. 19, 1918, File 9–16–19–51–292, DJ Control Files, Classified Subject Files, Correspondence, RG 60, NA.

40. Demaris, *The Director,* p. 53; *AG Report 1919,* p. 28.

41. Jensen, *Price of Vigilance,* p. 267.

Chapter 3:   The Red Years: The Lessons of Success
(*pp. 56–92*)

1. For a thorough account of the European revolution during 1919 and 1920, see Albert S. Lindemann, *The Red Years: European Socialism versus Bolshevism, 1919–1921* (Berkeley, Calif.: University of California Press, 1974), and David Mitchell, *1919: Red Mirage* (New York: Macmillan, 1970). See also John Dos Passos, in a June 1932 introduction to a reprint of *Three Soldiers* (1921), quoted in Alfred Kazin, *An American Procession* (New York: Knopf, 1984), p. 375.

2. Irving Howe and Lewis Coser, *The American Communist Party: A Critical History* (New York: Praeger, 1962), p. 26.

3. Joan M. Jensen, *The Price of Vigilance* (Chicago: Rand McNally, 1968), p. 262.

4. Robert K. Murray, *Red Scare: A Study in National Hysteria, 1919–1920* (New York: McGraw-Hill, 1964), pp. 63, 65.

5. Keeping the Legion at bay was a concern of Hoover's throughout his career; his worries about its capacity for vigilantism may have been as much caused by the example of the *Freikorps* as by the Centralia lynching.

6. Clemenceau of France was wounded by a "Bolshevik agent" on February 20, 1919 (Julian F. Jaffe, *Crusade Against Radicalism*, [Port Washington, N.Y.: Kennikat, 1972], p. 171). As commissioner of baseball, Landis would banish Shoeless Joe Jackson from baseball for life for his part in fixing the 1919 World Series even though Jackson had been acquitted by a jury (Murray, *Red Scare*, p. 71).

7. Such was the charge of Secretary of Labor Louis Post, who based his case on the fact that Hoover, despite the hundreds of thousands of dossiers collected on so-called radicals, was never able to track down the bomb-throwers. The reason, Post said, was that those who were guilty might not have been radicals. (Louis F. Post, *The Deportations Delirium of Nineteen-Twenty: A Personal Narrative of an Historic Official Experience* [New York: Da Capo, 1970; first published in 1923], p. 47.)

8. In April 1917, immediately after America entered the conflict, the Socialist party declared itself officially opposed to the American war effort. Prominent American Socialist leaders such as Victor Berger and Eugene Debs were indicted for violating the conscription or espionage statutes. The IWW also came out against the war, causing many to fear it would use political strikes to paralyze war industries. Leading anarchists—Emma Goldman and Alexander Berkman, for example—denounced the war and deliberately violated the draft laws to provoke a confrontation with the government.

9. Max Lowenthal, *The Federal Bureau of Investigation* (New York: William Sloane Associates, 1950), p. 36.

10. Ibid., p. 49; U.S. Senate, Committee on the Judiciary, *Bolshevik Propaganda, Hearings Before a Subcommittee of the Committee on the Judiciary*, Sen. Res. 439 and 469, 65th Cong., 3rd sess. (Feb. 11, 1919–Mar. 10, 1919), pp. 14, 16, 249.

11. Quoted in Lowenthal, *Federal Bureau of Investigation*, pp. 56, 57.

12. *The Liberator* (May 1919), quoted in Theodore Draper, *The Roots of American Communism* (New York: Viking, 1957), p. 110.

13. Murray, *Red Scare*, p. 25.

14. Jaffe, *Crusade Against Radicalism*, pp. 119, 120. The Lusk Committee Report (in four volumes), was published by the Senate of the State of New York, Joint Legislative Committee Investigating Radical Activities, *Revolutionary Radicalism* (Albany, N.Y.: J. Lyons, 1920).

15. Stanley Coben, *A. Mitchell Palmer: Politician* (New York: Columbia University Press, 1963), p. 206. Hoover's General Intelligence Division later published a detailed account of its investigation of this bombing, which it

concluded was the work of a Brooklyn-based group of Italian anarchists. See *Attorney General A. Mitchell Palmer on Charges,* pp. 157–165.

16. "Bielaski's resignation had taken effect on February 10. William Elby Allen, a graduate of the University of Texas who had been a United States Attorney and special assistant to O'Brian, took over as Acting Chief of the Bureau of Investigation" (Jensen, *The Price of Vigilance,* p. 262).

17. Coben, *A. Mitchell Palmer,* pp. 207, 211; Murray, *Red Scare,* p. 80; *New York Times,* June 4, 1919; *Washington Post,* June 19, 1919.

18. Coben, *A. Mitchell Palmer,* p. 207; *DJ Register, 1919,* p. 34.

19. Ovid Demaris, *The Director: An Oral Biography of J. Edgar Hoover* (New York: Harpers Magazine Press, 1975), p. 53. O'Brian stayed in the Justice Department until April 30. Since Woodrow Wilson did not decide to name Palmer attorney general until February 26, 1919, and since Palmer assumed the duties of the office on the effective date of Gregory's resignation, March 3, O'Brian must have spoken to Palmer during March or April (Coben, *A. Mitchell Palmer,* p. 154; Homer Cummings and Carl McFarland, *Federal Justice: Chapters in the History of Justice and the Federal Executive* [New York: Da Capo, 1970; originally published in 1937], p. 427).

20. Coben, *A. Mitchell Palmer,* p. 143; John G. Laylin, "Memorable International Cases and Friendships With John Lord O'Brian," *Buffalo Law Review, John Lord O'Brian Commemorative Issue* (Buffalo, N.Y.: University of Buffalo, 1974), p. 40.

21. John Lord O'Brian, interview by Peter C. Andrews, *Buffalo Courier Register* (May 3, 1972), quoted in *Memorial Tributes to J. Edgar Hoover* (Washington, D.C.: U.S. Government Printing Office, 1974), p. 155; *Biographical Data on Honorable J. Edgar Hoover,* a Masonic obituary, Hoover Memorabilia Collection, JEHF; Lynn Dumenil, *Freemasonry and American Culture* (Princeton, N.J.: Princeton University Press, 1985), and a review of Dumenil by Angus Paul, *Chronicle of Higher Education* (Mar. 13, 1985) p. 10; phone interview, Margaret Hoover Fennell, Jan. 30, 1985.

22. Coben, *A. Mitchell Palmer,* p. 197.

23. Coben says that this breakdown occurred on November 21, and that Palmer was back in Washington, D.C., by December 6 (Coben, *A. Mitchell Palmer,* p. 222).

24. Intelligence operations were formally suspended from 1924 until 1936, although it should not be supposed that all domestic intelligence operations were completely halted during this period. The Radical Division, according to the *DJ Register,* was located within the Bureau of Investigation, as was Hoover, its director, although Hoover also retained his rank within the Justice Department as special assistant to the attorney general.

25. For an example of a high-ranking Justice Department official's having to ask Hoover's permission to borrow an employee, see Creighton to Hoover, Dec. 20, 1919, DJ File 203557–63, RG 60, NA.

26. A card file of the publications read by Hoover's division exists in the National Archives, while a sample of the publications themselves can

be found in a collection in the Library of Congress. *Investigation Activities of the Department of Justice,* p. 10; *AG Report, 1920,* p. 179.

27. Dated December 8, 1919, but probably written several months earlier (*AG Report, 1919,* pp. 15–16).

28. On February 5, Gregory proposed that Congress authorize him to deport interned enemy aliens who seemed dangerous to him. It was because of O'Brian's concern that the wartime deportation regulations might be misused for political purposes that he delayed leaving the Justice Department until May 1 (Coben, *A. Mitchell Palmer,* p. 199; Jensen, *The Price of Vigilance,* p. 267).

29. Secretary of Labor Wilson was born in Scotland (William Preston, Jr., *Aliens and Dissenters* (Cambridge, Mass.: Harvard University Press, 1963), p. 206).

30. *AG Report, 1920,* p. 177.

31. The most important of these limitations involved the controversial "Rule 22" of the Immigration Bureau's Regulations. Originally, this limited an alien's right to counsel to those interrogations conducted after the initial interrogation (the most important for securing incriminating evidence) had been completed to the satisfaction of the government. On March 3, 1919, Secretary of Labor Wilson had revised Rule 22 to give aliens the right to counsel at the very beginning of any interrogation, much to the displeasure of the Immigration Bureau (Preston, *Aliens and Dissenters,* p. 212). The revised Rule 22 gave the Immigration Bureau and Radical Division so much difficulty during their interrogations of the aliens arrested in the November raids that Caminetti began to petition the secretary of labor for a return to the original restriction on the right to counsel. This was granted by Acting Secretary of Labor Abercrombie on December 30 (Preston, *Aliens and Dissenters,* p. 217). It is uncertain what role Hoover played in this agitation for a return to the more restrictive rule. On several occasions he wrote Caminetti asking him about the status of Rule 22 (Hoover to Caminetti, Dec. 17, 1919, DJ File 203557–38, and Dec. 18, 1919, DJ File 203557–45, RG 60, NA); there is reference to a letter dated November 11, 1919, from Hoover to Caminetti on this subject, but this letter seems to have been lost. However, during the hearings on the deportation raids, which were held from January 19 to March 3, 1921, and over which Senator Thomas Walsh presided, Hoover produced evidence that the initial request for a change had come from the legal counsel of the Labor Department and not from him, and that his letters simply asked that he be told which Rule 22 he would be expected to use. This testimony seemed to satisfy Walsh, who was by no means sympathetically disposed toward Hoover. See also Ralph de Toledano, *J. Edgar Hoover: The Man in His Time* (New Rochelle, N.Y.: Arlington House, 1973), p. 59.

32. Hoover to Burke, Feb. 21, 1920, DJ File 186701–14–82 1/2, RG 60, NA. Hoover and Palmer could, however, point to congressional intent, as expressed during the 1919 debate over the Justice Department's supplemen-

tal appropriation and the Immigration Bureau's appropriation. Some members of Congress made it clear that they expected and desired the Justice Department and Labor Department (to which the Immigration Bureau belonged) to cooperate in deporting radical aliens (Preston, *Aliens and Dissenters,* p. 211; Post, *Deportations Delirium,* p. 54).

33. What they wanted then was close to what Congress passed in 1940 with the Smith Act.

34. *Attorney General A. Mitchell Palmer on Charges,* pp. 14, 29; Preston, *Aliens and Dissenters,* p. 194.

35. Coben, *A. Mitchell Palmer,* p. 211; Murray, *Red Scare,* p. 202.

36. *Investigation Activities of the Department of Justice,* p. 14.

37. Ibid.

38. See Hoover to Palmer, May 25, 1920, DJ File 209264, and May 27, 1920, DJ File 209264, RG 60, NA; *Attorney General A. Mitchell Palmer on Charges,* p. 27; Murray, *Red Scare,* p. 230.

39. *Investigation Activities of the Department of Justice,* pp. 30, 31.

40. Ibid., p. 32.

41. Section 6, Fed. Penal Code of 1910; Coben, *A. Mitchell Palmer,* p. 217; *Attorney General A. Mitchell Palmer on Charges,* pp. 166.

42. Lowenthal, *Federal Bureau of Investigation,* p. 190, echoes the Bureau in accepting the lower figure, while Post, *Deportations Delirium,* p. 22, uses the higher; Coben, *A. Mitchell Palmer,* p. 219, citing U.S. House, Committee on Immigration and Naturalization, *IWW Deportation Cases* (66th Cong., 2nd sess., 1920, p. 79), says this meeting took place before October 1918. See also Murray, *Red Scare,* p. 206; *Investigation Activities of the Department of Justice,* p. 32; Coben, p. 218, citing *Charges of Illegal Practices of the Department of Justice,* pp. 7, 409; Coben also cites Wilson to Duncan, Apr. 22, 1920, W. B. Wilson Papers, Pennsylvania Historical Society.

43. Post, *Deportations Delirium,* p. 23. The Union of Russian Workers had been founded in 1907 and had its national headquarters at the Russian People's House, 133 East 15th Street in New York (Murray, *Red Scare,* p. 196). It had held its first national convention in Detroit in 1914 (Post, *Deportations Delirium,* p. 22). According to Post's information, the membership was 7,000 and the organization was founded in 1911. Hoover's Radical Division maintained that the Union had been founded in Russia by William Szaton, who was then the Soviet chief of police in Petrograd. According to an undercover agent working for Ohio Governor (and future presidential nominee) James M. Cox (see attachment to Cox to Palmer, Nov. 13, 1919, DJ File 203557–3 1/2, RG 60, NA), Trotsky had founded the group in 1906 when he was living on New York's Lower East Side.

44. Creighton to Caminetti (initialed JEH), July 30, 1919, DJ File 203557–1, RG 60, NA.

45. Hoover to Caminetti, Aug. 7, 1919, DJ File 203557–2, and Aug. 20, 1919, DJ File 203557–3, RG 60, NA.

46. *Investigation Activities of the Department of Justice,* p. 5. Palmer issued his reply on November 15, 1919.

47. Quoted in Coben, *A. Mitchell Palmer,* p. 214.

48. Ibid., p. 221; Hoover to Burke, Feb. 21, 1920, attached to Hoover to Burke, Mar. 16, 1920, DJ File 186701–14–824, RG 60, NA.

49. Coben, *A. Mitchell Palmer,* pp. 220, 221. Coben cites the *New York Times* and *New York World* for Nov. 8, 1919.

50. A photograph of the damage was reprinted in R. G. Brown et al., *Report Upon the Illegal Practices of the United States Department of Justice* (Washington, D.C.: National Popular Government League, 1920; reprinted New York: Arno, 1969), p. 17; Murray, *Red Scare,* p. 197.

51. Brown, *Illegal Practices of the Department of Justice,* p. 11.

52. See Sowers to Palmer, Nov. 14, 1919, DJ File 203557–8, RG 60, NA; Palmer's reply was *Investigation Activities of the Department of Justice;* Shorr to Palmer, Nov. 13, 1919, cited in Coben, *A. Mitchell Palmer,* p. 221.

53. Post, *Deportations Delirium,* p. 79.

54. Interrogation of Pete Mironovich, Nov. 18, 1919, DJ File 203557–14, RG 60, NA.

55. Murray, *Red Scare,* pp. 205, 206.

56. For media reactions to Goldman, see Candace Falk, *Love, Anarchy, and Emma Goldman* (New York: Holt, 1984), pp. 51, 58–59. One of Goldman's admirers then was Louis Post, who reluctantly had to sign the order for her deportation. He had written years before in his journal, *The Public,* that "I know no one who is kinder, more unselfish, or broader minded, and withal she has an indomitable courage both in word and deed." For his part, A. Mitchell Palmer said, "I do not need to inform you that there has probably never been in this country a woman who accomplished as much hurt to American morals and citizenship, particularly of the young, as Emma Goldman, so long a consort of the pervert, Alexander Berkman, with whom she was lately deported" (*Attorney General A. Mitchell Palmer on Charges,* p. 8; Falk, *Emma Goldman,* p. 47). Because of her commitment to freedom of thought she broke with bolshevism after her firsthand experience with repression under that regime after Hoover had sent her there. For writing *My Disillusionment in Russia* (New York: Doubleday, 1920) and *My Further Disillusionment in Russia* (New York: Doubleday, 1920) she was accused of being an American agent by William Z. Foster and an opportunist by Big Bill Haywood. Her literary agent even made a proposal, which Goldman rejected, to have the first of her books on Russia appear with an introduction by Hoover (Falk, *Emma Goldman,* pp. 326–327).

57. Hoover to Creighton, Aug. 23, 1919, DJ File 186233–13 sec. 3, and Hoover to Caminetti, Sept. 15, 1919, DJ File 186233–13–200, RG 60, NA.

58. The story is in *National Magazine* (Mar. 1925) in a scrapbook in the Hoover Memorabilia Collection, RG 65, NA, and also in a scrapbook in OCPA.

59. There are other inaccuracies in this story that cast doubt on the anonymous writer's reliability. For instance, the Haymarket riot occurred in 1886, and while Goldman was outraged by the trial and execution of the anarchists, she did not become publicly involved in politics until seven years later, at the time of Berkman's attack on Henry Clay Frick. The most likely explanation, however, is that Hoover had so thoroughly immersed himself in Goldman's writings during the preparation of his brief that he was able to describe her and her words so vividly that the reporter assumed Hoover had done personally what had actually been the work of his agents. It would have been natural for a reporter to seize any chance to create a human interest story out of such a sensational case (*National Magazine* [Mar. 1925]).

60. Goldman refused to answer any questions at the hearing on the grounds that she was actually a citizen, and hence outside the jurisdiction of the immigration authorities (*New York Times,* Sept. 19, p. 11; 26, p. 11; 28, 1919; Oct. 28, 1919, p. 32). In a letter to Francis G. Caffrey, the U.S. attorney for New York, Hoover implied that he presented oral arguments at the hearing based on new evidence that "I introduced without incorporating the same in my brief" (Hoover to Caffrey, Dec. 5, 1919, DJ File 186233–13–224, RG 60, NA).

61. *Investigation Activities of the Department of Justice,* pp. 35–38.

62. Ibid., p. 39.

63. Ibid., p. 41.

64. Ibid., p. 42.

65. Ibid., p. 43.

66. Ibid., pp. 48, 57.

67. Ibid., pp. 48, 50, 56–57.

68. Ibid., p. 50.

69. Ibid., pp. 51, 109.

70. *New York Times,* Nov. 30, 1919, p. 30, and Dec. 9, 1919, p. 19; Hoover to Caffrey, Dec. 5, 1919, DJ File 186233–13–224, RG 60, NA; Post, *Deportations Delirium,* p. 18; unidentified New York newspaper, Dec. 9, 1919, Hoover Memorabilia Collection, RG 65, NA. For a letter of Hoover's indicating that he was present at the hearing on December 9, see Hoover to Carter, Dec. 13, 1919, DJ File 186233–13–239, RG 60, NA.

71. Abercrombie to Secretary of War, Nov. 25, 1919, DJ File 203557, following 38; Hoover to Coxe, Dec. 17, 1919, DJ File 205492–5 between 2 and 3; Hoover to Poole, Dec. 24, 1919, DJ File 202600–65–2, RG 60, NA.

72. Post, *Deportations Delirium,* p. 27.

73. *Washington Post,* Dec. 22, 1919.

74. William N. Vaile of Colorado, "Deportation of Anarchist Aliens," *Congressional Record,* Jan. 5, 1920.

75. *New York Tribune,* Dec. 22, 1919, Hoover Memorabilia Collection, RG 65, NA.

76. Ibid. The *Tribune* credited Hoover with being in charge of the operation, saying that "he, with Immigration Commissioner Anthony Caminetti and Chief William A. Flynn of the secret service, supervised the large job of getting the 249 anarchists to Ellis Island from various parts of the country in which they had been apprehended and in putting them aboard the transport Buford, which sailed at 6 A.M. yesterday from Sandy Hook for some point in bolsheviki Russia."

77. Unidentified newspaper clipping, Hoover Memorabilia Collection, RG 65, NA.

78. Palmer to Grouitch (initialed JEH), Apr. 30, 1920, JD File 202600–59–37, RG 60, NA.

79. See Hoover to Caminetti, Nov. 7, 21, 22, 25, 26, 28, 1919; Dec. 1, 2, 4, 5, 12, 18, 1919, all DJ File 203557, RG 60, NA. On most days there were more than one letter between the two officials.

80. Hoover to Creighton, Dec. 4, 1919, cited by David Williams, "The Bureau of Investigation and Its Critics, 1919–1921: The Origins of Federal Political Surveillance," *The Journal of American History* 68 (Dec. 1981): 568; Hoover to Caminetti, Dec. 11, 1919, DJ File 203557–28; Hoover to Spencer, Dec. 11, 1919, DJ File 203557–29; Assistant Commissioner of Immigration to Hoover, Dec. 12, 1919, DJ File 203557–31 1/2, all RG 60, NA.

81. Louis Post saw this kind of vocabulary as an indication of contempt for constitutional rights and a conviction that the end justifies the means in politics (Post, *Deportations Delirium* p. 308). See also Hoover to Caminetti, Dec. 17, 1919, DJ File 203557–37, RG 60, NA.

82. For an original and insightful analysis of the Red Scare in these terms, see Stanley Coben, "A Study in Nativism: The American Red Scare of 1919–1920," *Political Science Quarterly* 79 (Mar. 1964):52–75. For the classic analysis of rituals of solidarity, particularly as they involve crime and punishment, see Emile Durkheim, *The Division of Labor in Society* (New York: Free Press, 1964; originally published in France in 1893).

83. Frank J. Donner, *The Age of Surveillance* (New York: Knopf, 1980), p. 31; James D. Horan, *The Pinkertons* (New York: Bonanza, 1967); Allan Pinkerton, *The Mollie Maguires and the Detectives* (New York, 1878).

84. *JD Register, 1924,* p. 12; Baughman obituary, in the Society of Former FBI Agents newsletter, *The Grapevine,* Apr. 1972; Fred J. Cook, *The FBI Nobody Knows* (New York: Macmillan, 1964), p. 75, citing Jack Alexander, "The Director," *The New Yorker,* Sept. 25, 1937; Oct. 2, 9, 1937. Alumni Affairs Office, George Washington University School of Law, and *The Grapevine,* Apr. 1972.

85. Spellacy to Slater, Dec. 22, 1919, DJ File 203557–57, RG 60, NA.

86. Phone interview, Margaret Hoover Fennell, Jan. 30, 1985; Hoover Memorabilia Collection, JEHF.

Chapter 4: The Red Years: The Lessons of Failure
(*pp. 93–129*)

1. Theodore Draper, *The Roots of American Communism* (New York: Viking, 1957), p. 137.
2. *Attorney General A. Mitchell Palmer on Charges,* p. 386.
3. Ibid., pp. 312, 322.
4. Ibid., p. 364; Don Whitehead, *The F.B.I. Story* (New York: Random House, 1956), p. 44; Draper, *American Communism,* p. 158.
5. *Attorney General A. Mitchell Palmer on Charges,* p. 323.
6. The memorandum brief on the Communist party is printed in its entirety in *J. Edgar Hoover Speaks Concerning Communism,* ed. James D. Bales (Washington, D.C.: Capitol Hill Press, 1970), pp. 266–288. It is also in the files of the Research Unit, External Affairs Division, FBI.
7. *Attorney General A. Mitchell Palmer on Charges,* p. 321.
8. Ibid., pp. 329–330.
9. Ibid., p. 327.
10. Foster had not yet joined the Party (Robert K. Murray, *Red Scare: A Study in National Hysteria, 1919–1920* [New York: McGraw Hill, 1964], pp. 142, 165; Draper, *American Communism,* p. 199).
11. Draper, *American Communism,* p. 152.
12. *Attorney General A. Mitchell Palmer on Charges,* p. 331.
13. The figure of 60,000 is based on the Party's own estimates. If other sources are to be believed, there were as few as 27,000. Theodore Draper tends to accept the lower figure, Robert K. Murray the higher (Draper, *American Communism,* pp. 189–190; Robert K. Murray, *Red Scare: A Study in National Hysteria, 1919–1920* [New York: McGraw-Hill, 1964], p. 53). Probably no more than 10 percent of the combined membership of the Communist parties could speak English; the actual number may have been far fewer (Draper, *American Communism,* p. 190).
14. *Attorney General A. Mitchell Palmer on Charges,* p. 377.
15. Draper, *American Communism,* p. 162; *Attorney General A. Mitchell Palmer on Charges,* p. 449.
16. Hoover to Caminetti, Jan. 13, 1920, DJ File 205492–157, RG 60, NA.
17. *Attorney General A. Mitchell Palmer on Charges,* p. 452.
18. Harold Lasswell later put forward an analysis of international conflict as a struggle between the ideologies of "nationalism" and "proletarianism" (Harold D. Lasswell, *World Politics and Personal Insecurity* [New York: Free Press, 1965]); *Attorney General A. Mitchell Palmer on Charges* p. 452.
19. Hoover to Caminetti, Dec. 22, 1919, DJ File 205492–6; Dec. 24, 1919, DJ File 205492–9; Dec. 24, 1919, DJ File 205492–10, all RG 60, NA.

20. Caminetti to Hoover, Dec. 24, 1919, DJ File 205492–15, RG 60, NA.

21. William Preston, Jr., *Aliens and Dissenters* (Cambridge, Mass.: Harvard University Press, 1963), p. 212; Hoover to Caminetti, Dec. 17, 1919, DJ File 203557–38, RG 60, NA. After the raids, Hoover and the Justice Department were accused of having engineered this harsh deprivation of aliens' right to counsel. Hoover defended himself to the satisfaction of senators investigating the episode by presenting testimony and evidence that Abercrombie had made the change at the request of the Labor Department's own counsel (Ralph de Toledano, *J. Edgar Hoover: The Man in His Time* [New Rochelle, N.Y.: Arlington House, 1973], p. 59.) Hoover's letters to Caminetti on this subject before the raid were certainly intended to pressure the Immigration Bureau to return to the old rule, but no surviving letter contains a specific request from Hoover for this change. Hoover's confidence in his position in this regard at the Senate hearings of December 1920 probably meant that, technically speaking, he never did make such a request. (For Hoover's detailed denial that he had initiated the request for the change in Rule 22, see Palmer to Sterling [initialed JEH], Mar. 3, 1921, DJ File 209115–38, RG 60, NA.)

22. According to Post, Wilson authorized arrests of both Communist and Communist Labor party members upon probable-cause proof of membership. Wilson certainly had Hoover's brief on the Communist party before him when he made this decision, but there is no certain proof that he had Hoover's Communist Labor brief (which Hoover had sent to Caminetti that day). It is unlikely, however, that Wilson would have rendered a decision on the Communist Labor party unless there was a request for warrants against Communist Labor party members before him, and in Hoover's cover letter, which accompanied the request, Hoover said his brief on the Communist Labor party would be sent with the warrants. It is likely, therefore, that Hoover proceeded with his plans for arresting members of the two parties only after learning both briefs had been approved by Wilson at the December 24 conference (Louis B. Post, *The Deportations Delirium of Nineteen-Twenty: A Personal Narrative of an Historic Official Experience* [New York: Da Capo, 1970; first published in 1923], p. 85). See also Hoover to Caminetti, Dec. 24, 1919, DJ File 205492–10, RG 60, NA. On the basis of almost the same admittedly ambiguous evidence, Stanley Coben constructs an altogether different chronology. Based on the fact that Caminetti's letter to Hoover of December 24 mentioned only a decision involving a Communist party member (Marion Bieznuk), he concludes that this conference was the December 24 meeting, and that a decision had been rendered only on Communist party members. He contends that Hoover "rashly" decided on his own to proceed with a roundup of Communist Labor party members as well on the "assumption" that Communist Labor party members were deportable (Stanley Coben, *A. Mitchell Palmer: Politician* [New York: Columbia University Press, 1963],

p. 224). He assumes that Hoover wrote his letter of December 24 (cited above) in reply to Caminetti's of the same day. I feel, however, that Hoover's was probably written first and that the messages were exchanged rapidly by means of messenger and supplemented by personal conversations of the sort mentioned in Caminetti's December 24 letter. I feel there is no reason to doubt Post's statement that at the Christmas Eve meeting Wilson specifically authorized warrants for the Communist Labor as well as the Communist party, since Post's statement occurs in a document in which he was presenting every possible fact that might discredit Hoover and Palmer.

23. Murray, *Red Scare*, p. 213; Hoover to Caminetti, Dec. 27, 1919, DJ File 205492–14, and Dec. 31, 1919, DJ File 205492 following 14, RG 60, NA; Coben, *A. Mitchell Palmer*, p. 226.

24. Hoover to Wilson (initialed JEH), Jan. 2, 1920, DJ File 205492–243, RG 60, NA; Baker to author, Apr. 11, 1985, Table of FBI Personnel Levels; Joan M. Jensen, *The Price of Vigilance* (Chicago: Rand McNally, 1968), p. 283.

25. Hoover to Chief Clerk, Jan. 2, 1920, DJ File 205492, RG 60, NA.

26. Murray, *Red Scare*, p. 213. See also Judge George Anderson's questioning of Boston Commissioner of Immigration Skeffington in *Colyer* vs. *Skeffington*, reprinted in R. G. Brown et al., *Report Upon the Illegal Practices of the United States Department of Justice* (New York: Arno, 1969; originally published, 1920), p. 46. For Hoover's and Baughman's warrant requests, see DJ File 205492, passim, RG 60, NA.

27. Judge George Anderson, quoted by Max Lowenthal, *The Federal Bureau of Investigation* (New York: William Sloan Associates, 1950), p. 207.

28. This was a result that had been foreseen by the aliens' chief attorney, George Vanderveer, and by officials within the Justice and Labor departments such as Byron Uhl and Franklin K. Lane.

29. Murray, *Red Scare*, p. 218.

30. *New York Times*, Jan. 4, 1920, in *Scrapbook*, Hoover Memorabilia Collection, RG 65, NA.

31. Hoover to Bowen, Dec. 24, 1919, DJ File 205492–8; Hoover to (George F.) Lamb, Feb. 6, 1920, DJ File 205492–21, both RG 60, NA. There is nothing to suggest he ever got this list of "silk-stockinged men and women," or that such a list ever existed.

32. Post, *Deportations Delirium*, p. 285; Hoover to (A. J.) Carter, (State Department), Jan. 7, 1920, DJ File 205492–41, RG 60, NA.

33. *Attorney General A. Mitchell Palmer on Charges*, pp. 283, 287, 288. According to Hoover to Schell, Jan. 26, 1920, DJ File 205492–326, RG 60, NA, Hoover attended the Senate hearings on Martens's activities in late January and early February.

34. In the aftermath of the raids, Hoover was attacked for using high bail to keep the aliens imprisoned unconstitutionally. He defended himself by claiming his only consideration was fixing an amount sufficient to "secure

the attendance of the person concerned" (*Attorney General A. Mitchell Palmer on Charges,* p. 37). Letters in the Justice Department files clearly contradict this claim. Complaining to Caminetti about the release of a radical named A. Dimitrishin on a bail of $1,000, Hoover said that, subsequent to his release, Dimitrishin told a radical gathering that "it will not be long before we will be able to overthrow the present form of government in this country." Hoover then asked that bail be raised to $5,000, because the person had been a "considerable amount of trouble to the local officers of the Bureau of Investigation." His reason for asking Caminetti to raise bail in this case was obviously to silence Dimitrishin's political opinions and to curtail his right of assembly. He was not simply making sure of his appearance at future hearings (Hoover to Caminetti, Jan. 15, 1920, DJ File 205492–20, RG 60, NA).

35. Hoover to Stone, Jan. 17, 1920, DJ File 205492–226, RG 60, NA.

36. Hoover to Stone, Jan. 23, 1920, DJ File 205492–296, RG 60, NA.

37. Palmer to (W. L.) Fuehrer (initialed JEH), Jan. 12, 1920, DJ File 205492–89, RG 60, NA.

38. These are on Reels 16–18 of *U.S. Military Intelligence Reports: Surveillance of Radicals in the United States, 1917–1941* (Frederick, Md.: University Publications, 1984), hereafter referred to as *General Intelligence Bulletin.*

39. *General Intelligence Bulletin,* March 20, 1920.

40. Ibid., Feb. 15–21, 1920, p. 44; Feb. 21–27, 1920, p. 39. (The two-minute course on patriotism was in a section devoted to "Counter Radical Activities.")

41. Hoover to Kenyon, Jan. 22, 1920, DJ File 205492–281; Hoover to A. Johnson, Jan. 22, 1920, DJ File 205492–280; and Hoover to W. H. King, Jan. 22, 1920, DJ File 205492–279, all RG 60, NA; *Attorney General A. Mitchell Palmer on Charges,* p. 155.

42. See also Palmer to Abbott, Jan. 27, 1920, DJ File 205492–338 1/2, RG 60, NA, which is also reprinted in Brown, *Illegal Practices of the Department of Justice,* pp. 64–65. Among the publications included with the letter were Louis Fraina's description of the program and platform of the Communist party, the Manifesto of the Third International, the Manifesto of the Communist party of America, and an example of "Russian Bolshevik propaganda among our soldiers in Siberia." The Justice Department helpfully noted that "striking passages in these exhibits are marked for convenience."

43. *Attorney General A. Mitchell Palmer on Charges,* p. 221.

44. Ibid., pp. 238, 239.

45. Ibid., p. 244.

46. Coben, *A. Mitchell Palmer,* pp. 241, 242, 244; Palmer to Gagnier, Jan. 29, 1920, DJ File 202600–59–20, drafted by JEH, and Hoover to Attorney General, Jan. 28, 1920, DJ File 202600–59, both RG 60, NA.

47. Hoover to Carter, Jan. 28, 1920, DJ File 205492–364; Hoover to Hurley, May 5, 1920, DJ File 202600–59–38; Hoover to A. Rorke, Feb. 11, 1920, DJ Control Files, Classified Subject Files, Correspondence, 9–12–

770–2; Hoover to Fisher, Oct. 24, 1919, DJ Control Files, Classified Subject Files, Correspondence, JD 9–12–799; Hoover to Black, May 13, 1920, DJ File 205492–664, all RG 60, NA.

48. Hoover to Russian Division, Department of State, Sept. 7, 1920, DJ File 202600–70; Hoover to Hurley, July 22, 1920, DJ File 205492–685; Hoover to Marlborough Churchill, July 22, 1920, DJ File 205492–686, all RG 60, NA.

49. Hoover to Burke, Feb. 21, 1920, DJ File 186701–14, RG 60, NA.

50. Ibid.

51. Palmer to Wilson, Jan. 2, 1920 (initialed JEH), DJ File 205492–243, RG 60, NA.

52. *New York American,* Jan. 22, 1920, in *Scrapbook,* Hoover Memorabilia Collection, RG 65, NA.

53. *New York World,* Jan. 22, 1920, in *Scrapbook,* Hoover Memorabilia Collection, RG 65, NA.

54. *New York Times,* Jan. 27, 1920, in *Scrapbook,* Hoover Memorabilia Collection, RG 65, NA.

55. Hoover to Churchill, Jan. 23, 1920, DJ File 205492–294, RG 60, NA. See also David Williams, "The Bureau of Investigation and Its Critics, 1919–1921: The Origins of Federal Political Surveillance," *Journal of American History* 68 (December 1981):570–571. Hale would again enrage Hoover during the Labor Department hearings on the Communist Labor party. He was one of the twelve lawyers who would issue a pamphlet on the illegal activities of the Justice Department during the raids.

56. Hoover to Caminetti, Feb. 2, 1920, DJ File 205492–391, RG 60, NA; Preston, *Aliens and Dissenters,* p. 222.

57. Post took over from Abercrombie, who resigned to run for the Senate seat from Alabama (Post, *Deportations Delirium,* pp. 79, 148–149).

58. Emma Goldman, *Living My Life* (New York: Knopf, 1931), p. 712.

59. Post, *Deportations Delirium,* p. 152.

60. Ibid., p. 155.

61. Ibid., p. 167.

62. Ibid., p. 170. In March, Hoover was interviewed about the radical situation:

> Radical agitators are still at work in many parts of the United States, according to Hoover who a few months ago discovered that the Communist party of the United States had 40,000 active members. The Party now is working along the same lines, Hoover said, as the Communist Labor party and the United Communist party. "The United Communist party is going in for secret work," said Hoover, "where formerly it agitated openly for overthrow of the government. The party has secret headquarters and secret printing plants. Recently it issued a pamphlet under the caption: Rules for Underground Work. We obtained a copy of the rules, which were supposed to be secret. They are much the same as those used in Russia in the time of the czar." [Unknown newspaper, Mar. 29, 1920, in *Scrapbook,* Hoover Memorabilia Collection, RG 65, NA]

63. *Boston Post,* Apr. 14, 1920, in *Scrapbook,* Hoover Memorabilia Collection, RG 65, NA.

64. *Boston Globe,* Apr. 7, 1920; *Boston Transcript,* Apr. 7, 1920; *Boston Record American,* Apr. 7, 1920, all in *Scrapbook,* Hoover Memorabilia Collection, RG 65, NA, which also contains a story on President Wilson's daughter, the wife of a Harvard Law professor, who appeared to watch the hearing and express her sympathy for the defendants.

65. See Draper, *American Communism,* pp. 226–232; *New York Tribune,* Apr. 25, 1920, in *Scrapbook,* Hoover Memorabilia Collection, RG 65, NA.

66. *Washington Post,* Apr. 25, 1920, in *Scrapbook,* Hoover Memorabilia Collection, RG 65, NA.

67. Murray, *Red Scare,* p. 249.

68. Hoover to Caminetti, June 14, 1920, DJ Files 205492–676 and 205492–677, RG 60, NA.

69. Coben, *A. Mitchell Palmer,* p. 235.

70. Post, *Deportations Delirium,* p. 168.

71. Quoted in Coben, *A. Mitchell Palmer,* p. 233; Preston, *Aliens and Dissenters,* p. 225.

72. Coben, *A. Mitchell Palmer,* p. 238.

73. Brown, *Illegal Practices of the Department of Justice,* pp. 3, 6, 8.

74. Hoover to Palmer, May 5, 1920, DJ File 209264–3(?) and May 27, 1920, DJ File JD 209264, RG 60, NA.

75. Hoover to Caminetti, June 5, 1920, DJ File 209264, RG 60, NA.

76. *Scrapbook,* Hoover Memorabilia Collection, RG 65, NA.

77. Coben, *A. Mitchell Palmer,* p. 251.

78. U.S. Senate, Committee on the Judiciary, *Charges of Illegal Practices of the Department of Justice,* 66th Cong. 3rd sess., Jan. 16–Mar. 3, 1921, p. 19. This was the hearing to look into charges raised by the Lawyers Committee whose report had been published by the National Popular Government League (cited by Lowenthal, *Federal Bureau of Investigation,* p. 191). It was not until February 5, 1923, that the reports of these inquiries were published, and that only after the subcommittee had voted not to issue any official report. The reports issued by individual senators (Walsh and Sterling, and Walsh's reply to Sterling) are in the Congressional Record for Feb. 5, 1923, pp. 3051–3073.

79. *Scrapbook,* Hoover Memorabilia Collection, RG 65, NA.

80. Murray, *Red Scare,* p. 241.

81. Albert S. Lindemann, *The Red Years: European Socialism versus Bolshevism, 1919–1921* (Berkeley, Calif.: University of California Press, 1974), p. 132.

82. Draper, *American Communism,* p. 275.

83. Irving Howe and Lewis Coser, *The American Communist Party* (New York: Praeger, 1962), pp. 91, 92. The problem is that it is difficult to establish exactly how many Communists there actually were when the radical factions

of the Socialist party were at their strongest. Estimates of the combined membership of the two parties at their formation in August and September 1919 range from 88,000 to 60,000, but many of these members, possibly the majority, were members of the various language federations of the Socialist party and were "automatically" transferred to the rolls of the Communist parties once they were organized. According to the Parties' own statistics, the membership had dropped to 38,623 by December. The left wing, in the course of formally organizing itself into Communist parties, had lost three-fifths of its membership even before the Palmer raids. Hoover's raids were directed against a Communist movement that was already losing its mass base (Howe and Coser, *The American Communist Party*, pp. 91–93).

84. Howe and Coser, *The American Communist Party*, pp. 60, 92.

85. "The Radical Division of the Department of Justice," in *Attorney General A. Mitchell Palmer on Charges*, p. 177.

86. Murray, *Red Scare*, p. 259.

87. On December 1, 1922, Hoover was the subject of newspaper attention when he rushed to New York to grill a suspect in the case who had been captured in Warsaw. According to the *New York World*, Hoover "questioned Lindenfeld for hours, then gave orders that he be locked in a room alone and be guarded day and night." The Justice Department later reluctantly admitted that Lindenfeld was a double agent who had been working for the Bureau as an informer (*St. Louis Star*, Mar. 2, 1922, and *New York World*, Dec. 2, 1922, Hoover Memorabilia Collection, RG 65, NA; Lowenthal, *Federal Bureau of Investigation*, p. 276).

88. Sanders to Fuller, July 30, 1927, Communist Party File, Series 1, CCP; O. K. Fraenkel, *The Sacco-Vanzetti Case* (New York: Knopf, 1931), p. 5, cited in Lowenthal, *Federal Bureau of Investigation*, p. 280.

89. *Attorney General A. Mitchell Palmer on Charges*, p. 328.

90. Hoover to Ridgely, Oct. 11, 1919, DJ File 198940, RG 60, NA, included in *Marcus Garvey and Universal Negro Improvement Association Papers*, Vol. 2, ed. Robert A. Hill (Berkeley: University of California Press, 1983), p. 72. For an admirably researched discussion of this case, see Robert A. Hill, " 'The Foremost Radical Among His Race': Marcus Garvey and the Black Scare, 1918–1921," *Prologue* 16 (Winter 1984): 215–231.

91. DJ File 202600–63, RG 60, NA, has correspondence reflecting the interest of the Bureau in black radicalism.

Chapter 5: The Assistant Director
(*pp. 130–143*)

1. Burns to Hoover, May 22, 1922, J. Edgar Hoover Personnel File 67–561, Section #2, FBI. Hoover's personnel file is not a personnel file in the usual sense (a record of commendations, letters of censure, and evalua-

tions); it contains instead an odd collection of items, perhaps gathered at various times, to be parceled out to biographers and feature story writers.

2. *Biographical Data on Honorable J. Edgar Hoover,* a Masonic obituary, Hoover Memorabilia Collection, JEHF; *Washington Herald,* Dec. 23, 1924, and *National Magazine,* Mar. 1925, in *Scrapbook,* Hoover Memorabilia Collection, RG 65, NA.

3. Phone interview, Margaret Hoover Fennell, Apr. 16, 1986; Ovid Demaris, *The Director: An Oral Biography of J. Edgar Hoover* (New York: Harpers Magazine Press, 1975), p. 44.

4. Phone interview, Margaret Hoover Fennell, Apr. 15, 1986.

5. Demaris, *The Director,* p. 8.

6. This language dated from March 3, 1871, and had been repeated annually. The Department of Justice itself had been founded only eight months earlier, in 1870, although the office of attorney general was one of the four original offices of the cabinet in 1789, along with state, war, and the treasury. See FBI, *Abridged History of the Federal Bureau of Investigation,* 1983, Research Unit, OCPA. The best source of information about the early Bureau is an internal Bureau document, *History of the Bureau of Investigation,* prepared by Special Agent Charles Appel, Nov. 18, 1930, OCPA. The most detailed account of the establishment of the Bureau is Willard B. Gatewood, *Theodore Roosevelt and the Art of Controversy* (Baton Rouge: Louisiana University Press, 1970), pp. 236–287. See also Harry Overstreet and Bonaro Overstreet, *The FBI in Our Open Society* (New York: Norton, 1969). Also authoritative is Homer S. Cummings and Carl McFarland, *Federal Justice: Chapters in the History of Justice in the Federal Executive* (New York: Da Capo, 1970; originally published in 1937). Don Whitehead's *The F.B.I. Story* (New York: Random House, 1956) is an authorized history, prepared under the supervision of Hoover and his publicity chief, Louis Nichols. It contains some valuable information on the early Bureau, but since Hoover's view was that Bureau history was divided into an old and new (after May 10, 1924) testament, only the new dispensation had any relevance to his FBI story. In contrast, Max Lowenthal's *The Federal Bureau of Investigation* (New York: William Sloan Associates, 1950) traces the less creditable activities of Hoover's Bureau back to the circumstances of its origins. His book, like Fred J. Cook's *The FBI Nobody Knows* (New York: Macmillan, 1964), was subjected to searing criticism from Hoover and the Bureau, which encouraged Harry and Bonaro Overstreet to write their own volume to refute Lowenthal and Cook. Most other Bureau histories concentrate on the Hoover period, while Sanford J. Ungar's *FBI* (Boston: Atlantic Monthly Press, 1976) focuses on the post-Hoover era. The raw materials for the Bureau's early history are the Justice Department and FBI files at the National Archives (RG 60 and RG 65) and the microfilm files of the Bureau of Investigation from 1908 to 1922, also at the National Archives (RG 65).

7. See Gatewood, *Theodore Roosevelt,* Chap. 8; Appel, *History of the Bureau of Investigation,* p. 4; Overstreet and Overstreet, *The FBI in Our Open Society,* pp. 17–27.

8. For TR's charges, see Overstreet and Overstreet, *The FBI in Our Open Society,* p. 28. Appel states that the organization of the Bureau took place "about" July 1. Preliminary arrangements for the organization of the Bureau began on June 24, 1908, with the appointment of Stanley W. Finch as chief examiner of the Department of Justice and on July 26, 1908, when Bonaparte directed the Department to refer all investigations to Finch (Appel, *History of the Bureau of Investigation,* p. 4; Cook, *The FBI Nobody Knows,* p. 51). The Overstreets make the original figure to be twenty-three, perhaps not counting all of the land frauds and peonage case investigators (Overstreet and Overstreet, *The FBI in Our Open Society,* p. 27). Gatewood makes the original number twenty-two by not counting the examiners (Gatewood, *Theodore Roosevelt,* p. 254).

9. These two functions might be called "elite discipline" and "symbolic politics," in which leaders seek out "dramaturgical jousts with public problems [to] make the world understandable and convey the promise of collective accomplishment to masses who are bewildered, uncertain, and alone" (Murray Edelman, *The Symbolic Uses of Politics* [Urbana, Ill.: University of Illinois, 1964], p. 91).

10. Lowenthal, *Federal Bureau of Investigation,* p. 15; J. Edgar Hoover, "Federal Bureau of Investigation," *Daughters of the American Revolution Magazine,* Ca. July 1935, p. 81, OCPA; the Hoover quote on vice is from Lowenthal, *Federal Bureau of Investigation,* p. 19; Appel, *History of the Bureau of Investigation,* p. 7.

11. On Flynn, Lowenthal, *The Federal Bureau of Investigation,* p. 72; on Burns, Gene Caesar, *Incredible Detective* (Englewood Cliffs, N.J.: Prentice Hall, 1968), pp. 179, 188.

12. Cf. Durkheim: "As soon as the news of a crime gets abroad, the people unite." Durkheim felt that crime, by offending the collective conscience ("the totality of beliefs and sentiments common to average citizens of the same society"), is a reminder to citizens that they have a collective conscience and form a moral community. According to this view, the crime, the criminal, and his punishment all combine to form a powerful ritual of cultural solidarity that exerts an almost magnetic fascination on the public (Emile Durkheim, *The Division of Labor in Society* [New York: Free Press, 1964; originally published in France in 1893], pp. 79, 104).

13. Hoover to Donovan, Apr. 8, 1928, cited in Whitehead, *The F.B.I. Story,* p. 332.

14. Lowenthal, *Federal Bureau of Investigation,* pp. 269–271; Baker to Power, Apr. 11, 1985, memo on personnel and budget levels of FBI, 1908–1985.

15. Senate Select Committee, *Final Report,* Book III, p. 387.

16. David Williams, "The Bureau of Investigation and Its Critics, 1919–1921: The Origins of Federal Political Surveillance," *Journal of American History* 68 (December 1981):577, citing Lamb to Hoover, Dec. 24, 1920, Bureau Section File 204048; Hale Dossier, Old German File 379228; Bureau Section File 209115, all on microfilm, RG 65, NA; Peter Irons, " 'Fighting Fair': Zechariah Chafee, Jr., the Department of Justice, and the 'Trial at the Harvard Club,' " *Harvard Law Review* 94 (April 1981):1205–1236. See also Dominic Candeloro, "Louis F. Post and the Red Scare of 1920," *Prologue* 11 (Spring 1979):40–55, esp. p. 52; Hoover to Keenan, May 4, 1934, DJ File 133149, RG 60, NA.

17. For O'Hare, see Hoover to Baley, Apr. 25, 1921, and [Agent] to Hoover, June 18, 1921, DJ Control Files, Classified Subject, Correspondence 9–19–603–108 and –113, RG 60, NA, and for Garvey, see Robert A. Hill, " 'The Foremost Radical Among His Race': Marcus Garvey and the Black Scare, 1918–1921," *Prologue* 16 (Winter 1984):215–231; *New York Times,* Dec. 9, 1922 and Apr. 10, 1923, cited in Michal R. Belknap, "The Mechanics of Repression: J. Edgar Hoover, the Bureau of Investigation and the Radicals 1917–1925," *Crime and Social Justice* 7 (Spring-Summer 1977):52; *New York Times,* Apr. 4, 1921, in *Scrapbook,* Hoover Memorabilia Collection, RG 65, NA; for federal-state cooperation, see Stewart to Cannon, May 2, 1921, DJ File 9–12–734–51, RG 60, NA, cited in Belknap, "Mechanics of Repression," p. 52.

18. See story in *New York Times,* Apr. 8, 1923; George F. Ruch, who left the Bureau to join the Frick Coal Company as a security officer, was Hoover's "principal assistant" in his study of communism (Whitehead, *The F.B.I. Story,* p. 331). Ruch and Hoover had met at George Washington, and Ruch remained "one of Hoover's closest friends" until his death in 1938 (Richard Whitney, *Reds in America* [New York: Beckwith, 1924]. See also Jacob Spolansky, *The Communist Trail in America* (New York: Macmillan, 1951), pp. 23–30.

19. Lowenthal, *Federal Bureau of Investigation,* p. 279.

20. Irving Howe and Lewis Coser, *The American Communist Party* (New York: Praeger, 1962), p. 419; Theodore Draper, *The Roots of American Communism* (New York: Viking, 1957), p. 373.

21. Francis Russell, *The Shadow of Blooming Grove: Warren G. Harding and His Times* (New York: McGraw-Hill, 1968), p. 547.

22. See letter from president of B & O to Clark, Aug. 7, 1922, Communist Party File, Series 1, CCP; Lowenthal, *Federal Bureau of Investigation,* pp. 283, 288 (on p. 283, Lowenthal has evidence of Hoover's role in coordinating the investigation of the strike).

23. Whitehead, *The F.B.I. Story,* p. 62.

24. Cook, *The FBI Nobody Knows,* p. 141.

25. Ibid., p. 144; Hoover to Donovan, Apr. 4, 1928, cited by Whitehead, *The F.B.I. Story,* p. 332.

26. J. Edgar Hoover, *Persons in Hiding* (Boston: Little Brown, 1938), p. 255.

27. In 1925, the Bureau of Investigation managed to have Means convicted of violating the Prohibition Amendment. After his release in 1928 he wrote an amazing exposé of Harding's death, claiming the president had been murdered by his wife (Gaston B. Means, *The Strange Death of President Harding* [New York: Gould, 1930]). After collecting his royalties, Means repudiated the book. Many adventures later, all a credit to his nerve and the limitless gullibility of his victims, he managed to rob Evalyn McLean of the *Washington Post* family of $100,000 by promising her he could solve the Lindbergh kidnapping.

28. Hoover told the story of Gaston Means in a December 1936 *American Magazine* story that was reprinted in the *Reader's Digest* in March 1937 and then as a chapter in *Persons in Hiding*. Without saying it in so many words, Hoover implied that Means represented the entire Bureau before 1924: "Other than the contribution of being a horrible example the life of Gaston Means presents little that is high-minded" (Hoover, *Persons in Hiding*, p. 267).

29. Whitehead, *The F.B.I. Story*, p. 67. For more information on Richey, see the Larry Richey Papers, HHL. The Willebrandt quote is from Mason, *Harlan F. Stone: Pillar of the Law* (New York: Viking, 1956), p. 159; the mention of Irey is in the *Washington Herald*, May 13, 1924.

30. Alpheus Thomas Mason, *Harlan Fiske Stone, Pillar of the Law* (New York: Viking, 1954), p. 150.

Chapter 6: The Progressive Years
(*pp. 144–178*)

1. Don Whitehead, *The F.B.I. Story* (New York: Random House, 1956), pp. 70–71.

2. See Nathan Douthit, "Police Professionalism and the War Against Crime in the United States, 1920s–1930s," in *Police Forces in History*, ed. G. L. Mosse (Beverly Hills, Calif.: Sage, 1974).

3. Richard Hofstadter, *The Age of Reform: From Bryan to F.D.R.* (New York: Knopf, 1968), p. 5. Hofstadter also noted "how overwhelmingly urban and middle-class they were. Amongst entirely native-born Protestants, they had an extraordinarily high representation of professional men and college graduates" (p. 144). J. Edgar Hoover's resemblance to Hofstadter's ideal progressive type is uncanny, even to the detail of Masonic membership (p. 145).

4. "Friendly Advice," unknown paper, circa 1924, in *Scrapbook*, Hoover Memorabilia Collection, RG 65, NA. Despite everything, Burns *was* an honest man. He had been fired for telling the truth—that he had sent agents to

Montana to investigate Burton Wheeler. Burns had had no reason to question Daugherty's order to investigate Wheeler. The charges against Wheeler were not totally groundless, and his guilt or innocence involved highly technical interpretations of the facts and the law. When Harlan Stone took over the Justice Department, he reviewed the evidence against Wheeler and ordered that the case be carried to trial. Burns's error was to remain silent when Daugherty falsely said that the Justice Department had had no hand in the Montana investigation. When the Senate learned the truth from Burns, it appeared as if he had helped cover up Daugherty's dishonesty. (And he had!) It would be a rare political appointee who would rush to expose his superior when there was no clear illegality involved and when the charges were made by his political enemies. But when Burns resigned (under pressure from Stone), considering these circumstances, it was interpreted as an admission of some sort of wrongdoing, so he left Washington with his integrity suspect and his reputation ruined.

5. *National Magazine,* Mar. 1925, and *Pittsburgh Press,* Jan. 27, 1925, both in *Scrapbook,* Hoover Memorabilia Collection, RG 65, NA; "A New Kind of Government Sleuth in Washington," *Literary Digest,* Jan. 24, 1925, Research Unit, OCPA.

6. *Baltimore Evening Sun,* Dec. 26, 1924, in *Scrapbook,* Hoover Memorabilia Collection, RG 65, NA.

7. Testimony by Assistant Attorney General John W. H. Crim, in U.S. Senate, Select Committee on Investigation of the Attorney General, *Investigation of Hon. Harry M. Daugherty, formerly Attorney General of the United States,* 68th Cong., 1st sess., Sen. Res. 157, 1924, Vol. III, p. 2570, 2584–5, quoted in Max Lowenthal, *The Federal Bureau of Investigation* (New York: William Sloane Associates, 1950), pp. 299–300; Alpheus Thomas Mason, *Harlan Fiske Stone: Pillar of the Law* (New York: Viking, 1956), p. 113; U.S. Senate, Committee on the Judiciary, *Charges of Illegal Practices of the Department of Justice,* 66th Cong., 3rd sess., 1921, cited in Senate Select Committee, *Final Report,* Book III, p. 389. Fred J. Cook, *The FBI Nobody Knows* (New York: Macmillan, 1964), p. 138.

8. According to Hoover's version of events, it was *he* who suggested these guidelines to Stone (Whitehead, *The F.B.I. Story,* p. 67). Ralph de Toledano claims Hoover drafted the rules for Stone's signature (Ralph de Toledano, *J. Edgar Hoover: The Man in His Time* [New Rochelle, N.Y.: Arlington House, 1973], p. 72). There is no way of definitively establishing the provenance of the guidelines. One of the conditions was that the staff of the Bureau would be reduced as far "as is consistent with the proper performance of its duties." This hardly sounds like a condition *any* bureaucrat would set as his price for accepting a job. For the guidelines, see Stone to Hoover, May 13, 1924, quoted in Alpheus Thomas Mason, *Harlan Fiske Stone, Pillar of the Law* (New York: Viking, 1954) p. 151.

9. Cook, *The FBI Nobody Knows,* p. 138; Hoover to Ridgely, May 14,

1925, quoted in Senate Select Committee, *Final Report,* Book III, p. 390; *Pittsburgh Press,* Jan. 27, 1925.

10. Baldwin to Stone, Aug. 6, 1924, JEH Personnel File, FBI File 67–561, FOIA Reading Room, FBI.

11. Stone to Hoover, Aug. 7, 1924, JEH Personnel File, FBI File 67–561, FOIA Reading Room, FBI. See also Harrison E. Salisbury, "The Strange Correspondence of Morris Ernst and John Edgar Hoover, 1939–1964," *The Nation,* Dec. 1, 1984, pp. 575–589.

12. Speech by Matthew Woll, Dec. 15, 1926; Stevenson to Easley, Apr. 30, 1927; Easley to Clark, May 28, 1927, Communist Party File, Series 1, CCP.

13. Joan Hoff Wilson, *Herbert Hoover: Forgotten Progressive* (Boston: Little, Brown, 1975), pp. 49, 57.

14. Part of the Bureau of Standards, this division held 1,200 conferences between 1921 and 1928 to persuade American manufacturers to adopt common measurements for their products (Wilson, *Herbert Hoover,* p. 110).

15. Hofstadter, *The Age of Reform,* p. 204.

16. Hofstadter argues that progressivism was "in considerable part colored by the reaction to this immigrant stream among the native elements of the population." Hence he finds in progressives "much that was retrograde and delusive, a little that was vicious, and a good deal that was comic" (Hofstadter, *The Age of Reform,* pp. 5, 11). For social control progressivism, see Wilson, *Herbert Hoover,* p. 50.

17. Hoover, speech to IACP, July 14, 1925, OCPA.

18. Whitehead, *The F.B.I. Story,* pp. 68–69.

19. For details, see the annual reports of the attorney general, portions of which are quoted in de Toledano, *J. Edgar Hoover,* pp. 89–91. See also Baker to Powers, Apr. 11, 1985, memo on Bureau personnel statistics; Hoover to Attorney General, Feb. 6, 1933, "Justice Department Accomplishments," Taylor-Gates Collection, HHL.

20. Rex Collier, "Crime Detection Is Taught to Prospective U.S. Agents," *Washington Post,* July 8, 190, OCPA; Charles Appel, *History of the Bureau of Investigation,* Nov. 18, 1930, p. 16, OCPA.

21. *Fellowship Forum,* Jan. 3, 1925, in *Scrapbook,* Hoover Memorabilia Collection, RG 65, NA. Hostile testimony to the contrary, there is little persuasive evidence that Hoover was anti-Semitic or anti-Catholic. If anything, there was an overrepresentation of Catholics in the Bureau, though there was, and is, probably an overrepresentation of Catholics in any police force. Compared to other police forces, the FBI probably had more than the predictable number of Jews (which was nonetheless small). Over the years, some of the Bureau's top executives were Jewish, and for a long time the Identification Division had an especially high proportion of Jewish officials. According to a Jewish agent (who afterward worked for the American Jewish Committee, and so was unlikely to ignore evidence of anti-Semitism),

special efforts were made by the Bureau while he was there (the thirties and forties) to accommodate Jews who wanted to observe religious holidays. The thirties were also great years for Jewish athletes. He recalls that the Bureau's basketball team in Washington's federal employee league was nearly all Jewish, and that the Bureau seemed to actively recruit Jewish ballplayers (author's phone interview, Milton Ellerin, Apr. 30, 1985).

22. Appel, *History of the Bureau of Investigation,* passim.

23. Ibid.; Hoover to Attorney General, Feb. 6, 1933, "Justice Department Accomplishments," Taylor-Gates Collection, HHL.

24. Bayliss to Mapes, Mar. 26, 1929, "Justice—FBI, 1929," Presidential Papers, Cabinet Officers Series, HHL.

25. Ibid.

26. Mitchell to Newton, Apr. 11, 1929, "Justice—FBI, 1929," Presidential Papers, Cabinet Officers Series, HHL; IACP to Attorney General, June 27, 1929, JEH Personnel File, FBI File 67–561, FOIA Reading Room, FBI.

27. *Washington Brevities,* Oct. 8, 1932, OCPA.

28. Attorney General to Harding, Nov. 28, 1921, "Bureau of Investigation" (Reel 139), WGHP; Appel, *History of the Bureau of Investigation,* pp. 13–14.

29. Hoover, speech to IACP, July 14, 1925, p. 6, OCPA.

30. Whitehead, *The F.B.I. Story,* p. 135; *Washington Post,* May 24, 1925, OCPA; Uthai Vincent Wilcox in unknown paper, circa 1927, OCPA.

31. Appel, *History of the Bureau of Investigation.*

32. Hoover to Stone, June 24, 1924, DJ File 62–41–306, and Stone to Hoover, June 26, 1924, DJ File 62–41–306, RG 60, NA.

33. Hoover, speech to IACP, July 14, 1925, OCPA.

34. Phone interview, Margaret Hoover Fennell, Apr. 15, 1986; Ugo Carusi interview; Ovid Demaris, *The Director: An Oral Biography of J. Edgar Hoover* (New York: Harpers Magazine Press, 1975), p. 57.

35. Demaris, *The Director,* p. 7.

36. Phone interview, Margaret Hoover Fennell, Apr. 15, 1986; Demaris, *The Director,* p. 7.

37. Demaris, *The Director,* pp. 41, 44; Demaris has the inventory of Hoover's possessions at the time of his death, pp. 339–396. See also *New York Times,* Mar. 5, 1932, p. 8, for mention of a collection of "old glassware and spinning wheels."

38. Phone interview, Margaret Hoover Fennell, Apr. 15, 1986.

39. Bureau legend later developed that Hoover called himself "J. Edgar" to avoid this confusion, but of course his family had always called him that. (Sometimes the agents gave the story a moral by making the other J.E. a "deadbeat.") See *Cincinnati Enquirer,* Dec. 6, 1928, for a photo story on six of the Hoovers (including J. Edgar and his brother) who were prominent in Washington in 1928. A story in the *Washington Star,* Nov. 25, 1926, profiled both of the J. E. Hoovers along with other prominent Hoovers.

For the bicycle story, see unidentified paper, Mar. 21, 1925, Hoover Memorabilia Collection, RG 65, NA.

40. *Washington Times,* Feb. 22, 1929, OCPA. On May 16, 1931, Hoover was placed in charge of another probe of the District's police force, this one on charges of brutality (*Scrapbook,* Hoover Memorabilia Collection, RG 65, NA).

41. Collier to Powers, Apr. 20, 1976. See also *Washington Post,* Oct. 13, 1929.

42. Interview, Rex Collier, Jan. 27, 1976.

43. Hoover to Ridgely, May 14, 1925; Reeves to Hoover, Sept. 29, 1925; Hoover to Reeves, Oct. 7, 1925, in Senate Select Committee, *Final Report,* Book III, p. 390.

44. In 1925, one of Coolidge's aides asked Hoover to find out about a "Bureau for the Investigation of Financial Fraud" in Newark, but phrased the request so apologetically as to make it clear both knew that the request bordered on impropriety: "I wish you could secure for me a confidential report. I, first of all, have no wish to injure an honest man. . . . You will understand I am not asking that any definite action be taken. . . . I leave this matter to your kindly discretion." Hoover replied with the written equivalent of a smile and a wink: "I have . . . issued positive instructions that any inquiries are to be of a strictly confidential nature so that no 'leak' is to ensue." There was another episode in 1925 in which an assistant attorney general asked Hoover to provide general information about an individual's political affiliations. This done, Hoover was told that no further investigation was needed (Clark to Hoover, Dec. 23, 1925, and Hoover to Clark, Dec. 24, 1925, in Series I, Number 101, CCP; Hoover to Marshall, Nov. 27, 1925, DJ File 230351–1, RG 60, NA). The Bureau had been currying favor with presidents by supplying them with tidbits of political information long before Hoover took charge, particularly during the end of Burns's tenure, when he was trying to persuade Coolidge and Stone to let him keep his job. Burns would send Coolidge flattering reports from his agents about the president's political strength. When he heard that prominent individuals had decided to support Coolidge's reelection, he also passed that along. This sort of political operation evidently ceased under Herbert Hoover and did not resume again until the Roosevelt administration (Burns to Slemp, Mar. 10, 1924, and Burns to Clark, May 3, 1924, in Bureau of Investigation File, Series 1, CCP).

45. For a detailed survey of this type of activity in Herbert Hoover's administration, see Kenneth O'Reilly, "Herbert Hoover and the FBI," *Annals of Iowa,* Summer 1983, pp. 46–63. See also Hoover to Richey, Nov. 21, 1929, "Sentinels of the Republic," Presidential Papers Subject File, HHL.

46. Newton to Hoover, Feb. 15, 1930; Hoover to Newton, Feb. 18, 1930, "American Citizens Political Awakening, 1929–1930"; Hoover to Richey, abstract, Dec. 11, 1929, "American Civil Liberties Union"; Hoover to Sisson,

Apr. 9, 1930, "Colored Question," all in Presidential Papers Subject File, HHL. Hoover to Carusi, May 23, 1930, "Countries, Italy, Correspondence," Presidential Papers, Foreign Affairs, HHL. Hoover to Attorney General, Sept. 12, 1931, "Moorhead, H—Moos, A.," Presidential Papers, President's Secretary's File, HHL.

47. Hoover to Attorney General, Oct. 10, 1931, "Menh.—Menl.," Presidential Papers, President's Secretary's File, HHL.

48. O'Reilly, "Herbert Hoover and the FBI," p. 54; Hoover to Richey, Oct. 30, 1931, "Navy League of the U.S., Investigation," Presidential Papers Subject File, HHL.

49. See, for example, the many letters from Ralph M. Easley of the National Civic Federation to the White House, for example Easley to Welliver, Feb. 28, 1925, Communist Party File Series I, CCP, and Easley to H. C. Hoover, June 5, 1930, "Communist—Correspondence, 1929, March–July," Presidential Papers Subject File, HHL. Also petitions from patriotic organizations to the White House that the Communist party be prosecuted under the Logan Act, Kilbreth to Slemp, Oct. 29, 1923, Communist Party File, Series 1, CCP.

50. Hughes to Coolidge, May 23, 24, 1924, and Jan. 24, 1925, Communist Party File, Series I, CCP. After Hughes left the State Department for the Supreme Court, his successor, Frank Kellogg, became the White House's anti-Communist watchdog (Kellogg to Coolidge, May 7, 1925, Communist Party File, Series 1, CCP).

51. Hoover described this brief as follows:

In January 1924 the Senate passed a resolution inquiring as to the question of the recognition of the Soviet Government. The Secretary of State requested the Department of Justice to prepare and submit to him a memorandum as to the communistic activities in the United States emanating from or directed by the Third International and therefore practically traceable to the Soviet Government. There was prepared in the Department of Justice at that time, and submitted to the Secretary of State, who in turn transmitted it to the Senate, a brief of approximately 400 to 500 pages, setting forth in detail what has been carried on in this country by the communistic groups among the children, among the churches, among the labor organizations, and in practically all walks of life. It was a complete summary. [Hoover testimony before House Appropriations Committee, Justice Department Appropriations for fiscal 1926, Dec. 16, 1924, p. 74, OCPA.]

According to Don Whitehead, "Hoover sat with Secretary Hughes at the witness table. . . . The Senate Foreign Relations Subcommittee refrained from acting favorably on the Senate resolution to recognize Soviet Russia" (Whitehead, *The FBI Story,* p. 350). Hoover evidently had maintained his reputation as the federal government's man to see about communism. The published transcript of these hearings—U.S. Senate, Subcommittee of the Foreign Relations Committee, *Hearings Regarding Recognition of Russia,* 68th Cong., 1st sess., 1924—does not show either Hughes or Hoover as appearing. Hughes is represented only by a letter and by the testimony of the experts in his Russian Division. There seem to have been executive sessions, and it was probably then that Hoover and Hughes appeared.

52. For the relevant passage in Hughes's statement, see Charles Chesney Hyde, "Charles Evans Hughes," in *The American Secretaries of State and their Diplomacy,* ed. S. F. Bemis (New York: Knopf, 1928), Vol. X, p. 287. Hughes's statement was on July 1, 1924. One group that made such a request was called the Woman Patriot (Kilbreth to Slemp, Oct. 29, 1923, Communist Party File, Series 1, CCP).

53. Hoover to House Appropriations Committee, Justice Department Appropriations for fiscal 1926, Dec. 16, 1924, p. 74, OCPA. See also Senate Select Committee, *Final Report,* Book III, p. 388, citing *FBI Digested History,* Feb. 1, 1940.

54. Hoover to Stone, Dec. 13, 1924, in Select Committee, *Final Report,* Book III, p. 390.

55. Ralph Easley, like Hoover, represents an anticommunism that has its origin in cultural, not economic, convictions. Easley was a Herbert Hoover-style progressive who devoted his life to the ideal of cooperation between labor, capital, and the public, and to the elimination of conflict from American society. When attaining the dream of national consensus eluded him, he looked for someone to blame. Communists became a symbol of the principle of conflict and of the tendency of history to move in uncongenial directions (Marguerite Green, *The National Civic Federation and the American Labor Movement, 1900–1925* [Westport, Conn.: Greenwood, 1973]). For the pamphlet, see Hunter to Saunders, Jan. 24, 1927, Communist Party File, Series 1, CCP. The speech was by Matthew Woll, "Subversive Forces in Our Country," New York Chamber of Commerce, Dec. 15, 1926, Communist Party File, Series 1, CCP.

56. Easley to Clark, May 28, 1927, Communist Party File, Series 1, CCP.

57. Easley to Clark, May 28, 1927, Communist Party File, Series 1, CCP; Easley to Luhring, Feb. 23, 1928, DJ File 202600–59–68, RG 60, NA.

58. Easley to Herbert Hoover, Sept. 26, 1929; Apr. 11, 19, 1930; May 10, 20, 1930; Feb. 24, 1931; Apr. 13, 1931; Oct. 30, 1931; Dec. 4, 1931. For the mention of Means, see Easley to Herbert Hoover, May 1930, "Communist—Correspondence," Presidential Papers Subject File, HHL.

59. U.S. House, Special Committee to Investigate Communist Activities in the U.S., *Investigation of Communist Propaganda,* 71st Cong., 2nd sess., 1930, Part 2, Vol. 1, p. 36, passim; Frank J. Donner, *The Age of Surveillance* (New York: Knopf, 1980), p. 49.

60. *Washington Star,* June 13, 1930, in *Scrapbook,* Hoover Memorabilia Collection, RG 65, NA.

61. Mitchell to Dodds, Dec. 2, 1931, DJ File 202600–59, RG 60, NA.

62. There were later reports that the White House's charges of Commu-

nist influence in the March came from the Bureau, but Military Intelligence was actually the source (Donald J. Lisio, *The President and Protest: Hoover, Conspiracy, and the Bonus Riot* [Columbia, Mo.: University of Missouri Press, 1973]). See also Joan M. Jensen, *Military Surveillance of Civilians in America* (Morristown, N.J.: General Learning Press, 1975), pp. 23–24, cited in Senate Select Committee, *Final Report,* Book III, p. 390; "Bonus March Conditions," Aug. 1, 1932, and "World War Veterans—Bonus Reports, Depositions, Statements," Presidential Papers Subject File, HHL. On September 1, 1932, Hoover sent Richey a rough draft of the analysis of the results of the search. Of the 5,091 veterans arrested, the Bureau had located the fingerprints of 4,364, and 24.4 percent of these had police records—Hoover included 187 "charges dismissed" in this group (Hoover to Richey, Sept. 1, 1932, and Hoover to Dodds, Sept. 10, 1932, "World War Veterans—Bonus, Reports, Depositions, Statements," Presidential Papers Subject File, HHL).

63. Senate Select Committee, *Final Report,* Book III, p. 391.

64. *DJ Register, 1927,* p. 8.

65. "Vocation Record," Apr. 12, 1945, Tolson Personnel File, FBI File 67–9524, FOIA Reading Room, FBI.

66. Whitehead, *The F.B.I. Story,* p. 120.

67. "Assignment History," circa July 1, 1956, Tolson Personnel File, FBI File 67–9524, FOIA Reading Room, FBI.

68. Ibid.; *Cedar Rapids Gazette,* June 7, 1931.

69. Appel, *History of the Bureau of Investigation,* p. 22.

70. "Assignment History," circa July 1, 1956, Tolson Personnel File, FBI File 67–9524, FOIA Reading Room, FBI.

71. See voucher for air travel, Sept. 2, 1937–Sept. 26, 1937, Hoover to McClure, Oct. 6, 1937, FBI File 66–801–229, and Tolson Memo, July 1, 1938, FBI File 67–9524–266, FOIA Reading Room, FBI, and photos of the three, September 1937, in Portland, Oregon, Hoover Memorabilia Collection, JEHF. For the Summit vacation, see *Herald of Westchester,* Nov. 24, 1944. For an idea of Baughman's role under Tolson, see Hoover to Tolson and Clegg, Nov. 12, 1935, FBI File 67–9524–214, FOIA Reading Room, FBI. Baughman was in Quantico by 1935.

72. Unknown Uniontown, Pennsylvania, newspaper, July 26, 1930, OCPA. For the crash, see many clippings, May 16, 1931, in *Scrapbook,* Hoover Memorabilia Collection, RG 65, NA.

73. Photos are in Hoover Memorabilia Collection, JEHF.

74. Hoover O&C File #33, Conroy to Tolson, July 5, 1944, marked "queer and derogatory." See also Tolson to Hoover, June 30, 1943, Hoover O&C File #75. An item dated June 20, 1951, Hoover O&C File #113, describes an investigation of a beautician who had spread rumors that Hoover was "queer." "Joseph Bryant III," Louis B. Nichols O&C File (the visit took place on June 3, 1955).

75. By 1930, Capone was a national celebrity, and a Chicago school of

journalism voted him "one of the ten outstanding personages of the world—the characters that actually made history" (John Cobler, *Capone* [New York: Putnam, 1971], p. 313). Capone shared the list with such figures as Charles Lindbergh, Admiral Richard Byrd, George Bernard Shaw, golfer Bobby Jones, Gandhi, Herbert Hoover, Albert Einstein, and Henry Ford.

76. Quoted in "Gangland's Challenge to Our Civilization," *Literary Digest* 107 (Oct. 25, 1930):8.

77. See *The Challenge of Crime in a Free Society: A Report by the President's Commission on Law Enforcement and Administration of Justice* (New York: Avon, 1968), pp. 101–105.

78. *Literary Digest* 111 (Oct. 31, 1931):6. See also Cobler, *Capone;* Geoffrey Perret, *America in the Twenties* (New York: Simon and Schuster, 1982), p. 393.

79. *New York Herald Tribune,* Mar. 3, 1932, p. 16.

80. Herbert Hoover had used other agencies besides the Bureau of Investigation to improve law enforcement, and they all followed the progressive formula. In 1929, the president had made Sanford Bates the first superintendent of the Federal Bureau of Prisons (located in the Justice Department), so that Bates, the man who reformed Massachusetts's notorious Deer Island prison, could "set a standard of penology against which all other America prisons would be judged." He had appointed George W. Wickersham, Taft's attorney general, to study the problems of law enforcement, particularly prohibition. The Wickersham Commission's monumental report, released at the end of 1930, was one of the major accomplishments of the Hoover administration, a milestone in the development of law enforcement professionalism (Perret, *America in the Twenties,* p. 320, 405–406). J. Edgar Hoover had a running feud with Bates and was always on the alert for ways to embarrass him. In 1931, Hoover's agents uncovered lax conditions at the federal prisons in Atlanta and Leavenworth, and the investigation received widespread coverage (*New York Daily News,* July 10, 1931, in *Scrapbook,* Hoover Memorabilia Collection, RG 65, NA). *New York Times,* Mar. 5, 1932, p. 1.

81. *New York Times,* Mar. 5, 1932, p. 1.

82. Ibid.

83. Ibid.

84. *Literary Digest* 113 (May 28, 1932):7.

85. For a perceptive analysis of the cultural significance of these and the following films, see Andrew Bergman, *We're in the Money* (New York: New York University Press, 1972).

86. *New York Times,* Feb. 28, 1930, p. 2; Mar. 32, 1930, sec. 2, p. 9; Dec. 19, 1930, p. 18; Mar. 13, 1931, p. 2; Aug. 25, 1931, p. 1; Sept. 15, 1931, p. 3; Apr. 10, 1932, p. 22; Aug. 15, 1933, p. 1; Oct. 10, 1933, p. 29. For the reaction to the Baumes Law sentence of life for a shoplifter, see *New York Times,* Feb. 7, 1930, p. 1; Aug. 15, 1933, p. 1.

87. In 1933, Hollywood contributed a cycle of movies glorifying vigilante

action against crime: *This Day and Age* (1933), *Gabriel Over the White House* (1933), and *The President Vanishes* (1934), all fantasies of direct, extralegal punishment of criminals. See Bergman, *We're in the Money,* Chap. 9, for an analysis of the "mob" cycle of films. For Dick Tracy, see Ron Goulart, *Line Up, Tough Guys* (Nashville, Tenn.: Sherbourne Press, 1966), p. 73.

Chapter 7: The New Deal FBI
(pp. 179–227)

1. Hoover, "Police Problems," *St. John's Law Review,* Dec. 1932, p. 55; he also wrote in this essay that "a lifetime is none too long a period in which to acquire that comprehensive grasp of conditions necessary for the most effective, constructive discharge of the duties of this position." For a survey of the FBI under FDR, see Kenneth O'Reilly, "A New Deal for the FBI: The Roosevelt Administration, Crime Control and National Security," *Journal of American History* 69 (Dec. 1982):638–658.

2. Hoover went to Walsh's colleague Burton Wheeler about this time and said that "he played no part in the reprisals against me [Wheeler]," holding Assistant Attorney General William J. Donovan, later chief of the OSS and Hoover's lifelong rival, responsible. Wheeler said he accepted this explanation (Fred J. Cook, *The FBI Nobody Knows* [New York: Macmillan, 1964], p. 144). There is some evidence that Walsh *had* had a change of heart about Hoover. After Walsh's death, his nephew, a Washington attorney, wrote that "shortly before he [Walsh] was to assume the post of Attorney General, he told his brother, Mr. John Walsh, and me [John Wattawa], that after careful consideration he had decided to retain Mr. J. Edgar Hoover in the position of director of the Bureau of Investigation" (Don Whitehead, *The F.B.I. Story* [New York: Random House, 1956], pp. 111, 336).

3. Cummings had represented Connecticut on the Democratic National Committee from 1900 to 1925 and had been one of Roosevelt's floor leaders at the 1932 convention (Paul W. Ward, "Hacking to Justice with Cummings," *Nation* 141 [July 3, 1935]:14–16).

4. FDR's inaugural address threatened that "in the event that the Congress shall fail, and in the event that the national emergency is still critical, I shall not evade the clear course of duty that will then confront me. I shall ask the Congress for the one remaining instrument to meet the crisis— broad Executive power to wage war against the emergency, as great as the power that would be given to me if we were in fact invaded by a foreign foe."

5. Leo C. Rosten, "Men Like War," *Harpers* 171 (June 1935):192, 195. FDR told the country he was going "to cement our society, rich and poor, manual worker and brain worker, into a voluntary brotherhood of freemen,

standing together, striving together, for the common good of all." He was going to provide the "unity of purpose that is best for the nation as a whole . . . among many discordant elements." His government would be "the outward expression of the unity and leadership of all groups." James MacGregor Burns argues that "the extent to which Roosevelt took the role of bipartisan leader during 1933 and 1934 has not been fully appreciated by scholars." Burns calls Roosevelt's policies during those years a " 'middle way' incorporating main lines of action of previous administrations, both Democratic and Republican, reflecting bipartisan support, and exploiting, of course, the atmosphere of crisis and fear" (Burns, *Roosevelt: the Lion and the Fox* [New York: Harcourt Brace, 1956], p. 609).

6. Cummings called the New Deal a political movement led by a "government in action" (Homer S. Cummings, "Modern Tendencies and the Law," speech before the American Bar Association, Aug. 32, 1933, in *New York Times,* Sept. 1, 1933).

7. *New York Times,* June 6, 1933, p. 6. For Cummings's anticrime rhetoric, see his telegram to a youth-against-crime rally at New York's Carnegie Hall on June 2, 1933, that "any public gathering to further the ends of law and order and to strengthen the safeguards of the citizen in his guaranteed rights under constitutional government has a meaning and a message to all worthy citizens" (*New York Times,* June 17, 1933, p. 28).

8. On March 18, a charity for crippled children asked Roosevelt for a letter of encouragement. Roosevelt waited for a report from Hoover on the group's bona fides before he responded, and this was the beginning of a steady stream of requests from FDR for personal favors (Eckstein to FDR, Mar. 18, 1933, Official File 10-B [Justice Department—FBI], FDRL).

9. FDR to Frankfurter, Apr. 22, 1933, with reply, Frankfurter to FDR, Apr. 26, 1933, in *Roosevelt and Frankfurter, Their Correspondence, 1925–1945,* ed. Max Freedman (Boston: Little Brown, 1967), p. 129; see also Arthur M. Schlesinger, Jr., *Robert Kennedy and His Times* (Boston: Houghton Mifflin, 1978), p. 246; Garvan to FDR, June 16, 1933, President's Personal Files, 1985, FDRL.

10. The Executive Order was #6610, Organization of Executive Agencies. Stories had both Jim Farley and Louis Howe lobbying against Hoover. Years later, reports surfaced that Hoover had been so worried about Farley that he had his agents follow him and tap his phones. This may or may not have been true. Later (starting around 1940), Hoover did tap Farley's phones at FDR's request, and it may have been the later episode that created suspicion that Hoover had also investigated Farley on the earlier occasion (Ray Tucker, *World Telegram,* June 14, 1940; Ralph de Toledano, *J. Edgar Hoover: The Man in His Time* [New Rochelle, N.Y.: Arlington House, 1973], p. 99; Ted Morgan, *FDR: A Biography* [New York: Simon and Schuster, 1985], p. 523). Morgan thinks this was about May 1941, and that Hoover was actually tapping the phone of his old antagonist, newsman Ray Tucker,

in an effort to overhear his conversation with Farley. For Hoover's reports to FDR on Farley, see Hoover to Watson, Official Files 10-B, FBI Numbered Report 1171A, and Hoover to Hopkins, Aug. 9, 1942, Official Files 10-B, FBI Numbered Report 2231A, FDRL.

11. De Toledano, *J. Edgar Hoover*, p. 101; Whitehead, *The F.B.I. Story*, p. 91.

12. *New York Times*, June 18, 1933, pp. 1, 18.

13. Ibid., July 3, 1933, p. 1.

14. Charles Francis Coe, *New York Times*, July 13, 1933, sec. 8, p. 2.

15. *New York Times*, July 30, 1933, p. 2; *AG Report, 1934*, p. 133.

16. *Colliers* 92 (Aug. 19, 1933):49; *Washington Herald*, Aug. 28, 1933.

17. Courtney Ryley Cooper, "Getting the Jump on Crime," *American Magazine* 116 (Aug. 1933):24, 25. The August issue would have been on the newsstands in mid-July, so it would have been written by the first of July at the latest.

18. Whitehead, *The F.B.I. Story*, p. 97.

19. For a detailed account of the case, see John Toland, *The Dillinger Days* (New York: Random House, 1963), pp. 82–102.

20. Toland, *The Dillinger Days*, p. 86.

21. For example, in *Persons in Hiding*, which Cooper wrote for Hoover, there is no mention that the Fort Worth detectives ever got in touch with the Bureau; the case is solved strictly by means of Urschel's clues (J. Edgar Hoover, *Persons in Hiding* [Boston: Little Brown, 1938], p. 157).

22. *New York Times*, Sept. 12, 1933, p. 3. In the early accounts of the story, the AP gave credit for the capture to the Memphis detectives. The *Washington Star*'s rewrites made Hoover's special agent in charge, William Rorer, the hero of the case (*New York Journal*, Sept. 26, 1933, p. 1, and *Washington Star*, Sept. 26, 1933, p. 1). The *Star*'s rewrite of the AP story added that SAC Rorer immediately telephoned word of the capture to Hoover. The *Star*'s own story said that Rorer was carrying out "Hoover's plan" and that the key to the capture was a planeload of agents from around the country who had converged on Memphis when the Bureau learned of the Kellys' whereabouts.

23. *New York Times*, Sept. 29, 1933.

24. Cummings to Keenan, Aug. 1, 1933, quoted in *Homer Cummings, Selected Papers*, ed. Carl Brent Swisher (New York: Da Capo, 1973; originally published in 1939), p. 29; *New York Times*, Oct. 13, 1933, p. 1. There were many stories about Alcatraz at the end of 1933 and early in 1934. For example, see " 'America's Devil's Island'—and some Others," *Real Detective*, Jan. 1934, p. 26.

25. *New York Times*, Mar. 20, 1934, p. 46.

26. Robert Cromie and Joseph Pinkson, *Dillinger: A Short and Violent Life* (New York: McGraw-Hill, 1962), p. 223.

27. Cromie and Pinkson, *Dillinger*, p. 169.

28. *New York Times,* Apr. 24, 1934, p. 1; Apr. 25, 1935, p. 3; May 24, 1934, p. 2.

29. Ibid., May 19, 1934, p. 1.

30. Toland, *The Dillinger Days,* p. 307; *Washington Star,* June 29, 1934, p. 1; July 9, 1934, p. 1; July 21, 1934, p. 1; *Time,* May 7, 1934, pp. 18–21.

31. *Time,* May 7, 1934, p. 18; Whitehead, *The F.B.I. Story,* p. 104; quoted by Milton S. Mayer, "Myth of the 'G-Men'," *Forum* 94 (Sept. 1935):145.

32. Toland, *The Dillinger Days,* p. 320.

33. Description of Hoover based on interviews with headquarters agents by Toland, in *The Dillinger Days,* p. 322; Hoover to Tolson, July 25, 1934, FBI File 67–9524–167, casts some doubt on the effectiveness of the communications between Chicago and Washington.

34. *San Francisco Chronicle,* July 23, 1934, p. 1.

35. Cowley had not even fired his weapon; FBI legend says that the death bullet came from the gun of Special Agent Charles Winfield. See also *New York Evening Journal,* July 24, 1934, pp. 1, 26; William C. Sullivan, quoted by Ovid Demaris, *The Director: An Oral Biography of J. Edgar Hoover* (New York: Harpers Magazine Press, 1975), p. 81; *Washington Star,* Sept. 2, 1934, p. 1; *Time,* Oct. 29, 1934, p. 11.

36. *Washington Star,* July 24, 1934, p. 1. The statement was carried over network radio.

37. Collier's series ran in the *Washington Star* from July 26, to July 31, 1934.

38. Jack Alexander, "Profile: The Director (I)," *New Yorker,* Sept. 25, 1937, p. 20.

39. All references are from stories in the *Washington Star,* Sept. 23, 1934, pp. 1, 2.

40. *New York Evening Journal,* Oct. 23, 1934, p. 10; *Washington Star,* Oct. 23, 1934, pp. 1, 3.

41. *New York Evening Journal,* Nov. 28, 1934, pp. 1, 2.

42. Ibid., p. 1; *New York American,* Nov. 29, 1934, p. 1.

43. Late in 1934, Cummings adopted Hoover's proposal for the new name, Federal Bureau of Investigation, made official on July 1, 1935.

44. Cummings to Dean, Nov. 8, 1934, in Swisher, *Cummings, Selected Papers,* p. 50.

45. In sociological jargon, his prestige was achieved, not ascribed.

46. In December 1934, Cummings had decided to give the Bureau its definitive title (Hoover to House Appropriations Committee, Dec. 18, 1934, p. 76) and the change became official on July 1, 1935 (*Significant Dates in FBI History,* OCPA, p. 10).

47. The books were *Ten Thousand Public Enemies* (1935), *Here's to Crime* (1937), and *Persons in Hiding* (1938, with Hoover listed as author). The movies were *Persons in Hiding* (1939), *Undercover Doctor* (1939), *Parole Fixer* (1940), and *Queen of the Mob* (1940).

48. Courtney Ryley Cooper, "Getting the Jump on Crime," *American Magazine* 116 (Aug. 1933):23–25, 100–101. Cooper's first FBI feature, this was the story that appeared while Hoover was waiting out Cummings's decision as to his future.

49. Ibid., p. 25.

50. Ibid., p. 100.

51. Courtney Ryley Cooper, "Crime Trap," *American Magazine* 116 (Nov. 1933):64–66, 94–98.

52. Courtney Ryley Cooper, *Ten Thousand Public Enemies* (New York: Blue Ribbon Books, 1935). These "ten thousand" were supposedly the especially dangerous criminals whose capture required special care, equipment, arms, and press releases. The title was supposed to refute the charge that the Bureau concentrated all its efforts on the short list of "public enemies."

53. Ibid., p. 46.

54. For a discussion of law enforcement's gratitude for Hoover's leadership at this time, see Nathan Douthit, "Police Professionalism and the War Against Crime in the United States, 1920s—30s," in *Police Forces in History,* ed. G. L. Mosse (Beverly Hills, Calif.: Sage, 1974), pp. 332–333.

55. Hoover to Criminal Law Section, Annual Meeting of the American Bar Association, Aug. 30, 1934, OCPA.

56. For a good discussion of film censorship, see Murray Shumach, *The Face on the Cutting Room Floor* (New York: William Morrow, 1964). The Payne Study was a twelve-volume study on the social effects of movies conducted by the National Committee for the Study of Social Values, named after the Payne Foundation that supported the research. Particularly important were Herbert Blumer and Philip M. Hauser, *Movies, Delinquency and Crime* (New York: Macmillan, 1933), and Henry James Forman, *Our Movie Made Children* (New York: Macmillan, 1933). For background on the study, see Robert Sklar, *Movie-Made America* (New York: Random House, 1975), p. 134. For an analysis of the effect of the study, see Garth Jowett, *Film, The Democratic Art* (Boston: Little, Brown, 1975), p. 227. The Legion of Decency (April 1934) grew out of a campaign launched by the Catholic bishops partly in response to the Payne Study, and partly in response to a papal command. Within a few weeks, over 7 million Catholics had taken a pledge to avoid movies that "glorify crime and criminals" (Shumach, *The Face on the Cutting Room Floor,* p. 84 and *Commonweal* 20 [May 18, 1934]:58). Report to the IACP by Peter J. Siccardi, president, quoted in Olga Martin, *Hollywood's Movie Commandments* (New York: H. W. Wilson, 1937), pp. 112, 135. A *G-Men* script is in the film archive collection of the State Historical Society of Wisconsin in Madison, which has a special strength in materials relating to Warner Bros. and RKO films.

57. Hoover, "The Adventure of Scientific Crime Control," Kalamazoo College, June 14, 1937, reprinted in *Vital Speeches,* July 1, 1937, pp. 559–562.

58. Hoover speech to Hi-Y Clubs of America, carried over network radio, June 22, 1936, OCPA.

59. Interview, Rex Collier, Jan. 1, 1976.

60. Lord to Collier, July 23, 1935, in possession of author. Evidently this ratified a working arrangement already in place. See FBI memo dated Sept. 23, 1935, OCPA.

61. All quotes are from scripts in possession of author.

62. For background on "Gangbusters," see Jim Harmon, *The Great Radio Heroes* (New York: Ace, 1967), p. 33, passim. Interview, Phillipa Lord (Lord's daughter), July 27, 1976.

63. Alexander, "The Director (I)," p. 20.

64. Rex Collier was again the writer, the illustrator was Kemp Starrett, and the Ledger Syndicate was distributor. Hoover and Tolson reviewed the strip at every stage of production. "War on Crime" promotional flyer, in possession of author.

65. For a full discussion of this and other G-man pulps, see Richard Powers, *G-Men: Hoover's FBI in American Popular Culture* (Carbondale, Ill.: University of Southern Illinois Press, 1983), Chap. 9.

66. C. K. M. Scanlon, "Give 'Em Hell," *G-Men*, Jan. 1937, p. 22.

67. Jack Kofoed, "Famous Cases of J. Edgar Hoover," *G-Men*, November 1935. *G-Men* was one of the two main G-man pulps (the other was *The Feds*), but there were many more. See Powers, *G-Men,* Chap. 9 for a full discussion.

68. *The Feds,* Sept. 1937. Besides the magazines devoted exclusively to the heroics of Hoover and the FBI, other adventure pulps developed FBI features in the late thirties. *Blue Book* had a series on the adventures of Special Agent James "Duke" Ashby, frankly modeled after Hoover (Robert R. Mill, "Shock Troops of Justice," *Blue Book,* Sept. 1935, inside front cover, p. 4).

69. Frederick L. Collins, *The FBI in Peace and War* (New York: Putnam, 1943), p. 287. Hoover also told this story in his *Persons in Hiding* pp. 70–72.

70. *Time,* Aug. 8, 1949, p. 15; *Washington Star,* May 2, 1936, p. 12 and May 16, 1936.

71. *New York Evening Journal,* May 2, 1936, p. 1.

72. Ibid., May 8, 1936, p. 1; *New York Times,* Dec. 15, 1936, p. 1.

73. This story has been told often (de Toledano, *J. Edgar Hoover,* p. 145). The last of Hoover's own cases was when he and Tolson arrested escaped convict "Terrible Roger" Touhy on December 29, 1942. The Bureau had tried but failed to convict Touhy in the Hamm kidnapping, but had managed to convict him, perhaps wrongly, for the Jake Factor kidnapping, 1942.

74. Hoover, address to Hi-Y Clubs of America, June 22, 1936, OCPA.

75. Ibid.

76. Hoover, "Patriotism and the War Against Crime," speech to the

DAR, May 23, 1936, reprinted by the Government Printing Office, SUDOC 67689–36.

77. Hoover, address to Hi-Y Clubs.

78. Hoover, "Modern Problems of Law Enforcement," speech to the annual meeting of the IACP, Atlantic City, N.J., July 9, 1935, in *Vital Speeches,* July 29, 1935, p. 682; Hoover, "Crime's Challenge to Society," speech to American Hotel Association, Nov. 9, 1937, OCPA.

79. Hoover, "Patriotism and the War Against Crime." Compare to Hofstadter's analysis of status resentment in his essays "The Pseudo-Conservative—1954," in his *The Paranoid Style in American Politics* (Chicago: University of Chicago Press, 1979) and "The Status Revolution and Progressive Leaders" in his *The Age of Reform* (New York: Vintage, 1955).

80. Hoover, "Soldiers—In Peacetime," speech to the American Legion, Sept. 19, 1938, OCPA. For the same sentiments in some of the very same words, see Hoover, "The Criminals' Code," speech to the Civic Organizations of Martinsburg, West Virginia, Oct. 20, 1938, OCPA. Hoover, "Fifty Years of Crime: Corruption Begets Corruption," speech to National Fifty Years in Business Club, Nashville, Tenn., May 20, 1939, in *Vital Speeches,* June 1, 1939, pp. 505–509.

81. Hoover, "Fifty Years of Crime"; Hoover, "An Adventure in Public Service," speech at Drake University, carried over Mutual Broadcasting, June 3, 1940, OCPA; Hoover, "Patriotism and the War Against Crime."

82. Hoover, "The Criminals' Code."

83. Hoover, speech to Economic Club, at Detroit, Mich., Nov. 14, 1938, OCPA.

84. Hoover, "Fifty Years of Crime."

85. Ibid.

86. Ibid.

87. Burns, *Roosevelt: The Lion and the Fox,* p. 371.

88. Francis Biddle, *In Brief Authority* (Garden City: Doubleday, 1967), pp. 164, 166.

89. Biddle, *In Brief Authority,* p. 258.

90. Biddle, *In Brief Authority,* p. 327.

91. There was a slight misunderstanding between the two men in April 1938, when the FBI, Military Intelligence, and Naval Intelligence were all competing to investigate German espionage. The State Department objected to FBI press releases on German spies, so Cummings ordered Hoover not to issue any more of them on these cases. Hoover, however, was on vacation in Florida, and when his aides read him the order over the phone, he thought Cummings wanted *all* press releases halted, and so, according to Cummings, he "clamped down on all publicity," to the wonder of the Justice Department press corps, "thereby creating an awkward situation." The problem was easily straightened out when Hoover returned to Washington (Apr. 11, 1938, "Personal and Political Diary of Homer S. Cummings," Cummings Papers, Uni-

versity of Virginia Library). On the Court Packing fight, see Swisher, *Cummings, Selected Papers,* pp. 146–154, 170–175, 215, and Morgan, *FDR,* p. 469.

92. Gordon W. Prange, *Pearl Harbor: The Verdict of History* (New York: McGraw-Hill, 1986), p. 306 (Prange cites the Stimson diary for Feb. 13, 1941); Biddle, *In Brief Authority,* p. 257.

93. Swisher, *Cummings, Selected Papers,* pp. 56–60. See also Hoover to Topeka *Daily Capital,* 1936, quoted in Whitehead, *The F.B.I. Story,* p. 150.

94. Nichols to Hoover, May 17, 1937, following FBI File 67–39021–169.

95. Baker to Powers, Apr. 11, 1985.

96. Hoover to Tolson, Nov. 8, 1934, FBI File 67–168–238. See also Hoover to Nathan and Tolson, Oct. 4, 1932, FBI File 67–883–174; Hoover to Tolson, July 25, 1934, FBI File 67–9524–116; Hoover to Tolson, Sept. 1, 1934, FBI File 67–9524–173, and Sept. 7, 1934, FBI File 67–15585–106.

97. Hoover to Tolson, Oct. 10, 1935, FBI File 67–9524–203; Nov. 12, 1935, FBI File 67–9524–215.

98. Hoover to Tolson, Oct. 22, 1935, FBI File 67–9524–208; Hoover to Tolson and Edwards, June 8, 1935, FBI File 67–9524–192.

99. Hoover to Tolson, et al., Nov. 12, 1935, FBI File 67–80008–(1)–1.

100. Hoover to Tolson, Mar. 11, 1935, FBI File 67–9524–186.

101. Hoover to Tolson, et al., July 5, 1935, FBI File 67–9524–195. Their replies, predictably, were that there were no policies with which they disagreed, but that if they thought of any they would let him know (Clegg to Hoover, July 6, 1935, FBI File 67–6524–204; Tolson to Hoover, July 6, 1935, FBI File 67–9524–196).

102. Hoover to Tolson, May 6, 1936, FBI File 67–9524–232; Jan. 18, 1937, FBI File 67–9524–245; Jan. 4, 1943, FBI File 67–9524–?

103. Hoover to Nichols, Aug. 6, 1937, FBI File 67–39–21–194.

104. Nichols to Hoover, Nov. 5, 1935, FBI File 67–39021–62; Nichols to [deleted], June 17, 1937, FBI File 67–39021–181; Nichols to Hoover, July 17, 1943, FBI File 67–39021–332; Joseph Schott, *No Left Turns* (New York: Praeger, 1975), p. 28.

105. Joseph to Tolson, Dec. 5, 1935, FBI File 67–39021–60; July 7, 1935, FBI File 67–39021–82. Apparently he had other nervous breakdowns later. See also Clegg to Hoover, Mar. 7, 1935, FBI File 67–026–6; Hoover to Nichols, Nov. 15, 1939, FBI File 67–39021–288; Hoover to [deleted], July 17, 1936, FBI File 67–39021–87; Nichols to Hoover, Aug. 6, 1936, FBI File 67–39021–92.

106. Hoover to Purvis, July 23, 1934, FBI File 67–7489–270.

107. "The successful termination of the hunt for Floyd was, I know, in large part due to the splendid work performed by you in directing the

activities of the Division in Ohio. The courage and efficiency of the representatives of the Division will I know prove to be of great value in the work which we are all attempting to do in connection with the current warfare against the criminal element" (Hoover to Purvis, Oct. 23, 1934, FBI File 67–7489–299). Summary of Inspection, Dec. 6, 1934, FBI File 67–342–515 and FBI File 67–342–515x.

108. Hoover to Purvis, Mar. 9, 1935, FBI File 67–7489–343; Purvis to Hoover, Mar. 12, 1935, FBI File 67–7489–352; Nathan to Hoover, Apr. 8, 1935, FBI File 67–7489–353.

109. Suydam to Nathan, July 12, 1935, FBI File 67–7489–364. Suydam was Cummings's press secretary; Nathan was acting director while Hoover and Tolson were on vacation in Atlantic City. Hoover to the files, July 12, 1935, FBI File 67–7489–368.

110. Melvin Purvis, *American Agent* (Garden City: Doubleday, 1936).

111. In this capacity, Special Agent in Charge Dunn gave technical advice to the producers of *Mary Burns, Fugitive, Snatched,* and *Show Them No Mercy;* Hoover to Tolson, July 16, 1935, FBI File 67–7489–387; Hoover had spoken to Charles C. Pettijohn of the Motion Pictures Producers and Distributers of America; Dunn to Hoover, File 67–7489–401, Sept. 21, 1935, FBI File 67–7489–420; and Oct. 31, 1935, FBI File 67–7489–437; Tolson to Hoover, Jan. 26, 1938, FBI File 67–7489–513.

112. For a discussion of the Junior G-Men craze, see Powers, *G-Men.* Later Purvis worked as an announcer on the unofficial radio show "Top Secrets of the F.B.I."

113. FBI File 80–84–74; memos to Hoover, Jan. 12, 19, 1938, FBI File 80–84–74; Smith to Hoover, Feb. 2, 1936, FBI File 67–7489–254; memo to Hoover, circa June 1937, File 67–7489–484.

114. Powers, *G-Men,* p. 131; memo to Hoover, Mar. 18, 1937, FBI File 67–7489–506.

115. Mason to Nichols, Dec. 18, 1944, FBI File 62–73866–2; Nichols to Tolson, Feb. 2, 1945, FBI File 67–7489–546, marginal note from Hoover; newspaper clipping from *Washington Times Herald,* with marginal note, Feb. 6, 1948, FBI File 67–7489.

116. Tamm to Hoover, Feb. 3, 1936, FBI File 67–7489–455; Inspection Division to Hoover, Oct. 4, 1935, FBI File 67–1617–488; the agent in question had delivered the remarks to the inspector, who passed them on to Hoover; memo to Hoover, Dec. 10, 1935, FBI File 67–7489–446; Lester to Hoover, Mar. 23, 1936, FBI File 67–7489–469.

117. Webb to Glavin, Mar. 26, 1951, FBI File 62–73866–8.

118. DeLoach to Mohr, Feb. 29, 1960; Rosanne, Melvin, Jr., Alison, and Christopher Purvis to Hoover, Mar. 7, 1960, FBI File 7487–585.

119. Senate Select Committee, *Final Report, Book III,* "Martin Luther King, Jr., Case Study," p. 139.

Chapter 8: The FBI Front
(*pp. 228–274*)

1. Don Whitehead, *The F.B.I. Story* (New York: Random House, 1956), pp. 161, 162; Hoover to Cowley, May 10, 1934, Senate Select Committee, *Final Report*, Book III, p. 25. At this stage, Hoover was still calling this kind of work a "so-called intelligence investigation," and stressed that this was not the Bureau's *own* project, but was a service provided to outside agencies: the State Department or the White House. For a brilliant panoramic survey of the FBI under Roosevelt, including the most important issues regarding the development of the Bureau's national security apparatus, see Kenneth O'Reilly, "A New Deal for the FBI: The Roosevelt Administration, Crime Control and National Security," *Journal of American History* 69 (Dec. 1982):638–658.

2. Hoover memo, Aug. 24, 1936, Senate Select Committee, *Final Report*, Book III, p. 394.

3. Hoover memos, Aug. 24, 25, 1936, Senate Select Committee, *Final Report*, Book III, p. 395.

4. Whitehead, *The F.B.I. Story*, p. 158. According to Ralph de Toledano, the word Hull used was "cocksuckers" (de Toledano, *J. Edgar Hoover, The Man in His Time* [New Rochelle, N.Y.: Arlington House, 1973], p. 152). This important episode is discussed in general terms in Senate Select Committee, *Final Report*, Book III, pp. 395, 396.

5. Whitehead, *The F.B.I. Story*, p. 159. Cummings was out of Washington at the time of the crucial meetings between Hull, FDR, and Hoover. Upon his return, Cummings was informed by Hoover and gave his approval (Hoover to Tamm, "Strictly Confidential," Sept. 10, 1936, Senate Select Committee, *Final Report*, Book III, p. 396). The chronology of these events is more clearly stated in Whitehead, *The F.B.I. Story*, p. 159.

6. Some scholars have argued that the 1916 statute permitting Bureau investigations upon request of the secretary of state envisioned only close-ended specific investigations, not the creation of a vast domestic intelligence machinery. Frank Donner says, "[N]o one could persuasively claim—although the Bureau has not hesitated to do so—that Secretary Hull requested an investigation in 1936 which permanently empowered it to conduct domestic intelligence investigations" (Donner, *The Age of Surveillance* [New York: Knopf, 1980], p. 54). Agreeing with Donner are Thomas I. Emerson, "Remarks" in John T. Elliff, "The Scope and Basis of FBI Data Collection," in Pat Watters and Stephen Gillers, *Investigating the FBI* (Garden City: Doubleday, 1973), p. 294; Athan Theoharis, *Spying on Americans* (Philadelphia: Temple University Press, 1978), p. 70. There is also dispute over whether Hoover exceeded FDR's mandate to look into foreign-linked movements when he told the attorney general the president wanted him to gather information on the "radical situation" and "subversive activities, including communism

and fascism" (Hoover to Tamm, Sept. 10, 1936, Senate Select Committee, *Final Report,* Book III, p. 396). Hoover's instructions to his agents ordered them to collect information on "subversive activities on the part of any individual or organization" (Hoover to Field Offices, Sept. 5, 1936, Senate Select Committee, *Final Report,* Book III, p. 396). The sticking point is the word *subversive,* which has no common or legal definition, but in context Roosevelt, Hoover, and his attorney generals all used it to refer to "radical" activities that were potentially dangerous without being in violation of any specific law (in contrast to espionage and sabotage, which *were* federal crimes). Despite the immediate threat of fascism, most of the Bureau's targets were Communists (Hoover to Field Offices, Sept. 5, 1936, and Tamm to Hoover, Aug. 28, 1936, Senate Select Committee, *Final Report,* Book III, pp. 396, 397; also Senate Select Committee, *Hearings,* Vol. 6, FBI, p. 562).

7. Hoover to Cummings, Oct. 10, 1938, enclosed with Cummings to FDR, Oct. 20, 1938, Senate Select Committee, *Final Report,* Book III, p. 398. In this memo, Hoover also told Cummings he believed that any future expansion of intelligence work that might be necessary might also be covered under the secretary of state's request. The FBI later claimed that Hoover was relying on the State Department request only to justify the use of funds, but Hoover's statement here seems more like a search for legal authority than a quest for funds not subject to legal restrictions. For two different FBI studies after Hoover's death examining the Bureau's authority for intelligence work, see Director to Attorney General, Aug. 7, 1973, and "An Analysis of FBI Domestic Security Intelligence Investigations: Authority, Official Attitudes, and Activities in Historic Perspective," Oct. 28, 1975, Senate Select Committee, *Hearings,* Vol. 6, FBI, pp. 540–546, 547–575.

8. Robert Sherwood, *Roosevelt and Hopkins* (New York: Harper, 1948), p. 274.

9. Sept. 18, 1936, "Personal and Political Diary of Homer S. Cummings," Cummings Papers, University of Virginia Library; Hoover to Cummings, June 22, 1938, President's Secretary's File, Department of Justice, FDRL; Hoover to Attorney General, Jan. 30, 1937; July 31, 1937; Aug. 1, 1937, Official File 10-B, FDRL, cited in O'Reilly, "A New Deal for the FBI," p. 647.

10. *New York Journal American,* Feb. 22, 1938, p. 3; Feb. 28, 1938, p. 1.

11. Ibid., May 9, 1938, p. 4; May 12, 1938, pp. 1, 2; June 20, 1938, p. 1. The report was entitled "Investigation . . . Nazi Training Camps in the United States," Dec. 31, 1937, cited in Kenneth O'Reilly, *Hoover and the Un-Americans* (Philadelphia: Temple University Press, 1983), p. 307.

12. Cummings to FDR, with Hoover memo, Oct. 20, 1938, Senate Select Committee, *Final Report,* Book III, p. 399. See also memos from Hoover, Nov. 7, 1938; Hoover to Acting Assistant to the Attorney General, May 5, 1939; Keenan to Agencies, Feb. 7, 1939; Hoover to Murphy, Mar. 16, 1939; Hoover to Attorney General, Mar. 16, 1939; Tamm to Hoover, May 31,

1939; Murphy to FDR, June 17, 1939, all in Senate Select Committee, *Final Report,* Book III, pp. 399–402. Roosevelt's key memo read:

> It is my desire that the investigation of all espionage, counterespionage, and sabotage matters be controlled and handled by the Federal Bureau of Investigation of the Department of Justice, the Military Intelligence Division of the War Department, and the Office of Naval Intelligence in the Navy Department. The directors of these three agencies are to function as a committee to coordinate their activities.
>
> No investigations should be conducted by any investigative agency of the Government into matters involving actually or potentially any espionage, counterespionage, or sabotage, except by the three agencies mentioned above.
>
> I shall be glad if you will instruct the heads of all other investigative agencies than the three named, to refer immediately to the nearest office of the Federal Bureau of Investigation any data, information, or material that may come to their notice bearing directly or indirectly on espionage, counterespionage, or sabotage. [FDR to Agency Heads, June 26, 1939, Senate Select Committee, *Final Report,* Book III, p. 403.]

13. Hoover to Attorney General, Sept. 6, 1939, Senate Select Committee, *Final Report,* Book III, p. 404.

14. Statement of the president, Sept. 6, 1939, Senate Select Committee, *Final Report,* Book III, p. 404. The first paragraph of this September 6 directive seems to restrict the Bureau to investigating violations of the law (espionage, sabotage, violations of the neutrality laws). In the last paragraph, however, the Bureau is empowered to collect information gathered by other agencies relating not only to violations of the law, but also *subversive activities.* According to an internal FBI memo, the Bureau had expected that the president's message would give the Bureau this formal authority to investigate "subversion" as a supplement to the oral instructions of 1936 and 1938 (Tamm, Memo for the File, Sept. 6, 1939, Senate Select Committee, *Final Report,* Book III, p. 404). Roosevelt may not have regarded the distinction as important because he expected Hoover to provide him with the "broad picture" of "subversive activities in the United States, particularly Fascism and Communism."

15. Proclamation, Sept. 8, 1939, 54 Stat. 2643; Executive Order No. 8247, Sept. 8, 1939; *Emergency Supplemental Appropriation Bill, 1940; Supplemental National Defense Appropriations,* 1941; Hearings Before the House Committee on Appropriations, June 6, 1940, p. 180, cited in Senate Select Committee, *Final Report,* Book III, pp. 405, 407, 408.

16. *Justice Department Appropriation Bill,* 1941, Hearings Before the House Committee on Appropriations, Jan. 5, 1940, p. 151, in Senate Select Committee, *Final Report,* Book III, pp. 407, 414; Report of the New York City Field Office, Oct. 22, 1941, summarized in Justice Department memo from Brodie to Quinn, Oct. 9, 1947, Senate Select Committee, *Final Report,* Book III, p. 415. The navy asked Hoover to look into a protest by black mess attendants against racial discrimination. After that the Bureau kept an informant in the NAACP to discover whether there were any connections

between it and "the communist party and other communist-controlled organizations." The Bureau reported that "there is a strong tendency for the NAACP to steer clear of Communistic activities. Nevertheless there is a strong movement on the part of the Communists to attempt to dominate this group through an infiltration of Communistic doctrines. Consequently the activities of the NAACP will be closely observed and scrutinized in the future" (Report of Oklahoma Field Office, Sept. 19, 1941, Senate Select Committee, *Final Report,* Book III, p. 416).

17. In 1943, Attorney General Biddle officially ordered the program terminated, but Hoover, in what seems to have been a notable act of insubordination, ordered the list continued under another name. An alternative explanation is that Roosevelt ordered Hoover to ignore Biddle's order, which would have been in keeping with the sort of arrangement that had evolved governing the relationships between Hoover and his attorney generals. There was a bureaucratic as well as an ideological reason for Hoover's insistence on maintaining such a detention list in defiance of orders. There were several imaginable circumstances in which Hoover might be ordered to round up radicals, and if he did not have lists ready based on investigations, he would have to rely on denunciations furnished by enemies and political rivals of the targets.

18. Hoover to Field Offices, Aug. 14, 1943, Senate Select Committee, *Final Report,* Book III, p. 421.

19. FDR to Hoover, June 14, 1940, Official File 10-B, FDRL.

20. Hoover to FDR, June 18, 1940, President's Personal Files, FDRL.

21. The June 14 letter had no legal validity, and it was never cited by Hoover or the Bureau, but it might have been valuable if Roosevelt had ever tried to disavow responsibility for Hoover's actions.

22. Jack Alexander, "Profile: The Director," *New Yorker,* Sept. 25, 1937, and Oct. 2, 9, 1937, condensed in *Reader's Digest,* Dec. 1937, p. 42–45; Kenneth G. Crawford, "J. Edgar Hoover," *Nation,* Feb. 27, 1937, pp. 232–234. The *Nation* blasted Hoover for his continued friendship with George Ruch, who was now in charge of plant security for the Frick industrial interests (July 7, 1936, p. 60). It also hoped FBI surveillance of "fifth columnists" might block private vigilante activity (June 29, 1940, p. 772). See also Kenneth Crawford's series on Hoover in *Nation,* Feb. 27, 1937, pp. 232–234, and Mar. 6, 1937, pp. 262–264.

23. The law involved was Sec. 22 Title 18 U.S.C., cited in Whitehead, *The F.B.I. Story,* p. 340. The arrests of the Abraham Lincoln Brigade veterans were part of a general crackdown on foreign-oriented extremist groups. Between December and March, the department charged several Russian agents with failing to register, and in January 1940 arrested seventeen members of the Christian Front on charges of conspiring to overthrow the government (Robert J. Goldstein, *Political Repression in Modern America* [Cambridge, Mass.: Schenckman/Two Continents, 1978], p. 249).

24. Whitehead, *The F.B.I. Story*, p. 176.

25. *Nation*, May 11, 1940, p. 585.

26. Ibid., "Our Lawless G-Men," Mar. 2, 1940, pp. 296–297.

27. Hoover told the White House that Franz Boas, who had protested the Lincoln Brigade arrests, was not a Communist but belonged to suspect organizations like the New School for Social Research and the World Association for the Advancement of Atheism (Hoover to Watson, Apr. 13, 1940, Official File 10-B, FBI Numbered Report 55, FDRL). On December 6, 1940, he told the president that the Communist party had begun a peace campaign, which he called "a typical Communist stratagem" (Hoover to Watson, Dec. 6, 1940, Official File 10-B, FBI Numbered Report 520, FDRL). The Lindbergh anecdote is in Ted Morgan, *FDR: A Biography* (New York: Simon and Schuster, 1985), p. 523. There are many accounts of FDR's Press Banquet endorsement of Hoover, for instance Whitehead, *The F.B.I. Story*, p. 180.

28. Biddle to Hoover, confidential memorandum, Oct. 9, 1941, Senate Select Committee, *Final Report*, Book III, p. 281. Biddle described department doctrine that held that wiretapping without divulgence was permissible, that all the courts had done was to make evidence gathered through wiretapping inadmissible in court.

29. FDR to Jackson, May 21, 1940, Senate Select Committee, *Final Report*, Book III, p. 279. Hoover may have appealed directly to Roosevelt to overrule Jackson's ban. Roosevelt did not hesitate to bypass his attorney general when dealing with Hoover. (He encouraged the director to begin sedition investigations despite Biddle's orders prohibiting them without his express permission [Early to Roosevelt, Mar. 20, 1942, President's Secretary's File, Justice Department, 1938–1944, FDRL].) Roosevelt did not discourage Hoover from coming directly to him with his problems. A few months after FDR's May directive, Hoover annoyed Secretary of War Stimson by bringing the president his complaints about General Sherman Miles, head of Military Intelligence. In his diary, Stimson called Hoover a prima donna, and felt the episode showed how he "poisons the mind of the President." Jackson told Stimson he "had found Hoover a most difficult person to deal with" (Stimson Diary, Feb. 12, 1941, Feb. 13, 1941, in Gordon W. Prange, *Pearl Harbor: The Verdict of History* [New York: McGraw-Hill, 1986], p. 306). Prange says the ability of Hoover, who merely headed "a division at staff level," to "go directly to the White House and almost force the reassignment of the head of G-2, indicates both the depth of his ego and the potency of his influence" (Prange, *Pearl Harbor*, p. 306). Arthur Schlesinger, Jr., says it was pressure from Secretary of the Treasury Morgenthau that persuaded Roosevelt to issue his May 1940 directive (Arthur M. Schlesinger, Jr., *Robert Kennedy and His Times* [Boston: Houghton Mifflin, 1978], p. 252, citing Joseph Lash, *Roosevelt and Churchill, 1939–1941* [New York: Norton, 1976], p. 119). According to Francis Biddle, who followed Jackson as attorney general, Jackson did not like the policy and so turned the matter over to

Hoover without examining each case; Biddle, on the other hand, made it his business to review every one of Hoover's requests (Francis Biddle, *In Brief Authority* [Garden City: Doubleday, 1967], p. 67).

30. Hoover to Katzenbach, Sept 14, 1965, Senate Select Committee, *Final Report,* Book III, pp. 286–287.

31. Under Nixon, Hoover instituted a formal program, "Inlet," to provide him with political tidbits to offer the president.

32. Hoover to Watson, Mar. 7, 1940, Official File 10-B, FBI Numbered Report 46, FDRL.

33. Hoover to Watson, Jan. 8, 1941, Official File 10-B, FBI Numbered Report 576, FDRL.

34. For Chambers's charges, see Berle's notes in Adolf Berle Papers, U.S. Committee on Un-American Activities, FDRL, as well as discussions in Allen Weinstein, *Perjury: The Hiss-Chambers Case* (New York: Knopf, 1978), and de Toledano, *J. Edgar Hoover,* p. 222. See also Hoover to Hopkins, May 7, 1943, Oct. 14, 1943, on British discoveries of Communist spy rings, Hopkins Papers, FBI Communist party, FDRL; Hoover to Watson, Mar. 14, 1944, Official File 10-B, FBI Numbered Report 2513; Biddle to FDR, Apr. 1, 1944, Biddle Papers, FBI, FDRL. The two Smith Act prosecutions during the war period were twenty-nine members of the Socialist Workers (Trotskyite) party in 1941 and thirty-nine "native fascists" in New York in 1944. Ironically, the Communist party applauded both prosecutions.

35. Whitehead, *The F.B.I. Story,* p. 182. The organization chart of the FBI at this time had two assistants to the director, Edward A. Tamm and Clyde Tolson. Tamm was in charge of the Laboratory, the Investigative, and the Security divisions; Identification, Training and Inspection, Administrative, and the Records and Communications divisions were under Tolson (Hoover to Tolson et al., Dec. 15, 1942, FBI File 67–80008–52).

36. Executive Order 9066. For an exemplary treatment of the Japanese-American internment, see Peter Irons, *Justice at War* (New York: Oxford, 1983).

37. Hoover to Watson, Dec. 7, 1941, Official File 10-B, FBI Numbered Report 1028, FDRL.

38. Morgan, *FDR,* p. 621.

39. Statement of the President, Sept. 6, 1939, Senate Select Committee, *Final Report,* Book III, p. 404; Memorandum Prepared by Assistant Secretary of State Berle, June 24, 1940, and Approved by the President, Official File 10-B, Justice Department, FBI, FDRL; Whitehead, *The F.B.I. Story,* p. 186.

40. Hoover to Early, Dec. 12, 1941, Stephen Early Papers, FBI, FDRL.

41. Ibid.

42. John Toland's *Infamy* (New York: Berkley, 1983) gives a sympathetic hearing to the arguments of Safford and others who believed Pearl Harbor was the result of a conspiracy at the highest level of the American government (a conviction Toland came to share).

43. Prange, *Pearl Harbor,* p. 329.

44. Whitehead, *The F.B.I. Story,* p. 186.

45. John O'Donnell, *Washington Times Herald,* circa Dec. 29, 1941, following Hoover to Early, Dec. 29, 1941, Stephen Early Papers, FBI, FDRL.

46. Hoover to Early, Dec. 29, 1941, Stephen Early Papers, FBI, FDRL.

47. Hoover to Watson, Jan. 5, 1942, Official File 10-B, FBI Numbered Report 1097, FDRL. Using clues from these messages, the Bureau identified and obtained a conviction for spying of a German national, Otto Kuehn, who was sentenced to be shot, a penalty commuted to fifty years at hard labor (Whitehead, *The F.B.I. Story,* p. 190).

48. Whitehead, *The F.B.I. Story,* p. 187.

49. Hoover to Watson, Jan. 5, 1942, Official File 10-B, FBI Numbered Report 1097, FDRL.

50. Prange, *Pearl Harbor,* pp. 651–652.

51. Sir John Masterman, inventor of the British "Double Cross System," later wrote that it was "surely a fair deduction that the questionnaire indicated very clearly that in the event of the United States being at war, Pearl Harbor would be the first point attacked and that plans for this attack were at an advanced stage in the summer of 1941" (J. C. Masterman, *The Double Cross System in the War of 1939 to 1945* [New York, 1972], pp. 79–80, cited in William Stevenson, *A Man Called Intrepid* [New York: Harcourt Brace, 1976], p. 260).

52. Dusko Popov, *Spy Counter-Spy* (New York, 1974), pp. 119, 203, cited in Prange, *Pearl Harbor,* p. 307. Actually, Hoover passed on an edited version of the Popov questionnaire to the White House as a demonstration of the German microdot technique. He turned the full Popov report over to Naval Intelligence, and the FBI cooperated with ONI to use Popov to send false data to the Germans. For both sides of this controversy, see John F. Bratzel and Leslie B. Rout, Jr., "Pearl Harbor, Microdots, and J. Edgar Hoover," *American Historical Review,* Dec. 1982, pp. 1346–1347, and John Estel, "Hoover Shared Spy Disclosure on Pearl Harbor," *Pittsburgh Post-Gazette,* Apr. 1, 1982. Also Prange, *Pearl Harbor,* pp. 310–311, 609.

53. Popov's claim is in *Spy Counter-Spy,* pp. 190–191, cited (with apparent agreement) by Toland, *Infamy,* p. 15. A more convincing argument is that Popov's questionnaire pointed toward sabotage at Pearl, not a sneak attack (Prange, *Pearl Harbor,* pp. 305–311, esp. p. 310).

54. For example, Hoover ruefully sent along a report that Japanese diplomats in Lima, Peru, had failed to appear for their weekly golf game on Sunday, December 7 (Hoover to Watson, Dec. 17, 1941, Official File 10-B, FBI Numbered Report 1057, FDRL).

55. Stevenson, *Intrepid,* p. 256. For a detailed analysis of the "signal-noise ratio," see Roberta Wohlstetter, *Pearl Harbor: Warning and Decision* (Stanford, Calif.: Stanford University Press, 1962), and the selection from it, "Signals and Noise: The Intelligence Picture" in *Pearl Harbor, Roosevelt*

and the Coming of the War, ed. George M. Waller (Boston: D. C. Heath, 1965), pp. 83–94. Wohlstetter notes that during the first week in December all American Far Eastern embassies were ordered to destroy their codes, but this was not a signal that the U.S. was preparing a sneak attack on Japan.

56. Hoover to Watson(?), July 26, 1940, FBI Numbered Report 244; Hoover to Watson, Aug. 30, 1940, FBI Numbered Report 291; FDR to Watson, Sept. 18, 1940, FBI Numbered Report 315A; Hoover to Watson, Nov. 15, 1940, FBI Numbered Report 465, all Official File 10-B FDRL.

57. Hoover to Watson, Feb. 19, 1941, FBI Numbered Report 648, reported that Japanese ships had received secret instructions that "probably pertain to action to be taken in case the ships are caught on the high seas or near a foreign enemy port upon the outbreak of war"; Hoover to Watson, Oct. 29, 1941, FBI Numbered Report 956; Hoover to Watson, Nov. 13, 1941, FBI Numbered Report 979; Hoover to Watson, Nov. 22, 1941, FBI Numbered Report 994; Hoover to Watson, Nov. 29, 1941, FBI Numbered Report 1010A; Hoover to Watson, Dec. 2, 1941, FBI Numbered Report 1016A, all Official File 10-B, FDRL.

58. Whitehead, The F.B.I. Story, pp. 187, 190, 343–344.

59. de Toledano, J. Edgar Hoover, p. 176; phone interview, de Toledano, Jan. 16, 1986. John Toland provides an uncorroborated report of a private talk Hoover supposedly gave early in 1942 to a group of congressmen and government officials at the Army-Navy Club in Washington. Supposedly, Hoover regaled the group with the "specific" warnings Roosevelt had received and ignored that an attack on Pearl was imminent (letter, Colonel Carlton G. Ketchum to Toland, in Toland, Infamy, p. 343; Ketchum's autobiography is The Recollections of Colonel Retread, 1942–1945 [Pittsburgh, Pa.: Hart, 1976]). When other scholars pressed Ketchum for corroboration, he was unable to furnish any. Donald Goldstein, one of the scholars who completed Prange's Pearl Harbor, interviewed Ketchum and concluded he was "not reliable" (phone interview, Goldstein, Jan. 16, 1986).

60. FDR ordered Hoover to take "charge of all censorship arrangements pending such further measures as I shall presently take" (Presidential Memorandum to Secretary of State et al., Dec. 8, 1941, Official File 10–B, FBI 1941, FDRL). On December 9, Hoover stopped the New York Times from printing a story that detailed the extent of the losses at Pearl, and he had to use threats to keep Drew Pearson from running a similar story a few days later (Hoover to Watson, Dec. 9, 1941, Official File 10–B, FBI Numbered Report 1038; Early to Hoover, Hoover to Early, Dec. 12, 1941, Early Papers, FBI, FDRL). See also Hoover to Watson, Dec. 9, 1941, with attached memorandum, Dec. 8, 1941, Official File 10–B, FBI Numbered Report 1039, FDRL, and Whitehead, The F.B.I. Story, pp. 184–185.

61. Whitehead, The F.B.I. Story, p. 188.

62. Ibid., p. 189.

63. Irons, *Justice at War,* p. 23.

64. Ibid., pp. 27, 28, 41, 60, 61. Irons points out that Hoover raised no objection to letting the army have his detention list, but he insisted his agents attach specific recommendations to each name so that "if there is any howl afterward we will not be left holding the bag" if attacked by "the Civil Liberties crowd" (Irons, *Justice at War,* p. 28).

65. Biddle, *In Brief Authority,* p. 219.

66. Federal Bureau of Investigation Survey of Japanese Relocation Centers, p. 5 (Ca. 1943), Hopkins Papers, Japanese Relocation, FDRL. In addition to the injustice done the Japanese-Americans, the evacuation established a fearsome precedent. In 1981, John J. McCloy defended the evacuation before a congressional commission, drawing the following analogy: "I don't want to be alarmist . . . but within 90 miles right now of our shore" was Cuba. In the case of a war, "Wouldn't you think seriously about moving those people out if there was a raid there?" (Irons, *Justice at War,* p. 353).

67. During the war, for example, Hoover had insisted on a clear statement that the FBI was in charge of any joint intelligence operation in the United States.

68. This is from a letter Berle wrote to Hoover, Sept. 17, 1946, Adolf Berle Papers, "H," FDRL. See also Whitehead, *The F.B.I. Story,* p. 210.

69. Whitehead, *The F.B.I. Story,* p. 212. Hoover's South American operations put him in constant contact with William Stephenson, the "Man Called Intrepid" who headed British Intelligence in the United States, with his offices at Rockefeller Center, in the same building where Nelson Rockefeller directed Latin American economic warfare. For a generally favorable assessment of Hoover's performance in South America, see Leslie B. Rout, Jr., and John F. Bratzel, *The Shadow War: German Espionage and American Counterespionage in Latin America During World War II* (Frederick, Md.: University Publications, 1986).

70. Whitehead, *The F.B.I. Story,* pp. 224, 347.

71. *United States Dependency on South America,* Hopkins Papers, FBI Cuba, FDRL.

72. *Axis Aspirations Through South America,* Apr. 1, 1942, Hopkins Papers, Latin American Misc., FDRL.

73. Hoover, "Problems of Law Enforcement," speech to the IACP, Oct. 10, 1939, *Vital Speeches,* Nov. 1, 1939, pp. 54–57; Hoover, "Our Future," Notre Dame Graduation, May 10, 1942, OCPA; Hoover, "An American's Privilege," annual banquet of the Holland Society of New York, Nov. 9, 1942, OCPA.

74. Whitehead, *The F.B.I. Story,* p. 208. Hoover's quest for publicity puzzled his British counterespionage partners, since they came out of a tradition that kept secret operations secret. The British claimed that "he lived by publicity," while they themselves "avoided publicity at all costs. Inevitably the FBI got the credit." The FBI "handled some information with reckless

disregard for consequences. By trumpeting successes, they tipped off the enemy" (Stevenson, *Intrepid,* pp. 269, 374). But publicity was essential for Hoover to fulfill his wartime responsibilities, just as it had been a vital part of the Justice Department's anticrime campaign.

75. J. Edgar Hoover, "Stamping Out the Spies," *American Magazine,* Jan. 1940, p. 83.

76. The film was directed by Hoover's favorite director, Louis De Rochemont (*The House on 92nd Street*); quotes are from the press release for *The FBI Front,* New York Public Library of the Performing Arts.

77. Frederick L. Collins, *The FBI in Peace and War* (New York: Putnams, 1943), pp. 257, 258, 259.

78. Hoover, "The Call of Americanism," speech to the Michigan Bankers Association, June 19, 1940.

79. Carlos Clarens, "Hooverville West: The Hollywood G-Man, 1934–45," *Film Comment,* May–June 1977, pp. 10–16. The Bureau endorsed a 1949 reissue of *G-Men,* this time with the FBI seal right after the Warner logo. *House on 92nd Street* dramatized the case of William Sebold, a German-American (in the movie an undercover FBI agent, William Eythe) forced by the Gestapo to set up a spy radio station on Long Island. The real Sebold went to the FBI, which set him up with a radio transmitter to broadcast disinformation back to Gestapo headquarters in Hamburg. Sebold also led the Bureau to the Manhattan headquarters of the Nazi spy ring headed by Fritz Duquesne (the "House on 92nd Street"). The beautiful spy queen was Signe Hasso (doubling in a trouser part as the Nazi spy chief). The father-son relationship (Lloyd Nolan and Eythe) between older and younger agents was a fixture of official FBI entertainment. Powers, *G-Men,* p. 222.

80. Whitehead, *The F.B.I. Story,* p. 193. For the story of the capture of the submarine saboteurs, see Whitehead, *The F.B.I. Story,* pp. 199–206. For the decision to publicize their capture, and FDR's determination to execute them (after a military trial in which Hoover took part), see Biddle, *In Brief Authority,* pp. 328, 330.

81. Whitehead, *The F.B.I. Story,* p. 209; Hoover to Watson, May 9, 1941, and Watson to Hoover, May 13, 1941, Official File 10–B, FBI Numbered Report 766, FDRL. FDR had Watson tell Hoover, "Keep up the good work, boy!"

82. Whitehead, *The F.B.I. Story,* p. 207. This left Hoover open to charges that the Bureau once again was engaged in labor spying. See reports on General Motors and Allis Chalmers, both Hoover to Watson, May 15, 1941, FBI Numbered Report 776, and May 17, 1941, FBI Numbered Report 778. See also Hoover to Watson, Nov. 15, 1940, FBI Numbered Report 460, and Hoover to Hopkins, July 18, 1942, FBI Numbered Report 2216A, all in Official File 10-B; Rowe to FDR, June 26, 1941, President's Secretary's File, Justice Department, all FDRL.

83. Hoover to Hopkins, June 30, 1942, Hopkins Papers, FBI Charts,

FDRL; Whitehead, *The F.B.I. Story,* pp. 208–209; Athan Theoharis, "The FBI and the American Legion Contact Program, 1940–1966," *Political Science Quarterly,* Summer 1985, pp. 271–286; microfilms of FBI files of the program are reproduced in *The FBI American Legion Contact Program,* ed. Athan Theoharis, Scholarly Resources, Wilmington, Del. See also Belmont to Baumgardner, June 22, 1960, FBI File 66–9330–389; and Hoover to Tamm and Clegg, Nov. 18, 1940, FBI File 66–9330–2. The number of contacts is from Theoharis, "American Legion Contact Program," p. 278.

84. Whose members were The Atom, The Sandman, The Spectre, The Flash, Hawkman, Dr. Fate, the Green Lantern, Hour Man, and, occasionally, Superman and Batman (see Richard Gid Powers, *G-Men: Hoover's FBI in American Popular Culture* [Carbondale, Ill.: University of Southern Illinois Press, 1983], pp. 156–159).

85. Collins, *The FBI in Peace and War,* pp. 285–286, 290–291.

86. Hoover kept up his energetic schedule of public speaking during the war. More often than not, Hoover's speeches were read into the *Congressional Record,* which made them available as free reprint material for newspapers and magazines across the country, especially rural papers that filled their pages from the public domain. His addresses were regularly reprinted in *Vital Speeches* and were often picked up by the radio networks for national broadcast. His warnings that the public could expect a "post war crime wave" may have reflected his nervousness about the possibility of having to cut back the FBI to prewar levels, which would have meant letting go four out of five agents.

87. Note that Hoover could use the success of his spy hunting operations (organizational function) to defend his monopoly over the security field against any competitors (bureaucratic function); quotes are from Hoover, "The Test of Citizenship," speech to the DAR, Apr. 18, 1940, *Vital Speeches,* May 1, 1940.

88. Hoover, "The Test of Citizenship"; "Your Call to Duty," Commencement, Rutgers, May 23, 1943, OCPA. For an attack on parole and its supporters, see *New York Herald Tribune,* July 12, 1935; on Bates, see *Pittsburgh Press,* July 31, 1935. For Hitler and parole, see Collins, *The FBI in Peace and War,* p. 285.

89. Hoover, "A Nation's Call to Duty," commencement, St. John's University Law School, June 11, 1942, OCPA; See also Hoover, "Your Call to Duty."

90. Hoover, "An American's Privilege," annual banquet of the Holland Society of New York, Nov. 9, 1942, OCPA.

91. Hoover, "An Adventure in Public Service," Drake University, Mutual Broadcasting, June 3, 1940, OCPA.

92. Hoover, "Your Call to Duty."

93. Hoover, "Our Duty to Youth," Annual Banquet of the Boys Clubs of America, May 4, 1944, OCPA, FBI.

94. Hoover, "Our Duty to Youth."

95. Ovid Demaris, *The Director: An Oral Biography of J. Edgar Hoover* (New York: Harpers Magazine Press, 1975), pp. 6, 35–36. Hoover's brother, Dickerson, would die on October 23, 1944.

96. Tolson to Hoover, Nov. 6, 1940, FBI File 67–9524–277.

97. Hoover to "Clyde," Oct. 21, 1943, FBI File 67–9524–289 (Handwritten note: Letter personally handed Mr. Tolson by Director 10–21–43).

98. Hoover, "Americans of Tomorrow," 99th Anniversary of YMCA, CBS Network, Oct. 12, 1943, OCPA; Hoover, "Our Duty to Youth"; Hoover, "Our Future" Commencement, Notre Dame, May 10, 1942.

99. Hoover, "Your Call to Duty," "Our Duty to Youth," and "Our Future."

100. Hoover, "Your Call to Duty" and "Our Duty to Youth."

101. Hoover, "Our Duty to Youth."

102. Ibid.

103. Herbert Hoover to J. Edgar Hoover, Oct. 4, 1943, "Herbert Hoover FBI File," General Accession, HHL. Hoover, "The Man I Want My Son to Be," *Parents Magazine,* Feb. 1940, p. 15.

104. *Washington Star,* Aug. 2, 1939.

105. Hoover, "America's Duty to the Future," New York Federation of Women's Clubs, May 3, 1940, OCPA; Hoover, "An American's Privilege. " "Your Call to Duty," and "A Nation's Call to Duty," commencement, St. John's University Law School, June 11, 1942, OCPA, FBI.

106. See Biddle, *In Brief Authority,* p. 190, for flattery by Biddle that backfired; Hoover to Watson, Jan. 15, 1942, FBI 1942, Official File 10-B; Hoover to Hopkins, Dec. 8, 1944, Hopkins Papers, FBI Brazil, FDRL.

107. Hoover to Watson, July 22, 1943, President's Personal File 4819, J. Edgar Hoover, Van Buren (Arkansas) *Post Argus,* May 21, 1943.

108. Reports were furnished on Sumner Welles, Thomas Corcoran, and Donald Nelson; see Theoharis, *Spying on Americans,* p. 159. For FDR's reaction, see Robert E. Sherwood, *Roosevelt and Hopkins* (New York: Harpers, 1948), p. 250.

109. Hoover to Watson, Sept. 3, 1943, Official File 10–B, FBI Numbered Report 2405, FDRL; Morgan, *FDR,* pp. 676–686. For other political investigations see Early to FDR, Mar. 20, 1942, and FDR to Hoover, Jan. 21, 1942, asking Hoover to use war emergency to clean up "vile" publications, both President's Secretary's File, Justice Department. See also FDR to Hoover, May 4, 1942, Cross Reference 1933–1945, Official File 10–B, requesting an investigation of Hamilton Fish. (All FDRL.)

110. FDR to Eleanor Roosevelt, June 17, 1942, President's Secretary's File, Justice 1938–1944, FDRL; Eleanor Roosevelt to FDR, Mar. 12, 1943, under Bjoze, Jack, Cross Reference 1933–1945, Official File 10–B, FDRL. ER made a similar remark in 1941 about Hoover after a fouled-up FBI investigation of her secretary, Edith Helm (Morgan, *FDR,* p. 674).

111. Morgan, *FDR,* p. 672.

112. Hoover O&C File 103; Morgan, *FDR,* pp. 669–673.

113. Morgan, who gives this episode a thoughtful analysis, also tends to be skeptical that the events, as reported to the FBI, ever took place (Morgan, *FDR,* p. 673).

114. Hoover set up this filing system on October 1, 1941 (Hoover memo, Oct. 1, 1941, U.S. House, Committee on Government Operations, *Hearing into the Destruction of Former FBI Director J. Edgar Hoover's Files and FBI Recordkeeping,* 94th Cong., 1st sess., 1975). In many instances, as in the O&C files on John and Robert Kennedy, much of the malicious gossip was referred to Hoover by the subjects themselves, who wanted to know if anything could be done to have it stopped. There is no proof that any of the O&C material (or the destroyed Personal and Confidential File material) was ever actually used for improper purposes. As a technical point, the material used to harass Martin Luther King, Jr., was developed in the course of investigations authorized by the Kennedy and Johnson administrations. Although no written records were kept of the Bureau's efforts to spread the sexually incriminating recordings of King throughout the government and the media, other steps in this outrageous conspiracy were recorded in the central files. It is also not at all unusual for an official to maintain separate files in his office for his personal and his official correspondence, and the more political an official is, the more difficult it will be to draw a clear line between the two. The general rule is that official records, which must be filed and may not be destroyed, are those developed in the normal course of the operations of the agency, or those that are essential to the activities of the agency. For an exhaustive examination of the deceptive filing Hoover developed to conceal illegal surveillance techniques, see Athan G. Theoharis, "In House Cover-up: Researching FBI Files," in *Beyond the Hiss Case,* ed. Athan G. Theoharis (Philadelphia: Temple University Press, 1982), pp. 20–77.

115. For a view on this from an unlikely source, see Kim Philby, quoted in Stevenson, *Intrepid,* p. 161.

116. For the intelligence confusion, see Bradley F. Smith, *The Shadow Warriors* (New York: Basic, 1983), pp. 67, 68. See also Anthony Cave Brown, *The Last Hero: Wild Bill Donovan* (New York: Times Books, 1982), p. 160, 161.

117. Smith, *The Shadow Warriors,* p. 63.

118. Brown, *The Last Hero,* pp. 160, 165; Thomas F. Troy, *Donovan and the CIA* (Washington, D.C.: CIA, 1981), p. 47; Stevenson, *Intrepid,* p. 328.

119. Foxworth to Tamm, July 3, 1941, Kermit Roosevelt File, Nichols O&C Files, FBI.

120. Tamm to Hoover, July 3, 1941; Donegan to Hoover, July 4, 1941, Kermit Roosevelt File, Nichols O&C Files, FBI.

121. Tamm to Hoover, July 4, 1941; Foxworth to Hoover, July 4, 1941, Kermit Roosevelt File, Nichols O&C Files, FBI.

122. Hoover to Watson, July 5, 1941, Kermit Roosevelt File, Nichols O&C Files, FBI.

123. Foxworth to Hoover, July 4, 1941, Kermit Roosevelt File, Nichols O&C Files, FBI. This is marked, "Informative memorandum, not to be sent to files section," a very early example of an FBI "Do Not File" file.

124. "Memorandum" July 5, 1941, Kermit Roosevelt File (evidently a verbatim transcript of a recording of the call), Nichols O&C File, FBI.

125. Brown, *The Last Hero,* pp. 164–165.

126. Smith, *The Shadow Warriors,* pp. 77, 80.

127. Brown, *The Last Hero,* p. 222.

128. Ibid., p. 209.

129. This follows the account of Donald Downes, *The Scarlet Thread* (London: Derek Verschoyle, 1953), pp. 91–97. Anthony Cave Brown adds some details. He says that when the OSS agents tried to flee, the FBI arrested them and took them to FBI headquarters for questioning. Downes had to call Donovan before the Bureau would release him and his group. The FBI kept the Spanish cipher data, which it would release only to Military Intelligence, not to Donovan. Hoover knew how to extract the last morsel of good out of something like this, and tried to have the OSS agents indicted on criminal charges. Donovan had to send Downes and the other burglars out of the country to escape American jurisdiction (Brown, *The Last Hero,* pp. 229–230).

130. Brown, *The Last Hero,* p. 338; Smith, *The Shadow Warriors,* p. 340.

131. Smith, *The Shadow Warriors,* pp. 341, 342.

132. Ibid., p. 344.

133. Ibid., p. 346. Operational cooperation between the NKVD and OSS in Germany did proceed, however, with the approval of the JCS.

134. Quoted in Brown, *The Last Hero,* pp. 614–615. The complete letter is in Whitehead, *The F.B.I. Story,* p. 347.

135. Rowe to Biddle, Oct. 31, 1942, Biddle Papers, James Rowe, FDRL.

136. Brown, *The Last Hero,* p. 626; Troy, *Donovan and the CIA,* p. 225. There were also other proposals on the table as the Joint Chiefs of Staff tried to make a decision about postwar intelligence; see Smith, *The Shadow Warriors,* p. 398.

137. Brown, *The Last Hero,* p. 627. There were, however, conflicting reports that Military Intelligence had leaked the report. Trohan himself claimed that he was "called by Steve Early, the President's secretary, given the [Donovan] documents, and told that 'FDR wanted the story out,'" but there is reason to be skeptical about anything Trohan said about Roosevelt (whom he hated) or Hoover (with whom he enjoyed a friendly and profitable relationship). Despite Trohan's statements, it makes more sense to conclude,

since Hoover benefited the most from the defeat of Donovan's plan, that he was the most likely suspect (Brown, *The Last Hero,* p. 631; Smith, *The Shadow Warriors,* p. 400); Troy also entertains some speculations in this direction, but tends toward suspecting Hoover, who had the "motive, the means and the ability to carry out the deed" (Troy, *Donovan and the CIA,* p. 260); Thomas Powers (*The Man Who Kept the Secrets* [New York: Knopf, 1979] p. 27), claims that Hoover "personally handed" the documents to Trohan. Trohan's denial of any Hoover involvement is to be doubted, since it was his practice generally to conceal his close relationship with Hoover. In his autobiography he does not mention his close, almost symbiotic relationship with Hoover throughout his career, reflected in the voluminous correspondence in the Walter Trohan papers at the Herbert Hoover Library. His autobiography mentions J. Edgar Hoover only in the most favorable light, leading to a suspicion that if Hoover had done the leaking, Trohan would have denied it. Furthermore, Trohan was a classic Roosevelt-hater, willing to retell any story if it would damage Roosevelt or his memory. Roosevelt was aware of this, but since Early liked Trohan, that part is believable. See Walter Trohan, *Political Animals* (Garden City: Doubleday, 1975), p. 165, for his attitude toward Roosevelt and Early.

138. News clippings, "Pearl Harbor," Nichols O&C Files.

Chapter 9:   Domestic Security for the Cold War
(*pp. 275–311*)

1. Ralph de Toledano, *J. Edgar Hoover: The Man in His Time* (New Rochelle, N.Y.: Arlington House, 1973), p. 256.

2. For the reports on Truman's criticism of Hoover, see the clippings from the *Washington Times Herald,* Feb. 4, 7, 1942, in "Pearl Harbor," Nichols O&C File, FBI. Truman says Biddle offered to resign; Biddle says he was fired (Harry S. Truman, *Memoirs: Year of Decisions* [Garden City: Doubleday, 1955], Vol. I, p. 325). For Hoover's attitude toward Biddle, see Tom Clark's remarks in Ovid Demaris, *The Director: An Oral Biography of J. Edgar Hoover* (New York: Harpers Magazine Press, 1975), p. 133. For the report that Hoover intimidated Clark, see interview, Pat Collins in Demaris, *The Director,* p. 135.

3. Hoover, "The Reconversion of Law Enforcement," speech to IACP, Dec. 10, 1945, OCPA. Hoover kept Roosevelt supplied with memos on Communist party activities throughout the war (see Spingarn to Wilson, May 4, 1942, Internal Security File, Spingarn Papers; Hoover to Watson, June 16, 1943, Justice Department, White House Central Files, HSTL; Hoover to Hopkins, July 22, 1942, Aug. 22, 1942, Sept. 26, 1942, Nov. 9, 1942, all FBI Communist Party, Hopkins Papers, FDRL; Hoover to Watson, Feb.

26, 1942, FBI Numbered Report 1119, Sept. 3, 1943, FBI Numbered Report 2405, Oct. 27, 1943, FBI Numbered Report 2435, May 17, 1944, FBI Numbered Report 2536, and Hoover to Hopkins, Dec. 26, 1943, FBI Numbered Report 2461B, Official File 10–B, FDRL; Biddle to FDR, Apr. 23, 1943, Justice Francis Biddle, President's Secretary's File, FDRL; Hoover to Berle, Oct. 8, 1943, Justice Department J. Edgar Hoover, President's Secretary's File, FDRL; Hoover to Hopkins, Jan. 13, 1944, FBI Cuba, Hopkins Papers, FDRL). His monthly General Intelligence Surveys were largely devoted to Communist activities (see General Intelligence Survey, Mar. 1942, Nov. 1942, Hopkins Papers, FDRL; General Intelligence Summary, Dept. 1944, FBI 1944–1945, Official File 10-B, p. 272). One of the last of these sent to the White House before Roosevelt's death reported that many locals of the Party were close to bankruptcy, that membership was low, and that a membership drive was getting off to a slow start, and in some locals, was not starting at all (General Intelligence Survey, Mar. 1945, Hopkins Papers, FDRL). Hoover had sent FDR reports on Communist spy rings in England (Hoover to Watson, Oct. 14, 1943, FBI Numbered Report 2433A, Official File 10–B, FDRL); had a wiretap on Tass's lines from Washington to the Soviet Union (Hoover to Hopkins, FBI Numbered Report 2516A, Official File 10–B, FDRL); and a spy in the Russian Government Purchasing Commission (Hoover to Biddle, Mar. 30, 1944, FBI, Biddle Papers, FDRL).

4. He told Truman the Russians had a deadline of February 1, 1946, to buy equipment from the United States; they wanted information on the atomic bomb by January 1, 1946 (Hoover to Vaughan, Jan. 4, 1946, Subject File FBI P, President's Secretary's File, HSTL). For the Easter crisis memo, see Hoover to Attorney General, Subject File Communist, President's Secretary's File, HSTL. For the uprisings in France, see Hoover to Vaughan, Feb. 15, 1946, Subject File FBI H, President's Secretary's File, HSTL. For more war warnings, see Hoover to Attorney General, Oct. 12, 1946, Subject File FBI S, President's Secretary's File, HSTL; Hoover to Vaughan, Mar. 25, 1946, Subject File FBI, President's Secretary's File, HSTL; Hoover to Attorney General, June 20, 1946, Hoover to Vaughan, July 30, 1946, and Hoover to Allen, Sept. 10, 1946, all in Subject File FBI Communist, HSTL. For the quoted memos, see Hoover to Allen, Feb. 24, 1947, and Hoover to Vaughan, Aug. 21, 1947, Subject File FBI, President's Secretary's File, HSTL.

5. Irving Howe and Lewis Coser, *The American Communist Party* (New York: Praeger, 1962), pp. 437–449. The report about Stalin's demise is in Hoover to Vaughan, Nov. 19, 1945, Subject File FBI S, President's Secretary's File, HSTL.

6. Hoover to Vaughan, Oct. 6, 1947, Subject File FBI N, President's Secretary's File, HSTL.

7. For a balanced and detailed treatment of the case, see Earl Latham, *The Communist Controversy in Washington* (Cambridge, Mass.: Harvard University Press, 1966), pp. 203–216. Also see the *Nation,* June 17, 1950.

Harvey Klehr and Ronald Radosh's "Anatomy of a Fix" (*New Republic,* Apr. 21, 1986) traces the methods used by the influential Washington lawyer Tom Corcoran, who intervened to have charges against John Stuart Service dropped. Klehr and Radosh surmise the motive for the Justice Department's reluctance to prosecute the case was to avoid providing opponents of Chiang Kai-shek a forum for publicizing the failures of the administration's China policy. For Hoover's resentment of Clark and the Justice Department, see Nichols to Hoover, Feb. 24, 1955, FBI File 94–3–4–317–366, in which Nichols says it would be not "in good taste to express our real feelings on Tom Clark," and Hoover to Tolson et al., May 31, 1950, "Jaffe II," Nichols O&C File, FBI. While Radosh thinks Hoover acquiesced in the cover-up to avoid revealing the wiretaps he was maintaining on Thomas Corcoran at Truman's request, Louis Nichols informed Peyton Ford on May 29, 1950, that while the Bureau did not want to admit the wiretapping, it was prepared to do so "and point out we were ordered to do this." Given Hoover's dislike for Truman and Clark, he probably would not have minded revealing that he had been tapping one of Truman's enemies on orders from the White House (Nichols to file [?], May 29, 1950, "Jaffe I," Nichols O&C File, FBI).

8. A detailed version of Bentley testimony is in "Underground Soviet Espionage Organization (NKVD) in Agencies of the United States Government," Oct. 21, 1946, Justice Department, White House Central Files, HSTL; Allen Weinstein, *Perjury* (New York: Knopf, 1978), pp. 347, 356; de Toledano, *J. Edgar Hoover,* p. 249.

9. Hoover to Vaughan, Nov. 8, 1945, Subject File FBI S, and Hoover to Vaughan, Feb. 1, 1946, Subject File FBI W, President's Secretary's File, HSTL. The Oct. 21, 1946, memo is cited above.

10. Walter Goodman, *The Committee: The Extraordinary Career of the House Committee on Un-American Activities* (New York: Farrar, Straus, 1968), pp. 125, 126, 131, 135, 141; George Seldes, *Witch Hunt* (New York: Modern Age, 1940), pp. 153–160; Weinstein, *Perjury,* p. 341, comments on the "general ineptitude" of the Bureau in investigating Soviet espionage during the war.

11. Hoover to Allen, May 29, 1946, Subject File FBI Atomic Bomb, President's Secretary's Files, HSTL.

12. Comments by the Church Committee staff that "detention . . . solely on the basis of race was exactly what the . . . Program was designed to prevent" are irrelevant. In the conflict with the Soviet Union that Hoover foresaw, the use of ethnic categories would not have been a possibility (Senate Select Committee, *Final Report,* Book III, p. 417.

13. Hoover's cold war custodial detention programs originated in a June 1940 discussion between Hoover, Attorney General Jackson, and Secretary of War Stimson over emergency plans for dealing with alien enemies. Jackson had the Justice Department, not the Bureau, assume this responsibility, and they stayed within the department until 1943, when Biddle ordered the pro-

gram terminated. Hoover, however, disobeyed and ordered that the program be continued under the new name of Security Index (Senate Select Committee, *Final Report,* Book III, pp. 418, 420–421). Hoover told Clark, the Security Index included "known members of the Communist Party, USA; strongly suspected members of the Communist party; and persons who have given evidence through their activities, utterances and affiliations of their adherence to the aims and objectives of the party and the Soviet Union (Ladd to Hoover, Feb. 27, 1946; Hoover to Attorney General, Mar. 8, 1946, and Sept. 5, 1946, cited in Senate Select Committee, *Final Report,* Book III, pp. 430, 438.)

14. Ladd to Hoover, Feb. 27, 1946, in Senate Select Committee, *Final Report,* Book III, p. 430.

15. For an exhaustive description of the development of this effort to influence public opinion through the media, see Kenneth O'Reilly, *Hoover and the Un-Americans* (Philadelphia: Temple, 1983), pp. 75–100 and passim.

16. Robert Justin Goldstein, *Political Repression in America* (Cambridge, Mass.: Schenkman/Two Continents, 1978), p. 295, who also cites Peter H. Irons, "American Business and the Origins of McCarthyism: The Cold War Crusade of the United States Chamber of Commerce," in *The Specter: Original Essays on the Cold War and the Origins of McCarthyism,* eds. Robert Griffith and Athan Theoharis, (New York: New Viewpoints, 1974), pp. 72–89; David Caute, *The Great Fear: the Anti-Communist Purge Under Truman and Eisenhower* (New York: Simon and Schuster, 1978), p. 26; Goldstein, *Political Repression in America,* p. 295.

17. Senate Select Committee, *Final Report,* Book III, pp. 431–435.

18. Director to Vanech, Jan. 3, 1947, Report of the Temporary Commission, Vanech Papers, HSTL; Minutes, Temporary Commission, Jan. 17, 1947, Stephen Spingarn Papers, President's Temporary Commission, HSTL; memo, Clark to Vanech, Feb. 14, 1947, HST Papers, Official File 252-I, HSTL, reprinted in Athan Theoharis, *The Truman Presidency: The Origins of the Imperial Presidency and the National Security State* (Stanfordville, N.Y.: Coleman, 1979), pp. 253–256.

19. Hoover to Clark, Mar. 19, 1947, FBI Loyalty File, Vanech Papers, HSTL; Memo for the Files, Stephen Spingarn, Feb. 20, 1947, Spingarn Papers, President's Temporary Commission, HSTL, cited in Theoharis, *The Truman Presidency,* p. 256. What later became known as the Attorney General's List was part of the Loyalty Program. The program called on the attorney general to "designate . . . totalitarian, fascist, communist, or subversive" organizations. "Membership in, affiliation with, or sympathetic association with" any such organization would constitute reason for removal from federal employment or cause a person to be barred from employment. In April 1947, Hoover advised Clark that the department should "bring up to date its material on the illegal status of the Communist Party" and also update the antiquated list originally drawn up by Biddle for use in Hatch Act and Smith Act prosecutions. The new Attorney General's List, based on suggestions from Hoover, was released in December 1947. By March 1948, it con-

tained eighty-seven organizations, and by November 1950, 197. The Attorney General's List served as one of the most effective weapons of HUAC, the Loyalty Board, and private red hunters. It was used as well by the Truman administration to intimidate groups opposed to its new foreign policy of Communist containment and confrontation (Executive Order 9835, Mar. 21, 1947, Charles Murphy Files, HSTL, reprinted in Theoharis, *The Truman Presidency,* pp. 257–261; O'Reilly, *Hoover and the Un-Americans,* p. 117; Goldstein, *Political Repression in America,* p. 311).

20. Roosevelt had always been able to limit the damage caused by HUAC's forerunner, the Dies Committee, but Truman did not have FDR's ability to overawe congressmen, and, more importantly, the Dies Committee had been a Democratic committee. In 1947, HUAC was under the control of Republicans who smelled presidential blood on the water in November 1947 and were going into a feeding frenzy in anticipation of 1948. The new chairman was a Republican, J. Parnell Thomas of New Jersey, but the brains and energy were supplied by that rising star in the anti-Communist firmament, Richard M. Nixon, the young congressman from California. Hoover to Clark, Mar. 18, 1947, FBI Loyalty File, Vanech Papers, HSTL. Hoover told Truman in June 1946 that to accept an invitation from HUAC would place an "impossible burden" on the FBI (Wood to HST, June 12, 1946; Vaughan to Hoover, June 17, 1946; Hoover to Vaughan, June 19, 1946; Vaughan to Wood, July 8, 1946, Official File 10-B HSTL). Nichols to Tolson, Mar. 18, 19, 1947, HUAC File # 1439 and 1440, cited in O'Reilly, *Hoover and the Un-Americans,* p. 115.

21. O'Reilly, *Hoover and the Un-Americans,* p. 116.

22. Demaris, *The Director,* p. 121.

23. Latham, *The Communist Controversy,* pp. 373–393. All quotes are from Hoover's testimony before HUAC, reprinted in the *Congressional Record, Appendix* (Mar. 28, 1947, p. A1409–A1412).

24. Hoover to Attorney General, Mar. 31, 1947, Loyalty Commission, Vanech Papers, HSTL.

25. Senate Select Committee, *Final Report,* Book III, p. 434.

26. Hoover to Vaughan, Nov. 13, 1946, Hf-Hz, General File, HSTL. Hoover's general policy seems to have been to help a president by furnishing information about his rivals within his party, but not to get involved in spying on the other major party.

27. O'Reilly, *Hoover and the Un-Americans,* p. 109.

28. *Newsweek,* June 9, 1947, p. 30.

29. Ladd to Hoover, Jan. 22, 1948; Hoover told the attorney general that in his opinion Congress would "readily" pass this legislation, Hoover to Attorney General, Jan. 27, 1948, both in Senate Select Committee, *Final Report,* Book III, p. 439.

30. Gil Green, *Cold War Fugitive* (New York: International Publishers, 1984), p. 26.

31. Michal R. Belknap, *Cold War Political Justice: The Smith Act, the*

Communist Party, and American Civil Liberties (Westport, Conn.: Greenwood, 1977), p. 46. For a "review" of the FBI's treatment of Communist theory and organization, see Green, *Cold War Fugitive*. Green, one of the eleven convicted at the Foley Square trial, comments that "like the man whose sole interest in literature was to search for erotic passages, the FBI 'historians' had combed through the many works of Marx, Engels, and Lenin, and the often turgid writings of lesser Marxists or self-styled Marxists for every mention of violence or forceful overthrow. Yet, significantly, they could not cite a single case of the advocacy or use of violence on the part of Communists in the United States" (Green, *Cold War Fugitive*, p. 25).

32. For the stops and starts of Clark's hesitant policy here, see Ronald Radosh and Joyce Milton, *The Rosenberg File: A Search for the Truth* (New York: Holt, 1983), p. 83, and Belknap, *Cold War Political Justice*, p. 48. Hoover based his proposal on a recommendation from the head of the Bureau's Intelligence Division that the Bureau "work earnestly to urge prosecution of important officials and functionaries of the Communist Party [under the Smith Act] . . . Prosecution of Party officials and responsible functionaries would, in turn, result in a judicial precedent being set that the Communist Party as an organization is illegal; that it advocates the overthrow of the government by force and violence; and finally that the patriotism of Communists is not directed towards the United States but towards the Soviet Union and world Communism" (Hoover to Attorney General, Jan. 27, 1948; and Ladd to Hoover, Jan. 22, 1948, Senate Select Committee, *Final Report*, Book III, p. 439). The indictment was that the twelve had conspired with each other and others to "organize as the Communist Party of the United States, a society, group and assembly of persons who reach and advocate the overthrow and destruction of the Government of the United States by force and violence, and knowingly and willfully to advocate and teach the duty and necessity of overthrowing and destroying the Government of the United States by force, which said acts are prohibited by . . . the Smith Act" (Belknap, *Cold War Political Justice*, pp. 48, 51).

33. From the Gil Green FBI file, quoted in Gil Green, *Cold War Fugitive*, p. 27. The file itself is in the Tamiment Library, N.Y.U.

34. Theodore Draper, *The Roots of American Communism* (New York: Viking, 1957), pp. 227–232.

35. Belknap, *Cold War Political Justice*, p. 156.

36. Weinstein, *Perjury*, p. 340–341, 351. Chambers first talked to Adolf Berle in the State Department in 1939, and had incorrectly assumed that Berle had passed the information along to the FBI. Actually the FBI did not get Berle's memo until 1943.

37. Weinstein, *Perjury*, p. 357.

38. Ibid., pp. 357, 359, 365–367. There is an obvious similarity between the Hoover-Truman arrangement regarding Hiss, and Truman's erroneous

recollections of another deal he thought he had worked out to handle the Harry Dexter White case. Truman, speaking carelessly, may have confused the two cases.

39. Ibid., p. 6.

40. Ibid., p. 15.

41. Murphy's record was clean (Ibid., p. 411).

42. U.S. House Resolution 262, 81st Cong., 1st sess., cited in Max Lowenthal, *The Federal Bureau of Investigation* (New York: William Sloan Associates, 1950), p. 546.

43. Allen Weinstein concludes, "The body of available evidence proves that he did in fact perjure himself when describing his secret dealings with Chambers, so that the jurors in the second trial made no mistake in finding Alger Hiss guilty as charged" (Weinstein, *Perjury,* p. 565).

44. Weinstein, *Perjury,* pp. 507, 513; Latham, *The Communist Controversy,* p. 10.

45. Undated Hoover memos, "Director," Nichols O&C File, FBI.

46. Richard Nixon, Jan. 26, 1950, *Congressional Record,* 81st Cong., 2nd sess., pp. 999–1000, reprinted in Theoharis, *The Truman Presidency,* p. 355.

47. Daniel Yergin quotes a former senior FBI official who said Kaufman "was historically pro-Hoover. . . . Why, Hoover was like Jesus Christ to him." (Maybe some irony there!) Kaufman had had personal contact with Hoover when Kaufman worked in the Justice Department as special assistant to the attorney general (Radosh and Milton, *The Rosenberg File,* p. 288). See also Transcript of Record, *United States of America* v. *Julius Rosenberg, Ethel Rosenberg, Anatoli A. Yakovlev, David Greenglass and Morton Sobell,* U.S. District Court, Southern District of New York, C. 134–245, Mar. 6–Apr. 6, 1951, pp. 1613–1614, quoted in Whitehead, *The F.B.I. Story* (New York: Random House, 1956), p. 317, and Radosh and Milton, *The Rosenberg File,* pp. 283–284.

48. In the most exhaustive and unprejudiced examination of the case to date, Ronald Radosh and Joyce Milton conclude that the "evidence is compelling that Julius Rosenberg, amateur though he may have been, managed over a period of years to become the coordinator of an extensive espionage operation whose contacts were well placed to pass on information on top-secret military projects in the fields of radar and aeronautics. Ethel Rosenberg probably knew of and supported her husband's endeavors. . . . [W]hile the Rosenbergs were not the victims of a frame-up, they were indeed hapless scapegoats of a propaganda war—a war in which their deaths would be counted as a victory for both sides" (Radosh and Milton, *The Rosenberg File,* p. 452). For Kaufman's public praise, see H. Montgomery Hyde, *The Atom Bomb Spies* (London: Hamish Hamilton, 1980), p. 183. For Kaufman's private congratulations ("The FBI did a fabulous job on this case, an outstanding job, and that he could not find the proper adjectives for it . . . he feels

very secure 'knowing we have an FBI.' ''), see Radosh and Milton, *The Rosenberg File,* p. 285.

49. Agents were stationed around the homes of the suspected remaining members of the Rosenberg spy ring in case they heard Julius had confessed and decided to flee (several of these suspects had already left the country). The agents had a thirteen-page memo with the questions they should ask Julius if they got the chance. One of them shows just how little confidence the Bureau had in its case against Ethel: "Was your wife cognizant of your activities?" The FBI's files are conclusive on the point that while the Bureau was convinced of Julius's major role in Soviet espionage, Ethel's role was to be the bait in "J. Edgar Hoover's extraordinary gamble" to make Julius talk (Radosh and Milton, *The Rosenberg File,* pp. 416–417).

50. Hoover to McGrath, July 19, 1950, and Hoover to SAC San Francisco, Mar. 24, 1952, Sarant File, cited in Radosh and Milton, *The Rosenberg File,* pp. 99, 575. Radosh and Milton argue convincingly that Greenglass's information did have value for the Russians: It allowed them to verify independently the authenticity of Fuchs's data, and it gave them a back-up source of information during several months when Fuchs had dropped out of sight and the Russians did not know whether he was going to continue to spy for them (Radosh and Milton, *The Rosenberg File,* pp. 444–445). See also J. Edgar Hoover, "The Crime of the Century: The Case of the A-Bomb Spies," *Reader's Digest,* May 1951, pp. 149, 150.

51. Radosh and Milton, *The Rosenberg File,* p. 280.

52. Hoover to Brownell, May 22, 1953, Radosh and Milton, *The Rosenberg File,* p. 376.

53. Hoover, "The Crime of the Century," pp. 149, 150, 168. Hoover also took care to point out that it was not until "three years later that the FBI got authority to guard atomic secrets."

54. Hoover also kept his distance from Westbrook Pegler, a fellow anti-Communist and frequent recipient of HUAC leaks and therefore, indirectly, of material from the FBI. Pegler tried to get Hoover to approve a loyalty oath for ex-Communists to sign to prove they had returned to loyal Americanism. Pegler was so irresponsible that it would have been foolish for Hoover to cultivate a close relationship, and Pegler resented Hoover's coldness (Pegler to McGuiness, Sept. 18, 1950, Pegler Papers, HHL). For the Spingarn effort, see Fitzgerald to Steelman, Aug. 18, 1950, Internal Security File National Defense and Individual Rights, Vol. II, Spingarn Papers, HSTL. See also Ken Hechler, *Working With Truman: A Personal Memoir of the White House Years* (New York: Putnam's, 1982), pp. 200 and 201 for reference to Murphy, Rosenman, and Morse. The offer to Hoover is in Donald Hansen Oral History, p. 44, OH-8, HSTL. According to Robert Donovan, the offer was made to McGrath, Hoover, and the chairman of the Civil Service Commission, Robert Ramspeck, to serve as a group to investigate corruption (Robert Donovan, *Tumultuous Years: The Presidency of Harry S. Truman, 1949–1953* [New

York: Norton, 1982], p. 376). For an inside view of the Coplon case, see Robert J. Lamphere, *The FBI–KGB War* (New York: Random House, 1986), p. 116–117.

55. Hechler, *Working with Truman,* p. 202; Nichols to Tolson, Apr. 11, 1952, "James P. McInerney," Nichols O&C File, FBI.

56. Max Lowenthal, *Federal Bureau of Investigation.* For the story of White House interest and involvement in Lowenthal's project, see George M. Elsey Oral History, p. 461, OH 128, HSTL. In Lowenthal to Hopkins, May 14, 1950, Official File 10-B HSTL, Lowenthal asks for White House help in getting early copies of the *FBI Law Enforcement Bulletins* from the rare book rooms of the Library of Congress. Although Elsey tried to claim that Truman did not agree with Lowenthal about the Bureau ("The President was just tolerant, shrugged his shoulder, tended to laugh it off and say, 'Oh, Max is that way' "), Truman wrote Lowenthal to congratulate him for his "wonderful service to the country" and wrote him that he "got a great kick out of reading . . . [the] manuscript and making notes on the margin." Truman, however, kept his satisfaction to himself; when asked about the book at a press conference, he said that he had not read it (Elsey Oral History, HSTL; Truman to Lowenthal, June 17, 1950, President's Personal Files—Max Lowenthal; Truman to Lowenthal, June 22, 1950, President's Secretary's Files-General [Max Lowenthal], HSTL, cited in O'Reilly, *Hoover and the Un-Americans,* p. 140).

57. See Louis Nichols Briefing, Pegler Papers, Subject—Communism—Max Lowenthal, HSTL; Hoover to Trohan, Nov. 28, 1950, in which Hoover commented that "the whole thing makes neither rhyme nor reason and it would certainly be interesting if we had the full facts behind, not only the author's motive, but that of the publisher." Six years later Pegler and Trohan discussed the possibility with Nichols of finding out whether Lowenthal had gotten money from AMTORG, perhaps opening him to charges of violating the Voorhis Act (Trohan to Pegler, Mar. 28, 1956, Subject—Communism—Max Lowenthal, Pegler Papers, HHL). Dondero's speech is in the *Congressional Record* for Sept. 1, 1950. Pegler's copy of Dondero's speech in the Hoover library bears the handwritten note "From Nichols FBI."

58. Dick to HST, Jan. 22, 1951, Official File 10-B, HSTL. For a general account of the Bureau reaction to Lowenthal's book, see "The FBI Reviews a Book," *Nation,* Jan. 27, 1951, p. 86.

59. Harry Overstreet and Bonaro Overstreet, *The FBI in Our Open Society* (New York: Norton, 1969), pp. 218–234; Fred J. Cook, *The FBI Nobody Knows* (New York: Macmillan, 1964).

60. Hechler, *Working with Truman,* pp. 185–188; Truman, *Memoirs,* Vol. II, pp. 272–273; "Witch Hunting and Hysteria," Internal Security File, Vol. III, Spingarn Papers, HSTL. There was, the study contended, a relatively permanent undercurrent of "hate and intolerance" in America. Periodically this surfaced as a outburst of intolerance against new objects of popular

hysteria. Truman was reassured to learn that after each of these periods, "the common sense of the American people soon began to tire of the alarms of the extremists" as they had "more serious things to think about" (Truman, *Memoirs,* Vol. II, pp. 272–273).

61. Hofstadter and those who, like Seymour Martin Lipset, adopted his approach saw the new anticommunism as "status politics" (as opposed to "interest politics"), which concerned itself with battles for shares of the national wealth. "Political life," wrote Hofstadter, "is not simply an arena in which the conflicting interests of various social groups in concrete material gains are fought out; it is also an arena into which status aspirations and frustrations are, as the psychologists would say, projected. It is at this point that the issues of politics, or the pretended issues of politics, become interwoven with and dependent upon the personal problems of individuals. We have, at all times, two kinds of processes going on in inextricable connection with each other: *interest politics,* the clash of material aims and needs among various groups and blocs; and *status politics,* the clash of various projective rationalizations arising from status aspirations and other personal motives (Richard Hofstadter, "The Pseudo-Conservative Revolt," in *The Radical Right,* ed. Daniel Bell [Garden City: Anchor, 1964], p. 84).

62. Hoover before Senate Internal Security Subcommittee, Nov. 17, 1953, quoted almost in its entirety in de Toledano, *J. Edgar Hoover,* p. 248.

63. Compare this to Ignazio Silone's famous prediction that "the final conflict will be between the Communists and the ex-Communists" in Weinstein, *Perjury,* p. 520; J. Edgar Hoover, "Secularism, Breeder of Crime," speech to Conference of Methodist Ministers, Evanston, Ill., Nov. 26, 1947, OCPA.

Chapter 10: The Eisenhower Presidency
(*pp. 312–352*)

1. Walter Goodman, *The Committee: The Extraordinary Career of the House Committee on Un-American Activities* (New York: Farrar, Straus, 1968), p. 417.

2. The two-Truman-era cases that had particularly frustrated Hoover were the administration's refusal to push the prosecution of the Amerasia case, and the Justice Department's willingness to furnish the court with raw and embarrassing FBI files during Judith Coplon's espionage trial in 1949. Hoover also felt that Truman had him in mind when he harped on civil liberties at a time when he should have been stressing law enforcement; one instance was when he warned Tom Clark against "prosecuting officers becoming prosecuting officers" (Harry S. Truman, *Memoirs: Year of Decisions* [Garden City: Doubleday, 1955], Vol. I, p. 325.)

3. Interview, Herbert Brownell, May 6, 1986; interview, William Rogers,

in Ovid Demaris, *The Director: An Oral Biography of J. Edgar Hoover* (New York: Harpers Magazine Press, 1975), pp. 151–152; Hoover's evaluation of Eisenhower and Herbert Hoover, whom he called a "great man," but not, specifically, a great president, was in *Nation's Business,* Jan. 1972, pp. 32–33.

4. Ralph de Toledano, *J. Edgar Hoover: The Man in His Time* (New Rochelle, N.Y.: Arlington House, 1973), p. 27.

5. Mark Felt, *The FBI Pyramid: From the Inside* (New York: Putnam's, 1979), p. 47.

6. Ibid., p. 53.

7. According to the pastor of the National Presbyterian Church, during the fifties Hoover was able to play an active role on these boards, but before and after Eisenhower the press of duties made him turn down these outside assignments (phone interview, Edward L. R. Elson, May 1, 1986).

8. Dwight D. Eisenhower, *Mandate for Change, 1953–1956* (Garden City: Doubleday, 1963), p. 90.

9. During the summer of 1953, Arthur Sulzberger of the *New York Times* said Eisenhower should come up with an objective test to determine loyalty. While Eisenhower had Brownell turn the idea over to Hoover, he was too shrewd to imagine that there was anything to this bizarre brainstorm. Instead, he turned it into a small gesture of his regard for the director's expertise (Eisenhower to Brownell, Brownell 1952–1955, Administrative Series, Papers as President of the United States, DDEL).

10. Louis Nichols had helped Brownell during the 1948 presidential campaign Brownell managed for Thomas Dewey. Hoover maintained one direct line to the White House by virtue of his chairmanship of the Interdepartmental Intelligence Committee, established by the National Security Council in 1949. This let Hoover report directly to the White House liaison of the National Security Council, bypassing the attorney general, so he could provide the White House with the same kind of unevaluated intelligence he had sent earlier to Larry Richey, Steve Early, Harry Hopkins, Larry Vaughan, and George Allen. This situation continued until President Kennedy put his attorney general, Robert Kennedy, in charge of the IIC (Senate Select Committee, *Final Report,* Book III, p. 458. Demaris, *The Director,* p. 148; Hoover to Rogers, Jan. 3, 1953; Apr. 10, 11, 1956; May 3, 1956; Jan. 3, 1957; Apr. 3, 1958; June 27, 1958; Nov. 7, 1958; June 17, 1959, and Rogers to Hoover, Dec. 9, 21, 1954, FBI Correspondence to and from Mr. Hoover, Rogers Papers, DDEL. By the end of the administration, Eisenhower was sending Hoover "Dear Edgar" letters. See also Eisenhower to Hoover, Mar. 28, 1960, FBI, Confidential File, WHCF, DDEL, requesting an informal evaluation of a sermon Eisenhower objected to.

11. Rogers informed Hoover that if these employees had been hired, "there might well have resulted serious prejudice to the best interests of the United States, and, at the very least, there would certainly have resulted

acute embarrassment to the President" (Rogers to Hoover, Dec. 21, 1953, FBI Correspondence to and from Mr. Hoover, Rogers Papers, DDEL).

12. This summary follows Parmet, *Eisenhower*, p. 256. See also Athan Theoharis, *Spying on Americans* (Philadelphia: Temple University Press, 1978), pp. 208, 210; the Eisenhower Loyalty Program was Executive Order 10450 of April 27, 1953; Stephen E. Ambrose, *Eisenhower, The President* (New York: Simon and Schuster, 1984), p. 46.

13. Ambrose, *Eisenhower, The President,* p. 64; David M. Oshinsky, *A Conspiracy So Immense: The World of Joe McCarthy* (New York: Free Press, 1983), p. 146; Parmet, *Eisenhower,* p. 343.

14. Parmet, *Eisenhower,* p. 335.

15. Oshinsky, *A Conspiracy So Immense,* p. 147.

16. Truman may have been confusing the White and Hiss cases. In the Hiss case there was an understanding to let Hiss continue with the State Department while the investigation proceeded.

17. Interview, Herbert Brownell, May 6, 1986; Hoover's SISS appearance is quoted at length in de Toledano, *J. Edgar Hoover,* p. 256.

18. Quoted in Oshinsky, *A Conspiracy So Immense,* p. 349.

19. Matthews's charges were in the July 1953 issue of *American Mercury;* Oshinsky, *A Conspiracy So Immense,* p. 57, gives the rundown on McCarthy's staff.

20. Oshinsky, *A Conspiracy So Immense,* pp. 117, 257, 321. In November 1953, when Senator Karl Mundt casually told a Utah dinner audience that the Bureau leaked information about Communists to Congress, Hoover had Mundt deny that this was true, and that he had even made the statement.

21. Ibid., p. 117.

22. Quoted in I. F. Stone, "The J. Edgar Hoover–McCarthy Axis," Sept. 5, 1953, in I. F. Stone, *The Haunted Fifties* (New York: Vintage, 1969), pp. 23–24.

23. Oshinsky, *A Conspiracy So Immense,* p. 430.

24. Sullivan to Hoover, Oct. 6, 1971, in William C. Sullivan with Bill Brown, *The Bureau: My Thirty Years in Hoover's FBI* (New York: Norton, 1979), pp. 268–269.

25. Demaris, *The Director,* p. 37.

26. Just about all the reports Hoover ever made on black organizations called attention to the potential for Communist infiltration.

27. "The Communist Party and the Negro," Feb. 1953, Office of the Special Assistant for National Security Affairs (SANSA), White House Office, DDEL; Hoover to Anderson, Oct. 6, 1955, FBI S(1), SANSA White House Office; Hoover to Anderson, Mar. 6, 1957, FBI O-R(1), SANSA, White House Office, DDEL.

28. In his memoirs, Eisenhower gave himself the benefit of hindsight. He said in principle he did not comment on court decisions, but that "in this case I definitely agreed with the unanimous decision" (Dwight D. Eisen-

hower, *The White House Years: Waging Peace, 1956–1961* [Garden City: Doubleday, 1965], p. 150).

29. Untitled, Mar. 5, 1947, FBI File 66–6200–44–?. In 1944, Hoover ordered his aides not to proceed in civil rights cases "until we have received specific approval of or direction from the Department in view of the highly controversial character of these matters. However, when we do receive authority to proceed, we should see that action is immediately taken and that the investigation is then vigorously presented so that no dereliction may be attributed to the Bureau in the handling of such cases" (Hoover to Tolson, Tamm, and Rosen, Apr. 5, 1944, FBI File 66–6200–44–10).

30. Hoover complained that while "it is incumbent to the effective working of democracy that the perpetrators of such offenses [lynchings] should be apprehended and prosecuted for their crimes," he pointed out to his superiors that "under the present circumstances it appears that the work of the Department and the Bureau is completely ineffective both as a deterrent and as a punitive force." Later he told the attorney general that "an increasingly large number of people are taking a critical attitude toward the Department because of its failure to 'get results' in these cases" and so "I feel it is a mistake for the Department and the Bureau to enter these mob violence cases unless and until there is some showing of a Federal violation" (Director to Attorney General, Sept. 12, 1946, FBI File 66–6200–44–?, and Sept. 17, 1946, FBI File 66–6200–44–?; Untitled, Mar. 5, 1947, FBI File 66–6200–44–?).

31. For analogous attacks by Martin Luther King, Jr., see David J. Garrow, *The FBI and Martin Luther King, Jr.: From "Solo" to Memphis* (New York: Norton, 1981), pp. 54–55. See also Tolson to Hoover, and Hoover margin comments, Nov. 22, 1955, FBI File 66–6600–44–377; Belmont to Tolson, Rosen to Tolson, Mar. 1, 1957, FBI File 66–6600–44–?.

32. Bureau Bulletin #66, Series 1947, Nov. 6, 1947, FBI File 66–6200–44–?; SAC Letter # 144, Series 1947, Nov. 12, 1947, FBI File 66–6200–44–?; Untitled, Oct. 29, 1952, FBI File 66–6200–44–?.

33. SAC Letter # 55–59, Sept. 20, 1955, FBI File 66–6200–44; "The FBI and Civil Rights," Sept. 1955, "Based on a memorandum from W. C. Sullivan to Mr. A. H. Belmont," in FBI File 66–6200–44.

34. Eisenhower, *Waging Peace,* pp. 151–152. This was in March 1956.

35. Monitor Radio Program, Dec. 5, 1955, DJ File 144–012, cited by Scott Rafferty, *Federal Protection of Civil Rights Against Acts of Violence* (unpublished Princeton B.A. thesis, 1976), pp. 36–37, JFKL.

36. For the Till case, see Don Whitehead, *The F.B.I. Story* (New York: Random House, 1956), pp. 257–258. The laws were Section 51 and 52, Title 18 of the U.S.C. (now 18 U.S.C. 241 and 242), which had been interpreted (particularly in *Screws* v. *U.S.* [1945]) to apply only when officials "under color of law" acted with specific intent to deny a person a specific constitutional right. Another difficulty with federal civil rights enforcement was the

Supreme Court doctrine that the Fourteenth Amendment did not extend all but only the most essential constitutional rights to the states (Alfred Kelly et al., *The American Constitution* [New York: Norton, 1983], p. 618–619). For Brownell's actions, interview, May 6, 1986.

37. There were two Hoovers at this meeting, with Under Secretary of State Herbert C. Hoover, Jr., representing Dulles. The uncomplimentary characterization was from Sanford J. Ungar, *FBI* (Boston: Little, Brown, 1975), p. 408. Quotes are from handwritten notes of cabinet meeting, Mar. 9, 1956, Office of Staff Secretary, Cabinet Series, White House Office; Cabinet Meeting of Mar. 9, 1956, Cabinet Series, Papers as President of the United States, DDEL; Eisenhower, *Waging Peace,* p. 161.

38. For Brownell's plans, see Parmet, *Eisenhower,* pp. 445–446.

39. Ibid., p. 554, quoting Tiffany to Morgan, Nov. 2, 1959, Morgan Papers, DDEL.

40. "The challenge for America in 1960," John Doar wrote in 1975, "was the destruction of the caste system itself. At the outset, few men had fully perceived this fact" (John Doar and Dorothy Landsberg, *The Performance of the FBI in Investigating Violations of Federal Laws Protecting the Right to Vote—1960–1967,* in Senate Select Committee, *Hearings,* Vol. 6, FBI, p. 948.

41. Fred J. Cook, *The FBI Nobody Knows* (New York: Macmillan, 1964), p. 227. For rumors of an implicit agreement between the FBI and organized crime to stay out of each other's way, see interview, George Allen, in Demaris, *The Director,* p. 23; also Hank Messick, *John Edgar Hoover: An Inquiry into the Life and Times of John Edgar Hoover and His Relationship to the Continuing Partnership of Crime, Business and Politics* (New York: David McKay, 1972). To say that this thesis is dubious is to put it mildly.

42. James Q. Wilson, *The Investigators: Managing FBI and Narcotics Agents* (New York: Basic Books, 1978), p. 170. Wilson adds, "In my view it is the desire for autonomy, and not for large budgets, new powers, or additional employees, that is the dominant motive of public executives" (Wilson, *The Investigators,* p. 165).

43. Demaris, *The Director,* p. 150.

44. Wilson, *The Investigators,* p. 170.

45. Cook, *The FBI Nobody Knows,* p. 229; Arthur M. Schlesinger, Jr., *Robert Kennedy and His Times* (Boston: Houghton Mifflin, 1978), p. 264. It should be noted, however, that the agents assigned to security in New York also have to handle Soviet and Eastern bloc espionage agents under U.N. diplomatic cover, an enormous job.

46. Cook, *The FBI Nobody Knows,* p. 230; Sanford Ungar, *FBI* (Boston: Atlantic Monthly, 1975), pp. 392–393. For an account of the struggle within the Bureau to get Hoover to change the Bureau line on the Mafia's nonexistence, see Sullivan, *The Bureau,* p. 121.

47. For the Brownell memo, see Attorney General to Director, May

20, 1954, Senate Select Committee, *Final Report,* Book III, p. 297. For Brownell's clarification, interview, May 6, 1986.

48. Robert Justin Goldstein, *Political Repression in Modern America, from 1870 to the Present* (Cambridge, Mass.: Schenkman/Two Continents, 1978), p. 341; "Role of Communist Party USA in Soviet Intelligence," Feb. 20, 1953, Staff Files, SANSA, DDEL. Hoover kept pounding away at this theme: a monograph of 1954 proved that "the Communist Party, USA, since its founding in 1919, has pledged and given its unqualified and undeviating allegiance and loyalty to the U.S.S.R. rather than to the United States" (Hoover to Cutler, Dec. 22, 1954, enclosing "Allegiance of the Communist Party, USA, to the Soviet Union," Staff Files, SANSA, DDEL).

49. Hoover to Cutler, Mar. 18, 1953, Staff Files, SANSA, DDEL. The FBI Series of the Office of the Special Assistant for National Security Affairs at the Eisenhower Library contains the following titles, some consisting of more than one volume:

1953

The Communist Party Line
Polish Intelligence Activities in the United States
The Communist Party and American Labor
The Sabotage Plans and Potential of the Communist Party, USA
Soviet Intelligence Targets in the United States
Charts, Communist Front Organizations
Soviet Intelligence Travel and Entry Techniques
The Communist Party USA versus Earl Russell Browder and Browderism
Communist Strategy and Tactics, Part I—General Principles Governing Communist Strategy and Tactics
Role of the Communist Party USA in Soviet Intelligence
The Communist Party and the Negro
FBI Liaison Activities

1954

Communist Party U.S.A. Summary—Activities
The Communist Party Line
Communist Work Among American Youth
Allegiance of the Communist Party USA to the Soviet Union
Communication Methods of the Communist Party USA
The Communist Press in the United States
The Communist Party U.S.A.—Funds and Finances
Potentialities of Chinese Communist Intelligence Activities in the United States
The Educational Program of the Communist Party, USA
The Communist Party USA and Its Tactic "Peaceful" Coexistence
The Nationalist Party of Puerto Rico

1955

The Communist Party Line
Communist Party U.S.A., Summary—Activities
Summary Brief, Donald Duart MacLean, Guy Francis De Moncy Burgess, Harold Adrian Russell Philby
Charts re Communist Party USA—Communist Youth
Communist Party U.S.A.—The Underground Apparatus

The Menace of Communism in the United States Today
Communist Infiltration of the American Merchant Marine
Discipline in the Communist Party, U.S.A.
The Socialist Workers Party
Communist Party U.S.A.—School System
The Communist Front Movement in the United States
Soviet Military, Naval and Air Representatives in the United States—Covert
  Operational Methods

1956
Communist Party, U.S.A. Summary—Activities
The Communist Party Line
Communist Propaganda in the United States, Theory, Objectives, and Organiza-
  tion
The Communist Party and the Negro
Charts re Current Communist Subversion and Espionage

1957
Communist Party, USA, Activities
Communist Party Line
Communist Propaganda in the United States
Soviet Illegal Espionage in the United States
Lenin's Revolutionary Thoughts
Leninism—Stalinism, The Deadly Parallel
Communist Propaganda in the United States, Demonstrations
The Communist Party and Social Reform
Communist Press, U.S.A., Statements Directed Against American Society, 1920–
  1924
Communism versus the Jewish People

1958
Communist Party Activities
Communist Party Line
Ku Klux Klan
Communist Press, USA, Statements Directed Against American Society
Communist Propaganda in the United States

1959
Communist Party Activities

1960
Nation of Islam
Communist Party Line and Activities

50. Goldstein, *Political Repression in America,* p. 402; Michal R. Belknap,
*Cold War Political Justice: The Smith Act, the Communist Party, and American
Civil Liberties* (Westport, Conn.: Greenwood, 1977), p. 261, quoting Hoover's
1958 annual report.

51. Senate Select Committee, *Final Report,* Book III, p. 449.

52. In *Yates,* Justice Harlan ruled that a Smith Act conviction was valid
only when it was proven that what was advocated was not a mere "abstract
doctrine of forcible overthrow" but "action to that end, by the use of language
reasonably and ordinarily calculated to incite persons to that end." There
must be advocacy of doctrine and not simply advocacy of action. This effec-

tively ended Smith Act prosecutions under the "advocacy" clause. In 1961, the Court's *Scales* decision made convictions under the membership clause equally unlikely. Like Secretary of Labor Wilson and Louis Post long before, the Supreme Court held that a person was liable only for "knowing" participation in a proscribed organization, and not merely for passive membership (Kelly et al., *The American Constitution,* p. 596).

53. Belknap, *Cold War Political Justice,* p. 155.

54. Hoover to Seaton, June 26, 1957, FBI, Seaton Papers, DDEL.

55. The timing of COINTELPRO later puzzled the Church Committee, because *Yates* was not announced until June 17, 1957 while COINTELPRO began in 1956. It was actually the Court's granting of certiorari for Yates in late 1955 and the department's reaction to it in March 1956 that effectively took the Smith Act out of the Bureau's arsenal (Senate Select Committee, *Final Report,* Book III, pp. 7, 10; Senate Select Committee, *Hearings,* Vol. 6, FBI, pp. 70–71).

56. Senate Select Committee, *Final Report, Book III,* pp. 15, 17; John Crewdson, "Seeing Red," *Sunday: The Chicago Tribune Magazine,* Mar. 2, 1986, p. 10. Former Chicago Special Agent Wesley Swearington says that although the Bureau admitted to 238 burglaries from the end of World War II until official termination of the technique in 1966, he personally participated in more than 500, and that was only one agent in one city, Chicago.

57. Belmont to Boardman, Aug. 28, 1956, Senate Select Committee, *Hearings,* Vol. 6, FBI, pp. 21, 372–376; Director to SAC, Chicago, Nov. 23, 1956, FBI File 100–3–104–? (COINTELPRO–CPUSA file).

58. Senate Select Committee, *Final Report,* Book III, pp. 33–61, 45, 58. (The accusation of homosexuality was never made since the agents withdrew their request for permission to proceed when they learned that the individual stopped working for the party.) Frank J. Donner, *The Age of Surveillance* (New York: Knopf, 1980), p. 187. Donner also gives an account of the case of William Albertson, a Communist leader whose life was destroyed by an FBI plot to frame him as an FBI spy (Donner, *Age of Surveillance,* p. 192–194).

59. Belknap, *Cold War Political Justice,* pp. 190, 197; Peter L. Steinberg, *The Great "Red Menace": United States Prosecution of American Communists, 1947–1952* (Westport, Conn.: Greenwood, 1984), p. 281. While specifics of COINTELPRO were kept secret, Hoover did notify his superiors in general terms of the program. Minutes of Cabinet Meeting, Nov. 6, 1958, Cabinet Series, Papers as President of the United States, DDEL; Hoover to Attorney General, May 8, 1958, in Senate Select Committee, *Hearings,* Vol. 6, FBI, p. 819; interview, Herbert Brownell, May 6, 1986; FBI memo to Select Committee, Jan. 12, 1976, in Senate Select Committee, *Hearings,* Vol. 6, FBI, pp. 992–994; Senate Select Committee, *Final Report,* Book III, pp. 11, 70–71. The Senate Committee found that Hoover notified Secretary of State Rusk in 1961, and the Appropriations Committee in 1961, 1963, 1966, and

1967. On the other hand, evidently no one outside the Bureau was notified about the SWP, Black Nationalist, or New Left COINTELPROs.

60. 68 Stat. 775 (1954) and 50 U.S.C. 841–844, Senate Select Committee, *Final Report,* Book III, p. 428; Kelly et al., *The American Constitution,* p. 588.

61. Senate Select Committee, *Final Report,* Book III, p. 62.

62. Sidney Hook, *Heresy, Yes—Conspiracy, No* (New York: John Day, 1953), p. 22. In his *Age of Surveillance,* Frank J. Donner called COINTEL-PRO "a nativist version of the English judgment of outlawry: 'It is the right and duty of every man to pursue him, to ravage his lands, to hunt him down like a wild beast and slay him; for a wilde beast he is; not merely is he a "friendless man," he is a wolf. . . . In these words the courts decreed outlawry.' The FBI treated the subject as though he or she wore a wolf's head; but, while the label of outlawry was the execution of a decree by a tribunal, here the Bureau constituted itself the secret instrument of a tribal system of justice directed against people it had itself defined as enemies and outcasts." (Donner, *Age of Surveillance,* p. 180).

63. Hoover was less than frank about the new form COMINFIL was taking, still referring to it as an intelligence operation. 1960 FBI Manual, Section 87, pp. 5–10, cited in Senate Select Committee, *Final Report,* Book III, p. 449; Annual Reports for 1958 (p. 338) and 1964 (p. 375), cited in Senate Select Committee, *Final Report,* Book III, p. 449.

64. Senate Select Committee, *Final Report,* Book III, pp. 450–451; note on memo from Assistant Attorney General Yeagley to Hoover, July 15, 1959, Senate Select Committee, *Final Report,* Book III, p. 453; Note on Donahue to Belmont, June 17, 1959, and Hoover to Attorney General, Sept. 9, 1960, Senate Select Committee, *Final Report,* Book III, p. 453.

65. The Church Committee was puzzled about why "a law enforcement agency" transformed itself "into a law violator." One agent said, "At this time [the mid-1950s] there was a general philosophy, too, the general attitude of the public at this time was you did not have to worry about Communism because the FBI would take care of it. Leave it to the FBI. I hardly knew an agent who would ever go to a social affair or something, if he were introduced as FBI, the comment would be, 'we feel very good because we know you are handling the threat.' We were handling the threat with what directives and statutes were available. There did not seem to be any strong interest of anybody to give us stronger or better defined statutes" (Senate Select Committee, *Final Report,* Book III, p. 10). The Church Committee distrusted the Bureau's explanation that it had been frustration with the Supreme Court's weakening of the Smith Act as a weapon that had led to COINTELPRO. The committee concluded that Hoover had turned the FBI into an organization so attuned to the fight against communism, that the Supreme Court had left it nowhere legally to go. One agent explained, "The FBI's counterintelligence program came up because there was a point—if you have anything

in the FBI you have an action-oriented group of people who see something happening and want to do something to take its place" (Senate Select Committee, *Final Report,* Book III, p. 11). See also interview, Herbert Brownell, May 6, 1986.

66. Attorney General to President, Oct. 6, 1956, Brownell 1952–1955 (5), Administrative Series, Papers as President of the United States, DDEL. Hoover also contributed a summary to a HUAC "expose" of anti-Stalinism called *The Great Pretense.* (Walter Goodman, *The Committee,* p. 397). On Nov. 6, 1958, Hoover gave the cabinet a special briefing on Soviet espionage. See also Hoover to Cutler, Jan. 16, 1958, forwarding "Real Meaning of 'Peaceful Co-existence,' " FBI O-R (1), Staff Files, SANSA, DDEL. This study was abstracted by Robert Cutler's assistant for his information. See also Hoover to Gray, Oct. 23, 1958, FBI C(4), Staff Files, SANSA, DDEL. Hoover to Jackson, Sept. 18, 1956, enclosing "Communist Press, USA, Statements Directed Against American Society, September–December, 1919," FBI Series, Staff Files, SANSA, DDEL.

67. Hoover to Cutler, June 11, 1957, enclosing "The Communist party and Social Reform," FBI Series, Staff Files, SANSA, DDEL.

68. A team of five agents in the Research Section put together what Sullivan called "a serious study of communism." The project was then taken over by Louis Nichols, who gave it to one of the writers in his Crime Records Division, Fern Stukenbroeker, to add anecdotal and human interest material. Finally, according to Nichols, he himself "did the finished writing with the help of another chap." This "other chap" was probably the William I. Nichols of *This Week:* There are two plugs for that magazine in *Masters,* one for an article by Hoover, another for a piece in which ex-Vice President Henry Wallace apologized for associating with Communists when he ran for the presidency in 1948 on the Progressive party ticket (Sullivan, *The Bureau,* p. 91; Demaris, *The Director,* pp. 90–91). There exists a handwritten speech by Hoover in OCPA dated Dec. 10, 1956. His style and that of his ghostwriters were so similar it is impossible to tell that speech from one by an agent writer in Crime Records.

69. Demaris, *The Director,* pp. 13–20; 90.

70. J. Edgar Hoover, *Masters of Deceit* (New York: Holt, 1958), p. 357. Louis Nichols readily admitted that he worked closely with Whitehead, but said the writing and editing were Whitehead's. Interview, Louis B. Nichols, June 26, 1975.

71. Kenneth O'Reilly and Athan G. Theoharis, "The FBI, the Congress, and McCarthyism, in *Beyond the Hiss Case: The FBI, Congress and the Cold War,* ed. Athan Theoharis (Philadelphia: Temple, 1982), p. 373. Don Whitehead also wrote *Attack on Terror: The FBI Against the Ku Klux Klan in Mississippi* (New York: Funk and Wagnalls, 1970).

72. Whitehead, *The F.B.I. Story,* pp. 323, 328.

73. Bosley Crowther, *New York Times,* Oct. 4, 1959, sec. 2, p. 1.

74. Mervyn LeRoy, quoted in Demaris, *The Director*, p. 68.

75. Goodman, *The Committee*, pp. 416, 419.

76. Ibid., pp. 418, 427, 428.

77. Ibid., pp. 431, 433.

78. Kenneth O'Reilly, *Hoover and the Un-Americans* (Philadelphia: Temple, 1983), pp. 262–270; Goodman, *The Committee*, p. 434.

79. A California assemblyman charged that Hoover had lied about the riots and went on to say, in a letter to Hoover, that his "pamphlet, published and distributed by the HUAC, clearly implies that there was not legitimate reason for any non-Communist to oppose the Committee hearing. Many San Franciscans considered that a political judgment which was unfounded in fact and also outside the rightful scope of the supposedly non-political function of your office" (Cook, *The FBI Nobody Knows*, p. 404; Goodman, *The Committee*, p. 434, referring specifically to HUAC).

80. de Toledano, *J. Edgar Hoover*, p. 259; Whitehead, *The F.B.I. Story*, p. 251.

Chapter 11: Kennedy Justice
(pp. 353–392)

1. Victor Navasky, *Kennedy Justice* (New York: Atheneum, 1971), p. 6; Arthur M. Schlesinger, Jr., *Robert Kennedy and His Times* (Boston: Houghton Mifflin, 1978), p. 260 (hereafter referred to as *RFK*).

2. Arthur M. Schlesinger, Jr., *A Thousand Days* (Boston: Houghton Mifflin, 1965), p. 125.

3. To complete the comparison, Vice President Lyndon Baines Johnson was nine years older than Kennedy, but thirteen years younger than Hoover. For the age of the cabinet, see Herbert S. Parmet, *JFK: the Presidency of John F. Kennedy* (New York: Dial, 1983), p. 63.

4. Norman Mailer, *The Presidential Papers* (New York: Berkley, 1963), pp. 6–7. In these essays Mailer calls the FBI the "only absolute organization in America . . . a high church for the true mediocre" (Mailer, *The Presidential Papers*, p. 129).

5. Schlesinger, *RFK*, p. 256.

6. Norman Ollestad, *Inside the FBI* (New York: Lancer, 1967), p. 17.

7. Jack Levine's forty-four-page *Memo on the FBI* is enclosed with a letter, Levine to Miller, Jan. 23, 1962, JFKL. Herbert J. Miller, Jr., was assistant attorney general in charge of the Criminal Division.

8. Edwin Guthman, *We Band of Brothers* (New York: Harper and Row, 1964), p. 266.

9. Parmet, *JFK*, p. 60. The friends who recommended the firings were Bill Walton and Ben Bradlee (Schlesinger, *RFK*, p. 256).

10. Herbert Parmet, *Jack: The Struggles of John F. Kennedy* (New York:

Dial, 1980), p. 510; Schlesinger, *RFK*, pp. 111, 112. The dispute was over Annie Lee Moss. Despite his role as counsel for the enemies who brought McCarthy down, Kennedy retained a fondness for the senator and often defended him in conversations with his friends.

11. Schlesinger, *RFK*, p. 230; Navasky, *Kennedy Justice*, p. 4; Ovid Demaris, *The Director: An Oral Biography of J. Edgar Hoover* (New York: Harpers Magazine Press, 1975), p. 183.

12. Parmet, *Jack*, pp. 88, 90, 91.

13. Richard Bissell, in charge of CIA attempts to get rid of Castro, reported in 1975 that he was "chewed out" by John and Robert Kennedy in the cabinet room for "sitting on his ass" instead of getting rid of Castro (Henry Hurt, *Reasonable Doubt* [New York: Holt, Rinehart and Winston, 1985], p. 316).

14. Parmet, *JFK*, pp. 126, 127. Hoover's meeting with RFK about CIA efforts to hire Giancana through Robert Maheu is described in Hoover to Tolson et al., May 19, 1962, Senate Select *Final Report*, Book V, Assassination of JFK, p. 11.

15. Parmet, *JFK*, p. 128.

16. Levine, *Memo on the FBI*, p. 3, JFKL. Much of the evidence on the Hoover–Robert Kennedy relationship is anecdotal and must be approached with caution. In 1966, an open fight erupted between Hoover and the Robert Kennedy camp over whether or not the attorney general had been notified that the FBI was using illegal microphone surveillance in organized crime investigations. By that time, Hoover was a fully committed Lyndon Johnson loyalist, so in addition to all his other motives for attacking Kennedy, he also had the desire to defend the president. The Kennedy partisans had a reciprocal need to discredit Hoover.

17. William L. O'Neill, *Coming Apart: An Informal History of America in the 1960s* (New York: Quadrangle, 1971), p. 46.

18. William W. Turner, *Hoover's FBI, The Men and the Myth* (New York: Dell, 1971), pp. 241–242, 292.

19. Turner, *Hoover's FBI*, p. 243; the "secret society" model is from Navasky, *Kennedy Justice*, p. 15, passim.

20. Demaris, *The Director*, p. 67; interview, Louis Nichols, June 26, 1975.

21. In his will Hoover left the two "J. Edgars" rings as personal mementos. The will is reprinted in Demaris, *The Director*, p. 333.

22. Navasky, *Kennedy Justice*, pp. 87–88.

23. Phone interview, Edward L. R. Elson, May 1, 1986; Hoover to Robert Kennedy, Nov. 20, 1962, Personal Papers of RFK, General Correspondence, Hoover, J. Edgar, JFKL.

24. Hoover quotation is from January 1961 issue of the *FBI Law Enforcement Bulletin*, quoted by Schlesinger, *RFK*, p. 409. The discussion of the Juvenile Delinquency Act also follows Schlesinger, *RFK*, p. 411.

25. Schlesinger, *RFK*, p. 413.

26. Ibid., p. 269; Navasky, *Kennedy Justice,* p. 26.

27. Schlesinger, *RFK,* p. 264.

28. Guthman, *We Band of Brothers,* p. 266.

29. Kennedy was in favor of court-ordered wiretapping for criminal investigations and urged Congress, unsuccessfully, to pass such legislation. The taps he approved while he was attorney general were almost exclusively for national security cases (Schlesinger, *RFK,* p. 271). See also Guthman, *We Band of Brothers,* p. 263. The dispute surfaced in 1966, and is carefully discussed in Navasky, *Kennedy Justice,* p. 80.

30. Navasky, *Kennedy Justice,* p. 81; Schlesinger, *RFK,* p. 269.

31. Ollestad, *Inside the FBI,* p. 129; Levine, *Memo on the FBI,* p. 7, JFKL.

32. Schlesinger remarks that even to call this tokenism "would have been wild overstatement" (Schlesinger, *RFK,* p. 292).

33. Navasky, *Kennedy Justice,* p. 100.

34. For John F. Kennedy's dilemmas in the area of civil rights, see Schlesinger, *A Thousand Days,* p. 930; John Doar and Dorothy Landsberg, *The Performance of the FBI in Investigating Violations of Federal Laws Protecting the Right to Vote—1960–1967,* U.S. Senate, Select Committee to Study Governmental Operations with Respect to Intelligence, *Hearings,* Vol. 6, FBI, 94th Cong., 1st sess., p. 948.

35. David J. Garrow, *The FBI and Martin Luther King, Jr.: From "Solo" to Memphis* (New York: Norton, 1981), p. 41. The other principal source for this discussion is Senate Select Committee, *Final Report,* Book III, p. 79–184, "Dr. Martin Luther King, Jr., A Case Study." The FBI's source was one of the Bureau's most trusted informants on the Party, code-named "Solo."

36. Both Navasky, *Kennedy Justice,* p. 152, and Schlesinger, *RFK,* p. 359, point out the possible connection between the White case and the Kennedys' response to the allegations about King.

37. Garrow, *FBI and Martin Luther King, Jr.,* p. 45.

38. Ibid., p. 55.

39. Executive Committee to Director, Nov. 22, 1955, FBI File, 66–6200–?, in Max Rafferty Papers, JFKL; Garrow, *FBI and Martin Luther King, Jr.,* p. 56. The fact that Hoover and DeLoach tried to approach King means that they had not yet written him off as hopeless since there are many memos in which Hoover orders his men not to waste their time trying to straighten someone out once he decided the person was his enemy.

40. Garrow, *FBI and Martin Luther King, Jr.,* p. 59.

41. Sullivan was born in 1912 on a farm near Bolton, Massachusetts. He obtained a degree in education from American University and taught in Bolton. He then worked for the Internal Revenue Service in Boston before joining the FBI in August 1941. He worked in counterintelligence during the war until he became ill while on a special assignment in Spain and was

transferred to the Domestic Security Division in Washington, D.C., where he spent the rest of his career. See William C. Sullivan with Bill Brown, *The Bureau: My Thirty Years in Hoover's FBI* (New York: Norton, 1979), passim, esp. 14–46; obituary, *New York Times,* Nov. 10, 1977, p. D13; Sanford Ungar, *FBI* (Boston: Atlantic Monthly, 1975), pp. 295–312; Demaris, *The Director,* pp. 76–97, passim.

42. Mark Felt, *The FBI Pyramid: From the Inside* (New York: Putnam's, 1979), p. 142.

43. Sullivan to Belmont, Oct. 9, 1956, FBI File 100–3–104, sec. 2; Director to SAC, Chicago, Nov. 23, 1956, all in Rafferty Papers, JFKL.

44. Felt, *The FBI Pyramid,* p. 111.

45. Senate Select Committee, *Final Report,* Book III, "King," p. 106.

46. Hoover note on memo from Baumgardner to Sullivan, Aug. 23, 1963, Senate Select Committee, *Final Report,* Book III, "King," pp. 105–106.

47. Arthur M. Schlesinger, Jr., who knew Sullivan long before Sullivan left the Bureau, told me he did not hear Sullivan criticize Hoover in conversations with him prior to Sullivan's being fired in 1971; the change in attitude afterward was marked (telephone interview, Arthur M. Schlesinger, Jr., June 4, 1986; Sullivan testimony, Nov. 1, 1975, in Senate Select Committee, *Final Report,* Book III, p. 107).

48. Hoover comments on Baumgartner to Sullivan, Aug. 26, 29, 1963, Senate Select Committee, *Final Report,* Book III, p. 107.

49. Sullivan testimony, Nov. 1, 1975, p. 20, Senate Select Committee, *Final Report,* Book III, p. 120.

50. Sullivan to Belmont, Aug. 30, 1963, Senate Select Committee, *Final Report,* Book III, "King," p. 108.

51. Baumgartner to Sullivan, Sept. 16, 1963, Senate Select Committee, *Final Report,* Book III, p. 108.

52. Hoover's marginal notes on Baumgartner to Sullivan, Sept. 16, 1963, Senate Select Committee, *Final Report,* Book III, "King," p. 109.

53. Sullivan testimony, Nov. 1, 1975, p. 46, quoted in Senate Select Committee, *Final Report,* Book III, p. 109.

54. Hoover marginal note on memorandum from Tolson to Hoover, Sept. 18, 1963, Senate Select Committee, *Final Report,* Book, III, "King," p. 109.

55. Sullivan testimony, Nov. 1, 1975, p. 30, Senate Select Committee, *Final Report,* Book III, "King," p. 109.

56. The Church Committee characterized Sullivan's testimony as "only one side of the story." It raised the possibility that Sullivan had been trying to maneuver Hoover into supporting increased domestic intelligence programs. The third, and most likely, possibility, ignored by the Church Committee, is that Hoover really wanted to know the truth, since he was going to have to defend his position against media cross-examination (Senate Select Committee, *Final Report,* Book III, "King," p. 111).

57. Senate Select Committee, *Final Report,* Book III, pp. 131–132; Garrow, *FBI and Martin Luther King, Jr.,* pp. 74–75.

58. Turner, *Hoover's FBI,* p. 61 and passim. Many more of these anecdotes can be found in Joseph Schott, *No Left Turns* (New York: Praeger, 1975).

59. Ollestad, *Inside the FBI,* p. 54.

60. Ibid., p. 89.

61. Levine, *Memo on the FBI,* JFKL. Levine, a graduate of New York University Law School, joined the FBI in September 1960 and left less than a year later. He told his story to Fred J. Cook, who made it part of his *The FBI Nobody Knows* (New York: Macmillan, 1964), pp. 1–48.

62. Schlesinger, *RFK,* p. 608.

63. Hoover to Johnson, Nov. 23, 1963, preliminary report; Katzenbach to Moyers, Nov. 26, 1963, Senate Select Committee, *Final Report,* Book V, Assassination of JFK, p. 23.

64. Senate Select Committee, *Final Report,* Book V, Assassination of JFK, pp. 13–20.

65. Hoover to Belmont, Dec. 10, 1963, Senate Select Committee, *Final Report,* Book V, Assassination of JFK, p. 23, and p. 5. The Church Committee later thought it was obvious that Hoover's great concern was possible criticism of the Bureau's handling of Oswald's security case (p. 47). See also Hurt, *Reasonable Doubt,* p. 32.

66. Senate Select Committee, *Final Report,* Book V, Assassination of JFK, p. 89.

67. Ibid., p. 92.

68. William C. Sullivan said that the reason Hoover was in such a rush to discipline the agents was so that if the Warren Commission did break through his defenses he could show he had cracked down on the offenders (Sullivan, *The Bureau,* p. 52).

69. Hoover, handwritten note on DeLoach to Mohr, Sept. 25, 1964, and Gale to Tolson, Sept. 30, 1964, Senate Select Committee, *Final Report,* Book V, Assassination of JFK, pp. 53, 54.

70. Hoover note on Sullivan to Belmont, Sept 24, 1964, and Hoover note on Belmont to Tolson, Oct. 1, 1964, Senate Select Committee, *Final Report,* Book V, Assassination of JFK, pp. 52–55.

71. Hoover, Administrative Cover Sheet from FBI Supervisor to Gale, Oct. 12, 1964; Hoover note on Rosen to Belmont, Oct. 2, 1964, Senate Select Committee, *Final Report,* Book V, Assassination of JFK, pp. 53, 55. The FBI kept separate books on its critiques of the Warren Commission, tallying up as serious blunders actions that it defended before the commission. For example, the Bureau noted that it had "by letter to the Commission indicated that the facts did not warrant placing a stop on the passport as our investigation disclosed no evidence that Oswald was acting under the instructions or on behalf of any foreign Government or instrumentality thereof. Inspector feels it was proper at that time to take this 'public' position. However, it is

felt that with Oswald's background we should have had a stop on his passport, particularly since we did not know definitely whether or not he had any intelligence assignments at that time" (Gale to Tolson, Sept. 30, 1964, Senate Select Committee, *Final Report,* Book V, Assassination of JFK, p. 54).

72. In Hoover's jargon, "smear" simply meant criticism of the Bureau, true or false. Hoover note on DeLoach to Mohr, Oct. 6, 1964, Senate Select Committee, *Final Report,* Book V, Assassination of JFK, p. 57.

73. Schlesinger, *RFK,* p. 616.

74. Jones to DeLoach, Feb. 1, 1963, FBI File 67–561–?; DeLoach to Mohr, Feb. 7, 1963, FBI File 67–561–?, Hoover Personnel File.

75. Schlesinger, *RFK,* p. 629, vouches for the telephone story, which evidently had wide currency in the Bureau (Schott, *No Left Turns,* p. 204– 205, and Turner, *Hoover's FBI,* both tell it); Ralph de Toledano, *J. Edgar Hoover: The Man in His Time* (New Rochelle, N.Y.: Arlington House, 1973), p. 308, says it is a fabrication.

76. Guthman, *We Band of Brothers,* p. 266; Hoover to Robert Kennedy, Jan. 9, 1964; Robert Kennedy to Hoover, May 12, 1964, Robert Kennedy note on Hoover to Robert Kennedy, May 13, 1964, General Correspondence, Hoover, J. Edgar, Personal Papers of Robert Kennedy, JFKL.

77. Schlesinger, *RFK,* pp. 629–630; Guthman, *We Band of Brothers,* p. 658.

Chapter 12: LBJ's FBI

(*pp. 393–438*)

1. Ovid Demaris, *The Director: An Oral Biography of J. Edgar Hoover* (New York: Harpers Magazine Press, 1975), p. 232. When Demaris asked Ramsey Clark about this statement by Johnson, Clark said he doubted if Johnson had said it, or, if he had said it, that he meant it: "I think he kind of enjoyed having him around. He was always extremely cordial to Mr. Hoover, always anxious to have him involved."

2. Hoover to Johnson, Mar. 15, 1964, FG 135–6, WHCF; Hoover to Johnson, May 10, 1966, Name File: Hoover, J. Edgar, WHCF, LBJL.

3. *Nation's Business,* Jan. 1972.

4. Demaris, *The Director,* p. 232. For the story of Hoover's visit in 1959 to the LBJ ranch, see Joseph Schott, *No Left Turns* (New York: Praeger, 1975), pp. 172, 1984; see letter of thanks from Hoover to Johnson, Nov. 10, 1959, LBJ Famous Names Box J. Edgar Hoover, WHCF, LBJL. For friendly correspondence between Hoover and Johnson, see Johnson to Hoover, May 6, 1958, LBJ Famous Names Box J. Edgar Hoover. Compare the warm tone of the LBJ letters to the correct but perhaps condescending JFK correspondence, JFK to Hoover, June 9, 1962, and Sept. 26, 1962, Name File: Hoover, J. Edgar, WHCF, JFKL.

5. Hoover, "Off the record remarks," informal reception for editors of Georgia and Michigan newspapers, Apr. 15, 1965, OCPA. Hoover was criticizing the Warren Commission's recommendations for improving the protection of the president.

6. Tucker to Johnson, Oct. 12, 1966; Morrison to Clinton, July 23, 1965; Russell Kirk column, Dec. 12, 1964; Burford to Johnson, Dec. 16, 1964, Name File: Hoover, J. Edgar, WHCF, LBJL.

7. LBJ Phone Diary, LBJL; Sanford J. Ungar, *FBI* (Boston: Atlantic Monthly Press, 1976), p. 292.

8. Callahan to Mohr, Feb. 18, 1959, FBI File 67–561–?, Hoover Personnel File, FBI. For instances of Bureau sensitivity to the age issue, see reaction to a critical "Man in the Street" interview about the reappointment, Jones to DeLoach, May 14, 1964, FBI File 67–561–356, Hoover Personnel File, FBI.

9. Executive Order 11154, May 8, 1965, in Ralph de Toledano, *J. Edgar Hoover: The Man in His Time* (New Rochelle, N.Y.: Arlington House, 1973), p. 301. Also see Tolson to LBJ, May 18, 1964, Name File: DeLoach, Cartha D., WHCF, LBJL, thanking the president for a picture of the ceremony.

10. Manuscript, Robert Spivack, "Watch on the Potomac," Dec. 14, 1966, and H. H. Wilson to the President, Dec. 13, 1966, EX JL, Dec. 12, 1963–July 31, 1967, WHCF, LBJL.

11. Arthur M. Schlesinger, *Robert Kennedy and His Times* (Boston: Houghton, Mifflin, 1978), p. 260 (hereafter referred to as *RFK*), citing interviews of RFK by Anthony Lewis and John Bartlow Martin at the Oral History Program, JFKL.

12. Ungar, *FBI,* p. 282. DeLoach arranged for Walter Trohan to speak at the American Legion convention, and wrote a speech for him (DeLoach to Trohan, Sept. 14, 1964, DeLoach, Trohan Papers, HHL). See also James to LBJ, Feb. 22, 1966, Diary Back-up, LBJL.

13. Schlesinger, *RFK,* pp. 663–664; Ungar, *FBI,* p. 288; Staff Report: Political Abuse and the FBI," DeLoach to Jenkins, Aug. 25, 1964, and DeLoach to Mohr, Aug. 29, 1964, "Morning Summary of Activities, Democratic National Convention," Senate Select Committee, *Hearings,* Vol. 6, FBI, pp. 476, 623–637, 714–717; DeLoach to Moyers, Sept. 14, 1964, Name File: DeLoach, Cartha D., WHCF, LBJL.

14. Statement of the President, Oct. 15, 1964, Jenkins File, LBJL; William C. Sullivan, *The Bureau* (New York: Norton, 1979), pp. 68–70; Ungar, *FBI,* p. 291; "Addendum to Staff Report on Political Abuse and the FBI: The Johnson Administration and Mrs. Anna Chennault," Senate Select Committee, *Hearings,* Vol. 6, FBI, pp. 483–484.

15. Hoover to Watson, Sept. 15, 1965, Hoover, J. Edgar, Macy Papers, LBJL.

16. Richard Harris, *Justice: the Crisis of Law, Order, and Freedom in America* (New York: Avon, 1970; first published in 1969), p. 53.

17. "Daniel J. Freed, "Proposed District of Columbia Crime Control Program," Oct. 12, 1967; see [H. Rowan] Gaither: Crime-General, and Crime General—Juvenile Delinquency, Presidential Task Forces, Gaither Papers, LBJL.

18. Harris, *Justice,* p. 56. Nicholas Katzenbach later said that one of the reasons he left the Justice Department was that he found it so unpleasant working with Hoover (Senate Select Committee, *Hearings,* Vol. 6, FBI, p. 202).

19. Hoover, speech to former special agents of the FBI, Sept. 28, 1967, p. 4, OCPA.

20. John T. Elliff, *Crime, Justice, and the Attorney General: The Justice Department in the 1960s* (Beverly Hills, Calif.: Sage, 1971), p. 122.

21. See Watson to LBJ, Nov. 30, 1965, JL, WHCF; "Wiretaps," Administrative History, Department of Justice, Vol. III, LBJL; "Warrantless FBI Electronic Surveillance," Senate Select Committee, *Final Report,* Book III, pp. 271–351, esp. 285, 310; Pub Law 90–351, June 1968. Hoover to Katzenbach, Sept. 14, 1965, Senate Select Committee, *Final Report,* Book III, p. 287; Athan Theoharis, *Spying on Americans* (Philadelphia: Temple, University Press, 1978), pp. 113. In 1964, Hoover also ended mail covers and trash covers) (Robert Justin Goldstein, *Political Repression in Modern America* (Cambridge, Mass.: Schenkman/Two Continents, 1978], p. 443). Johnson's order banning wiretaps was drafted by Katzenbach on April 8, 1965, to take effect July 1 (White to Moyers, Apr. 10, 1965; Katzenbach to LBJ, Apr. 8, 1965; Busby to Moyers, Apr. 20, 1965, Justice Department, Moyers File, LBJL). Hoover ended mail covers on September 29, 1965; he ended surreptitious entries on July 19, 1966 (Sullivan to DeLoach, July 19, 1966, p. 3, Senate Select Committee, *Final Report,* Book III, p. 365).

22. Belmont to Tolson, Feb. 27, 1965, Senate Select Committee, *Final Report,* Book III, p. 670.

23. Statement in early 1964 before House Appropriations Committee, opposing FBI takeover of Federal narcotics enforcement, cited in Ungar, *FBI,* p. 421.

24. Hoover, "Faith, Freedom and Law," speech to Michigan State Bar Association, June 8, 1967, OCPA; "Off the record remarks."

25. Hoover, "Faith, Freedom and Law."

26. Hoover, "Off the record remarks."

27. Elliff, *Crime, Justice, and the Attorney General,* p. 38.

28. Hoover, "Off the record remarks"; speech to former special agents of the FBI, Sept. 28, 1967.

29. Hoover, "Time for Decision," "Sword of Loyola" Award Dinner, Chicago, Nov. 24, 1964.

30. Hoover to Tolson et al., Aug. 19, 1966, FBI File 67–9524–?, Tolson Personnel File, FBI.

31. Hoover, "Our Heritage of Greatness," Dec. 12, 1964, speech to the Pennsylvania Society, OCPA.

32. Hoover, "Faith, Freedom and Law," "Off the record remarks."

33. Eric Goldman, *The Tragedy of Lyndon Johnson* (New York: Knopf, 1969), p. 499.

34. John Doar and Dorothy Landsberg, *Performance of the FBI in Investigating Violations of Federal Laws Protecting the Right to Vote—1960–1967,* in Senate Select Committee, *Hearings,* Vol. 6, FBI, p. 950; interview, Ramsey Clark, ca. 1975, in Demaris, *The Director,* p. 232.

35. Hoover to Jenkins, July 17, 1964, FG 135–6, WHCF, LBJL.

36. LBJ to Hoover, July 13, 1964, Name File: Hoover, J. Edgar, WHCF, LBJL.

37. Statement by the President, Mar. 26, 1965, Appointment File Backup, LBJL. See also Hoover to Tolson, Mar. 26, 1965, FBI File 67–9524–?, Tolson Personnel File, FBI, in which Hoover told Katzenbach that he had had an informant in the murder car, had the houses of the suspects under surveillance, and wanted to move fast so they didn't get away. Sullivan was in Selma directing the investigation.

38. Hoover to Tolson et al., Mar. 26, 1965, FBI File 67–9524–?, Tolson Personnel File, FBI.

39. Hoover, "Off the record remarks."

40. Ibid.; phone conversation with Birch Bayh; Hoover to Tolson et al., July 6, 1966, FBI File 67–9524–?, Tolson Personnel File, FBI.

41. Hoover, "Our Heritage of Greatness," "Time for Decision."

42. Hoover, "Our Heritage of Greatness."

43. Doar and Landsberg, *Performance of the FBI,* Senate Select Committee, *Hearings,* Vol. 6, FBI, p. 936.

44. Senate Select Committee, *Final Report,* Book III, p. 27.

45. Doar and Landsberg, *Performance of the FBI,* in Senate Select Committee, *Hearings,* Vol. 6, FBI, p. 985. See also Senate Select Committee, *Final Report,* Book III, pp. 471–475.

46. Senate Select Committee, *Final Report,* Book III, p. 471; *Hearings,* Vol. 6, FBI, p. 378. Goldstein, *Political Repression in Modern America,* p. 445.

47. George C. Moore testimony, Nov. 3, 1975, p. 31, Senate Select Committee, *Final Report,* Book III, pp. 18, 19; Katzenbach testimony, *Hearings,* Vol. 6, FBI, p. 219; Hoover, "Off-the-record remarks."

48. Hoover to SACs, Sept. 2, 1964, and Oct. 12, 1964, Senate Select Committee, *Hearings,* Vol. 6, FBI, pp. 377–382.

49. Baumgardner to Sullivan, Sept. 16, 1963. This intensification was announced to the field in an October 1, 1963, memorandum (Hoover to SACs, Oct. 1, 1963). See also Sullivan to Belmont, Dec. 24, 1963, and Hoover to Atlanta Field Office, Apr. 1, 1964, Senate Select Committee, *Final Report,* Book III, pp. 108, 111, 134.

50. Hoover note on UPI Press Release, Dec. 29, 1963; Sullivan to Belmont, Jan. 8, 1964, Senate Select Committee, *Final Report,* Book III, pp. 135, 136. See also David Garrow for a thorough discussion of these FBI

plots: *The FBI and Martin Luther King, Jr.: From "Solo" to Memphis* (New York: Norton, 1981), pp. 101–150, esp. 106.

51. Hoover to SAC, Atlanta, Aug. 28, 1964, and Hoover, FBI memo, Aug. 28, 1964, Senate Select Committee, *Final Report*, Book III, pp. 138, 139.

52. Garrow, *The FBI and Martin Luther King, Jr.*, pp. 107–109.

53. Ibid., p. 114.

54. Baumgartner to Sullivan, Aug. 31, 1964; Hoover's note on UPI Release, Sept. 8, 1964; and *New York Herald Tribune*, Sept. 19, 1964, in Senate Select Committee, *Final Report*, Book III, p. 143. For a full description of the Hoover-Spellman relationship, see John Cooney, *The American Pope* (New York: Times Books, 1984). The two men were strikingly similar in age, appearance, political and religious beliefs, organizational skills, closeness to their mothers, even in the persisting rumors of their homosexuality.

55. DeLoach memo, Nov. 18, 1964; DeLoach testimony, Nov. 25, 1975; Senate Select Committee, *Final Report*, Book III, p. 157.

56. Interview, Cartha DeLoach, Mar. 10, 1975.

57. *New York Times*, Nov. 11, 1964, in Senate Select Committee, *Final Report*, Book III, p. 157.

58. Hoover notes on Rosen to Belmont, Nov. 20, 1964, Senate Select Committee, *Final Report*, Book III, p. 158.

59. A copy was found in Sullivan's files after he left the Bureau. Sullivan later said he could not recall ever having seen the letter, but that it was "possible" he had something to do with it, but could not remember (Senate Select Committee, *Final Report*, Book III, p. 160).

60. Senate Select Committee, *Final Report*, Book III, p. 152. Arthur Schlesinger's comment was that "Hoover seems to have taken leave of his sense that November" (Schlesinger, *RFK*, p. 364).

61. Senate Select Committee, *Final Report*, Book III, pp. 165–167; Hoover, "Off the record remarks."

62. For one such poll, see *Washington Post*, Feb. 17, 1965, for a Harris Poll that showed 50 percent of respondents backing Hoover, only 16 percent King. The poll concluded that "Hoover is, in the estimate of most people, what he has been for at least a generation: a powerful symbol of law and order, a pillar of security in an uncertain nation and world" (FBI File 67–561–?, Hoover Personnel File, FBI). For White House mail on affair, Hopkins to White, Nov. 27, 1964, FG 135–6, WHCF, LBJL.

63. Interview, Ramsey Clark in Demaris, *The Director*, p. 230.

64. Hoover to Jenkins, Sept. 25, 1964, and Moyers to Valenti, Sept. 26, 1964, Crime and Delinquency, Moyers Papers, LBJL; Senate Select Committee, *Final Report*, Book III, p. 475.

65. Hoover to Tolson, et al., July 25, 1967, FBI File 67–9524, Tolson Personnel File.

66. Hoover to Tolson et al., July 25, 1967, July 26, 1967, and Hoover,

Memorandum for Personal Files, July 31, 1967, FBI File 67–9524, Tolson Personnel File.

67. Senate Select Committee, *Final Report,* Book III, pp. 492–493; Goldstein, *Political Repression in Modern America,* p. 450.

68. Senate Select Committee, *Final Report,* Book III, p. 179.

69. Hoover to SAC, Albany, Aug. 25, 1967, Senate Select Committee, *Hearings,* Vol. 6, FBI, p. 383; Senate Select Committee, *Final Report,* Book III, pp. 3, 20, 21, 180.

70. Hoover to SACs, Mar. 4, 1968, Senate Select Committee, *Final Report, Book III,* p. 180; Senate Select Committee, *Hearings,* Vol. 6, FBI, pp. 387–390.

71. Senate Select Committee, *Final Report,* Book III, p. 189.

72. Hoover, "Turbulence on Campus," *PTA Magazine,* Feb 1966, p. 4.

73. Hoover memo, Apr. 28, 1965, Senate Select Committee, *Final Report,* Book III, p. 485.

74. Ibid.; Goldstein, *Political Repression in Modern America,* p. 449. The resulting intelligence gathering effort was called the VIDEM (Vietnam Demonstration) program, and it disseminated intelligence about demonstrations to the White House and other interested government agencies (SAC letter, Mar. 26, 1968, Senate Select Committee, *Final Report,* Book III, pp. 488, 491).

75. Goldstein, *Political Repression in Modern America,* p. 430. See also *FBI Director's Report,* 1968, p. 56, FBI Narrative History, Documentary Supplement, LBJL.

76. Hoover, "Turbulence on Campus"; Goldstein, *Political Repression in Modern America,* p. 438.

77. Senate Select Committee, *Final Report,* Book III, p. 489; Goldman, *The Tragedy of Lyndon Johnson,* p. 500.

78. The Bureau also continued its practice of placing material in the hands of friendly journalists, such as Walter Trohan of the *Chicago Tribune,* to "expose" Communist influence in the antiwar movement (Goldstein, *Political Repression in Modern America,* p. 438). See also DeLoach to LBJ, July 10, 1967, FG 135–6, WHCF, LBJL; Hoover, statement to House Appropriations Committee, 1967, p. 93, FBI Narrative History, Documentary Supplement, LBJL.

79. Senate Select Committee, *Final Report,* Book III, p. 519; Goldstein, *Political Repression in Modern America,* p. 458.

80. Goldstein, *Political Repression in Modern America,* p. 449.

81. Charles D. Brennan testimony, Sept. 25, 1975, Senate Select Committee, *Final Report,* Book III, p. 524.

82. Ibid., p. 525.

83. Brennan to Sullivan, May 9, 1968, Senate Select Committee, *Final Report,* Book III, p. 24.

84. SAC letter, May 21, 1968, Senate Select Committee, *Final Report,* Book III, p. 506.

85. SAC letter, Apr. 2, 1968, Senate Select Committee, *Final Report, Book III*, pp. 26, 507.

86. Headquarters to SACs, May 23, 1968, and July 6, 1968, Senate Select Committee, *Final Report, Book III*, pp. 24, 26.

87. Senate Select Committee, *Final Report, Book III*, p. 511; Goldstein, *Political Repression in Modern America*, pp. 452–453; Senate Select Committee, *Hearings*, Vol. 6, FBI, p. 371, for examples of COINTELPRO—New Left operations, see pp. 812–813; Senate Select Committee, *Final Report, Book II*, pp. 88–89.

88. For these and other examples see Frank J. Donner, *The Age of Surveillance* (New York: Knopf, 1980), pp. 432–440.

89. Garrow and Donner both argue that throughout his career Hoover's basic motivation was resistance to cultural change, and that it was the threat to traditional culture represented by King and by radicals that provoked him to action. In the opinion of Felt, DeLoach, and John Mohr, the COINTELPRO operations were strictly Sullivan programs. Mohr said COINTELPRO "was Sullivan, that was engineered by Sullivan. He was behind most of that. . . . Principally, it was intelligence gathering, but it also included harassment." Sullivan had no particular apologies to make: "I think it was a fine program. I can't understand all the damn misinformation that's been put out about it. . . . [T]he essence of it is this: Are you going to spend millions of taxpayer dollars going around ringing doorbells and asking questions of people who know nothing, or are you going to very systematically and very carefully penetrate these organizations like the Ku Klux Klan and the Black Panthers and disrupt them from within at a cost of almost nothing, and that's precisely what we did, we disrupted them. . . . It's a rough, tough business." According to Sullivan's chief deputy, the "acquiescence" of Hoover and the Executive Conference was "grudging" (Demaris, *The Director*, p. 325; Brennan testimony, Senate Select Committee, *Final Report, Book III*, pp. 527–528.)

But even if Sullivan was the motivating force behind the COINTELPROs (and there is no question about that), it is also true that Hoover supervised these operations very closely, not only approving them in broad outline, but insisting on personal supervision over individual harassment operations. Hoover was not Sullivan's creature; Sullivan was his.

After Sullivan left the Bureau under fire in 1971, his stability deteriorated, and he alternated between defending the COINTELPRO operations as patriotic triumph (although sometimes he claimed that pressure from agents in the field forced him to create the program), and blaming COINTELPRO on an evil and malevolent Hoover. Sullivan is, moreover, the sole source for some of the most damning accusations of Hoover as a vulgar racial bigot (calling Martin Luther King, Jr., a "burrhead"), an anti-Semite, even a voyeur obsessed by the sex lives of his enemies. But despite the quotability of Sullivan's opinions, his reliability is open to question. Sullivan often claims knowledge about events when he was not present, while it is not hard to catch him in factual errors even when he was an eyewitness (see a story Sullivan told one way in his *The Bureau,* p. 116, and another way in an interview in Demaris, *The Director,* p. 236).

90. Hoover to LBJ, Apr. 1, 1968, Name File, Hoover, J. Edgar, LBJL.

91. Hoover to Tolson et al., June 20, 1968, FBI File 65–9524–?, Tolson Personnel File, FBI.

92. *FBI Law Enforcement Bulletin,* Aug. 1968, FG 135–6, WHCF, LBJL.

93. Davidson to Callahan, July 23, 1962, FBI File 67–9524–392; DeLoach to Mohr, Mar. 1, 1965, FBI File 67–9524–461; in his approaches to John Macy, head of Civil Service Commission, DeLoach implied that the only reason Tolson had not gotten it before was because of Kennedy's prejudice against Hoover. (See also Hoover to LBJ, June 2, 1965, FG 135–6, WHCF, LBJL.

94. Hoover O&C File, #6, FBI; interview, Efrem Zimbalist, Jr., in Demaris, *The Director,* p. 71; Richard Gid Powers, *G-Men: Hoover's FBI in American Popular Culture* (Carbondale, Ill.: Southern Illinois, 1983), pp. 245, 246.

95. Interview, Ramsey Clark, in Demaris, *The Director,* p. 238.

Chapter 13: The Nixon Years
(*pp. 439–485*)

1. At a briefing on December 12, 1968 (Richard Nixon, *The Memoirs of Richard Nixon* [New York: Grosset & Dunlap, 1978], p. 358).

2. John Ehrlichman, *Witness to Power* (New York: Simon and Schuster, 1982), p. 156.

3. According to Nixon, the help was from a "lower-level agent," but it is known that Louis Nichols handled the contacts (Nixon, *Memoirs,* p. 58).

4. Ehrlichman, *Witness to Power,* pp. 156, 157, 163.

5. Ibid., p. 168.

6. FBI executive John Mohr called the situation under Nixon "weird because, actually, I think that of all the presidents that he served under, Hoover was closer to Nixon than any other one, yet there were more people in the White House that were out gunning for Hoover than in any other administration that I can remember" (interview, John Mohr, in Ovid Demaris, *The Director: An Oral Biography of J. Edgar Hoover* [New York: Harpers Magazine Press, 1975], p. 307). According to Ehrlichman, "as far as Nixon was concerned, his grant of direct Presidential access to Hoover was symbolic. It bestowed on Hoover the access the Kennedys had denied him. But once the gesture had been made, it became Bob Haldeman's assignment to create a process to protect Nixon from Hoover exercising that power" (Ehrlichman, *Witness to Power,* p. 157).

7. Ehrlichman, *Witness to Power,* p. 159.

8. Ibid., p. 156.

9. Ibid., p. 158.

10. For a neighbor's reaction, and the anecdote about photographing the layout of Hoover's pictures, see *Washington Sunday Star*, May 7, 1972, in U.S. Senate, *Memorial Tributes to J. Edgar Hoover in the Congress of the United States and Various Articles and Editorials Relating to His Life and Work*, 94th Cong., 2nd sess., 1974, p. 229.

11. Ehrlichman, *Witness to Power*, p. 160; Demaris, *The Director*, p. 42.

12. Ehrlichman, *Witness to Power*, pp. 160, 161.

13. Ibid., p. 160.

14. Theodore White, *Breach of Faith: The Fall of Richard Nixon* (New York: Atheneum, 1975), p. 97. Nixon did criticize Hoover to his aides for his growing timidity and excessive caution (Ehrlichman, *Witness to Power*, p. 164).

15. That is Tom Charles Huston's theory, paraphrased in Demaris, *The Director*, p. 251.

16. December 12, 1968 briefing, Nixon, *Memoirs*, p. 358. In its dependence on secrecy, American policy in Asia under Nixon and Johnson betrayed its origins in the reliance of the Eisenhower and Kennedy administrations on secret counterinsurgency rather than conventional warfare as an instrument of foreign policy. Secrecy was, says Tad Szulc, "one of Nixon's principal instruments in the evolution and conduct of America's foreign affairs" (Szulc, *The Illusion of Peace* [New York: Viking, 1978], p. 803).

17. White, *Breach of Faith*, p. 78; Nixon, *Memoirs*, p. 366.

18. Theodore White says Nixon learned, at the beginning of his career, that there were buttons that could be pushed to set off public reactions. "You won by attack—you picked a nameless few and frightened the voters; or you picked a well-known name and dissected it and pinned a catch-tag on it" (White, *Breach of Faith*, pp. 62–63).

19. Presidential Counselor Daniel Patrick Moynihan told Nixon the late sixties were like the Weimar Republic in Germany when the inability of the Weimar liberals to put down disorders had paved the way for Hitler. "Your task is clear," Moynihan told Nixon, "to restore the authority of American institutions." But Nixon hardly needed Moynihan to tell him that (Dan Rather and Gary Paul Gates, *The Palace Guard* [New York: Warner, 1975], p. 93).

20. Nixon, *Memoirs*, p. 386.

21. Ibid., p. 387. Nixon's assertion that wiretapping was urged on him by Hoover has to be taken with a grain of salt in light of Hoover's subsequent near-panic over their danger.

22. Ibid., p. 388.

23. Hoover to Tolson, DeLoach, Sullivan, and Bishop, May 9, 1969 (three memos), and Kissinger testimony in *Halperin* v. *Kissinger*, Civ. No.

1187–73 (D.D.C.), Jan. 12, 1976, p. 18, in Senate Select Committee, *Final Report,* Book III, p. 324; Nixon, *Memoirs,* p. 388; Demaris, *The Director,* p. 252.

24. The *"Keith"* decision was *U.S.* v. *U.S. District Court,* 407 U.S. 297 (1972). The memos from Hoover to Mitchell requesting authority, bearing Mitchell's signature, are in House Select Committee, *Hearings,* Part 3, pp. 1208–1220. Mitchell later denied having signed the memos, but offered no convincing alternative explanation for the existence of the signed authorizations.

25. Haig deposition, *Halperin* v. *Kissinger,* Civ. No. 1187–73 (D.D.C.), Oct. 25, 1974, pp. 9–10, in Senate Select Committee, *Final Report,* Book III, p. 325.

26. Mark Felt, *The FBI Pyramid: From the Inside* (New York: Putnam's, 1979), pp. 143, 144; Demaris, *The Director,* p. 260.

27. "Unfortunately none of these wiretaps turned up any proof linking anyone in the government to a specific national security leak" (Nixon, *Memoirs,* p. 389); Senate Select Committee, *Final Report,* Book III, pp. 323, 336.

28. White, *Breach of Faith,* pp. 128, 129. This account follows White, pp. 129–132. Notes on Nixon's talks with students are in Nixon, *Memoirs,* p. 464.

29. J. Edgar Hoover, "Modern Day Campus Attilas or the SDS in Action," *Phi Kappa Epsilon,* Spring 1970, p. 46.

30. Ibid., pp. 42, 46; One example of how Hoover burned himself by attacking students in his late years was his "The SDS and the High Schools, a Study in Student Extremism," *The PTA Magazine,* Jan., Feb., Mar., 1970. The March issue has the readers' replies.

31. Hoover to Tolson et al., May 11, 1970; phone conversation with Egil Krogh, May 11, 1970, FBI File 67–9524, Tolson Personnel File, FBI; Hoover to Tolson et al., May 11, 1970, FBI File 44–54339, Kent State File, FBI.

32. Hoover to Helms, Mar. 31, 1970, Senate Select Committee, *Hearings,* Vol. 2, Huston Plan, pp. 354–356.

33. Nixon, *Memoirs,* p. 471.

34. Ibid., p. 472.

35. Ibid., p. 471. For an account of the disagreement with the CIA that led to the end of formal liaison between the two agencies (the Riha case, Feb. 26, 1970), see Felt, *The FBI Pyramid,* pp. 78–79.

36. White, *Breach of Faith,* p. 133; Athan Theoharis, *Spying on Americans* (Philadelphia: Temple University Press, 1978), pp. 16–17; Nixon, *Memoirs,* p. 473.

37. See the description of the meeting and Bennett's remarks to the committee staff in Senate Select Committee, *Final Report,* Book III, p. 937. Sullivan says that after the meeting Hoover was "visibly upset" and called

him into his office. "I've just returned from the White House," he said. "They don't like our performance, our intelligence operation. On top of that," he went on, "all the heads of the intelligence community were there . . . Richard Helms, Admiral Gayler, and the others." Hoover was really depressed as he continued, "They're making up a committee of the heads of the different intelligence agencies and they're going to make me the chairman" (William C. Sullivan, *The Bureau: My Thirty Years in Hoover's FBI* [New York: Norton, 1979], p. 209).

38. Sullivan, *The Bureau,* pp. 204, 206. Felt also believed Hoover's curtailment of surveillance techniques was the origin of his feud with Sullivan (Felt, *The FBI Pyramid,* pp. 106, 112). According to his colleagues, Sullivan was "genuinely concerned that the FBI was not doing enough to combat and disrupt the violence-oriented segments of the New Left. He sincerely believed that the restrictions placed on him by Hoover impaired the Bureau's ability to protect the citizens of the United States." He would go to fellow executive Mark Felt and say, "The Boss is wrong!" Assistant to the Director John Mohr also thought "the Huston plan evolved as a result of Hoover discontinuing what we call 'dirty tricks' stuff. Sullivan always thought that Hoover was wrong in doing that. Personally, I thought Hoover was right, that the time had come when the American people just wouldn't put up with that stuff, and as it turned out, Hoover was right. . . . He didn't want to be identified with this stuff [the Huston plan]" (interview, John Mohr, in Demaris, *The Director,* p. 310; Felt, *The FBI Pyramid,* p. 114).

39. Sullivan, *The Bureau,* p. 211.

40. Demaris, *The Director,* p. 294. The reference to the Palmer raids is from Demaris's Mohr interview, p. 314.

41. This follows the account of the Church Committee staff, and Hoover's reaction is related by Sullivan, who, by the time he testified before the Church Committee (November 1, 1975), was trying to discredit Hoover (Senate Select Committee, *Final Report,* Book III, p. 942).

42. The document is reproduced in Senate Select Committee, *Hearings,* Vol. 2, Huston Plan, pp. 141–188.

43. Willard and Sullivan interviews, in Senate Select Committee, *Final Report,* Book III, p. 944, 945; Sullivan, *The FBI Pyramid,* p. 214.

44. Huston to Haldeman, July 1970, Senate Select Committee, *Hearings,* Vol. 2, Huston Plan, p. 189.

45. Nixon, *Memoirs,* p. 474; Haldeman to Huston, July 14, 1970, Senate Select Committee, *Hearings,* Vol. 2, Huston Plan, p. 198.

46. Senate Select Committee, *Final Report,* Book III, p. 956.

47. Sullivan says when Hoover learned Nixon had approved the plan in spite of his objections, he "went through the ceiling." "That hippie [his nickname for the somewhat long-haired Huston] is behind this," he began. "Well, they're not going to put the responsibility on me. . . . and I just won't take it any more. I'll only accept the recommendations outlined in this draft

if the President orders me to. And I'll only carry them out if someone else—the President, the attorney general—takes the responsibility" (Senate Select Committee, *Final Report,* Book III, p. 956; Sullivan, *The Bureau,* p. 211; interview, William Sullivan, in Demaris, *The Director,* p. 312). Arthur M. Schlesinger, Jr., *Imperial Presidency* (Boston: Houghton Mifflin, 1973), p. 274: "It may well be that he did not care all that much about civil liberties, but he did care supremely about the professional reputation of the FBI." Sullivan thought Hoover's real objection was the degree of interagency cooperation the plan envisioned, and the call for periodic review of intelligence operations (Sullivan, *The Bureau,* p. 212).

48. Hoover told Mitchell that "despite my clear-cut and specific opposition to the lifting of the various investigative restraints referred to above and to the creation of a permanent interagency committee on domestic intelligence, the FBI is prepared to implement the instructions of the White House at your direction. Of course we would continue to seek your [Mitchell's] specific authorization, where appropriate, to utilize the various sensitive investigative techniques involved in individual cases" (Hoover to Mitchell, July 25, 1970, Senate Select Committee, *Final Report,* Book III, p. 957).

49. Senate Select Committee, *Final Report,* Book III, p. 956; Nixon, *Memoirs,* pp. 474–475.

50. Huston's complaints are in his memo to Haldeman, Aug. 5, 1970, Senate Select Committee, *Hearings,* Vol. 2, Huston Plan, pp. 249–253. After the demise of the Huston Plan, Hoover continued to fight efforts to revive the discarded techniques. He told Gayler and Helms that he was "not at all enthusiastic" about resuming mail covers. All that remained of the Huston plan was a powerless Intelligence Evaluation Committee with Hoover at its head, which John Dean said he had to represent as meaningless to Hoover and Mitchell, and significant to Haldeman and Ehrlichman. On February 3, 1971, Hoover notified Mitchell that he would not even lend the single agent to the Intelligence Evaluation Committee that John Dean had recommended. "Although we are unable to provide any personnel support," he said scornfully, "you may be assured of our continuing full cooperation" (Hoover, Memo for Files, Apr. 12, 1971, Senate Select Committee, *Final Report,* Book III, p. 978).

51. See "King," Hoover O&C File 23, for an effort to persuade Sen. Scott not to honor King, May 22, 1968; Hoover to Tolson et al., June 19, 1969, FBI File 67–9524, Tolson Personnel File. The Panther Directives were Nov. 25, 1968, and Jan. 30, 1969 (Senate Select Committee, *Final Report,* Book III, p. 22). See also Sanford J. Ungar, *FBI* (Boston: Atlantic Monthly Press, 1975), p. 465.

52. Ungar, *FBI,* p. 466: "It is fair to say that the FBI was shopping around for a law enforcement unit that was willing to conduct a raid that it, the Bureau, wanted to see carried out, but had no legal pretext for staging on its own.

53. Ehrlichman, *Witness to Power,* p. 164. For a thorough account of

the Seberg case, see David Richards, *Played Out: The Jean Seberg Story* (New York: Playboy, 1981).

54. Richards, *Played Out,* p. 237.

55. Ibid., p. 238.

56. It has not been established whether the source of Haber's article was in fact the Bureau, but it seems very likely. See Richards, *Played Out,* p. 240.

57. Attachment to William Sullivan memorandum to Cartha DeLoach, June 6, 1970, Senate Select Committee, *Hearings,* Vol. 2, Huston Plan, Exhibit 9, quoted in Senate Select Committee, *Final Report,* Book III, p. 939.

58. Interviews, Mark Felt and John Mohr, in Demaris, *The Director,* p. 314. See also Felt, *The FBI Pyramid,* pp. 116–117.

59. Headquarters to SACs, May 23, 1968, and July 6, 1968, Senate Select Committee, *Final Report,* Book III, pp. 24, 26.

60. Sullivan, *The Bureau,* pp. 148, 266.

61. There is some confusion as to when Sullivan actually assumed his new position. Sullivan later said he replaced DeLoach in June, but DeLoach was still active in the fight against the Huston plan at the Bureau in July. For memos showing how Sullivan protected himself with both sides by posing as promoter or foe of the plan depending on the audience, see Senate Select Committee, *Final Report,* Book III, pp. 965–966.

62. Demaris, *The Director,* pp. 274, 327; Sullivan, *The Bureau,* p. 203. The speculation about Hoover's motives in promoting Sullivan is my own.

63. Felt *The FBI Pyramid,* p. 93.

64. Ungar, *FBI,* p. 139.

65. Felt, *The FBI Pyramid,* pp. 88, 98.

66. Theoharis, *Spying on Americans,* pp. 149, 152.

67. Hoover to Tolson et al., Apr. 6, 1971 (five memos) record phone calls from Kleindienst, Hugh Scott, and Haldeman. Edmund Muskie and Gaylord Nelson of Wisconsin denounced Hoover for having FBI agents at Earth Day activities. Muskie charged that there were some forty to sixty reports covering Earth Day demonstrations. Hoover said fifty offices did report on fifty-seven rallies; however, in all but four cases the FBI simply picked up information from outside sources and passed it to Washington (Hoover to Tolson et al., Apr. 15, 1971, all FBI File 67–9524, Tolson Personnel File, FBI). Nelson called for a special committee to investigate the FBI (the motion died, and was reintroduced in 1973, 1974, and 1975; the Senate Select Committee was finally established in May 1976).

68. Hoover to Tolson et al., Apr. 28, 1971, FBI File 67–9524, Tolson Personnel File; Pat Gillers and Stephen Watters, *Investigating the FBI* (Garden City: Doubleday, 1973), pp. 474–475.

69. Theoharis, *Spying on Americans,* p. 150.

70. Felt, *The FBI Pyramid,* p. 130; interview, John Mohr, in Demaris, *The Director,* p. 222; Sullivan, *The FBI Pyramid,* p. 203.

71. Felt, *The FBI Pyramid,* p. 88; Jack Nelson and Ronald J. Ostrow,

The FBI and the Berrigans (New York: Coward, McCann, 1972), pp. 19–20.

72. Sullivan, *The Bureau,* p. 154.

73. Hoover to Tolson et al., Apr. 5, 1971, FBI File 67–9524, Tolson Personnel File, FBI.

74. Nixon, *Memoirs,* pp. 508, 513.

75. Felt, *The FBI Pyramid,* p. 131.

76. Sullivan to Hoover, June 7, 1971, and Beaver to Hoover, June 18, 1971, Senate Select Committee, *Final Report,* Book III, p. 540; Felt, *The FBI Pyramid,* p. 132.

77. Nixon, *Memoirs,* p. 513.

78. Ibid., p. 514.

79. Ibid., p. 513. According to Ehrlichman, "the administration would have been far better off if Mr. Hoover had been retired earlier, predating this episode, because many, many of the problems that we encountered were as a result of Mr. Hoover's very fixed views, very sincere. He was alert and he was sincere, he was patriotic, but he was certainly fixed in his views, and it made operation very, very difficult. Now, when you run across a situation where you have a retirement of that kind that is politically sensitive and difficult, sometimes the decision is made to postpone the retirement, and when that happens, then you simply have to find other ways of doing things" (quoted in Demaris, *The Director,* p. 304). A member of the Watergate Committee, Senator Lowell Weicker, concluded that Hoover was slated for removal because "both the White House and elements within his own Bureau, specifically William Sullivan, obviously didn't think that he was the most cooperative person in the world in going along with the rather unconstitutional methods and procedures which they advocated. They didn't think he was tough enough for what they wanted to do" (Lowell Weicker, quoted in Demaris, *The Director,* p. 305). On the burglary of the psychiatrist's office, see interview, John Mohr, in Demaris, *The Director,* p. 307, and Nixon, *Memoirs,* p. 514.

80. Felt, *The FBI Pyramid,* p. 133.

81. Interview, Mark Felt, in Demaris, *The Director,* p. 271; Executives Conference Memorandum, June 2, 1971, Senate Select Committee, *Final Report,* Book III, p. 539.

82. Nixon, *Memoirs,* p. 596. In *The Director* (p. 260), Demaris mentions Mitchell's testimony that Hoover had opposed placing and continuing these taps (John Dean agrees), and that Sullivan at this time was "a little nuts." The real danger to the administration here was that Ellsberg had "walked in" on the Halperin wiretap and this would endanger the trial of Ellsberg if it became known.

83. See Sullivan, *The Bureau,* p. 244; Felt, *The FBI Pyramid,* pp. 138, 140.

84. Felt, *The FBI Pyramid,* pp. 1, 140.

85. Felt, *The FBI Pyramid,* p. 142. In 1972, after Hoover's death, Sullivan was brought back to the Justice Department to run the Office of National Narcotics Intelligence, and he annoyed the Bureau by hiring some renegade agents like Jack Shaw, whom Hoover had forced to quit when he wrote a paper at John Jay College criticizing Bureau policies.

86. Ralph de Toledano, *J. Edgar Hoover: The Man in His Time* (New Rochelle, N.Y.: Arlington House, 1973), p. 367.

87. Ehrlichman, *Witness to Power,* p. 166. According to DeLoach, Nixon wanted to get Hoover out of the Bureau by making him a window dressing "Director Emeritus," and Kleindienst recommended this to Nixon (interview, Richard Kleindienst, in Demaris, *The Director,* p. 244). See also Nixon, *Memoirs,* pp. 596, 597.

88. Nixon, *Memoirs,* pp. 597–598.

89. Ehrlichman, *Witness to Power,* p. 166.

90. Nixon, *Memoirs,* pp. 598–599.

91. Ehrlichman, *Witness to Power,* p. 166.

92. John W. Dean III, *Blind Ambition* (New York: Pocket Books, 1977; originally published in 1976), p. 46.

93. Ibid., p. 50; Felt, *The FBI Pyramid,* p. 170.

94. Felt, *The FBI Pyramid,* pp. 170, 173, 174.

95. "Political realism," John Dean says, and not the "fear of blackmail," was what kept Nixon from firing Hoover (Dean, *Blind Ambition,* p. 51).

96. Dean, *Blind Ambition,* p. 50.

97. For the description of Hoover's last day, see Felt, *The FBI Pyramid,* p. 178. Felt's account is the most reliable, but there are discrepancies between his and other firsthand accounts.

98. Hoover, "Message from the Director," May 1, 1972, reprinted in Senate, *Memorial Tributes,* p. 14. Felt somewhat improves Hoover's actual schedule by saying that Hoover customarily worked until six-thirty or seven in the evening; DeLoach and one of Hoover's neighbors say that he usually left earlier. Judging by the time he usually got home, Hoover normally left shortly before six. For the report that Hoover was leaving for work later and returning earlier, see *Washington Star,* May 7, 1972, and interview, Cartha DeLoach, Mar. 10, 1975.

99. *Washington Post,* May 3, 1972; Felt, *The FBI Pyramid,* p. 176.

100. Felt, *The FBI Pyramid,* p. 178; DeLoach to Trohan, June 21, 1972, Hoover, J. Edgar, Walter Trohan Papers, HCHL.

101. For the military plan for the ceremonies, see FBI File 67–561, Hoover Personnel File.

102. Allen got Senator Ernest Hollings of South Carolina, who said Hoover had told him he did not want the building named after him, to concede most buildings in Washington were monstrosities. His point was that if the Senate let the aesthetic standards of honorees stand in the way, it would never manage to name any buildings (see remarks of Allen and

Hollings, "Proceedings in the Senate," May 2, 1972, in *Memorial Tributes,* pp. 2, 3).

103. Don Clausen remarks in House, Senate, *Memorial Tributes,* pp. 137–139.

104. Savannah *Morning News,* May 4, 1972, and Augusta *Chronicle,* May 3, 1972, both in Senate, *Memorial Tributes,* pp. 300, 305.

105. Columbus, Georgia, *Enquirer,* May 3, 1972, in Senate, *Memorial Tributes,* p. 302.

106. Ungar, *FBI,* p. 273; Demaris, *The Director,* p. 9.

107. Felt, *The FBI Pyramid,* p. 183.

108. Elson's and Nixon's remarks are in Senate, *Memorial Tributes,* pp. xix–xxviii; Felt, *The FBI Pyramid,* p. 185; Lawrence Van Gelder, Tolson obituary, *New York Times,* Apr. 15, 1975; story of burial, *Washington Evening Star,* May 5, 1972, in *Memorial Tributes,* p. 229. Tolson died on April 14, 1975.

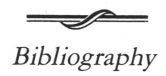

Bibliography

STUDYING THE LIFE OF J. Edgar Hoover presents difficulties that go beyond the normally complicated process of working with government records. One of Hoover's principal ways of managing his Bureau was by writing marginal comments on the memos that crossed his desk, usually vigorously expressed, often contributing valuable insights to his thoughts and feelings. As long as there are unreleased FBI files, it is likely that there will be Hoover documents still unexamined. The FBI's efficient filing and cross-referencing system makes much research relatively straightforward once the relevant file has been located and released by way of an FOIA request. There is no sure way, however, of locating the memos and marginalia of Hoover that are scattered everywhere, so to understand Hoover's life, *all* the files are relevant.

Since Hoover scholars have to grapple with a nearly uncontrollable mass of materials, they need all the help they can get. The place to start is with the guide to FBI research put out by the Research Unit of the Office of Congressional and Public Affairs of the FBI (OCPA), *Conducting Research in FBI Records,* which provides guidance in making Freedom of Information and other requests to the Bureau, as well as listing major holdings of FBI materials in other archives. Another important guide is a publication of the National Archives and Record Service, *Appraisal of the Records of the Federal Bureau of Investigation* (available from the National Archives on microfiche). The next step is to consult the citations of leading FBI scholars to locate files that have already proven valuable, and for locating archives where copies of files are kept. The most valuable resource is the multivolume report of the Senate Select Committee to Study Governmental Operations with Respect to Intelligence Activities (the Church Committee). Beyond this, the brilliant investigations of Athan Theoharis, Kenneth O'Reilly, Joan Jensen, William Preston, Stanley Coben, David Garrow, Allen Weinstein, Ronald Radosh, and Joyce Milton (noted below) are invaluable guides to the files.

Many FBI files important for the study of Hoover have already been released and are available at the FOIA reading room at the FBI; many of these have also been microfilmed and are available from Scholarly Resources, Wilmington, Delaware. Examples of those released and microfilmed are the files on Kent State, Watergate, Marcus Garvey, Martin Luther King, Jr., Malcolm X, SCLC, J. Robert Oppenheimer, Albert Einstein, HUAC, the American Legion Contact Program, COINTELPRO, the Committee on Public Justice, FBI Manuals of Instruction, Investigative Procedures and Guidelines, and FBI Filing and Records Procedures.

Besides these files, there is a great deal of important Hoover material in the sensitive files once kept in the offices of Hoover and his public relations chief, Louis B. Nichols: These are available in the FOIA reading room as the Hoover and Nichols Official and Confidential Files. Another important resource is the personnel files of Hoover himself and the key agents and officials who worked with him. Already released, and available at the FOIA reading room, are the personnel files of Hoover himself and of Louis B. Nichols, Melvin Purvis, and (most importantly), Clyde Tolson. In his last years, Hoover routinely wrote extremely detailed memos (probably transcriptions of tapes) of many important meetings and phone calls and then distributed them to his key executives. Large numbers of these lodged in Tolson's file.

The early records of the FBI (1908 to 1922) are in the National Archives (Record Group 65) on difficult-to-read microfilm (the first 111 files are the index, and there is a brief guide, *Investigative Case Files of the Bureau of Investigation 1908–1922* available from the Archives.) There is an enormous amount of Hoover material here, and also in the Archives Justice Department files (Record Group 60). One can find a running record of Hoover's communications with the Justice Department, and Justice Department duplicates of cases that were selected (or considered) for prosecution, in certain instances as late as the 1940s. The computerized index to the Emma Goldman Papers at Berkeley helps point to Hoover material in these early records. Many Hoover documents may be found in the subversive activities files 202600 and 202492 in RG 60.

The best guide to Hoover's public activities is the Hoover Memorabilia Collection in the National Archives (Record Group 65), whose 243 boxes contain scrapbooks of newspaper articles on Hoover that his office maintained for his information and use. A critical counterpoint to this collection is the back files of the *Nation* magazine, which, particularly under editor Carey McWilliams, pestered Hoover from the late thirties until his death, calling attention to the more outrageous and outlandish of the director's deeds and misdeeds. The Archives' Still Picture Collection also has an enormous number of Hoover photos, including many personal pictures. For Hoover's speeches and writings, see the bibliographies by Frank Donner in his *Age of Surveillance* and by the author in his *G-Men: Hoover's FBI in American Popular Culture.* The research unit of the OCPA has a large collection of Hoover speeches, and many of them can also be found in the Public Affairs files of Record Group 60 in the National Archives, and reprinted in *Vital Speeches.*

All of the libraries of the presidents Hoover served contain vital Hoover material, so the Hoover biographer must travel to the Herbert Hoover Library, the FDR Library, the Harry S Truman Library, the Eisenhower Library, the Kennedy Library, and the Johnson Library. They all have general finding aids to J. Edgar Hoover documents. The Calvin Coolidge and Warren G. Harding Papers have many Hoover items, and there are a few more in the Woodrow Wilson Papers (all on microfilm). Other collections with important Hoover holdings are the University of Virginia (Homer Stillé Cummings), University of Buffalo Law School (John Lord O'Brian), the Historical Society of Pennsylvania (Secretary of Labor Wilson), and the Tamiment Library at NYU. The John Jay library in New York has a good collection of the microfilmed files. The District of Columbia Public Library (the Martin Luther King Library) has the files of the *Washington Star,* and the reports of the public school system, as well as the city directories and detailed maps necessary for placing events.

The Library of Congress has a sample (on microfilm) of the radical periodicals collected by Hoover's Radical Division in 1919 (Microfilm #122; a finding aid is available in the microfilm room). The library's records of the chief clerk's office has documents on Hoover's employment when he worked for the library. Another important resource for this period is *Surveillance of Radicals in the United States, 1917–*

1941, a microfilm collection published by University Publications of America, Frederick, MD. On Reels 16 through 18 there is an almost complete set of Hoover's *General Intelligence Bulletins* from 1920 to 1921.

Most of Hoover's personal records were destroyed after his death by Helen Gandy and Clyde Tolson. What survived is in the eighty-five cartons of the Hoover Memorabilia Collection, which is owned by the J. Edgar Hoover Foundation and temporarily housed at the J. Edgar Hoover Library at the Freedoms Foundation at Valley Forge, Pennsylvania. Besides hundreds of gifts and knickknacks from Hoover's home, there are personal items, such as his christening robe and Masonic apron, many childhood pictures, letters to Hoover from his parents, Hoover's diaries from high school, high school papers and notebooks (including some debate notes), his law school notebooks (twenty-five volumes), and many photos, including hundreds of photos Hoover took of Tolson, mostly on trips during the thirties and forties. The inventory of the collection at the library can serve as a finding aid.

Besides the histories of the Bureau by Max Lowenthal, Don White-head, Fred J. Cook, and Sanford Ungar, and Ralph de Toledano's biography, the published works that throw most light on Hoover are the memoirs of retired FBI officials William C. Sullivan and Mark Felt, and the rich collection of interviews in Ovid Demaris's *The Director.*

Government Reports and Publications

Annual *Reports* of the Attorney General.

Annual *Testimony* of the FBI Director Before the House Appropriations Committee.

Comptroller General of the United States. *FBI Domestic Intelligence Operations: An Uncertain Future.* Nov. 9, 1977. GGD-78-10.

———. *FBI Domestic Intelligence Operations—Their Purpose and Scope: Issues That Need to Be Resolved.* Feb. 24, 1976. GGD-76-50.

Congressional Record. Feb. 5, 1923, pp. 3051–3073. (Reports by Senators Walsh and Sterling, and Walsh's reply to Sterling on the Palmer raids.)

FBI Annual Reports.

General Intelligence Bulletin. Reels 16–18 of *U.S. Military Intelligence Reports: Surveillance of Radicals in the United States, 1917–1941.* Frederick, Md.: University Publications, 1984?.

National Advisory Commission on Civil Disorders. *Report.* New York: Bantam, 1968.

National Archives. *Appraisal of the Records of the Federal Bureau of Investigation:*

A Report to Honorable Harold H. Greene, United States District Court for the District of Columbia. 1981.

National Commission on the Causes and Prevention of Violence. *Rights in Conflict.* [The Walker Report on the 1968 Chicago riots.] New York: Bantam, 1968.

President's Commission on Law Enforcement and Administration of Justice. *The Challenge of Crime in a Free Society.* New York: Avon, 1968.

Registers of the Justice Department.

Research Unit, Office of Congressional and Public Affairs. Federal Bureau of Investigation. *Conducting Research in FBI Records. 1986.*

Senate of the State of New York, Joint Legislative Committee Investigating Radical Activities, Revolutionary Radicalism. Albany, N.Y.: J. Lyons, 1920.

U.S. House, Committee on Government Operations. *Inquiry into the Destruction of Former FBI Director J. Edgar Hoover's Files and FBI Recordkeeping.* 94th Cong., 1st sess.

U.S. House, Committee on Rules. *Attorney General A. Mitchell Palmer on Charges Made Against Department of Justice by Louis F. Post and Others.* 65th Cong., 2nd sess., June 1, 1920.

U.S. House, Select Committee on Intelligence. *Hearings,* U.S. Intelligence Agencies and Activities: Domestic Intelligence Programs, Part 3. 94th Cong. 1st sess.

U.S. House, Special Committee to Investigate Communist Activities in the U.S. *Investigation of Communist Propaganda.* 71st Cong., 2nd sess., 1930, Part 2, Vol. 1.

U.S. Senate, Committee on the Judiciary. *Bolshevik Propaganda, Hearings Before a Subcommittee of the Committee on the Judiciary.* Sen. Res. 439 and 469, 65th Cong., 3rd sess. (Feb. 11, 1919–March 10, 1919).

————. *Charges of Illegal Practices of the Department of Justice.* 66th Cong., 3rd sess., Jan. 16–Mar. 3, 1921.

————. *Hearing,* Freedom of the Press. 92nd Cong., 1st and 2nd sess.

U.S. Senate. *Investigation Activities of the Department of Justice, Letter from the Attorney General, Transmitting in Response to a Senate Resolution of October 17, 1919, a Report on the Activities of the Bureau of Investigation of the Department of Justice against Persons Advising Anarchy, Sedition, and the Forcible Overthrow of the Government.* 66th Cong., 1st sess., Nov. 15, 1919.

U.S. Senate. *Memorial Tributes to J. Edgar Hoover in the Congress of the United States and Various Articles and Editorials Relating to His Life and Work.* 94th Cong., 2nd sess., 1974.

U.S. Senate, Select Committee on Investigation of the Attorney General. *Investigation of Hon. Harry M. Daugherty, formerly Attorney General of the United States.* 68th Cong., 1st sess., S. Res. 157, 1924, Vol. III.

U.S. Senate, Select Committee to Study Governmental Operations with Respect to Intelligence Activities. *Final Report,* Intelligence Activities and the Rights of Americans, Book II. 94th Cong., 2nd sess., Report No. 94–755.

————. *Final Report,* Supplementary Reports on Intelligence Activities, Book IV. 94th Cong., 2nd sess., Report No. 94–755.

————. *Final Report,* The Investigation of the Assassination of President John F. Kennedy: Performance of the Intelligence Agencies, Book V. 94th Cong., 2nd sess., Report No. 94–755, Serial 13133–5.

_____. *Final Report,* Supplementary Detailed Staff Reports on Intelligence Activities and the Rights of Americans, Book III. 94th Cong., 2nd sess., Report No. 94–755, Serial 13133–5.

_____. *Hearings,* Huston Plan, Vol. 2. 94th Cong., 1st sess., Sept. 23, 24, 25, 1975, pp. 354–356.

_____. *Hearings,* Vol. 6, FBI. 94th Cong., 1st. sess.

Books

Abridged History of the Federal Bureau of Investigation. c. 1983. OCPA.

ADLER, BILL, ed. *Kids' Letters to the FBI.* Englewood Cliffs, N.J.: Prentice-Hall, 1966.

AMBROSE, STEPHEN E. *Eisenhower, The President.* New York: Simon and Schuster, 1984.

American Friends Service Committee. *Anatomy of Anti-Communism.* New York: Hill and Wang, 1969.

Appel, Special Agent Charles. *History of the Bureau of Investigation.* Nov. 18, 1930. OCPA, FBI.

BALES, JAMES D., ed. *J. Edgar Hoover Speaks Concerning Communism.* Washington, D.C.: Capitol Hill Press, 1970.

BALTZELL, DIGBY. *The Protestant Establishment: Aristocracy and Caste in America.* New York: Vintage, 1964.

BELKNAP, MICHAL R. *Cold War Political Justice: The Smith Act, the Communist Party, and American Civil Liberties.* Westport, Conn.: Greenwood, 1977.

BELL, DANIEL, ed. *The Radical Right.* New York: Anchor, 1964; originally published in 1955.

BERGMAN, ANDREW. *We're in the Money.* New York: New York University Press, 1972.

BERLE, ADOLF; BERLE, BEATRICE; AND JACOBS, TRAVIS; eds. *Navigating the Rapids.* New York: Harcourt Brace, 1973.

BIDDLE, FRANCIS. *In Brief Authority.* Garden City, N.Y.: Doubleday, 1962.

BLUMER, HERBERT, AND HAUSER, PHILIP M. *Movies, Delinquency and Crime.* New York: Macmillan, 1933.

BONTECOU, ELEANOR. *The Federal Loyalty-Security Program.* Ithaca, N.Y.: Cornell University Press, 1953.

BROWN, ANTHONY CAVE. *The Last Hero: Wild Bill Donovan.* New York: Times Books, 1982.

BROWN, R. G., et al. *Illegal Practices of the Justice Department.* Washington, D.C.: National Popular Government League, May 1920.

BURNS, JAMES MACGREGOR. *Roosevelt: The Lion and the Fox.* New York: Harcourt Brace, 1956.

CAESAR, GENE. *Incredible Detective.* Englewood Cliffs, N.J.: Prentice-Hall, 1968. (A life of William Burns.)

CAUTE, DAVID. *The Great Fear: The Anti-Communist Purge Under Truman and Eisenhower.* New York: Simon and Schuster, 1978.

Centennial History of Central High School. Washington, D.C.: Alumni Association of Central High School, 1976.

CHESTER, REV. JOHN, D. D. *Discourse Delivered at the Funeral Services of Mrs. Anna Hitz in the Metropolitan Presbyterian Church of Washington, D.C., on March 8, 1883.* Washington, D.C.: Beresford, 1883.

COBEN, STANLEY. *A. Mitchell Palmer, Politician.* New York: Columbia University Press, 1963.

COBLER, JOHN. *Capone.* New York: Putnam's, 1971.

COLLINS, FREDERICK L. *The FBI in Peace and War.* New York: Putnam's, 1943.

COOK, FRED J. *The F.B.I. Nobody Knows.* New York: Macmillan, 1964.

COONEY, JOHN. *The American Pope.* New York: Times Books, 1984.

COOPER, COURTNEY RYLEY. *Ten Thousand Public Enemies.* New York: Blue Ribbon Books, 1935.

COWAN, PAUL, et al. *State Secrets.* New York: Holt, Rinehart and Winston, 1974.

CRAWFORD, ALAN. *Thunder on the Right: The New Right and the Politics of Resentment.* New York: Pantheon, 1980.

CROMIE, ROBERT, AND PINKSON, JOSEPH. *Dillinger: A Short and Violent Life.* New York: McGraw-Hill, 1962.

CUMMINGS, HOMER, AND McFARLAND, CARL. *Federal Justice: Chapters in the History of Justice in the Federal Executive.* New York: Da Capo, 1970; originally published in 1937.

DEAN, JOHN W., III. *Blind Ambition.* New York: Pocket Books, 1977; originally published in 1976.

DEMARIS, OVID. *The Director: An Oral Biography of J. Edgar Hoover.* New York: Harper's Magazine Press, 1975.

DE TOLEDANO, RALPH. *J. Edgar Hoover: The Man in His Time.* New Rochelle, N.Y.: Arlington House, 1973.

Digested History of the FBI. Feb. 1, 1940. OCPA, FBI.

DONNER, FRANK J. *The Age of Surveillance.* New York: Knopf, 1980.

DONOVAN, ROBERT J. *Conflict and Crisis: The Presidency of Harry S Truman, 1945–1948.* New York: Norton, 1977.

———. *Tumultuous Years: The Presidency of Harry S Truman, 1949–1953.* New York: Norton, 1982.

DOWNES, DONALD. *The Scarlet Thread.* London: Derek Verschoyle, 1953.

DRAPER, THEODORE. *The Roots of American Communism.* New York: Viking, 1957.

DUBOFSKY, MELVYN, AND THEOHARIS, ATHAN. *Imperial Democracy: The United States since 1945.* Englewood Cliffs, N.J.: Prentice-Hall, 1983.

DUMENIL, LYNN. *Freemasonry and American Culture.* Princeton, N.J.: Princeton University Press, 1985.

DURKHEIM, EMILE. *The Division of Labor in Society.* New York: Free Press, 1964; written in 1893.

EASTMAN, MAX. *Reflections on the Failure of Socialism.* New York: Devin-Adair, 1962.

EDELMAN, MURRAY. *The Symbolic Uses of Politics.* Urbana, Ill.: University of Illinois Press, 1964.

EHRLICHMAN, JOHN. *Witness to Power.* New York: Simon and Schuster, 1982.

EISENHOWER, DWIGHT D. *Mandate for Change: 1953–1956.* Garden City, N.Y.: Doubleday, 1963.

————. *The White House Years: Waging Peace, 1956–1961.* Garden City, N.Y.: Doubleday, 1965.

ELLIFF, JOHN T. *Crime, Dissent, and the Attorney General: The Justice Department in the 1960s.* Beverly Hills, Calif.: Sage, 1971.

FALK, CANDACE. *Love, Anarchy, and Emma Goldman.* New York: Holt, Rinehart and Winston, 1984.

FELT, MARK. *The FBI Pyramid.* New York: Putnam's, 1979.

FORMAN, HENRY JAMES. *Our Movie Made Children.* New York: Macmillan, 1933.

FRAENKEL, O. K. *The Sacco-Vanzetti Case.* New York: Knopf, 1931.

FREEDMAN, MAX, ed. *Roosevelt and Frankfurter: Their Correspondence.* Boston: Little, Brown, 1967.

GARROW, DAVID J. *The FBI and Martin Luther King, Jr.: From "Solo" to Memphis.* New York: Norton, 1981.

GATEWOOD, WILLARD B. *Theodore Roosevelt and the Art of Controversy.* Baton Rouge: Louisiana University Press, 1970.

GITLOW, BENJAMIN. *The Whole of Their Lives.* New York: Scribner's, 1948.

GOLDMAN, EMMA. *Living My Life.* New York: Knopf, 1931.

GOLDMAN, ERIC. *The Tragedy of Lyndon Johnson.* New York: Knopf, 1969.

GOLDSTEIN, ROBERT J. *Political Repression in Modern America.* Cambridge, Mass.: Schenckman/Two Continents, 1978.

GOODMAN, WALTER. *The Committee: The Extraordinary Career of the House Committee on Un-American Activities.* New York: Farrar, Straus, 1968.

GOULART, RON. *Line Up, Tough Guys.* Nashville, Tenn.: Sherbourne Press, 1966.

GREEN, CONSTANCE MCLAUGHLIN. *Washington: Capital City, 1879–1950* Princeton, N.J.: Princeton University Press, 1963.

GREEN, GIL. *Cold War Fugitive.* New York: International Publishers, 1984.

GREENE, NATHANAEL. *European Socialism Since World War I.* Chicago: Quadrangle, 1971.

GRIFFITH, ROBERT, AND THEOHARIS, ATHAN. *The Specter: Original Essays on the Cold War and the Origins of McCarthyism.* New York: New Viewpoints, 1974.

GUTHMAN, EDWIN. *We Band of Brothers.* New York: Harper and Row, 1964.

HALPERIN, MORTON H., et al. *The Lawless State: The Crimes of the U.S. Intelligence Agencies.* New York: Penguin, 1976.

HANDY, ROBERT T. *A Christian America: Protestant Hopes and Historical Realities.* New York: Oxford University Press, 1984.

HARMON, JIM. *The Great Radio Heroes.* New York: Ace, 1967.

HARRIS, RICHARD. *Justice: The Crisis of Law, Order, and Freedom in America.* New York: Avon, 1970; originally published in 1969.

HECHLER, KEN. *Working with Truman: A Personal Memoir of the White House Years.* New York: Putnam's, 1982.

Here's to Old Central. Washington, D.C.: Alumni Association of Central High, 1967.

HIGHAM, JOHN. *Strangers in the Land: Patterns of American Nativism, 1860–1925.* New York: Atheneum, 1973.

HILL, ROBERT A., ed. *Marcus Garvey and Universal Negro Improvement Association Papers.* Vol. 2. Berkeley, Calif.: University of California Press, 1983.

HOOK, SIDNEY. *Heresy, Yes—Conspiracy, No.* New York: John Day, 1953.

HOOVER, J. EDGAR. *Persons in Hiding.* Boston: Little Brown, 1938.

———. *Masters of Deceit.* New York: Henry Holt, 1958.

———. *A Study of Communism.* New York: Holt, Rinehart and Winston, 1962

———. *J. Edgar Hoover on Communism.* New York: Random House, 1969.

———. *J. Edgar Hoover Speaks.* Edited by James D. Bales. Washington, D.C.: Capitol Hill, 1971.

HORAN, JAMES D. *The Pinkertons.* New York: Bonanza, 1967.

HOWE, IRVING, AND COSER, LEWIS. *The American Communist Party: A Critical History.* New York: Praeger, 1962.

HUIE, WILLIAM BRADFORD. *Three Lives for Mississippi.* New York: Signet, 1968.

HURT, HENRY. *Reasonable Doubt.* New York: Holt, Rinehart and Winston, 1985.

HYDE, H. MONTGOMERY. *The Atom Bomb Spies.* London: Hamish Hamilton, 1980.

ICKES, HAROLD L. *The Secret Diaries.* New York: Simon and Schuster, 1954.

IRONS, PETER. *Justice at War.* New York: Oxford University Press, 1983.

JAFFE, JULIAN F. *Crusade Against Radicalism.* Port Washington, N.Y.: Kennikat, 1972.

JENSEN, JOAN M. *The Price of Vigilance.* Chicago: Rand McNally, 1968.

———. *Military Surveillance of Civilians in America.* Morristown, N.J.: General Learning Press, 1975.

JOHNSON, LYNDON BAINES. *The Vantage Point.* New York: Holt, Rinehart and Winston, 1971.

JOWETT, GARTH. *Film, The Democratic Art.* Boston: Little, Brown, 1975.

KAYSER, ELMER LOUIS. *Bricks Without Straw: The Evolution of George Washington University.* New York: Appleton-Century-Croft, 1970.

KEARNS, DORIS. *Lyndon Johnson and the American Dream.* New York: Harper and Row, 1976.

KELLY, ALFRED, et al. *The American Constitution.* New York: Norton, 1983.

KEMPTON, MURRAY. *Part of Our Time: Some Monuments and Ruins of the Thirties.* New York: Simon and Schuster, 1955.

KIMBALL, PENN. *The File: The Chilling True Account of Government Spying on an Innocent Man.* New York: Harcourt Brace, 1983.

KLEINDIENST, RICHARD. *Justice: The Memoirs of an Attorney General.* Ottawa, Ill.: Jameson, 1985.

KUTLER, STANLEY I. *The American Inquisition: Justice and Order in the Cold War.* New York: Hill and Wang, 1982.

LASCH, CHRISTOPHER. *The Agony of the American Left.* New York: Vintage, 1969.

LATHAM, EARL. *The Communist Controversy in Washington.* Cambridge, Mass.: Harvard University Press, 1966.

LEWIS, EUGENE. *Public Entrepreneurship: Toward a Theory of Bureaucratic Political Power.* Bloomington, Ind.: Indiana University Press, 1984.

LINDEMANN, ALBERT S. *The Red Years: European Socialism versus Bolshevism, 1919–1921.* Berkeley, Calif.: University of California Press, 1974.

LISIO, DONALD J. *The President and Protest: Hoover, Conspiracy and the Bonus Riot.* Columbia, Mo.: University of Missouri Press, 1973.

LOWENTHAL, MAX. *The Federal Bureau of Investigation.* New York: William Sloane Associates, 1950.

LYNN, ROBERT W., AND WRIGHT, ELLIOTT. *The Big Little School: Two Hundred Years of the Sunday School.* New York: Harper and Row, 1971.

MACDONALD, J. FRED. *Television and the Red Menace: The Video Road to Vietnam.* New York: Praeger, 1985.

MAILER, NORMAN. *The Presidential Papers.* New York: Berkley, 1963.

MARTIN, OLGA. *Hollywood's Movie Commandments* New York: H. W. Wilson, 1937.

MASON, ALPHEUS THOMAS. *Harlan Fiske Stone: Pillar of the Law.* New York: Viking, 1956.

Masonic Obituary. J. Edgar Hoover Memorabilia Collection. Freedoms Foundation, Valley Forge, Pennsylvania.

MASTERMAN, J. C. *The Double Cross System in the War of 1939 to 1945.* New Haven: Yale University Press: 1972.

MITCHELL, DAVID. *1919: Red Mirage.* New York: Macmillan, 1970.

MORGAN, RICHARD E. *Domestic Intelligence: Monitoring Dissent in America.* Austin, Tex.: University of Texas Press, 1980.

MORGAN, TED. *FDR: A Biography.* New York: Simon and Schuster, 1985.

MURRAY, ROBERT K. *Red Scare: A Study in National Hysteria, 1919–1920.* New York: McGraw-Hill, 1964.

NAVASKY, VICTOR. *Kennedy Justice.* New York: Atheneum, 1971.

_____. *Law Enforcement: The Federal Role.* New York: McGraw-Hill, 1976.

_____. *Naming Names.* New York: Viking, 1980.

NELSON, JACK, AND OSTROW, RONALD J. *The FBI and the Berrigans.* New York: Coward, McCann, 1972.

NIXON, RICHARD. *The Memoirs of Richard Nixon.* New York: Grosset & Dunlap, 1978.

O'NEILL, WILLIAM L. *Coming Apart: An Informal History of America in the 1960s.* New York: Quadrangle, 1971.

O'REILLY, KENNETH. *Hoover and the Un-Americans.* Philadelphia: Temple University Press, 1983.

OLLESTAD, NORMAN. *Inside the FBI.* New York: Lancer, 1968.

OSHINSKY, DAVID M. *A Conspiracy So Immense: The World of Joe McCarthy.* New York: Free Press, 1983.

OVERSTREET, HARRY, AND OVERSTREET, BONARO. *The FBI in Our Open Society.* New York: Norton, 1969.

PARMET, HERBERT S. *Eisenhower and the American Crusades.* New York: Macmillan, 1972.

———. *Jack: The Struggles of John F. Kennedy.* New York: Dial, 1980.

———. *JFK: The Presidency of John F. Kennedy.* New York: Dial, 1983.

PERKUS, CATHY, ed. *COINTELPRO: The FBI's Secret War on Political Freedom.* New York: Monad, 1975.

PERRETT, GEOFFREY. *Days of Sadness, Years of Triumph.* New York: Coward, McCann, 1973.

———. *Dream of Greatness.* New York: Coward, McCann, 1979.

———. *America in the Twenties.* New York: Simon and Schuster, 1982.

PHILBRICK, HERBERT. *I Led Three Lives: Citizen, "Communist," Counterspy.* New York: McGraw-Hill, 1952.

PINKERTON, ALLAN. *The Mollie Maguires and the Detectives.* New York: G. W. Carleton, 1877.

POPOV, DUSKO. *Spy Counter-Spy.* New York: Grosset & Dunlap, 1974.

POST, LOUIS F. *The Deportations Delirium of Nineteen-Twenty: A Personal Narrative of an Historic Official Experience.* New York: Da Capo, 1970; originally published in 1923.

POWERS, RICHARD GID. *G-Men: Hoover's FBI in American Popular Culture.* Carbondale, Ill.: Southern Illinois University Press, 1983.

POWERS, THOMAS. *The Man Who Kept the Secrets.* New York: Knopf, 1979.

PRANGE, GORDON W. *Pearl Harbor: The Verdict of History.* New York: McGraw-Hill, 1986.

PRESTON, WILLIAM, JR. *Aliens and Dissenters.* Cambridge, Mass.: Harvard University Press, 1963.

PURVIS, MELVIN. *American Agent.* Garden City, N.Y.: Doubleday, 1936.

RADOSH, RONALD, AND MILTON, JOYCE. *The Rosenberg File: A Search for the Truth.* New York: Holt, Rinehart and Winston, 1983.

RATHER, DAN, AND GATES, GARY PAUL. *The Palace Guard.* New York: Warner, 1975.

RICHARDS, DAVID. *Played Out: The Jean Seberg Story.* New York: Playboy, 1981.

ROUT, LESLIE B., AND BRATZEL, JOHN F. *The Shadow War: German Espionage and United States Counterespionage in Latin America During World War II.* Frederick, Md.: University Publications, 1986.

RUSSELL, FRANCIS. *The Shadow of Blooming Grove: Warren G. Harding and His Times.* New York: McGraw-Hill, 1968.

SCHLESINGER, ARTHUR M., JR. *The Vital Center: The Politics of Freedom.* New York: Houghton, Mifflin, 1949.

———. *A Thousand Days.* Boston: Houghton, Mifflin, 1965.

———. *The Imperial Presidency.* Boston: Houghton, Mifflin, 1973.

———. *Robert Kennedy and His Times.* Boston: Houghton, Mifflin, 1978.

SCHOTT, JOSEPH. *No Left Turns.* New York: Praeger, 1975.

SELDES, GEORGE. *Witch Hunt.* New York: Modern Age, 1940.

SHERWOOD, ROBERT. *Roosevelt and Hopkins.* New York: Harper and Row, 1948.

SHILS, EDWARD W. *The Torment of Secrecy: The Background and Consequences of American Security Policies.* Glencoe: Free Press, 1956.

SHUMACH, MURRAY. *The Face on the Cutting-Room Floor.* New York: William Morrow, 1964.

Significant Dates in FBI History. Jan. 2, 1985. OCPA, FBI.

SKLAR, ROBERT. *Movie-Made America.* New York: Random House, 1975.

SMITH, BRADLEY F. *The Shadow Warriors.* New York: Basic, 1983.

SMITH, RICHARD NORTON. *An Uncommon Man: The Triumph of Herbert Hoover.* New York: Simon and Schuster, 1984.

SPOLANSKY, JACOB. *The Communist Trail in America.* New York: Macmillan, 1951.

STEINBERG, PETER L. *The Great "Red Menace": United States Prosecution of American Communists, 1947–1952.* Westport, Conn.: Greenwood, 1984.

STEVENSON, WILLIAM. *A Man Called Intrepid.* New York: Harcourt, Brace, 1976.

STONE, I. F. *The Haunted Fifties.* New York: Vintage, 1969.

————. *The Truman Era.* New York: Vintage, 1973.

STRIPLING, ROBERT E. *The Red Plot Against America.* New York: Bell, 1949.

SULLIVAN, WILLIAM C. *The Bureau: My Thirty Years in Hoover's FBI.* New York: Norton, 1979.

SUMMERS, ANTHONY. *Goddess: The Secret Lives of Marilyn Monroe.* New York: Macmillan, 1985.

SWISHER, CARL BRENT, ed. *Homer Cummings, Selected Papers.* New York: Da Capo, 1973; originally published in 1939.

SZULC, TAD. *The Illusion of Peace.* New York: Viking, 1978.

THEOHARIS, ATHAN. *The Truman Presidency: The Origins of the Imperial Presidency and the National Security State.* Stanfordville, N.Y.: Coleman, 1979.

————, ed. *Beyond the Hiss Case.* Philadelphia: Temple University Press, 1982.

TOLAND, JOHN. *The Dillinger Days.* New York: Random House, 1963.

————. *Infamy.* New York: Berkley, 1983.

TROHAN, WALTER. *Political Animals.* Garden City, N.Y.: Doubleday, 1975.

TROY, THOMAS F. *Donovan and the CIA.* Washington, D.C.: CIA, 1981.

TRUMAN, HARRY S. *Memoirs.* 2 vols. Garden City, N.Y.: Doubleday, 1955, 1956.

TURNER, WILLIAM W. *Hoover's FBI, The Men and the Myth.* New York: Dell, 1971.

UNGAR, SANFORD J. *FBI.* Boston: Atlantic Monthly Press, 1976.

WALLER, GEORGE M., (ed.) *Pearl Harbor, Roosevelt and the Coming of the War.* Boston: D. C. Heath, 1965.

WATTERS, PAT, AND GILLERS, STEPHEN. *Investigating the FBI.* Garden City, N.Y.: Doubleday, 1973.

WEINSTEIN, ALLEN. *Perjury: The Hiss-Chambers Case.* New York: Knopf, 1978.

WEINSTEIN, JAMES. *The Decline of Socialism in America, 1912–1925.* New York: Monthly Review Press, 1967.

WEYL, NATHANIEL. *The Battle Against Disloyalty.* New York: Crowell, 1951.

WHITE, THEODORE. *Breach of Faith: The Fall of Richard Nixon.* New York: Atheneum.

WHITEHEAD, DON. *The F.B.I. Story.* New York: Random House, 1956.

_____. *Attack on Terror: The FBI Against the Ku Klux Klan in Mississippi.* New York: Funk and Wagnalls, 1970.

WHITNEY, RICHARD. *Reds in America.* New York: Beckwith, 1924.

WILSON, JAMES Q. *The Investigators: Managing FBI and Narcotics Agents.* New York: Basic Books, 1978.

WILSON, JOAN HOFF. *Herbert Hoover: Forgotten Progressive.* Boston: Little, Brown, 1975.

WOHLSTETTER, ROBERTA. *Pearl Harbor: Warning and Decision.* Stanford, Calif.: Stanford University Press, 1962.

WOLFE, ALAN. *The Seamy Side of Democracy: Repression in America.* New York: David McKay, 1973.

WOODWARD, C. VANN. *The Strange Career of Jim Crow.* New York: Oxford, 1955.

WRIGHT, RICHARD O., ed. *Whose FBI?* La Salle, Ill.: Open Court, 1974.

Articles

ALEXANDER, JACK. "Profiles: The Director." *New Yorker* 13 (Sept. 25, 1937):20–25; 13 (Oct. 2, 1937):22–27; 13 (Oct. 9, 1937):42–45. Condensed in *Reader's Digest,* December 1937, pp. 42–45.

" 'America's Devil's Island'—and Some Others." *Literary Digest* 119 (Oct. 28, 1933):34.

"A New Kind of Government Sleuth in Washington." *Literary Digest* 84 (Jan. 24, 1925):44–46.

BELKNAP, MICHAL R. "The Mechanics of Repression: J. Edgar Hoover, the Bureau of Investigation and the Radicals 1917–1925." *Crime and Social Justice* 7 (Spring–Summer 1977):49–58.

BRATZEL, JOHN F., AND ROUT, LESLIE, JR. "Pearl Harbor, Microdots, and J. Edgar Hoover." *American Historical Review* 87 (Dec. 1982):1346–1347.

CANDELORO, DOMINIC. "Louis F. Post and the Red Scare of 1920." *Prologue* 11 (Spring 1979):40–55.

CLARENS, CARLOS. "Hooverville West: The Hollywood G-Man, 1934–45." *Film Comment* 3 (May–June 1977):10–16.

COBEN, STANLEY. "A Study in Nativism: The American Red Scare of 1919–1920." *Political Science Quarterly* 79 (Mar. 1964):52–75.

COHN, ROY. "Could He Walk on Water?" *Esquire* 78 (Nov. 1972):117–119.

COOPER, COURTNEY RYLEY. "Crime Trap." *American Magazine* 116 (Nov. 1933):64–66, 94–98.

_____. "Getting the Jump on Crime." *American Magazine* 116 (Aug. 1933):23–25.

CRAWFORD, KENNETH G. "J. Edgar Hoover." *Nation,* Feb. 27, 1937, pp. 232–234.

CREWDSON, JOHN. "Seeing Red; An FBI 'Commie Hunter' Rebels at Illegal Tactics." *Sunday: The Chicago Tribune Magazine,* Mar. 2, 1986.

DOS PASSOS, JOHN. "Introduction," June 1932, to a reprint of *Three Soldiers* (1921), quoted in Alfred Kazin, *An American Procession.* New York: Knopf, 1984.

DOUTHIT, NATHAN. "Police Professionalism and the War Against Crime in the United States, 1920s–1930s." Mosse, G. L. *Police Forces in History.* Beverly Hills, Calif.: Sage, 1974.

ELSON, EDWARD L. R. "The J. Edgar Hoover You Ought to Know, by His Pastor." N.C.: The General Commission on Chaplains, 1950.

ESTEL, JOHN. "Hoover Shared Spy Disclosure on Pearl Harbor." *Pittsburgh Post-Gazette,* April 1, 1982, p. 28.

"Head of the Secret Service." *National Magazine,* Mar. 1925. In *Scrapbook.* Hoover Memorabilia Collection, RG 65, NA.

HILL, ROBERT A. " 'The Foremost Radical Among His Race': Marcus Garvey and the Black Scare, 1918–1921." *Prologue* 16 (Winter 1984):215–231.

HOFSTADTER, RICHARD. "The Pseudo-Conservative Revolt." In *The Radical Right,* edited by Daniel Bell. Garden City, N.Y.: Anchor, 1964.

———. *The Age of Reform: From Bryan to F.D.R.* New York: Knopf, 1968.

HOOVER, J. EDGAR. " 'The FBI'—Looking Back from our Seventh Season." *TV Guide,* May 20, 1972, p. 28.

IRONS, PETER. " 'Fighting Fair': Zechariah Chafee, Jr., the Department of Justice, and the 'Trial at the Harvard Club.' " *Harvard Law Review* 94 (Apr. 1981):1205–1236.

IRONS, PETER. "American Business and the Origins of McCarthyism: The Cold War Crusade of the United States Chamber of Commerce." In *The Specter: Original Essays on the Cold War and the Origins of McCarthyism.* Edited by Robert Griffith and Athan Theoharis. New York: New Viewpoints, 1974.

KELLY, SEAN. "The Love Song of J. Edgar Hoover." In *National Lampoon's This Side of Parodies.* New York: Warner Paperbacks, 1974.

KIMBALL, PENN. "The History of *The Nation* According to the F.B.I." *The Nation* 242 (Mar. 22, 1986):399–426.

KLEHR, HARVEY, AND RADOSH, RONALD. "Anatomy of a Fix: the Untold Story of the 'Amerasia' Case." *The New Republic* 194 (Apr. 21, 1986):18–21.

KOFOED, JACK. "Famous Cases of J. Edgar Hoover: the Dillinger Mob." *G-Men.* 9 (Oct. 1935):82–88; 103.

MAYER, MILTON. "Myth of the 'G Men'." *Forum* 94 (Sept. 1935):144–148.

MCAULIFFE, MARY S. "Dwight D. Eisenhower and Wolf Ladejinsky: The Politics of the Declining Red Scare." *Prologue* 14 (Fall 1982):109–128.

O'NEILL, HESTER. "Life and Career of J. Edgar Hoover: Thirty Years on the Job." *American Boy and Open Road* 36 (May 1954):2–4; 36 (June 1954):4–5; 36 (July 1954):8; 38–39; 36 (Sept. 1954):8; 22–23.

O'REILLY, KENNETH. "A New Deal for the FBI: The Roosevelt Administration, Crime Control and National Security." *Journal of American History* 69 (Dec. 1982):638–658.

———. "Herbert Hoover and the FBI." *Annals of Iowa,* Summer 1983, pp. 46–63.

OSHINSKY, DAVID M. "Fort Monmouth and McCarthy: The Victims Remember." *New Jersey History* 100 (Spring/Summer 1982):1–14.

ROSTEN, LEO O. "Men Like War." *Harpers* 171 (June 1935):183–197.

SALISBURY, HARRISON E. "The Strange Correspondence of Morris Ernst and John Edgar Hoover, 1939–1964." *The Nation* 239 (Dec. 1, 1984):575–589.

SAYRE, NORA. "Cold War Cinema, I, II." *The Nation* 228 (Feb. 24, 1979):213–217, 228 (Mar. 3, 1979):245–248.

SEAGLE, WILLIAM. "The American National Police." *Harpers* 169 (Nov. 1934):752–761.

THEOHARIS, ATHAN. "The FBI and the American Legion Contact Program, 1940–1966." *Political Science Quarterly* 100 (Summer 1985):271–286.

TUCKER, RAY. "Hst! Who's That!" *Colliers* 92 (Aug. 19, 1933):15, 49.

WEINSTEIN, ALLEN. "The Symbolism of Subversion: Notes on Cold War Icons." *Journal of American Studies* 6 (Aug. 1972):165–180.

WILLIAMS, DAVID. "The Bureau of Investigation and Its Critics, 1919–1921: The Origins of Federal Political Surveillance." *Journal of American History* 68 (Dec. 1981):570–571.

WILSON, JAMES Q. "Buggings, Break-ins & the FBI." *Commentary* 65 (June 1978):52–58.

Index

607